GOODREADING GUIDE

GUIDE

EIGHTH EDITION

EDITED BY NICK RENNISON

A & C Black • London

First published 2009

A & C Black Publishers Limited
36 Soho Square
London W1D 3QY
www.acblack.com

Copyright © Nick Rennison 2009

Nick Rennison has asserted his rights under the Copyright, Designs
and Patents Act, 1988, to be identified as the author of this work.

A CIP catalogue record for this book is available from the
British Library.

ISBN: 978 1 4081 1395 0

Typeset in 8.5pt on 12pt Meta-Light

Printed and bound in Great Britain by
CPI Cox & Wyman, Reading, RG1 8EX

CONTENTS

HOWTOUSETHISBOOK iiii

INTRODUCTION vii

FIVEFORTHEFUTURE 1

AUTHORENTRIESA–Z 5

STARTPOINTS

Autobiography 26 • Biography 46 • Crime 103 • Historical Novels 214 • History 218 • Letters and Diaries 274 • Poetry 354 • Science Fiction and Fantasy 394 • Thrillers 439 • Travel 448

READONATHEME

Adolescence 7 • Africa 7 • All the World's a Stage 11 • Altered States (Chemical Fiction) 12 • Ancient Greece and Rome 15 • The Animal Kingdom 16 • Art for Whose Sake? 17 • Australia 25 • Author, Author! 25 • Autobiographies and Memoirs (Ghosted!) 26 • Before the Novel 42 • The Bible 45 • Black Britons 50 • Bloomsbury Lives 51 • Booze and Boozers 51 • Bridget Jones and Friends 56 • Canada 71 • The Caribbean 73 • Children 84 • China and Hong Kong 84 • Cities: New World 86 • Cities: Old World 86 • Classic Detection 89 • Comedy Thrillers 94 • Culture Clash 102 • Cyber Fiction 102 • Deep South, USA 114 • Depression and Psychiatry 117 • Dreaming Spires 127 • Eccentric Families 132 • Echoes of Empire 132 • Egypt 135 • The Elderly 136 • Fantasy Adventure 142 • Fantasy Societies 143 • The Film Business 149 • Film of the Book, Book of the Film 149 • First World War 150 • Future Societies 169 • Gay/Lesbian Fiction 172 • Good and Evil 182 • Great (Classic) Detectives 189 • High Adventure 210 • Higher (?) Education 210 • Historical Adventure 214 • Horror 226 • The Human Comedy 230 • India 232 • Ireland 232 • Israel 236 • Japan 240 •

Journalism 243 • Larger Than Life 262 • Latin America 262 • London 282 • Madness 293 • Many Generations 301 • The Middle Ages 308 • Money 316 • Music 325 • New York 330 • Other Peoples, Other Times 341 • Parents and Children 344 • Past and Present 344 • Places 352 • Police Procedural 353 • Politics 354 • Private Eyes 361 • Publish and Be Damned 364 • Renaissance Europe 371 • Rescued Lives 373 • Revisiting One's Past 374 • Rewriting History 374 • The Rhythm of Nature 376 • Roman Catholicism 381 • Russia 386 • Schools 394 • Science Writing 397 • Scotland 399 • Sequels 403 • Sex 404 • Ships and the Sea 407 • Shipwreck 408 • Short Stories 408 • The Sixties 413 • Slaves and the Slave Trade 413 • Small-Town Life, USA 414 • South Africa 418 • Spies and Double Agents 419 • Sporting Tales 420 • Teenagers 432 • Terrorists/Freedom Fighters 433 • Trains 447 • Victorian England 462 • Village and Countryside 463 • Wales 466 • War: Behind the Lines 467 • Weepies 472 • The West (The Great American Frontier) 479 • The Wilderness 483

LITERARYTRIVIA

Five Strange Authorial Deaths 20 • The First Ten Penguin Paperbacks Ever Published (in 1935) 30 • Five Proposed Titles for Famous Novels 76 • Five Authors Who Were Jailbirds 139 • Five Curious Pseudonyms 156 • Five Banned Books 176 • Five Writers Who Suffered from Insanity 205 • Five Writers Who Were Killers 249 • Five Famous People Who Wrote a Single Novel 266 • Five Memorable Books That Never Existed 313 • Ten Winners of the Diagram Prize for the Oddest Title of the Year 338 • Five Curious Book Dedications 383 • Five Sporting Writers 392 • Ten Nobel Laureates Few People Now Read 435 • Ten Fictional Places 475

HIDDENGEM

Edmund Gosse – *Father and Son* (1907) 29
A.J.A. Symons – *The Quest for Corvo* (1934) 48
Donald E. Westlake – *The Hot Rock* (1970) 94
John Franklin Bardin – *The Deadly Percheron* (1946) 103
Daniel Woodrell – *The Death of Sweet Mister* (2002) 106
Hope Mirrlees – *Lud-in-the-Mist* (1926) 143
Mika Waltari – *The Egyptian* (1949) 217

H.F.M. Prescott – *The Man on a Donkey* (1952) 217
James Boswell – *London Journal* (1950) 276
Charles G. Finney – *The Circus of Dr Lao* (1935) 397
Geoffrey Household – *Rogue Male* (1939) 441
Apsley Cherry-Garrard – *The Worst Journey in the World* (1922) 450

PRIZELISTS 494

INDEX 503

HOWTOUSETHISBOOK

The Bloomsbury Good Reading Guide seeks to answer two main questions: 'Which book should I read?' and 'Which book should I read next?' The bulk of the text consists of articles on more than 400 authors, describing the kind of books they wrote, listing titles and suggesting books (by the same authors and by others) which might make interesting follow-ups. For the first time I have included a section (**Five for the Future**) at the beginning of the A–Z entries which draws attention to five authors who have recently published first novels that suggest they have remarkable careers ahead of them. Scattered through this guide are over a hundred **Read on a Theme** menus of suggested reading. These are straightforward lists of between six and twelve books of a similar kind, from *Adolescence* to *The Wilderness*. There are also eleven double-page features, **Startpoints**, each of which covers a particular category of reading, with a large number of suggestions and follow-ups. In alphabetical sequence, they are: *Autobiography, Biography, Crime, Historical Novels, History, Letters* and *Diaries, Poetry, Science Fiction and Fantasy, Science Writing, Thrillers* and *Travel*. In addition there are a dozen **Hidden Gems** highlighted, books which have been undeservedly forgotten over the years. At random points you will also find **Literary Trivia** lists, ranging from *Five Authors Who Were Jailbirds* to *Ten Fictional Places*. These have no particular connection to the entries and are intended solely as (hopefully) entertaining interludes. The book concludes with several lists of winners of major literary prizes, including the Man Booker and the Pulitzer.

The text contains no literary criticism. I wanted to describe books, not to be clever at their expense. In particular, I have tried to avoid ranking authors by 'literary merit', on assessments of whether their work is 'great' or 'light'.

All books mentioned in the *Good Reading Guide* were written in English or are widely available in translation. I have tried to cover as wide a range of writers of English as possible, and have included authors from Australia, Canada, New Zealand, the Republic of Ireland, South Africa and the USA, as well as the UK. Books originally written in a foreign language are listed by their English titles. Original titles follow in brackets where they may be familiar to readers or where they may be used from some English editions.

In this eighth edition of the *Good Reading Guide* I have updated entries to include books that have been published (and alas, deaths that have occurred) since the last edition, and I have revised entries (some substantially), included new titles and menus and added nearly fifty authors new to the guide. To accommodate these changes I have, regretfully, excluded a small number of writers who appeared in earlier editions but whose popularity has waned significantly. I welcome ideas, comments and suggestions for any future editions. Please write to me, care of the publishers.

KEY TO THE SYMBOLS

◆ Other books by the same author

◪ Similar books by other authors

≫ A book by an author who features in the *Good Reading Guide*

ACKNOWLEDGEMENTS

The cut-off date for inclusion in this eighth edition of the *Good Reading Guide* was June 2009. The final choice of books and authors, the comments and the text have been my responsibility. I take the blame. But many people have helped. This is the fourth edition of the *Good Reading Guide* in which the revisions and changes have not been made by the original author, the late Kenneth McLeish. However, a great deal of the book remains, in essence, his work. Many of the entries he wrote for earlier editions were so concise, witty, informative and insightful that it has always seemed both presumptuous and unnecessary to change them. Susan Osborne has a knowledge of contemporary fiction second to none and the Read on a Theme menus have benefited enormously from her many suggestions. Steve Andrews is a walking encyclopedia of information and opinion about science fiction, and I am grateful for his advice and suggestions in a genre where I make no claims to expertise. Richard Shephard contributed many suggestions for Read Ons in American fiction and outlined the entries on half a dozen contemporary American novelists for me. I am very grateful to all three of them and to the many other people who have, over the years, suggested new authors and books to me. To name Eve Gorton, Noel Murphy, Hugh Pemberton, Gordon Kerr, Travis Elborough, Niamh Marnham, John Magrath, Kevin Chappell, Linda Pattenden, Peter French, Brian Grist, Lucinda Rennison and Paul Skinner is to mention only a few. To name more would be to run the risk of sounding like an Oscar-winning actor thanking his entire acquaintance for contributions to his career. But many others have done for me what this *Good Reading Guide* hopes to do for anybody who uses it – pointed me in the direction of rewarding and enjoyable books which I would not otherwise have had the good fortune to read. At A&C Black Jenny Ridout and Inderjeet Garcha have been excellent and supportive editors on this project. *The Good Reading Guide* is a book that demands great skill and patience from the person copy-editing it. On this eighth edition I have been lucky to have had the help of Judy Tither and her work on it is much appreciated. Without her editing skills the book would not have appeared on bookshop shelves in time and I am very grateful for all she did.

Nick Rennison
July 2009

INTRODUCTION

There are more books published each year than ever before. Walk into any large branch of the major book retailers and the shelves stretch into the distance, great vistas of novels and biographies, histories and whodunits, romances and fantasies searching for a readership. The sight is stimulating to any lover of books but also daunting. How are the keenest of readers to choose from the vast numbers of books on offer? Like explorers in some limitless, landmarkless new continent, they hardly know where to turn. *The Good Reading Guide* is an attempt to provide signposts and indicate pathways through the landscape.

Paradoxically, despite the fact that more titles appear than ever before, there are those who claim that books may be an endangered species. They are not under threat in the way they have been before. Books have regularly faced the wrath of cultural dictators in past centuries. The Nazis were by no means the only burners of books. Ideologues of all kinds have seen books as potentially subversive and attempted to curb their influence. Yet books and literature have survived their attentions.

Today's threat to books, it is said, is twofold. Both parts come in the shape of technology. First, it may be that the printed page is set to go the way of the illuminated manuscript in the fifteenth century. The interactive CDs of the early 1990s were only the harbingers of momentous changes in the ways in which words and information can be accessed. The extraordinary growth of the internet has seen more and more texts available through a PC screen. It is no longer necessary to go to a bookshop or a library to track down literature as different as a Shakespeare play and a novel by Edgar Rice Burroughs, a poem by Tennyson and a Sherlock Holmes short story. You can locate, if you wish, the work of the Church Fathers or Jane Austen's *Pride and Prejudice*, the *Book of Mormon* or Cervantes in Spanish in a matter of moments. They are all out there in the rapidly expanding realm of cyberspace. The way in which we read may well be changing. The latest generation of small book-sized e-readers enable you to read in an armchair, or sitting in bed, instead of bolt upright at a table. Today's children, brought up from infancy to use computers as tools for both learning and entertainment, may well find scrolling a handier way to move through a text than turning pages. So books themselves, as physical objects, may be about to change but this is not a cause for overmuch alarmist hand-wringing. They have changed before. If they change again, there will be those who cling to the old ways just as there were doubtless those in the late Middle Ages who swore by the handwritten manuscript and refused to countenance the new-fangled creations of Gutenberg and Caxton. Yet, for the majority who embrace the new technologies, the content will be the same. It will only be the form in which that content is presented that has changed.

The second way in which technology might be viewed as a threat to the book in general, and the novel in particular, may seem more insidious. It is safe to assume that there will never come a time when we don't need and demand stories of some kind. There have been many attempts to define the essential qualities of *Homo sapiens* – man the tool-maker, man the hunter and so on. A better way might to be talk of man the storyteller. Every human culture that has ever existed has needed stories and narratives to help its members give meaning and coherence to their lives. Books have been one effective way of presenting these stories but, Jeremiahs insist, the last hundred years have seen the development of others which have overtaken the printed word. We live in an age where 'fiction' means, mainly, films, TV soaps, drama series, sitcoms, computer games. These new media fulfil our inherent need for stories. Literary fiction, fiction in the written word, is a minority pleasure and will soon be as dead as a dodo.

So it is claimed. But it seems unlikely. There are many ways in which the stories we have always told ourselves give meaning to our lives. In mythology and religious texts, for example, they provide an explanation for our place and purpose in the world. Just as importantly, stories can engage the emotions and draw us out of the narrow sphere of self into an engagement with others. The usual way to 'live' our emotions, to release their potential, is by sharing them, by communication with other people. Each individual's emotional make-up is as unique – as personal – as a gene pattern, but we spend our whole lives trying to match them with others, and we draw strength and comfort both from the similarities we find and from the differences. Two of the most exciting activities of human life are finding occasions for such emotional dialogue, and pondering the results. We talk to parents, lovers, children, friends, strangers, in a constant attempt to find out their feelings, to measure our response to life against theirs. It is a form of growth, of education. The more we find in common with others, the more we learn about ourselves. Stories, and particularly the stories we read, form a parallel path to this understanding of ourselves and others. As long as this remains true, fiction in the form of written texts, however they are presented to us, seems safe.

The BBC poll for the Big Read in 2003 proved the point. The response was enormous and the range of books in the list the BBC released showed just how many different types of fiction continued to engage our attention. Look down the list (see page 494) and the evidence is clear. There are the classics (Dickens, Tolstoy, Jane Austen and, among twentieth-century writers, Orwell, Steinbeck and F. Scott Fitzgerald), which have proved themselves over many years and seem likely to occur in such polls for as long as pollsters continue to invite our suggestions for the world's greatest books. There are the books which exemplify that much-discussed crossover between adult and children's literature such as the Harry Potter books and the Philip Pullman trilogy. Like the children's classics (*The Wind in the Willows* and *Alice in Wonderland*) that also appear in the list, they win their place because of the ways in which they delight and enthral us with the very basic power of narrative, of storytelling. And there are, happily, the one-off books which resist all the ebbs and flows of fashion and continue to find an audience. Who would have thought that a 1914 novel about the trials and tribulations of a group of painters and decorators in Edwardian England, the only fiction by an Irish socialist called Robert Noonan, would still inspire readers in the twenty-first century? Yet there sits Noonan's book, *The Ragged Trousered Philanthropists* (published under his pseudonym Robert Tressell), alongside the Brontës, Salman Rushdie and Dostoevsky.

As Tressell's book shows, fiction is the ideal way to enter the emotional experi-ence of a vast range of people, from all countries, all periods, all kinds of society. I know Dickens's London, R.K. Narayan's India, Peter Carey's Australia, the 'mean streets' walked by American private eyes, even the future dystopias of William Gibson, as well as I know my own neighbourhood – not because I've been there but because I recognize the way people feel in them and the way the authors distil those feelings into words. This is not cosy escapism, nor living one's life 'vicariously'. It is an enlargement of the necessarily narrow horizons of our own small lives. The world of books is boundless, and is crammed with human beings of every profession, viewpoint, character, moral and ethical persuasion. It covers not only everything that has happened in 'real' human existence, but the infinite possibilities of the imagination. To anyone standing outside, this can seem bewildering. But, as any reader knows, once you start exploring, the experience becomes ever more addictive and enriching. *The Good Reading Guide* aims to offer as large a range of entry paths into undiscovered worlds as possible.

FIVEFORTHEFUTURE

ADAMSON, Gil (born 1961)

Canadian poet and novelist

Gil Adamson is a Canadian poet whose verse has been widely published in the last twenty years but her first novel, *The Outlander*, was not published in the UK until the beginning of 2009. With its originality of expression and its disdain for cliché and the commonplace, it immediately marked Adamson out as a writer to watch. The year is 1903 and Mary Boulton has just shot her husband. Young and half-deranged by the tragedy, the widow (as the narrative insistently describes her) flees from civilization and into the Canadian backwoods. She is chased relentlessly by her husband's brothers, red-haired twins intent on revenge. After joining forces with a reclusive mountain man, and enjoying an unexpectedly intense relationship with him, she settles in a remote mining township where an eccentric minister, the Reverend Bonnycastle, becomes her protector. However, her new-found home is built (literally) on shifting ground and the hunters have not given up the chase. The widow's difficult journey is not yet over. What makes *The Outlander* so memorable is not so much the tale of Mary Boulton's troubled journey through the wilderness (although that is compelling enough) but the language in which it is described. Adamson's first novel is recognisably the work of someone who loves language and savours its ability to re-imagine the world.

📖Read on

◻ Stef Penney, *The Tenderness of Wolves*, Guy Vanderhaeghe, *The Last Crossing*.

HARKAWAY, Nick (born 1972)

British novelist

Nick Harkaway is the pseudonym adopted by Nicholas Cornwell, the son of ❯❯ John Le Carré when, after a successful career as a screenwriter, he published his first novel, *The Gone Away World*, in 2008. The book is an enormously ambitious work of post-apocalyptic SF. Most of the world has been rendered uninhabitable in the Go Away War. Survivors of the war huddle together in the Livable Zone, narrow strips of land which hug the sides of the Jorgmund Pipe. The Pipe is a network of life-support systems pumping out FOX, the mysterious substance which counteracts the bad effects of the devastating superweapon which made the world uninhabitable in the first place. The Civil Freebooting Company, a gang of libertarian troubleshooters led by a charismatic hero called Gonzo Lubitsch, is given the task of extinguishing a fire which threatens the integrity of the Pipe. As they set off to douse the flames, the book abruptly changes direction and plunges readers into the past histories of Gonzo and his men and into the story of how the Go Away War made them who they are. Madly inventive and often very funny, Harkaway's novel was probably the only one published in 2008 that could be legitimately compared (as it was) to both the work of Salman Rushdie and a Mad Max movie.

Read on

◘ ›› China Miéville, *The City and the City*; ›› Neal Stephenson, *Anathem*.

JONES, Sadie (born 1968)
British novelist

Sadie Jones worked for a number of years as a screenwriter before she published her first novel, *The Outcast*, in 2008. The book is set in the 1950s and focuses on Lewis Aldridge who becomes a victim of the hypocrisy and repression that characterise Waterford, the small commuter belt town in the Home Counties where he grows up. As a boy, Lewis is traumatised by his mother's accidental drowning but he discovers that his father, who soon remarries, has little understanding of his grief. The neighbours want only to ignore the whole messy business. As he grows up, Lewis becomes increasingly disaffected and estranged from his father and stepmother. His grief and rage can only be expressed through self-harming, boozing and acts of minor juvenile delinquency which eventually land him in jail. When he emerges from prison and returns to Waterford, the stage is set for another series of confrontations with the small-minded community which has already condemned him. Jones's elegantly written debut novel brings to vivid life both her alienated and damaged protagonist and the people, intent only on maintaining the social status quo, who turn their backs on him.

Read on

◘ ❯❯ Ian McEwan, *Atonement*; Kate Morton, *The House at Riverton*.

RAISIN, Ross (born 1979)

British novelist

Sam Marsdyke is a gangling misfit, nicknamed 'Lankenstein' at school, who works for his father on his isolated Yorkshire hill farm. Expelled from school after what might or might not have been a sexual assault on a fellow pupil, he spends much of his time trudging the hills and brooding on the frustrations and indignities of his life. When a new family moves into the area, the teenage daughter takes centre stage in Marsdyke's fantasies. The girl is lonely herself, exiled from the world she has previously known, and unwittingly she encourages Sam in his delusions. She confides in him her own unhappiness and her plans of escape. The two abscond across the moors and idle teenage disaffection begins to transform itself into something more sinister. *God's Own Country*, which was published in 2008, is the first novel by Ross Raisin, a Yorkshire-born author who won the *Sunday Times* Young Writer of the Year Award the following year. What distinguishes Raisin's book from other first novels of recent years is the narrative voice in which it is told. His odd, isolated and eventually unbalanced protagonist tells his own story and Sam Marsdyke, who blends Yorkshire dialect and colloquialism with flights of imagination and verbal fancy, is like no other character in contemporary fiction. He is both very funny and very disturbing. Raisin's act of fictional ventriloquism in first creating and then sustaining Marsdyke's inner voice suggests that he is a writer with an exciting future ahead of him.

Read on

◘ Sarah Hall, *Haweswater*; Edward Hogan, *Blackmoor*; Patrick McCabe, *The Butcher Boy*.

WROBLEWSKI, David (born 1959)
US novelist

The Story of Edgar Sawtelle was published in 2008 but its author, David Wroblewski, had been working on it for more than a decade. The work shows in the masterly way he unfolds the narrative of his first novel and in the beauty of its prose. Edgar Sawtelle is a mute teenager with an affinity for the dogs which his family breeds on a remote Wisconsin farm. His world is shattered by the sudden and mysterious death of his father and by the affair that later develops between his mother and his uncle. The suspicion that his uncle had something to do with his father's death grows until Edgar can no longer bear to remain at home. He makes the decision to head for Canada with three of the dogs. They never quite make it to the border but, in self-imposed exile from the farm, they discover how to fend for themselves. Joining forces with an eccentric loner named Henry Lamb, Edgar and the dogs seem to have found a new home but the pull of the old one proves too much for the boy. He returns for a final Oedipal confrontation with his mother and her lover. With its echoes of works from *Hamlet* to *Huckleberry Finn*, *The Story of Edgar Sawtelle* is a book that pays tribute to the literary past but it is also a novel of refreshing originality.

Read on

◻ ›› Peter Matthiessen, *Shadow Country*; Ron Rash, *Serena*.

AUTHORENTRIESA–Z

ACKROYD, Peter (born 1949)
British writer

Ackroyd is a biographer as well as a novelist – his much-acclaimed *Dickens* is a rich reconstruction of the novelist's life – and his fiction benefits from a researcher's eye for extraordinary and revealing detail about the past. Often, he blends a modern story with a historical one, and characters from the past move in and out of the contemporary narrative like ghosts. He sets many stories in London (he is the author of *London: A Biography*), and superbly evokes its people and atmosphere, both today and in different periods of the past.

HAWKSMOOR (1985)
This remains the most exhilarating and adventurous of Ackroyd's explorations of a London in which past and present endlessly intertwine. A contemporary detective (the namesake of the seventeenth-century architect) is driven towards a mystical encounter with forces from the past through his investigations of a series of murders in London churches. Part of the narrative is written in a prose which demonstrates Ackroyd's chameleon-like ability to mimic the English of past centuries and its rhythms.

Ackroyd's other novels include Chatterton *(about the eighteenth-century literary forger who committed suicide at the age of 17),* The House of Doctor Dee *(in which the central character inherits a Clerkenwell house once owned by the Elizabethan magus John Dee),* Dan Leno and the Limehouse Golem *(blending the stories of the real Dan Leno, 'the funniest man in England' in nineteenth-century music hall, such literary figures as George Gissing and Karl Marx, and the mysterious serial killer of the 1890s nicknamed the Limehouse Golem),* The Lambs of London *(in which he provides his own fictional version of the lives of Charles and Mary Lamb) and* The Casebook of Victor Frankenstein *(an offbeat re-telling of Mary Shelley's story). He has also written poetry, biographies of T.S. Eliot, William Blake, Sir Thomas More, Shakespeare and Edgar Allan Poe and, in addition to his London 'biography', a characteristically idiosyncratic investigation of the English imagination entitled* Albion.

5

📖**Read on**

◘ to *Hawksmoor*: David Liss, *A Conspiracy of Paper*; Iain Pears, *An Instance of the Fingerpost*; ›› Iain Sinclair, *White Chappell, Scarlet Tracings*.

◘ to Ackroyd's work in general: ›› Michael Moorcock, *Mother London*; ›› Iain Sinclair, *Downriver*; ›› Rose Tremain, *Restoration*; ›› Jeanette Winterson, *Sexing the Cherry*.

ADAMS, Douglas (1952–2001)
British novelist

Adams began his career as a radio joke-writer, and also worked for the TV science fiction series *Doctor Who*. He made his name with a series of genial science fiction spoofs, beginning with *The Hitchhiker's Guide to the Galaxy* (1979). In this, Earthman Arthur Dent, informed that his planet is about to be vapourized to make room for a hyperspace bypass, escapes by stowing away on an alien spacecraft. This is the beginning of a wild journey through time and space, in the course of which he meets the super-cool President of the Galaxy, Zaphod Beeblebrox, discusses the coastline of Norway with Slartibartfast (who won prizes for designing it), watches the apocalyptic floor-show in the Restaurant at the End of the Universe, and discovers the answer to the 'ultimate question about life, the universe and everything'. The other Hitchhiker books (self-contained sequels) are *The Restaurant at the End of the Universe*; *Life, the Universe and Everything*; *So Long, and Thanks for All the Fish* and *Mostly Harmless*.

In 1987 Adams began a second series, this time starring an intergalactic private eye named Dirk Gently. The Gently books are *Dirk Gently's Holistic Detective Agency* and *The Long Dark Teatime of the Soul*. In his later years Adams largely turned away from the printed page to concentrate on projects in other media but the Hitchhiker books remain as the most inspired of all science fiction spoofs.

📖**Read on**

◘ science fiction spoofs in similarly lunatic vein: ›› Harry Harrison, *The Stainless Steel Rat*; Robert Asprin, *Phules Company*.

◘ fantasy spoofs: ›› Terry Pratchett, *The Colour of Magic*; Robert Asprin, *Another Fine Myth*; Robert Rankin, *The Anti-Pope* (and others in the Brentford series); Jasper Fforde, *The Eyre Affair*.

READ ON A THEME:

ADOLESCENCE
Alain-Fournier, *Le Grand Meaulnes*
›› Beryl Bainbridge, *A Quiet Life*
Colette, *The Ripening Seed*
Miles Franklin, *My Brilliant Career*
Jane Gardam, *Bilgewater*
Lesley Glaister, *Digging to Australia*
S.E. Hinton, *That Was Then, This is Now*
›› Rose Tremain, *The Way I Found Her*
›› Antonia White, *Frost in May*
›› Edmund White, *A Boy's Own Story*

See also: Children; Eccentric Families; Parents and Children; Schools; Teenagers

READ ON A THEME:

AFRICA
Chinua Achebe, *Things Fall Apart*
Ronan Bennett, *The Catastrophist*
Paul Bowles, *The Sheltering Sky*
›› William Boyd, *A Good Man in Africa*
Justin Cartwright, *Masai Dreaming*
Giles Foden, *The Last King of Scotland*
›› Nadine Gordimer, *None to Accompany Me*
Abdulrazak Gurnah, *Paradise*
›› Barbara Kingsolver, *The Poisonwood Bible*
›› V.S. Naipaul, *In a Free State*
Ben Okri, *The Famished Road*
Wole Soyinka, *The Season of Anomie*
›› Evelyn Waugh, *Scoop*

AKUNIN, Boris (born 1956)
Russian novelist

Working under the pseudonym of Boris Akunin, the Russian academic Grigory Chkhartishvili (an expert on Japanese culture) has written a series of crime novels that have become wildly popular not only in his own country but around the world. In Erast Fandorin, government special investigator in late nineteenth century Imperial Russia, Akunin has created a character so protean that he can play his part in almost any type of crime fiction from imitation Agatha Christie to espionage thriller. Refusing to take the improbable twists and turns of his plots too seriously, the Russian writer has produced stories which not only pay tongue-in-cheek homage to genre fiction of the past but also have their own individual charm.

THE WINTER QUEEN (2003)
Fandorin made his first appearance, as a naive young police investigator, in a story that begins dramatically with a public suicide in a Moscow park, and he is soon propelled into the company of enigmatic and beautiful women, devious conspirators and a most unlikely Svengali intent on world domination. He is sent to London and there uncovers what he believes to be treachery on an epic scale. Hastening back to Russia he finds that he has got everything upside down and back to front. In a breathless denouement he defeats the forces arrayed against him but only at great personal cost.

The other Fandorin novels to appear in English (there are more awaiting translation) are The Turkish Gambit, Murder on the Leviathan, The Death of Achilles, Special Assignments, The State Counsellor, The Coronation *and* The She Lover of Death. *He has also written three novels about a gauche but resourceful nun in late nineteenth-century Russia who finds herself at the centre of a series of mysteries* – Pelagia and the White Bulldog, Pelagia and the Black Monk *and* Pelagia and the Red Rooster.

🕮Read on
♦ *Pelagia and the White Bulldog* (on a ramshackle family estate where Chekhovian characters idle away their days, the owner's prized white bulldogs are found dead and only Sister Pelagia can work out what their deaths portend).
◻ David Dickinson, *Death on the Nevskii Prospekt*; Jason Goodwin, *The Janissary Tree*; Frank Tallis, *Mortal Mischief*.

ALI, Monica (born 1967)

Bangladeshi-born British novelist

Monica Ali's *Brick Lane*, the story of a young Bangladeshi woman arriving in London to face an arranged marriage with a man twenty years her senior, became a bestseller when it was first published in 2003. It was not difficult to see why it was so successful. Here was an ambitious and absorbing narrative, filled with characters that engaged readers' emotions and attentions, set against the backdrop of a community which had hitherto been inadequately represented in British fiction. *Brick Lane* had many of the reassuring qualities of old-fashioned fiction but it also provided the shock of the new in that it gave a voice to people who had been voiceless. Nazneen, isolated in an East End tower block, speaking no English and obliged to rely on her ineffectual husband, is a character to whom readers can respond and her evolution from shy, tongue-tied teenager to strong and independent woman is at the heart of the book. Since *Brick Lane* propelled her into the limelight, Ali has published two further novels. *Alentejo Blue* took her a long way from Brick Lane with its stories of the assorted inhabitants, both native and ex-pat English, of a Portuguese village named Mamarrosa; *In the Kitchen* returned her to polyglot London in a narrative that focused on a chef in a posh hotel, presiding over a melting pot of staff from all over the world.

🕮 Read on

◻ Nadeem Aslam, *Maps for Lost Lovers*; Romesh Gunesenkera, *The Match*; ❯❯ Zadie Smith, *White Teeth*; Meera Syal, *Anita and Me*.

ALLENDE, Isabel (born 1942)

Peruvian-born Chilean novelist

Allende's first novel, *The House of the Spirits* (1985), was a glowing family tapestry in the magic-realist manner of ❯❯ Márquez's *One Hundred Years of Solitude*, spanning five generations and thronged with larger-than-life characters and supernatural events. She followed this vein in *Eva Luna*, which is particularly evocative of life on a decaying hacienda deep in the tropical bush. *Of Love and Shadows* (see below) added politics to the magic-realist mixture, to devastating effect. *Paula* is a moving account of the death of Allende's daughter which opens out into the story of her own life and the political tragedies of Chile. *The Sum of Our Days* is a memoir of family and friends.

OF LOVE AND SHADOWS (1987)

Irene Beltrán, a journalist, and her photographer-lover Francisco Leal are investigating the disappearance of a disturbed, possibly saintly adolescent. In the jackbooted dictatorship in which they live, however, the child is not simply missing but 'disappeared', one of thousands snatched by the authorities who will never be seen again. Allende surrounds her main characters with a web of fantastic personal history in true magic-realist style. But the further the investigators thread their way through the sadism and ruthlessness of the labyrinthine fascist state, the more fact begins to swallow fairytale. The investigators themselves begin to lose reality – their love affair becomes a swooning parody of romantic fiction – but what they discover grows more and more uncomfortably like real South American life, like nightmare fleshed.

Allende's other books include The Stories of Eva Luna *(a set of long short stories which forms a pendant to Eva Luna),* Daughter of Fortune, Portrait in Sepia *(two novels which have the same setting and some of the same characters as* The House of the Spirits*),* City of the Beasts *and* Zorro, *her own take on the legend of the swashbuckling, masked hero.*

🕮 Read on

Alejo Carpentier, *The Chase*; Stephen Dobyns, *The Two Deaths of Señora Puccini*; Oscar Hijuelos, *The Fourteen Sisters of Emilio Montez O'Brien*; ›› Paulo Coelho, *The Alchemist*; ›› Mario Vargas Llosa, *Captain Pantoja and the Special Service* gives a more farcical view of Allende's terrifying, haunted world.

ALLINGHAM, Margery (1905–66)
British novelist

Allingham wrote 'crime fiction' only in the sense that each of her books contains the step-by-step solution of a crime, and that their hero, Albert Campion, is an amateur detective whose amiable manner conceals laser intelligence and ironclad moral integrity. But instead of confining Campion within the boundaries of the detective-story genre, Allingham put him in whatever kind of novel she felt like writing. Her best book is *The Tiger in the Smoke*, set in an atmospheric, cobble-stones-and-alleyways London filled with low-life characters as vivid as any in ›› Dickens. Like all Allingham's novels, it is not a conventional whodunit, although it contains plenty of mysteries that demand solutions. Jack Havoc, the 'tiger' of the title, escapes from jail and the hunt for this violent convict takes place in an eerie and fog-enshrouded London that Allingham brilliantly evokes.

Allingham's other Campion books include More Work for the Undertakers, Sweet Danger, Traitor's Purse, Police at the Funeral, Hide My Eyes, Look to the Lady *and the short-story collections* Mr Campion and Others *and* Take Two at Bedtime.

📖Read on
◆ *Death of a Ghost* (set in London's eccentric art community and involving – what else? – forged paintings); *The Beckoning Lady*.
◻ Michael Innes, *The Daffodil Affair*; Edmund Crispin, *The Case of the Gilded Fly*; H.R.F. Keating, *A Rush on the Ultimate*; ›› P.D. James, *A Taste for Death*.

READ ON A THEME:

ALL THE WORLD'S A STAGE (books about theatre)
›› Beryl Bainbridge, *An Awfully Big Adventure*
   Caryl Brahms and S.J. Simon, *A Bullet in the Ballet*
›› Angela Carter, *Wise Children*
›› Robertson Davies, *Tempest-Tost*
›› Charles Dickens, *Nicholas Nickleby* (Nicholas's adventures with the Crummles)
›› Thomas Keneally, *The Playmaker*
›› Ngaio Marsh, *Opening Night*
›› J.B. Priestley, *The Good Companions*
›› Mary Renault, *The Mask of Apollo*
›› Barry Unsworth, *Morality Play*

READ ON A THEME:

ALTERED STATES (CHEMICAL FICTION)
   M. Ageyev, *Novel with Cocaine*
   Nelson Algren, *The Man with the Golden Arm*
>> J.G. Ballard, *Cocaine Nights*
>> William S. Burroughs, *Junky*
>> Bret Easton Ellis, *Glamorama*
   Donald Goines, *Dopefiend*
>> Jay McInerney, *The Story of My Life*
   Kevin Sampson, *Powder*
   Hubert Selby Jr, *Requiem for a Dream*
   Alexander Trocchi, *Cain's Book*
>> Irvine Welsh, *Trainspotting*

AMIS, Kingsley (1922–95)
British writer of novels, poems and non-fiction

In the 1950s, when Amis's writing career began, British writers of all kinds – the 'angry young men' – had begun to rant in plays, films and novels about the unfairness, snobbishness and priggishness of life. Whingeing became an artistic form – and Amis's novels showed its funny side. The working-class hero of *Lucky Jim* (1954) tries to conform with his madrigal-singing, right-newspaper-reading, wine-savouring university colleagues, and in the process shows them up for the pretentious fools they are. The central character of *That Uncertain Feeling*, a small-town librarian, thinks that devastating sexual charm will carry him to the pinnacle of local society; the results are farcical. The hero of *Take a Girl Like You* (1960) finds it hard to persuade anyone else in his circle that 'free love' and 'the swinging sixties' are the good things glossy magazines crack them up to be. In the 1960s and 1970s Amis's farcical fires burned low. He began to affect a ponderous, self-consciously right-wing fuddy-duddiness, and abandoned satire for books of other kinds (a ghost story, a James Bond spy story and several science fiction books). In the 1980s, however, he returned to the satirical muttering he always did better than any of his imitators – and his later books (beginning with *The Old Devils*, see below) are among his funniest.

THE OLD DEVILS (1986)

A group of old men, acquaintances for over forty years, meet daily in a Welsh bar to grumble. They are obsessed by failure, their own and the world's. They are especially vitriolic about other people's success – and their discomfort with the world is brought to a peak when one of their 'friends', a famous TV Welshman and an expert on a Dylan-Thomasish poet, comes to settle in the town.

The best of Amis's comic novels not mentioned above are One Fat Englishman, Ending Up, The Folks Who Live on the Hill, Jake's Thing, Stanley and the Women *and* Difficulties With Girls *(a 1988 sequel to* Take a Girl Like You*).* The Anti-Death League *is about a top-secret army unit whose aim is to abolish death and* The Alteration *is set in a fantasy contemporary Britain in which the Reformation never happened and the Catholic Church is all-powerful. His* Memoirs *contain gleefully malicious pen portraits of two dozen former friends.*

🕮Read on

◆ *Jake's Thing*; *Stanley and the Women.*

▫ Malcolm Bradbury, *Eating People is Wrong*; ⟩⟩ A.N. Wilson, *Love Unknown*; Christopher Hope, *Serenity House*; ⟩⟩ Tom Sharpe, *Porterhouse Blue*; ⟩⟩ William Boyd, *A Good Man in Africa*; ⟩⟩ Howard Jacobson, *Peeping Tom*; William Cooper, *Scenes from Provincial Life.*

AMIS, Martin (born 1949)

British novelist

The novels of Amis *fils* are icily satirical, cold with rage at the physical and moral sleaziness of the human race. His characters' preoccupations are sex, drugs, money and success, and they are tormented by failure to win, or keep, all four. ⟩⟩ F. Scott Fitzgerald found similar prancing emptiness in the 'gay young things' of the 1920s. Amis matches those writers' bilious wit and parades his dazzlingly inventive prose style in his pages but adds a pungent view of his own: that the entire generation born after the creation of nuclear weapons is maimed beyond cure, a race of psychotic moral mutants. Few contemporary writers treat such repulsive subject matter so dazzlingly. Amis's novels are compulsively nasty, superbly hard to like.

MONEY (1984)

This is the 'suicide note' of an obese, deranged and despairing film director, stumbling through a New York inferno of fast food, pornography, violence and moronic greed. He is a lunatic in a world that has gone mad; when he opens his mouth to scream, his voice is drowned in the mega-metropolitan carnival, the dance of death that is (for Amis, at least) contemporary America.

Amis's other novels are The Rachel Papers, Dead Babies, Other People, London Fields, Success, Time's Arrow, The Information, Night Train, Yellow Dog *and* House of Meetings. The Moronic Inferno *is a bilious travelogue about the USA, a marvellously raw, non-fiction counterpart to* Money. Experience *is a remarkable memoir, particularly affecting and moving (not words usually applied to Amis's work) in its portrait of his relationship with his father,* ›› Kingsley Amis. War Against Cliché *is a collection from thirty years of literary journalism.* Koba the Dread *is a curious and not very successful work of non-fiction in which an appalled account of Stalin's career is mingled with Amis's ongoing debate with his late father.* The Second Plane *collects his writings about 9/11 and its aftermath.*

⬃Read on

◆ *London Fields* (about a man in apocalypse-hurtling 1999 London trying to write a novel about a woman trying to arrange her murder by a slob of a man fantasizing about winning the world darts championship).

◻ Terence Blacker, *Fixx*; ›› Iain Banks, *The Wasp Factory*; Madison Smartt Bell, *The Year of Silence*; ›› Saul Bellow, *Mr Sammler's Planet*; ›› Jay McInerney, *Model Behaviour*; ›› Will Self, *My Idea of Fun*; ›› Vladimir Nabokov, *Despair*.

READ ON A THEME

ANCIENT GREECE AND ROME
Greece:

Hilary Bailey, *Cassandra, Princess of Troy*
>> William Golding, *The Double Tongue*
Tom Holt, *Olympiad*
Naomi Mitchison, *The Corn King and the Spring Queen*
Steven Pressfield, *Gates of Fire*
>> Mary Renault, *The King Must Die*
>> Gore Vidal, *Creation*

Rome:
>> Lindsey Davis, *The Iron Hand of Mars*
>> Robert Graves, *I, Claudius*
Allan Massie, *Tiberius*
>> Steven Saylor, *Roman Blood*
Thornton Wilder, *The Ides of March*
David Wishart, *Ovid*
Marguerite Yourcenar, *Memoirs of Hadrian*

See also: The Bible; The Middle Ages; Other Peoples, Other Times; Renaissance Europe

ANGELOU, Maya (born 1928)
American autobiographer and poet

As a young woman, Maya Angelou was a singer and actress, touring the world in *Porgy and Bess* and working in New York nightclubs. In the 1960s she became a civil rights activist and spent five years in Africa as a journalist and teacher. Today she is one of America's most respected poets and writers. Her finest work is the reconstruction of her own past life she has made in her volumes of autobiography. Angelou has triumphed in these not only because she has a lively prose style and writes of extraordinary characters and unusual locations, but because she has succeeded in making her own life seem somehow emblematic of an entire black generation's progress from the segregation and oppression of the 1930s through the campaign for civil rights to the present day.

I KNOW WHY THE CAGED BIRD SINGS (1969)

The first of Maya Angelou's five volumes of autobiography records the traumas and tribulations of her upbringing in the American Deep South during the 1930s. Poignantly recording her struggle to forge her own identity and to triumph over the obstacles of being black and poor in a racist society, the book is a scathing indictment of injustice which also manages to be a document of hope and conviction that even the worst of circumstances can be left behind.

Maya Angelou's other autobiographical works are Gather Together in My Name, Singin' and Swingin' and Gettin' Merry Like Christmas, The Heart of a Woman *and* All God's Children Need Travelling Shoes.

⊌Read on

◘ Alex Haley, *Roots*; Zora Neale Hurston, *Their Eyes Were Watching God* (a novel first published in the 1930s which tells the story of a strong black woman triumphing over the odds); ›› Alice Walker, *The Color Purple*.

READONATHEME

THE ANIMAL KINGDOM
   Richard Adams, *Watership Down*
   Aeron Clement, *The Cold Moons*
›› Louis de Bernières, *Red Dog*
   Paul Gallico, *The Snow Goose*
›› Kenneth Grahame, *The Wind in the Willows*
›› Ernest Hemingway, *Fiesta/The Sun Also Rises*
   William Horwood, *Duncton Wood*
   Jack London, *The Call of the Wild*
   Henry Williamson, *Tarka the Otter*

ARNOTT, Jake (born 1961)
British novelist

Pulp fiction combines with immaculately researched social history in Jake Arnott's trilogy of novels set in London's gangster underworld and featuring the homosexual East End racketeer, Harry Starks. Harry first appeared in *The Long Firm* (1999) which made use of five different narrators, each with a different perspective on the gangster, to chart his rise and fall. Arnott's second novel, *He Kills Coppers*, opens in the summer of 1966, as London basks in the sun and enjoys the aftermath of England's World Cup victory. Again making use of several different narrators, Arnott unfolds a gripping story of the seedier side of the swinging sixties. In *truecrime* the setting is the 1990s but the effects of Harry Sparks's gangland reign are still being felt as a young actress, discovering that her father was one of the crime boss's victims, decides she wants revenge on him. The three books have very varied stories to tell but they are held together as a trilogy by the recurring characters (Harry Sparks is only one of many) whose lives we witness, by the pace of Arnott's narrative and by his time-travelling ability to resurrect the sights, sounds and smells of the recent past.

📖 Read on
◆ *Johnny Come Home* (set in a 1970s London where glam rock and political activism meet and collide); *The Devil's Paintbrush* (Arnott travels further back into the past in this story of an encounter between legendary occultist Aleister Crowley and a disgraced imperial hero in the Paris of 1903 and its consequences).
◘ ≫ Christopher Brookmyre, *Quite Ugly One Morning*; Ken Bruen, *London Boulevard*; Simon Kernick, *The Murder Exchange*.

READ ON A THEME

ART FOR ART'S SAKE
Books about art, artists and the art world

≫ Margery Allingham, *Death of a Ghost*
　 Joyce Cary, *The Horse's Mouth*
≫ Tracy Chevalier, *Girl with a Pearl Earring*
≫ Michael Frayn, *Headlong*

Lesley Glaister, *Sheer Blue Bliss*
>> Alan Hollinghurst, *The Folding Star*
Wyndham Lewis, *Tarr*
Shena Mackay, *The Artist's Widow*
>> W. Somerset Maugham, *The Moon and Sixpence*
>> Arturo Pérez-Reverte, *The Flanders Panel*
Irving Stone, *The Agony and the Ecstasy*

ASIMOV, Isaac (1920–92)

US writer of novels, short stories and non-fiction

Asimov published his first story at nineteen, and went on to write over three hundred books, ranging from Bible guides and history textbooks to the science fiction novels and stories for which he is best known. Much of his most seminal science fiction work was written in the 1940s when he (and others) came under the editorial wing of John W. Campbell, the pulp magazine man under whose aegis Golden Age science fiction developed. Strongly plotted and concentrating on ideas more than style, Asimov's novels and stories invite the reader to collaborate in the unfolding of concepts like the famous 'three laws of robotics'.

THE FOUNDATION SAGA (1951–93)

The first three books, a self-contained trilogy, appeared in the 1950s; Asimov added the remaining volumes thirty years later. The Saga is 'space opera' (science fiction soap opera) on a huge scale, an account of political manoeuvrings among nations and civilizations of the far future. Hari Seldon, a professor of psychohistory (statistical and psychological prediction of the future) foresees a disastrous era of war in the galactic empire, and establishes two Foundations on the galaxy's edge, dedicated to safeguarding civilized knowledge until it is again required. The Saga describes the nature and work of each Foundation, their uniting to defeat external threat (from an alien intelligence, the Mule) and their subsequent internecine struggles.

The Foundation novels are Foundation, Foundation and Empire *and* Second Foundation. *Books in the continuation series are* Prelude to Foundation, Foundation's Edge, Foundation and Earth *and the posthumous* Forward the

Foundation. *Asimov's other science fiction novels include* Pebble in the Sky, The Stars Like Dust *and* The Currents of Space.

⛉Read on

◆ Asimov's other major achievement is the robot sequence of books: *I, Robot, The Rest of the Robots, The Caves of Steel, The Naked Sun* and *The Robots of Dawn*.

◘ to the Foundation Saga: ›› Iain M. Banks, *Consider Phlebas* (and the other Culture novels); Gordon R. Dickson, *Tactics of Mistake* (and others in the Dorsai sequence); ›› Robert Heinlein, *The Man Who Sold the Moon*; Peter F. Hamilton, *The Reality Dysfunction*.

◘ other examples of Golden Age, John W. Campbell-inspired science fiction: ›› Robert Heinlein, *Methuselah's Children*; A.E. Van Vogt, *The Voyage of the Space Beagle*.

ATKINSON, Kate (born 1951)
British novelist

Kate Atkinson writes family sagas but they are family sagas unlike any others to be found on the shelves of a library or bookshop. The narrative bounces back and forth between decades, the language and imagery are often poetical and allusive, boundaries between what is real and what is unreal blur. Eccentricity and quirkiness intrude on ordinary lower-middle-class domesticity and the books are often very funny. Her first novel, *Behind the Scenes at the Museum* (1994), is the story of Ruby Lennox, growing up in the family home above a pet shop in York in the 1950s and 1960s. Her womanizing father and her disgruntled mother, dreaming of a Hollywood glamour that would have been preferable to Yorkshire home life, are strongly created characters, as are the other members of the family. Ruby reaches back into the past in search of explanations for family flaws and frailties and the narrative zigzags between the generations, from her great-grandmother's affair with a French photographer to the unruly circumstances of her own life. Kate Atkinson has since written five further novels – *Human Croquet*, the extravagantly told story of a family whose glory days are in the past, *Emotionally Weird*, about a mother and daughter holed up in a decaying family home and telling one another stories of their own and others' lives, and *Case Histories, One Good Turn* and *When Will There Be Good News*, three idiosyncratic but gripping crime novels featuring private investigator Jackson Brodie. *Not the End of the World* is a collection of short stories.

Read on
◆ *Human Croquet*; *Case Histories*

◘ ›› Angela Carter, *Wise Children*; ›› Margaret Atwood, *The Blind Assassin*; Esther Freud, *Gaglow*; Liz Jensen, *The Ninth Life of Louis Drax*; ›› Zadie Smith, *White Teeth*.

LITERARY TRIVIA 1:

FIVE STRANGE AUTHORIAL DEATHS

Pietro Aretino
The sixteenth-century Italian satirist is said to have fallen off his theatre seat laughing and banged his head on the floor with fatal consequences.

›› Arnold Bennett
The author of novels set in his native Potteries died of typhoid as a result of drinking water in a French hotel in a failed attempt to prove it was safe to drink it.

Rainer Maria Rilke
The German poet died of blood poisoning after pricking himself on the thorn of a rose he had picked for a woman friend.

Tennessee Williams
The American playwright choked to death on the plastic top from a nasal spray.

Aeschylus
According to an ancient tradition, the Greek playwright died in Sicily in 456 BC when an eagle, flying high in the sky, mistook his bald head for a stone and dropped a tortoise on it in the hope of breaking open the shell.

ATWOOD, Margaret (born 1939)

Canadian writer of novels, short stories and poems

Atwood is a poet as well as a novelist, and her gifts of precise observation and exact description illuminate all her work. She is fascinated by the balance of power between person and person, and by the way our apparently coherent actions and sayings actually float on a sea of turbulent unseen emotion. Her books often follow the progress of relationships, or of one person's self-discovery. The heroine of *Life Before Man*, for example, is caught up in a sexual quadrilateral (one of whose members, her lover, has just committed suicide), and our interest is as much in seeing how she copes with her own chaotic feelings as in the progress of the affair itself. In *Cat's Eye* a middle-aged painter returns to Toronto, remembers her dismal childhood and adolescence there, and finally comes to terms with the bully who made her life miserable as a schoolchild and with that bully's appalling, manipulative mother. In *The Blind Assassin* an elderly woman attempts to understand the secret history of her family and to unravel the enigma of her sister's death many decades before. Many writers have tackled similar themes, but Atwood's books give a unique impression that each moment, each feeling, is being looked at through a microscope, as if the swirling, nagging 'real' world has been momentarily put aside for something more urgent which may just – her characters consistently put hope above experience – make sense of it.

THE HANDMAID'S TALE (1985)

This dazzling dystopian novel, at once Atwood's most savage book and a departure from her usual Canadian stamping grounds, is set in the twenty-first-century Republic of Gilead. In this benighted state, fundamentalist Christianity rules and the laws are those of Genesis. Women are chattels: they have no identity, no privacy and no happiness except what men permit them. Offred, for example, is a Handmaid, and her life is devoted to one duty only: breeding. In Gilead public prayers and hangings are the norm; individuality – even looking openly into a man's face or reading a woman's magazine – is punished by mutilation, banishment or death. The book shows Offred's struggle to keep her sanity and her identity in such a situation, and her equivocal relationship with the feminist Underground which may be Gilead's only hope.

Atwood's other novels include Surfacing, The Edible Woman, Bodily Harm, The Robber Bride, Alias Grace, Oryx and Crake, *in which she returns to the dystopian science fiction of* The Handmaid's Tale, *and* The Penelopiad, *a playful retelling of the myth of Odysseus and Penelope.* Dancing Girls, Wilderness Tips, Bluebeard's Egg *and* Moral Disorder *contain short stories.* The Journals of Susannah Moodie *and* True Stories *are poetry collections, and her* Selected Poems *are also available.*

⮂Read on
◆ *Alias Grace* (an exploration of women's sexuality and social roles wrapped up in a gripping story of a nineteenth-century housemaid who may or may not have been a murderess).

◘ to *The Handmaid's Tale*: ›› George Orwell, *Nineteen Eighty-four*.

◘ to *Cat's Eye*: ›› Bernice Rubens, *Our Father*; Lynne Reid Banks, *Children at the Gate*; ›› Alison Lurie, *Imaginary Friends*.

◘ to Atwood's work in general: ›› Doris Lessing, *Martha Quest*; ›› Nadine Gordimer, *A Sport of Nature*; ›› Saul Bellow, *Herzog*.

AUSTEN, Jane (1775–1817)
British novelist

Austen loved the theatre, and the nearest equivalents to her novels, for pace and verve, are the social comedies of such writers as Sheridan or Goldsmith. The kind of novels popular at the time were epic panoramas (like those of ›› Sir Walter Scott), showing the human race strutting and swaggering amid stormy weather in vast, romantic landscapes. Austen preferred a narrower focus, concentrating on a handful of people busy about their own domestic concerns. Her books are about the bonds which draw families together and the ambitions and feelings (usually caused by grown-up children seeking marriage partners) which divide them. Her plots fall into 'acts', like plays, and her dialogue is as precise and witty as in any comedy of the time. But she offers a delight available to no playwright: that of the author's own voice, setting the scene, commenting on and shaping events. She is like a bright-eyed, sharp-tongued relative sitting in a corner of the room watching the rest of the family bustle.

PRIDE AND PREJUDICE (1813)
Genteel Mr and Mrs Bennet and their five grown-up daughters are thrown into confusion when two rich, marriageable young men come to live in the neighbour-

hood. The comedy of the story comes from Mrs Bennet's mother-hen-like attempts at matchmaking, and the way fate and the young people's own inclinations make things turn out entirely differently from her plans. The more serious sections of the novel show the developing relationship between Elizabeth Bennet, the second daughter, and cold, proud Mr Darcy. Although secondary characters (henpecked Mr Bennet, snobbish Lady Catherine de Bourgh, Elizabeth's romantic younger sister Lydia, the dashing army officer Wickham and the toady Mr Collins) steal the limelight whenever they appear, the book hinges on half a dozen magnificent set-piece scenes between Elizabeth and Darcy, the two headstrong young people the reader longs to see realizing their love for one another and falling into one another's arms.

Austen's completed novels are: Northanger Abbey *(a spoof of romantic melodrama, unlike any of her other books),* Sense and Sensibility, Pride and Prejudice, Mansfield Park, Emma *and* Persuasion. *She also left a number of unfinished works, including* The Watsons *(completed by Joan Aiken) and* Sanditon *(finished by Marie Dobbs).*

⮎Read on

♦ *Emma* (about a young woman so eager to manage other people's lives that she fails, for a long time, to realize where her own true happiness lies); *Mansfield Park* (a darker comedy about a girl brought up by a rich, charming family who is at first dazzled by their easy brilliance, then comes to see that they are selfish and foolish, and finally, by unassuming persistence, wins through to the happiness we have hoped for her).

◻ to *Pride and Prejudice*: Emma Tennant, *Pemberley* (ripely romantic sequel, not terribly Austenish but fun for Elizabeth/Darcy lovers); ▶▶ Mrs Gaskell, *Wives and Daughters*.

◻ to *Mansfield Park*. Joan Aiken, *Mansfield Revisited* — the best of many attempts to use Austen's characters and equal Austen's style.

◻ to Austen's work in general: ▶▶ William Thackeray, *Vanity Fair*; ▶▶ E.M. Forster, *A Room With a View*; ▶▶ Alison Lurie, *Only Children*; ▶▶ Barbara Pym, *Excellent Women*; the short stories of ▶▶ Anton Chekhov and ▶▶ Katherine Mansfield.

AUSTER, Paul (born 1947)
US writer

Auster's first book, *Squeeze Play* (1982), was a pastiche of a crime novel and his key work, *The New York Trilogy* (1987, although the individual books appeared separately in 1985 and 1986 as *City of Glass*, *Ghosts* and *The Locked Room*), is also a sly deconstruction job on the detective novel. The trilogy is a more complex narrative than *Squeeze Play*, one in which reader, author and sleuth seem to exchange roles in a strange kind of free-for-all. In the first segment, Quinn, a writer of detective stories, is summoned by someone who wants to get hold of a character called Paul Auster. *Ghosts* sees a detective named Blue hired by White to tail Black and, again, identities seem elastic and fluid. The third volume has the narrator following a friend, the writer Fanshawe, who has vanished, leaving behind not only his writing but also his wife and child. Before long, the mysterious Fanshawe is the one doing the following and the narrator the one being pursued.

Auster's other novels include In the Country of Last Things *(in which a woman searches for her brother in a crumbling, post-apocalyptic city),* The Music of Chance *(in which a professional gambler drifts across America winning and losing at cards),* Mr Vertigo, Moon Palace, The Invention of Solitude, Oracle Night, The Brooklyn Follies *and* Travels in the Scriptorium. The Art of Hunger *consists of essays, largely on literary subjects.* True Tales of American Life, *edited by Auster, is a compelling selection of autobiographical accounts by 'ordinary' Americans.*

☜Read on
♦ *The Invention of Solitude*; *Man in the Dark* (in which the central character imagines a dystopian version of recent American history).
◘ Robert Coover, *Ghost Town* (undermines the Western genre just as Auster undermines the detective story); ≫ Don DeLillo, *Running Dog*; ≫ Thomas Pynchon, *The Crying of Lot 49*; ≫ Michael Chabon, *The Mysteries of Pittsburgh*; Cameron McCabe, *The Face on the Cutting Room Floor* (very different in style and setting but also takes apart the conventions of the detective story to great effect).

READONATHEME:

AUSTRALIA

Murray Bail, *Eucalyptus*
>> Peter Carey, *The True History of the Kelly Gang*
>> Bruce Chatwin, *The Songlines*
Richard Flanagan, *Gould's Book of Fish*
Miles Franklin, *My Brilliant Career*
>> Howard Jacobson, *Redback*
>> Thomas Keneally, *Woman of the Inner Sea*
>> David Malouf, *Remembering Babylon*
H.H. Richardson, *The Getting of Wisdom*
>> Jane Rogers, *Promised Lands*
Nevil Shute, *A Town Like Alice*
>> Patrick White, *A Fringe of Leaves*
>> Tim Winton, *Cloudstreet*

READONATHEME:

AUTHOR, AUTHOR!

Novels featuring famous writers

>> Julian Barnes, *Arthur & George* (Sir Arthur Conan Doyle)
>> Anthony Burgess, *Nothing Like the Sun* (William Shakespeare)
Frederick Busch, *The Night Inspector* (Herman Melville)
>> Tracy Chevalier, *Burning Bright* (William Blake)
>> Helen Dunmore, *Counting the Stars* (Catullus)
Carlos Fuentes, *The Old Gringo* (Ambrose Bierce)
>> Michèle Roberts, *Fair Exchange* (William Wordsworth)
>> Steven Saylor, *A Twist at the End* (O. Henry)
C. K. Stead, *Mansfield* (Katherine Mansfield)
>> Colm Toibin, *The Master* (Henry James)

READ ON A THEME

AUTOBIOGRAPHIES AND MEMOIRS (GHOSTED!)

Margaret George, *The Memoirs of Cleopatra*
>> Robert Graves, *I, Claudius*
>> Joseph Heller, *God Knows* (King David of Israel)
Stephen Marlowe, *The Memoirs of Christopher Columbus*
Rosalind Miles, *I, Elizabeth*
Jude Morgan, *The King's Touch* (Duke of Monmouth)
Robert Nye, *The Voyage of the Destiny* (Sir Walter Raleigh)
Augusto Roa Bastos, *I, The Supreme* (Francia, dictator of Paraguay)

STARTPOINT

AUTOBIOGRAPHY

Writing an autobiography gives you the chance to relive your own life – and to edit it to suit yourself. Although we readers may think that an auto-biography allows us inside the writer's head, this is an illusion. We see only what we are allowed to see, and who is to tell how much is fiction, how much is fact? Often the better known the person, the less interesting the book. Generals' and politicians' memories tend to rehash old battles; showbiz autobiographies tend to revive old triumphs and pay off old scores. Some writers, as different as Maya Angelou and Laurie Lee, have made a speciality out of autobiography and because their books concentrate on place and other people's characters as much as their own, they are often the most enjoyable of all.

>> **Amis, Martin**, ***Experience* (2000)**. The *enfant terrible* of English fiction has now reached middle age, and this reflective book, moving in its medita-tions on time and loss, is one of the results. Very candid, funny and revealing.

>> **Angelou, Maya**, ***I Know Why the Caged Bird Sings* (1969)**. Singer, dancer and black rights activist tells scathing story of growing up in racist Southern USA. Also: *Gather Together in My Name*; *Singin' and Swingin'*

and Gettin' Merry Like Christmas; *The Heart of a Woman*; *All God's Children Need Travelling Shoes*.

Beah, Ishmael, *A Long Way Gone* **(2007)**. Beah recalls his brutalised childhood and his experiences as a boy soldier in the civil wars in Sierra Leone. A mesmerising, eye-opening account of how he lost his true self amidst all the violence and struggled to regain it.

Brittain, Vera, *Testament of Youth* **(1933)**. Upper-middle-class young woman becomes battlefield nurse in the First World War and finds her attitudes to herself and her society completely changed. Also: *Testament of Friendship*; *Testament of Experience*.

Burroughs, Augusten, *Running with Scissors* **(2002)**. Memoir of growing up in a spectacularly dysfunctional American family, in which each potentially harrowing event in an alarming upbringing is transformed into a further episode in a kind of surreal sitcom.

Chang, Jung, *Wild Swans* **(1991)**. The author grew up in Mao's China, only escaping to study abroad after the Cultural Revolution. Through her own story and those of her mother and grandmother, she tells the unhappy story of China in the twentieth century.

Douglass, Frederick, *Narrative of the Life of an American Slave* **(1845)**. Moving recollections of life as a slave in the pre-Civil War South by man who went on to become the first great African American orator and leader.

Durrell, Gerald, *My Family and Other Animals* **(1956)**. Idyllic childhood of young naturalist in 1930s Corfu. The animals are described with zestful seriousness; the humans (including brother ›› Lawrence) are like the cast of some eccentric farce. Also: *A Zoo in My Luggage*; *Birds, Beasts and Relatives*.

Feynman, Richard, *Surely You're Joking, Mr Feynman* **(1985)**. Endearing, entertaining and intellectually stretching memoir by Nobel Prize-winning physicist who added new realms of meaning to the word 'eccentric'.

Frame, Janet, *An Autobiography* **(1990)**. Compendium of three books: *To the Island*, about growing up in rural New Zealand, *An Angel At My Table*, a scarring account of eight years in a mental hospital, and *The Envoy From Mirror City*, about trying to make a career as a writer, falling in love and finding happiness at last.

Gray, Simon, *The Smoking Diaries* **(2004)**. The late playwright's journals, wickedly observant of the faults and foibles of himself and others, are addictively readable and mordantly funny. Followed by *The Year of the Jouncer* and *The Last Cigarette*.

Keenan, Brian, *An Evil Cradling* **(1992)**. Keenan turns his terrible experiences as a hostage in Beirut into a luminous, beautifully written account of suffering, friendship and forgiveness.

>> Lee, Laurie, *Cider With Rosie* **(1959)**. A childhood in rural Gloucestershire is recalled with a loving exactness that never strays into unthinking nostalgia.

>> Levi, Primo, *If This is a Man* **(1987)**. Levi's unsparing memoir of life in Auschwitz forces us to contemplate both the depths and the heights of the human spirit.

McCourt, Frank, *Angela's Ashes* **(1996)**. Compelling story of surviving, with humour and humanity intact, a childhood spent in poverty and deprivation in 1930s and 1940s Limerick. Sometimes harrowing, often very funny. *'Tis* is a sequel continuing McCourt's story after he emigrated to New York as a young man.

Wolff, Tobias, *This Boy's Life* **(1999)**. How to survive the perils and pleasures of a typical American adolescence (in the 1950s) when you're living in a very untypical family.

Also recommended: Andrea Ashworth, *Once in a House on Fire*; Diana Athill, *Somewhere Towards the End*; Brendan Behan, *Borstal Boy*; >> Bruce Chatwin, *What Am I Doing Here?*; Paula Fox, *Borrowed Finery*; >> Robert Graves, *Goodbye to All That*; P.J. Kavanagh, *The Perfect Stranger*; Eric

Lomax, *The Railway Man*; ›› Vladimir Nabokov, *Speak, Memory*; John Peel, *Margrave of the Marshes*; Gwen Raverat, *Period Piece*; Lorna Sage, *Bad Blood*; Wole Soyinka, *Ake*; Peter Ustinov, *Dear Me*; Joan Wyndham, *Love Lessons*.

HIDDENGEM:

EDMUND GOSSE – *FATHER AND SON* (1907)

More than a century after its first publication this remains a classic account of two generations clashing and tells the story of Gosse's relationship with his God-fearing, terrifying father and his attempts to fashion his own character. Philip Gosse was a distinguished nineteenth-century zoologist who refused to accept the ideas of his contemporary Charles Darwin and clung tenaciously to the tenets of fundamental Christianity. As his son struggles to assert himself in the face of his father's formidable presence, an extraordinary portrait emerges of a Victorian family life like no other.

BAINBRIDGE, Beryl (born 1934)
British novelist

In British music-hall and stand-up comedy, there is a tradition of using flat, unemotional words to recount the disasters that happen to perfectly ordinary people, whose boring lives conceal passions and aspirations the speaker can only hint at. Bainbridge's short, dialogue-filled novels do the same thing in print. They are horror stories told like everyday gossip, and their downbeat wit and plain style are essential to the effect. *The Bottle-factory Outing*, for example, is about two women, pathologically jealous of one another, who share a flat and make plans for the seductions and other delights of a works outing – which turns out darkly different from anything either suspected. In several books, Bainbridge uses real historical characters, imagining for them the same kind of chance-ridden, often desperate lives as those of her invented people. *Young Adolf* sends Hitler to a tatty 1919 Liverpool boarding house filled with Bainbridge eccentrics. *The Birthday Boys* is a retelling, a chapter by each of the men involved, of Scott's disastrous 1910–12 Antarctic expedition.

MASTER GEORGIE (1998)

The best and bleakest of Bainbridge's historical fictions, this is the story of Liverpudlian surgeon and photographer George Hardy, who volunteers to take his medical skills to the war in the Crimea. Accompanied by an eccentric entourage of family and friends, including Myrtle, his adoring adoptive sister, and Dr Potter, his increasingly troubled brother-in-law, George flounders through the death and disease of the war in search of meanings that aren't there. Told in a series of narrative voices – including those of Myrtle and Dr Potter – this is a dark, laconic and moving story that long remains in the mind.

Bainbridge's other novels include A Quiet Life, Harriet Said, The Dressmaker, Sweet William, Injury Time, Watson's Apology *and* According to Queeney, *another of Bainbridge's offbeat historical fictions in which Dr Johnson is seen through the often unforgiving eyes of the daughter of a woman with whom he is conducting an intense but platonic relationship.*

✥Read on

◆ *An Awfully Big Adventure* (set in shabby provincial theatre in the bleak 1950s); *Every Man For Himself* (Bainbridge's typically idiosyncratic take on the Titanic disaster).
◘ Paul Bailey, *Sugar Cane*; ›› Ian McEwan, *The Cement Garden*; Alice Thomas Ellis, *The Inn at the Edge of the World*; ›› Hilary Mantel, *The Giant O'Brien*.

LITERARY TRIVIA 2:

THE FIRST TEN PENGUIN PAPERBACKS EVER PUBLISHED (in 1935)

André Maurois: *Ariel* (a book about the poet Shelley that was actually numbered as the very first Penguin)
›› Agatha Christie: *The Mysterious Affair at Styles*
Susan Ertz: *Madame Claire*
›› Ernest Hemingway: *A Farewell to Arms*
Eric Linklater: *Poet's Pub*
Compton Mackenzie: *Carnival*
Beverley Nichols: *Twenty Five*
›› Dorothy L. Sayers: *The Unpleasantness at the Bellona Club*
Mary Webb: *Gone to Earth*
E.H. Young: *William*

BAKER, Nicholson (born 1957)
US writer

The minutiae of life, the tiny details that form the background to most fiction, are brought into the foreground in the early novels of Nicholson Baker. Little happens in a conventional narrative sense but the reader's interest is held by Baker's playfulness with language, his odd, oblique observations and his digressions. In *Room Temperature* the novel's only action (if that is the right word) is the feeding of a baby. *The Mezzanine* centres on the short escalator journey of an office worker to the floor on which he works. This makes the books sound dull and they are anything but. They are short books and Baker crams them with the most extraordinary, offbeat information and speculation, often contained in elaborate footnotes in which the word count substantially outmatches that in the main text. After his early novels, Baker gained a certain notoriety by turning his obsessive attention to sex. *Vox*, explicitly detailed about the delights of telephone sex, was followed by *The Fermata*, the story of an office temp, Arno Strine, who has the ability to freeze time at the snap of his fingers. He uses this ability to explore erotic possibilities not otherwise available to him, undressing women at will, playing sexual practical jokes on those frozen. Some readers will find Baker's knowing ironies and reflections, his stream of consciousness for the designer-label generation deeply irritating. Others will be beguiled by his wit, the attention he gives to the everyday and the way books like *Room Temperature* and *The Mezzanine* reveal the idle, insignificant internal monologues and debates we all conduct as we go about our lives.

Baker's other books (fiction and non-fiction) include U and I, The Size of Thoughts, The Everlasting Story of Nory, Double Fold, A Box of Matches *(in which he returns to the obsessive scrutiny of ephemera that characterized his first books),* Checkpoint *and* Human Smoke, *a long and controversial volume which re-examines some of our myths about the Second World War.*

📖Read on

◘ to *The Fermata*: ›› Will Self, *Cock and Bull*.
◘ to Baker's other fiction: ›› John Updike, *Couples*; ›› Paul Auster, *The New York Trilogy*; Donald Antrim, *The Hundred Brothers*; Gilbert Sorrentino, *Imaginative Qualities of Actual Things*.

BALDWIN, James (1924–87)

US writer of novels, plays and non-fiction

In a series of non-fiction books (*Notes of a Native Son*, *The Fire Next Time*, *No Name in the Street*), Baldwin described the fury and despair of alienated American blacks, urging revolution as the only way to maintain racial identity in a hostile environment. His plays and novels tackle the same theme, but add two more, equally passionate: the way fundamentalist Christianity is a destructive force, and the quest for sexual identity in an amoral world. *Go Tell it on the Mountain* is a novel about a poor Harlem family torn apart by the pressures of born-again Christianity. *Another Country* shows people living lives of increasing desperation in a corrupt, all-engulfing and terrifying New York. *Giovanni's Room* (1956) is about an American in Paris, having to choose between his mistress and his (male) lover.

Baldwin's other novels are Tell Me How Long the Train's Been Gone, If Beale Street Could Talk *and* Just Above My Head; Going to Meet the Man *is a collection of short stories;* The Evidence of Things Not Seen *is a book about a notorious series of child murders in Atlanta in the early 1980s.*

🕮 Read on

▫ Ralph Ellison, *Invisible Man* (a rootless black American travels the USA in search of identity, and finally – as the book becomes increasingly surreal – continues his quest in hell); Richard Wright, *Native Son* (first published in 1940, the story of a young black man driven to crime and murder by racism and deprivation); Chester Himes, *Cotton Comes to Harlem* and his other detective novels (set in a wildly vibrant and violent Harlem and, crime plots apart, are as unsparing as any of Baldwin's books); ▸▸ Maya Angelou's autobiographical sequence, beginning with *I Know Why the Caged Bird Sings* (sunnier reactions to equally abrasive Southern US black experience).

▫ books as bleak as Baldwin's about the conjunction of sex, violence and despair: Jean Genet, *Querelle of Brest*; John Rechy, *City of Night*; John Edgar Wideman, *A Glance Away*.

BALLARD, J.G. (James Graham) (1930–2009)
British novelist

Ballard's pessimism about the human race, with our capacity for violence and destruction, reveals itself in novels which are usually designated science fiction but which stretch the limits of the genre almost to breaking point. Each of these novels takes an aspect of the way we treat the planet, and each other, and extends it towards catastrophe. In some books (e.g. *The Drowned World*, about the melting of the polar ice-caps) human actions trigger natural disaster. In others (e.g. *Concrete Island*, about a man trapped on a motorway island, and *High Rise*, about the effects on human nature of living in ever-higher tower-blocks) we laboriously reconstruct the world as a single, megalopolitan prison cell. *Crash*, which gained a new notoriety as a consequence of David Cronenberg's 1996 film version, delves into dark realms of the psyche in its examination of the sexual allure of car crashes and adds new realms of meaning to the word 'auto-eroticism'. Apart from science fiction, Ballard is best known for *Empire of the Sun* (1984), a powerful auto-biographical novel about a young teenager in a Second World War Japanese internment camp, and its sequel *The Kindness of Women* (1991), about the same boy as a young adult looking for love in post-war England. The novels of his later years straddle the gap between social analysis and social prediction in their depictions of sex and drugs-fuelled decadence. In *Cocaine Nights* the investigation of a fatal fire in an upmarket Spanish resort reveals violence and anarchy lurking beneath a civilized veneer. The apparently utopian business community in the south of France in *Super-Cannes*, 'an ideas laboratory for the new millennium', is the setting for unsettling mind-games and eventual violence.

Ballard's other novels include Hello America *(about European explorers of the future rediscovering a long-abandoned USA),* The Atrocity Exhibition, Millennium People *and* Kingdom Come. The Terminal Beach, Myths of the Near Future, Low-flying Aircraft *and the linked volume* The Vermilion Sands, *and* War Fever *are collections of short stories.* Miracles of Life, *subtitled 'Shanghai to Shepperton', is an autobiography published in the last year of his life.*

📖Read on
♦ *The Day of Creation* (about a scientist trying to find water in drought-stricken Africa, who sees a new river appear miraculously, becomes obsessed with it, and travels up it to find its source and hopefully understand himself); *Rushing to*

Paradise (about a post-apocalypse utopia run by a mad, fundamentalist feminist).
◘ ≫ William S. Burroughs, *The Soft Machine*; ≫ Will Self, *How the Dead Live*; ≫ Philip K. Dick, *Valis*.

BALZAC, Honoré de (1799–1850)
French novelist

Photography was invented during Balzac's lifetime, and there was talk of using it to produce an encyclopedia of human types, catching each trade, profession and character in a suitable setting and at a particularly revealing moment. Balzac determined to do much the same thing in prose: to write a set of novels which would include people of every possible kind, described so minutely that the reader could envisage them as clearly as if they had been photographed. He called the project *The Human Comedy* (*La Comédie Humaine*), and although he died before completing it, it still runs to some 90 pieces of fiction – which can be read separately – and includes over 2,000 different characters.

OLD GORIOT (LE PÈRE GORIOT) (1834)
Goriot is a lonely old man obsessed by love for his two married daughters. He lives in a seedy Parisian boarding-house (whose contents and inhabitants Balzac meticulously describes), and gradually sells all his possessions, and even cuts down on food, to try to buy his daughters' love with presents. They treat him with a contempt he never notices – in fact everyone despises him except Rastignac, a student living in the same house. Goriot's death-bed scene, where he clutches Rastignac's hand thinking that his daughters have come to visit him at last, is one of Balzac's most moving passages, a deliberate evocation of King Lear's death in Shakespeare's play.

The best-known novels from The Human Comedy *are* César Birotteau *(about a shopkeeper destroyed by ambition),* Eugénie Grandet *(a love story, one of Balzac's few books with a happy ending),* Cousin Bette *(about a man whose obsessive philandering tears his family apart) and its companion volume* Cousin Pons. Droll Tales (Contes drolatiques) *is a set of farcical short stories, similar to those in Giovanni Boccaccio's* Decameron *or* The Arabian Nights.

📖Read on

◆ *The Curé of Tours* (like *Le Père Goriot*, a detailed and moving study of desolate old age).

▫ to Balzac's power and emotional bleakness: ›› Émile Zola, *Nana*; François Mauriac, *The Woman of the Pharisees*; Theodore Dreiser, *An American Tragedy*; ›› Carson McCullers, *The Ballad of the Sad Café*.

▫ to his vision of the 'ant-hill of human aspiration', the senseless, self-destructive bustle of affairs: ›› Charles Dickens, *Dombey and Son*; ›› George Gissing, *New Grub Street*.

BANKS, Iain (born 1954)

British novelist

As Iain Banks, Banks writes literary novels, each of them fuelled with dark, obsessive imaginings. His first novel, *The Wasp Factory* (1984), was a disturbing but compelling announcement of his themes. It is the story, in his own words, of Frank Cauldhame, a teenage killer, living with his father on a remote Scottish island where he practises bizarre sacrificial rituals to protect himself against perceived threats. Extremely graphic in its description of blood, death and violence, it is not a book for the queasy but creates its own imagined world with great power. *The Bridge* (1986) explores the fantasies of a man about to die after a car crash – and is set partly on a nightmarish Forth Bridge, partly in the hero's memories of his Scottish childhood, and partly in a mad sword-and-sorcery fantasy adventure into which his fevered imagination projects him. *The Business* (1999) is a tale of corruption and conspiracy in a shadowy, centuries-old organization devoted to the making of money. As Iain M. Banks, Banks writes science fiction, filled with the same wild humour and bizarre imagination. The Culture novels tell of a future society in which technological advance has created super-beings of great longevity and almost limitless capacities. The advanced inhabitants of the Culture come into contact and often conflict with other less-developed societies throughout the galaxies. Banks's science fiction is basically space opera but with an intelligence and sophistication space opera doesn't usually possess.

The other novels he has written as Iain Banks are Walking on Glass, Canal Dreams, Espedair Street, The Crow Road, Complicity, Whit, A Song of Stone, Dead Air *and* The Steep Approach to Garbadale. *The Culture novels are* Consider

Phlebas, The Player of Games, Use of Weapons, Excession, Inversions, Look to Windward *and* Matter. Against a Dark Background, Feersum Endjinn *and* The Algebraist *are three SF novels not set in the Culture.*

ᗰRead on
◘ to Banks's literary novels: ›› Ian McEwan, *The Comfort of Strangers*; ›› Martin Amis, *The Information*; Clive Barker, *The Damnation Game*; ›› Alasdair Gray, *Lanark*.
◘ to his science fiction: Peter F. Hamilton, *The Reality Dysfunction*; Ken McLeod, *The Star Fraction*.

BANVILLE, JOHN (born 1945)
Irish novelist

John Banville is one of the most inventive and intellectually exhilarating novelists of his generation. He uses his fiction to explore the intricate connections between past and present, our shifting and fluctuating sense of personal identity and the personalities of others, and the varying ways we interpret the world and create (or fail to create) our place in it. *Doctor Copernicus* brings to life the Polish/German priest whose theories undermined medieval ideas about man's position in the universe. It was followed by *Kepler* and *The Newton Letter*, a story largely set in contemporary Ireland but with a central character obsessed by writing a biography of Isaac Newton. In the twenty-five years since these three interconnected books (sometimes known as the 'Revolutions Trilogy') were published, Banville has continued to produce fiction which plays sophisticated games with its readers, often undermining or challenging our ideas about narratives and the reliability of narrators. In *The Book of Evidence*, Freddie Montgomery, the narrator, is a man of culture, intelligence and self-awareness. He is also a murderer. The novel is Freddie's chilling dissection of his life and how it has led him to the killing. Half confession and half the self-conscious creation of a persona that may or may not reflect his inner self, Freddie's marshalling of the evidence in his case is another example of Banville's fascination with the unreliable narrator and with mysteries of human motivation.

THE SEA (2005)

Art historian Max Morden is in mourning for his wife, recently dead from cancer, and he returns to a small Irish seaside resort he had visited as a boy. Fastidious and ever so slightly pretentious, Max views the little town and its present-day inhabitants with morose disdain while travelling back in his own mind to the days of his marriage and to the summer in his boyhood when he met the much-admired Grace family. Slowly both narrative and narrator wind towards the revelation of what really happened in the past.

Banville's other novels include Ghosts *and* Athena *(two titles which link with* The Book of Evidence *to form a loose trilogy),* Mefisto, The Untouchable, Eclipse *and* Shroud. *In the last few years, using the pseudonym 'Benjamin Black', he has written two crime novels* (Christine Falls *and* The Silver Swan) *set in 1950s Dublin and a contemporary thriller,* The Lemur.

📖 Read on

◆ *The Untouchable* (a fictional version of the story of the Cambridge spy Anthony Blunt).

◘ to 'The Revolutions Trilogy': >> Peter Ackroyd, *Hawksmoor*; Malcolm Bradbury, *To the Hermitage.*

◘ to *The Book of Evidence*: >> John Lanchester, *The Debt to Pleasure*; >> Vladimir Nabokov, *Lolita.*

◘ to Banville's fiction in general: John McGahern, *That They May Face the Rising Sun*; >> Graham Swift, *Ever After*; >> W.G. Sebald, *The Emigrants.*

BARKER, Nicola (born 1966)

British novelist

A reviewer once described Nicola Barker as having 'a determinedly perverse and ungovernable imagination' and her novels and stories, unmistakably offbeat and quirky, are certainly unlike those of almost any other contemporary novelist. Usually set in some of the least glamorous and scenically attractive areas of contemporary Britain – Palmers Green, the Isle of Sheppey, Canvey Island – her books present a contrast between the mundane, if indefinably sinister, topography and the oddballs who people it: furtive pornographers, a teenage giantess, stalkers and pseudo-religious sages, a man who feeds his right hand to an owl. Her characters are those who, through choice or fate, fail to fit in to society. They are all weirdly memorable, as is Barker's elaborate prose style which is rich in darkly comic metaphor and simile and packed with punning playfulness.

BEHINDLINGS (2002)

The Behindlings, a group of assorted misfits and grotesques, have their own guru in the shape of Wesley, the enigmatic central character. Half down-and-out and half charismatic trickster, Wesley shapes the lives of his followers through a bizarre kind of treasure hunt he is orchestrating. He hands out portentous clues; they track his nomadic wanderings around the country. Arriving in Canvey Island, with a selection of Behindlings in tow, Wesley begins his self-appointed task of turning the everyday world upside down.

📖 Read on

◆ *Wide Open* (a roll-call of eccentrics and walking wounded gather on the Isle of Sheppey in search of redemption and escape from the demons that haunt them). Nicola Barker's other novels are *Reversed Forecast, Small Holdings, Five Miles from Outer Hope, Clear* and *Darkmans. The Three Button Trick* is a collection of short stories.

◘ ≫ A.L. Kennedy, *So I Am Glad*; Magnus Mills, *The Restraint of Beasts*; Ali Smith, *The Accidental.*

BARKER, Pat (born 1943)

British novelist

Barker's early novels told, in a no-nonsense, brisk way, about the lives of ordinary people, usually women, poor and in the north of England. In the 1990s she used the same blunt precision on a completely different subject, the experience of fighting men in the First World War, and produced the award-winning trilogy of *Regeneration, The Eye in the Door* and *The Ghost Road*. Mixing wholly fictional characters like the anti-heroic Billy Prior with real characters such as the poets Siegfried Sassoon and Wilfred Owen and the psychiatrist William Rivers, Barker succeeded in re-imagining the First World War for a new generation of readers. These novels enter into the heads of young men forced to cause, endure and deal with horrors beyond imagining: in short, not the bravado but the waste of war. Our grandparents or great-grandparents brought back tales like these, and Owen turned them into lacerating poems; Barker's books strip away time and distance, giving voices to shadows and the inarticulate, so that you feel that this is exactly what it must have been like to live these nightmares. After completing her First World War trilogy Pat Barker returned to something like the territory of her earlier fiction with *Another World* and *Border Crossing*, in which a child psychiatrist working in the north of England is drawn back into a terrible crime in the past. *Double Vision* again took war as its subject, in a story of a man struggling to come to terms with his experiences in 1990s Sarajevo. Her most recent novel, *Life Class* (2007), returns to the era of her famous trilogy in a story of students at the Slade School of Art in 1914 and their experiences of love and war.

✥Read on

◆ Barker's earlier novels include *Union Street* (filmed as *Stanley and Iris*, with Robert de Niro and Jane Fonda) and the particularly fine *Blow Your House Down*.

▣ to the trilogy: Erich Maria Remarque, *All Quiet on the Western Front* (renowned 1930s novel about German squaddies in the First World War); ›› Sebastian Faulks, *Birdsong*; ›› Norman Mailer, *The Naked and the Dead* (about bewildered young airmen in the Second World War).

▣ to Barker's work in general: ›› Helen Dunmore, *With Your Crooked Heart*; ›› Margaret Forster, *Mother Can You Hear Me?*; Jane Gardam, *Bilgewater*; Anne Fine, *Telling Liddy*.

BARNES, Julian (born 1946)
British novelist

Barnes worked as editorial assistant on the Oxford English Dictionary, and as a drama critic, before becoming a full-time writer in his early thirties. After two enjoyable but ordinary novels, *Metroland* and *Before She Met Me*, he hit form in 1984 with *Flaubert's Parrot*. This is a dazzlingly ironical book about a biographer of ›› Flaubert so obsessed with his subject, so eager to investigate every piece of fluff on Flaubert's carpet or tea-stain on his crockery, that the quest utterly and ludicrously swallows his own identity. Other cunningly contrived fictions have followed in the two decades since *Flaubert's Parrot*. In the linked stories of *A History of the World in 10½ Chapters* (1989), Barnes describes a number of skin-of-the-teeth escapes for the human race, epic voyages from life-threatening reality to one mirage of the radiant future after another: Noah's Ark, the raft of the Medusa, a boatful of Jewish refugees, a film crew in the Amazon rain forest. The book also meditates on love – which, in Barnes's most ironical shift of all, may be the solution to the human dilemma, a solution all his characters are too self-obsessed to see. *England, England* (1998) is a knowing, sophisticated and often very funny satire on ideas of Englishness. A megalomaniac tycoon creates a theme-park England on the Isle of Wight, filled with all those things deemed quintessentially English, and the fantasy land gradually supersedes the real England. In *Arthur and George* (2005), Barnes takes the real story of Arthur Conan Doyle and his attempts to win justice for George Edalji, a wrongly imprisoned solicitor, and creates an elegant narrative of two very different men whose lives collide.

As well as novels under his own name, Barnes has also written private-eye thrillers as Dan Kavanagh. They include Duffy, Going to the Dogs *and* Putting the Boot In. Cross Channel *and* The Lemon Table *are collections of meaty short stories,* Something to Declare *a selection of essays which explore his delight in France and French culture;* Nothing to Be Frightened Of *is a memoir.*

❧Read on

◘ to *Flaubert's Parrot*: ➤➤ Vladimir Nabokov, *Pale Fire*; ➤➤ A.S. Byatt, *The Biographer's Tale.*

◘ to *A History of the World in 10½ Chapters*: ➤➤ Michèle Roberts, *The Book of Mrs Noah.*

◘ to Barnes's other works: ➤➤ Jonathan Coe, *What a Carve Up!*; ➤➤ Ian McEwan, *Enduring Love*; ➤➤ John Lanchester, *The Debt to Pleasure.*

BECKETT, Samuel (1906–89)
Irish writer

Novelist, poet and playwright, Beckett produced work both in French and English, issuing translations as he went along. Most of his novels, and his best-known play *Waiting for Godot*, first appeared in French. As a young man he was ➤➤ Joyce's secretary, and his work owes debts to the monologue which ends *Ulysses* and to the dream-narratives of *Finnegans Wake*. His subject is the futility of human existence, and his characters (the narrators of his books) are tramps, cripples and the insane. His works would be unendurably bleak – many readers find them so –

if they were not lit with a fantastical, death-defying black humour and marked by an almost obsessive interest in the potential and limits of language.

Beckett's main novels are Murphy, Watt *and the trilogy* Molloy, Malone Dies *and* The Unnameable. *His plays include* Waiting for Godot, Endgame, Krapp's Last Tape *and* Happy Days. *His poems are in* Collected Poems in English and French. More Pricks than Kicks *is a collection of early, Joycean short stories.*

☟Read on

◘ ≫ James Joyce, *Ulysses*; Julio Cortazar, *Hopscotch*; Georges Perec, *A Void*; B.S. Johnson, *House Mother Normal*.

BEEVOR, Antony (born 1946)
British historian

Antony Beevor was in the army before becoming a writer and his non-fiction books (he also published four novels in the 1970s and 1980s) are often military history written with a profound sympathy for the ordinary soldiers forced to do the actual fighting in time of war. Beevor's two finest achievements to date deal with the Second World War. In both he provides a sweeping narrative of terrible events without ever losing sight of the individuals caught up in them. *Stalingrad* is a moving account of the ferocious battle for the Soviet city which became a turning point in the war. *Berlin – The Downfall 1945* looks at the bloody *Götterdämmerung* that brought the Second World War in Europe to an end as Allied armies closed in on Berlin from all sides. Both books will satisfy those readers interested in the large-scale tactics and strategy of warfare and those who are drawn to the small-scale human dramas of people struggling to survive in the worst of circumstances.

Antony Beevor's other books include The Battle for Spain, Crete: The Battle and the Resistance, Paris After the Liberation *(with Artemis Cooper) and* D-Day.

☟Read on

◆ *The Mystery of Olga Chekhova* (the intriguing story of a Russian woman who became a film star in Berlin and a spy for the Soviets).
◘ William Craig, *Enemy at the Gates: The Battle for Stalingrad*; Max Hastings, *Armageddon: The Battle for Germany*; Richard Overy, *Russia's War*.

READ ON A THEME

BEFORE THE NOVEL
The novel as we know it was perfected in the eighteenth century. These books preceded it – but are novels in all but name.

Apuleius (second century), *The Golden Ass*
John Bunyan (seventeenth century), *Pilgrim's Progress*
Miguel de Cervantes (sixteenth century), *Don Quixote*
Thomas Malory (fifteenth century), *Morte d'Arthur*
Thomas Nashe (sixteenth century), *The Unfortunate Traveller*
Petronius (first century), *Satyricon*
➤➤ François Rabelais (sixteenth century), *Gargantua and Pantagruel*

BELLOW, Saul (1915–2005)
US novelist and playwright

In Bellow's view, one of the most unexpected aspects of life in the modern world, and particularly in the post-Christian West, is that many people have lost all sense of psychological and philosophical identity. All Bellow's leading characters feel alienated from society. Some are content to suffer; others try to assert themselves, to invent an identity and live up to it – an attempt which is usually both bizarre and doomed. The hero of *The Adventures of Augie March*, trying to model himself on one of ➤➤ Hemingway's men of action, takes his girlfriend lizard-hunting in Mexico with a tame eagle, and is amazed when she leaves him. The hero of *Henderson the Rain King* goes on safari to darkest Africa, only to be taken prisoner by a remote people who think him a god-king and mark him for sacrifice. All of Bellow's fiction is written in a rich and expansive prose and the exuberance of his imagination, clear both in description and in the creation of character, adds life and energy to what is already philosophically intriguing.

HUMBOLDT'S GIFT (1975)
The book's hero, Charlie Citrine, is a wisecracking, streetwise failure. He is a writer whose inspiration has run out, a husband whose wife is divorcing him and whose mistress despises him, an educated man terrified of brainwork. Unexpectedly, a

legacy from a dead friend, a drunken, bawdy poet, turns out to be not the worthless pile of paper everyone imagines but a scenario which forms the basis for a hugely successful film. Wealth is now added to Citrine's problems, and he is battened on by tax officials, accountants, salesmen and an unsuccessful crook who tries to extort from him first money and then friendship. As the novel proceeds, Citrine keeps nerving himself to make the decision – any decision – that will focus his life, and is hampered each time by ludicrous circumstances and by the contrast between his own inadequacy and the memory of his larger-than-life, dead friend.

Bellow's other full-length novels are Mr Sammler's Planet, Herzog, The Dean's December *and* More Die of Heartbreak. *Publication of* Ravelstein, *a novel of mortality and friendship, in 2000 showed that old age had brought little diminution of Bellow's creative zest and imagination.* Dangling Man, The Victim, Seize the Day, A Theft, The Bellarosa Connection *and* The Actual *are mid-length novellas, and his short stories are collected in* Mosby's Memoirs, Something to Remember Me By *and* Him With the Foot in His Mouth. It All Adds Up *is a fat, juicy collection of non-fiction.*

⛟Read on

◆ *Herzog* (about a panic-stricken intellectual who revisits the scenes of his past life trying to find clues to his psychological identity – cue for a magnificent travelogue through the city of Chicago, Bellow's consistent inspiration and this book's other central 'character').

◘ to Bellow's theme of people searching for identity: ▸▸ Albert Camus, *The Fall (La Chute)*; ▸▸ William Golding, *The Paper Men*; Bernard Malamud, *A New Life*; ▸▸ Margaret Atwood, *Surfacing*.

◘ to Bellow's work in general: ▸▸ Philip Roth, *American Pastoral*; Henry Roth, *Call It Sleep*; ▸▸ Mordecai Richler, *Barney's Version*.

BENNETT, Arnold (1867–1931)
British novelist and non-fiction writer

Bennett worked as a journalist (he once edited *Woman's Own*), and then spent eight years in Paris, setting himself up as playwright, novelist and essayist. He was a workaholic, writing hundreds of thousands of words each year, and much of his output was potboiling. But his best novels and stories, set in the area he called 'the

Five Towns' (Stoke-on-Trent and its surrounding conurbations), are masterpieces. They deal in a realistic way with the lives and aspirations of ordinary people (factory hands, shop assistants, housewives) but are full of disarming optimism and fantasy. Bennett's characters have ambitions; they travel, they read, they dream. Apart from the Five Towns novels his best-known works are two books originally written as magazine serials: *The Card* (about a bouncy young man whose japes outrage provincial society but who ends up as mayor) and *The Grand Babylon Hotel*, a set of linked stories about the guests and staff in a luxury hotel.

THE OLD WIVES' TALE (1908)

The lives of two sisters are contrasted: vivacious Sophia and steady Constance. Sophia feels constricted by life in the Five Towns, falls for a handsome wastrel and elopes with him to Paris, where he deserts her. Constance meanwhile marries a clerk in her father's shop, and settles to a life of bored domesticity. The novel charts the sisters' lives, and includes memorable scenes of the 1870 siege of Paris in the Franco-Prussian War. Its concluding section unites the sisters and shows, as their lives draw to a close, that those lives were all they had, that neither achieved anything or made any impact on the world.

The Five Towns novels are Anna of the Five Towns, The Old Wives' Tale, Clayhanger, Hilda Lessways, These Twain *and* The Roll Call. Riceyman Steps, *which tells the tragedy of a miserly secondhand bookseller in London's Clerkenwell, is grimmer and more* >> Zolaesque.

⬦Read on

♦ *Clayhanger*; *Riceyman Steps*.

▣ >> D.H. Lawrence, *The Rainbow*; >> H.G. Wells, *Ann Veronica*; Theodore Dreiser, *Sister Carrie*; >> W. Somerset Maugham, *Of Human Bondage*; >> J.B. Priestley, *Angel Pavement*.

READ ON A THEME

THE BIBLE
Old Testament
Anita Diamant, *The Red Tent*
Jenny Diski, *Only Human*
>> Joseph Heller, *God Knows*
>> Howard Jacobson, *The Very Model of a Man*
>> Thomas Mann, *Joseph and His Brothers*
>> Jeanette Winterson, *Boating for Beginners*

New Testament
>> Anthony Burgess, *The Kingdom of the Wicked*
>> Jim Crace, *Quarantine*
>> Norman Mailer, *The Gospel According to the Son*
George Moore, *The Brook Kerith*
>> Michèle Roberts, *The Wild Girl*
Jose Saramago, *The Gospel According to Jesus Christ*
Henryk Sienkiewicz, *Quo Vadis?*

See also: Ancient Greece and Rome; Other Peoples, Other Times

BINCHY, MAEVE (born 1940)
Irish novelist

Maeve Binchy is usually classified as a romance writer, but this classification can obscure her skill and versatility. Many romance writers appear to write the same novel over and over again. Every Maeve Binchy novel is different, although all demonstrate her humour and humanity. Whether writing about a family in a small Irish village (*The Glass Lake*), a Dublin woman who only becomes her true self when she spends time away from Dublin and her home (*Tara Road*) or two old friends whose friendship becomes something more as they struggle to achieve their ambition of running the best catering company in Dublin (*Scarlet Feather*), Binchy provides affectionate and compelling tapestries of ordinary people's lives and loves.

Maeve Binchy's other novels include Circle of Friends, Echoes, Evening Class, The Firefly Summer, Light a Penny Candle, Silver Wedding, Quentins, Whitethorn Woods *and* Heart and Soul. The Lilac Bus *is a set of linked short stories about the passengers who travel regularly on a small country bus.* Victoria Line, Central Line *is a collection of short stories about passengers on the London Underground.*

📖 Read on
◆ *Echoes*.

◘ Rosamunde Pilcher, *The Shell Seekers*; Edna O'Brien, *The Country Girls*; Patricia Scanlan, *Promises, Promises*; Clare Boylan, *Holy Pictures*; Cathy Kelly, *She's the One*; ›› Marian Keyes, *Watermelon*.

STARTPOINT

BIOGRAPHY
Next to fiction, biography is the most popular of all forms of literature. More 'Lives' are written, bought and borrowed from libraries than at any other time in history; some people read nothing else. Some biographies are works of documentary history, with every phrase checked and verified from first-hand accounts. Others set out to explain their subject, to puzzle out his or her psychological identity as well as narrating the life. Others again (the celeb biographies which enjoy their brief shelf-life) are chiefly for fans: memoirs or snapshots whose main purpose is to remind, not tell. The best biographies, perhaps, do all these jobs at once, so that you end up entertained as well as informed, enriched by what you read.

›› **Ackroyd, Peter,** *The Life of Thomas More* **(1998)**. Novelist and biographer of several great Londoners (Dickens, Blake) turns his attention to the man for all seasons and comes up with a novel but convincing portrait.

Boswell, James, *The Life of Samuel Johnson* **(1791)**. Classic known by all but read by few. Wonderful, word-by-word accounts of Johnson's table talk, evocative scene-setting, full of personal affection for its subject. Like a window thrown open on eighteenth-century London.

Ellmann, Richard, *James Joyce* (1968). Magisterial interpretation of the life and work of Ireland's greatest novelist and exile.

Hodges, Andrew, *Alan Turing: The Enigma* (1983). The troubled life of the Second World War code-breaker and pioneering computer genius whose homosexuality (at a time when its physical expression was illegal) led to tragedy is brilliantly and movingly reconstructed.

>> Holmes, Richard, *Coleridge: Early Visions* (1989) and ***Coleridge: Darker Reflections* (1998)**. Two vividly readable volumes which bring to life the pathos and achievement of Coleridge's struggle to subdue his addiction and fulfil the extraordinary promise of his youth.

>> Holroyd, Michael, *Lytton Strachey* (1968). **>>** Strachey was himself an innovative biographer (*Eminent Victorians*, 1918), but is also interesting as a member of the Bloomsbury Group, an extraordinarily self-obsessed collection of early twentieth-century British writers, artists, critics, autobiographers, biographers and diarists. Holroyd brilliantly untangles their relationships, while still managing to focus on Strachey.

Kershaw, Ian, *Hitler: Hubris 1889–1936* (1998) and ***Hitler: Nemesis 1936–1945* (2000)**. After nearly 50 years Alan Bullock's biography of Hitler has finally been supplanted as the standard work by Kershaw's chilling, two-volume examination of the creation and career of a tyrant.

Lahr, John, *Prick Up Your Ears* (1978). The short life and violent death of legendary playwright Joe Orton evoked, together with his claustrophobic and eventually fatal relationship with Kenneth Halliwell.

Macintyre, Ben, *Agent Zigzag* (2007) The scarcely credible story of Eddie Chapman, a criminal and conman who became one of the greatest double agents of the Second World War, is told in hugely entertaining style.

Motion, Andrew, *Philip Larkin* (1993). Motion, himself a poet and a friend and colleague of Larkin, undertook the difficult task of a biography of an intensely private man and produced one of the best lives of a poet in years.

Sobel, Dava, *Longitude* (1996). Sobel created what became almost a subgenre of biography with this short but compelling account of the clockmaker John Harrison and his search for an accurate means of measuring longitude at sea.

Spurling, Hilary, *The Unknown Matisse* (1998) and *Matisse the Master* (2005). Two brilliantly researched and written volumes which trace the progress of the life and art of one of the twentieth century's greatest painters.

Tillyard, Stella, *Aristocrats* (1994). Entertaining and successful multi-biography in which Tillyard recreates the upper-class eighteenth-century world of the four Lennox sisters.

>> Uglow, Jenny, *Hogarth* (1997). The eighteenth-century London in which Hogarth found the subjects of his art is vividly recreated in this portrait of a man and his times.

Also recommended: Jung Chang and Jon Halliday, *Mao: The Unknown Story*; Amanda Foreman, *Georgiana, Duchess of Devonshire*; Antonia Fraser, *Cromwell: Our Chief of Men*; Patrick French, *Younghusband*; >> Victoria Glendinning, *Jonathan Swift*; Fiona McCarthy, *Byron: Life and Legend*; Simon Sebag Montefiore, *Young Stalin*; >> Charles Nicholl, *Leonardo da Vinci: Flights of the Mind*; James Palmer, *The Bloody White Baron*; Graham Robb, *Rimbaud*; Gitta Sereny, *Albert Speer*; >> D. J. Taylor, *Orwell: The Life*; >> Claire Tomalin, *Samuel Pepys: The Unequalled Self.*

HIDDENGEM:

A.J.A. SYMONS – *THE QUEST FOR CORVO* (1934)

Frederick Rolfe, the self-styled Baron Corvo, was one of the oddest writers ever to put pen to paper and his 1904 novel *Hadrian the Seventh*, in which a failed priest named George Rose, clearly modelled on Rolfe himself, is elected Pope, is a bizarre mixture of authorial paranoia and extravagantly ornate and memorable prose. Symons's book, which honestly reveals the biographer's own difficulties in separating the truth from the elaborate fantasies in which Rolfe cloaked his own life, remains a compelling read.

BLACKBURN, Julia (born 1948)

British writer

Julia Blackburn's first book was a biography of the eccentric English naturalist Charles Waterton and her later works have continued to show an interest in the offbeat and the unusual, and in the lives of those who march to the sound of a different drum. With an unpretentious ease, her books cross the barriers often needlessly erected between genres. Her two novels (*The Book of Colour* and *The Leper's Companions*) employ vivid and sensuous prose to evoke worlds distant in either time or space but her non-fiction works also make use of techniques usually associated with fiction. *Daisy Bates in the Desert*, for example, is the 'true' story of a remarkable Australian woman who lived and worked with the Aborigines of South Australia in the early years of the twentieth century but Blackburn endeavours to convey the thoughts, dreams and fantasies of her subject with the kind of freedom a novelist is allowed with fictional characters. The result is a book that, in its subversive originality, is difficult to pigeonhole or categorize. A more recent book, *With Billie*, uses a series of interviews conducted by an earlier prospective biographer to create an unconventional portrait of the jazz singer Billie Holiday. *The Three of Us* is a memoir which describes her upbringing and her troubled relationship with her father, the poet Thomas Blackburn, and her mother.

✥Read on

◆ *The Emperor's Last Island* (a visit to Saint Helena is the starting point for a book that describes the island today and resurrects its past as the last home of Napoleon Bonaparte).

◘ to *The Emperor's Last Island*: Dea Birkett, *Serpent in Paradise* (about a visit to Pitcairn Island); Jean Paul Kauffmann, *The Black Room at Longwood*.

◘ to Blackburn's non fiction in general: Jenny Diski, *Skating to Antarctica*.

◘ to her novels: ❯❯ Hilary Mantel, *The Giant O'Brien*.

BLACK BRITONS
Diran Adebayo, *Some Kind of Black*
>> Monica Ali, *Brick Lane*
David Dabydeen, *The Intended*
Bernardine Evaristo, *The Emperor's Babe*
Jackie Kay, *Trumpet*
>> Hanif Kureishi, *The Buddha of Suburbia*
>> Andrea Levy, *Never Far From Nowhere*
Samuel Selvon, *The Lonely Londoners*
Meera Syal, *Anita and Me*
>> Zadie Smith, *White Teeth*
Stephen Thompson, *Toy Soldiers*

BLISHEN, Edward (1920–96)
British writer

From the 1950s to the 1990s, Edward Blishen wrote a succession of memoirs, each one focusing on a particular aspect of his life. Chatty, informal and often very funny, these books combine to create a self-portrait of the author as a mildly bemused spectator of the ups and downs of his own life. Blishen's first major success, *Roaring Boys* (1955), recorded his experiences teaching in a tough secondary modern school and further books dealt with his time working the land as a pacifist in the Second World War (*A Cack-Handed War*), his relationship with his father (*Sorry, Dad*) and his everyday life as a freelance broadcaster and writer (*The Disturbance Fee*).

Edward Blishen's other books include Shaky Relations, Donkey Work, A Nest of Teachers, The Penny World, This Right Soft Lot, Uncommon Entrance *and* Mind How You Go, *his final work of autobiography which takes a rueful, poignantly comic look at the perils and indignities of old age. He was also a prolific writer and editor of books for children.*

Read on

◻ ❯❯ Michael Holroyd, *Mosaic*; George Melly, *Rum, Bum and Concertina*; ❯❯ Eric Newby, *Something Wholesale*; Philip Oakes, *Dwellers All in Time and Space*.

BLOOMSBURY LIVES

Jane Dunn, *Virginia Woolf and Vanessa Bell: A Very Close Conspiracy*
Leon Edel, *Bloomsbury: A House of Lions*
P.N. Furbank, *E.M. Forster: A Life*
Angelica Garnett, *Deceived with Kindness*
Gretchen Gerzina, *Carrington*
❯❯ Victoria Glendinning, *Leonard Woolf*
❯❯ Michael Holroyd, *Lytton Strachey*
Hermione Lee, *Virginia Woolf*
Frances Partridge, *Love in Bloomsbury*
Frances Spalding, *Vanessa Bell*

BOOZE AND BOOZERS

Charles Bukowski, *Tales of Ordinary Madness*
Joyce Cary, *The Horse's Mouth*
❯❯ Graham Greene, *The Power and the Glory*
Patrick Hamilton, *Hangover Square*
Charles Jackson, *The Lost Weekend*
❯❯ Malcolm Lowry, *Under the Volcano*
❯❯ Flann O'Brien, *The Poor Mouth*
George Pelecanos, *Down by the River Where the Dead Men Go*
Budd Schulberg, *The Disenchanted*

BORGES, Jorge Luis (1899–1987)
Argentinian short story writer and poet

Until the 1950s Borges worked as a librarian and was an admired poet. He had to give up librarianship when he went blind, but he always claimed that the 'darkness of his eyes' enabled him to see better in his writings. In the 1950s his 'fictions' began to appear in English, and his reputation spread worldwide. A Borges 'fiction' is a short prose piece, ranging in length from a paragraph to a half-dozen pages. Some are short stories, in the manner of ≫ Kipling, Chesterton or ≫ Kafka (whom Borges translated into Spanish). Others are tiny surrealist meditations, zen-like philosophical riddles or prose-poetry. A twentieth-century writer produces a version of Don Quixote for modern times – and it is identical, word for word, to the original. A man meets a mysterious stranger by a riverside, and finds that the stranger is himself. The library of the Tower of Babel is meticulously described. *Labyrinths* is a generous anthology of Borges's work, and gives the flavour particularly of the 'fictions'.

Borges's stories and fictions are in A Universal History of Infamy, Fictions, The Aleph, Dreamings, The Book of Sand *and* Doctor Brodie's Report. *His* Selected Poems *were published in English translation in 1972.*

⮽Read on
◆ *The Book of Imaginary Beings* (descriptions of 120 fanciful creatures from the weirder recesses of the world's imagination: the chimera, the Cheshire cat, the chonchon, the lunar hare, the elephant that foretold Buddha's birth, the 36 lamed wufniks, Haokah the thunder-god, Youwakee the flying girl, and so on).
◘ ≫ Gabriel García Márquez, *Innocent Erendira*; G.K. Chesterton, *The Man Who Was Thursday*; Robert Coover, *Pricksongs and Descants*; ≫ Italo Calvino, *Invisible Cities*.

BOWEN, Elizabeth (1899–1973)
Irish novelist and short story writer

Although Bowen's themes were emotional – loneliness, longing for love, lack of communication – she wrote in a brisk and faintly eccentric style (italicizing the most unlikely words, for example) which gives her stories an exhilarating feeling of detachment from the events and reactions they describe. She was especially skilful at evoking atmosphere in houses or locales – London streets and tube stations during the 1940s Blitz (the setting of 'Mysterious Kor', possibly her finest short story), for example, become places of eerie fantasy rather than reality. Her concern, despite her characters' craving to preserve the social niceties, was to show 'life with the lid off' – and this, coupled with the unpredictability of her writing style, constantly edges her plots from realism through dream to nightmare.

THE DEATH OF THE HEART (1938)

Portia, a naïve sixteen-year-old orphan (in a more modern book she might be twelve or thirteen) goes to live with her stuffy half-brother and his brittle, insecure wife in fashionable 1930s London. Her innocence is in marked contrast to their world-weary sophistication, and they are as exasperated with her as she is with them. Then she falls in what she imagines to be love, and all parties are launched on an ever-bumpier emotional ride.

Bowen's other novels include The House in Paris, The Heat of the Day, A World of Love *and* Eva Trout. *Her short stories are published in* Encounters, Ann Lee's, Joining Charles, The Cat Jumps *and the Second World War collections* Look at All Those Roses *and* The Demon Lover. Bowen's Court *is an idiosyncratic but compelling account of her Anglo-Irish family's history.*

☝Read on

◆ *The Heat of the Day* (in which a doomed love affair is conducted against the backdrop of Second World War London); *Eva Trout.*
◘ to Bowen's novels: ➤ Henry James, *The Wings of the Dove*; ➤ Angus Wilson, *The Middle Age of Mrs Eliot*; ➤ Iris Murdoch, *The Sandcastle.*
◘ to Bowen's short stories: ➤ Elizabeth Taylor, *A Dedicated Man*; ➤ John Fowles, *The Ebony Tower*; ➤ William Trevor, *The Collected Stories.*

BOYD, William (born 1952)
British novelist and screenwriter

Boyd began his career as an Oxford don and a film critic. His early books were serious farces, in the manner of ➤ Waugh's *A Handful of Dust* or *Sword of Honour*. He is particularly biting about ruling-class English idiocy, and the grotesquely inappropriate settings in which it flourishes. *A Good Man in Africa*, for example, detailed the last limp flourishes of colonialism through its portrait of Morgan Leafy, drunken and corrupt representative of Her Majesty's government in the imaginary African state of Kinjanja. In more recent novels Boyd has turned his attention to contemporary London (in *Armadillo*) and also returned to the fictional autobiography form he used so successfully in *The New Confessions* (see below). In *Any Human Heart* an ageing writer looks back on his life and the world in which it has been spent.

THE NEW CONFESSIONS (1987)

The 'autobiography' of John James Todd, from inept adolescence at a hearty Scottish school, through ludicrous and ghastly First World War experiences, to a roller coaster career as one of the founding geniuses of German silent cinema. Throughout his life, Todd is obsessed by making a nine-hour epic based on Rousseau's *Confessions*, and is frustrated at every turn: by the coming of sound, the rise of Hitler, the Second World War and McCarthyism. There are plenty of farcical incidents, but this is none the less a substantial, sombre study of a man in thrall to his own glittering opinion of his past.

Boyd's other books include the novels An Ice Cream War, *set in the forgotten African campaigns of the First World War,* Stars and Bars, Brazzaville Beach, The Blue Afternoon *and* Restless, *a complicated story of espionage and deceit.* On the Yankee Station, The Destiny of Natalie 'X' and Other Stories *and* Fascination *are volumes of short stories.* Nat Tate: An American Artist *is a short, spoof biography which gleefully highlights the idiocies and pretensions of the art world.* Bamboo *is a huge collection of Boyd's reviews and non-fiction writings over a thirty-year period.*

🐢Read on

◆ *An Ice-Cream War*; *Any Human Heart*.
◘ to the early books: ➤➤ Anthony Powell, *What's Become of Waring?*; Malcolm Bradbury, *Stepping Westward*.
◘ to *The New Confessions*: ➤➤ Adam Thorpe, *Still*; ➤➤ Robertson Davies, *What's Bred in the Bone*.
◘ to *Armadillo*: ➤➤ Martin Amis, *The Information*.

BRAGG, Melvyn (born 1939)
British writer

One of the best-known faces on arts TV for the last forty years, Bragg has written some twenty novels, all meatily readable and all dealing with aspects of Englishness. His earlier books are set in his native Lake District, and explore themes of country life and the coming of industrialization in ways reminiscent of ▸▸ Thomas Hardy or ▸▸ D.H. Lawrence, recast in a more contemporary prose style. Typical titles are *The Hired Man*, *Josh Lawton* and *Kingdom Come*. *The Maid of Buttermere* re-tells the story (familiar to Wordsworth and Coleridge) of a late eighteenth-century Lakeland beauty who was seduced by a bigamist and impostor. *Crystal Rooms* is a scathing portrait of the Thatcher London of the 1980s, complete with fat-cat politicians, Garrick Club mediafolk, orphans begging in the streets, cynical stockbrokers and corrupt police. *Credo* was a very different novel from any Bragg had previously written, but was the result of a long-cherished ambition to tell the story of the Christianization of the north of England in the seventh century. The result is one of the most satisfying historical novels of the last two decades, rich in detail, character and conviction. In recent, autobiographical fiction (*The Soldier's Return*, *A Son of War*, *Crossing the Line* and *Remember Me*) Bragg gives a version of his own and his father's lives in the story of Sam Richardson, scarred by the Second World War, and his son Joe who moves from Cumbria via Oxford to the bright lights of London.

⛫Read on

◆ *The Soldier's Return*.

◻ to *Crystal Rooms*: ▸▸ Martin Amis, *London Fields*; ▸▸ Jonathan Coe, *What a Carve Up!*

◻ to Bragg's Cumbria-set books: Stanley Middleton, *The Daysman*; David Storey, *Saville*; ▸▸ D.H. Lawrence, *Sons and Lovers*.

BRIDGET JONES AND FRIENDS
Helen Fielding, *Bridget Jones's Diary*
Katie Fforde, *Living Dangerously*
Jane Green, *Life Swap*
Lisa Jewell, *Ralph's Party*
>> Marian Keyes, *Lucy Sullivan Is Getting Married*
Sophie Kinsella, *The Undomestic Goddess*
Jill Mansell, *The One You Really Want*
Freya North, *Love Rules*
Alexandra Potter, *Be Careful What You Wish For*
Fiona Walker, *Tongue in Cheek*

BRINK, André (born 1935)
South African novelist

In the South Africa of the apartheid era it was impossible for an honest novelist to ignore the central tenet of crude racial injustice on which society was founded. All the country's finest novelists, from >> Nadine Gordimer to >> J.M. Coetzee, had to find their own fictional means to confront it. André Brink's novels have told very different stories in very different forms and voices. *An Instant in the Wind* is an historical novel of great poignancy, set in the eighteenth century, in which the wife of an explorer and a black runaway slave are stranded in the South African wilderness and embark on a doomed love affair as they trek painfully back towards the Cape. In *A Dry White Season* an ordinary, decent man is drawn ever further into a quagmire of state corruption when he persists in the investigation of the death of a man he knew in police custody. Both these and Brink's other novels of the 1970s and 1980s represent, in some ways, his responses to the iniquities of apartheid. In the new South Africa Brink has continued to find interesting ways of exploring his country's past and present. In *Imaginings of Sand* South Africa is on the verge of its first democratic elections and an exile returns to the deathbed of her 103-year-old grandmother. Through her grandmother and the stories she tells, both personal and national, the returned exile learns new truths about the oppressions and deceits of history.

Andre Brink's other novels include Rumours of Rain, A Chain of Voices, An Act of Terror, Devil's Valley, Praying Mantis, The Blue Door *and* Other Lives. A Fork in the Road *is a recently published memoir.*

📖Read on
◘ ❯❯ J.M. Coetzee, *In the Heart of the Country*; ❯❯ Nadine Gordimer, *The Late Bourgeois World*; Breyten Breytenbach, *A Season in Paradise*; Alan Paton, *Cry, The Beloved Country*.

BRONTË, Charlotte (1816–55)

BRONTË, Emily (1818–48)
British novelists

Much has been made of the Brontës' claustrophobic life in the parsonage at Haworth in Yorkshire, and of the way they compensated for a restricted and stuffy daily routine by inventing wildly romantic stories. Their Haworth life was first described by a novelist (❯❯ Mrs Gaskell), and is as evocative as any fiction of the time. In some ways it colours our opinion of their work: for example, if the third sister, Anne, had not been a Brontë, few people would nowadays remember her novels, which are pale shadows of her sisters' books. But Charlotte and Emily need no biographical boosting. They were geniuses, with a (remarkably similar) fantastical imagination, a robust, melodramatic view of what a 'good story' ought to be, and a pre-Freudian understanding of the dark places of the soul. Their brooding landscapes and old, dark houses may have been drawn from life, but what they made of them was an original, elaborate and self-consistent world, as turbulent as dreams.

JANE EYRE (by Charlotte Brontë, 1847)
The plot is a romantic extravaganza about a poor governess who falls in love with her employer Mr Rochester, is prevented from marrying him by the dark secret which shadows him, and only finds happiness on the last page, after a sequence of melodramatic and unlikely coincidences. The book's power is in its counterpointing of real and psychological events. We read about storms, fires, wild-eyed creatures gibbering in attics and branches tapping at the windows – but what we are really being shown is the turmoil in Jane's own soul, the maturing of a personality. This

emotional progress, magnificently described, unifies the book and transmutes even its silliest events to gold.

WUTHERING HEIGHTS (by Emily Brontë, 1847)

The story begins in the 1770s, when a rich Yorkshire landowner, Earnshaw, brings home a half-wild, sullen foundling he names Heathcliff. Heathcliff grows up alongside Earnshaw's own children, and falls in love with Cathy, the daughter. But he overhears her saying that she will never marry him because she is socially above him – and the rest of the novel deals with his elaborate revenge on her whole family and the way the emotional poison is eventually neutralized. As in *Jane Eyre*, desolate moorland and lonely, rain-lashed houses are used as symbols of the passions in the characters' hearts. Heathcliff, in particular, is depicted as if he were a genuine 'child of nature', the offspring not of human beings but of the monstrous mating of darkness, stone and storm.

All three sisters wrote Wordsworthy, nature-haunted poetry. Emily's only completed novel was Wuthering Heights; *Charlotte's were* Jane Eyre, The Professor *and* Villette; *Anne's were* Agnes Grey *and* The Tenant of Wildfell Hall.

📖Read on

◆ to *Jane Eyre*: *Wuthering Heights*.

◆ to *Wuthering Heights*: *Jane Eyre*.

◘ to *Jane Eyre*: ▸▸ Daphne Du Maurier, *Rebecca*; ▸▸ Jean Rhys, *Wide Sargasso Sea* (a prequel, the story of the first Mrs Rochester); ▸▸ Margaret Mitchell, *Gone With the Wind*; George Douglas Brown, *The House With the Green Shutters*.

◘ to *Wuthering Heights*: Lin Haire-Sargeant, *Heathcliff* (romance sequel); R.D. Blackmore, *Lorna Doone*; ▸▸ Thomas Hardy, *Tess of the d'Urbervilles*; ▸▸ Iris Murdoch, *The Unicorn* (about the turbulent passions of a more modern heroine).

BROOKMYRE, Christopher (born 1968)
British novelist

A crime writer like no other, Brookmyre mixes slapstick farce, violent action and a cynical perspective on the ways of the rich and the powerful. His first novel, *Quite Ugly One Morning* (1996), introduced his recurring character Jack Parlabane, a drink-swigging, unillusioned journalist who regularly finds himself involved in murder investigations. Parlabane is not an unfamiliar type in crime fiction but he is saved from cliché by the detail of the Scottish setting in which he operates and by Brookmyre's disenchanted views of Scottish society and politics that inform all the plots. In the second novel, *Country of the Blind*, for example, the murder of a newspaper tycoon, apparently in a burglary gone badly wrong, turns out to be much more than it seems and involves Parlabane in a spectacular web of corruption that stretches from the Scottish Secretary of State downwards. Brookmyre has also written several non-Parlabane books, all equally inventive and with settings as diverse as an oil rig turned tourist spot and a pre-millennium California filled with the deranged and the dangerous.

Brookmyre's other novels are One Fine Day in the Middle of the Night, Not the End of the World, Boiling a Frog, A Big Boy Did It and Ran Away, The Sacred Art of Stealing, Be My Enemy, All Fun and Games Until Somebody Loses an Eye, A Tale Etched in Blood and Hard Black Pencil, The Attack of the Unsinkable Rubber Ducks *and* A Snowball in Hell.

☀Read on

♦ *One Fine Day in the Middle of the Night* (incompetent terrorists take over an international resort on an old oil rig).

◘ ≫ Jake Arnott, *The Long Firm*; Colin Bateman, *Divorcing Jack*; Nicholas Blincoe, *Acid Casuals*; Zane Radcliffe, *Big Jessie*.

BROOKNER, Anita (born 1928)
British novelist

Anita Brookner's novels are written in a stylish, witty, undemonstrative prose – one exactly suiting the characters of her people. They are middle-aged, upper-middle-class women (professors, librarians, novelists): well-off, well-tailored, well-organized and desperately lonely. Something has blighted their emotional lives, leaving them to order their comfortable, bleak existences as best they can, to fill their days. The books reveal what brought them to their condition – usually the actions of others: husbands, parents or friends – but only occasionally show that the problem can be resolved.

LOOK AT ME (1983)

Frances Hinton, librarian at a medical research institute, lives a disciplined, unvarying existence which she compares wistfully with what she imagines to be the exuberant, exciting lives of the research workers and others who use the library. She is 'taken up' by one of the most brilliant men, dazzling as a comet, and by his emotionally extrovert wife. She falls in love and imagines that she is loved in return. But what looks like being a sentimental education in fact teaches her only that all human beings are islands, and that unless we hoard our inner lives and treasure our privacy, we will lose even what peace of mind we have.

Brookner's other novels include A Start in Life, Providence, Hôtel du Lac, A Friend from England, Latecomers, A Family Romance, Falling Slowly, Undue Influence, The Rules of Engagement, The Next Big Thing, Leaving Home *and* Strangers. *Anita Brookner is an expert on eighteenth- and nineteenth-century French art, and has published books about the painters Watteau, Greuze and David.* Soundings *is a collection of art history essays.*

ＲRead on

◆ *Hôtel du Lac*; *A Family Romance*.

◘ Elizabeth Jane Howard, *Something in Disguise*; Edward Candy, *Scene Changing*; ›› A.S. Byatt, *The Virgin in the Garden*; Jenny Diski, *Rainforest*; Susan Fromberg Shaeffer, *The Injured Party*.

BROOKS, Geraldine (born 1955)
Australian born US novelist

Brooks was an award-winning foreign correspondent before she turned to fiction but, rather than mine her experiences in the trouble spots of the world for her novels, she has ventured back into the past in search of stories to tell. Her first novel, *Year of Wonders*, followed the lives of the inhabitants of a seventeenth-century Derbyshire village as they struggled to retain their humanity in the face of an epidemic of the plague. *March*, her second novel, won the Pulitzer Prize for Fiction. It takes as its starting point Louisa May Alcott's *Little Women* but tells its story from the viewpoint not of any of the female characters but of the March girls' father who joins the Union army as a chaplain. An ardent abolitionist, he soon finds his naïve ideas about the brotherhood of all men undermined by the behaviour of the soldiers in his spiritual care. The racism and mindless brutality he witnesses shake his idealism and his body is all but broken by the physical illnesses he endures. As Brooks's narrative progresses, he is forced to find new ways of living with himself and of re-establishing contact with loved ones who cannot begin to understand what he has experienced. *March* takes a much-loved classic and, by changing readers' perspectives, gives it an added and powerful resonance.

Brooks has written one other novel, People of the Book, *and two works of non-fiction –* Nine Parts of Desire, *which explores the experiences of women in Muslim societies, and* Foreign Correspondence, *which chronicles her search as an adult for the pen-pals of her childhood.*

🕮Read on
◆ *People of the Book* (Brooks's most recent novel records the journey through history and through the world of a Hebrew manuscript, a mysterious codex known as the Sarajevo Haggadah).
◻ Joan Brady, *Theory of War*; Charles Frazier, *Cold Mountain*; Mark Slouka, *God's Fool*.

BRYSON, Bill (born 1951)
American travel writer

Bill Bryson was an American journalist and writer living in England who had had some success with books on the quirks of the English language when he hit the jackpot with his first travel book, *The Lost Continent* (1989) which opens with the memorable lines, 'I come from Des Moines, Iowa. Somebody had to.' The book chronicled his return to the small-town America which he had left behind and was painfully funny about what he found there. His second account of his travels, *Neither Here Nor There* (1991), was the story of the author as innocent abroad in Europe, alternately bewildered and amused by the behaviour of the locals. By viewing Germans, Swedes, French and English as an eccentric anthropologist might tribesmen from the hinterlands of Papua New Guinea, Bryson produced a book that was both very funny and surprisingly revealing of the realities of modern Europe. Presenting himself as ordinary bloke rather than veteran traveller, he is often more perceptive than many other writers with more exalted ideas of their own status. And he gives the reader significantly more laughs per page. Bryson followed his first two triumphs with several other books (*Notes from a Small Island, A Walk in the Woods, Down Under*) in the same vein but just as it seemed as if he had settled into a comfortable, if predictable, groove, he surprised many people by changing direction from travel literature to popular science. Bryson is no scientist himself but *A Short History of Nearly Everything* (2003), shows how skilful he is at turning his own voyage of discovery into one that readers can follow and enjoy. His most recent books have been a memoir of growing up in Iowa in the 1950s, *The Life and Times of the Thunderbolt Kid* and a short biography of Shakespeare.

⮑Read on

◘ to the travel books: Pete McCarthy, *The Road to McCarthy*; Tim Moore, *French Revolutions*; ⟫ Eric Newby, *A Short Walk in the Hindu Kush*.
◘ to *A Short History of Nearly Everything*: ⟫ Melvyn Bragg, *On Giants' Shoulders*; Richard Fortey, *Life: An Unauthorised Biography*.

BUCHAN, John (1875–1940)
British novelist

John Buchan combined a literary career with a life in public service, culminating in a five-year period as governor-general of Canada. As befits the works of an imperial administrator, his many novels celebrate British pluck and derring-do. His thrillers play virtuoso variations on the same basic plot. A stiff-upper-lipped hero (often Richard Hannay) discovers a conspiracy to End Civilization As We Know It, and sets out single-handed, or with the help of a few trusted friends, to frustrate it. He is chased (often by the police as well as by the criminals), and wins through only by a combination of physical courage and absolute moral certainty. The pleasure of Buchan's novels is enhanced by the magnificently described wild countryside he sets them in (usually the Scottish highlands or the plains of southern Africa), and by their splendid gallery of minor characters, the shopkeepers, tramps, local bobbies and landladies who help his heroes, often at enormous (if shrugged-off) personal risk.

THE THIRTY-NINE STEPS (1915)
Richard Hannay, returning from South Africa, is told by a chance American acquaintance of a plot to invade England. Soon afterwards the American is killed and Hannay is framed for his murder. To escape two manhunts, one by the

conspirators and the other by the police, he takes to the hills, and only after three hundred pages of breathtaking peril and hair's-breadth escapes does he succeed in saving his country and clearing his name.

Buchan's other thrillers include Huntingtower, John McNab *and* Witchwood *(all set in Scotland), and the Hannay books* Greenmantle, Mr Standfast, The Three Hostages *and* The Island of Sheep. *He also wrote a number of lively historical novels including* The Free Fishers, *set at the time of the Napoleonic Wars,* Midwinter, *a story of Bonnie Prince Charlie's Jacobite Rebellion which includes a young Samuel Johnson as a character, and* The Blanket of the Dark, *an ingenious narrative built round a rightful heir to the Tudor throne and a plot to assassinate Henry VIII.*

⏃Read on

◆ *Greenmantle*; *Mr Standfast*; *Prester John* (an African adventure as exciting and bizarre as anything by ❯❯ H. Rider Haggard).
◘ Erskine Childers, *The Riddle of the Sands*; Geoffrey Household, *Rogue Male.*

BULGAKOV, Mikhail (1891–1940)
Russian novelist and dramatist

During his lifetime Bulgakov was known primarily as a dramatist and a number of his plays were performed at the Moscow Arts Theatre with Stalin among the audience. In private, Bulgakov was fiercely critical of the Soviet regime and wrote a sequence of satirical works mocking its attempts to reshape society. None of these could be published at the time they were written and Bulgakov made great efforts to leave the Soviet Union but these were always thwarted, often on Stalin's personal intervention. Only after the deaths of Bulgakov himself and of the dictator did the writer's hidden manuscripts start to trickle into print and he is now considered one of the greatest Russian authors of the twentieth century.

THE MASTER AND MARGARITA (1967)
Although it had circulated in samizdat form for many years, Bulgakov's masterpiece was not properly published until decades after his death. Beginning with the arrival in Moscow of the Devil, disguised as a black magician named Woland, *The Master*

and Margarita opens out into a many-layered narrative involving a persecuted and paranoid genius (The Master), who has written an unpublished novel about Pontius Pilate, and his one true love (Margarita) who enters into a pact with the Devil to redeem her lover. Flitting between competing stories (we get to read some of the Master's novel as well as witnessing the Devil's trickery in Moscow), the book is an extraordinary work, part fantasy and part satire but wholly original.

Bulgakov's other works include Heart of a Dog, *a surreal novella in which a dog gains human intelligence as the result of experimentation by an archetypal mad professor, and* The White Guard, *a book which reflects his own experiences in the Russian Civil War.*

⮒Read on

◘ J.A.E. Curtis (ed.), *Manuscripts Don't Burn* (a life of Bulgakov largely constructed from his own diaries and letters); ›› Nikolai Gogol, *Dead Souls*; Victor Pelevin, *The Clay Machine Gun* (a contemporary novel which shares Bulgakov's surreal sense of humour).

BURGESS, Anthony (1917–93)
British novelist and non-fiction writer

Originally a composer, Burgess began writing books in his mid-thirties, and poured out literary works of every kind, from introductions to ›› James Joyce to film scripts, from opera libretti to book reviews. Above all he wrote several dozen novels, of a diversity few other twentieth-century writers have ever equalled. They range from fictionalized biographies of Shakespeare (*Nothing Like the Sun*) and the early Christian missionaries (*The Kingdom of the Wicked*) to farce (the four Enderby stories, of which *Inside Mr Enderby* is the first and *Enderby's Dark Lady* is the funniest), from experimental novels (*The Napoleon Symphony*, about Napoleon, borrows its form from Beethoven's Eroica Symphony) to semi-autobiographical stories about expatriate Britons in the Far East (*The Malayan Trilogy*). The literary demands of Burgess's books vary as widely as their contents: the way he finds a form and style to suit each new inspiration is one of the most brilliant features of his work.

A CLOCKWORK ORANGE (1962)

In a grim future Britain, society is divided into the haves, who live in security-screened mansions in leafy countryside, and the have-nots, who swagger in gangs through the decaying cities, gorging themselves on violence. The book is narrated by the leader of one such gang, and is written in a private language, a mixture of standard English, cockney slang and Russian. (Burgess provides a glossary, but after a few pages the language is easy enough to follow, and its strangeness adds to the feeling of alienation which pervades the book.) The young man has committed a horrific crime, breaking into a house, beating up its owner and raping his wife, and the police are 'rehabilitating' him. His true 'crime', however, was not action but thought – he aspired to a way of life, of culture, from which his class and lack of money should have barred him – and Burgess leaves us wondering whether his 'cure' will work, since he is not a brute beast (as the authorities claim) but rather the individuality in human beings which society has chosen to repress.

Burgess's other novels include, among many others, a reflection on what he sees as the death throes of modern Western civilization, 1985, *a gentler,* ›› *Priestleyish book about provincial English in the early twentieth century,* The Piano Players; *and* A Dead Man in Deptford *(an atmospheric novel about Christopher Marlowe – and Elizabethan theatre and espionage).* Little Wilson and Big God *and* You've Had Your Time *are autobiography,* Mozart and the Wolf Gang *is a 'celebration' written for the bicentenary year of Mozart's death,* Urgent Copy *and* Homage to Qwert Yuiop *are collections of reviews and literary articles.* The Devil's Mode *is a collection of short stories.*

Read on

◆ *Earthly Powers* (a blockbuster embracing every kind of twentieth-century 'evil', from homosexual betrayal to genocide, and the Church's reluctance or inability to stand aside from it).

◘ to *A Clockwork Orange*: ›› Aldous Huxley, *Brave New World*; ›› Margaret Atwood, *The Handmaid's Tale*; ›› Russell Hoban, *Riddley Walker*.

◘ to Burgess's historical novels: ›› Michèle Roberts, *The Wild Girl*; Patricia Finney, *Firedrake's Eye*.

◘ to the Enderby comedies: ›› David Lodge, *Small World*; Peter De Vries, *Reuben, Reuben*.

BURROUGHS, WILLIAM S. (1914–97)
US novelist and writer

Norman Mailer, with characteristic extravagance, once said that William Burroughs was one of the few modern American writers who 'might, conceivably, be possessed of genius'. Certainly Burroughs's personal torments – his addictions, his accidental killing of his wife in a drunken game – were transformed in the creation of a body of work that is unlike any other in American literature. Burroughs himself firmly believed in the idea of possession, although he was more often likely to believe himself possessed by evil spirits rather than genius. With one or two exceptions (*Junky*, for instance, is a relatively straightforward account of heroin addiction) Burroughs's work defies the straitjackets of conventional forms. His books are not so much novels as weirdly visionary allegories of the 'outsider' battling against personal demons and the repressive forces of society. Burroughs's adoption of the famous 'cut-up' technique (in which he took texts by himself and others, cut them up into fragments and randomly re-pasted them together) results in books that are bizarre collages of words, images and metaphors. Combine the cut-up technique with Burroughs's magpie raiding of material from sources as diverse as Mayan culture, pop art, assorted conspiracy theories, the work of Wilhelm Reich and science fiction and the outcome is his own unique brand of literature. Burroughs's books are at once baffling, obscene, haunting, funny and liberating.

THE NAKED LUNCH (1959)
More than forty years after it was written, Burroughs's account of an addict's descent into a lurid hell of his own making and his own imaginings retains the power to shock and surprise the reader. The narrator Bill Lee travels his own *via dolorosa* from New York to Tangiers and into a hallucinatory fantasy world, the Interzone, where the forces of darkness and the forces of individual freedom do battle. The book has no conventional narrative form but is a surreal mélange of bitter satire, vividly described nightmares, weird characters (human, animal and insect), opinionated rants and jarringly juxtaposed fragments of text.

Burroughs's other works include The Soft Machine, The Ticket That Exploded, Nova Express, The Wild Boys, The Last Words of Dutch Schultz, Cities of the Red Night, The Place of Dead Roads *and* The Western Lands.

🐙**Read on**

♦ *The Wild Boys*.

◘ ≫ J.G. Ballard, *The Atrocity Exhibition*; Hubert Selby Jr, *Last Exit to Brooklyn*; Alexander Trocchi, *Cain's Book*.

BYATT, A.S. (Antonia Susan) (born 1936)
British novelist

Byatt was a university teacher for twenty years. Her work has many particularly 'academic' qualities: it is erudite, thoroughly researched and coolly authoritative. But it also springs surprises: she deals with intellectuals from the professional and upper middle classes, and shows how their conceits and self-control are undermined by passions and enthusiasms as hard to discipline as they are unexpected. *Shadow of a Sun* (1964) and *The Game* (1967) are each about women who feel eclipsed by more successful relatives: a novelist father in the first book, a sister in the second. (Byatt's sister is ≫ Margaret Drabble.) *The Virgin in the Garden* and its sequel *Still Life* are about two sisters balancing their passion for English literature and their belief that the truth about emotions and ideas is to be found in books, with their discovery that real life, real experience, has many surprises and even more to offer them. *Babel Tower* follows some of the characters from these two novels into the turbulent personal and political world of the early 1960s and the *roman fleuve* seemed to have reached a conclusion with a fourth book, *A Whistling Woman*, published in 2001.

POSSESSION (1990)
In this Booker Prize-winning novel Byatt unravels the interlocking lives of two present-day literary researchers who are themselves tracking the lives of two interlocking Victorian poets. As the two academics discover that the nineteenth-century writers, Randolph Ash and Charlotte LaMotte, shared an illicit but all-consuming passion, they themselves stretch the emotional bonds they have placed upon their lives. This imaginative and engaging mixture of literary pastiche, detective story, romance and fairytale remains Byatt's most substantial, most rewarding book.

Byatt's other novels are The Biographer's Tale *which revisits the relationship between literary scholars and the writers they study that was one of the subjects of* Possession *and* The Children's Book. Angels and Insects *consists of two linked short novels, set in Victorian England and splendid on the clash between claustrophobic etiquette and the thrusting intellectual excitement of the time.* The Djinn in the Nightingale's Eye *is made up of retellings of five fairytales;* The Matisse Stories, Sugar and Other Stories, Elementals *and* The Little Black Book of Stories *are all volumes of short stories.*

☞Read on

◆ *Angels and Insects*.
◘ ≫ Angus Wilson, *Anglo-Saxon Attitudes*; ≫ Iris Murdoch, *The Sea, The Sea*; Elizabeth Jane Howard, *Falling*; ≫ Carol Shields, *Mary Swann*.

BYRON, Robert (1905–41)
British travel writer

The 1930s was a decade that saw the publication of many classic works of travel literature (≫ Evelyn Waugh and ≫ Graham Greene, for example, both produced memorable writing in the genre) but critics usually agree that one book from the period outshone all others. Robert Byron's *The Road to Oxiana* is uniquely different from all previous travel writing. 'What *Ulysses* is to the novel between the wars and what *The Waste Land* is to poetry,' Paul Fussell wrote, 'so *The Road to Oxiana* is to the travel book.' An extraordinary mélange of anecdote, eccentric erudition and sensually descriptive prose, Byron's book is an account of a journey which begins in Venice, takes him through the Middle East and on to Oxiana, the country around the River Oxus which forms the boundary between Afghanistan and what was then the Soviet Union. Ahead of his time in his appreciation of Islamic culture (particularly its architecture), Byron was a traveller who managed to be both opinionated and open-minded and he also possessed a remarkable gift for the apposite phrase or unexpected image which illuminated the places he visited. He was killed in the Second World War at the age of only thirty five, when the ship on which he was travelling was torpedoed by a German U-boat, but *The Road to Oxiana* survives as a record of an original and intriguing sensibility.

The Road to Oxiana *is Byron's best-known book by far but he also wrote another account of travel in remote spots,* First Russia, Then Tibet, *and* The Station, *a characteristically offbeat description of a journey to the monasteries of Mount Athos.*

📖 Read on
◆ *The Station.*
◘ ➤➤ Bruce Chatwin, *In Patagonia* (Chatwin was a devotee of Byron's writing and it shows); ➤➤ William Dalrymple, *In Xanadu*; ➤➤ Peter Fleming, *News from Tartary.*

CALVINO, Italo (1923–85)
Italian novelist and short story writer

Calvino's first works followed the grim neo-realist tradition of the late 1940s, treating contemporary subjects in an unsparing, documentary way. But in the 1950s he decided to change his style, to write (as he put it) the kind of stories he himself might want to read. These were fantastic, surrealist tales, drawing on medieval legend, fairy stories, science fiction and the work of such twentieth-century experimental writers as ➤➤ Kafka and ➤➤ Borges. The style is lucid and poetic; the events, however bizarre their starting point, follow each other logically and persuasively, and the overall effect is magical. The people in *The Castle of Crossed Destinies* are struck magically dumb and have to tell each other stories using nothing but tarot cards. In *The Baron in the Trees*, the full-length novel which together with two long stories makes up the volume entitled *Our Ancestors*, a boy abandons the ground for the treetops and – in one of Calvino's most sustained and lyrical *tours de force* – lives an entire, fulfilled life without ever coming down to earth. *If On a Winter's Night a Traveller*, a sequence of interacting chapters from novels that never quite transform themselves into conventional narratives, is a playful examination (half post-modernist meta-fiction, half old-fashioned shaggy dog story) of the pleasures of books and reading. In *Invisible Cities* Marco Polo invents fantasy cities to tickle the imagination of Kubla Khan. Calvino's wide-eyed, bizarre fantasy has been imitated but never surpassed; he is one of the most entrancing writers of the twentieth century.

Calvino's neo-realist books are The Path to the Nest of Spiders *(a novel) and* Adam, One Afternoon *(short stories). His fantasies are collected in* T Zero, Cosmicomics, Invisible Cities, Our Ancestors, The Castle of Crossed Destinies, Mr

Palomar *and* The Watcher and Other Stories. Under the Jaguar Sun *(unfinished at his death) contains three stories on taste, hearing and smell, part of a projected set on the five senses.* Numbers in the Dark *is a posthumous collection of short 'fables', dialogues, essays and other gleanings from newspapers and magazines – an addict's treasure-hoard.* Italian Folktales *reworks traditional material in a similar, uniquely personal way.*

⮩Read on

◘ ❯❯ Thomas Mann, *The Holy Sinner*; ❯❯ Jim Crace, *Continent*; Donald Barthelme, *Snow White*.

◘ Good short-story follow-ups: ❯❯ Jorge Luis Borges, *Fictions*; ❯❯ Angela Carter, *The Bloody Chamber*.

CAMUS, Albert (1913–60)

French novelist and non-fiction writer

Throughout his life, in newspaper articles, plays, essays and novels, Camus explored the position of what he called *l'homme révolté*, the rebel or misfit who feels out of tune with the spirit of the times. His characters recoil from the values of society. They believe that our innermost being is compromised by conformity, and that we can only liberate our true selves if we choose our own attitude to life, our day-to-day philosophy. Camus compared the human condition to that of Sisyphus in Greek myth, forever rolling a stone up a hill only to have it crash back down every time it reached the top – and said that the way to cope with this situation was to abandon ambition and concentrate on the here and now. But despite his uncompromising philosophy, his books are anything but difficult. His descriptions of sun-saturated Algeria (in *The Outsider/L'Étranger*), rainy Amsterdam (in *The Fall/La Chute*) or disease-ridden, rotting Oran (in *The Plague/La Peste*) are fast-moving and evocative and he shows the way inner desolation racks his heroes with such intensity that we sympathize with every instant of their predicament and long, like them, for them to break through into acceptance, into happiness.

THE PLAGUE (La Peste) (1947)

Plague ravages the Algerian town of Oran. Quarantined from the outside world, the citizens cope with their tragedy as best they can, either clinging to the outward forms of social life (petty city ordinances; the formalities of religion) or pathetically, helplessly suffering. (For Camus's original readers, the novel was an allegory of France under wartime Nazi occupation.) At the heart of the story are Dr Rieux (the storyteller) and a group of other intellectuals. Each has different feelings about death, and for each of them the plague is not only a daily reality, an external event which has to be endured, but a philosophical catalyst, forcing them to decide what they think about the world and their place in it.

As well as in novels, Camus set out his philosophy in two substantial essays, The Rebel (L'Homme révolté) *and* The Myth of Sisyphus. *His plays are* Caligula, Cross Purpose, The Just Assassins *and* State of Siege *(a stage version of* The Plague*).* Exile and the Kingdom *is a collection of short stories.* The First Man *is a fascinating autobiographical sketch (childhood in Algiers), written in fictional form and posthumously published.*

⌇Read on
◆ *The Fall.*
◻ ❯❯ Saul Bellow, *The Victim*; ❯❯ Hermann Hesse, *Rosshalde*; ❯❯ William Golding, *The Spire*; Simone de Beauvoir, *The Mandarins*; Paul Bowles, *The Sheltering Sky*; ❯❯ Jean-Paul Sartre, *Nausea/Nausée*

READ ON A THEME:

CANADA
❯❯ Margaret Atwood, *Surfacing*
    Marilyn Bowering, *Visible Worlds*
❯❯ Robertson Davies, *The Salterton Trilogy*
    Howard Engel, *The Cooperman Variations*
    Wayne Johnston, *The Colony of Unrequited Dreams*
    Margaret Laurence, *A Jest of God*
❯❯ Brian Moore, *Black Robe*
❯❯ Alice Munro, *Friend of My Youth* (short stories)
❯❯ Mordecai Richler, *Solomon Gursky Was Here*
❯❯ Carol Shields, *Larry's Party*
    Jane Urquhart, *Away*

CAREY, Peter (born 1943)
Australian novelist

A common theme of Australian writers, from Miles Franklin to ❯❯ Patrick White to ❯❯ Thomas Keneally, is the way discovering the vastness of the continent opens up psychological chasms in the souls of their leading characters. Carey follows this grand tradition, but instead of concentrating on Australian vistas, as most of these other writers do, he focuses on the inner torment and turmoil of his people, their precarious grasp on the condition of humanity. *Illywhacker* is the 'autobiography' of an outrageous boaster and liar, who has, it seems, personally supervised the entire history of white people in Australia. In *The True History of the Kelly Gang* Carey tackles the great Australian story, both 'true' and legendary, of the bushwhacker Ned Kelly. Told by the semi-literate Kelly himself, this is a dazzling recreation of the past. *Jack Maggs* skilfully mingles events copied from Dickens's life with a reworking of the plot of *Great Expectations* to create a new narrative that is both a powerful historical novel and a subtle examination of 'character' in life and in fiction.

OSCAR AND LUCINDA (1988)
Oscar Hopkins is a freak of nature: a clumsy, obstinate Anglican clergyman with a genius for gambling. Lucinda Leplastrier is an heiress who buys a glassworks in the hope that it will be her ticket to equality with men. Sadly, for this is the 1850s, both are constricted by the manners and bigotries of their time. They end up in Sydney, planning to transport a glass-and-steel church deep into the Outback – a gamble as ludicrous and as pointless as anything else in their anguished, unsatisfied lives. They think that they are taking on the whole continent of Australia; in fact their battles are chiefly against themselves.

Carey's other novels are Bliss, The Tax Inspector, The Unusual Life of Tristan Smith, My Life as a Fake, Theft *and* His Illegal Self. *He has also published a volume of* Collected Stories. Wrong About Japan *is an idiosyncratic account of Carey's encounters with contemporary Japan and its culture.*

⮒Read on
◆ *My Life as a Fake* (Carey tells of a poet who creates an alter ego that outruns its creator).
◻ to *Oscar and Lucinda*: Rupert Thomson, *Air and Fire*; ❯❯ Matthew Kneale, *English Passengers*.

■ to *The True History of the Kelly Gang*: ›› David Malouf, *The Conversations at Curlow Creek*; Desmond Barry, *The Chivalry of Crime* (Jesse James not Ned Kelly, southern states of the USA not Australia, but the same exploration of the dispossessed driven to crime).

■ to Carey's fiction generally: ›› Patrick White, *Voss*; ›› Thomas Keneally, *The Playmaker*; ›› Tim Winton, *Dirt Music*.

THE CARIBBEAN
Wilson Harris, *The Guyana Quartet*
Jamaica Kincaid, *At the Bottom of the River*
George Lamming, *In the Castle of My Skin*
›› Rosamond Lehmann, *A Sea-Grape Tree*
Earl Lovelace, *The Wine of Astonishment*
›› Andrea Levy, *Fruit of the Lemon*
›› Brian Moore, *No Other Life*
›› Toni Morrison, *Tar Baby*
Shiva Naipaul, *The Chip-Chip Gatherers*
›› V.S. Naipaul, *A Way in the World*
›› Caryl Phillips, *Cambridge*
›› Jean Rhys, *Wide Sargasso Sea*
›› Marina Warner, *Indigo*

CARR, Caleb (born 1955)
US novelist

Caleb Carr is the son of Lucien Carr, a legendary figure in the history of the Beat movement. He had only published one not-very-successful novel and a biography of the nineteenth-century American soldier-of-fortune Frederick Townsend Ward when *The Alienist* (see below) appeared and took the bestseller lists by storm. Since his triumph with this novel, Carr has produced a sequel which highlights his skill in bringing the seamier side of New York's history to life, a homage to Sherlock Holmes and (perhaps surprisingly) a science fiction novel.

THE ALIENIST (1994)

New York in the 1890s and a deranged murderer is butchering young transvestite prostitutes on the streets of the city. Commissioner of Police Theodore Roosevelt is on the case and he gives the job of tracking the killer down to an unconventional task force, led by a pioneer in the science of criminal psychology. Through the eyes of the book's narrator, a journalist named John Schuyler Moore, readers follow the twists and turns of the investigation as Laszlo Kreizler, the 'alienist' of the title, makes use of what were then cutting-edge scientific techniques to track down the killer. *The Alienist* is a book that deserves all the critical acclaim and the high paperback sales it has received. As a reconstruction of 1890s New York, as an exploration of crime, insanity and freewill, and as a compelling, page-turning crime novel, it works superbly.

Caleb Carr's other novels are The Angel of Darkness *(a sequel to* The Alienist, *featuring most of the same characters),* Killing Time *and* The Italian Secretary.

✥Read on
◆ *The Italian Secretary* (Carr provides a new adventure for Sherlock Holmes).
◻ Lawrence Goldstone, *The Anatomy of Deception*; John Maclachlan Gray, *The Fiend In Human*; ≫ Matthew Pearl, *The Dante Club*; Eric Zencey, *Panama*.

CARTER, Angela (1940–92)
British novelist and non-fiction writer

Carter's inspiration included fairytales, Jung's theory of the collective unconscious, horror movies and the fantasies of such writers as ≫ Poe and ≫ Mary Shelley. Above all, she was concerned with female sexuality and with men's sexual predations on women. Her early books range from Gothic reworkings of fairytales (*The Bloody Chamber*) to such surrealist nightmares as *The Passion of New Eve* (see Read On). The novels begin with dream-images and spiral quickly into fantasy. In the opening chapter of *The Magic Toyshop*, for example, fifteen-year-old Melanie walks in a garden at night in her mother's wedding dress – a common, if none too reassuring dream. Soon afterwards, however, Melanie's parents die, she is fostered by a mad toymaker-uncle, and the book climaxes when she is forced to re-enact the myth of Leda and the Swan with a life-sized puppet-swan. Later novels like *Nights at the Circus* (see below) and *Wise Children* (1991) give full rein to Carter's gifts for the baroquely imagined, the theatrical and the picaresque.

NIGHTS AT THE CIRCUS (1984)

Walser, a reporter, is investigating the claims of Fevvers, a winged trapeze artist who may or may not be an angel disguised as a blowsy, turn-of-the-century circus artiste. The story begins with wide-eyed accounts of Fevvers' early life in a brothel, the object of strange and violent male lusts, and continues as she and Walser tour Russia with Colonel Kearney's magic, surreal circus. At first *Nights at the Circus* seems to be jollying up Carter's usual fascination for digging in the darker corners of society, and its gusto and wit continue to the end. But as the story proceeds, events become ever more sinister, and human endeavour is shown more and more to be a hopeless, grubby farce.

Carter's other novels are Shadow Dance, Several Perceptions, Heroes and Villains, Love *and* The Infernal Desire Machines of Dr Hoffman. The Sadeian Woman *is non-fiction, a study of the social and sexual potential of women.* Fireworks, Black Venus *and* American Ghosts and Old World Wonders *collect short stories (among her most disturbing works);* Nothing Sacred *and* Expletives Deleted *collect essays and journalism.*

Read on
◆ *The Passion of New Eve*. (In a near-future USA where armies of blacks, feminists and pubescent children are waging guerrilla war, the young man Evelyn hides in the California desert, only to be kidnapped by devotees of the multi-breasted, all-engulfing Earth Mother, who rapes him, castrates him and remakes him as a woman, Eve).
◘ to *Nights at the Circus*: ›› Jeanette Winterson, *Sexing the Cherry*.
◘ to Carter's work in general: D.M. Thomas, *The White Hotel*; ›› Margaret Atwood, *The Handmaid's Tale*; ›› Kate Atkinson, *Human Croquet*.

CARVER, Raymond (1939–88)
US writer

Once described as 'America's laureate of the dispossessed', Raymond Carver wrote about ordinary-seeming people in the drab rooms, fly-blown diners and dusty streets of boring middle America. Nothing is happening, the people are leading mundane lives – preparing to go out, feeding a neighbour's cat, watching a quarrel in a car park – and yet there is an air of hovering, inescapable disaster. Carver describes atmosphere in brief, poetic phrases; his dialogue is like snippets of real, overheard conversation, tantalizingly incomplete; the effect is unsettling and satisfying, all at once. His collections are *Will You Please Be Quiet, Please*; *What We Talk About When We Talk About Love*; *Where I'm Calling From*; *Cathedral* and *Elephant and Other Stories*. *Fires* and *No Heroics Please* contain poems, essays and other writings, as well as stories. Carver's poems, published in several volumes in his lifetime, are collected in one volume in *All of Us*. *Call If You Need Me* is a posthumous grab-bag of Carver material, including five stories never previously published, several that had never before been collected and all his non-fiction prose.

Read on
◻ to contemporaries of Carver: Richard Ford, *Rock Springs*; Tobias Wolff, *The Collected Stories*; André Dubus, *Finding a Girl in America*.
◻ to classic short story writers whom Carver matches for intensity and precision: ›› Anton Chekhov, *Lady with a Lap Dog*; ›› Katherine Mansfield, *In a German Pension*; William Maxwell, *All the Days and Nights*.

LITERARY TRIVIA 3:

FIVE PROPOSED TITLES FOR FAMOUS NOVELS
Incident at West Egg (*The Great Gatsby*)
›› Scott Fitzgerald always found settling on a title for a novel difficult and went through a number of options for his most famous book, including 'The High-Bouncing Lover', 'Under Red, White and Blue' and this one.

Catch-18 (*Catch-22*)
>> Joseph Heller wanted the dilemma that gives his classic anti-war satire its name to be Catch-18 but Leon Uris had just published a novel called Mila 18, set in the Warsaw Ghetto, and Heller's publishers, keen to avoid confusion, asked him to change the number.

Ba! Ba! Black Sheep (*Gone with the Wind*)
>> Margaret Mitchell's Civil War epic could have ended up with this title or with several other options, including 'Tote the Weary Load' and 'Bugles Sang True'. It seems unlikely that it would have been quite so successful if it had been finally published under any of them.

The Sea Cook (*Treasure Island*)
Long John Silver, the cook aboard the *Hispaniola*, is the most memorable character in the classic adventure story and >> Robert Louis Stevenson's original idea was to name the novel for him.

A Jewish Patient Begins His Analysis (*Portnoy's Complaint*)
The opening section of >> Philip Roth's famous novel was originally published in *Esquire* magazine under this baldly descriptive title and Roth originally intended that the entire work should appear under it.

CATHER, Willa (1876–1947)
US novelist

Most of Cather's books are set in the south-western USA, and are about settlers (often European immigrants) coming to terms with the wilderness. But there is no Hollywood melodrama: her interests are in the contrast between civilized feelings and the wild natural environment, in psychological growth and change. In two characteristic books, *My Antonia* and *A Lost Lady*, the central female characters (the ones who change) are described by men who have watched them, and loved them, from a distance since childhood – a device which allowed Cather the objective, emotional distance from her characters that she preferred. This objectivity and the elegance of her style are two of the most enjoyable features of her books. Her sentences seem placid and unhurried: every event, every description seems to be given the same measured treatment. But nothing is extraneous. Every phrase has emotional or philosophical resonance, and after a few pages the reader is drawn into the narrative, hypnotized by nuance.

DEATH COMES FOR THE ARCHBISHOP (1927)

Based on true events, and on diaries and letters by real people, this novel tells of two French Catholic missionaries to New Mexico in the second half of the nineteenth century. The book is partly about landscape, and contains magnificent descriptions of the desert. But it is mainly concerned with relationships: between the two priests, friends for many years, between the humans and their animals (who have to carry them on long, lonely desert journeys from one Christian settlement to another), and between the missionaries' ancient European culture and the stripped-to-essentials, 'primitive' habits of life and mind of their New Mexican flock.

Two of Cather's novels, The Song of the Lark *and* Lucy Gayheart, *are about young women torn between the claims of family life and an artistic, musical career.* O Pioneers!, *like* My Antonía, *is about foreign immigrants settling in the wilderness. The main character of* The Professor's House *is a successful academic who suddenly feels that he has failed, that lack of danger (emotional, intellectual or physical) has blighted his life. Other novels are* One of Ours *and* My Mortal Enemy. Obscure Destinies *is a collection of short stories.*

⮐Read on

◆ *Shadows on the Rock* (a quiet book about the impact of the North American wilderness on Europeans, this time seventeenth-century settlers in Quebec).
◻ Sarah Orne Jewett, *The Country of the Pointed Firs* (Jewett was an American writer of the previous generation to whom Cather paid particular tribute); ❯❯ Edith Wharton, *Ethan Frome*; William Maxwell, *Time Will Darken It.*

CHABON, Michael (born 1963)

US novelist

Chabon was only twenty-five when he published his debut novel, *The Mysteries of Pittsburgh*, which followed the fortunes of young student Art Bechstein as he ricocheted between a relationship with the flamboyantly charming Arthur Lecomte and an affair with a mysterious and beautiful girl named Phlox. It became a bestseller and its success was such that Chabon, like many another writer, found it difficult to produce a second novel to match it. It was seven years before *Wonder Boys* was published and this turned out to be a quirky comedy about a writer finding it difficult to write a second novel to match his first. Chabon has since found much inspiration in genre and juvenile fiction, the themes and motifs of which he reworks for his own ends. *The Amazing Adventures of Kavalier and Clay* makes use of comic book heroics in its story of two Jewish cousins who taste success in the Golden Age of Comics when they create a superhero named The Escapist; *The Yiddish Policemen's Union* travels into the kind of alternate history more familiar from science fiction than mainstream literature with its story set in an Alaska that has become a homeland for Jews who fled Nazi persecution during World War II; *Gentlemen of the Road*, about two Jewish outlaws in tenth-century Khazaria, is a knowing version of swash and buckle stories from the past.

Chabon's other books are The Final Solution *(a novel),* Summerland *(a fantasy for young adults),* A Model World *and* Werewolves in their Youth *(collections of short stories), and* Maps and Legends *(a volume of essays).*

☜Read on

◘ Joshua Ferris, *Then We Came to the End*; Jonathan Safran Foer, *Extremely Loud and Incredibly Close*; Jonathan Lethem, *Motherless Brooklyn*.

CHANDLER, Raymond (1888–1959)

US novelist

Born in the USA, Chandler was brought to England as a boy and educated at Dulwich College (also the alma mater of ❯❯ P.G. Wodehouse). After a false start in England as a poet and literary journalist and war service in France, Chandler returned to the USA. He became a successful executive in the oil industry until a fondness for the bottle resulted in unemployment. Broke and out of work, Chandler began writing stories for pulp magazines like *Black Mask*, treating violence, prostitution and betrayal in the cynical, hardboiled style popular in films of the time. His ambition was to replace the kind of detective novels then fashionable (stories of bizarre crimes solved by wildly eccentric detectives, distantly modelled on Sherlock Holmes: see ▸▸ Christie and ▸▸ Sayers) with books about realistic crimes, investigated in a plausible way by a detective who would be ordinary, with recognizable human hopes, fears and reactions. Philip Marlowe (Chandler's private-eye hero) is an honest, conscientious man who sweats, cowers and lusts just like anyone else. He narrates the stories himself, in the wisecracking, deadpan style – 'I was neat, clean, shaved and sober, and I didn't care who knew it. I was everything the well-dressed private detective ought to be. I was calling on four million dollars.' – that has become the target of a thousand parodies in the decades since Chandler first perfected it. Emphasizing atmosphere and character even more than plot – 'the ideal mystery is one you would read if the end was missing,' he once remarked – Chandler's novels were among the first to alert more snobbish critics to the potential of genre fiction. They remain great works of American literature, as readable and enjoyable as when they were first published.

FAREWELL, MY LOVELY (1940)

Marlowe, as often, is drifting with nothing particular to do when he is picked up (literally, by the scruff of the neck) by a muscle-bound ex-convict called Moose Malloy, memorably described as 'about as inconspicuous as a tarantula on a slice of angel food'. From this simple event, as ripples spread on a pond, the story grows to take in a priceless necklace, kidnapping, blackmail and murder – and at its heart, like the still centre of a whirlwind, Marlowe slouches from clue to clue, a martyr to his own curiosity, pushing open every door and investigating each alleyway even though he knows, from long experience, that painful or nasty surprises are all he will find.

Chandler's Marlowe novels are The Big Sleep, Farewell My Lovely, The High Window, The Lady in the Lake, The Little Sister, The Long Goodbye *and* Playback. Killer in the Rain *is a collection of short stories.* Poodle Springs, *an unfinished Marlowe novel, was completed in 1990 by Robert B. Parker, whose own Spenser private eye novels provide some of the closest contemporary equivalents to Chandler's wisecracking style.*

Read on

• *The Big Sleep*; *The Lady in the Lake*.

□ Robert B. Parker, *Perchance to Dream* (sequel to *The Big Sleep*). ❯❯ Dashiell Hammett, *The Maltese Falcon*; Ross Macdonald, *The Drowning Pool*; John D. Macdonald, *The Deep Blue Goodbye*.

CHATWIN, Bruce (1940–89)
British novelist and travel writer

A journalist, Chatwin wrote precise, brisk prose – and it utterly belies the contents of his books. Neither fiction nor fact, they straddle the borders between dream and reality, reportage and philosophy. He was fascinated by nomads and the dispossessed, and inserted himself into his work as narrator, as rudderless and amazed as any of his characters. *In Patagonia*, ostensibly a travel book, is a magpie's nest of history, anecdote and self-revelation, set in a South America which seems to shimmer between fantasy and reality. *On the Black Hill*, ostensibly a novel, is a meditation on loneliness and the interaction between landscape and personality, set in the remote Welsh hills. Chatwin's masterpiece, *The Songlines*, is a 'novel' about a white man, 'Bruce Chatwin', travelling in central Australia to investigate the Aboriginal songlines, the paths invisibly traced by the world's ancestors as they sang dream-reality into being. The book is raw with rage about both the whites ('caring people' and 'trash' alike) and the feckless, hopeless Aborigines, and most savage of all about its dogged, put-upon central character, a 1960s hippie floundering out of his depth and out of his time, lost in someone else's dream.

Chatwin's other novels are The Viceroy of Ouidah *and* Utz. What Am I Doing Here *is a fascinating collection of his journalism.*

Read on

• *The Viceroy of Ouidah* (about a slave trader exporting 'black gold' from West Africa to Brazil).

□ Keri Hulme, *The Bone People*; Chinua Achebe, *Things Fall Apart*; Carlos Fuentes, *The Old Gringo*.

CHEKHOV, Anton (1860–1904)

Russian short story writer and playwright

Chekhov paid his way through medical school by writing short comic articles for magazines; in his mid-twenties he began publishing more elaborate pieces, and by the time he was forty (and turning from stories to plays) he was considered one of the finest of all Russian prose writers. Many of his stories are first-person monologues – he said that he was inspired by the sort of things people tell doctors during consultations, or penitents murmur at confession – and, like such monologues, they often reveal far more than the speaker intends. We hear symptoms, as it were, and from them diagnose a whole sick life. In other stories it is as if Chekhov were sitting beside us, drawing our attention to people moving about in the distance, and commenting in a quiet, compassionate way on their motives and feelings. Sympathetic detachment is the essence of his art: reading his stories (like watching his plays) is like looking through a window into other people's lives. The stories have been collected in a number of volumes, including *The Lady with a Lap Dog*, *The Fiancé and Other Stories*, *The Duel and Other Stories* and *The Kiss and Other Stories*.

🕮 Read on

◆ of Chekhov's plays, the nearest in mood to his stories are *Uncle Vanya* and *The Seagull* (Michael Frayn's translations are recommended).
▢ ▸▸ Ivan Turgenev, *Sketches from a Hunter's Album*; ▸▸ Guy de Maupassant, *Selected Stories*; ▸▸ Katherine Mansfield, *In a German Pension*; ▸▸ Raymond Carver, *Where I'm Calling From* (Carver was a great admirer of Chekhov).

CHEVALIER, Tracy (born 1962)

US/British novelist

Born in America but a long-time resident of Britain, Tracy Chevalier had published one novel (*The Virgin Blue*) without setting bookshop tills ringing before her historical fiction set in seventeenth-century Holland, *Girl with a Pearl Earring*, was published in 1999. It became a bestseller and the basis for an Oscar-nominated movie. The novel cleverly takes a well-known painting by Vermeer and provides a story to explain the enigmatic woman who appears in it. Griet is sixteen when she arrives in Vermeer's household to act as a maid and is slowly drawn, despite the difference in age and social class, into an increasingly intimate relationship with her master, eventually acting as his muse and his model. The novel's portrait of the world reflected in classic Dutch painting and of Vermeer's household, thrown into confusion by the arrival of Griet, is moving and convincing. Chevalier's next novel, *Falling Angels*, moved forward several centuries, the events taking place in the years immediately after Queen Victoria's death as two families struggle to deal with the demands of the new century. *The Lady and the Unicorn* takes another work of art, the late fifteenth-century tapestries known as the Lady and the Unicorn cycle, and uses it as the hook on which to hang a story of star-crossed lovers, the artist who created the tapestries and the daughter of the man who commissioned them. Her most recent novel, *Burning Bright*, follows the story of two children in late eighteenth-century London and their entanglement in the life of their neighbour, the poet and painter William Blake.

Read on

◘ Deborah Moggach, *Tulip Fever*; Salley Vickers, *Miss Garnet's Angel*; Susan Vreeland, *Girl in Hyacinth Blue*.

CHILD, Lee (born 1954)
British novelist

Born in Britain, Lee Child (real name Jim Grant) had a successful career in TV there before moving to the USA in 1998, the year after the publication of *Killing Floor* his first novel and the book in which Jack Reacher made his first appearance. While living in the USA, Child has produced a succession of novels with the same protagonist, all of which have now proved to be huge bestsellers. Since his debut in *Killing Floor*, Jack Reacher has shown himself the archetypal macho hero – taciturn, prone to violence and fond of weaponry and gadgetry. *Persuader* (2003), the seventh in the series, is a typical title, told by Reacher in the first person, in which he infiltrates the organisation of a drug lord, and, by slaughtering more or less every male and seducing every female, further establishes his credentials as the twenty-first century equivalent of ›› Ian Fleming's James Bond. From the opening chapter, with an attempted kidnapping that is not quite what it seems, Child does what he always does and throws readers into the deep end of the action. The Reacher books are not subtle and they are not the work of a great prose stylist but they are relentlessly fast-paced and exciting.

The other Jack Reacher novels are Die Trying, Tripwire, The Visitor, Echo Burning, Without Fail, The Enemy, One Shot, The Hard Way, Bad Luck and Trouble, Nothing to Lose *and* Gone Tomorrow.

📖 Read on

▫ David Baldacci, *Last Man Standing*; Jeffery Deaver, *The Bone Collector*; James Patterson, *Along Came a Spider*; John Sandford, *Dark Side of the Moon*.

READ ON A THEME

CHILDREN
- ›› Margaret Atwood, *Cat's Eye*
- ›› Roddy Doyle, *Paddy Clarke Ha Ha Ha*
- Esther Freud, *Hideous Kinky*
- ›› William Golding, *Lord of the Flies*
- L.P. Hartley, *Eustace and Hilda*
- Richard Hughes, *A High Wind in Jamaica*
- Harper Lee, *To Kill a Mockingbird*
- Shena Mackay, *The Orchard on Fire*
- ›› Nancy Mitford, *The Blessing*
- ›› Marcel Proust, *Swann's Way* (Part One of *Remembrance of Things Past*)
- ›› Mark Twain, *The Adventures of Tom Sawyer*

See also: Adolescence; Parents and Children; Teenagers

READ ON A THEME

CHINA AND HONG KONG
- Pearl S. Buck, *The Good Earth*
- Jung Chang, *Wild Swans*
- James Clavell, *Taipan*
- Wei Hui, *Shanghai Baby*
- ›› John Lanchester, *Fragrant Harbour*

Timothy Mo, *An Insular Possession*
Wang Shuo, *Playing for Thrills*
>> Amy Tan, *The Joy Luck Club* (Chinese women's lives both in China and America)
>> Paul Theroux, *Kowloon Tong*
Hong Ying, *Daughter of the River*

CHRISTIE, Agatha (1890–1976)
British novelist

Ingenuity is the essence of Christie's detective stories. She confined herself largely to two detectives, pompous Poirot and elderly, inquisitive Miss Marple. Nowadays, as well as her plots, it is the period detail of her books which fascinates: her English villages, spa hotels, 1930s cruise ships and, above all, country houses are caught like flies in amber. She chronicles a vanished pre-Second World War, upper-middle-class Britain with an accuracy which is enhanced rather than diminished by the staginess of her characters and plots.

THE MURDER AT THE VICARAGE (1930)
This typical Miss Marple story is set in a picture-postcard English village riven by gossip and inhabited by as unlikely a collection of eccentrics as even Christie ever threw together. Everyone could be guilty of murder, and Miss Marple's investigation is so gently persistent, so self-effacingly efficient, that one trembles in case she ends up as victim rather than as sleuth.

Among the best known of Christie's detective novels are The Murder of Roger Ackroyd, Murder on the Orient Express, The ABC Murders, Death on the Nile, Appointment with Death, The Moving Finger, The Crooked House, They Do It with Mirrors *and* 4.50 From Paddington. *She also wrote stage plays (including* The Mousetrap, *still breaking all records for longest West End run), an excellent Second World War espionage thriller* (N or M), *and six romantic novels under the pseudonym Mary Westmacott.*

Read on
♦ to *Murder at the Vicarage*: *A Murder is Announced*.

◘ Patricia Wentworth, *Miss Silver Intervenes*; Dorothy Simpson, *Wake the Dead*; ›› Ngaio Marsh, *Overture to Death*; ›› Margery Allingham, *The Crime at Black Dudley*.

READ ON A THEME:

CITIES: NEW WORLD
- ›› Saul Bellow, *Herzog* (Chicago)
- ›› James Ellroy, *LA Confidential* (Los Angeles)
- ›› Jay McInerney, *Bright Lights, Big City* (New York)
  Armistead Maupin, *Tales of the City* (San Francisco)
- ›› Mordecai Richler, *The Apprenticeship of Duddy Kravitz* (Montreal)
- ›› Colm Tóibín, *The Story of the Night* (Buenos Aires)
- ›› Edith Wharton, *The Age of Innocence* (New York)
- ›› Tom Wolfe, *The Bonfire of the Vanities* (New York)

CITIES: OLD WORLD
- ›› Margery Allingham, *The Tiger in the Smoke* (London)
  Louis Aragon, *Paris Peasant*
- ›› Lawrence Durrell, *The Alexandria Quartet*
- ›› Mrs Gaskell, *Mary Barton* (Manchester)
- ›› Victor Hugo, *The Hunchback of Notre Dame* (Paris)
  Ivan Klima, *My Golden Trades* (Prague)
- ›› James Joyce, *Dubliners*
- ›› Christopher Isherwood, *Goodbye to Berlin*

CLANCY, Tom (born 1947)
US novelist

For a generation of thriller writers the Cold War, with its superpower confrontation and its elaborate, deadly games of espionage and counter-espionage, provided superb plot material and Tom Clancy's first few books successfully mined this rich vein. *The Hunt for Red October* (1984), the story of a desperate attempt by a

Russian submarine to defect to the West, made good use of Cold War rivalries and allowed Clancy to deploy his own knowledge of naval history and technology. In this first book, he also demonstrated his gift for gripping narrative. Yet, in the years after his bestselling debut, the potential in Cold War plots was clearly waning. The march of history was making them seem a little old-hat. Clancy saw this coming and, with a resourcefulness worthy of his ongoing character Jack Ryan, a CIA analyst who eventually becomes President, he turned his attention to other trouble spots of the world. *Patriot Games* pitches Ryan into the turbulent waters of Irish politics; *Clear and Present Danger* has him battling the drug barons of Colombia; *The Sum of All Fears* imagines a nightmare scenario in which a nuclear weapon falls into the hands of Middle Eastern terrorists. Tight plotting and vivid characterization remain the most important ingredients in all of Clancy's novels.

His other novels include Red Storm Rising, The Cardinal of the Kremlin, Without Remorse, Debt of Honour, Executive Orders, The Bear and the Dragon, Red Rabbit *and* The Teeth of the Tiger. *In recent years he has given his name and an undisclosed (probably small) level of creative input to a series of stories set in the worlds of the Internet and virtual reality* (Net Force) *and to a series about the exploits of a shadowy government organization* (Op-Centre). *He has also written non-fiction on his favourite topics of naval and military technology.*

🕮Read on

◆ *The Bear and the Dragon* (President Jack Ryan spends one thousand pages battling a succession of international crises).
◘ ≫ Frederick Forsyth, *The Fist of God*; Clive Cussler, *Deep Six*; Harold Coyle, *God's Children*; Campbell Armstrong, *Jigsaw*; Stephen Leather, *The Double Tap*; Stephen Coonts, *Liberty*.

CLARKE, Arthur C. (Charles) (1917–2008)
British writer of novels, short stories and non-fiction

Apart from ≫ Asimov, Clarke is the best 'real' scientist among classic science fiction writers. His subject is space travel, and his 1940s and 1950s non-fiction books and articles predicted, in accurate detail, many things which have since happened, such as the invention of communications satellites, the first moon landing and the development of laser space weaponry. He begins a fictional story with existing scientific fact or theory, and then extends it logically; even his wildest fantasies thus seem rooted in the possible. His main themes are the colonization from Earth of other planets and visits to Earth by explorers from distant galaxies. His stories bustle with the detail of space travel and setting up home in alien environments, and he is particularly interested in the psychological stress on people faced with the unknown and with the relationship between human beings and high technology. These ideas outweigh sometimes wooden character drawing and creaky plots.

RENDEZVOUS WITH RAMA (1973)

Like Clarke's story 'The Sentinel', which was the basis for Kubrick's film *2001: A Space Odyssey*, this novel is the story of man's contact with an enigmatic alien artefact. An enormous and seemingly abandoned spaceship drifts into our solar system. When humans explore Rama, they find their imaginations overwhelmed by its mystery and possible significance. The novel is a fine example of Clarke's capacity to evoke a sense of awe and to lead us to wonder about our own small place in the vastness of time and space.

Clarke's other novels include Childhood's End, The City and the Stars, A Fall of Moondust, Imperial Earth *and* The Fountains of Paradise. *In the last twenty years of his life, Clarke co-authored a number of novels, including titles in the* 2001 *and* Rama *sequences, with Gentry Lee and Stephen Baxter.* Astounding Days *is autobiography, excellent on why Clarke writes and how his career began.* The Collected Stories of Arthur C. Clarke, *appropriately published in 2001, gathered together more than a hundred of his SF short stories, many of them classics of the genre.*

Read on

◆ *2001: A Space Odyssey; 2010: Odyssey Two.*

◘ to *2001*: Algis Budrys, *Rogue Moon*; Robert Holdstock, *Earthwind*; Stanislaw Lem, *Solaris*.

◘ Greg Bear, *Eon*; Larry Niven, *Ringworld*.

CLASSIC DETECTION
Nicholas Blake, *The Beast Must Die*
G.K. Chesterton, *The Innocence of Father Brown*
Edmund Crispin, *Love Lies Bleeding*
Michael Innes, *Death at the President's Lodging*
>> P.D. James, *The Skull Beneath the Skin*
>> Ngaio Marsh, *Surfeit of Lampreys*
Gladys Mitchell, *Laurels are Poison*
>> Dorothy L. Sayers, *Murder Must Advertise*
Patricia Wentworth, *Latter End*

See also: Great (Classic) Detectives; Police Procedural; Private Eyes

COBEN, Harlan (born 1962)
US novelist

Coben first came to notice as the author of a series of crime stories featuring the sports agent turned private investigator Myron Bolitar. Bolitar was a character in the wisecracking tradition of the American private eye and the books in which he appeared were all fast-paced, funny and entertaining. In 2001, Coben turned away from his series character to write a number of stand-alone mysteries which have all the virtues of the Bolitar books but concentrate even more on the twists and turns of ingenious plotting. *Tell No One*, the first non-Bolitar novel he had written since the early 1990s, started with its protagonist receiving an e-mail that appeared to come from his wife, supposedly murdered eight years earlier, and went on to pile mystery upon mystery in a satisfying tangle before the truth was revealed. Other books followed, including *Hold Tight* (see below) in which similarly baffling events are gradually provided with rational explanations.

HOLD TIGHT (2008)
Sixteen-year-old Adam Baye goes missing shortly after the suicide of his best friend. Who was the mysterious correspondent sending him e-mails before he went? And what dangers may now threaten other local teenagers? Coben keeps the reader guessing in a thriller that unearths dark secrets in a seemingly ordinary neighbourhood.

The Myron Bolitar novels are Deal Breaker, Drop Shot, Fade Away, Back Spin, One False Move, The Final Detail, Darkest Fear, Promise Me *and* Long Lost. *His other fiction includes* No Second Chance, Just One Look *and* The Woods.

⩭Read on

◆ *Deal Breaker* (the first of the Myron Bolitar novels).

◘ to the Myron Bolitar novels: Robert Crais, *The Monkey's Raincoat*; Robert Ferrigno, *Heartbreaker*.

◘ to Coben's other fiction: ❯❯ Michael Connelly, *The Poet*; Jonathan Kellerman, *When the Bough Breaks*.

COE, Jonathan (born 1961)
British novelist

Jonathan Coe is one of the funniest and cleverest novelists of his generation and his fiction, although readily accessible and readable, plays ingeniously with the possibilities of the novel. His narratives move back and forth in time and space. They contain stories within stories and a multitude of perspectives which Coe weaves into sophisticated fictional tapestries. His books are in a long tradition of English comic fiction and make use of every device from scathing satire to downright slapstick but they are also, in the best sense of the word, experimental. He plays with readers' expectations of what a novel might be and uses every form of fictional device available to him to move his story forward. *The Rotters' Club* might, in précis, sound like a conventional enough account of the progress of four school friends through adolescence and growing pains in the 1970s. The book is achingly exact in its period detail. It is also strikingly original in the way Coe shifts the narrative duties from character to character and places into his story diary entries, articles from the school newspaper – and, in one section, a thirty-page, single-sentence monologue – without ever appearing to strain for effect or to indulge in fictional games to no purpose. *The Closed Circle* is a sequel to *The Rotters' Club* which catches up with what a quarter of a century has done to the central characters.

WHAT A CARVE UP! (1994)
Taking its name from a 1962 horror-comedy movie, *What a Carve Up!* is a deliciously unforgiving satire of the rampant materialism of the 1980s, focusing on one family – the spectacularly unlovely Winshaws. Different members of the clan –

an arms dealer selling weapons to Saddam Hussein, a banker with a finger in every financially fishy pie, a journalist with no moral scruples whatsoever – represent, individually and collectively, all that was wrong about the country in that low, dishonest decade. Reclusive novelist Michael Owen is commissioned to write a family biography and his growing conviction that the Winshaws have ruined his life persuades him to take his revenge upon them by acting out the film with which he is obsessed, murdering each member of the family in a way that makes the punishment fit the crime.

Coe's other novels are A Touch of Love, The Accidental Woman, The Dwarves of Death, The House of Sleep *and* The Rain Before It Falls. Like a Fiery Elephant *is a biography of the British experimental novelist of the 1960s, B.S. Johnson.*

🐟Read on
♦ *The House of Sleep*.
◘ ⟩⟩ William Boyd, *Armadillo*; ⟩⟩ Tibor Fischer, *The Thought Gang*; John Preston, *Ghosting*; Geoff Nicholson, *The Errol Flynn Novel*.

COELHO, Paulo (born 1947)
Brazilian novelist

In terms of sales alone, Paulo Coelho is South America's most successful novelist by far, his work translated into dozens of languages and selling millions of copies worldwide. Often derided by sophisticated critics appalled by the popularity of his simple, parable-like stories, Coelho reaches out to readers in search of fiction that combines page-turning narrative with a spiritual message. His novels are not subtle and they are not complicated but they are not meant to be. They are intended to entertain and enlighten, providing readers with an uplifting hope that life might just be the way it seems in the books. For millions of people around the world, they work their own particular magic.

THE ALCHEMIST (1988)
Subtitled 'A Fable About Following Your Dreams', Coelho's heartening story tells of an Andalusian shepherd boy who dreams of a treasure in a far-off land and sets off in search of it. Santiago's meeting with the alchemist who becomes his guru opens his eyes to the real meanings of life, love and suffering.

Other novels by Coelho include The Pilgrimage, By the River Piedra, I Sat Down and Wept, Veronika Decides to Die, The Devil and Miss Prym, The Zahir *and* The Witch of Portobello.

⌇Read on

◆ *Veronika Decides to Die* (a woman only discovers the true value of life as she faces her impending death).

▢ Richard Bach, *Jonathan Livingstone Seagull*; Jostein Gaarder, *Sophie's World*; James Redfield, *The Celestine Prophecy*; Antoine de Saint Exupéry, *The Little Prince*.

COETZEE, J.M. (John Maxwell) (born 1940)
South African novelist

Only two writers have won the Booker Prize for Fiction twice. One is ❯❯ Peter Carey; the other is the South African novelist J.M. Coetzee. Coetzee has since been awarded the 2003 Nobel Prize for Literature. Since publishing his first fiction in 1974 Coetzee has produced a series of memorably bleak portraits of individual lives caught up in the political maelstrom of South Africa. His books are not comfortable reading – he is too honest and unillusioned to provide that – but they are beautifully written, concise and elegant laments for lives shaped and often shattered by political events. Unlike many modern novelists, Coetzee is unafraid of allegory and his novels have some of the simple, unadorned power of parables. In *The Life and Times of Michael K*, an Everyman figure, the gardener Michael K (the echo of ❯❯ Kafka is clear) struggles to retain his dignity and worth amid a country torn apart by civil war. Setting off from the city to return with his mother to her rural birthplace, he suffers her death, imprisonment in a labour camp and the constant uncertainties of a land of anarchy and yet, at the end of the novel, he has still managed to survive. *Age of Iron* takes the form of a series of letters from an elderly South African woman, dying of cancer, to her daughter in America. A former classics professor, she is obliged to reassess her own life, the society in which she has lived and her own complicity in its evils.

DISGRACE (1999)
The central character of *Disgrace*, the second of Coetzee's novels to win the Booker, is David Lurie, a middle-aged university professor. Lurie has twice failed in marriage and he seduces his young female students with cynical regularity, while

still proclaiming his faith in the 'romance' that fuelled the Romantic poets he loves. After one particularly joyless sexual encounter – very nearly a rape – the student complains to the university authorities and Lurie, asked to apologise, instead resigns. Largely unrepentant, he goes to stay with his daughter on her farm in a remote part of South Africa. There he and his daughter, striving to come to some sense of accommodation with one another, are the victims of a brutal attack that changes them both. *Disgrace* is a daring novel – daring in creating an unsympathetic narrator, daring in its willingness to tackle sensitive issues of gender and race and daring in presenting an unflinchingly pessimistic view of the effect political change can have on personal relationships.

Coetzee's other novels include Dusklands *(actually two novellas),* In the Heart of the Country, Waiting for the Barbarians, Foe, The Master of Petersburg, Youth, Elizabeth Costello, Slow Man, Youth *and* Diary of a Bad Year. *Stranger Shores and* Inner Workings *are collections of essays,* Boyhood *a memoir of growing up in provincial South Africa.*

🕮Read on

♠ *The Master of Petersburg* (Coetzee moves out of South Africa and into nineteenth-century Russia in this novel based on incidents in the life of ≫ Dostoevsky).

◘ ≫ André Brink, *A Dry White Season*; Bessie Head, *A Question of Power*; Justin Cartwright, *White Lightning*.

COLLINS, Wilkie (1824–89)
British novelist

In England in the 1860s, a new genre of fiction emerged which became known as 'sensation fiction'. With its antecedents in the Gothic and 'Newgate' novels of earlier decades, 'sensation fiction' peered beneath the surface gentility of Victorian domesticity and revealed a world of bigamy, madness, murder and violence supposedly lurking there. It was all too much for some critics. One described the genre as 'unspeakably disgusting' and castigated its 'ravenous appetite for carrion'. The best known purveyor of 'sensation fiction' was Wilkie Collins and two novels by him are the finest examples of it. *The Woman in White*, published in 1860, is a melodramatic and complicated tale of a conspiracy to dispossess an heiress of her money, filled with dark secrets of lunacy, illegitimacy and mistaken identities and made memorable by its suave and sinister Italian villain, Count Fosco. *The Moonstone*, published eight years later, is a similarly elaborate tale of intrigue and mystery which focuses on a fabulous diamond, looted from a Hindu shrine, and the trouble it brings to those back in England who come into its possession.

Other novels by Wilkie Collins include Hide and Seek, Armadale, The Dead Secret, No Name, The Law and the Lady *and* Man and Wife.

📚Read on
◆ *No Name* (a young woman struggles to regain her place in society after discovering that she is illegitimate).
▫ Mary Elizabeth Braddon, *Lady Audley's Secret*; ≫ Charles Dickens, *Bleak House*; Sheridan Le Fanu, *Uncle Silas*.

READ ON A THEME:

COMEDY THRILLERS
Eric Ambler, *Passage of Arms*
Lawrence Block, *The Burglar Who Thought He Was Bogart*
≫ Christopher Brookmyre, *One Fine Day in the Middle of the Night*
Richard Condon, *Prizzi's Honour*
Janet Evanovich, *One for the Money*
Peter Guttridge, *The Once and Future Con*
≫ Carl Hiaasen, *Double Whammy*
Greg McDonald, *Fletch*
Lawrence Sanders, *McNally's Secret*

HIDDEN GEM:

DONALD E. WESTLAKE – *THE HOT ROCK* (1970)
Under a series of pseudonyms such as Richard Stark and Tucker Coe, Donald E. Westlake wrote dozens of hard-boiled crime stories and private eye novels. Under his own name, he produced the kind of books for which he ought to be much better known than he is – comedy thrillers which are

among the funniest ever written. Most feature the incompetent burglar John Dortmunder and his gang of highly dysfunctional associates. *The Hot Rock* was the first in the series and shows our hero handpicking a bunch of bunglers to assist and hinder him in the heist of a fabulously valuable emerald. Everything that could go wrong, does go wrong as Dortmunder and his hapless sidekicks fail miserably to make crime pay.

CONNELLY, Michael (born 1956)
US novelist

Michael Connelly is one of the very best of the newer breed of crime writers. Many of his books feature Hieronymus 'Harry' Bosch, a world-weary detective in the LAPD. A Vietnam veteran and former 'tunnel rat', Bosch has a personal history that's harsh, complex and fascinating. Working from the Hollywood division in a superbly realized Los Angeles, Bosch is a very good cop in that he solves crimes and puts the criminals away, but not so good in that he invariably faces suspension by his antagonistic, pen-pushing superiors. Bosch is a maverick who works to his own rules and code of honour rather than that of the system. Although maverick cops with drink problems and dysfunctional love lives are standard fare, Bosch is different. Connelly has succeeded in making him a sympathetic and compelling character, partly through his dry humour and partly because the reader knows, whatever the odds, that Bosch will be right – that he is the moral centre of the fiction and the authority he is always prepared to defy is self-serving.

The Bosch books are The Black Echo, The Black Ice, The Concrete Blonde, The Last Coyote, Trunk Music, Angels Flight, A Darkness More Than Night, City of Bones, Lost Light, The Narrows, The Closers, Echo Park *and* The Overlook. *Connelly's other, non-Bosch novels are* The Poet, Blood Work, Void Moon, The Lincoln Lawyer *and* The Scarecrow. The Brass Verdict *features the central character from* The Lincoln Lawyer *working in tandem with Harry Bosch.*

📖Read on
◻ James Lee Burke, *Black Cherry Blues*; Robert Crais, *LA Requiem*; Jeffery Deaver, *The Bone Collector*; Jonathan Kellerman, *Flesh and Blood*; ❯❯ Dennis Lehane, *Prayers for Rain*.

CONRAD, Joseph (1857–1924)
Polish/British novelist

Born in Poland, Conrad ran away to sea at seventeen and ended up a captain in the merchant navy and a naturalized British subject. He retired from the sea after twenty years and spent the rest of his life as a writer. There was at the time (1890s–1910s) a strong tradition of sea-stories, using the dangers and tensions of long voyages and the wonders of the worlds sailors visited as metaphors for human life. Most of this writing was straightforward adventure, with little subtlety; Conrad used its conventions for deeper literary ends. He was interested in 'driven' individuals, people whose psychology or circumstances force them to extreme behaviour, and the sea-story form exactly suited this idea. His books often begin as 'yarns', set in exotic locations and among the mixed (and mixed-up) human types who crew ocean-going ships. But before long psychology takes over, and the plot loses its straightforwardness and becomes an exploration of compulsion, obsession and neurosis.

HEART OF DARKNESS (from YOUTH, 1902)
This one hundred and twenty-page story begins as a yarn: Marlow, a sea captain, tells of a journey he once made up the Congo river to bring down a stranded steamer. He became fascinated by stories of an ivory merchant, a white man called Kurtz who lived deep in the jungle and was said to have supernatural powers. Marlow set out to find Kurtz, and the journey took him deeper and deeper into the heart not only of the Dark Continent, but into the darkness of the human soul. (Francis Ford Coppola's 1970s film *Apocalypse Now* updated this story to the Vietnam War, making points about American colonialism as savage as Conrad's denunciation of the ivory trade.)

Conrad's major novels are Lord Jim, The Nigger of the Narcissus, Nostromo, The Secret Agent *and* Under Western Eyes. *His short story collections (an excellent introduction to his work) are* Tales of Unrest, Youth, Typhoon, A Set of Six, 'Twixt Land and Sea, Within the Tides *and* Tales of Hearsay.

✥Read on
◆ *Typhoon* (which deals with corruption and exploitation of a different kind, this time using as its metaphor a passenger steamer caught in a typhoon in the China Sea); *The Secret Agent* (about the conflict between innocence and corruption among a group of terrorists in 1900s London).

□ ›› Robert Edric, *The Book of the Heathen* (a modern novelist examines Conradian themes in the Conradian setting of 1890s Belgian Congo); ›› Graham Greene, *The Comedians*; ›› Herman Melville, *Billy Budd, Foretopman*; ›› Paul Theroux, *The Mosquito Coast*; B. Traven, *The Treasure of the Sierra Madre.*

COOKSON, Catherine (1906–98)
British novelist

Catherine Cookson, née Katie Ann McMullen, wrote warm-hearted romances about 'ordinary people' dealing with the 'ordinary' emotions of love and longing that affect us all. She set most of them in the north-east of England (Tyneside) where she was born, and showed how her characters coped with the harsh conditions of life in the area in the nineteenth century and the early decades of the twentieth. She grouped many of her novels in series, for example the Mary Ann books (beginning with *A Grand Man*) and the Mallen trilogy (*The Mallen Girl*, *The Mallen Litter* and *The Mallen Streak*). The heroine of *Tilly Trotter*, *Tilly Trotter Wed* and *Tilly Trotter Widowed* (a characteristic series, written in the 1960s) is a poor but spirited girl in 1930s County Durham who becomes the mistress of the owner of the 'big house', emigrates to America when he dies, and returns in middle age to find happiness at last in her beloved native country. *Kate Hannigan's Daughter*, published after her death, brought her remarkable career as perhaps the most popular British writer of her time to a fitting conclusion by being a sequel to *Kate Hannigan*, her very first novel, published more than fifty years earlier.

Cookson's books include, among many others, The Invisible Cord, The Gambling Man, The Black Candle, The Harrogate Secret, The Tinker's Girl, The Obsession, The Thursday Friend *and* A House Divided. *She also wrote as* Catherine Marchant; *titles include* Heritage of Folly, The Fen Tiger, The Mists of Memory, Miss Martha Mary Crawford *and* The Slow Awakening.

⮷Read on
□ Tessa Barclay, *Dayton and Daughter*; Emma Blair, *An Apple from Eden*; Josephine Cox, *Looking Back*; Sheelagh Kelly, *A Long Way from Heaven* (and others set in Victorian York); Pamela Oldfield, *All Our Tomorrows*; Mary Jane Staples, *Echoes of Yesterday* (and others in the series about the Adams family of Walworth).

CORNWELL, Bernard (born 1944)

British novelist

Although he has published other series of historical fiction – including a trilogy set in the Hundred Years War and a sequence focusing on Alfred the Great and his wars against the Vikings – Bernard Cornwell remains best known for the Sharpe books, set in the Napoleonic Wars and tracing the rise from the ranks of Richard Sharpe. Cornwell's fiction has the old-fashioned virtues of writers like ›› C.S. Forester and ›› John Buchan. His historical research is impeccable but unobtrusive. His capacity to sustain a suspenseful and exciting narrative and his gift for vivid description of military action are admirable. And his hero, flawed but likeable, retains the reader's sympathies. We want to know what will happen next to Sharpe and how he will deal with it. Modern readers demand a racier package than the readers of Forester and Buchan did, and Cornwell is willing enough to supply it, but essentially he is the inheritor of their tradition and the best contemporary exponent of it.

The Sharpe books cover the years 1799 to 1821. In chronological order (although not the order in which Cornwell wrote and published them), they are: Sharpe's Tiger, Sharpe's Triumph, Sharpe's Fortress, Sharpe's Trafalgar, Sharpe's Prey, Sharpe's Rifles, Sharpe's Havoc, Sharpe's Eagle, Sharpe's Gold, Sharpe's Escape, Sharpe's Battle, Sharpe's Fury, Sharpe's Company, Sharpe's Sword, Sharpe's Enemy, Sharpe's Honour, Sharpe's Regiment, Sharpe's Siege, Sharpe's Revenge, Sharpe's Waterloo *and* Sharpe's Devil.

⮑Read on

◆ *The Winter King* (the first in the trilogy based on the Arthurian legends, the others being *Enemy of God* and *Excalibur*); *The Last Kingdom* (the first of Cornwell's books set in Alfred's England).

◻ ›› Patrick O'Brian, *Master and Commander* (and the other Aubrey/Maturin books); ›› C.S. Forester, *Mr Midshipman Hornblower*; Allan Mallinson, *A Close Run Thing*; Richard Howard, *Bonaparte's Sons*.

CORNWELL, Patricia (born 1952)
US writer

Each of Cornwell's Scarpetta thrillers begins with the discovery of a gruesomely mutilated body, which is then sent to Kay Scarpetta, Chief Medical Examiner of Richmond, Virginia. Scarpetta's post-mortem is the beginning of a spiral of serial killing, political machinations (she is not popular with corrupt official colleagues), personal involvement and nail-biting suspense. A favourite secondary character is her niece Lucy, a brilliant adolescent whose computer wizardry is equalled only by her social awkwardness. Since 1991 and the publication of *Post-Mortem*, the first of the Scarpetta books, Cornwell's combination of clinical and forensic expertise with tight plotting has made her books unputdownable.

POINT OF ORIGIN (1998)
Grisly murder comes once again to Scarpetta's home town of Richmond and once again Scarpetta's past returns to dog her. A farmhouse in Virginia has been destroyed in a fire and the remains of a body found there reveal clear signs of brutal murder. Meanwhile Carrie Grethen, a killer who tangled with Scarpetta in *The Body Farm*, has escaped from a psychiatric hospital and is sending Kay cryptic messages threatening revenge.

The other Scarpetta novels (best read in sequence, though self-contained) are Post-Mortem, Body of Evidence, All That Remains, Cruel and Unusual, The Body Farm, From Potter's Field, Cause of Death, Unnatural Exposure, Black Notice, The Last Precinct, Blow Fly, Trace, Predator, Book of the Dead *and* Scarpetta. Hornet's Nest, Southern Cross, Isle of Dogs, At Risk *and* The Front *are non-Scarpetta novels. Patricia Cornwell has also written a non-fiction work,* Portrait of a Killer, *in which she claims to have definitively identified the man who was Jack the Ripper.*

Read on
◻ Jonathan Kellerman, *Over the Edge*; Carol O'Connell, *Mallory's Oracle*; ›› Kathy Reichs, *Déjà Dead*; Tess Gerritsen, *The Surgeon*; Linda Fairstein, *The Bone Vault*.

COUPLAND, Douglas (born 1961)

Canadian novelist

Only a handful of writers get the chance to attach a lasting label to an entire generation. Gertrude Stein called the young people of the 1920s jazz era the 'Lost Generation' and the name stuck. **»** Jack Kerouac (supposedly) coined the phrase 'Beat Generation' to describe his own group of boho drop-outs disillusioned with the materialism of 1950s America and instantly became, in the eyes of the media, the spokesman of youth. And Douglas Coupland, in calling his darkly ironic stories of three twenty-somethings caught up in dead-end jobs in the service industry *Generation X* (1991), gave a name and a human face to a demographic trend. The danger of naming a generation, as Kerouac cruelly and tragically found out, is that you might never outgrow it; Coupland has recognized this and, in the years since *Generation X*, he has continued to expand the range of his fiction and the subjects it tackles. In a dozen further novels he has proved that there is much more to his writings than the phrase he coined for his first.

GIRLFRIEND IN A COMA (1998)

Coupland uses an imaginative conceit to illuminate the compromises and limitations that life imposes on a group of high-school friends. One of them, Karen, goes into a coma in 1979 and only re-emerges twenty years later. An adolescent in the body of a woman approaching middle age, she is suddenly witness to the changes two decades have made to her friends. Her Rip Van Winkle-like astonishment at hi-tech culture on the cusp of the millennium and her unjaded insights into the hollowness of the lives her friends are now leading are skilfully conveyed to the reader, clear instances of how much Coupland has matured as a writer since his generation-defining debut.

Douglas Coupland's other works of fiction are Shampoo Planet, Microserfs *(in which he turned his comic eye on the enclosed world of Silicon Valley programmers, trapped in a kind of perpetual adolescence),* Life After God, Miss Wyoming, All Families Are Psychotic, Hey Nostradamus *(which, despite its jokey-sounding title, is a subtle account of the aftermath of a Columbine-like school massacre),* Eleanor Rigby, jPod *and* The Gum Thief. Polaroids from the Dead *is a collection of stories and essays.*

Read on

♦ *Hey Nostradamus*.

◘ Dave Eggers, *You Shall Know Our Velocity*; ›› William Gibson, *Virtual Light*; ››
Jay McInerney, *Story of My Life*; Douglas Rushkoff, *The Ecstasy Club*.

CRACE, Jim (born 1940)
British writer

The settings of Crace's early books (*Arcadia, Continent*) are almost familiar: the
forests, mountains, seas, villages and cities of our own real world. But they seem
half-glimpsed, recognizable and strange all at once, like reality seen in dream.
There is no history. Past and present exist in the same moment, the realities of
medieval life and those of today blurring into one another. He is a prose poet,
selecting just the aspects of life he needs, and letting the unsaid do as much work
as what is there. *The Gift of Stones* is a recreation, remarkable because so
understated and undemonstrative, of a Stone Age village and its inhabitants. In
Being Dead a middle-aged couple return to a beach where they first made love
thirty years before and become the victims of a casual killer. Undiscovered, their
bodies lie on the dunes and Crace charts, meticulously and dispassionately, their
disintegration. In Crace's hands this is neither morbid nor voyeuristic but instead
becomes a haunting and moving meditation on love, death and transience. His
most recent novel, *The Pesthouse,* is a dystopian fiction set in a future America
where social bonds have largely disintegrated.

ARCADIA (1992)
In a skyscraper tower above the ancient fruit and vegetable market lives Victor, the
eighty-year-old financier who began as a beggar in the streets below, and rose to
be barrow-boy, stallholder, landlord and finally owner of all he surveys. From his
eyric above the stalls he plans change, plans to make a brave new world in the
market – and only Rook, his impersonal personal assistant, and Anna, Rook's
mistress, have any influence on what happens next. The book relates Victor's early
life, tells what happens when he begins to remake his world, and shows us, in a
blur of tiny details, a picture of society as bustling and as grotesque as one of
Brueghel's or Bosch's crowded scenes.

🕮Read on
♦ *Continent, The Gift of Stones, Being Dead.*

◘ ≫ Italo Calvino, *The Baron in the Trees*; ≫ William Golding, *The Inheritors*; ≫ Andrew Miller, *Ingenious Pain*; ≫ Vladimir Nabokov, *Ada*.

READ ON A THEME

CULTURE CLASH
Chinua Achebe, *Things Fall Apart*
≫ E.M. Forster, *A Passage to India*
≫ William Golding, *The Inheritors*
Carlos Fuentes, *The Crystal Frontier*
≫ Graham Greene, *The Quiet American*
≫ Henry James, *The Europeans*
≫ Barbara Kingsolver, *The Poisonwood Bible*
≫ David Malouf, *Remembering Babylon*
Joseph Olshan, *A Warmer Season*
Meera Syal, *Anita and Me*
≫ Evelyn Waugh, *The Loved One*

READ ON A THEME

CYBER FICTION
Pat Cadigan, *Tea From an Empty Cup*
Richard Calder, *Malignos*
Greg Egan, *Permutation City*
≫ William Gibson, *Neuromancer*
Jeff Noon, *Vurt*
Michael Marshall Smith, *Only Forward*
≫ Neal Stephenson, *Snow Crash*
Bruce Sterling, *Holy Fire*
Tricia Sullivan, *Dreaming in Smoke*
Jack Womack, *Going, Going, Gone*

HIDDENGEM:

JOHN FRANKLIN BARDIN – *THE DEADLY PERCHERON* (1946)

The Deadly Percheron, possibly the most surreal crime novel ever written, begins in a psychiatrist's office where Dr George Matthews has a patient to see. The patient, who appears in most ways to be perfectly sane, has the strangest of stories to tell. He is employed by a group of little men, 'leprechauns', to wander the city streets and perform such unusual tasks as wearing flowers in his hair and handing out small change to passers by. His latest job is to deliver a percheron, a type of horse, to the apartment of a well-known actress. Unsurprisingly, Matthews assumes that his patient is delusional but he is forced to reconsider when he gets to meet one of the 'leprechauns' himself. When the actress is murdered, he is obliged to take his patient's story even more seriously. Slowly the strange events are rationally explained and the crime solved, although many readers will feel that the explanation is never as interesting or intriguing as the original scenes of weirdness.

STARTPOINT

CRIME

Crime fiction began in 1841 with Edgar Allan Poe's story *The Murders in the Rue Morgue*, and its popularity has never waned. Stories concentrate either on events leading up to the crime or on detection. Some crime-centred books are darkly psychological, exploring the mind of the criminal compelled towards the crime. Others are 'caper' novels, showing the detailed planning and execution of the crime and concentrating on the relationships of everyone involved. Many detection-centred books are procedural, following the investigation of a crime step by meticulous step. Others centre on the character of the detective (an eccentric genius; a dogged cop with a complicated private life; a private eye who is the guardian of morality and integrity in a corrupt world). In ninety-nine per cent of all crime fiction, from >> Arthur Conan Doyle's *The Hound of the Baskervilles* (1902) to the latest >> Kathy Reichs or >> Ian Rankin, the crime is murder. In the first heyday of crime fiction (the 1930s) people favoured 'snobbery with violence' (as in the books of ›› Dorothy L. Sayers) and 'locked room' mysteries (such as those of John Dickson Carr). Nowadays, in the second heyday, we prefer psychological thrillers (such as those of ›› Barbara Vine), procedurals (often set in the past, or abroad) and private eye stories.

Block, Lawrence, *The Burglar Who Thought He Was Bogart* (1995). Block has written a cherishable series of books about the amiable, witty burglar-cum-bookseller Bernie Rhodenbarr and this title, in which Bernie adopts the persona of Bogart, is one of the best.

Carr, John Dickson, *The Blind Barber* (1933). Classic tale of beautiful women, international playboys, priceless jewels, stolen films, diplomatic incidents and murder, set on a transatlantic liner. Wonderful sense of period; one of the most rollicking of all 'locked room' mysteries.

Crais, Robert, *The Monkey's Raincoat* (1987). The opening novel in a hugely enjoyable series of LA private-eye stories featuring wisecracking Elvis Cole and his dangerous sidekick Joe Pike.

›› Dexter, Colin, *The Jewel That Was Ours* (1991). Opera-loving loner Morse and his assistant Lewis investigate murder among a group of Americans doing the Oxford Heritage Tour.

›› Dibdin, Michael, *Dead Lagoon* (1994). Dibdin's policeman Aurelio Zen returns to his native Venice and finds himself anything but at home as he struggles to solve the disappearance of a wealthy American and to disentangle webs of deceit both personal and political.

›› Ellroy, James, *The Black Dahlia* (1987). The first in Ellroy's powerful LA Quartet, this fictionalized account of a famous sex murder from the 1940s reveals Ellroy's mastery of period, dialogue and characterization and his dark, obsessive imagination.

Grafton, Sue, *A Is for Alibi* (1986). The first of the 'alphabet' novels featuring the feisty female detective Kinsey Milhone. Move on to *B Is for Burglar*, *C Is for Corpse* and all the letters up to *U Is for Undertow* (so far).

>> Hill, Reginald, *Dialogues of the Dead* (2001). Hill skilfully weaves together the investigations of his two policemen, Dalziel and Pascoe, and the inner world of a serial killer who is a word-obsessed maniac intent on playing games with them.

Hjortsberg, William, *Falling Angel* (1979). Cult classic, memorably filmed in 1987 as Angel Heart by Alan Parker, in which seedy, hard-boiled hero Harry Angel homes in on some terrible truths. Trespassing rewardingly on other fiction genres (horror, fantasy), this is a crime novel like no other.

Lansdale, Joe, *The Bottoms* (2000). Deftly combining a murder mystery with an elegiac coming-of-age story, Lansdale's book is set in east Texas in the mid-1930s. Its narrator, Harry Crane, on the verge of his teenage years, has his life changed forever when he discovers a mutilated body in the river bottoms near his home.

>> Leon, Donna, *Death in a Strange Country* (1993). Commissario Brunetti, the protagonist in all of Leon's Venetian tales, finds his inquiries into the death of an American soldier on the mainland are blocked by high command.

Lovesey, Peter, *A Case of Spirits* (1975). Lovesey specializes in period detective stories. In this, nineteenth-century Sergeant Cribb investigates murder and spiritualism among the snobbish middle classes of suburban London.

Mitchell, Gladys, *Laurels Are Poison* (1942). Classic eccentric-detective tale, in which Mrs Lestrange Bradley, witch-like psychologist and sleuth, investigates the murder of the warden of an all-women teachers' training college.

Pelecanos, George, *Down by the River Where the Dead Men Go* (1998). Super-boozer and PI Nick Stefanos awakes from a bender in a public park to find a body being dumped in the river nearby. In a novel filled with pop-culture references and 1980s hedonism, he pursues the killers.

Peters, Ellis, *One Corpse Too Many* (1979). Ellis Peters wrote a series about worldly-wise monk and herbalist Brother Cadfael in which cosy crime met the Middle Ages. TV has now given her books an even wider readership than before. This one, in which monks burying the dead from a battle find one more body than they bargained for, shows Cadfael at his most likeable.

>> Rankin, Ian, *Black and Blue* (1997). Rankin provides a wonderfully wide-ranging panorama of contemporary Scotland as his series character, Rebus, investigates a series of killings which has echoes of a famous case from the past.

Stout, Rex, *Too Many Cooks* (1938). Classic story in which fat, woman-hating, orchid-growing genius Nero Wolfe and his legman Archie Goodwin investigate murder at a conference for master chefs at a West Virginia luxury hotel.

Also recommended: James Lee Burke, *Cadillac Jukebox*; K.C. Constantine, *The Man Who Liked to Look at Himself*; Edmund Crispin, *The Moving Toyshop*; Loren Estleman, *The Hours of the Virgin*; G.M. Ford, *Who in Hell is Wanda Fuca?*; George V. Higgins, *The Friends of Eddie Coyle*; Francis Iles, *Malice Aforethought*; Stuart Kaminsky, *Murder on the Yellow Brick Road*; John D. MacDonald, *The Deep Blue Goodbye*; Margaret Millar, *Beast in View*; James Sallis, *The Long-Legged Fly*; Julian Symons, *A Three Pipe Problem*; Josephine Tey, *The Daughter of Time*; Scott Turow, *Presumed Innocent*; Barbara Vine, *A Fatal Inversion*; Charles Willeford, *Miami Blues*; Margaret Yorke, *No Medals for the Major*.

See also: Allingham, Chandler, Christie, Classic Detection, Great lassic) Detectives, Hammett, Highsmith, Marsh, Police Procedural, Private Eyes, Rendell, Simenon.

HIDDENGEM:

DANIEL WOODRELL – *THE DEATH OF SWEET MISTER* (2002)

Narrator Shug, an overweight teenager in the Ozark Mountains of Missouri, is used by his brutish stepfather to carry out robberies that the stepfather, perilously close to a long jail sentence, no longer dares to do. Meanwhile Shug's mother, the desperately flirtatious Glenda, is trying to find a route out of the trap her life has become. Woodrell, the most offbeat and accomplished stylist in contemporary American crime fiction, is a writer who deserves bestseller status. There are no mysteries in a novel like *The Death of Sweet Mister* – beyond the eternal mysteries of the human heart – but Woodrell's unique prose and subtle characterisation give it qualities few other crime novels can match.

DALRYMPLE, William (born 1965)
British travel writer and historian

Dalrymple had just graduated from Cambridge when he published *In Xanadu* (1989), his precocious account of his student travels in the footsteps of Marco Polo. Trekking along the Silk Road through the trouble spots of Central Asia, he recorded his experiences with a wit and erudition that almost matched those of earlier travellers like ›› Robert Byron. Since his debut, Dalrymple has become one of the most admired and acclaimed of modern travel writers. *From the Holy Mountain* saw him travelling in the footsteps of a sixth-century Byzantine monk, John Moschos, who journeyed from Mount Athos in Greece to Egypt through what was then an almost entirely Christian Middle East. Dalrymple has lived in India for a number of years and he has published several books which reveal his understanding of and insight into the sub-continent. *City of Djinns* is a multi-faceted portrait of Delhi, based on his experiences of living in the city for a year; *The Age of Kali* is an uncomfortable and disturbing investigation of contemporary India in which Dalrymple does not allow his love for the country to blind him to the dangers of corruption, violence and social disintegration it faces. Dalrymple's more recent books have ventured into India's past. *White Mughals* looks at the surprisingly close interactions between British Imperialists and their Indian subjects in the pre-Victorian Raj, focusing on the love affair between an official in the East India Company and a Hyderabadi princess; *The Last Mughal* (2006) traces the demise of an Indian ruler and his dynasty in the aftermath of the Indian Mutiny.

⩨Read on
◘ to *In Xanadu*: ›› Robert Byron, *The Road to Oxiana*; Peter Hopkirk, *Foreign Devils on the Silk Road*.
◘ to the Indian books: Alexander Frater, *Chasing the Monsoon*; ›› Norman Lewis, *A Goddess in the Stones*; ›› V.S. Naipaul, *India: A Million Mutinies Now*; Mark Tully, *No Full Stops in India*.

DAVIES, Robertson (1913–95)

Canadian novelist, journalist and playwright

The deceptively gentle, expansive tone of Davies's satires belies their extraordinary subject matter. Davies's books, most of which fall into 'trilogies' are comedies of manners, many set in small university towns riven with gossip and pretension. *Tempest-tost* is about an amateur production of Shakespeare's *The Tempest* all but sabotaged by the unexpected, lacerating love of the middle-aged leading man for the girl who plays his daughter. *Leaven of Malice* follows the events that result from the placing in a provincial newspaper of the false announcement of an engagement. *A Mixture of Frailties* describes the chain of bizarre events after a woman leaves money to educate a girl in the arts, unless and until the woman's son sires a male heir. The three books together have been published as *The Salterton Trilogy*. *The Deptford Trilogy* begins with the throwing of a stone-filled snowball, and spirals out to cover three twentieth-century lives, interlocking in a dazzling, bizarre mosaic, involving medieval (and modern) saints, big business, Houdini, Jungian analysis, touring freak-shows and a barnstorming company of travelling actors.

THE CORNISH TRILOGY (1982)

The books in this trilogy, about members of the wealthy, eccentric Cornish family, are *The Rebel Angels, What's Bred in the Bone* and *The Lyre of Orpheus*. Hovering over the events, as puppeteers loom over marionettes, are guardian angels, devils and spirits of medieval mischief; we humans are not alone. Alternate chapters of *The Rebel Angels* are told by Father Darcourt, a professor of biblical Greek at a small, Roman Catholic, Canadian university, and Maria Magdalene Theotoky, a research student. The university is a quiet place, dedicated to placid scholarship and barbed common-room gossip. But Ms Theotoky is researching Rabelais, and the plot suddenly erupts with priceless manuscripts, bizarre lusts, devil worship, scatology, and a storm of passion and deceit against which no grove of academe could stand unbowed. *What's Bred in the Bone* is the life story of Francis Cornish, art expert, multi-millionaire, wartime spy and loner, whose search for himself, and for love, is hampered by his guardian devil Maimas. *The Lyre of Orpheus* tells of the recreation, in twentieth-century Canadian academe, of a lost Arthurian opera by the devil-inspired nineteenth-century romantic composer E.T.A. Hoffman.

The books in the 'Deptford' trilogy are Fifth Business, The Manticore *and* World of Wonders. *Davies's other two novels, published in the last years of his life, are* Murther and Walking Spirits *and* The Cunning Man.

📖 Read on

◆ *Murther and Walking Spirits*.

▫ to *The Rebel Angels*: ›› David Lodge, *Small World*; ›› Anthony Burgess, *Enderby's Dark Lady*.

▫ to *What's Bred in the Bone*: ›› Thomas Mann, *The Confessions of Felix Krull*.

▫ to *The Lyre of Orpheus*: D.J. Enright, *Academic Year*; Randall Jarrell, *Pictures from an Institution*.

▫ to Davies's work in general: ›› John Irving, *A Prayer for Owen Meany*.

DAVIS, Lindsey (born 1949)

British novelist

Lindsey Davis has combined unobtrusive scholarship and research with great storytelling skills in her series of crime novels set in ancient Rome. Her engaging hero Marcus Didius Falco, a private investigator walking the mean streets of the city in the time of the Emperor Vespasian, has appeared in eighteen books so far and there are undoubtedly many more to come. Falco begins the series as the archetypal tough-guy gumshoe transported to ancient Rome but he has developed into a much more complex and compelling character during subsequent books. Narrator of his own adventures, he has travelled far in stories which have taken him from the forbidding forests of Germany (*The Iron Hand of Mars*) to the tourist sites of Greece (*See Delphi and Die*) and from North Africa (*Two for the Lions*) to the Middle East (*Last Act in Palmyra*). He has spawned a number of imitators but he retains his position as one of the best of all private eyes from the ancient world.

THE SILVER PIGS (1989)

The first book in the series remains one of the best. Falco is despatched to one of the most godforsaken spots in the entire Roman Empire – Britain – to investigate a scam in the silver mines which are the colony's only major asset. Far from home, he shivers and shakes in the inhospitable climate and nearly meets an untimely end but he does get to meet the feisty senator's daughter Helena Justina who is to be his unlikely partner in love and adventure throughout future books.

The other Falco novels include Shadows in Bronze, Venus in Copper, A Dying Light in Corduba, A Body in the Bath House, Scandal Takes a Holiday, See Delphi and Die, Saturnalia *and* Alexandria. *Also set in Ancient Rome but a non-Falco novel is*

The Course of Honour which tells the story of the emperor Vespasian and his love affair with a freed slave.

⮒Read on
◆ *See Delphi and Die* (Falco and Helena investigate the fate of two newly weds who disappeared while visiting the Olympic Games).
◘ Rosemary Rowe, *The Germanicus Mosaic*; ❯❯ Steven Saylor, *Roman Blood* (the first novel to feature the other candidate for the role of ancient Rome's Philip Marlowe, Gordianus the Finder); Marilyn Todd, *I, Claudia*; David Wishart, *White Murder*.

DAWKINS, Richard (born 1941)
British science writer

Richard Dawkins came to public attention with *The Selfish Gene* (1976), in which he presented general readers as well as his fellow scientists with an overview of the ideas of neo-Darwinism and argued that genes are the basic units of life. Organisms of all kinds, including ourselves, exist primarily to ensure their survival. He has followed this ground-breaking book with a number of other works which explore his ideas about how evolution shapes the world. *The Blind Watchmaker* (Dawkins has a gift for eye-catching and memorable titles for his books) takes the eighteenth-century metaphor which compares the universe with a watch, both too complicated to exist without a creator, and turns it on its head. Natural selection is the blind watchmaker; no other creator is required. *Unweaving the Rainbow* (1998), a typically trenchant polemic directed against those who doubt the power of science to explain the universe, argues that scientific knowledge enhances rather than diminishes our sense of wonder. *The God Delusion* (2006), a huge bestseller, is his most sustained attack yet on what he sees as the irrationality of religion.

Richard Dawkins's other publications include River Out of Eden, Climbing Mount Improbable, A Devil's Chaplain *(a collection of essays),* The Ancestor's Tale *and* The Greatest Show on Earth.

⮒Read on
◆ *The Ancestor's Tale* (Dawkins's journey back through evolutionary time).

□ to *The God Delusion*: Christopher Hitchens, *God Is Not Great*.

□ to Dawkins's work in general: Susan Blackmore, *The Meme Machine*; Daniel Dennett, *Darwin's Dangerous Idea*; Matt Ridley, *The Red Queen*; Lewis Wolpert, *Six Impossible Things Before Breakfast*.

DEAKIN, Roger (1943–2006)
British writer and naturalist

The death of Roger Deakin in 2006 deprived the environmental movement of one of its most admired figures and his readers of one of the finest natural history writers of recent years. His sensitivity to the natural world and his ability to record his responses to it in memorable prose were first seen in *Waterlog*, published in 1999. This was a record of his journey from his home in East Anglia across the country to the Hebrides via a succession of rivers, lakes, estuaries, pools and canals. Swimming through the landscape and (literally) immersing himself in nature, Deakin found a new way of describing the British countryside and his book about his adventures in the water was full of insight and humour. Deakin planned to follow this book with *Wildwood*, a journey in search of what he called 'the residual magic of trees and wood' but, sadly, it was only to be published after his death. In a series of vivid chapters and vignettes, he moves from Britain (writing of nights spent sleeping in the woods on his own land or of joining friends on an island in the Thames to build a bender with bundles of hazel wood) to Central Asia where he seeks out the Ur-apple that is the ancestor of all the twenty thousand varieties of the tree currently in existence. As in *Waterlog*, Deakin demonstrates a haunting ability to draw readers into the experiences he describes through the precision and exact observation of his prose.

Deakin's only other book is Notes from Walnut Tree Farm, *a selection from the journals in which he recorded his thoughts on life, nature and literature.*

🕮Read on
□ Mark Cocker, *Crow Country*; Richard Mabey, *Beechcombings*; Robert Macfarlane, *The Wild Places*; Colin Tudge, *The Secret Lives of Trees*.

DE BERNIÈRES, Louis (born 1954)
British novelist

Louis de Bernières spent some of his earlier career as a teacher in South America and his early novels are both set there and borrow many of the 'magic realist' qualities of the continent's great modern authors like ›› Garcia Márquez and ›› Isabel Allende. *The War of Don Emmanuel's Nether Parts, Señor Vivo and the Coca Lord* and *The Troublesome Offspring of Cardinal Guzman* are the three volumes in a loosely connected trilogy which takes place in an imaginary South American republic where farce, violence and sexual passion intermingle. De Bernières's major success (sales in the millions, a movie-based on the book) came, however, with *Captain Corelli's Mandolin* – a novel that is very traditional in its virtues. It has strong characterization, a powerfully evoked setting and a story of pathos and drama that told of individual lives caught up by the larger forces of history. In the Second World War the Greek island of Cephalonia is occupied by an Italian force led by the amiable and civilized Captain Antonio Corelli. More interested in music and his mandolin than he is in potential military glory, Corelli is a gentlemanly invader and embarks on an intense love affair with the local doctor's daughter, Pelagia. Yet, as the war goes on, its horrors drawing ever closer to Cephalonia, the political and the personal become ever more difficult to disentangle and tragedy becomes inevitable. Since the enormous success of *Captain Corelli's Mandolin*, de Bernières has published *Red Dog*, a 'biography' of an Australian outback sheepdog, *Birds Without Wings*, another epic story of love and tragedy played out against the backdrop of the collapse of the Ottoman Empire during and immediately after the First World War, and *A Partisan's Daughter*.

Read on

◘ to the earlier novels: ›› Isabel Allende, *The House of the Spirits*; Laura Esquivel, *Like Water for Chocolate*; ›› Gabriel García Márquez, *One Hundred Years of Solitude*.

◘ to *Captain Corelli's Mandolin* and *Birds Without Wings*: Jeffrey Eugenides, *Middlesex*; ›› Sebastian Faulks, *Charlotte Gray*; Eric Linklater, *Private Angelo*.

DE BOTTON, Alain (born 1969)
British novelist and writer

Alain de Botton began his career with three novels (*Essays in Love, The Romantic Movement* and *Kiss and Tell*) which used a variety of narrative techniques to chart the difficulties of romantic relationships. All three mixed elements associated with fiction with those more usually used in non-fiction to produce their effects and de Botton soon decided to write a book which made no claim to fictional status at all. *How Proust Can Change Your Life* (1997) used the French novelist's epic fiction as the starting point for a witty variation on the self-help book, ransacking the pages of *Remembrance of Things Past* for nuggets of wisdom and trawling through Proust's life in search of the lessons it might provide. De Botton has his tongue firmly in his cheek throughout, as sections with titles like 'How to Suffer Successfully' suggest, but the result is a book that (curiously) is more useful as a guide to life's difficulties than most books in the genre he is parodying. Since the (perhaps unexpected) success of *How Proust Can Change Your Life*, de Botton seems to have abandoned fiction altogether in favour of more works which draw on his wide reading to provide witty guides to the problems of modern life. In *The Consolations of Philosophy* he takes six philosophers (Socrates, Epicurus, Seneca, Montaigne, Schopenhauer and Nietzsche) and gives them a new relevance to the conduct of our own everyday lives. Difficulties that can afflict us all (being poor, being unpopular, losing the love of one's life) are viewed through the prism of great thinkers from the past.

De Botton's other books are The Art of Travel, Status Anxiety, The Architecture of Happiness *and* The Pleasures and Sorrows of Work.

🕮 Read on

◘ to the novels: ➤➤ Julian Barnes, *Talking it Over*; Dan Rhodes, *Anthropology*; Adam Thirlwell, *Politics*.
◘ to *How Proust Can Change Your Life* and *The Consolations of Philosophy*: Simon Blackburn, *Truth: A Guide for the Perplexed*; A.C. Grayling, *The Meaning of Things*; Richard Layard, *Happiness: Lessons from a New Science*.

READONATHEME:

DEEP SOUTH, USA
James Lee Burke, *Cadillac Jukebox*
>> William Faulkner, *Absalom, Absalom!*
Fannie Flagg, *Fried Green Tomatoes at the Whistle Stop Café*
Joe R. Lansdale, *The Bottoms*
Harper Lee, *To Kill a Mockingbird*
>> Carson McCullers, *The Ballad of the Sad Café*
>> Margaret Mitchell, *Gone With the Wind*
Flannery O'Connor, *Wise Blood*
>> Mark Twain, *The Adventures of Huckleberry Finn*
>> Alice Walker, *The Color Purple*
Rebecca Wells, *Divine Secrets of the Ya-Ya Sisterhood*
>> Eudora Welty, *Delta Wedding*
Thomas Wolfe, *Look Homeward, Angel*

See also: Places; Small-Town Life, USA

DEFOE, Daniel (1660–1731)
British novelist and non-fiction writer

A journalist, Defoe wrote over five hundred essays, poems, political satires and other works, including a history of England, a handbook of good manners and a guidebook to Britain. In his sixties he began writing what he called 'romances': books which purported to be the autobiographies of people who had led unusual or adventurous lives (pirates, whores, treasure hunters) but which were really fiction and among the earliest English novels. Apart from his characters' proneness to theological and philosophical reflection (eminently skippable), his books lack the ponderousness of later eighteenth-century fiction. His fast-moving, simple prose and his journalist's talent for description give his work a freshness which belies its age.

ROBINSON CRUSOE (1719)
The germ of this story came from the autobiography of a real-life sailor, Alexander Selkirk, who was marooned on a deserted island in 1704. As often in his works,

Defoe was fascinated by the idea of the confrontation between civilization and barbarism, in this case by how a 'modern' European, filled with the knowledge and aspirations of the Age of Reason, might cope if all the trappings of civilization were stripped from him. Crusoe is allowed nothing but a few tools and other possessions saved from the shipwreck, and the resources of his own ingenuity. Later, after Crusoe has lived alone for twenty-six years, Defoe provides him with a companion, the 'savage' Friday, and so lets us see 'civilized' humanity through innocent, unsophisticated eyes.

Defoe's 'romances' include Moll Flanders *(set in the eighteenth-century criminal underworld),* The Life and Adventures of Mr Duncan Campbell *(whose hero is a deaf-and-dumb conjurer),* Captain Singleton *(whose hero is a pirate),* Memoirs of a Cavalier *and* Memoirs of Captain George Carleton *(whose heroes are swashbuckling soldiers-of-fortune), and – more serious –* A Journal of the Plague Year, *a day-by-day, first-person account of life during the Great Plague of London in 1664–5.*

🕮 Read on
‣ *The Further Adventures of Robinson Crusoe.*

◘ ≫ Henry Fielding, *Tom Jones*; ≫ William Golding, *Rites of Passage*; ≫ Patrick White, *Voss*. Michel Tournier's *The Other Friday*, and Jane Gardam's *Crusoe's Daughter* both play fascinating games with Robinson Crusoe's themes and plot, Tournier by retelling the story from Friday's point of view, and Gardam by focusing on a reclusive girl fixated on Robinson Crusoe who makes it her chief emotional resource. ≫ J.M. Coetzee's *Foe* gives an alternative account of how Robinson Crusoe came to be written, and of the 'real' events which might have inspired it – Friday and Crusoe are the sole survivors from a wrecked slave ship.

DEIGHTON, Len (born 1929)
British novelist

In the 1960s, fired by dislike of snobbish spy fantasies of the James Bond school, Deighton produced a series of books (beginning with *The Ipcress File*) showing spies as ordinary human beings, functionaries of a ridiculous and outdated bureaucracy in which requisitions for paper-clips could take precedence over analyses of the danger of nuclear war. He devised for them a documentary, 'dossier' technique, flooding the text with lists, letters, memoranda, meeting transcripts, diary entries and technical notes. Deighton went on to use this device in a series of devastatingly authentic-seeming novels on non-spy subjects.

BOMBER (1970)

In direct contrast to the stiff-upper-lip, jolly-good-show British war films of the 1950s, Deighton gives a blunt, detailed idea of what it was probably like to prepare for and make an RAF bombing raid in 1943. In this documentary novel he is particularly interested in the tensions between service and civilian personnel, the class divisions between officers and other ranks and the bumbling and paper-chasing which contrasted with, and sometimes jeopardized, the bravery of actual combat.

Deighton's spy novels include Funeral in Berlin, Horse Under Water, Spy Story, Mamista, City of Gold *and three trilogies:* Berlin Game, Moscow Set, London Match; Spy Hook, Spy Line, Spy Sinker *and* Faith, Hope, Charity. Close-Up *is a black satire on the film business.* Only When I Larf *is a comedy about confidence tricksters.* Violent Ward *is a sparky updating of the Marlowe, Lew Archer genre to 1990s L.A. His 'dossier' novels include* SS-GB, *a nightmarish vision of what might have happened if Britain had lost the Second World War and were now under Nazi rule.*

📖Read on

◘ to the spy stories: ►► John Le Carré, *The Spy Who Came in from the Cold*; Adam Hall, *The Quiller Memorandum*; Richard Condon, *The Manchurian Candidate*.
◘ to *Bomber*: Derek Robinson, *Piece of Cake*.
◘ to *SS-GB*: ►► Robert Harris, *Fatherland*.

DELILLO, Don (born 1936)
US writer

DeLillo's first novel, *Americana*, appeared in 1971 and set the mould for his later work, in that it satirized, with acute perceptiveness and a laconic wit, a particular strand of American culture – in this case, the television industry. Subsequent subjects have included football in *Endzone* (where, by drawing a parallel with this game and nuclear warfare, he examined the violence implicit in much US culture); the music business in *Great Jones St* and *Running Dog*; Wall Street finance (and terrorism) in *Players*; academia in *White Noise*. *Libra* is a brilliant meditation on the Kennedy assassination and *Mao II* investigates the heavy price of fame and media attention for a reclusive author. For some years, DeLillo himself proved reclusive and it looked as if *Mao II* (1991) might be his last book, but it was followed in 1997 by *Underworld*. A huge, sprawling epic, it was an immensely imaginative speculation based on actual historical events in which the Cold War came under DeLillo's penetrating gaze – specifically, the first nuclear bomb exploded by the USSR in the 1950s. Recalling *Endzone*, with its sly, playful teaming of sport and mass destruction, the book commences, in a typically bravura opening, with a scene at a baseball game when a figure in the crowds catches a ball hit by the batter. From there DeLillo takes the reader on a journey, backwards and forwards through time, across five decades of American life and culture in a panoramic book peopled by hundreds of characters, both real and fictional.

DeLillo's other work includes Ratner's Star, The Names, The Body Artist, Cosmopolis *and* Falling Man.

⮈Read on
■ to *Libra*: ❱❱ Norman Mailer, *Oswald's Story*.
◨ to *Underworld*: ❱❱ Thomas Pynchon, *Vineland*; E.L. Doctorow, *Ragtime*.
◨ to DeLillo's fiction in general: David Foster Wallace, *Infinite Jest*; Richard Powers, *The Gold Bug Variations*.

READ ON A THEME

DEPRESSION AND PSYCHIATRY
    Lisa Alther, *Other Women*
    Paul Bailey, *Peter Smart's Confessions*
❱❱ Doris Lessing, *The Golden Notebook*
    Wendy Perriam, *Fifty-minute Hour*
    H.H. Richardson, *Maurice Guest*
❱❱ J.D. Salinger, *Franny and Zooey*
    Paul Sayer, *The Comforts of Madness*

See also: Madness

DEXTER, Colin (born 1930)
British novelist

Since the days of Holmes and Watson there has been no surer ingredient of long-term success in detective fiction than an alliance between two apparently mismatched characters who are, in fact, devoted to one another. As the readers of his books – and the millions who have watched the TV films – know, Colin Dexter created just such an alliance in the partnership of Chief Inspector Morse and Detective Sergeant Lewis of the Oxford police. Morse is grumpy, intellectual, fond of booze, opera and crosswords, and a bachelor. Lewis is stolid, reliable, diligent but slightly unimaginative. Together they form a classic genius/sidekick duo. The third constant in the Morse books is Oxford. The city of dreaming spires provides the ideal setting for the complicated crimes Morse and Lewis investigate. However, plot, particularly in the early books, is not sacrificed to character and place. Dexter is a one-time national crossword champion and his narrative twists and turns have the ingenuity of the most cryptic of crossword clues.

The full-length Morse novels are: Last Bus to Woodstock, Last Seen Wearing, The Silent World of Nicholas Quinn, Service of All the Dead, The Dead of Jericho, The Riddle of the Third Mile, The Secret of Annexe 3, The Wench is Dead, The Jewel That Was Ours, The Way Through the Woods, The Daughters of Cain, Death is Now My Neighbour *and* The Remorseful Day. Morse's Greatest Mystery *is a collection of short stories, some about Morse, some not.*

⏚Read on
◘ ≫ Reginald Hill, *An Advancement of Learning*; John Harvey, *Easy Meat*; R.D. Wingfield, *A Touch of Frost* (one of a series that shares with Dexter's books TV success and a grumpy central character); Veronica Stallwood, *Oxford Exit*.

DIBDIN, Michael (1947–2007)
British novelist

Dibdin's early novels, including one in which the Victorian poet Robert Browning plays amateur detective in Florence, are enjoyable mixtures of authentic crime fiction and pastiche. His finest creation, however, and one of the most appealing protagonists in contemporary crime writing, is Aurelio Zen, Venetian investigator for the Criminalpol section of the Italian Ministry of the Interior. Zen, unlike the one-dimensional ciphers of so much detective fiction, is a rounded and convincing character. Struggling to maintain what moral integrity he can amid the labyrinthine bureaucracy and corruption of Italian society, he tries to unearth as much of the truth about the cases he is assigned as circumstances allow. Dibdin himself lived and worked in Italy for a number of years and the richness and unobtrusive detail of the Italian settings – Venice, Rome, the impoverished south – add to the pleasures of reading the novels.

CABAL (1992)

Cabal opens with startling suddenness as a man plummets to his death from the gallery in St Peter's, Rome while a priest is celebrating mass. The man is a gambler, playboy and prominent Catholic aristocrat and the initial assumption is that he committed suicide. Zen is brought in by the Vatican police force to rubber-stamp this verdict, but soon concludes that the case is not that simple. The dead man was involved in dubious financial skulduggery and, as murder begins to seem the likeliest option, potential witnesses join the ranks of the dead. Caught between the Vatican and his own superiors, Zen suspects far-reaching conspiracies and secret organizations ruthlessly intent on covering up their misdeeds.

The other Zen novels (each one self-contained) are Ratking, Vendetta, Dead Lagoon, Cosi Fan Tutti, A Long Finish, Blood Rain, And Then You Die, Medusa, Back to Bologna *and* End Games. *Dibdin's other books include* The Last Sherlock Holmes Story, Dark Spectre, Dirty Tricks, The Tryst *and* Thanksgiving.

⮑Read on

♦ *Dead Lagoon; Dirty Tricks.*

▣ to the Zen novels: ≫ Donna Leon, *The Death of Faith* (one of another crime series with an Italian setting and central character); Iain Pears, *Giotto's Hand*; ≫ Ian Rankin, *The Hanging Garden*; ≫ Reginald Hill, *Bones and Silence*.

▣ to *The Last Sherlock Holmes Story*; Julian Symons, *A Three-Pipe Problem*; Jamyang Norbu, *The Mandala of Sherlock Holmes*.

▣ to non-Zen crime stories: Nicci French, *Beneath the Skin*; Barbara Vine, *The House of Stairs* (see ≫ Ruth Rendell).

DICK, Philip K. (Kendred) (1928–82)
US novelist and short story writer

Dick used standard science fiction ideas – androids, alternative worlds, aliens – to write novels about the hinges between fantasy and reality, madness and sanity, paranoia and true perception. For a time in the 1960s, thanks to books like *The Three Stigmata of Palmer Eldritch*, which deals with the effects of mind-altering drugs on our perception of reality and with the nature of that perception, he had a huge cult following and he continues to be much admired, often by readers who otherwise read little science fiction. His characters often teeter on the brink of insanity, struggling to understand the world in which they feel trapped. In one classic novel, *Do Androids Dream of Electric Sheep?* (later filmed as *Bladerunner*), their dilemma is entirely real, as they are not human beings at all but androids aspiring to humanity. Science fiction fans make high claims for Dick, and he is certainly a master of the genre. But his metaphorical transformation of well-worn ideas, and his bizarre humour, make him a pleasure not only for addicts, but for readers who would not normally cross the road to read science fiction.

THE MAN IN THE HIGH CASTLE (1962)
The rewriting of history is a standard idea in science fiction and, at first glance, *The Man in the High Castle* seems a standard example of the subgenre. The Axis powers have won the Second World War and the Japanese rule the USA. Yet Dick's book soon reveals itself as far more complicated and subtle than a straightforward work of alternative history. It is an interlocking, intermeshing web of possible realities. Dick feeds the reader a heady cocktail of fascism, Taoism, the I Ching (which he used as an aid in plotting the book), individual schizophrenia and mass paranoia.

Dick's other novels include The Penultimate Truth, A Maze of Death, Eye in the Sky, Ubik, Martian Time-Slip, A Scanner Darkly *(about how the dual life of a future-Earth narcotics agent causes him to lose hold of his own identity), and* Time Out of Joint. Valis, *about what happens when an ancient, extra-terrestrial satellite beams directly into the hero's brain the news that reality ended in the year 74 AD, is one of Dick's most challenging novels and draws on his own experiences of apparent contact with alien intelligences.*

℥Read on
◆ to *The Man in the High Castle*: *The Crack in Space*.
◆ to *Valis*: *Radio Free Albemuth*; *The Transmigration of Timothy Archer*.

◻ Other alternative history/science fiction: Norman Spinrad, *The Iron Dream*; Keith Roberts, *Pavane*.

◻ Drugs and altered perceptions: Brian Aldiss, *Barefoot in the Head*; K.W. Jeter, *Dr Adder*; ›› William S. Burroughs, *The Ticket That Exploded*.

DICKENS, Charles (1812–70)

British novelist

In his early twenties Dickens worked as a journalist, writing reports of law court proceedings and parliamentary debates, and short essays on the life and manners of the time (later collected as *Sketches by Boz*). After the startling success of his first novel *The Pickwick Papers*, when he was twenty five, he was able to make writing a full-time career and continued to be the most popular of Victorian novelists until his death. He composed large parts of his novels in dialogue, and was proud of his gift for showing character through speech alone; he also gave his minor characters (pot-boys, shop customers, carters, oystermen, toddlers) turns of speech or physical eccentricities to make them instantly memorable. These are theatrical techniques and Dickens was renowned for his love of the theatre. The vividness of his depiction of character is combined with a sustained commentary on human nature and society: Dickens consistently savaged the humbug and petty-mindedness of the very middle classes who bought his books, and said that human happiness comes not from law, religion, politics or social structures but from gratuitous, individual acts of kindness. In his later books, notably *Great Expectations* and *Our Mutual Friend*, savagery predominated over sentimentality to an extent rivalled only by ›› Zola.

DAVID COPPERFIELD (1849–50)

Dickens's own favourite among his novels, this tells the story (in the first person, as if an autobiography) of a boy growing up: his unhappy childhood and adolescence, his first jobs and first love affair, and the way he finally transmutes his experience into fiction and becomes a writer. As often in Dickens's books, subsidiary characters seem to steal the show: the grim Murdstones, the optimistic Micawbers, salt-of-the-earth Peggotty, feckless Steerforth and, above all, the viperish hypocrite Uriah Heep. But the book's chief interest is the developing character of Copperfield himself. Apparently passive, at other people's mercy, he learns and grows by each experience, maturing before our eyes.

Dickens's novels, in order of publication, are The Pickwick Papers, Oliver Twist, Nicholas Nickleby, The Old Curiosity Shop, Barnaby Rudge, Martin Chuzzlewit, Dombey and Son, David Copperfield, Bleak House, Hard Times, Little Dorrit, A Tale of Two Cities, Great Expectations, Our Mutual Friend *and the unfinished* The Mystery of Edwin Drood. *His shorter works include* A Christmas Carol, A Child's History of England *and three collections of articles:* Sketches by Boz, American Notes *and* The Uncommercial Traveller.

☲Read on

◆ *Nicholas Nickleby; Bleak House.*

◘ Novels of 'growing up', using a biographical framework to give a picture (documentary, satirical or both at once) of society: ›› Henry Fielding, *Tom Jones*; ›› W. Somerset Maugham, *Of Human Bondage*; ›› James Joyce, *Portrait of the Artist as a Young Man*.

◘ to Dickens's fiction in general: ›› William Makepeace Thackeray, *Pendennis*; ›› H.G. Wells, *Kipps*; Tobias Smollett, *The Adventures of Roderick Random*; ›› George Gissing, *The Nether World*.

DOSTOEVSKY, Fyodor (1821–81)
Russian novelist

Dostoevsky admired ›› Balzac and ›› Dickens, and set out to describe Russian characters and society in a similar way, creating atmosphere by a series of vivid evocations (verbal snapshots) of everything from people's skin and clothes to the texture of furniture or the gleam of rain on cobblestones. His characters are a gallery of 'types', particularly strong on the destitute, the suffering and the inadequate. He was fascinated by people driven to extreme behaviour by despair or lack of external moral guidance. Raskolnikov, the central character of *Crime and Punishment*, makes himself a moral outsider by committing murder. Myshkin in *The Idiot* is so tormented by the thought of his own inadequacy that he becomes the imbecile he thinks he is. Every member of the Karamazov family (in *The Brothers Karamazov*) is morally tainted, and only the youngest, a novice monk, is able to wrestle with his own evil nature and win. If Dostoevsky had been a twentieth-century writer his pessimistic view of human existence might have led him to surrealist black comedy in the vein of ›› Kafka; as it was, the psychological intensity of his books is closer to stage tragedy (*King Lear* or *Medea*, say) than to prose fiction, and has a similar all-engulfing power.

CRIME AND PUNISHMENT (1866)

Raskolnikov, a student driven to neurotic frenzy by his powerlessness to change the injustice of the world, decides to demonstrate the freedom of his soul by a single gratuitous act: murder. Instead of being liberated, however, he is enslaved by his own guilt-feelings, and the book describes, in a remorseless and clinical way, the disintegration of his personality. The part of his 'conscience' is embodied in Inspector Petrovich, who harries him like a Fury from ancient myth, goading and cajoling him to admit his guilt and so to purge his soul.

Dostoevsky's other books include Notes from the House of the Dead *(based on his own prison-camp experiences: he was a political dissident),* Winter Notes on Summer Experiences *(a horrifying account of the degenerate Europe he found while visiting the London World Exhibition of 1862), and the novels* Notes from Underground, The Gambler *and* The Possessed.

Read on

◆ *The Idiot*; *The Brothers Karamazov*.
◘ ❯❯ Victor Hugo, *Les Misérables*; ❯❯ Nathaniel Hawthorne, *The Scarlet Letter*; ❯❯ Joseph Conrad, *Under Western Eyes*; ❯❯ Albert Camus, *The Fall*; ❯❯ Vladimir Nabokov, *Despair*.

DOYLE, Arthur Conan (1859–1930)

British writer of novels, short stories and non-fiction

As a doctor with very few patients, Doyle began writing to improve his income. His main interest was military history, and he regarded his historical novels (e.g. *The White Company*, the story of a band of fourteenth-century knights-errant, or the Brigadier Gerard books, set during the Napoleonic Wars) as his best work. His Sherlock Holmes stories were meant as potboilers, and throughout his life he claimed to be embarrassed by their success. Famously, he attempted to finish Holmes off by sending him over the Reichenbach Falls in the clutches of his deadliest enemy, the criminal mastermind Professor Moriarty, but public pressure forced him to resurrect the cerebral, eccentric detective. The Holmes stories were published by *The Strand* magazine in the UK and by *Harper's* in the USA; these periodicals also serialized Doyle's Professor Challenger novels (beginning with *The Lost World*), about a flamboyant scientific genius and explorer, a blend of the heroes of ›› Jules Verne and ›› Rider Haggard.

THE MEMOIRS OF SHERLOCK HOLMES (1893)

In each of the eleven stories in this collection, Holmes is presented with a problem which seems insoluble – at least so far as his friend and chronicler Dr Watson can see – and solves it by a mixture of dazzling deductive reasoning and melodramatic adventure. Holmes is a master of disguise, an expert shot and boxer, a drug-taker, a neurotic introvert, a plausible liar who uses every trick to trap his suspects – and Doyle's style has a single-mindedness, an obsessiveness, which perfectly suits both Holmes's character and the mysteries he is set to solve.

Doyle's Holmes books are the novels A Study in Scarlet, The Sign of Four, The Hound of the Baskervilles *and* The Valley of Fear, *and the short-story collections* The Adventures of Sherlock Holmes, The Return of Sherlock Holmes, His Last Bow *and* The Case Book of Sherlock Holmes. *The Challenger books include* The Poison Belt *and* The Land of Mist, *and Doyle's historical novels, apart from those mentioned, include* Micah Clarke *(set during the Monmouth Rebellion of 1685 and its bloody aftermath),* Rodney Stone, *which takes place in the world of Regency prizefighting, and* Sir Nigel, *a prequel to* The White Company.

⮂Read on

♦ *The Case Book of Sherlock Holmes*; *The Lost World*.

◘ to Holmes: Nicholas Meyer, *The Seven-per-cent Solution* (one of the most convincing of many Holmes stories by others); G.K. Chesterton, *The Innocence of Father Brown* (and the other volumes of Father Brown stories); John Dickson Carr, *The Emperor's Snuff Box*; Arthur Morrison, *Martin Hewitt, Investigator*; August Derleth, *The Adventures of Solar Pons* (half-parody, half-homage in which a Holmes-like detective operates from rooms in Praed Street); Laurie King, *The Beekeeper's Apprentice* (first in a wonderfully witty and convincing series of books in which an astute young woman is trained by the retired Holmes in the art of deduction).

◘ to the historical fiction: ›› Alexandre Dumas, *The Queen's Necklace*; ›› R.L. Stevenson, *Kidnapped*; Rafael Sabatini, *Bellarion the Fortunate*.

DOYLE, Roddy (born 1958)

Irish writer

The families in Doyle's early books (epitomized by the Rabittes of the Barrytown trilogy) are large, endlessly ambitious and totally useless. They live in Dublin, scraping a living on welfare (and by other less official activities), and are always dreaming of the big time. The Barrytown books consist of *The Commitments* (made into an exuberant film by Alan Parker), *The Snapper* and *The Van*. The 1993 Booker Prize-winning *Paddy Clarke Ha Ha Ha* is set in the same type of working-class area of Dublin's northside as the Barrytown books and tells of the growing pains of its ten-year-old protagonist from his perspective. With *The Woman Who Walked Into Doors* (see below) Doyle indicated an ambition to extend his fictional range and this was confirmed by *A Star Called Henry*, the first of what is intended to be a trilogy re-examining the history of the Irish Republic through the eyes of Henry Smart. Born in the Dublin slums, Henry grows up quickly to play his part in the 1916 Easter Uprising (grittily and unromantically presented by Doyle) and to enter the violent politics of the civil war years as a hard and unillusioned fighter. The second part of the trilogy, *Oh, Play That Thing*, which takes Henry to America where he falls into the world of gangsters, speakeasies and jazz clubs, was published in 2004. In 2002 Doyle published his first work of non-fiction, *Rory and Ita*, the story of his parents and the changing Ireland they have experienced. *The Deportees* is a collection of short stories, published in 2008.

THE WOMAN WHO WALKED INTO DOORS (1996)

Paula Spencer is looking back on seventeen years of marriage to a violent man. Her husband now dead (shot by police), she is an alcoholic consumed by self-hatred and the self-image imposed on her by the men in her life. Doyle provides unflinching insights into Paula's inner life and her struggles to regain dignity and self-worth. Often as funny as his earlier books (despite its stark subject matter) *The Woman Who Walked Into Doors* is a remarkable feat of empathy and imagination. Doyle returned to the character in *Paula Spencer*, published in 2006.

Read on

◘ Patrick McCabe, *Breakfast on Pluto*; ▶▶ Joseph O'Connor, *Cowboys and Indians*; Dermot Bolger, *Father's Music*; Jeff Torrington, *Swing, Hammer, Swing* (for a working-class Glasgow as exuberant as Doyle's working-class Dublin); Sebastian Barry, *The Whereabouts of Eneas McNulty*.

DRABBLE, Margaret (born 1939)
British novelist and non-fiction writer

An admirer of ➤➤ George Eliot and ➤➤ Arnold Bennett, Drabble has updated their fictional ideas to the present day. Her books are crammed with the detail of everyday lives – fetching children from school, making gravy, taking intercity trains, washing tights – and are about 'ordinary' people: housewives, librarians, teachers, midwives. But Drabble, like Eliot and Bennett, is also interested in intellectual ideas, in describing the spirit of the times as well as their domestic detail. Her books centre on women's experience and tell us how middle-class girls of the late 1950s felt about their lives, how they went on in the 1960s to balance marriage, motherhood and careers, and how they coped in the 1970s, 1980s and 1990s with teenage children and rocky marriages. Drabble's sister is ➤➤ A.S. Byatt and she is married to ➤➤ Michael Holroyd.

THE RADIANT WAY (1987)
The lives of three women of similar age (late forties) and background (educated middle class) are contrasted in a brilliantly evoked mid-1980s Britain. All were born in the north of England: Liz has moved south and made a career as a Harley Street psychiatrist; her sister has stayed at home to look after their senile mother; Alix and her husband, failing to make a success in London, are returning north to regenerate their lives. The characters' contrasting experiences, and their middle-aged views of the way their younger ambitions have worked out, match the political and social feelings Drabble sees as typical of Britain in the 1980s, when the young adults of the flower-power generation are just beginning to feel that life has passed them by. Their stories are continued in two sequels, *A Natural Curiosity* and *The Gates of Ivory*.

Drabble's novels include The Garrick Year, The Millstone, A Summer Bird-Cage, The Realms of Gold, The Ice Age, The Witch of Exmoor, The Peppered Moth, The Seven Sisters, The Red Queen *and* The Sea Lady. *She has also written biographies of Wordsworth and* ➤➤ *Bennett and has acted as general editor of* The Oxford Companion to English Literature. The Pattern in the Carpet *is an idiosyncratic book of autobiographical reflections triggered by Drabble's fondness for jigsaw puzzles.*

📖Read on

♦ *The Garrick Year* (a moving study, set in the 1960s, of a woman trying to manage both marriage, to a rising actor, and the claims of her own career); *The Peppered Moth* (four generations of a family, from a young woman in an early twentieth-century mining village trying to escape to a more fulfilling world to a granddaughter who has still not quite reached it).

◘ ›› A.S. Byatt, *The Virgin in the Garden*; Penelope Mortimer, *The Pumpkin Eater*; Deborah Moggach, *Close to Home*; ›› Margaret Atwood, *The Edible Woman*; Joan Didion, *A Book of Common Prayer*; Mary Flanagan, *Trust*.

READ ON A THEME:

DREAMING SPIRES
Books set in Cambridge and Oxford universities

Max Beerbohm, *Zuleika Dobson*
›› Penelope Fitzgerald, *The Gate of Angels*
›› Barbara Pym, *Crampton Hodnett*
Frederic Raphael, *The Glittering Prizes*
Robert Robinson, *Landscape with Dead Dons*
›› Dorothy L. Sayers, *Gaudy Night*
J.I.M. Stewart, *The Gaudy* (and following four titles in the Staircase in Surrey series)
›› Tom Sharpe, *Porterhouse Blue*
C.P. Snow, *The Masters*

See also: Higher (?) Education

DUMAS, Alexandre (1802–70)

French writer of novels, plays, short stories and non-fiction

In his twenties Dumas worked as a civil service clerk; it was not until he was twenty nine that he was able to take up writing full-time. From then until his death, working with a team of assistants, he poured out over two hundred and fifty plays, novels, essays, books on history, travel and cooking and no fewer than twenty two volumes of memoirs. He was one of the most popular authors of his century, and the genre he specialized in, swashbuckling historical romance, has continued to enthrall many readers to the present day.

THE THREE MUSKETEERS (1844–45)

At the beginning of the seventeenth century d'Artagnan, a young country squire, goes to Paris to seek adventure. He makes friends with three of the King's musketeers (by the unusual method of challenging each of them to a duel on the same day) and the four become inseparable. D'Artagnan is accepted for royal service, and the musketeers throw themselves into the political intrigues centring on weak King Louis, his unhappy queen and her arch-enemies Cardinal Richelieu and the seductive, treacherous Milady. The story involves stolen jewels, masquerades, bluff and double bluff, and the musketeers gallop the length and breadth of France, duelling, drinking, wenching and making a thousand skin-of-the-teeth escapes. Although the book's style is old-fashioned, its breathless plot, its good humour and above all the wisecracking, bantering friendship between the four central characters, give it irresistible gusto.

Although Dumas was best known – and is now best remembered – for his Musketeers' adventures, he wrote fine novels set in other periods, notably The Queen's Necklace *and* The Countess of Charny *(both of which take place during the French Revolution) and* The Count of Monte Cristo, *about a man falsely imprisoned for helping the defeated Napoleon, who escapes, discovers hidden treasure and proceeds to hunt down the people who betrayed him.*

⛵Read on

◆ Dumas continued the Musketeers' adventures in *Twenty Years After*, *The Vicomte of Bragelonne* and *The Man in the Iron Mask*.

◻ old-fashioned swashbuckling stories: Rafael Sabatini, *Captain Blood*; Jeffery Farnol, *The Broad Highway*; Stanley J. Weyman, *Gentleman of France*; Baroness Orczy, *The Scarlet Pimpernel*.

◻ today's versions of swash and buckle: ›› George MacDonald Fraser, *Flashman*; ›› Bernard Cornwell, *Sharpe's Regiment*; Allan Mallinson, *The Nizam's Daughters*.

DU MAURIER, Daphne (1907–89)
British novelist and non-fiction writer

Although Du Maurier wrote novels and stories of many kinds, she is best known for a series of atmospheric romances set in the English West Country (Cornwall, Devon and Somerset) and drawing on the moorland landscape and seafaring associations of the area. In her best-loved book, *Rebecca*, a naïve girl marries Max de Winter, an enigmatic young widower, and goes to be mistress of his large country house Manderley, only to find it haunted by the mystery of his first wife's death. Solving that mystery (against the wishes of the sinister housekeeper Mrs Danvers) is the only way to bring happiness to the young girl (who is unnamed) and peace to her tormented husband – and the search leads her into a psychological labyrinth as threatening as the corridors of the dark old house itself.

Du Maurier's romances include Jamaica Inn, Frenchman's Creek, My Cousin Rachel *and* Mary Anne. *Her other novels include* The King's General, The Parasites, The Glassblowers, The Scapegoat *and* The House on the Strand. *The Birds and Other Stories includes the short story that was the basis for Hitchcock's classic film.* Don't Look Now and Other Stories *includes the novella/short story that inspired the 1973 movie directed by Nicolas Roeg. Daphne Du Maurier also wrote plays, biographies (of her family, Branwell Brontë and Francis Drake) and an autobiography,* The Shaping of a Writer/Myself When Young.

📖 Read on
♦ *Frenchman's Creek* (piracy and romance in Restoration Cornwall).
◘ ≫ Charlotte Brontë, *Jane Eyre*; ≫ Susan Hill, *Mrs de Winter* (a sequel to *Rebecca*); ≫ Philippa Gregory, *The Favoured Child*; Barbara Erskine, *House of Echoes*; Susan Howatch, *Penmarric*.

DUNMORE, Helen (born 1952)
British poet, novelist and short story writer

Helen Dunmore's fiction explores, in prose of a strong, lyrical sensuousness that reflects her gifts as a poet, the seductive charms and potential betrayals of intense love affairs. Her characters often harbour dark secrets or transgressive desires which threaten the stability of everyday life. Past events continue to echo in the present and to re-emerge, often to devastating effect. In *Talking to the Dead* Nina arrives at her sister's home to provide help after a difficult childbirth but is drawn into an affair with her brother-in-law. The relationship grows more obsessive, her sister retreats further into a private world and Nina finds disturbing memories of childhood and the death of a brother returning with new force. Set in Edwardian England, *A Spell of Winter* borrows elements of Gothic melodrama and the most sinister of fairytales in its story of a family that has been traumatized by the desertion of a mother. The father has been driven into an asylum and the two children, living in isolation in an eerily described country home, have found comfort in an incestuous relationship. *With Your Crooked Heart* adds dimension and depth to the cliché of the eternal triangle in its story of the stifling interrelationship of Louise with her husband Paul and his younger, charming, irresponsible brother. The settings of Dunmore's novels are various but all share the same sense of the enabling power and threatening danger of erotic love.

Helen Dunmore's other novels are Zennor in Darkness, Burning Bright, Your Blue-Eyed Boy, The Siege *(which recreates the horrors of the Siege of Leningrad in a story that none the less celebrates the power of love to endure them),* Mourning Ruby, House of Orphans *and* Counting the Stars *(set in ancient Rome and retelling the story of the relationship between the poet Catullus and his mistress Clodia).* Love of Fat Men *and* Ice Cream *are collections of short stories. She has also written several volumes of poetry and a number of books for children.*

🐢Read on

◆ *The Siege*.

▣ Alison Fell, *Mer de Glace*; Nicci French, *Killing Me Softly*; Lesley Glaister, *Honour Thy Father*; Linda Grant, *The Cast Iron Shore*.

DURRELL, Lawrence (1912–90)
British writer of novels, poems and non-fiction

Durrell lived most of his life out of Britain: in Greece, Egypt and France. As well as fiction, he wrote poetry and half a dozen non-fiction books about Greek islands: they are among his most enjoyable work, allowing scope for the impressionistic descriptions of landscape and character and the ruminations on love and life which sometimes clog his novels. In his fiction, he used experimental forms, constantly varying each story's structure and standpoint; this sets up a dialogue between writer and reader, a feeling of collaboration, which is one of the most exhilarating aspects of his work.

THE ALEXANDRIA QUARTET (1957–60)

Each book in the quartet, *Justine*, *Balthazar*, *Mountolive* and *Clea*, tells us part of the story: they give different viewpoints of the same events, and it is not until the end that every motive, every action, every twist of character becomes clear. The people are a group of friends and lovers, English, Greek and Egyptian, living in the turmoil of late-1930s Alexandria. At the centre is Darley, a teacher and would-be writer who observes events, partakes, but cannot explain. A main 'character' is the city of Alexandria itself. Durrell/Darley pretends to be giving accurate pictures of its souks, bars, palaces, brothels and crumbling embassies, but it is a dream city, a fantasy land where reality is subjective and events are only what you make of them.

His other novels include The Black Book, *two linked titles,* Tunc *and* Nunquam, *and the Avignon quincunx:* Monsieur, Livia, Constance, Sebastian *and* Quinx. *His island books include* Prospero's Cell *(about Corfu),* Reflections on a Marine Venus *(about Rhodes) and* Bitter Lemons *(about Cyprus).*

☜Read on

♦ *Tunc*; *Nunquam*.

❑ ≫ Olivia Manning's Balkan trilogy and Levant trilogy; ≫ John Fowles, *The Magus*; Henry Miller, *Tropic of Capricorn*; Gerald Durrell, *My Family and Other Animals* (for glimpses of 'Larry' as a young man, sharply observed by his little brother).

DYER, Geoff (born 1958)

British novelist, critic and travel writer

Although he has written both fiction and non-fiction, Geoff Dyer's best work defies easy categorisation and straddles the boundary between invention and reportage. *But Beautiful* is both a meditation on the power of jazz and a series of fictionalized portraits of some of the music's greatest practitioners, from Lester Young to Charlie Mingus. *The Missing of the Somme* weaves together our myths and memories of the First World War into a poignant examination of the way we remember our history and our dead.

Geoff Dyer's novels are The Colour of Memory, The Search, Paris Trance *and* Jeff in Venice, Death in Varanasi. *His other books include* Out of Sheer Rage *(an account of his travels in the wake of D.H. Lawrence),* The Ongoing Moment *(a very personal essay on photography) and* Yoga for People Who Can't Be Bothered. Anglo-English Attitudes *is a collection of reviews and essays.*

📖Read on
◆ *Out of Sheer Rage*.
▫ John Berger, *And Our Faces, My Heart, Brief as Photos*; ▸▸ Julia Blackburn, *With Billie*; Paul Fussell, *The Great War and Modern Memory*.

READ ON A THEME

ECCENTRIC FAMILIES
▸▸ Kate Atkinson, *Human Croquet*
   H.E. Bates, *The Darling Buds of May*
   Ivy Compton-Burnett, *A House and its Head*
▸▸ Roddy Doyle, *The Van*
   Lesley Glaister, *Honour Thy Father*
▸▸ John Irving, *The Hotel New Hampshire*
▸▸ Nancy Mitford, *The Pursuit of Love*
▸▸ Vladimir Nabokov, *Ada*
▸▸ Virginia Woolf, *To the Lighthouse*

See also: Many Generations; Parents and Children

READ ON A THEME

ECHOES OF EMPIRE
▸▸ J.G. Farrell, *The Singapore Grip*
   C.S. Godshalk, *Kalimantaan*
   Ruth Prawer Jhabvala, *Heat and Dust*
▸▸ Matthew Kneale, *English Passengers*

>> John Lanchester, *Fragrant Harbour*
Timothy Mo, *An Insular Possession*
>> V.S. Naipaul, *The Enigma of Arrival*
Paul Scott, *Staying On*

ECO, Umberto (born 1932)
Italian novelist

Before publishing his first novel in his late forties, Eco had carved out a substantial career for himself as an academic and was a well-known figure in the Italian intellectual and cultural world. Beginning as a medievalist with a particular interest in Thomas Aquinas, Eco moved into the emerging field of semiotics and became the first professor of the subject at one of Europe's oldest universities, Bologna. *The Name of the Rose* (see below) was an enormous success, selling millions of copies worldwide, and Eco was launched on a parallel career as a novelist. He has published four further novels. *Foucault's Pendulum* is a huge, sprawling narrative which uses crackpot conspiracy theories, particularly about the Knights Templar, as the starting point for a story of murder, esoterica and the mysteries of belief and reality. In *The Island of the Day Before* a seventeenth-century Italian nobleman is shipwrecked and finds refuge on another, apparently abandoned ship. As he explores the ship and begins to realize that he is not alone on it, Eco's tale opens out into another dazzling display of erudition and imagination. *Baudolino* is set at the time of the Fourth Crusade and is a characteristically wide-ranging mélange of fact, fable and invention centred on the eponymous narrator who sets off, ultimately, on a picaresque search for Prester John, the legendary Christian monarch said to reign in the Far East. *The Mysterious Flame of Queen Loana* is an illustrated novel about a man who suffers a stroke and loses his memory of everything in his life apart from the books he has read.

THE NAME OF THE ROSE (1983)
The framework of Eco's first novel is a murder mystery. A fourteenth-century monk, William of Baskerville, using methods of deduction which anticipate those of Sherlock Holmes, solves seven murders in the monastery he happens to be visiting. On this simple frame Eco weaves a wonderful tapestry of philosophy, intellectual jokes, extraordinary lore about monasticism, alchemy and religious belief.

Although *The Name of the Rose* tweaks and stimulates the intellect, it is anything but hard to read – largely due to Eco's beautifully clear prose and to his affection for even the tiniest detail of medieval life.

📖Read on

◘ ›› Italo Calvino, *Our Ancestors*; ›› Lawrence Norfolk, *The Pope's Rhinoceros*; John Barth, *The Sot-Weed Factor*; ›› William Golding, *The Spire*; ›› Hermann Hesse, *The Glass Bead Game*; Richard Zimler, *The Last Kabbalist of Lisbon*.

EDRIC, Robert (born 1956)
British novelist

Robert Edric is not a household name even in literary households but there is a case to be made that he is the most exciting and adventurous historical novelist of his generation. Certainly he is one of the most wide-ranging in his subject matter. He has written incisive and intelligent novels set in (among other places and times) the Belgian Congo at the height of exploitative imperialism (*The Book of the Heathen*), the Arctic wastes in the era of heroic European exploration (*The Broken Lands*) and a Swiss mountain resort in the aftermath of the First World War (*In Desolate Heaven*). The thread that runs through most of these disparate novels is Edric's interest in the uncomprehending, sometimes brutal attempts by Westerners to impose their own values on societies alien to them.

ELYSIUM (1995)
Elysium is another of Edric's rich explorations of the clash of cultures in imperial history, set in a nineteenth-century Tasmania where the indigenous population is about to be wiped out. Told as a mosaic of short scenes narrated by different voices and moving backwards and forwards in time, the book focuses on William Lanne, mockingly nicknamed 'King Billy' by the colonists, who becomes the last full-blooded aboriginal man. Caught between his own culture and a triumphalist imperialism whose victory he recognizes as inevitable, Lanne is a sympathetic character. His oppressors, from soldiers indulging in mindless violence to the scientist Fairfax, who sees him only as an exhibit in some ethnographical museum to be measured and classified, are united only in their refusal to see him as fully human.

Edric's other novels include In the Days of the American Museum, The Earth Made of Glass, The Sword Cabinet, Peacetime, Gathering the Water, The Kingdom of Ashes *and* In Zodiac Light. Cradle Song, Siren Song *and* Swan Song *are three interconnected crime novels featuring a Yorkshire private investigator.*

📖Read on

♦ *The Book of the Heathen*.

□ ≫ Jim Crace, *Signals of Distress*; Adam Foulds, *The Quickening Maze*; ≫ Matthew Kneale, *English Passengers*.

READ ON A THEME

EGYPT
Ancient:
   Paul Doherty, *The Mask of Ra*
≫ H. Rider Haggard, *Queen of the Dawn*
   Christian Jacq, *Son of Light*
≫ Norman Mailer, *Ancient Evenings*
≫ Wilbur Smith, *River God*
   Mika Waltari, *The Egyptian*

Modern:
≫ Lawrence Durrell, *Justine*
≫ Naguib Mahfouz, *Palace Walk*
≫ Olivia Manning, *The Danger Tree* (and the two further titles in the Levant trilogy)
   Michael Pearce, *The Mamur Zapt and the Spoils of Egypt*
≫ Elizabeth Peters, *Crocodile on the Sandbank*
   Robert Solé, *The Photographer's Wife*
   Ahdaf Soueif, *The Map of Love*

THE ELDERLY
>> Kingsley Amis, *Ending Up*
   Trezza Azzopardi, *Remember Me*
>> Honoré de Balzac, *Old Goriot*
>> Julian Barnes, *Staring at the Sun*
   Jenny Diski, *Happily Ever After*
>> Margaret Forster, *Have the Men Had Enough?*
>> Russell Hoban, *Angelica's Grotto*
   Christopher Hope, *Serenity House*
   Alan Isler, *The Prince of West End Avenue*
   Deborah Moggach, *These Foolish Things*
>> Muriel Spark, *Memento Mori*

ELIOT, George (1819–80)
British novelist

George Eliot was the pen-name of Marian Evans, a farm manager's daughter. She grew up in the stifling provincial pieties of middle-class Victorian England, but after her father's death became an atheist and freethinker, travelled abroad and set up home in London. She was at the heart of the liberal intellectual circles of her time: a supporter of Darwin and an admirer of William Morris and other early socialists. A similar receptivity to new ideas and disdain for convention mark her novels. They deal with the kind of moral issues (such as whether a 'good life' can be lived without religion, or if sexual happiness is essential to a successful marriage) which were rarely discussed in polite Victorian company and were even less common in literature. At the same time her books teem with realistic detail of provincial society, minutely observed. The combination of exact documentation of behaviour and character with unashamed discussion of ideas normally left unspoken was a heady one: she was one of the most widely read authors of her day.

MIDDLEMARCH (1871–72)
Two people try to break free from the petty-minded boredom of the English provincial town of Middlemarch. Dorothea Brooke marries because of intellectual

infatuation, only to find that her husband (an elderly scholar) is a domestic tyrant. Tertius Lydgate, a doctor struggling to introduce new medical ideas in a society which is deeply suspicious of them, marries for love, only to find that his wife's brainless following of fashion destroys his bank balance, his self-confidence and his social position.

Apart from Romola, *set in fifteenth-century Florence, all Eliot's novels have nineteenth-century English locations and characters. Her first book,* Scenes of Clerical Life, *contains three mid-length stories; it and the short novel* Silas Marner *(about a free-thinking country weaver tormented for his beliefs and for a crime he did not commit) are the most accessible of all her works. Her full-length novels are* Adam Bede, The Mill on the Floss, Felix Holt, Middlemarch *and* Daniel Deronda.

📖Read on
◆ *The Mill on the Floss* (about a brother and sister who are idyllically happy together as children, grow apart in adult life, and are finally, tragically reunited).
◘ matching Eliot's concern for the individual stifled by society: ❯❯ Gustave Flaubert, *Madame Bovary*; ❯❯ Mrs Gaskell, *North and South*; ❯❯ Thomas Hardy, *Jude the Obscure*; Benjamin Disraeli, *Sybil*; ❯❯ Arnold Bennett, *Anna of the Five Towns*.
◘ twentieth-century books combining social observation with 'issues' in an Eliot-like way, though their styles are entirely different: ❯❯ Margaret Drabble, *The Millstone*; Winifred Holtby, *South Riding*.

ELLIS, Bret Easton (born 1964)
US novelist

Controversy has raged over Bret Easton Ellis's novels, particularly *American Psycho* (see below) and there are diametrically opposed views of the blank tones his narrators employ to describe even the most viscerally violent and disturbing events. Are we reading the work of a deadpan satirist, revealing the moral shallowness of the age, or that of a voyeuristic misogynist? Ellis's most severe critics under-estimate the extent to which his style is consciously crafted and over-estimate the extent to which writer and fictional narrator must be identified. From his first novel (*Less Than Zero*, published in 1985 when he was 21) Ellis has shown his interest in people who are sleepwalking, morally and emotionally, through life and the narrator of *American Psycho* is a clear descendant of the spaced-out, over-indulged teenagers of that first book.

AMERICAN PSYCHO (1991)

Patrick Bateman is good-looking, intelligent and earns colossal sums of money working on Wall Street. His life, which he describes in careful detail, relentlessly namechecking the designer label clothing and accessories that help create the persona he presents to the world, appears to be an embodiment of the American Dream. Yet Bateman's inner life, and secret world, is one of appalling moral depravity. He mutilates and murders young women, acts which he describes with the same cool precision he applies to his wardrobe and toilette. *American Psycho* is a very disturbing book, graphic in its descriptions of violence and bodily dismemberment, and is not to be recommended to the squeamish or those in search of light reading. Ellis is not, however, writing violent pornography. His intent is to paint a portrait of moral nullity in the midst of material plenty, of a man who finds no meaning in life save conspicuous consumption and his own monstrous acts and desires. There is humour of the blackest kind in the disparity between Bateman as he appears to others and his terrible hidden world but, ultimately, this is a serious study of moral blankness.

Bret Easton Ellis's other books include The Rules of Attraction, Glamorama, The Informers *and* Lunar Park, *in which he uses a fictionalized version of his own experiences as a bestselling writer to examine questions of love, loss and the meaning of success.*

Read on

◘ to *American Psycho*: Dennis Cooper, *Frisk* (another exploration of death, desire and sadism, not for the squeamish); Jason Starr, *Cold Caller*; Poppy Z. Brite, *Exquisite Corpse* (a horror novel about necrophiliac serial killers, even more extreme than *American Psycho*, but admired by some as a portrayal of contemporary decadence).
◘ to the fiction in general: ▶ Jay McInerney, *Bright Lights, Big City*; ▶ Douglas Coupland, *Generation X*; ▶ Chuck Palahniuk, *Fight Club*; ▶ Michel Houellebecq, *Atomised*.

LITERARY TRIVIA 4:

FIVE AUTHORS WHO WERE JAILBIRDS
John Bunyan
The Pilgrim's Progress, for many years the bestselling English book after the Bible, was written in Bedford Gaol where Bunyan was imprisoned for twelve years for preaching without a licence.

>> Fyodor Dostoevsky
The Russian novelist was sentenced to death for revolutionary activities and was even placed in front of a firing squad before being reprieved at the last minute and sent to Siberia, where he spent four years in a prison camp.

Sir Thomas Malory
The author of the Arthurian chivalric romance *Le Morte D'Arthur* was not notably chivalrous himself. He served time in a number of jails in the 1450s for rape, extortion and attempted murder.

Joe Orton
Together with his partner, Kenneth Halliwell, the 1960s playwright was jailed for six months for defacing public library books. The pair pasted their own surreal and often obscene jacket blurbs into an assortment of books.

Paul Verlaine
The turbulent relationship between the two nineteenth-century French poets Paul Verlaine and Arthur Rimbaud ended when Verlaine shot and wounded his younger lover. He spent two years in a Belgian prison for the shooting.

ELLROY, James (born 1948)
US novelist

Few crime writers have been more obviously driven to the genre by their own personal demons than James Ellroy. As his luridly readable autobiography *My Dark Places* makes clear, his was not an all-American, apple-pie upbringing. His mother was murdered when he was ten years old and his adolescence and early manhood were overshadowed by drink, drugs and sexual obsessions. (Breaking into women's apartments in order to sniff their underwear is but one of the confessions he makes in the book.) More than most writers, his writing has clearly been a lifeline to some kind of sanity and self-respect. His first few novels were straightforward hardboiled cop thrillers, but *The Black Dahlia* was something else. Taking a famous unsolved murder of the 1940s – one with echoes of his own mother's killing – Ellroy created a dark and compelling narrative in which real-life individuals interact with bruised and obsessed characters of his own creation. It was the beginning of his best and most intense work, the books collectively known as the 'LA Quartet', which comprise an extraordinary retelling of California's secret history seen through the eyes of its corrupt and cynical police officers. Marshalling dozens of characters and a tangled web of competing plots and sub-plots, Ellroy creates his own alternative history of the decades in which American dreams began to turn to nightmares.

The books that form the LA Quartet are The Black Dahlia, The Big Nowhere, LA Confidential *and* White Jazz. *Ellroy's other novels include* Brown's Requiem, Blood on the Moon, Because the Night, American Tabloid *and* The Cold Six Thousand. My Dark Places *is an autobiography which chronicles his own years of seedy delinquency and his attempts to learn the truth about his mother's murder.* Destination: Morgue *is a collection of short pieces, mostly on true crime.*

🕮Read on
◆ *American Tabloid* (an ambitious attempt to use the crime genre to explore the dark side of American history in the run-up to the JFK assassination).
◘ ❯❯ Michael Connelly, *Blood Work*; James Lee Burke, *Cadillac Jukebox*; George Pelecanos, *King Suckerman*; Max Allan Collins, *Angel in Black* (for a less intense fictional take on the Black Dahlia case which obsesses Ellroy).
◘ to *American Tabloid*: ❯❯ Don DeLillo, *Libra*.

ENRIGHT, Anne (born 1962)
Irish novelist

From the publication of her first short stories in her early 1990s and the appearance of her first novel, *The Wig My Father Wore*, in 1995, Anne Enright swiftly won a reputation as one of the subtlest and most individually stylish of contemporary Irish writers. *The Wig My Father Wore*, which wittily combined realism and surrealism in its story of a young woman whose life is transformed by the arrival of an angel on her doorstep, was highly praised but Enright remained a writer too little known outside Ireland until her profile was raised dramatically when *The Gathering* won the Man Booker Prize in 2007. The story of a troubled Dublin family coming together to mourn the death of one of its members, the novel was praised by one reviewer for its 'exhilarating bleakness'. Certainly the bitter wit with which the protagonist Veronica Hegarty anatomises her own self and unearths from memory the reasons for her brother's suicide makes *The Gathering* a powerful and uncomfortable read.

Anne Enright's other novels are What Are You Like? *and* The Pleasure of Eliza Lynch. The Portable Virgin *(her first book) and* Yesterday's Weather *are collections of short stories.* Making Babies *consists of reflections on motherhood.*

🐱Read on
♦ *The Pleasure of Eliza Lynch* (an exuberant historical novel about a beautiful Irish adventuress who became the mistress of a nineteenth-century South American dictator).
◘ ›› John Banville, *The Sea*; Sebastian Barry, *Annie Dunne*; John McGahern, *Amongst Women*.

FABER, Michel (born 1960)
Dutch-born British novelist

Born in the Netherlands and brought up in Australia, Michel Faber moved to Scotland as a young man and it was a Scottish publisher which brought out *The Crimson Petal and the White*, a huge novel Faber had spent years writing. This epic narrative is the story of Sugar, a resourceful and strong-minded prostitute in Victorian London. As she journeys through the class-ridden sexual politics of the imperial capital, caught between dreams of personal freedom and the dubious security offered by a wealthy admirer, the brutal realities of nineteenth century society are revealed. Rather as ›› John Fowles did thirty years earlier in *The French Lieutenant's Woman*, Faber uses many of the themes and motifs of Victorian fiction but he gives them a distinctly modern, indeed post-modern, twist. The story of Sugar gives readers many of the satisfactions provided by the great novelists of the nineteenth century but Faber constantly reminds us that it is also the product of a contemporary sensibility. It all adds to the tension and interest of what the publisher, on its first appearance, cleverly described as 'the first great nineteenth century novel of the twenty-first century'.

Faber's other novels are Under the Skin*,* The Courage Consort *and* The Fire Gospel*.* The Hundred and Ninety Nine Steps *is a novella about a woman stumbling across mystery and a long-forgotten murder at an archaeological dig in Whitby.* Some Rain Must Fall *consists of short stories written while Faber was working on his magnum opus,* The Apple *is a collection of stories featuring characters from* The Crimson Petal and the White*,* The Fahrenheit Twins *another volume of stories.*

📖 Read on
◆ *The Fire Gospel* (a satirical story of an academic unleashing a fifth, unauthorised Gospel on the world).
▣ Michael Cox, *The Meaning of Night*; ›› John Fowles, *The French Lieutenant's Woman*; Charles Palliser, *The Quincunx*; ›› D.J. Taylor, *Kept: A Victorian Mystery*; ›› Sarah Waters, *Tipping the Velvet*.

READ ON A THEME:

FANTASY ADVENTURE
    Terry Brooks, *The Sword of Shannara* (and subsequent Shannara books)
›› Arthur Conan Doyle, *The Lost World*
    David Eddings, *The Belgariad Quintet*
›› Raymond E. Feist, *The Riftwar* series
    Terry Goodkind, *The Sword of Truth* sequence
    J.V. Jones, *The Baker's Boy* (and its two sequels)
›› Robert Jordan, *The Wheel of Time* series
    George R.R. Martin, *A Game of Thrones* (and its sequels)
›› J.R.R. Tolkien, *The Lord of the Rings*
›› Jules Verne, *Journey to the Centre of the Earth*

See also: Fantasy Societies; High Adventure

READONATHEME:

FANTASY SOCIETIES

>> Michael Frayn, *Sweet Dreams*
>> Alasdair Gray, *Lanark*
>> Aldous Huxley, *Island*
>> Ursula Le Guin, *The Earthsea Quartet*
   Tanith Lee, *Biting the Sun*
   Anne McCaffrey, *Dragonflight*
>> Mervyn Peake, *The Gormenghast Trilogy*
   Robert Silverberg, *Lord Valentine's Castle*
>> Jonathan Swift, *Gulliver's Travels*
>> H.G. Wells, *The Time Machine*
   Gene Wolfe, *The Book of the New Sun*

See also: Future Societies

HIDDENGEM:

HOPE MIRRLEES – *LUD-IN-THE-MIST* (1926)

The unlikely hero of this book is Nathaniel Chanticleer, honest burgher and sometime mayor of the port of Lud-in-the-Mist. The town is situated in Dorimare, a land which borders Fairyland. Over many years, the people of Dorimare have grown fearful and suspicious of their fairy neighbours and, in particular, they dread the influence of 'fairy fruit' which alters and enraptures all those who eat it or drink its juice. When Chanticleer stumbles upon an underground plot to smuggle the fairy fruit into Dorimare and discovers that his own children have been spirited away as a consequence of it, he becomes an unlikely knight errant, riding across the border into Fairyland to rescue them. Written by a woman who was on the fringes of the Bloomsbury Group, this is a delightful work of fantasy fiction which deserves a much larger readership than it has ever had.

FARRELL, J.G. (James Gordon) (1935–79)
British novelist

In his best novels, Farrell took his themes from imperial history. *Troubles*, set in Ireland after the First World War, is a barbed account of the Irish freedom struggle against the English. *The Siege of Krishnapur*, equally vitriolic and farcical – its tone is close at times to ➤ Heller's *Catch-22* – is set in 1850s India, during the so-called Mutiny. *The Singapore Grip* is a blockbuster about the Japanese capture of Malaya in the Second World War – for Farrell, the beginning of Britain's eclipse as a global power. Taken together, the three books are an indictment of Britain's attitude towards its empire: not so much thuggishness as boneheaded indifference, the unconcern of those who never imagine that others might resent their rule.

📖Read on
◘ to *Troubles*: Liam O'Flaherty, *The Informer*; Bernard MacLaverty, *Cal*.
◘ to *The Siege of Krishnapur*: John Masters, *Nightrunners of Bengal*; Julian Rathbone, *The Mutiny*; Giles Foden, *Ladysmith*.
◘ to *The Singapore Grip*: ➤ J.G. Ballard, *Empire of the Sun*; Timothy Mo, *An Insular Possession*.

FAULKNER, William (1897–1962)
US novelist and short story writer

Faulkner's work deals obsessively with a single theme: the moral degeneracy of the American Deep South. His characters are the descendants of the cotton barons of the time before the Civil War, and of the slaves who worked for them. The whites live in crumbling mansions, dress in finery handed down from previous generations and bolster their sagging self-esteem with snobbery, racism and drink. The blacks either fawn, as if slavery had never been abolished, or seethe in decaying slums on the edge of town. The air itself seems tainted: despair, lust, introversion and murder clog people's minds. It is a society without hope or comfort, and Faulkner describes it in a series of moral horror stories, compulsive and merciless.

THE SOUND AND THE FURY (1929)
The novel's theme is how moral decadence overwhelms two generations of the white Compson family. We see a brother and sister, Caddy and Quentin, growing up as

bright, happy adolescents, full of hope for the future, only to fall victims to the family taint and spiral into incest, nymphomania and suicide. One of their brothers, Jason, a morose bully, succeeds his father as head of the family and becomes a miser and a tyrant; their other brother Benjy has a mental age of two. In the second half of the book we see the corruption threatening to engulf Caddy's and Quentin's incestuous daughter, and her attempts to break free from the family curse. Large sections of the book are told as first-person narratives, by Caddy, Jason, Quentin and, eerily, the retarded Benjy – a tour de force of writing demanding concentration in the reader. A final strand of claustrophobia is added by the Compsons' negro servants: watching, always present, like the chorus of a particularly fraught Greek tragedy.

Faulkner's short stories are in two fat volumes, Collected Stories *and* Uncollected Stories. *His main Southern novels, a series set in the imaginary Yoknapatawpha County, Mississippi, are* Sartoris, Absalom, Absalom!, The Unvanquished *and the trilogy consisting of* The Hamlet, The Town *and* The Mansion. *His other books include* Intruder in the Dust, Light in August, The Reivers, Sanctuary *and two books in experimental styles,* As I Lay Dying *and* Requiem for a Nun.

Read on

◆ *Light in August* (a woman searches for the father of her unborn child and a man struggles to assert his divided identity in a society riven by racism); *Intruder in the Dust* (an adolescent awakens to adult responsibilities as he strives to repay a debt to an elderly black man accused of murder).

◘ to the Deep South novels: ›› Carson McCullers, *The Ballad of the Sad Café*; William Styron, *Lie Down in Darkness*; Harper Lee, *To Kill a Mockingbird*; Flannery O'Connor, *Wise Blood*.

◘ on the theme of the degenerate, collapsing family: ›› Thomas Mann, *Buddenbrooks*; Giuseppe Tomaso di Lampedusa, *The Leopard*; Ivy Compton-Burnett, *Mother and Son*.

FAULKS, Sebastian (born 1953)
British novelist

There are writers (nearly all men) who write with knowledge of, even enthusiasm for, war, the technology of warfare and the comradeship of men in battle. There are writers (mostly women) who are precisely observant of the subtlest nuances of the ebb and flow of romantic relationships. Other writers (men and women) are skilled at the evocation of place. Sebastian Faulks is an unusual writer in that he writes with equal power about love, war and landscape. His finest novel to date is *Birdsong* (see below). Before *Birdsong* Faulks had written three novels, *A Trick of the Light*, *The Girl at the Lion d'Or* (an atmospheric story of a woman in a small French provincial town in the 1930s, still carrying the weight of the past on her shoulders) and *A Fool's Alphabet*. Since the resounding commercial and critical success of *Birdsong* he has published *Charlotte Gray* (about a young woman journeying into occupied France in the Second World War in search of her lover and involving herself in the work of the Resistance), *On Green Dolphin Street*, set in Kennedy-era Washington, *Human Traces* (2005), which follows the fortunes of two pioneering psychiatrists across several decades of the late nineteenth and early twentieth centuries, the blackly comic *Engleby* and the James Bond novel, *Devil May Care*.

BIRDSONG (1993)

In 1910 a young Englishman, Stephen Wraysford, arrives in Amiens to stay with the Azaire family. Soon he is embarked upon an intense, convention-defying affair with Madame Azaire and, when it is discovered, the two leave together. The affair does not last and Stephen is left a cold and empty man by its failure, uncaring of what his future might be. History and politics decree that his future is to be the trenches of the Great War where he becomes an officer. Taking part in Ypres, the Somme and many of the major actions of the war, Stephen watches men die horribly all around him and discovers in himself a surprising, steely determination to survive. As the northern France he knew before the war becomes a quagmire and a slaughter-house, his past relationship with Madame Azaire resurfaces in an unexpected and disturbing way. No précis of *Birdsong* can do justice to the power of Faulks's writing both in its evocation of the overwhelming love affair and in its descriptions of the claustrophobia and terror of the trenches and battle. Imagining the unimaginable, Faulks creates a remarkable novel of individuals trapped in the coils of history.

Read on

◆ *Charlotte Gray*.

◘ ≫ Pat Barker, *Regeneration* (and its successors *The Eye in the Door* and *The Ghost Road*); ≫ Louis de Bernières, *Captain Corelli's Mandolin*; ≫ Ian McEwan, *Atonement*; Andrew Greig, *That Summer*.

FEIST, Raymond E. (Elias) (born 1945)
US novelist

Since Tolkien first launched the epic fantasy genre, there have been many writers who have trafficked in dwarves and elves, wise magicians and dragon lords. There have been many writers who have attempted to match his creation of a world-engulfing struggle between the forces of good and the forces of evil. Most have created pale echoes of Middle Earth and their books have travelled down roads well travelled already. One of the few who can genuinely claim to have created a rich and powerfully imagined fantasy world is Raymond E. Feist. Feist's *Riftwar Saga* is an ongoing series in which there are three-dimensional characters who grow and develop rather than cardboard cutouts, complex plots that bypass the clichés of the genre and an adult rather than adolescent awareness of how the politics of alternative realities might work. Chronicling the conflicts between the two cultures of Midkemia (Middle Earth meets the Middle Ages) and Kelewan (a kind of samurai state supported by magic), the *Riftwar Saga* is fantasy on a grand scale. One of Feist's cleverest ploys in the books is to turn our expectations on their head by shifting our perspectives on the different cultures he has invented. In the original trilogy our sympathies are enlisted on behalf of the Midkemians and the Kelewan are a ruthless, alien enemy. In the *Empire Trilogy* (co-written with Janny Wurts) we see events from the viewpoint of the Kelewan and much that was inexplicable in their behaviour is given a context.

The original Riftwar Saga consists of three novels – Magician, Silverthorn *and* A Darkness at Sethanon. *Feist's other books are largely grouped in trilogies and sequences, including the Empire Trilogy* (Daughter of the Empire, Servant of the Empire, Mistress of the Empire), *Legends of the Riftwar* (Honoured Enemy, Murder In LaMut, Jimmy the Hand) *and The Serpentwar Saga* (Shadow of a Dark Queen, Rise of a Merchant Prince, Rage of a Demon King, Shards of a Broken Crown). *Feist's most recent work is a sequence called the Darkwar Saga* (Flight of the Nighthawks, Into a Dark Realm, Wrath of a Mad God).

🐦 Read on

◻ nearly all the major works of modern fantasy writers are multi-volume sequences. The following are a few authors and the general titles of the series in which they have created worlds and landscapes to match those of Feist: David Eddings, The Belgariad books; ❯❯ Robert Jordan, The Wheel of Time series; Terry Brooks, The

Shannara series; David Gemmell, *Legend* and the other books in the Drenai Sagas; Terry Goodkind, The Sword of Truth series.

FIELDING, Henry (1707–54)
British novelist and playwright

Fielding's first successes were with satirical stage comedies but his plays proved too political for the authorities in Georgian England and they closed them down. He qualified as a magistrate and set up the Bow Street Runners, ancestors of the modern police force. He continued to write, but now turned to prose fiction, announcing that he meant to write an English equivalent of *Don Quixote*. His books are comic life-stories, following charming young people in a series of escapades as they journey from country house to inn, from farmyard to theatre box, from law court to bedroom, gathering experience and outwitting would-be predators at every step. Fielding's novels are long and leisurely: it is as if he is taking a stroll through English society, high and low, and everything he sees or hears reminds him of an anecdote, genial, unhurried and preposterous.

TOM JONES (1749)
Tom Jones is a foundling brought up by kindly Squire Allworthy. He is a personable, amorous young man, and his immorality finally makes Allworthy send him into the world to seek his fortune. The novel tells Tom's adventures, in and out of bed, as he wanders through England enjoying life as it comes, torn by the thought of his true love Sophia Western, but still ready to be seduced by every pretty girl he meets. The story is told in short chapters, like extended anecdotes, and Fielding keeps breaking off to address the reader directly, telling jokes, pointing morals and commenting on the life and manners of the time.

Fielding's other novels are Joseph Andrews *and* Amelia. A Journey from This World to the Next *and* The Life and Death of Jonathan Wild the Great *are short, savage satires: the second, for example, treats a notorious, real-life thief as if he were an epic hero.* Journal of a Voyage to Lisbon *is a fascinating travel diary about crossing the Bay of Biscay in a leaky, storm-tossed ship.*

Read on
♦ *Joseph Andrews* (a parody of the heroine-in-moral-danger novels of ➤➤ Samuel

Richardson: the story of a young man so beautiful that every woman he meets longs to entice him into bed).

◘ other picaresque adventures: Miguel de Cervantes, *Don Quixote*; ›› Laurence Sterne, *Tristram Shandy*.

◘ later books in a similarly relaxed, discursive vein: ›› H.G. Wells, *Kipps*; ›› Thomas Mann, *Confessions of Felix Krull*; ›› Saul Bellow, *The Adventures of Augie March*.

READ ON A THEME:

THE FILM BUSINESS

Dirk Bogarde, *West of Sunset*
Charles Bukowski, *Hollywood*
›› Len Deighton, *Close-Up*
John Gregory Dunne, *Playland*
›› F. Scott Fitzgerald, *The Last Tycoon*
›› Elmore Leonard, *Get Shorty*
Frederic Raphael, *California Time*
Theodore Roszak, *Flicker*
Budd Schulberg, *What Makes Sammy Run?*
Terry Southern, *Blue Movie*
Nathanael West, *The Day of the Locust*

READ ON A THEME:

FILM OF THE BOOK, BOOK OF THE FILM

Peter Benchley, *Jaws* (filmed in 1975 by Steven Spielberg)
James M. Cain, *Double Indemnity* (filmed in 1944 by Billy Wilder)
Howard Fast, *Spartacus* (filmed in 1960 by Stanley Kubrick)
›› C.S. Forester, *The African Queen* (filmed in 1951 by John Huston)
Winston Groom, *Forrest Gump* (filmed in 1994 by Robert Zemeckis)
Thomas Harris, *The Silence of the Lambs* (filmed in 1991 by Jonathan Demme)

>> Patricia Highsmith, *Strangers on a Train* (filmed in 1951 by Alfred Hitchcock)

Ken Kesey, *One Flew Over the Cuckoo's Nest* (filmed in 1975 by Milos Forman)

>> Michael Ondaatje, *The English Patient* (filmed in 1996 by Anthony Minghella)

Mario Puzo, *The Godfather* (filmed in 1972 by Francis Ford Coppola)

Walter Tevis, *The Hustler* (filmed in 1961 by Robert Rossen)

Charles Webb, *The Graduate* (filmed in 1967 by Mike Nichols)

READ ON A THEME

FIRST WORLD WAR

Henri Barbusse, *Under Fire*

>> Pat Barker, *Regeneration*

Ben Elton, *The First Casualty*

>> Sebastian Faulks, *Birdsong*

Timothy Findley, *The Wars*

>> Ernest Hemingway, *A Farewell to Arms*

>> Susan Hill, *Strange Meeting*

Frederic Manning, *Her Privates We* (later published in unexpurgated form as *The Middle Parts of Fortune*)

R.H. Mottram, *The Spanish Farm Trilogy*

Erich Maria Remarque, *All Quiet on the Western Front*

Derek Robinson, *Goshawk Squadron*

FISCHER, Tibor (born 1959)
British novelist

Don't Read This Book If You're Stupid is the self-consciously defiant title of a collection of short stories published by Tibor Fischer in 2000. It is a health warning that could be attached to all of Fischer's books. He really doesn't like stupidity. Most of us get annoyed or mildly irritated by the petty, everyday stupidities of ordinary life. Fischer gets outraged. He has the 'savage indignation' of the great satirists and his books are scathing, witty indictments of our follies. *The Thought Gang* is a dazzling display of linguistic and intellectual fireworks which tells the unlikely story of an out-of-work philosopher joining forces with a one-armed robber in a crime spree through France. Peppered with epigrams, puns and stylistic inventions, it is one of the funniest and most imaginative novels of the last twenty years. *The Collector Collector* is a darker and more misanthropic book but almost equally original. Its 'narrator' is an ancient Sumerian bowl, a clay vessel somehow made sentient and marked by a uniformly poor view of the human clay that has possessed it over the centuries. The narrative alternates between stories from four thousand years of human lust, greed and hypocrisy (as observed by the bowl) and a modern story of sexual and financial treacheries centred on the bowl's current owner. *Voyage to the End of the Room* tells the story of a computer graphics designer who has withdrawn into her South London flat, bringing the world into it through the media of satellite TV and the Internet, and yet still finds her past catching up with her.

Read on

◆ *Under the Frog* (Fischer's first novel, a black comedy about two members of a travelling basketball team in 1950s Hungary); *Good to Be God* (an unsuccessful con artist arrives in Miami and attempts to persuade its more gullible citizens that, despite all appearances, He is the Supreme Being).
▪ ≫ Will Self, *Great Apes*; ≫ Jonathan Coe, *What a Carve Up!*; ≫ John Lanchester, *The Debt to Pleasure*; ≫ David Mitchell, *number9dream*.

FITZGERALD, F. (Francis) Scott (1890–1940)
US novelist and short story writer

In the USA of the 1920s the earnestness which had been needed to win the First World War was replaced by giddy exhilaration. Jazz, bootleg liquor, drugs and sex seemed to be not merely pleasures, but symbols of a new, liberated age – and the fact that that age was clearly doomed, that the dancing would end in tears, gave every party, every spending spree, an edge of extra excitement, as if people were roller-skating on the brink of the abyss. Rich, handsome, athletic and talented, Fitzgerald not only wrote about this doomed high society, but was one of its leaders. In the 1930s, when the inevitable reckoning came – the Great Depression was paralleled in Fitzgerald's life by his wife's madness and his own alcoholism and bankruptcy – his books not unnaturally turned sour and sad. But his 1920s stories and novels told the legend of the Jazz Age with such glittering force that it is easy, now, to believe that all Americans, and not just a few thousand sophisticates, lived like that.

THE GREAT GATSBY (1925)

In a millionaire community on Long Island, the enigmatic bachelor Gatsby gives huge all-night parties at his mansion, orgies of dancing, drugs and sex, the season's most fashionable events. His fascinated neighbour, the book's narrator Nick Carraway, makes friends with him and begins unravelling the secrets of his personality. Carraway's intervention triggers revelations about Gatsby's criminal past, and a love affair between Gatsby and the wife of a wealthy oaf, Tom Buchanan; these in turn lead to further tragedy. At the end of the book Carraway sits alone outside Gatsby's deserted house, reflecting on the emptiness of the lives he has just described.

Fitzgerald's other novels are This Side of Paradise, The Beautiful and Damned, Tender is the Night *(a bitterly autobiographical tale of an alcoholic doctor and his insane wife on the French Riviera) and the unfinished* The Last Tycoon, *a satire on the Hollywood for which he wrote rubbish to earn money in his last desperate months of life.* The Collected Short Stories of F. Scott Fitzgerald *brings together his shorter works, including the novella* The Diamond as Big as the Ritz, *the Pat Hobby stories about a hack Hollywood screenwriter down on his luck and* The Curious Case of Benjamin Button, *recently made into a film by David Fincher.*

⮜Read on

◆ *The Beautiful and Damned* (about the doomed marriage of two bright young things, leaders of Jazz Age society, a book displaying fierce irony for today's readers given what we know of the eventual decay in Fitzgerald's own marriage).
◘ ≫ Evelyn Waugh, *Vile Bodies*; ≫ Anthony Powell, *Afternoon Men*; Anita Loos, *Gentlemen Prefer Blondes*; Dawn Powell, *A Time to be Born*.

FITZGERALD, Penelope (1916–2000)
British writer

Fitzgerald published her first novel, *The Golden Child*, in 1977 when she was sixty one, won the Booker Prize two years later with *Offshore*, and went on to publish seven more novels. Each is different in period, setting and characters, but all have the same wry style, the same feeling that Fitzgerald is a detached but not uninvolved spectator of the miseries and follies of her people, and the same 'hint of the sublime' (in one reviewer's florid praise). She shares these qualities with ➤➤ Jane Austen, and if Austen were writing today this is exactly the kind of barbed, wise prose she might produce. Two typical Fitzgerald books are *At Freddie's*, set in a Covent Garden stage school for precocious brats in the 1960s, and *The Gate of Angels*, about a young academic in a 1912 all-male college coming to terms with the torments of 'the mind-body problem' – that is, reconciling the Apollonian quest for truth with the Dionysian urge for emotional experience, not least of sex.

Fitzgerald's other novels are The Bookshop, Human Voices, Innocence, The Beginning of Spring *and* The Blue Flower *(a haunting recreation of life and love in the circle of the German Romantic poet Novalis).* The Means of Escape *is a collection of short stories. She also wrote prize-winning biographies:* Edward Burne-Jones, The Knox Brothers *(one of whom, E.V. Knox of Punch, was her father) and* Charlotte Mew and Her Friends.

📖Read on
◆ *Innocence* (set in Italy after the Second World War; about the problems and difficulties of trying to make other people happy).
◘ ➤➤ Beryl Bainbridge, *Every Man for Himself*; ➤➤ Rose Tremain, *Music & Silence*; ➤➤ Anne Tyler, *Morgan's Passing*; Salley Vickers, *Miss Garnet's Angel*; Jane Gardam, *God on the Rocks*; J.L. Carr, *A Month in the Country*.

FLAUBERT, Gustave (1821–80)
French novelist

Many of Flaubert's contemporary writers – even such 'realists' as ➤➤ Balzac and ➤➤ Dickens – believed that 'fiction' involved larger-than-life characters, events or emotions. Flaubert's ambition, by contrast, was to hold up a mirror to ordinary people in humdrum situations, to take the boring events of commonplace lives and make them interesting. He also avoided heightened language, wit, irony and the other devices novelists used to enliven their narrative. He worked to make his prose evenly paced and unobtrusive, taking its tensions and climaxes from the flow of events themselves. In doing so, he aimed to reveal by indirect means just how tempestuous and extraordinary everyday lives can be.

MADAME BOVARY (1857)

Emma, a romantic and foolish young woman, dreams of being swept away on clouds of ecstasy, either by a handsome lover or into the arms of the Church. She marries a small-town doctor and finds the routine of provincial life stifling and unfulfilling. She tries to bring excitement into her life by flirting, and is gradually trapped in pathetic and grubby love affairs, stealing from her husband to pay for her ever more eccentric whims. In the end, destroyed by her inability to live up to her own dreams, she kills herself – and everyone else's life goes on as if she had never existed.

Flaubert's other novels of ordinary French life are Sentimental Education (L'Éducation sentimentale) *and the unfinished* Bouvard and Pécuchet. Salammbô *applies the same techniques to a story of the Carthage of Hannibal's time, to bizarre effect, as if an archaeological treatise had been jumbled up with the script for a Hollywood epic film.* The Temptation of St Anthony *seeks to describe all the temptations, of flesh, spirit and will, which might assail a devout Roman Catholic;* Three Stories *contains* 'A Simple Heart', *one of the most moving of all Flaubert's works.*

⏾Read on

◆ *Sentimental Education* (about a young man who tries, like Emma Bovary, to spice his boring life with grand passions, and fails. A secondary strand in the book is the political situation leading up to the 1848 revolution – something as busy and sterile, in Flaubert's opinion, as his hero's attempts to find meaning in existence).

◻ Italo Svevo, *A Life*; ▸▸ Arnold Bennett, *Hilda Lessways*; ▸▸ Joseph Heller, *Something Happened*; ▸▸ Elizabeth Taylor, *A Wreath of Roses*; ▸▸ Iris Murdoch, *Under the Net*; ▸▸ R.K. Narayan, *The English Teacher*, though set in a society (provincial India) and a period (the 1950s) remote from Madame Bovary, and less than a quarter as long, magnificently matches Flaubert's insight into the way that the joys and sorrows of small lives, no less than large, can tear the heart.

FLEMING, Fergus (born 1959)
British historian

Over the last decade Fergus Fleming has written a series of compelling accounts of the adventures and misadventures of Europeans in the furthest flung corners of the world during the heroic age of exploration. Simultaneously alert both to the courage and endurance of these pioneers and to the ways in which their exploits can seem strange and even ridiculous to our ironic, slacker generation, Fleming's books are witty, readable and original. His first, *Barrow's Boys*, looked at the lives and expeditions of those nineteenth-century explorers despatched by Sir John Barrow, Second Secretary to the Admiralty, to fill in the blank spaces on the maps of either Africa or the Polar regions. He followed this with *Ninety Degrees North*, the story of the almost farcical rivalry that developed between men such as Robert Peary and Frederick Cook in the struggle to be the first to reach the North Pole. *Killing Dragons* is about the first mountaineers to attempt to conquer Alpine peaks in the nineteenth century; *The Sword and the Cross* looks at two contrasting French adventurers who played major roles in their country's gradual expansion into Saharan Africa.

Read on
◘ Sarah Murgatroyd, *The Dig Tree*; Nathaniel Philbrick, *Sea of Glory*; Anthony Sattin, *The Gates of Africa*.

FLEMING, Ian (1908–64)
British novelist

Fleming's James Bond books are like comic strips for adults: Bond is a super-hero who saves the world from spectacularly nasty, psychopathic master-criminals. Bond wins through by a mixture of supreme physical prowess and a late-Edwardian one-upmanship somewhat bizarre in the 1960s setting. Adult tastes are catered for less by psychological insight or intellectual depth than by frequent sex scenes (Bond, as well as everything else, is a super-stud) and by laconic, hardboiled wit. In everything but plot – over-the-top technology, larky dialogue, high-gloss violence – the Bond films give the exact flavour of Fleming's books.

The Bond novels include Goldfinger, Moonraker, Thunderball, From Russia With Love, Diamonds are Forever, Dr No, On Her Majesty's Secret Service, You Only Live Twice *and* The Man With the Golden Gun. Octopussy *is a collection of short stories.*

🖙 Read on
◆ *From Russia With Love.*
◘ in the 1960s, until ➤➤ Len Deighton and ➤➤ John Le Carré took the spy story in a different direction, there were a million Bond imitations and spoofs, of which some of the jolliest are by John Gardner, Fleming's official successor as chronicler of Bond. (A good example of Gardner at his best is *Scorpius*.) ➤➤ Sebastian Faulks has recently taken on the role of chronicler of Bond's adventures with *Devil May Care*. Charlie Higson has produced a series for young adults which features Bond as a schoolboy. *Silverfin* was the first of these.
◘ other Bond follow-ups: ➤➤ Robert Ludlum, *The Matarese Circle*.

LITERARY TRIVIA 5:

FIVE CURIOUS PSEUDONYMS
Count O'Blather (➤➤ Flann O'Brien)
Comic writer Flann O'Brien produced a monthly magazine in the 1930s under the title Blather, which he claimed was the work of one Count O'Blather and his simple-minded son Blazes. Flann O'Brien was also a pseudonym, although a less outlandish one, of the real author, Brian O'Nolan.

Hilarius Bogbinder (Søren Kierkegaard)
The Danish philosopher used many weird pseudonyms during his career, including this one, and regularly used one nom de plume to review books he had written under another.

Corno di Bassetto (George Bernard Shaw)
Shaw used this pseudonym, which is an Italian term for a type of clarinet, when he was producing regular music criticism in the 1880s and 1890s for the London press.

> **Miss Tickletoby** (>> William Makepeace Thackeray)
> Before he made his name with his novels, Thackeray published comic sketches and essays under countless pseudonyms. 'Miss Tickletoby's Lectures on English History' appeared in *Punch* in 1842.
>
> **Gom Gut** (>> Georges Simenon)
> The awesomely prolific crime novelist Georges Simenon published hundreds of novels, some written in a matter of days, under pseudonyms such as Gom Gut, Luc Dorsan and Christian Brulls.

FLEMING, Peter (1907–71)
British travel writer and historian

Peter Fleming's reputation has long languished in the shadow of that of his younger brother Ian (see above), creator of James Bond, but there are plenty of admirers who would say that the older brother's blend of detached irony and almost >> Wodehousian farce in far-flung territories is much more appealing than the espionage fantasies produced by his more famous sibling. Long before >> Redmond O'Hanlon was publishing his accounts of over-educated incompetents in wild places, Peter Fleming wrote *Brazilian Adventure*, his description of a 1932 expedition into the Amazonian jungle in search of Colonel Fawcett, a half-mad army officer who had disappeared seven years earlier while trying to locate a lost city supposedly peopled by white Indians. Any chance of tracking down the missing colonel vanishes almost before the expedition leaves England but Fleming chronicles the trials and tribulations of his band of naïve adventurers with tremendous wit and comic energy. His later books include other similarly ironic accounts of travels off the beaten path (*News from Tartary*, for example, describes his 1935 journey from Peking to Kashmir) and histories of imperial adventures in the Far East (*Bayonets to Lhasa* tells the story of Younghusband's expedition into Tibet in 1904; *The Siege at Peking* the tale of the Boxer Rebellion in China and the defence of the foreign legations in Peking).

Peter Fleming published many other books, including One's Company, The Flying Visit *(a novel in which Hitler pays Britain an unintended visit),* My Aunt's

Rhinoceros, The Gower Street Poltergeist *and* Goodbye to the Bombay Bowler *(all collections of essays)*, A Forgotten Journey *and* The Fate of Admiral Kolchak.

≋Read on

◆ *Bayonets to Lhasa*.

◘ to the travel books: David Grann, *The Lost City of Z*; Fitzroy Maclean, *Eastern Approaches*; ›› Redmond O'Hanlon, *In Trouble Again*; ›› Evelyn Waugh, *When the Going Was Good*.

◘ to the history books: Peter Hopkirk, *The Great Game*.

FORD, Ford Madox (1873–1939)
British novelist and non-fiction writer

Although Ford produced books of all kinds, from biographies to historical novels (*The Fifth Queen*, a Tudor trilogy), he is best remembered for *Parade's End* and *The Good Soldier*. *The Good Soldier* (1915) is a ›› Jamesian story about two couples who meet in a German hotel and become emotionally and sexually entwined, with devastating results for both themselves and the innocent young ward of one of them. The four novels of *Parade's End* (1924–28) tell how a country landowner, a young man rooted in the social and moral attitudes of the past, is forced by experience (as an officer in the First World War and as a reluctant participant in the freer sexual atmosphere of the post-war years) to slough off the skin of Victorian morality and come to terms, a dozen years later than everyone else, with twentieth-century values.

≋Read on

◘ Vita Sackville-West, *The Edwardians*; Isabel Colegate, *The Shooting Party*; ›› Kazuo Ishiguro, *An Artist of the Floating World* (setting the 'coming-to-terms' theme in post-war Japan).

FORESTER, C.S. (Cecil Scott) (1899–1966)
British novelist

Forester is best known for his Hornblower novels, about a career officer in the British navy of Nelson's time. The books are rich in the detail of life on wooden fighting ships, and the historical background is meticulous. Forester, however, gives Hornblower twentieth-century sensibilities (he is, for example, sickened by floggings and horrified by the brutality of war) which both flesh him out as a character and draw the reader into the story. The Hornblower series has overshadowed Forester's other books, which include two superb novels set during the Napoleonic Wars (*Death to the French* and *The Gun*), the psychological crime stories *Payment Deferred* and *Plain Murder*, and the comedy-thriller *The African Queen*, memorably filmed in the 1950s with Katharine Hepburn and Humphrey Bogart.

The core of the Hornblower series is a trilogy (The Happy Return, Flying Colours, Ship of the Line) *often published together as* Captain Horatio Hornblower. *Other books in the series fill in details of Hornblower's career, tracing his adventures over a quarter of a century. Typical titles are* Mr Midshipman Hornblower, Hornblower and the Atropos, Hornblower in the West Indies *and* Lord Hornblower.

☜Read on
- *The African Queen* (about a prissy missionary and a rough-diamond ship's captain who take a leaky old boat full of dynamite down an African river in the First World War to blow up an enemy convoy – and fall in love on the way).
- ◘ to the Hornblower books: ›› Patrick O'Brian, the Jack Aubrey stories, beginning with *Master and Commander*; ›› Bernard Cornwell, *Sharpe's Honour* (one of a series about an army officer at the time of the Peninsular War); Alexander Kent, *Richard Bolitho, Midshipman*; Richard Woodman, *The Eye of the Fleet*.

FORSTER, E.M. (Edward Morgan) (1879–1970)
British novelist

All Forster's novels were written in the 1900s (though *A Passage to India* was not published until 1924), and all are concerned with the crippling emotional reticence he considered typical of the Edwardian age. (Many were filmed in the 1980s and 1990s, with huge success.) Outwardly extrovert and competent, the Edwardians

(Forster thought) were afraid of intimacy. They replaced it with 'manners', and often even members of the same family, even husbands and wives, were inhibited from showing towards each other the kind of genuine feelings they revealed towards God, the flag or their pampered pets. Forster's plots all turn on the disastrous results of emotional inexperience, of people blundering about in each other's sensibilities. In *Where Angels Fear to Tread* an Edwardian family's inability to believe that an Italian can have true paternal feelings for his baby leads to a doomed expedition to Italy to kidnap the child. In *Howards End* a note from one friend to another, confessing love (in fact one snatched kiss in a garden), leads to a hurricane of emotional misunderstanding and disapproval that involves a dozen people and three generations. Forster, himself an emotional introvert (a self-deprecating homosexual), offers no solutions, but few writers have better described the problem. His intuition for emotional nuance and his compelling characterization (especially of women), give his books fascination despite their narrow focus.

A PASSAGE TO INDIA (1924)

Adela Quested leaves for India to get to know her fiancé Ronny before she marries him. Her openness of manner, and especially the way she treats Indians as equals, offends the stuffy British community. For her part, she is overwhelmed by India, and her stupefaction leads her to a moment of mental confusion during which she accuses an Indian friend, Dr Aziz, of molesting her on a visit to the Malabar Caves. In court, oppressed by the certainty of the English that Aziz must be guilty, she reruns the events at Malabar in her mind, and suddenly recants. Her behaviour has, however, made apparent the unbridgeable gulf between Indians and English under the Raj, not to mention the lack of communication between 'free spirits' such as herself and her more hidebound contemporaries.

Forster's other novels are The Longest Journey, A Room With a View *and* Maurice *(about a homosexual friendship; written in the 1910s but not published until the 1970s) He also published two collections of short stories,* The Celestial Omnibus *and* The Eternal Moment *in his lifetime.* The Life to Come, *another collection of shorter fiction, appeared two years after his death.* Aspects of the Novel *is a work of literary criticism.*

📖Read on

◆ *A Room With a View* (about the emotional awakening of a naïve English girl visiting Italy for the first time and realizing that there is a real world beyond Edwardian English convention).

◘ to *A Passage to India*: Ruth Prawer Jhabvala, *Heat and Dust*; Paul Scott, *The Raj Quartet*; M.M. Kaye, *The Far Pavilions*; Pankaj Mishra, *The Romantics*.
◘ to Forster's work in general: ›› Henry James, *The Wings of the Dove*; ›› Marcel Proust, *Within a Budding Grove* (Part Two of *Remembrance of Things Past*); L.P. Hartley, *The Go-Between*.

FORSTER, Margaret (born 1938)
British novelist

The film of Forster's novel, *Georgy Girl*, was one of the most characteristic British movies of the 1960s and the book was Forster's first major success. Its heroine (a perfectly ordinary girl desperate to sample the Swinging Sixties before they, or her own youth, disappear) was a neat alternative to other, more bubble-headed, fictional heroines of the time. Forster is outstanding at showing slow change in people's characters: the coming of maturity, the growth of wisdom, processes of human warmth or misery. Many of her best-known novels (for example *Marital Rites*, *Private Papers* and *Mother Can You Hear Me?*, all published in the 1980s), are about people trapped in relationships, who find an escape not because of outside events, but through their developing awareness of their own potential. Her style is patient, meticulous and absorbing.

LADY'S MAID (1990)
Elizabeth Wilson, a shy country girl, goes to London in the 1850s to become lady's maid to Elizabeth Barrett, a brilliant intellect trapped in the body of a feeble invalid. We see, from Wilson's point of view, the development of their relationship, as Barrett is warmed by Wilson's understated robustness of character, and Wilson learns from Barrett that she herself is a person, with a brain and character worth consideration. Then Robert Browning courts and marries Barrett, and the relationship, the mutual dependency between mistress and maid (or is it by now friend and friend?) is forever changed.

Forster's other novels include The Travels of Maudie Tipstaff, Have the Men Had Enough?, Mother's Boys, The Battle for Christabel, Shadow Baby, The Memory Box, Diary of an Ordinary Woman, Is There Anything You Want?, Keeping the World Away *and* Over. *She has also published two remarkable and revealing volumes about her own family and north of England background:* Hidden Lives *and* Precious Lives.

Read on

♦ *Private Papers*; *The Battle for Christabel*.
◘ ≫ Margaret Drabble, *The Garrick Year*; ≫ Anne Tyler, *Morgan's Passing*; ≫ Carol Shields, *The Stone Diaries*; Elizabeth Jolley, *Miss Peabody's Inheritance*; Nina Bawden, *Afternoon of a Good Woman*.

FORSYTH, Frederick (born 1938)
British novelist

Forsyth worked as a BBC reporter and a war correspondent, and his thrillers are as immediate and waffle-free as good news stories. They often include real people and events; only the hair-trigger tension of his plots makes actuality look tame. In *The Odessa File*, for example, a journalist covering the hunt for a war criminal uncovers a Nazi arms-smuggling conspiracy to help Arab terrorists in Israel. *The Day of the Jackal*, famously, follows a hired killer as he prepares to assassinate General de Gaulle. The details are fiction, but the story is as fresh as this morning's news.

Forsyth's other novels are The Devil's Alternative, The Fourth Protocol, The Dogs of War, The Negotiator, The Fist of God, Icon, Avenger *and* The Afghan. The Shepherd *is a short novel;* The Deceiver *contains four linked stories;* No Comebacks *and* The Veteran and other Stories *are collections of short stories.*

Read on

◘ Gerald Seymour, *The Walking Dead* (from another ex-news reporter); Jack Higgins, *The Eagle Has Landed*; Anthony Price, *Soldier No More*; Robert Ludlum, *The Bourne Identity*; Jean-Christophe Grangé, *The Flight of the Storks*.

FOWLES, John (1926–2005)

British novelist

Fowles worked as a teacher (of modern languages) until the success of *The Collector* (1963) made it possible for him to write full time. His main themes are obsession and delusion. The deranged hero of *The Collector* 'collects' a pretty girl as one might a butterfly. The heroes of *Daniel Martin* and *Mantissa* are authors deserted by the Muse, one a screenwriter corrupted by success, the other a novelist undergoing creative therapy at the hands (and other parts) of a seductive, feminist goddess. *A Maggot*, set in the eighteenth century, reworks a real-life murder investigation to take in erotic obsession, witchcraft, religious mania and flying saucers. Fowles further blurs the boundary between truth and fiction by using experimental techniques. He shifts between past and present, makes authorial asides and comments, and gives us two, three or half a dozen alternative versions of the same events. As with ▶▶ Lawrence Durrell, this experimentalism is coupled with ornate prose (sometimes in brilliant imitation of eighteenth- and nineteenth-century styles); few modern bestselling writers offer such a packed experience.

THE FRENCH LIEUTENANT'S WOMAN (1969)

The book's heart is a straightforward nineteenth-century story about the obsessive love between a rich man and an outcast, the 'French Lieutenant's woman' of the title. They meet in the seaside town of Lyme Regis; their affair scandalizes society; she runs away; he pursues her. Fowles's prose, likewise, is for much of the time straightforward and solid in the nineteenth-century manner. But he also plays games with the reader. He keeps interrupting the story to tell us things about Lyme Regis (home of Mary Anning the fossil collector), Darwin, Freudian psychology and the social customs of Victorian London. He claims that he has no idea what will happen next, that this is the characters' story, not his. He also supplies alternative endings, so that we can choose our own. These devices give the book an unexpectedness in marked contrast to its sober nineteenth-century heart – it is as if someone reading us ▶▶ George Eliot or ▶▶ Thackeray kept breaking off to perform conjuring tricks.

Apart from novels, Fowles published a story collection, The Ebony Tower, The Aristos, *a set of philosophical meditations, and* Wormholes, *a collection of non-fiction pieces. Two volumes of his stimulatingly cantankerous* Journals *have so far been published and there are probably more works to appear posthumously.*

🕮Read on

◆ *The Magus* (revised version recommended), about a man trying obsessively to find out if what he thinks he experiences is real or fantasy. Much of it involves magic and takes place on a mysterious Greek island – or seems to, for our perception of 'truth' and 'fiction' is as shifting as the character's.

◘ to *The French Lieutenant's Woman*: John Barth, *The Sot-Weed Factor*; John Berger, *G*; ❯❯ William Golding, *Rites of Passage*.

◘ to *The Magus*: ❯❯ Lawrence Durrell, *The Dark Labyrinth/Cefalù*; D.M. Thomas, *The White Hotel*.

FRANCIS, Dick (born 1920)
British novelist

Authenticity is a priceless commodity in crime fiction and thriller writing. Pick up any Dick Francis novel and it is immediately apparent that he knows the world of racing inside out and is familiar with the characters who people it. It is this authenticity (and his ability to fashion a tightly constructed plot) that has kept him a bestselling writer for forty years. Francis was champion jockey in 1953/4 and was riding the Queen Mother's horse Devon Loch in the 1956 Grand National when it fell so mysteriously with victory in sight. In a later fall Francis was badly injured and forced to give up riding. He turned to journalism and, in 1962, published his first novel, *Dead Cert*. More than forty others have followed, all of them providing that first-hand knowledge of the racing game which fans so much enjoy.

Dick Francis's many other novels include For Kicks, Blood Sport, Bonecrack, High Stakes, Reflex, Bolt, The Edge, Comeback, Wild Horses, Come to Grief, To the Hilt, 10lb Penalty, Second Wind, Shattered *and* Straight.

🕮Read on

◆ *Bonecrack*; *Hot Money*.

◘ John Francome, *Lifeline*; Stephen Dobyns, *Saratoga Fleshpot* (racing crime with a US setting); Richard Pitman, *Hunted*.

FRANZEN, Jonathan (born 1959)

US novelist

Franzen has published only three novels in twenty years but, with the publication of *The Corrections* in 2001 he established himself as one of the leading figures in contemporary American fiction. He also caused something of a media stir by throwing away the opportunity to appear on *The Oprah Winfrey Show* (she had chosen *The Corrections* for her massively influential book club) and harvest the resulting sales of his work. Anyone who had actually read *The Corrections* would have been aware that Franzen was deeply ambivalent about many aspects of the TV and celebrity culture which Oprah represented. The novel is a large and ambitious story of one family seen against the backdrop of the last half-century of American history. The lives of the Lamberts – Alfred and Enid and their three children, Denise, Gary and Chip – are anatomized in intimate detail and, as Franzen lays them bare, they provide him with opportunities to examine very nearly every aspect of contemporary American culture.

Franzen's other two novels are The Twenty-Seventh City, *a labyrinthine literary thriller set in his home town of St Louis, Missouri and* Strong Motion *in which the story of one dysfunctional family and a sinister plot involving a mysterious series of earthquakes in Boston come together.* How to be Alone *is a collection of essays and* The Discomfort Zone *is a funny and intimate memoir of his coming-of-age in an apparently ordinary American family.*

📖Read on

◻ to the fiction: ▶▶ Michael Chabon, *Wonder Boys*; Jeffrey Eugenides, *Middlesex*; David Foster Wallace, *Infinite Jest*.

◼ to *The Discomfort Zone*: Dave Eggers, *A Heartbreaking Work of Staggering Genius*.

FRASER, George MacDonald (1925–2008)
British writer

Fraser's literary career was shaped by his brilliant idea of taking Flashman, the bully from the nineteenth-century boarding-school novel *Tom Brown's Schooldays* and recording his further adventures throughout a long life. In the original book he was just an adolescent thug; in Fraser's hands he becomes sexy, sly and, although an irredeemable coward and cad, an unlikely hero of the British empire. He progresses through the ranks of the British army and plays his part in such events as the Indian Mutiny, the Charge of the Light Brigade, the Crimean War and Little Big Horn. There are a dozen books, all told in the voice of Flashman himself, and all are equally enjoyable. Typical is *Flashman and the Angel of the Lord*, in which Flashman gets mixed up with the American anti-slavery campaign and its Harper's Ferry hero John Brown (the man whose soul, in the song, goes marchin' on).

The Flashman books are, in order of publication, Flashman, Royal Flash, Flash for Freedom, Flashman at the Charge, Flashman in the Great Game, Flashman's Lady, Flashman and the Redskins, Flashman and the Dragon, Flashman and the Mountain of Light, Flashman and the Angel of the Lord, Flashman and the Tiger *and* Flashman on the March.

📖Read on
◆ *The Candlemass Road* (non-Flashman: a swashbuckling novel set on the bandit-ridden Scots–English borders at the time of Mary Queen of Scots).
◘ ❯❯ Bernard Cornwell, *Sharpe's Honour*; Allan Mallinson, *A Close-Run Thing*; ❯❯ J.G. Farrell, *The Siege of Krishnapur*; Julian Rathbone, *A Very English Agent*.

FRAYN, Michael (born 1933)
British novelist and playwright

Michael Frayn began his career as a writer of urbanely satirical columns in various newspapers and his early novels, published in the 1960s and 1970s, were in the same vein as his journalism – deft and amusing exposés of the foibles and follies of the time. A Fleet Street hack makes a bid for TV celebrity with disastrous consequences (*Towards the End of the Morning*); Heaven turns out to be rather like the blandest dreams of it entertained by Guardian-reading liberals (*Sweet Dreams*); an institution of 'automation research' examines the ways in which computers can take over repetitive human tasks like praying and compiling newspaper reports (*The Tin Men*). From the mid-1970s onwards, Frayn's creative energy went into writing for the theatre more than into fiction but, in the last few years, he has returned to the novel to great effect. *Headlong* and *Spies* (see below) are often as funny as the earlier fiction but they possess a depth of characterization and a melancholy irony that the satirical works didn't have (indeed didn't need). The two recent novels, particularly *Headlong*, have elements of the farce that is never far away in Frayn's view of the world but they are also subtle portraits of how our hopes and aspirations and beliefs so rarely coincide with reality.

SPIES (2002)

As an old man, Stephen Wheatley returns to the suburban streets of his wartime childhood. As he walks them he recalls a story in which the fantasy games he played during those years came into abrupt and painful contact with adult reality. Stephen and his closest friend pretended to believe that the friend's mother was a German spy, shadowing her about the streets, even reading her diary. Frayn's delicately and subtly written novel gradually tracks the boy Stephen's realization that his friend's mother does indeed have secrets to hide but they are not the ones he naïvely imagined.

Frayn's other fiction includes The Russian Interpreter, The Trick of It *and* A Landing on the Sun.

📖Read on

◆ *Headlong* (an art historian believes he has made the discovery of the century and sets out to try and exploit it).

◻ to the early novels: ≫ Anthony Burgess, *Enderby's Dark Lady*; ≫ Evelyn Waugh, *The Loved One*.

◻ to *Spies*: Mick Jackson, *Five Boys*.

◻ to *Headlong*: ≫ Arturo Pérez Reverte, *The Flanders Panel*; Lesley Glaister, *Sheer Blue Bliss*.

FURST, Alan (born 1941)
US novelist

With the end of the Cold War, many writers of spy fiction lost their plots. When the Iron Curtain and the Berlin Wall came down, what was there left to provide the material for their stories? The American writer Alan Furst, however, had already been clever enough to look further back into the past for his scenarios. In 1988, he had published *Night Soldiers*, about a young Bulgarian working in the Soviet espionage network in the 1930s, and it was to be only the first of a series of novels set in the years just before and after the outbreak of World War II. All of the books are marked by wide research, subtle plotting and an acute awareness of the ways in which his characters are often forced into their actions by the circumstances of war and by their own fears and desires. There are few heroes in Furst's fiction, only ordinary men and women struggling to cope in extraordinary times but his books outshine all save the very best examples of the genre in which he has chosen to write.

THE POLISH OFFICER (1995)
Captain Alexander de Milja is a Polish officer and gentleman but, when Alan Furst's novel opens in 1939, his country has hardly any army left in which to claim command, and gentlemanliness has become a virtue of little use. De Milja joins the fight against Nazism, working as an intelligence agent in occupied Europe. After shadowy missions in Paris and the Channel ports, he is sent back to Eastern Europe for one more job ...

Furst's other espionage and Second World War novels include Dark Star, The World at Night, Red Gold, Kingdom of Shadows, Dark Voyage *and* Spies of Warsaw.

▱Read on
▫ David Downing, *Zoo Station*; Philip Kerr, *March Violets* (crime fiction set in Nazi Berlin); Henry Porter, *Brandenburg*.

READONATHEME:

FUTURE SOCIETIES

>> Margaret Atwood, *The Handmaid's Tale*
>> Iain M. Banks, *Consider Phlebas*
>> Angela Carter, *The Passion of New Eve*
>> Philip K. Dick, *The Man in the High Castle*
>> Robert Graves, *Seven Days in New Crete*
>> Russell Hoban, *Riddley Walker*
>> Aldous Huxley, *Brave New World*
>> P.D. James, *Children of Men*
   Paul Johnston, *Body Politic*
   Walter M. Miller Jr, *A Canticle for Leibowitz*
   William Morris, *News from Nowhere*
>> George Orwell, *Nineteen Eighty-four*
>> John Wyndham, *The Chrysalids*

See also: Fantasy Societies

GAIMAN, Neil (born 1960)
British novelist

Gaiman first came to attention as the writer of graphic novels. *The Sandman*, which appeared in multiple volumes between 1989 and 1996, was part of a renaissance of the comic book tradition which was spearheaded by such writers as Alan Moore and Frank Miller. In 1990 he collaborated with >> Terry Pratchett on the writing of *Good Omens*, a novel which turned the idea of impending apocalypse into high comedy, and *Neverwhere*, a weird vision of an alternative London, which began life as a TV series, was published as a novel in 1996. Perhaps Gaiman's most imaginative and successful novel so far is *American Gods* (2001) in which the protagonist, an ex-con named Shadow, meets up with the mysterious Mr Wednesday and is employed as his bodyguard. As Shadow learns more about his employer and eventually embarks on a bizarre road trip across America with him, it becomes apparent that Wednesday is not a man but one of the old gods brought across the Atlantic many centuries before and now intent upon battle with the new deities of consumerism and the media. *American Gods* is a picaresque fantasy in which the dark dreams of *The Sandman* and the comic chaos of *Good Omens* combine.

Gaiman's work in comics, outside the Sandman volumes, includes The Books of Magic, The Tragical Comedy or Comical Tragedy of Mr Punch, Death: The High Cost of Living *and* Death: The Time of Your Life. *His other novels are* Stardust *and* Anansi Boys. Smoke and Mirrors *and* Fragile Things *are collections of shorter fiction.* Coraline *and* The Graveyard Book *are novels for children.*

☜Read on
♦ *Neverwhere* (Gaiman's everyman hero Richard Mayhew leaves the world of London Above and plunges into the strange, parallel universe of London Below where a rich assortment of oddball and memorable characters, from the dandyish Marquis de Carabas to the sinister assassins, Mr Croup and Mr Vandemar, walk the streets).
◘ to the comic books: Frank Miller, *Batman: The Dark Knight Returns*; Alan Moore, *The League of Extraordinary Gentlemen*.
◘ to the novels: ›› Michael Chabon, *The Amazing Adventures of Kavalier and Clay*; M. John Harrison, *The Course of the Heart*; Diana Wynne Jones, *Eight Days of Luke* (a children's novel in which the central character meets figures who prove to be incarnations of the Norse gods); ›› Stephen King, *The Gunslinger*.

GARFIELD, Simon (born 1960)
British writer

Simon Garfield is a journalist who has published a wide variety of non-fiction works in the last twenty years, many of which began as stories for the newspapers. *The Wrestling*, for example, was an investigation, both very funny and surprisingly touching, into the rise and fall of old-fashioned British wrestling and its stars, from Mick McManus to Giant Haystacks. He has also written historical biographies. *Mauve*, a book in the style of Dava Sobel's *Longitude*, tells the entertaining story of the forgotten Victorian chemist William Perkin, who created the synthetic dye that kick-started a worldwide industry. *The Error World* is a more personal book, a memoir which focuses on Garfield's own interest in rare stamps but has much that is witty and insightful to say about male obsessiveness and the urge to collect and classify.

Simon Garfield's other books are Our Hidden Lives, We Are At War ***and*** Private Battles ***(three selections from the diaries of ordinary people),*** The Last Journey of William Huskisson, The Nation's Favourite, The End of Innocence, Mini ***and*** Exposure ***(the life of the talented and self-destructive photographer Bob Carlos Clarke).***

Read on

◆ ***Our Hidden Lives*** (Garfield trawled through the archives of Mass Observation to produce this selection from the diaries the pioneering social research organisation asked ordinary people to keep in the 1940s).

◘ Richard Fortey, ***Dry Store Room No. 1: The Secret Life of the Natural History Museum***; Helen Morgan, ***Blue Mauritius: The Hunt for the World's Most Valuable Stamps***; ›› Simon Winchester, ***The Surgeon of Crowthorne.***

GASKELL, Mrs (Elizabeth Cleghorn) (1810–65)

British novelist

For a century after her death, Gaskell was chiefly remembered for a biography of her friend ›› Charlotte Brontë, and for *Cranford* (1853), a gently malicious book about middle-class life in a provincial town. (It reads like a collaboration between ›› Austen and ›› Trollope, without being quite as good as either.) But she was actually a novelist of a far tougher kind. She was a friend of ›› Dickens and ›› George Eliot, and shared their interest in social themes, particularly the way men treat women and the plight of the urban poor. She lived in Manchester, and wrote pungently about life among the 'dark Satanic mills' (as Blake had called them) which her southern readers had until then imagined were figments of the revolutionary imagination. Her novels were discussed in Parliament and led to social reform, a result that greatly pleased her. They survive today less as social documents than as powerful stories of people struggling against their environment or the indifference of others.

MARY BARTON (1848)

Mary's father is a mill-hand employed by the unfeeling Henry Carson. He is also a staunch fighter for workers' rights. When the mill-owners ignore their workers' requests for better treatment, the men decide to murder Carson as a warning to his class, and nominate Barton to fire the gun. Mary's beloved Jem Wilson is arrested for the crime, and Mary has to face the agony of proving his innocence by incriminating her father.

Gaskell's novels Ruth, Cousin Phyllis *and* Wives and Daughters *concern the relationship between the sexes.* Sylvia's Lovers*, an unsmiling tale set in Whitby in the eighteenth century, is about a man snatched by the press gang.* North and South*, like* Mary Barton*, is about class war.* My Lady Ludlow *and* Cousin Phillis *are novellas;* Lois the Witch*, a long short story, is set during the Salem witch-hunts of the seventeenth century.*

Read on

◆ *North and South* (in which a southern minister goes to preach God's word in a northern mill town, and his wife and daughter become involved in the class struggle – a concern greatly complicated when the daughter falls in love with a mill-owner's son).

◘ ›› Charlotte Brontë, *Shirley*; ›› Charles Dickens, *Hard Times*; ›› Émile Zola, *Germinal*; ›› Arnold Bennett, *Clayhanger*; ›› D.H. Lawrence, *Sons and Lovers*; Lewis Grassic Gibbon, *A Scots Quair* (a saga of three generations coping with harsh conditions on West Highland crofts and in industrial Glasgow during the 1920s General Strike).

READ ON A THEME

GAY/LESBIAN FICTION
›› James Baldwin, *Giovanni's Room*
Djuna Barnes, *Nightwood*
Emma Donoghue, *Stir Fry*
Radclyffe Hall, *The Well of Loneliness*
›› Alan Hollinghurst, *The Swimming-Pool Library*
David Leavitt, *The Lost Language of Cranes*
Adam Mars Jones, *Monopolies of Loss*
Armistead Maupin, *Tales of the City*
›› Colm Tóibín, *The Story of the Night*
›› Edmund White, *A Boy's Own Story*
Christopher Whyte, *The Gay Decameron*
›› Jeanette Winterson, *Oranges Are Not the Only Fruit*

GHOSH, Amitav (born 1956)

Indian novelist

As a novelist Amitav Ghosh has made superbly effective use of both Indian history and Indian geography in the telling of his stories. The land itself always has a role to play in his fiction. *The Hungry Tide*, for example, is set in the vast area of islands, ocean and mangrove forest in the Bay of Bengal known as the Sundarbans which is where three very different people (an American-Indian marine biologist, a native fisherman, an egotistical translator from New Delhi) come together. With their unsettling landscape and troubled history, the Sundarbans become the setting for a journey into the heart of the tidal lands that changes all three central characters. Both *The Glass Palace* (see below) and *Sea of Poppies*, his most recent work and the first in a proposed trilogy, delve into the troubled and ambivalent history of the relationships between the British and the indigenous peoples of Asia for their complex and rewarding narratives.

THE GLASS PALACE (2000)

In 1885, Rajkumar, an Indian boy stranded in Mandalay, is witness to the invasion that began British rule in Burma and sent the last native king into exile. As looters pour into the king's glass palace, Rajkumar catches a glimpse of one of the maids in the royal household. This becomes the starting point for an exhilarating saga of lives and loves unfolding against the backdrop of more than a hundred eventful years of Burmese history.

Ghosh's other novels are The Circle of Reason, The Shadow Lines *and* The Calcutta Chromosome. In an Antique Land *is an account of his experiences when he moved from India to Egypt to live and study. He has also published several works of non-fiction of which the most recent is* Incendiary Circumstances.

⮒Read on

◆ *Sea of Poppies* (the first of what will be a trilogy, this is set in the Far East at the time of the Opium Wars).

◻ Tash Aw, *The Harmony Silk Factory*.

GIBSON, William (born 1948)
US novelist

In the history of science fiction there has been a handful of books which have redefined the genre for a new generation of readers. One of these is William Gibson's *Neuromancer* (see below). Gibson is often dubbed the father of cyberpunk but critics do not always agree on what a definition of cyberpunk might be. In truth, what Gibson did was what the best science fiction writers have always done. He took contemporary scientific and technological developments, seized upon potential implications and projected them imaginatively into the future. In the case of *Neuromancer*, and the books that followed it in a loosely connected trilogy, *Count Zero* and *Mona Lisa Overdrive*, it was computer technology and the newly developing internet. In his books since the trilogy, Gibson has turned his attention to other subjects. In *Idoru*, with its emphasis on the blankness of media celebrity, and *All Tomorrow's Parties* he has shown another quality of the best science fiction writers. While ostensibly writing fantasies of the future, he is using the freedom the genre gives him to reflect, obliquely, the realities of modern society. His most recent novels, *Pattern Recognition* and *Spook Country*, have been described as his first forays into contemporary society but it is a measure of the way Gibson's earlier novels mirrored today as much as they predicted the future that the world of these later books seems seamlessly connected to the worlds created in his other fiction.

NEUROMANCER (1984)

The time is the mid twenty-first century. Case, once a master hacker able to project his consciousness into cyberspace (a term Gibson invented), is now a low-life addict in the massive urban sprawl of Japan. He is given a chance to redeem himself when a group of shadowy corporate conspirators offers him the means to regain the buzz that travelling cyberspace provided. The plot of *Neuromancer* is clichéd enough, familiar from dozens of thrillers, but what give the book its strength are the enormous energy of Gibson's imaginative construction of the world in which his anti-hero operates and the originality of the language he uses. In prose that deftly combines streetwise slang and techno-vocabulary (often his own inventions) he describes a nightmarish future in which personal relationships have been irrevocably compromised by materialism and hope lies in release from the meat of the body into the exhilarating ether of cyberspace.

⬥Read on
◆ *Idoru*.
❑ ⟫ Philip K. Dick, *Do Androids Dream of Electric Sheep?*; Jeff Noon, *Vurt*; ⟫ Neal Stephenson, *Snow Crash*; Bruce Sterling, *Heavy Weather*; Tricia Sullivan, *Someone to Watch Over Me*.

GIDE, André (1861–1951)
French novelist, poet and non-fiction writer

The heroes in Gide's novels seek the truth about themselves, the core of their being, and they do it by considering and rejecting all religious, social, sexual and intellectual conventions. Sometimes a quest results in the happiness of self-knowledge, but often the young men – Gide was not over-interested in young women – find, when they reach the core of themselves, that there is nothing there at all. In *The Immoralist* (1902), for example, Michel, a young intellectual, nearly dies of tuberculosis, and his brush with death changes his character. He rejects his former convention-ridden life in favour of living each moment for itself, of doing exactly what he pleases. As his personality flowers, that of his beloved wife begins to wither, leaving him to agonize over whether his actions have led to psychic liberation or to a surrender to selfishness.

Gide's other fiction includes Strait is the Gate (La Porte étroite), The Vatican Cellars, Isabelle, The Pastoral Symphony (La Symphonie pastorale) *and* The Counterfeiters. *His non-fiction works on similar themes include* If It Die (Si le grain ne meurt), Et nunc manet in te/Madeleine *and* Journals.

⬥Read on
◆ *Strait is the Gate*; *The Vatican Cellars* (a more extrovert romp than most of Gide's other fiction involving murder, the kidnapping of the Pope and a frantic chase across Europe).
❑ ⟫ Hermann Hesse, *Peter Camenzind*; Joris-Karl Huysmans, *Against Nature*; Frederick Rolfe, *The Desire and Pursuit of the Whole*; ⟫ Aldous Huxley, *Eyeless in Gaza*.

LITERARY TRIVIA 6:

FIVE BANNED BOOKS
Alice's Adventures in Wonderland
In 1931, the Governor of Hunan Province in China, distressed by the supposedly disrespectful idea of animals using human language, banned Lewis Carroll's classic children's fantasy and ordered copies of it destroyed.

Black Beauty
Putting the words 'black' and 'beauty' together in a book title was thought too racy by South Africa's old apartheid regime and Anna Sewell's famous story of a horse's life was banned.

Fahrenheit 451
In 1992, students at a California school received copies of Ray Bradbury's science fiction masterpiece in which potentially corrupting words like 'hell' and 'damn' had been blacked out. Ironically, the book is set in a future society in which books are censored.

Animal Farm
>> George Orwell's political allegory seems to annoy just about everybody. As a vicious satire on Stalinism, it was banned in the Soviet Union for many years as 'anti-communist' but, in some US states, it has been banned from public libraries for being too 'pro-communist'.

Lady Chatterley's Lover
>> D.H. Lawrence's novel was barred from publication for decades because of its sexual explicitness. In 1960, Penguin Books faced prosecution when they tried to publish it. 'Is this the sort of book you would want your wife or servants to read?', the jury at the ensuing trial was famously asked. It seems it was and it became a bestseller.

GISSING, George (1857–1903)

British novelist

Gissing's fiction, with its strong sympathies for the poor and for society's outsiders, was shaped by his own experiences of rejection and humiliation. His promising career as a classical scholar was cut short in 1876 when he was convicted of theft. He had stolen money from his college cloakroom in order, he hoped, to reclaim from the streets a young prostitute with whom he had fallen in love. He failed but, after serving a short period of imprisonment, he married the woman. His marriage became another social and economic burden that the novelist had to bear. Beginning with *Workers in the Dawn* (1880), Gissing wrote nearly twenty novels in his relatively short career in which characters struggle against poverty, injustice and the constraints of traditional morality. The typical Gissing hero is a man like Reardon in *New Grub Street* (see below), sensitive and intelligent but condemned to a life in which his gifts are little recognized. With a relish that is almost sadistic (or masochistic, if one considers how much he identified with his central characters), Gissing charts his hero's decline and eventual fall.

NEW GRUB STREET (1891)

Gissing's most famous novel is a painfully accurate portrait, as insightful today as it was in the 1890s, of the vicissitudes and indignities of the literary life. The two central characters of the novel stand at each end of the literary spectrum as Gissing envisages it. Edward Reardon, clearly a version of Gissing himself, is a fine writer but he is hampered by poverty and by marriage to a woman who cannot sympathise with his art. Jasper Milvain is a glib and facile reviewer with his eye firmly set on worldly success. Milvain's inexorable rise contrasts with Reardon's inevitable decline.

Gissing's other novels include The Nether World, The Odd Women, In the Year of the Jubilee, The Whirlpool *and* The Private Papers of Henry Ryecroft. By the Ionian Sea *is his account of his travels in Southern Italy in the late 1890s.*

☜Read on

◆ *The Odd Women* (single women in 1890s London struggle to find success and self-esteem in a society that often appears to scorn them).

◘ ⟩⟩ Thomas Hardy, *Jude the Obscure*; Arthur Morrison, *A Child of the Jago*; Robert Tressell, *The Ragged Trousered Philanthropists*; ⟩⟩ H.G. Wells, *The History of Mr Polly*.

GLENDINNING, Victoria (born 1937)
British biographer and novelist

Victoria Glendinning's earlier biographies were all of women writers (Elizabeth Bowen, Edith Sitwell and Rebecca West) and all demonstrated an acute sense of both the challenges her subjects faced in trying to make their voices heard and the courage they showed in succeeding. *Trollope* was another story of a struggle for achievement, chronicling the Victorian novelist's rise from unconsidered younger son of a famous mother to his status as one of the most respected and prodigiously productive writers of his time. *Jonathan Swift* analyses the complex and difficult personality of the satirist and poet best known for writing *Gulliver's Travels*. Glendinning's most recent book is a biography is a life of Leonard Woolf, the husband of Virginia. Her novels are *The Grown-Ups*, *Electricity* and *Flight*. Of these, the most interesting is *Electricity*, set in the 1880s when new forces, from the campaign for women's rights to electricity itself, were overturning the High Victorian view of the world and Glendinning's heroine finds her own life similarly overturned.

📖Read on

◘ to the biographies: ›› Peter Ackroyd, *Dickens*; ›› Claire Tomalin, *The Life and Death of Mary Wollstonecraft*.

◘ to the novels: Isabel Colegate, *The Shooting Party*; Jane Gardam, *God on the Rocks*; Angela Huth, *Easy Silence*.

GOETHE, Johann Wolfgang von (1749–1832)
German writer of novels, poems, plays and non-fiction

As well as being a writer, Goethe was a politician, lawyer, theatre manager, philosopher and scientist. His genius expressed itself in restless intellectual energy: he never heard an idea without wanting to develop it. In his writing, he took the nearest convenient form – Shakespearean or Greek tragedy, letters, biography – and crammed it with philosophical and political reflections, discussions and suggestions. During his lifetime he was regarded as an innovator, forming European thought; with hindsight he seems rather to have caught ideas in the air – humanism, romanticism, political libertarianism – expanded them and given them wide circulation.

THE SORROWS OF YOUNG WERTHER (DIE LEIDEN DES JUNGEN WERTHERS) (1774)

Werther is a melancholic artist out of tune with the times and with himself. Through a series of letters he tells the story of his growing, indeed obsessive, love for Lotte, who is engaged to another man, Albert. All Werther's attempts to distract himself from the pain his love causes him prove ineffectual and eventually he kills himself with Albert's pistol. One of the earliest works to announce the arrival of the new spirit of Romanticism, Goethe's book was astonishingly successful throughout Europe. Young men dressed like Werther and memorized long parts of the novel; copycat suicides were recorded.

Goethe is best known for his poetry, and for such plays as Egmont, Iphigenia in Tauris, Götz von Berlichingen/Ironhand *and* Faust. *Apart from* The Sorrows of Young Werther, *his novels are* Wilhelm Meister *and* Elective Affinities.

📖Read on

♦ *Elective Affinities (Die Wahlverwandtschaften)* is a heartless, amoral book about a married couple, each of whom has a love affair.
■ to *Wilhelm Meister*: Miguel de Cervantes, *Don Quixote*; ▶▶ Thomas Mann, *The Magic Mountain*.
◘ to *Elective Affinities*: Christina Stead, *The Man Who Loved Children*.
◘ to *The Sorrows of Young Werther*: ▶▶ Hermann Hesse, *Gertrud*.

GOGOL, Nikolai Vasilevich (1809–52)
Russian writer of novels, short stories and plays

The despair which seems to hover over much Russian fiction was replaced in Gogol by hilarity: he was a twentieth-century surrealist ahead of his time, a forerunner of ▶▶ Kafka and Ionesco. His best-known work, the stage farce *The Government Inspector*, is about a confidence trickster mistaken for a high official by a village of pompous fools. In one of his stories a nose takes on a malign, satirical life independent of its owner's will; in another a man saves for years to buy a new coat, only to be mugged and robbed the first time he wears it. Gogol's preferred form was the short story – he was terrified of writer's block. He struggled for a dozen years to finish his one long book, *Dead Souls*, and in 1852, convinced by a religious adviser that the second (unpublished) half of the book was 'sinful' and that if he went on writing he would go to hell, he burned the manuscript and fasted until he died.

DEAD SOULS (1842)

In nineteenth-century Russia landowners estimated their wealth not only by the land they owned, but also by the number of their serfs, or slaves. Chichikov, a confidence trickster, realizes that serfs who die between official censuses are not legally dead until the next census, and so still count as property. He travels the length and breadth of Russia, buying 'dead souls' from landowners, and becomes – on paper at least – one of the wealthiest men in the country. Gogol uses this simple story as the basis for a set of farcical character studies: he saw the book as a portrait gallery of contemporary Russia, and filled it with short, self-contained comic episodes. He also wrote, with ironical pointedness, that Chichikov's journey stands for the journey of every human being through life: we move on, never sure of what is coming next, relieved each time that whatever it was we did, we got away with it.

Gogol's most surreal short stories are 'Diary of a Madman', 'Nevski Prospekt', 'The Portrait', 'The Nose' *and* 'The Overcoat'. *His collections* Evenings on a Farm, Mirgorod *and* Arabesques *are more farce than surrealism, short sketches about tongue-tied suitors, credulous peasants and feather-headed, pretty girls.*

🕮Read on

◘ Gogol's sinister brilliance is matched in the short stories of ►► Franz Kafka, Saki and Roald Dahl; his gentler comic stories are like ►► Anton Chekhov's.
◘ to *Dead Souls*: Ivan Goncharov, *Oblomov* (about a man so alienated from the world that he decides to spend the rest of his life in bed); ►► Franz Kafka, *America*; ►► Jaroslav Hasek, *The Good Soldier Svejk*; Bernard Malamud, *The Fixer*; Miguel de Cervantes, *Don Quixote*.

GOLDING, William (1911–93)

British novelist

Golding worked in the theatre and served in the Royal Navy in the Second World War. He worked as a schoolmaster until *Lord of the Flies* brought him international fame in 1954. The story of that book (about choirboys reverting to savagery after being marooned on a desert island) is typical of all his work: an exploration of the dark side of human nature. He believed that *Homo sapiens* is corrupt, that we destroy more than we create, that we are devilish without redemption. But instead of baldly stating this philosophy, he dressed it in allegories of the most unusual and fantastical kind. He pictured the devil engulfing not only choirboys on an island, but also (in other novels) a drowning sailor, a tribe of Neanderthal people, the dean of a medieval cathedral, a boy growing up in 1960s Britain, and a group of eighteenth-century people sailing towards Australia. He evoked each of these situations with absolute conviction: few writers were better at suggesting the feel, taste, smell and sound of things, the texture of experience.

THE SPIRE (1964)

Inspired by a vision, Dean Jocelin commissions for his cathedral a four hundred-foot spire. (Although the cathedral is unnamed, much of the background is drawn from the building of Salisbury Cathedral's spire, still the tallest in England.) Jocelin intends his spire as proof of human aspirations towards God; his enemies see it as a symbol of vanity, the devil's work. The master-builder points out that, as the cathedral's foundations are inadequate, the tower will bring the whole building crashing down. Jocelin overrides all objections, the work proceeds – Golding gives fascinating, vertigo-inducing detail of medieval building techniques – and the higher the spire rises the more people are destroyed. In the end the struggle between God and the devil takes over Jocelin's own self. In truly medieval manner, his brain and body become a battleground, and the issue moves from the tower to questions of his own moral integrity and saintliness.

Golding's other novels are Lord of the Flies, Pincher Martin, Free Fall, The Pyramid, Darkness Visible, *a trilogy about an ill-assorted cargo of passengers on a voyage to Australia in the eighteenth century* (Rites of Passage, Close Quarters and Fire Down Below, *also collected in one volume as* To the Ends of the Earth), The Paper Men *and the unfinished* The Double Tongue *(fictional 'memoirs' of a sybil at ancient Delphi).* The Scorpion God *is a collection of three long stories, one based on his stage comedy* The Brass Butterfly, *about a crazy inventor trying to interest a decadent Roman ruler of Egypt in steam power.*

☜Read on

◆ *The Inheritors* (a brilliantly imagined story of the coming of *Homo sapiens*, seen from the standpoint of the gentle ape-people they exterminate).
◻ to *The Spire*: Peter Benson, *Odo's Hanging* (about the clash between Bishop Odo, commissioning a wall-hanging to commemorate the accession of William the

Conqueror, and Tuvold, the genius-craftsman who wants to do things his way); ❯❯ Hermann Hesse, *Narziss and Goldmund* (which parallels both the good/evil theme and the medieval craft-background of *The Spire*).

◘ to *Lord of the Flies*: Marianne Wiggins, *John Dollar*; Richard Hughes, *A High Wind in Jamaica*.

◘ to the Australian trilogy: ❯❯ Barry Unsworth, *Sacred Hunger*; ❯❯ Thomas Keneally, *The Playmaker*.

READ**ONA**THEME:

GOOD AND EVIL
The devil at large
❯❯ Mikhail Bulgakov, *The Master and Margarita*
❯❯ John Fowles, *A Maggot*
❯❯ Stephen King, *Carrie*
❯❯ Doris Lessing, *The Fifth Child*
    Ira Levin, *Rosemary's Baby*
❯❯ Ian McEwan, *The Comfort of Strangers*
❯❯ I.B. Singer, *Satan in Goray*
❯❯ John Updike, *The Witches of Eastwick*
❯❯ Fay Weldon, *The Life and Loves of a She-Devil*

GORDIMER, Nadine (born 1923)
South African novelist and short story writer

Gordimer makes life in South Africa (and especially among the tormented liberal whites who are her main characters) an objective background for subjective choice. Her concerns are the diversity of human nature, and the way our moral and psychological personality is revealed in what we do. She also, magnificently, evokes the vastness and beauty of Africa. Like other South African writers (Alan Paton, Laurens van der Post, ❯❯ André Brink) she gives the continent a kind of mystical identity; its indigenous inhabitants understand this completely, but it gives the incoming whites (who can only dimly perceive it) an unsettling sense of their own inadequacy, as if they are made second-class citizens not by other people's laws but by the very place they live in.

A SPORT OF NATURE (1987)

From adolescence rich, white Hillela is dominated by politics and sex, and combines the two: sex is a source of power, politics gives orgasmic satisfaction. She is attracted by, and attracts, powerful men of all professions and races – and progressively moves out of the orbit of whites to a leading position in the black revolutionary movement. The book ends with the success of the revolution, the establishment of majority rule – and with doubts sown in the reader's mind about Hillela herself. Has she really identified as wholly with the blacks as she hoped, or does she remain the 'sport of nature', or freak, of the book's title?

Gordimer's other novels are The Lying Days, A World of Strangers, Occasion for Loving, The Late Bourgeois World, A Guest of Honour, Burger's Daughter, The Conservationist, July's People, My Son's Story, None to Accompany Me, The House Gun, The Pickup *and* Get a Life. *Her many short story collections include* Not For Publication, Why Haven't You Written?, Jump, Loot *and* Beethoven Was One-Sixteenth Black. The Essential Gesture *and* Living in Hope *and* History *contain sharp, thoughtful essays.*

✑Read on

◆ *The House Gun* (a study of a liberal-minded but politically uncommitted couple forced into a confrontation with social violence when their son is accused of murder).

◘ ›› André Brink, *Rumours of Rain* (about redneck Afrikaanerdom); ›› J.M. Coetzee, *In the Heart of the Country*; Alan Paton, *Cry, the Beloved Country* (a moving book about the harmony between ancient Zulu culture and the land, and the discord brought by invading whites).

GOULD, Stephen Jay (1941–2002)
US science writer

Few people in the last fifty years have written about the history of science and its contemporary practice with greater elegance and erudition than Stephen Jay Gould. He published several book-length works, including *Wonderful Life* (an eye-opening account of the dizzying variety of fossils found in the Burgess Shale deposits in the Canadian Rockies, and what that said about the nature of evolution), but he was at his best as an essayist. For many years he wrote a regular column in the American *Natural History* magazine where the freedom he was given to range as widely as he liked produced dozens and dozens of short essays which throw light on both the highways and the byways of science, particularly biology and palaeontology. Whether writing about Darwin's role on the voyage of the *Beagle* or the feeding habits of flamingos, snails that change sex or the Piltdown Man hoax, Gould showed his remarkable ability to lead readers gently from small, seemingly insignificant details towards larger questions and debates.

The ten collections of Gould's essays from Natural History *are* Ever Since Darwin, The Panda's Thumb, Hen's Teeth and Horse's Toes, The Flamingo's Smile, Bully for Brontosaurus, Eight Little Piggies, Dinosaur in a Haystack, Leonardo's Mountain of Clams and the Diet of Worms, The Lying Stones of Marrakech *and* I Have Landed.

〰Read on
♦ *Time's Arrow, Time's Cycle* (Gould's examination of the history of our discovery of the vast stretches of geological time reveals how we use myth, metaphor and measurement to make sense of the world).
◻ Richard Fortey, *Trilobite: Eyewitness to Evolution*; Armand Marie Leroi, *Mutants* (a book which looks at human oddities and freaks and what they tell us about evolution with the same insight and understanding that Gould shows in his essays); Matt Ridley, *Genome*; Edward O. Wilson, *The Diversity of Life*.

GRAHAME, Kenneth (1859–1932)
British writer

Graham worked for many years at the Bank of England, where he rose through the ranks to a senior position before taking early retirement. However, beneath the surface of conventional City man lurked a sensitive and imaginative dreamer who wrote essays for 1890s periodicals like 'The Yellow Book' and yearned for an idyllic world of childhood from which he believed that adult life had exiled him. In 1908, after he had retired from the Bank, he published *The Wind in the Willows*, a book which began as a series of stories he told his young son and which rapidly established itself as a children's classic. *The Wind in the Willows* is the story of

Ratty and his friend Mole and their assorted adventures on their beloved riverbank. Together they mess about on boats, venture into the Wild Wood, have a mystical encounter with the 'Piper at the Gates of Dawn' and, together with Mr Badger, are witnesses to the outrageous behaviour of the obstreperous Toad of Toad Hall. *The Wind in the Willows* is a book that combines fantasy (anthropomorphised animals behaving remarkably like good middle-class Edwardians of Kenneth Grahame's acquaintance) and the everyday (a beautifully evoked English countryside) to very special effect. It continues to beguile both children and adults more than a century after it was written.

Kenneth Grahame's only other significant publications are The Golden Age, *a collection of short pieces about childhood and its sequel,* Dream Days, *which includes the well-known children's story 'The Reluctant Dragon'.*

⮒Read on
◻ A.A. Milne, *Winnie-the-Pooh*; Jan Needle, *Wild Wood* (the story Grahame tells re-told from the point of view of the despised stoats and weasels)

GRASS, Günter (born 1927)
German writer of novels, plays and non-fiction

In his twenties Grass worked as a graphic artist, stage designer and jazz musician; he took up writing full time only after his novel *The Tin Drum* (*Die Blechtrommel*, 1959) was a bestseller, when he was thirty-two. Politics are the main subject of his books: he grapples with what has happened in Germany over the last half-century, and what is happening now. He uses a framework of absurdity, blending real events with wild black fantasy, collapsing history (so that time is like a well from which you draw not systematically but at random), and making his characters allegorical figures like the people in cartoons. The leading character in *The Tin Drum*, for example, symbolizes the German people: a child who chooses to stop growing at the age of three, and who spends forty years banging a toy drum and giggling as the procession of Nazism and post-war reconstruction passes by. For Grass, the human condition is 'absurd': not only ridiculous but morally and philosophically out of focus. His books offer no solutions, but they point out the problems with enormous, malicious glee.

THE FLOUNDER (DER BUTT) (1977)

The wife and husband from a Grimm fairytale move through the entire history of the human race, popping up in this period or that, playing each role by the conventions of its time, and endlessly, affably arguing about gender dominance. They are aided or hindered by a talking fish from the same fairytale: it takes now her side, now his. Finally the fish is ordered to defend itself before a late twentieth-century feminist tribunal, and the whole male/female business is thrashed out in a hearing as preposterous as the trial in *Alice in Wonderland*. The fact that this book is about sexual rather than German politics makes it one of Grass's most accessible novels to non-German readers, and it is also wonderfully enlivened with puns, poems, satires and recipes.

Grass's other novels include Cat and Mouse, Dog Years, From the Diary of a Snail, The Meeting at Telgte, Headbirths, The Rat, The Call of the Toad *and* Crabwalk. My Century *(1999) is a collection of linked stories, each one appropriate to a particular year of the twentieth century.* Peeling the Onion *is a recently published memoir.*

᎒Read on

◆ *Crabwalk* (this story of a man trying to learn the truth about the 1945 sinking by a Soviet submarine of a ship full of German refugees shows Grass still struggling creatively with the legacy of his country's twentieth-century history).

◘ other books similarly reinventing the human race, tossing all human knowledge and invention into a single fantastic melting pot: Thornton Wilder, *The Eighth Day*; ›› Kurt Vonnegut, *Galápagos*; ›› J.G. Ballard, *The Unlimited Dream Company*; ›› Jeanette Winterson, *The Passion*.

GRAVES, Robert (1895–1985)
British novelist, poet and non-fiction writer

Graves's main interests were myth and poetry. He wrote a bestselling version of the Greek myths, a controversial account of the Bible stories as myth, and *The White Goddess* (1948–52), a study of poetic inspiration. Throughout his life he composed poetry (much of it autobiographical), and his love poems in particular are much admired. He claimed that his novels were potboilers, written to finance 'real' work, but their quality and craftsmanship belie this description. Most are historical, reimagining characters of the past – from the author of the Odyssey to Jesus – as people with markedly twentieth-century sensibilities, able to view the events of their own lives, as it were, with hindsight. His books are like psychological documentaries, as if we are looking directly into his characters' minds.

I, CLAUDIUS (1934)

This novel and its sequel, *Claudius the God*, purport to be the autobiography of the fourth Roman emperor. Disabled and epileptic, he is regarded by everyone as a fool and ignored; he thus survives the myriad political and dynastic intrigues of the first fifty years of the Roman empire, the reigns of his three dangerous predecessors. He is finally made emperor himself, in a palace coup – and proceeds to rule with a blend of wisdom, guile and ruthlessness which he describes with fascinated relish. The story ends – typically for Graves – with a real document, an account by a Roman satirist of the 'Pumpkinification of Claudius', the arrival of the stammering, limping fool of an emperor in Olympus, home of the gods and of his own terrifying, deified relatives.

Graves's other novels include Count Belisarius *(set in sixth-century Byzantium),* Sergeant Lamb of the Ninth *and* Proceed, Sergeant Lamb *(about the American War of Independence),* Wife to Mr Milton *(set in Puritan England, and written in a brilliant pastiche of seventeenth-century prose),* Homer's Daughter *(set in prehistoric Greece), and* King Jesus *(about the life and death of Christ).* Seven Days in New Crete *is an urbane future-fantasy, and* Goodbye to All That *is autobiography, moving from a tormented account of Graves's time as an officer in the First World War to malicious glimpses of Oxford life and the literary London of the 1920s.*

⌣Read on

◘ to *I, Claudius*: David Wishart, *I, Virgil* (about the Roman Civil War, Caesar's assassination, Antony and Cleopatra, the rise of Augustus – a kind of prequel to *I, Claudius*); ›› Robert Harris, *Pompeii*; ›› Steven Saylor, *Roman Blood*; Naomi Mitchison, *The Corn King and the Spring Queen*; Allan Massie, *Tiberius*.

◘ books of similar gusto, on non-classical subjects: Frederick Rolfe, *Hadrian the Seventh* (about a waspish inadequate who is elected Pope); Augusto Roa Bastos, *I, The Supreme* (the 'autobiography' of a deranged nineteenth-century Paraguayan dictator); ›› Gore Vidal, *Kalki* (about an insane Vietnam veteran who imagines himself Kalki, the Hindu god whose coming will end the present cycle of human existence).

GRAY, Alasdair (born 1934)
British writer

Founding father of the renaissance of Scottish literature in the past two decades, Alasdair Gray has demonstrated his erudition, playful wit and skill as an illustrator and designer in a series of books that have ranged from gothic fantasy to dark eroticism. Gray loves all aspects of the writing, reading and making of books. His own are packed with allusion and parody, arcane snippets of literary knowledge, experiments with form and style. He jumps into the midst of his own fiction to offer justifications for the developments in it. He starts novels with 'Book 3', includes a 'Prologue' after a hundred pages and then moves on to 'Book 1'. He takes literary and sub-literary genres like science fiction and pornography and plays unexpected games with readers' expectations of what they will offer. Gray is involved closely with the design of his works and, like a modern version of a medieval illuminator, he scatters his illustrations through his text. Even errata slips provide food for Gray's comic imagination. 'This erratum slip has been placed in this book in error' reads one sandwiched between the pages of one of his books. Gray has published a number of excellent books in the last twenty years. *Poor Things*, an imaginative Victorian pastiche which tells of the creation of a kind of female Frankenstein's monster in nineteenth-century Glasgow, deservedly won the Guardian Fiction Prize when it first appeared. *A History Maker*, set in a twenty-third-century world where war has become an elaborate board game, is Gray's extremely idiosyncratic but enjoyable version of a science fiction novel. However, Alasdair Gray's major achievement, the book that gave a new confidence to Scottish literature, remains *Lanark*. Moving between the two worlds of 1950s Glasgow, where Duncan Thaw struggles to find love and fulfil his artistic vision, and the strange city of Unthank where the dead Thaw is reincarnated as Lanark, the book is an imaginative tour de force, a place where fantasy and realism collide to startling effect.

Gray's other books include 1982, Janine, The Fall of Kelvin Walker, Something Leather *and* Old Men in Love *(all novels),* Unlikely Stories, Mostly *and* The Ends of Our Tethers *(two volumes of stories) and* The Book of Prefaces.

📖Read on
◆ *Poor Things*.
▫ James Kelman, *How Late it Was, How Late*; Jeff Torrington, *Swing, Hammer, Swing*; ▸▸ Flann O'Brien, *At Swim-Two-Birds* (for the same mixture of erudition and

playfulness); >> Jorge Luis Borges's stories (which have very different settings but demonstrate a similar love for the arcana and byways of literature).

READ ON A THEME

GREAT (CLASSIC) DETECTIVES

John Dickson Carr, *Death Watch* (Gideon Fell)
>> Agatha Christie, *Murder on the Orient Express* (Hercule Poirot)
>> Arthur Conan Doyle, *The Hound of the Baskervilles* (Sherlock Holmes)
Michael Innes, *Hamlet, Revenge!* (Inspector Appleby)
>> Ngaio Marsh, *Death and the Dancing Footman* (Chief Inspector Roderick Alleyn)
>> Dorothy L. Sayers, *The Nine Tailors* (Lord Peter Wimsey)
>> Georges Simenon, *Maigret and the Headless Corpse*
Rex Stout, *Murder by the Book* (Nero Wolfe)

See also: Classic Detection, Private Eyes

GREENE, Graham (1904–91)
British writer of novels, plays and non-fiction

In the 1930s Greene wrote several thrillers influenced by >> Buchan and by action films of the time: they include *Stamboul Train* (set on the Orient Express), *A Gun for Sale/This Gun for Hire* (about the manhunt for a political assassin) and *The Confidential Agent* (about left-wing politics in a right-wing state). This period of his writing culminated in atmospheric film scripts, of which the best (later novelized) was *The Third Man*. But thrillers – and, later, comedies such as *Our Man in Havana, Travels With My Aunt* and *Monsignor Quixote* – always took second place, at least in Greene's own estimation, to his Catholic novels. These are all concerned with people tormented by their own moral failure and by the longing for God's forgiveness. The settings are often the tropics; the political situations are unstable; the heroes are second-rank functionaries despised by their superiors. Two novels, *Brighton Rock* (1938, about a petty criminal in 1930s Brighton) and

The Human Factor (written forty years later, about the minor-public-school loyalties and betrayals of the British intelligence services), set similar searches for grace in a soulless, down-at-heel Britain. Despite the Catholic overtones of these books, which non-believers may find unconvincing, Greene's plots are fascinating, and his evocation of character and place is marvellous.

THE HEART OF THE MATTER (1948)

Scobie, Captain of Police in a God-forsaken African colony during the Second World War, is a decent, honest man. His wife Louise, tormented by memories of their dead daughter and by her own isolation from the rest of the British community, begs him to send her away to South Africa – and because of a mixture of pity for her misery and anguish at his inability to make her happy, he breaks police rules and borrows money from a suspected diamond smuggler. From that lapse onwards, everything Scobie does ends in disaster, and there is nothing he can do but watch himself, appalled but helpless, as he plunges remorselessly towards damnation.

Greene's other novels include The End of the Affair, The Quiet American, A Burnt-out Case, The Comedians, The Honorary Consul, Doctor Fischer of Geneva *and* The Captain and the Enemy. *His short stories (many of them 'comedies of the sexual life', as he called them) are collected in* Twenty-one Stories, May We Borrow Your Husband? *and* The Last Word. *He also wrote travel books and plays and a fascinating book intended as a 'substitute for autobiography',* A World of My Own, *recounting his dreams.*

🕮Read on

◆ *The Power and the Glory* (a lacerating story, set in Mexico during a left-wing revolution, about a drunken, self-hating priest who struggles against his own fear and the persecution of the revolutionaries to take God to the peasants).

▫ 'psychic thrillers', similarly showing people driven to the edge of breakdown and beyond, by circumstances, their surroundings or consciousness of their own moral failings: ▸▸ Malcolm Lowry, *Under the Volcano*; ▸▸ Joseph Conrad, *Nostromo*; B. Traven, *The Treasure of the Sierra Madre*.

▫ to other aspects of Greene's fictional world: ▸▸ John Le Carré, *The Honourable Schoolboy*; Patrick Hamilton, *Hangover Square*.

GREER, Germaine (born 1939)

Australian critic and essayist

Germaine Greer came to the world's attention with the publication of *The Female Eunuch* (1970), wittiest and most pugnacious of all feminist polemics, which continues to be a liberating read for both women and men. Charting the ways in which traditional, patriarchal ideas about the relations between the sexes oppress us all, Greer's book takes no prisoners as it turns accepted wisdom about the roles of men and women on its head. In the decades since *The Female Eunuch*, Greer has written books on a wide variety of other subjects. *The Obstacle Race* is a passionate, lucidly argued and widely researched explanation of why women painters have been unable to scale the same heights as male artists. *Sex and Destiny*, in its controversial investigation of the politics of fertility in the developed and developing world, seemed, to some, to go back on the opinions she had voiced so vigorously in *The Female Eunuch*, but it is written with the same wit and commitment. *The Whole Woman* returns, thirty years on, to many of the issues that Greer raised in her first book.

Germaine Greer's other books include The Change, Daddy, We Hardly Knew You, Shakespeare: A Very Short Introduction, The Boy, Whitefella, Jump Up *and* Shakespeare's Wife. The Madwoman's Underclothes *is a collection of her essays and reviews.*

🕮 Read on

◆ *Daddy, We Hardly Knew You* (a memoir of her upbringing and of her absent father).
◘ to *The Female Eunuch*: Simone de Beauvoir, *The Second Sex*; Susan Faludi, *Backlash*; Betty Friedan, *The Feminine Mystique*; Kate Millett, *Sexual Politics*.
◘ to *The Obstacle Race*: Rozsika Parker and Griselda Pollock, *Old Mistresses*.
◘ to *Daddy, We Hardly Knew You*: Sally Morgan, *My Place*.

GREGORY, Philippa (born 1954)
British novelist

Philippa Gregory writes historical fiction set in a range of places and periods from the Middle Ages to the eighteenth century but there is no doubt that the years of the Tudor monarchs have provided her with the canvas for her finest novels. Few historical novels have been more popular in recent years than her 2001 book *The Other Boleyn Girl* which concentrates on Mary Boleyn, sister of the more famous Anne, but tells the story of the entire family and its tragic ambitions. The tale, of course, is a familiar one but Gregory gives it a new vitality. *The Other Boleyn Girl* succeeds because it combines the page-turning qualities of the bestselling bodice-ripper with genuinely deep and wide-ranging historical research. Gregory takes readers into the heart of the claustrophobic Tudor court through the convincing detail and dialogue she provides but, once she has got them there, she also unfolds a narrative that seizes their attention and holds it to the end.

The other books in the Tudor series are The Queen's Fool, The Virgin's Lover, The Constant Princess, The Boleyn Inheritance *and* The Other Queen. *The Wideacre trilogy* (Wideacre, The Favoured Child *and* Meridon) *is set in the eighteenth century.* Earthly Joys *and* Virgin Earth *are two novels based on the lives of the adventurous seventeenth-century botanists and plant-hunters, the Tradescants. The recently published novel* The White Queen *is the first in a new series of books set during the Wars of the Roses.*

📖 Read on
◆ *The Other Queen* (Mary, Queen of Scots); *The Queen's Fool* (Hannah Verde, the queen's fool of the title, is servant to Bloody Mary and has to struggle to survive amidst the dangers of the Tudor court).
▫ Margaret Campbell Barnes, *Brief Gaudy Hour* (evergreen novel about Anne Boleyn first published in the 1940s); Rosalind Miles, *I, Elizabeth*; Anya Seton, *Katherine*; Reay Tannahill, *Fatal Majesty*; Alison Weir, *Innocent Traitor* (Lady Jane Grey).

GRENVILLE, Kate (born 1950)
Australian novelist

One of the subtlest and most engaging Australian novelists of her generation, Kate Grenville has written with great insight about both the past and the present of her country. *The Idea of Perfection*, her novel about two unlikely lovers in a small New South Wales town, won the Orange Prize for Fiction in 2001. Shortlisted for the Man Booker Prize, *The Secret River* (2005) reconstructs the early days of white Australia and tells the story of Will and Sal Thornhill, transported from London to New South Wales. In the harsh sunlight of a distant land, they are forced not only to build new lives for themselves but also to confront the alarming otherness of the Aboriginal peoples already inhabiting it. Will, a fundamentally decent man, struggles to reconcile his desire to possess a piece of land which can be 'the blank page on which a man might write a new life' and his desire to live in peace with neighbours both white and black. In the end he finds it impossible to do so and is forced into a decision which involves him in an act of terrible violence that haunts him for the rest of his life. Through the story of Sal and Will, Grenville movingly highlights the human losses and gains involved in the creation of white Australia.

Kate Grenville's earlier novels are Lilian's Story, Dreamhouse, Joan Makes History *and* Dark Places. *Her first book,* Bearded Ladies, *was a collection of short stories; her most recent one,* The Lieutenant, *is set, like* The Secret River *in the first years of white settlement in Australia and tells the story of a soldier who arrives on the First Fleet and his poignant relationship with an Aboriginal child.*

📖Read on
♦ *Lilian's Story* (one woman's journey from troubled middle-class upbringing to life as an eccentric, Shakespeare-quoting bag-lady on the streets of Sydney),
◘ to *The Secret River*: Carol Birch, *Scapegallows*; ›› Thomas Keneally, *The Playmaker*; ›› Jane Rogers, *Promised Lands*.
◘ to Kate Grenville's fiction in general: Murray Bail, *Eucalyptus*; Michelle de Kretser, *The Lost Dog*; Tim Winton, *Cloudstreet*.

GRISHAM, John (born 1955)

US writer

Before turning to fiction, Grisham practised law and he has become the most successful writer of the legal thriller genre in which lawyers play central roles and the
intricacies of the law often provide the fuel for the plot. His first novel, *A Time to Kill*
(1989), with its story of a lawyer defending a black father who has killed his
daughter's rapists, had many of what would be later recognized as the classic
ingredients of a Grisham plot. But it was with his second book, *The Firm*, that
Grisham really hit his stride and propelled himself into the bestseller ranks. The
central character is a brilliant and ambitious young lawyer who joins a prominent
law firm and gradually discovers that it is a front for the Mafia, working solely for
the benefit of organized crime. The novel follows his attempts to break free of the
dangerous web in which the firm has entangled him. Grisham cranks up the tension
with great skill and the legal details are neatly dovetailed into a plot that twists and
turns with satisfying suspense. For many of his fans this remains Grisham's best
book but he has followed it with a number of other thrillers that are almost equally
engrossing. In *The Client*, for example, a senator has been the victim of a Mafia
hitman and a small boy, the only person who knows the identity of the killer,
becomes the innocent centre of a legal battle. *A Painted House* shows a desire to
get away from the courtroom and is a nostalgic story of a boy growing up in the
rural Midwest in the 1950s. His change of pace and style surprised many of his
readers although he has since returned to the expertly crafted legal thrillers for
which he will always be best known.

Grisham's other legal thrillers include The Partner, The Pelican Brief, The
Runaway Jury, The Summons, The King of Torts, The Last Juror, The Broker, The
Appeal *and* The Associate. Bleachers *and* Playing for Pizza *are two feelgood
novels centred on American football.*

☕Read on

◆ *The Runaway Jury*.
◘ Scott Turow, *Presumed Innocent*; James Patterson, *Along Came a Spider*;
Michael Crichton, *Rising Sun*; Steve Martini, *The Attorney*.

GUTERSON, David (born 1956)

US novelist

By combining elements of both courtroom drama and murder mystery with an evocative recreation of a particular community caught at a particular moment in its history, David Guterson produced one of the most satisfying bestsellers of the 1990s. *Snow Falling on Cedars* (1994) is set on an island off the north-west coast of America in the 1950s. A fisherman has been murdered on his boat and a man stands in the dock of the courtroom, accused of the murder. The man is Kabuo Miyamoto, a member of the large Japanese community on the island. Watching the proceedings is Ishmael Chambers, owner of the local newspaper, a lonely man whose only love has been for a woman who refused him and later became Miyamoto's wife. As the trial moves forward, with the inherent tension that courtroom dramas in fiction and film so often possess, the story also moves back in time to Chambers's failed love affair, to the war and the racial tensions it released on the island. Piece by piece, Guterson builds up his picture of an entire community, living precariously in a harsh landscape that the novel brilliantly evokes. And he does so while both maintaining the reader's interest in the whodunit elements of his plot and exploring a drama of clashing cultures and values. For any novelist it would be a major achievement. For a first novelist it is remarkable.

Guterson has also written a collection of short stories, The Country Ahead of Us, The Country Behind *and three other novels.* East of the Mountains *is about a terminally ill man who sets out on a journey into the mountains which becomes a journey into his own past;* Our Lady of the Forest *tells the story of a troubled teenage girl whose visions of the Virgin Mary disrupt the small community in which she lives;* The Other *traces the lives of two old friends as they take very different paths over thirty years.*

🕮Read on

◘ ›› Amy Tan, *The Joy Luck Club*; ›› Annie Proulx, *The Shipping News*; Charles Frazier, *Cold Mountain*; Arthur Golden, *Memoirs of a Geisha*.

HAGGARD, H. (Henry) Rider (1856–1925)
British novelist

Haggard's novels are adventure fantasies set in wildly exotic locations: the geysers and glaciers of Iceland (*Erik Bright-eyes*), the South American jungle (*Montezuma's Daughter*) or – most commonly of all – Darkest Africa, a continent of the imagination as fabulous as the setting of Sinbad's adventures in *The Arabian Nights*. (Haggard knew what he was writing about: in his twenties he was a colonial administrator in the Transvaal.) In *King Solomon's Mines* (1885), Haggard's best-known book, Allan Quatermain leads a safari in search of the fabulous treasure beyond Africa's Solomon Mountains, a treasure which has already claimed a thousand lives. Desert heat, jungle, hostile warrior tribes and ice-caves in the mountains must all be faced, to say nothing of black magic, cannibalism and the guile and treachery of members of Quatermain's own party. Hokum? The best.

⮒Read on
◆ *She* (Englishmen head into the heart of Africa and discover a lost people ruled over by a fabulously beautiful and seemingly immortal queen); *Allan Quatermain* (the first of several sequels to *King Solomon's Mines*).
◻ ≫ John Buchan, *Prester John*; ≫ Jules Verne, *Around the World in Eighty Days*; ≫ Rudyard Kipling, *Kim*; ≫ Wilbur Smith, *A Falcon Flies*.

HAMMETT, Dashiell (1894–1961)
US writer of novels, short stories and screenplays

A former private detective, Hammett wrote stories and serials for pulp magazines, and later became a Hollywood scriptwriter. He perfected the private eye story, in which kidnappings, thefts and murders are investigated by laconic, wisecracking individuals who are always just on the side of the angels and just one step ahead of the police. His best-known detectives are Sam Spade (made famous by Humphrey Bogart), the urbane Nick Charles (star of William Powell's 'Thin Man' films) and the Continental Op.

Hammett's novels are The Dain Curse, Red Harvest, The Maltese Falcon, The Glass Key *and* The Thin Man; *his story collections include* The Continental Op *and* The Big Knockover and Other Stories.

Read on

◘ ›› Raymond Chandler, *The Lady in the Lake*; James M. Cain, *Double Indemnity*; Ross Macdonald, *The Drowning Pool*; Jim Thompson, *The Killer Inside Me*.

HARDY, Thomas (1840–1928)
British novelist and poet

As a young man Hardy worked as an ecclesiastical architect, sketching and surveying country churches. This work intensified his love of the old ways of the countryside, patterns of life and customs which dated from feudal times. This is the background to his novels (which are all set in south-western England, the ancient kingdom of Wessex). He describes the minutiae of farming and village life with the exactness of a museum curator, and his characters' habits of mind are rooted in the ebb and flow of the seasons, in the unending cycle of tending for their animals and caring for the land. Life is unhurried but inexorable: Hardy's people are owned by their environment. They are also subject to a range of violent passions and emotions – Hardy thought of human beings as the playthings of destiny, struggling against the indifferent and inexplicable forces of nature and fate – and the placid continuum of existence is the setting for such irrational psychological forces as jealousy, intolerance and revenge. Hardy's bleakness and pessimism were much criticized, and in 1895 he gave up novels to concentrate on poetry.

FAR FROM THE MADDING CROWD (1874)
The shepherd Gabriel Oak works for Bathsheba Everdene, and loves her. Bathsheba's head is turned by dashing Sergeant Troy, who marries her and then deserts her, letting her believe that he is dead. Bathsheba now agrees to marry Boldwood, a yeoman farmer, unimaginative and dull, who has secretly loved her for years. Then Troy comes back and claims his wife – provoking a crisis and the resolution of the uneasy relationship between Oak and Bathsheba which has simmered all this time.

Hardy's other novels include Under the Greenwood Tree, A Pair of Blue Eyes, The Return of the Native, The Trumpet Major, The Mayor of Casterbridge, The Woodlanders, Tess of the D'Urbervilles *and* Jude the Obscure. *He wrote an epic drama set during the Napoleonic Wars,* The Dynasts, *and several books of poetry including* Satires of Circumstance, Moments of Vision *and* Winter Words.

📖 Read on

◆ *The Mayor of Casterbridge* (Michael Henchard rises to become rich and respected but his past returns to bring him down); *Tess of the D'Urbervilles*.

▣ on similar themes, in a similar style: ▶▶ George Eliot, *Adam Bede*; ▶▶ Mrs Gaskell, *Ruth*; ▶▶ Edith Wharton, *Ethan Frome*; ▶▶ Melvyn Bragg, *The Hired Man*.

▣ further away in period or manner or setting, but equally atmospheric: ▶▶ John Fowles, *The French Lieutenant's Woman*; Halldor Laxness, *Independent People*.

HARRIS, Joanne (born 1964)
British novelist

Joanne Harris had published two earlier novels in the late 1980s and early 1990s but she had made little impact on the bestseller lists until the appearance of *Chocolat* in 1999. This charming and deceptively simple story tells of a mysterious young woman, Vianne Rocher, and her daughter arriving in a small village in the south of France to open a chocolate shop. Their coming throws the village into confusion and turmoil as the decadent pleasures Vianne's shop offers threaten to overturn the rules by which the isolated community is regulated. The parish priest, Father Reynaud, becomes the sworn foe of all the chocolate shop offers, but Vianne's influence only spreads − a battered wife finds the courage to leave her husband; shy young couples declare their love. As Easter approaches, the traditional religious rites of Reynaud's church face the challenge of Vianne's chocolate festival and the village is divided down the middle. *Chocolat* works both as the story of a small community riven by conflict and as a fable of the perennial struggle between dogmatic self-denial and the pleasures of the flesh.

Since the success of Chocolat, *Harris has published other novels, including* Blackberry Wine, Five Quarters of the Orange, Coastliners *and* Gentlemen and Players. The Lollipop Shoes *is a follow-up to* Chocolat *which returns to the characters of Vianne Rocher and her daughter, now living in Montmartre in Paris and embarking on a friendship with a charming visitor to their chocolate shop who is not all she seems.* Runemarks *is a children's fantasy novel.*

📖 Read on

◆ *Gentlemen and Players* (in a story reminiscent of a darker version of *Goodbye, Mr Chips*, James Hilton's 1930s classic, a master approaching retirement finds that resentments that have smouldered for years are about to erupt).

◘ ﹥﹥ Tracey Chevalier, *Girl with a Pearl Earring*; Laura Esquivel, *Like Water for Chocolate*; Salley Vickers, *Mr Golightly's Holiday*.

HARRIS, Robert (born 1957)
British writer

In his fiction Robert Harris shows all the best qualities he honed as a fine political journalist. He is exact in description, his eye for the telling detail which illuminates a scene is acute and his prose is precise but relaxed. The result is that his books have a plausibility that is sustained even when the plot is based on imaginative speculation. 'What if?', he asks and then provides an answer that convinces because it is rooted in everyday realities. Many writers, most of them working in the science fiction genre, have written alternative histories in which the Nazis won the Second World War. None has produced a portrait of what that alternative reality might have been like that matches the one Harris provides in *Fatherland* (1992). And he succeeds precisely because he rejects sweeping, generalized conjecture in favour of closely observed, mundane details. Within a short time we are immersed in Berlin 1964 as preparations begin to celebrate Hitler's seventy-fifth birthday. This is the day-to-day world of Kripo detective Xavier March and it rapidly becomes ours. The puzzling murder of a figure from the wartime past disturbs March's world. As he takes his investigation into territory his superiors would rather avoid, he edges towards truths about the Nazi world that we know but March doesn't.

Robert Harris's other novels are Enigma *(set in the Second World War code-breaking centre at Bletchley),* Archangel, Pompeii *(set in Ancient Rome at the time when a volcanic eruption is about to engulf the eponymous city),* Imperium *(another Ancient Roman thriller) and* The Ghost *(a political thriller focusing on a British prime minister who seems remarkably similar to Tony Blair). He has also written several works of non-fiction including* Selling Hitler, *the very funny and scarcely credible story of the forged Hitler diaries of the 1980s.*

📚Read on
♦ *Archangel* (centres on the search for a missing archive of Stalin's papers).
◘ ﹥﹥ Len Deighton, *SS-GB*; ﹥﹥ Frederick Forsyth, *The Odessa File*; Philip Kerr, *A Philosophical Investigation*; ﹥﹥ Alan Furst, *The World at Night*.

HAŠEK, Jaroslav (1883–1923)
Czech novelist and journalist

Hašek spent most of his youth as a dropout and a half-baked political activist. He served, reluctantly, in the First World War, was invalided out and returned to the journalistic career he had begun before the war. This career was as unpredictable as most other things in Hašek's boozy, disorganized life. He worked on an anarchist paper but was sacked for stealing the office bicycle. For a while he edited a magazine called *Animal World* but was again shown the door when it was discovered that he had been inventing animals about which to write. Hašek's masterpiece, the seven hundred-page comic novel *The Good Soldier Svejk*, makes hilarious use of all his early experiences. Svejk is the town drunk, a dog-catcher, who is conscripted into the Austrian army as the lowliest of privates. A moon-faced, brainless lump, he obeys every fatuous order and follows every regulation to the letter. The book follows his farcical army career, during which he rises to the dizzy heights of chaplain's batman, takes part in the First World War and sees the first skirmishes of the Russian revolution. He understands nothing of what is going on: food, drink and staying out of trouble are all that interest him. Hašek uses Svejk's blankness like a mirror, showing up officers, politicians and bureaucrats for the fools they are.

📖Read on
◆ *The Red Commissar* (a selection of Hašek's journalism and shorter works).
◘ Eric Linklater, *Private Angelo* (a genial satire on the Second World War); Thomas Berger, *Reinhart in Love* (a similarly light-hearted novel about a Svejkish American 'little man'); ›› Thomas Mann, *The Confessions of Felix Krull, Confidence Man* (about a confidence trickster travelling the spas and luxury hotels of Europe in the 1900s; though it lacks Hašekk's devastating view of war and politics, it exactly parallels his wide-eyed, amiable style); ›› Joseph Heller, *Catch-22* (a hilarious black-farce take on all Hašek's themes).

HAWTHORNE, NATHANIEL (1804–64)
US novelist

A member of a long-established New England family, Hawthorne was born in Salem, Massachusetts. Salem was, of course, the town in which the notorious witch-trials of the seventeenth century had taken place and Hawthorne was a direct descendant of one of the judges in the trial. Much of his work is concerned with his heritage of New England Puritanism. Many of his novels and stories struggle to understand the combination of personal moral rectitude with ferocious and pitiless intolerance of others that characterized both his ancestors and many of his contemporaries. Hawthorne wrote and published fiction throughout his adult life but his greatest achievements belong to an extraordinary burst of creativity in the late 1840s and early 1850s, which saw the publication of *The Scarlet Letter*, *The House of the Seven Gables* and *The Blithedale Romance*. Hawthorne's gifts can also be seen in many of his short stories, particularly 'Young Goodman Brown' (good and evil battling it out again in New England), 'The Maypole of Merry Mount' and 'Rappaccini's Daughter'.

THE SCARLET LETTER (1850)

This study of intolerance and humbug is set among the first Puritan settlers in North America. Hester Prynne has spent two years in Boston, waiting for her elderly husband to join her from England. In the meantime she has borne a love-child, Pearl, and the Puritans pillory her and brand her as an adulteress, making her wear the scarlet letter A embroidered on her clothes. Her husband arrives, discovers that her secret lover is a minister of the church, and mercilessly persecutes him for refusing to admit his guilt. Hester's husband and lover pursue their enmity to the end; they ignore Hester herself, who in the meantime lives an unobtrusive but truly Christian life helping the neighbours who once mistreated her.

📖 Read on

♦ *The House of the Seven Gables* (a similarly remorseless novel about a New England family cursed for generations because of their forebears' persecution of an innocent man for witchcraft); *The Blithedale Romance* (a satire, based on Hawthorne's own experience, about life in a Massachusetts utopian community).

◘ ▶▶ Aldous Huxley, *The Devils of Loudon* (about an outbreak of hysteria and demonic possession in a sixteenth-century French village); ▶▶ I.B. Singer, *Satan in Goray* (set in a medieval community of Polish Jews harassed by pogroms and torn apart by the appearance of a false messiah); ▶▶ Edgar Allan Poe, *Tales of Mystery and Imagination*.

HEINLEIN, Robert (1907–88)
US novelist

Heinlein's 1930s and 1940s writings were a bridge between early science fiction (>> Verne and >> Wells) and the present day. They are straightforward stories of space travel and the colonization of distant planets, and much of their detail has been overtaken by events. In the 1960s his novel *Stranger in a Strange Land* had a cult following because it seemed to be advocating a mystical union of humankind brought about by flower power, free love and hallucinatory drugs. His 1970s and 1980s books range from the serious *I Will Fear No Evil* to the ironical farce *Job*, akin to the bleakly hilarious fantasies of >> Joseph Heller and >> Kurt Vonnegut. Heinlein's work, especially gung-ho space-war classics like *Starship Troopers*, has been condemned as excessively right wing but there is no doubting Heinlein's imaginative range. His best-known books, the heart of his achievement, are a series of independent but linked novels about Lazarus Long, a man who has the ability to live forever, and who ends up as a kind of universal patriarch; everyone in existence is one of his descendants. Heinlein explores the personal and social problems of such a person, stirring in exotic and fascinating plot-ideas. In *Time Enough to Love*, for example, Lazarus Long, bored with life and contemplating suicide, is distracted by being allowed to try the forbidden experience of time travel. He goes back to 1917, fights in the First World War, meets himself as a six-year-old and falls in love with his own mother. Other books including Lazarus Long are *Methuselah's Children*, *The Number of the Beast* and *The Cat Who Walks Through Walls*.

📖Read on
♦ *Job* (a Bible-inspired story of a human being tormented by a practical-joking, malicious God and finally befriended by the devil).
◘ >> Isaac Asimov, *Foundation*; Orson Scott Card, *Ender's Game*; Ray Bradbury, *The Martian Chronicles*; Larry Niven, *Ringworld*.

HELLER, Joseph (1923–99)
US novelist

Throughout the 1950s, the escalation of the nuclear arms race produced in many people a feeling of desperate impotence. Faced with imminent apocalypse, the only possible option seemed to be hysterical, cynical laughter. By the early 1960s this mood was common in plays, comedians' routines, cartoons and satirical magazines, and Heller's first novel, *Catch-22*, expressed it perfectly. On the surface a wild farce about airmen in the Second World War, it shows human beings as both trapped in a detestable destiny and paradoxically liberated, by the absence of hope or choice, to do exactly as they please, to turn reality into fantasy. *Catch-22* was such an enormous critical and popular success that its shadow fell over the rest of Heller's career. As he once sardonically remarked, 'People say that, in the last thirty years, I haven't written a novel as good as *Catch-22*. True, but, then, nor has anyone else.' In fact, several of Heller's later novels are comic masterpieces in their own right.

CATCH-22 (1961)
A group of US bomber pilots is stationed on a Mediterranean island during the Second World War. Every time a man thinks he has flown his quota of bombing missions, high command doubles the number. There is no escape, and the reason is Catch-22: if you're sane enough to ask to be grounded because what you're doing is crazy, you're sane enough to fly. For all its bleak philosophy, *Catch-22* is brilliantly funny, particularly in its deadpan reporting of the lunatic, gung-ho US top brass, of Milo Minderbinder's extension to infinity of the rules of free-market enterprise (profiteering on everything from eggs to his comrades' lives), and of such pitiful victims of destiny as Major Major Major Major, a man haunted by his name.

Heller's other novels are Something Happened, Good as Gold, God Knows, Picture This *and* Closing Time. No Laughing Matter *is non-fiction, a blackly funny account of Heller's recovery from near-fatal illness.* Now and Then *is a memoir of growing up in Coney Island and of service in the US Air Force during the Second World War.*

✺Read on
◆ *Closing Time* is a sequel to *Catch-22*, in which Yossarian and his ex-comrades are facing old age, despair and death in the hell that is 1990s capitalist New York. Two other Heller novels centre on characters who are trapped. *Something Happened* shows a man in thrall to the routine and ordinariness of his life; in *God Knows* the

Old Testament King David is shackled by knowledge of the world's whole future history, and by his relationship with a wisecracking, cynical and unhelpful God. ('Where does it say nice?' asks God. 'Where does it say I have to be nice?')
◻ ❯❯ Jaroslav Hašek, *The Good Soldier Svejk*; ❯❯ Philip Roth, *Portnoy's Complaint*; ❯❯ John Kennedy Toole, *A Confederacy of Dunces*.

HEMINGWAY, Ernest (1898–1961)
US novelist and short story writer

Few great writers provoke such love/hate reactions as Hemingway: it seems impossible to read him without judging him. The reason is that, although he wrote some of the most evocative, persuasive prose of the century – as direct and compelling as the best journalism – many people find his subject matter and philosophy of life repellent. He believed that creatures, including human beings, are at their noblest when fighting for survival, and his novels and stories are therefore about boxing, big-game hunting, deep-sea fishing, bullfighting and, above all, war. Hemingway was aware himself of the defects and shortcomings of his macho philosophy, and most of his books are tinged with failure. His heroes rarely succeed in 'proving' themselves, their wars are futile, the emphasis is on pain, despair and death. But the dream remains, and is Hemingway's own dream. He spent his leisure time in exactly the activities he describes – precise details of how to fight bulls, hunt big game, box or fish are what he does best – and in 1961, feeling too old and sick to continue, he shot himself.

A FAREWELL TO ARMS (1929)
A US ambulance driver in Italy during the First World War is wounded and taken to hospital, where he falls in love with an English nurse. While he convalesces the couple are deliriously happy, but then he is commanded back to the front. She tells him that she is pregnant, and they decide that their only course is 'a farewell to arms', escaping from the war to neutral Switzerland.

Hemingway's other novels are The Torrents of Spring, The Sun Also Rises/Fiesta *(which includes a superb description of bull-running during the festival at Pamplona),* Green Hills of Africa, To Have and Have Not, For Whom the Bell Tolls *(set during the Spanish Civil War),* Across the River and Into the Trees *and* The Old Man and the Sea. *Several unrevised, unfinished books were published posthumously: most famous is* Islands in the Stream, *most recent is* True at First Light. *His short story collections include* In Our Time, Men Without Women *and* Winner Take Nothing. Death in the Afternoon *combines non-fiction descriptions of bullfighting with short stories on the same subject.* A Moveable Feast *is his memoir of happy days as a young, would-be writer in Paris in the early 1920s.*

🕮 Read on

◆ *The Old Man and the Sea* describes a duel to the death between the old Cuban fisherman Santiago and a gigantic marlin, the biggest fish he has ever tried to catch in his life. The book is short, and concentrates on Santiago, struggling not only with the marlin but his own failing powers, and kept going only by determination and a lifetime's skill.

◘ ❯❯ Graham Greene, *The Power and the Glory*; ❯❯ Norman Mailer, *The Naked and the Dead*; ❯❯ George Orwell, *Homage to Catalonia*; Jack London, *The Sea-wolf*.

LITERARY TRIVIA 7:

FIVE WRITERS WHO SUFFERED FROM INSANITY
❯❯ Jonathan Swift

The author of *Gulliver's Travels* was declared 'unsound in mind and memory' at the age of seventy five and confined to his house. He left money in his will to go to the founding of a hospital for the mentally ill in Dublin.

Charles Lamb

The essayist was briefly committed to an asylum in 1796 and, on his release, he wrote to his friend Coleridge that, 'I am got somewhat rational now and don't bite any more'. His sister Mary, who co-wrote *Tales from Shakespeare* with him, killed their mother in a fit of insanity and spent long periods of her life in an asylum.

Friedrich Nietzsche

The German philosopher lost his mental equilibrium in Turin in 1889 when he burst into uncontrollable tears after witnessing a man mistreat his horse. Nietzsche never recovered and spent the last eleven years of his life insane.

Ezra Pound

The American poet, who lived in Italy, was arrested after the Second World War for broadcasting pro-Fascist propaganda. Repatriated to America, he was judged to be insane and committed to an asylum rather than prison.

John Clare

The nineteenth-century poet spent the last years of his life in Northampton General Lunatic Asylum, suffering from severe delusions, and it was there that he wrote some of his best-known verse.

HENSHER, Philip (born 1965)
British novelist

Hensher's first three novels were malevolently witty, cleverly crafted comedies of modern mores, set in different parts of a seemingly corrupt and bankrupt Europe. *Other Lulus* juxtaposed a contemporary tale of love and betrayal involving an Austrian singer and her English musicologist husband with erudite speculations about the life of the composer Alban Berg and his opera *Lulu*. *Kitchen Venom* is the story of a distinguished parliamentary official whose secret life of afternoon sex with rent boys leads him into a maze of intrigue and death, all played out against the backdrop of the weird rites and rituals of Westminster. It won Hensher many admirers for its wit and sharpness but lost him his job as a clerk in the House of Commons. *Pleasured* is set in Berlin in the late 1980s and tells the story of two feckless drifters drawn into an unlikely plot to flood East Berlin with a supposedly liberating supply of Ecstasy tablets. The publication of *The Mulberry Empire* in 2002 marked a radical change in direction in Hensher's fiction. This is a historical novel of great ambition and scope, set in England and Afghanistan in the 1830s. Hensher marshals a large cast of characters and many different plot-lines to tell the story of a British officer and explorer, Alexander Burnes, caught up in an ill-fated attempt by the British to oust the Amir from government in Kabul and replace him with a régime more favourable to imperial expansion. The novel succeeds brilliantly in combining the epic sweep of some of the nineteenth-century novelists to which it pays knowing tribute (>> Dickens and >> Tolstoy among others) and a twenty-first-century irony about the pretensions of imperialism and European complacency. Since the appearance of *The Mulberry Empire*, Hensher has returned to the contemporary world with *The Fit*, a short satirical novel in which the orderly life of a professional indexer is disrupted by marital troubles and a terrible attack of the hiccups, and anatomised Britain in the 1970s and 1980s in *The Northern Clemency*.

⛁Read on

◘ to Hensher's first three novels: ›› Allan Hollinghurst, *The Swimming-Pool Library*; Neil Bartlett, *Ready to Catch Him Should He Fall*.
◘ to *The Mulberry Empire*: ›› J.G. Farrell, *The Siege of Krishnapur*; ›› Matthew Kneale, *English Passengers*.

HERBERT, Frank (1920–86)
US novelist

Herbert's work is dominated by the two thousand-page (six-novel) Dune series (1965–85), a science fiction epic whose scope and complexity dwarfs all rivals. Dune is a desert planet, inhabited by gigantic sand-worms which produce melange, a substance which inhibits ageing and gives knowledge of the past and future. The saga (each of the novels is self-contained) tells how Paul Atreides inherits Dune, has to win it from his enemies and then colonize it. It describes the 'greening' of a planet where water is the most precious of all commodities, and recounts the wars between the Atreides family and other interests (especially the powerful Bene Gesserit sisterhood, which is dedicated to harnessing the pure power of thought and so dispensing with science and technology). The books are partly a swaggering multi-generation saga, the apotheosis of space-opera, and partly a detailed and moving account of the inter-relationship between the colonists and their planet.

The first Dune trilogy is Dune, Dune Messiah *and* Children of Dune; *the second is* God Emperor of Dune, Heretics of Dune *and* Chapterhouse of Dune. *Herbert's many other books include* The Dragon in the Sea, The Whipping Star, The Dosadi Experiment, The Green Brain *and* The Santaroga Barrier.

⛁Read on

◘ to *Dune*: Brian Aldiss, *Helliconia Spring* and its sequels; Robert Silverberg, *Majipoor Chronicles*; Jack Vance, *Big Planet*.
◘ to *God Emperor of Dune*: Alfred Bester, *The Stars My Destination*; Philip José

Farmer, *Jesus on Mars*; Roger Zelazny, *Lord of Light*; Kim Stanley Robinson, A *Memory of Whiteness*.

HESSE, Hermann (1877–1962)
German/Swiss novelist and non-fiction writer

A poet and mystic, Hesse was influenced by Jung's ideas of the unconscious and the collective unconscious, and later by Buddhist philosophy. His most famous mystical novel, *The Glass Bead Game (Das Glasperlenspiel)*, is about a future utopia where all questions about life, morality and personality are covered by a monastic philosophical system centred on a zen-like game involving coloured beads and an abacus. Hesse's reputation for gentle, philosophical woolliness has obscured his true worth. His novels before *The Glass Bead Game* are spare, moving accounts of how people in psychological turmoil reach peace with themselves, either through their own efforts or with the help of friends and loved ones. He is something of a special taste, but few writers' works so reward their devotees.

Hesse's major novels are Gertrud, Peter Camenzind, Siddhartha *(about Buddha)*, Rosshalde, Steppenwolf, Narziss and Goldmund *and* The Glass Bead Game. *He also published shorter, more mystical fiction* (Knulp; Klingsor's Last Summer), *poetry, short stories, essays and letters.*

⏛Read on
♦ *Gertrud* (the story of a tragic love triangle between a girl and two young men who are close friends). *Steppenwolf* and *Narziss and Goldmund* are both about the divided self. In *Steppenwolf* a hopeless, middle-aged recluse is 'brought back' by the spiritual energy of three young people who may be dream-figures from his subconscious. In *Narziss and Goldmund* (set in medieval Europe) the conflict between flesh and spirit is symbolized by the two main characters, close friends, one carnal, one spiritual.
◘ Heinrich Böll, *The Clown*; ›› Kazuo Ishiguro, *An Artist of the Floating World*; Knut Hamsun, *Mysteries*.

HIAASEN, Carl (born 1953)

US journalist and novelist

Carl Hiaasen knows the world of which he writes with such black relish in his comedy thrillers. Born and raised in Florida, the setting for his books, he has worked as a journalist investigating the kinds of corruption and chicanery that provide the fuel on which his plots run. Hiaasen's novels have the suspense and mystery of the best crime fiction but it is safe to assume that what readers remember of them are the manic, comic energy, the grotesque villains (and, often, even more grotesque heroes) and the writer's ability to focus on one seemingly trivial incident, spinning out its consequences to logical but bizarre lengths. Only in a Hiaasen novel is a hit-man a seven-foot-tall Amish man. Only in a Hiaasen novel does a deranged bad guy spend the second half of the book with a dead dog's rotting head firmly embedded by the teeth in his forearm. And only a Hiaasen plot can begin with the theft of blue-tongued mango voles from the Kingdom of Thrills in Key Largo and escalate into an insane confrontation between environmentalists and a mobster developer that results in the total destruction of the Kingdom. As ≫ P.J. O'Rourke once pointed out (correctly): 'Reading Hiaasen will do more to damage the Florida tourist trade than anything except an actual visit to Florida.'

TOURIST SEASON (1986)

A band of anti-tourist terrorists is on the loose in Florida, led by a rogue newspaperman appalled by the destruction of the state's natural beauty and resources. The head of Miami's Chamber of Commerce has been found dead with a toy rubber alligator lodged in his throat. More murders follow. Another reporter turned private eye is given the job of tracking down the terrorists, a job that soon turns into one of Hiaasen's characteristic excursions along the wilder highways and byways of the Sunshine State. And beneath the mayhem, violence and dark farce, the author's serious environmental concerns are apparent.

Hiaasen's other novels are Double Whammy, Skin Tight, Native Tongue, Strip Tease, Stormy Weather, Lucky You, Sick Puppy, Basket Case, Skinny Dip *and* Nature Girl. *He has also written three novels with William Montalbano* (Powder Burns, Trap Line *and* A Death in China), *less anarchic than his solo fiction, and three recent novels for young adults,* Hoot, Flush *and* Scat.

Read on

◆ *Sick Puppy*.

◻ Lawrence Shames, *Sunburn*; Dave Barry, *Big Trouble*; Charles Willeford, *The Shark-Infested Custard*; Doug J. Swanson, *Dreamboat*; Charles Higson, *King of the Ants* (for an English version of Hiaasen's mix of grotesquerie, violence and comedy).

READ**ON**A THEME:

HIGH ADVENTURE
Boys' Own stories, past and present
›› John Buchan, *Huntingtower*
›› Alexandre Dumas, *The Three Musketeers*
   Ken Follett, *The Man From St Petersburg*
›› Frederick Forsyth, *The Day of the Jackal*
   Jean-Christophe Grangé, *Blood Red Rivers*
›› H. Rider Haggard, *King Solomon's Mines*
   Anthony Hope, *The Prisoner of Zenda*
   Stephen Hunter, *A Time to Hunt*
   Rafael Sabatini, *Captain Blood*
›› Wilbur Smith, *Birds of Prey*
   B. Traven, *The Treasure of the Sierra Madre*

See also: Historical Adventure; Spies and Double Agents; Terrorists/ Freedom Fighters

---

READ**ON**A THEME:

HIGHER (?) EDUCATION
   Malcolm Bradbury, *The History Man*
›› Robertson Davies, *The Rebel Angels*
   J.P. Donleavy, *The Ginger Man*
   Richard Gordon, *Doctor in the House*
›› Howard Jacobson, *Coming from Behind*
   Randall Jarrell, *Pictures From an Institution*
›› Alison Lurie, *The War Between the Tates*
›› Tom Sharpe, *Wilt*

See also: Dreaming Spires

HIGHSMITH, Patricia (1921–95)

US novelist and short story writer

Except for *The People Who Knock on the Door* (1982, about the disintegration of an 'ordinary' American family whose father becomes a born-again Christian), Highsmith's books are chiefly psychological thrillers. They show the planning and commission of horribly convincing, 'everyday' crimes, and the way murder erodes the murderer's moral identity. Few writers screw tension so tight in such functional, unemotional prose. Highsmith's most chilling insight is how close the criminally insane can be to people just like ourselves.

RIPLEY'S GAME (1974)

Ripley, who appears in several Highsmith books, is a charming American psychopath who lives in France. In this book, out of boredom, he sets up circumstances to snare an entirely innocent man into committing murder. But the murder victim is a Mafia boss, and soon assassins begin to hunt down both Ripley and his dupe. The plot is exciting, but Highsmith's main concern is the comparison between Ripley's icy amorality and the conscience-racked flailings of the man he corrupts.

Other Ripley books are The Talented Mr Ripley, Ripley Under Ground, The Boy Who Followed Ripley *and* Ripley Under Water. *Highsmith's other novels include* Strangers on a Train, The Two Faces of January, The Glass Cell, The Tremor of Forgery, Edith's Diary, Found in the Street, Small G: a Summer Idyll *and* Carol. The Animal-lover's Book of Beastly Murder, Mermaids on the Golf Course *and* Tales of Natural and Unnatural Catastrophes *contain short stories.*

📖 Read on

◆ the central character of *The Glass Cell* (a typical non-Ripley book) is a man released from prison after six years during which his character has been brutalized and his moral integrity destroyed. Tormented by the possibility of his wife's unfaithfulness, he sets out to discover the truth.

◘ Julian Symons, *The Man Who Killed Himself*; Barbara Vine (see ▶▶ Ruth Rendell), *A Fatal Inversion*; ▶▶ P.D. James, *The Skull Beneath the Skin*; ▶▶ Minette Walters, *The Echo*.

HILL, Reginald (born 1936)

British novelist

In his first novel, *A Clubbable Woman* (1970), Hill introduced the two characters who have been central to his books ever since – the aggressive, slobbish but shrewd Superintendent Dalziel and the eager, sensitive Inspector Pascoe. Each successive book has expanded our knowledge of the pair and shown Hill's increasingly confident use of humour, deft characterization and ingenious plotting to tell traditional crime stories in a contemporary setting. To many readers Reginald Hill is now the best crime writer in Britain.

ON BEULAH HEIGHT (1998)

During a hot summer a village re-emerges from the reservoir which had covered it fifteen years earlier. At the time the villagers were evacuated three girls were missing and so too was the man suspected of abducting them. Now he seems to have returned, another girl is missing and Dalziel is obliged to face once again the most demanding and puzzling of cases from his past. Hill produces a crime story of satisfying complexity and depth which also manages, unpretentiously, to say something about the power of the past to haunt the present.

Hill's other books include An Advancement of Learning, A Fairly Dangerous Thing, A Very Good Hater, Bones and Silence, *the cheekily named* Another Death in Venice, *the superbly comic* Pictures of Perfection, Arms and the Women, Dialogues of the Dead, Death's Jest-Book, Good Morning, Midnight, The Stranger House, The Death of Dalziel, A Cure for All Diseases *and* Midnight Fugue. *Hill has also written several novels about a Luton-based private investigator, Joe Sixsmith, and has published fiction under the pseudonyms Dick Morland, Patrick Ruell and Charles Underhill.*

📖 Read on

◻ ≫ Val McDermid, *A Place of Execution*; ≫ Colin Dexter, *Death is Now My Neighbour*; ≫ Ian Rankin, *The Falls*; ≫ Peter Robinson, *In a Dry Season*.

HILL, Susan (born 1942)
British writer

Susan Hill has written *Mrs de Winter* (a 1993 sequel to ›› Daphne Du Maurier's *Rebecca*), three ghost stories, *The Woman in Black, The Mist in the Mirror* and *The Man in the Picture*, and four crime stories featuring the cerebral and sensitive police officer Simon Serrailler (*The Various Haunts of Men, The Pure in Heart, The Risk of Darkness* and *The Vows of Silence*). Her other novels are mostly about emotional relationships. Often, the relationship is predatory: one partner (spouse, friend, lover or acquaintance) can only survive by engulfing the other, and the process is agonizing and deliberate. The exceptions are *In the Springtime of the Year*, in which a young woman, devastated by the death of her husband, is rescued from despair by the tranquil daily round of country life, and *Air and Angels*, a moving story of the love in Edwardian times of a lonely, middle-aged bachelor for a fifteen-year-old girl.

Hill's other novels include I'm the King of the Castle, Strange Meeting, The Bird of Night *and* The Service of the Clouds. The Albatross *and* The Beacon *are novellas and* A Bit of Singing and Dancing *and* The Boy Who Taught the Beekeeper to Read *contain short stories.* The Magic Apple Tree *and* Family *are autobiographical. She has also written radio plays and many children's books.*

⮧Read on
♦ *I'm the King of the Castle* (set in a gloomy Victorian mansion where one young boy gains tormenting power over another); *The Bird of Night.*
◘ to *I'm the King of the Castle*: ›› Henry James, *The Turn of the Screw*; ›› John Wyndham, *Chocky*; ›› William Golding, *Lord of the Flies.*
◘ to *In the Springtime of the Year*: ›› Penelope Lively, *Perfect Happiness.*
◘ to *Air and Angels*: ›› Penelope Fitzgerald, *The Gate of Angels.*

READ ON A THEME:

HISTORICAL ADVENTURE
- ➤➤ Bernard Cornwell, *Sharpe's Regiment*
- ➤➤ Alexandre Dumas, *The Count of Monte Cristo*
- ➤➤ C.S. Forester, *Mr Midshipman Hornblower*
- ➤➤ George MacDonald Fraser, *Flashman*
  Bjorn Larsson, *Long John Silver*
- ➤➤ Arturo Pérez-Reverte, *The Fencing Master*
  Derek Robinson, *Goshawk Squadron*
- ➤➤ R.L. Stevenson, *Kidnapped*

See also: High Adventure; Spies and Double Agents

START POINT

HISTORICAL NOVELS
For a writer, setting novels in the past is seductive. If you write about the present, readers know as much as you do – and judge you by what they know. But if you write about the past, you are often their main source of information. All you have to do is convince. Some writers stun their readers with research, showing every detail of clothes, food, manners and turns of phrase, and keeping strictly to such facts as are known. This kind of 'documentary' historical novel used to be more popular than any other, and there can be few great names or historical events which have not been used: the range is from the career of Julius Caesar (in Conn Iggulden's Emperor series) to the domestic life of Elizabeth Barrett Browning (in ➤➤ Margaret Forster's *Lady's Maid*), from Columbus's career (in Stephen Marlowe's *The Memoirs of Christopher Columbus*) to Scott's last polar expedition (in ➤➤ Beryl Bainbridge's *The Birthday Boys*). The second kind of novel puts the 'great' aside, and concentrates on ordinary people's lives. These books are, so to speak, 'true' novels which are given extra depth and colour by their setting in the past, by the way they show recognizable relationships, family life, hopes and fears in a context of historical events. This kind of historical novel, nowadays more popular than the other, ranges from 'literary' books

(such as >> Barry Unsworth's *Sacred Hunger*, set on an eighteenth-century slave ship) to crime novels (Ellis Peters's Brother Cadfael series, set in twelfth-century Shrewsbury and >> Lindsey Davis's Falco novels, set in the Roman Empire of Vespasian, for example) and romances and family sagas such as Sheelagh Kelly's series set in the slums of Victorian York.

Bennett, Ronan, *Havoc in its Third Year* (2004). In the 1630s the coroner of a small town in the North of England is drawn into the religious and political turmoil of the era and faces a cruel choice between justice and his own personal safety.

>> Carr, Caleb, The Alienist (1994). Pioneer psychiatrist (or alienist) teams up with unlikely group of social misfits to track down a serial killer in 1900 New York. Superbly researched and evocative book which combines for the reader the pleasures of historical and crime fiction.

Doctorow, E.L., *The March* (2005). General Sherman's march to the sea in the last days of the American Civil War is the setting for a novel which recreates the lives of ordinary people caught up in extraordinary events.

>> Graves, Robert, *Wife to Mr Milton* (1943). In Puritan London in the mid-seventeenth century, Mary Powell tells the story of her marriage to the poet and political secretary John Milton. Good on period detail, especially domestic; outstanding on the problems of being married to a morose, irascible genius who regards you not as a fellow human being but as a chattel.

>> Moore, Brian, *Black Robe* (1985). In the mid-seventeenth century, a Jesuit missionary is captured by North American Indians

Penman, Sharon Kay, *The Sunne in Splendour* (1982). Was Richard III the hunchbacked villain portrayed by Shakespeare or was he a good man betrayed by those he trusted during his lifetime and traduced by historians ever since? In her absorbing novel based on Richard's life, Penman clearly has no doubt that the king has been much-maligned.

Rathbone, Julian, *The Last English King* (1997). Tongue-in-cheek, deliberately anachronistic romp through the decline and fall of Anglo-Saxon

England, as revealed in the story of the only member of King Harold's elite bodyguard to survive the Battle of Hastings.

›› Renault, Mary, *The Mask of Apollo* (1966). Niko, a Greek actor of the fourth century BC, is used as a go-between by politicians trying to organize a political coup in Sicily. Complicated private life; fascinating theatre detail (Niko is a true luvvie); aromatic sense of sunny, blood-soaked ancient Greece.

›› Roberts, Michèle, *The Wild Girl* (1984). The events of the Gospels are told from a startlingly new point of view: that of Mary Magdalene.

Edward Rutherfurd, *London* (1997). Episodic but compelling, this book unfolds the history of England's capital through the lives of ordinary people down the centuries.

›› Seth, Vikram, *A Suitable Boy* (1993). Panoramic story of four families in 1950s India, just after independence from Britain. High hopes; bitter politics; fascinating clash of cultures; tragic, comic family life.

Shaara, Michael, *The Killer Angels* (1974). Pulitzer Prize-winning novel about the Battle of Gettysburg. Brings the reality of American Civil War battle-fields home like no fiction since Stephen Crane's *The Red Badge of Courage*.

Thompson, Harry, *This Thing of Darkness* (2005). The contrasting lives of two men, the young Charles Darwin, sailing as a naturalist on HMS *Beagle*, and the ship's captain, Robert Fitzroy, an evangelical Christian, form the basis for Thompson's vivid reconstruction of Victorian doubts and certainties.

›› Winterson, Jeanette, *The Passion* (1987). Surreal fantasy spinning off from the story of the peasant boy who became Napoleon's cook.

Richard Zimler, *The Last Kabbalist of Lisbon* (1998). A renowned scholar is murdered during an anti-Jewish pogrom in early sixteenth-century Lisbon and his nephew devotes himself to finding the killer.

Also recommended: Ivo Andric, *The Bridge Over the Drina*; Thomas Berger, *Little Big Man*; ›› Melvyn Bragg, *Credo*; ›› Anthony Burgess, *The Kingdom of the Wicked*; James Clavell, *Shogun*; Sarah Dunant, *In the Company of the Courtesan*; Margaret Elphinstone, *Voyageurs*; Ken Follett, *The Pillars of the Earth*; Douglas Galbraith, *The Rising Sun*; ›› Amitav Ghosh, *The Glass Palace*; Peter Ho Davies, *The Welsh Girl*; Ross Leckie, *Hannibal*; ›› Hilary Mantel, *The Giant O'Brien*; James Meek, *The People's Act of Love*; ›› Lawrence Norfolk, *Lemprière's Dictionary*; Iain Pears, *An Instance of the Fingerpost*; Steven Pressfield, *Gates of Fire*; James Robertson, *Joseph Knight*; ›› Sarah Waters, *Fingersmith*.

See also: Carey, Eco, Farrell, Fowles, Fraser, Keneally, Other Peoples, Other Times, Tolstoy, Tremain, Unsworth.

HIDDENGEM:

MIKA WALTARI – *THE EGYPTIAN* (1949)

Mika Waltari was a Finnish novelist whose *magnum opus, The Egyptian*, became a huge international success when it was first published. It was also made into a Hollywood epic in the 1950s. Its fame has faded in recent decades but it remains an exciting work of historical imagination, well worth reading. It is set in one of the most tumultuous periods in the history of Ancient Egypt and during the reign of Akhenaten, one of its most controversial pharaohs. Its central character is Sinuhe, once physician to the pharaoh, who tells the story of his life from exile. Through Sinuhe's eyes, readers get a highly-coloured reconstruction of an era of change and upheaval (Waltari's descriptions of the sex lives of the Ancient Egyptians, tame enough today, were considered particularly racy at the time of first publication) and of one man's search for meaning amidst apparent chaos.

HIDDENGEM:

H.F.M. PRESCOTT – *THE MAN ON A DONKEY* (1952)

The Man on a Donkey is not a book that would feature on everybody's list of the great works of the twentieth century. For long stretches of the five decades and more since it was published, it has been neglected and forgotten but it is a work of fiction that deserves far more attention and a wider readership than it has ever received. At the heart of this novel by Hilda Prescott is the popular protest in the North of England against Henry VIII's religious and social reforms which was known as the Pilgrimage of Grace. Through the stories of a small number of characters, from Robert Aske, the doomed leader of the rebellion against Henry's depredations, to a servant who has visions of Christ walking the land, she builds up a panoramic picture of one of the periods when the future of England hung in the balance. The struggle between conflicting visions of what the nation and the church should be ends at last in tragedy on a grand scale.

STARTPOINT

HISTORY

History, it seems, has never been more popular than it is now. On the TV, both ambitious series like Simon Schama's *History of Britain* and one-off documentaries on everything from Alexander the Great to everyday life in Edwardian England find an avid audience. Films and novels raid the past for subject matter. And books written by professional historians that are aimed not at their academic peers but at a general readership proliferate. The range of books which could be classified as 'popular history' is enormous. The following selection only scratches the surface. There are hundreds and hundreds of books which go a long way to proving the often-expressed opinion that the best stories are to be found not in fiction but in fact, not in the imaginary worlds of novelists but in the real worlds of the past.

>> **Beevor, Antony, *Stalingrad* (1998)**. The struggle for Stalingrad, the major turning point in the Second World War, is brilliantly reconstructed in a book which never forgets, amid the epic drama of the battle, the lives of the ordinary people caught up in it.

Brown, Dee, *Bury My Heart at Wounded Knee* (1970). The history of the American West as seen by the Indians whose way of life was destroyed. Culminating in the massacre at Wounded Knee in 1890, this is a moving account of a tragic clash of cultures.

Figes, Orlando, *A People's Tragedy* (1996). The tragedy of Figes's title is that of the Russian people whose lives were turned upside down, almost always for the worse, by the Revolution instigated by Lenin and his small band of Bolsheviks.

Fox, Robin Lane, *Pagans and Christians* (1986). The two centuries in which pagan Rome faced the ideological threat represented by the new Christian religion are brought vividly to life in a compelling and wide-ranging narrative.

Hibbert, Christopher, *The Rise and Fall of the House of Medici* (1974). Hibbert was one of Britain's finest popular historians for fifty years and this account of the Medici and their rule in Florence is one of his best books.

Holland, Tom, *Persian Fire* (2005). The David and Goliath confrontation between the mighty Persian empire and a loose confederation of Greek city-states in the fifth century BC is retold with enormous brio and bravura.

Holmes, Richard, *Sahib* (2005). A soldier's-eye view of the British military presence in India from the battles fought by Robert Clive through the heyday of the Raj and the sobering horrors of the Mutiny to the end of the nineteenth century.

>> Hughes, Robert, *The Fatal Shore* (1987). How Britain transported its convicts across the world and inadvertently created a great nation. The early history of Australia is recreated with passion and authority.

Keegan, John, *The Face of Battle* (1976). Few books have ever given readers so powerful a description of what warfare in the past was really like as Keegan's superb evocations of how men fought at Agincourt, Waterloo and the Somme.

>> Milton, Giles, *Nathaniel's Nutmeg* (1999). How the seventeenth-century conflict between the Dutch and the English over control of the nutmeg trade led, by roundabout means, to the making of modern New York.

Picard, Liza, *Restoration London* (1997). Picard's fascinating scrapbook of everyday life in the 1660s provides insights into the past that more academic tomes cannot. The first of several such compendia that Picard has written.

Porter, Roy, *Enlightenment* (2000). Porter draws on a huge range of material to paint a wonderful portrait of eighteenth-century England in all its complexity, drama and intellectual vitality.

Summerscale, Kate, *The Suspicions of Mr Whicher* (2008). Not only a remarkable reconstruction of the circumstances surrounding a famous nineteenth-century murder and its aftermath but a book which gives far more insight into Victorian life and literature than many weightier volumes.

Thomas, Hugh, *The Slave Trade* (1997). The horrors of the Atlantic slave trade and its four hundred-year history have never been so tellingly portrayed as they are in Thomas's magisterial history.

Thompson, E.P., *The Making of the English Working Classes* (1963). Thompson's classic book rescues from 'the condescension of posterity' the lives of the ordinary men and women in the late eighteenth and early nineteenth centuries who struggled to take charge of their own destinies.

Weir, Alison, *The Six Wives of Henry VIII* (1991). The familiar story of Bluff King Hal and his assorted wives is told with great narrative skill and biographical insight. Weir's other books on medieval and Tudor England are well worth investigating.

Also recommended: Saul David, *Zulu*; James Davidson, *Courtesans and Fishcakes*; Norman Davies, *Europe: A History*; Eamon Duffy, *The Stripping of the Altars*; Niall Ferguson, *Colossus: The Rise and Fall of the American Empire*; ❯❯ Fergus Fleming, *Barrow's Boys*; Antonia Fraser, *The Weaker Vessel*; Roy Hattersley, *The Edwardians*; Peter Heather, *The Fall of the Roman Empire*; Adam Hochschild, *Bury the Chains*; Lawrence James, *Raj*; Ronald Pearsall, *The Worm in the Bud*; Graham Robb, *The Discovery of France*; Andrew Roberts, *A History of the English-Speaking Peoples Since 1900*; Steven Runciman, *History of the Crusades*; Dominic Sandbrook, *Never Had it So Good*; ❯❯ Simon Schama, *Citizens*.

HOBAN, Russell (born 1925)
US/British novelist

Hoban first made his name with children's books but, over the last thirty-five years, he has published a number of idiosyncratic and highly imaginative novels for adults. Each one is different from his other works and all of them are largely unlike anything else being published in English. *Pilgermann* is told by a narrator who is, literally, a ghost writer, a phantasm of waves and particles, which remembers its time on earth – the eleventh century – but can also range in time through the centuries to the present day. In *Angelica's Grotto* an ageing art historian, trying to deal with the mutinies of his mind and body, finds himself drawn into new sexual territory by a pornographic website.

RIDDLEY WALKER (1980)
This is a future-fantasy, set in England generations after the nuclear holocaust. The society is primitive – making fire is still a problem, never mind organizing the rule of law – and the survivors are haunted by memories of the time before the bomb. Rags of old culture, technology and morality flap in their minds, as inexplicable and as powerful as myth. Their language, similarly – the one the book is written in – is shredded, reconstituted English: words coalesce, grammar has collapsed, new metaphors sprout like weeds. Although this style is difficult at first, it becomes perfectly comprehensible after a few pages, and before long the broken, patched-together words begin to seem like poetry, as Riddley, the storyteller, struggles to find ways to describe the pictures inside his mind.

Russell Hoban's other novels include The Lion of Boaz-Jachin and Jachin-Boaz, Kleinzeit, The Bat Tattoo, The Medusa Frequency, Her Name Was Lola, Come Dance With Me, Linger Awhile *and* My Tango with Barbara Strozzi.

☜Read on
◆ *The Lion of Boaz-Jachin and Jachin-Boaz*; *Kleinzeit.*
◘ to *Riddley Walker*: Walter M. Miller Jr, *A Canticle for Leibowitz*; ►► Anthony Burgess, *A Clockwork Orange.*
◘ to the imaginative realms of Hoban's fiction in general: ►► William Golding, *Pincher Martin*; ►► Italo Calvino, *Invisible Cities.*

HØEG, Peter (born 1957)
Danish novelist

The author biography on the English editions of Peter Høeg's books proclaims a more adventurous life than most desk-bound writers can claim. He has been, at different times, a dancer, an actor, a fencer, a sailor and a mountaineer. His fiction has shown a similar variety, an unwillingness to be pinned down by the restrictions of genre and the conventional pigeon-holes into which novelists are so regularly placed. His most famous novel, *Miss Smilla's Feeling for Snow*, is a thriller of great intelligence and depth. A small boy has apparently fallen to his death from an apartment block in snowbound Copenhagen. The police are satisfied it is an accident but the boy's neighbour is Smilla Jesperson, half-Danish, half-Inuit, who has an uncanny ability to read the stories that tracks in the snow can tell. And the story the boy's tracks tell suggests murder. In pursuit of the truth about the death, Smilla is led into realms of corruption, double-dealing and death, and she is forced to board a ship heading into dark waters off the coast of her native Greenland.

Peter Høeg's other novels are The History of Danish Dreams*,* Borderliners *(the story of three emotionally troubled children, trapped inside the Danish care system, who attempt to escape an experimental school and its oppressive, time-regulated regime),* The Woman and the Ape *(about an unlikely but liberating love affair between the dipsomaniac wife of a zoologist and an ape called Erasmus, significantly more intelligent than the human characters) and* The Quiet Girl. Tales of the Night *is a collection of stories which all take place, in different parts of the world, on the same night in 1929.*

☜Read on
◆ *The Woman and the Ape*.
◘ Kirstin Ekman, *Blackwater*; ▸▸ David Guterson, *Snow Falling on Cedars*; Yann Martel, *Life of Pi*.

HOLLINGHURST, Alan (born 1954)
British writer

Hollinghurst, who worked for many years on *The Times Literary Supplement*, gained immediate acclaim as a novelist with the publication in 1988 of *The*

Swimming-Pool Library. Centred on the relationship between a rich, cultured and promiscuous aristo and an ageing gay roué, it was an unembarrassedly open and very funny exploration of gay life, sex and love in pre-AIDS Britain. He has followed it with *The Folding Star*, a dark tale of sexual obsession and unrequited fantasies focusing on a young English teacher in Belgium, *The Spell*, the half-farcical, half-sad story of the entangled sex lives of four very different men and *The Line of Beauty* (see below), which won the 2004 Man Booker Prize for Fiction and was adapted for television to great acclaim.

THE LINE OF BEAUTY (2004)

Opening in 1983, *The Line of Beauty* charts the progress of its central character, Nick Guest, through a Thatcherite London obsessed by money, sex and the pursuit of power. Living in the Notting Hill home of an ambitious and charming Tory MP, father of an Oxford friend, Nick is plunged into the world of power politics which he observes with an appalled fascination. In the burgeoning London gay scene he also discovers love, sex and, as the 1980s move on, the growing shadows cast by AIDS. It seems entirely appropriate that Nick, amid all the excitements of his life, is struggling to complete a PhD on ➤➤ Henry James, for Hollinghurst's prose, with its cool elegance and erudition, is a modern match for that of the older master.

📚 Read on

◆ *The Swimming-Pool Library*.

▣ ➤➤ Edmund White, *A Boy's Own Story*; Neil Bartlett, *Mr Clive and Mr Page*; David Leavitt, *While England Sleeps*; ➤➤ Philip Hensher, *Kitchen Venom*.

HOLMES, Richard (born 1945)
British biographer

Two very different writers named Richard Holmes have books on the non-fiction shelves of bookshops and libraries to confuse the unwary reader. Military historian Richard Holmes has published widely on subjects ranging from the early life of Winston Churchill to the British soldier in India. Biographer Richard Holmes, with whom we are concerned here, is best known for his two-volume life of a Romantic poet – *Coleridge: Early Visions* and *Coleridge: Dark Reflections*. Few biographies can honestly claim to change the perception of their subjects radically. Holmes's portrait of Coleridge, usually seen as a lyric poet whose gift was rapidly destroyed by addiction but here presented as a man of much more substantial, lifelong achievements, did so. The biography of Coleridge was preceded by a life of another Romantic poet, *Shelley: The Pursuit*. Sandwiched between the two volumes on Coleridge was *Dr Johnson and Mr Savage*, which shone a spotlight on the early life of Samuel Johnson, chronicling his youthful friendship with the disreputable Grub Street poet Richard Savage. However, Holmes's most original work may well be a book in which biography and autobiography sit side by side. In *Footsteps*, travels through space trigger travels through time. In a series of essays, Holmes's own journeys through France and Italy lead him back to the lives of other writers in the past, from Wordsworth and Mary Wollstonecraft to ➤➤ Robert Louis Stevenson, who had traversed the same landscapes.

📖 Read on

◆ *Sidetracks* (a companion volume to *Footsteps* with similarly diverse contents); *The Age of Wonder* (a compelling account of the ways in which scientific experimenters and great poets interacted in England during the Romantic era).

◘ to the biographies: Fiona McCarthy, *Byron: Life and Legend*; Andrew Motion, *Keats*.

◘ to *Footsteps*: ➤➤ W.G. Sebald, *The Rings of Saturn* (a more sombre account of a journey in which past and present intermingle).

HOLROYD, Michael (born 1935)
British biographer

Michael Holroyd has been one of the most influential biographers in Britain over the last forty years and his biography of the Bloomsbury writer Lytton Strachey, which first appeared in two volumes in 1967 and 1968, has often been hailed as a landmark publication, remarkable both for its wide-ranging research and meticulous attention to detail. Two volumes on the flamboyant painter Augustus John followed in 1974 and 1975 and Holroyd was then engaged for more than a decade in a massive life of George Bernard Shaw. Four volumes, subtitled 'The Search for Love', 'The Pursuit of Power', 'The Lure of Fantasy' and 'The Last Laugh', eventually appeared between 1988 and 1992. The biographer turned autobiographer with *Basil Street Blues*, an account of the eccentricities of his upbringing and the uneasy relationship between his mismatched parents that managed to be both humorously anecdotal and strangely moving. *Works on Paper* is a collection of essays, many of them containing Holroyd's thoughts on the art of biography he has so long and so successfully practised.

☷Read on

◆ *Mosaic* (more Holroyd family secrets revealed); *A Strange Eventful History* (Holroyd's most recent biography chronicles the complicated lives of actors Henry Irving and Ellen Terry and their families).

▢ to the biographies: ›› Peter Ackroyd, *Blake*; ›› Victoria Glendinning, *Trollope*; Hermione Lee, *Virginia Woolf*; Norman Sherry, *The Life of Graham Greene* (three volumes).

▢ to *Basil Street Blues*: Alan Bennett, *Untold Stories*; Stephen Fry, *Moab is My Washpot*; Andrew Miller, *The Earl of Petticoat Lane*.

HORNBY, Nick (born 1957)
British writer

No one in the last twenty years has been as successful as Nick Hornby at portraying the emotional confusions and immaturities of a certain kind of white middle-class male. His first book, *Fever Pitch* (1992), an autobiographical account of his obsession with football in general and Arsenal FC in particular, was a bestseller. His first two novels cover similar emotional territory and do so in the same relaxed, easy and (often) very funny prose that marked *Fever Pitch*. *High Fidelity* has as its central character a thirtysomething record-store owner whose emotional life is a mess. Shying away from commitment, he hides his feelings behind relentless list-making ('my desert-island, all-time, top five most memorable split-ups in chronological order') and a superbly organized record collection. The book is an engaging chronicle of his slow, unwilling progression to something halfway resembling adult emotions. *About a Boy* records the life of Will Lightman, clinging to cool in north London and living off royalties from a jingle his father wrote decades earlier. Pretending to single fatherhood as a means of ingratiating himself with desirable single mothers, Will meets Fiona and, more importantly, her son Marcus. The terminally unhip Marcus latches on to Will who finds himself, at first very unwillingly, cast in the role of the father figure that he has been play-acting. Two boys together (one twelve, the other thirty-six), Marcus and Will begin to learn about emotional competence.

📖 Read on

◆ *How to Be Good* (in his third novel Hornby takes the ambitious step of choosing to narrate the story in a woman's voice); *A Long Way Down* (four very different characters, all intent on committing suicide, meet on a London rooftop on New Year's Eve and the story follows their attempts to help each other find reasons for living).

◻ Tony Parsons, *Man and Boy*; Tim Lott, *White City Blue*; Helen Fielding, *Bridget Jones's Diary* (for a similarly comic woman's viewpoint on thirtysomething relationship angst); Mike Gayle, *My Legendary Girlfriend*; William Sutcliffe, *The Love Hexagon* (twentysomethings having much the same relationship problems as Hornby's thirtysomethings).

READ ON A THEME:

HORROR

Clive Barker, *Books of Blood*
William Peter Blatty, *The Exorcist*
William Hope Hodgson, *The House on the Borderland*
Shirley Jackson, *The Haunting of Hill House*
➤➤ Stephen King, *Pet Sematary*
H.P. Lovecraft, *At the Mountains of Madness*
Richard Matheson, *I Am Legend*
Dan Simmons, *Song of Kali*
➤➤ Bram Stoker, *Dracula*
Peter Straub, *Ghost Story*

HOSSEINI, Khaled (born 1965)

Afghanistan-born US novelist

Khaled Hosseini has written two novels which have unfolded against the backdrop of Afghanistan's recent history. Both have been huge worldwide bestsellers. In *The Kite Runner* Amir looks back from exile in America and remembers his childhood and adolescence in Kabul. In particular he remembers the kite-fighting tournament that took place when he was twelve which was the both the occasion of his greatest childhood triumph and the trigger for a humiliating act of betrayal that still haunts him. A quarter of a century later his past is not dead and it draws him from the comfort of the new life he has created in America and back to an Afghanistan ravaged by years of war and poverty. Returning to his native country he embarks on a search for what he has lost and for the chance of self-forgiveness. In *A Thousand Splendid Suns* the focus moves to the women of Afghanistan. Mariam and Laila are two very different women who find themselves trapped in marriage to the same brutal and insensitive man. Imprisoned by the terrors of war and by the restrictions imposed on them in a Taliban-controlled Afghanistan, they have only the growing, sister-like love between them to cherish. Both of Hosseini's novels travel movingly through a landscape of suffering towards small moments of hope and redemption.

Read on

◘ Yasmina Khadra, *The Swallows of Kabul*; ➤➤ Michael Ondaatje, *Anil's Ghost*; Atiq Rahimi, *Earth and Ashes*.

HOUELLEBECQ, Michel (born 1958)
French novelist

Few writers anywhere in the world today are as controversial as Michel Houellebecq. Those who dislike his work accuse him of being a misogynist and a racist. They point to his apparent approval of sex tourism and his much-quoted statement that Islam is 'the stupidest religion' as evidence. His admirers, of whom there are many, sing his praises as a writer unafraid to tackle taboos and to use his fiction to question the most fundamental assumptions on which liberal, Western society is built. *Atomised*, first published in France in 1998, is the story of two half-brothers, one a cold intellectual, the other a priapic monster of lust, addicted to prostitutes and phone sex. Through the darkly satirical tale of their lives, Houellebecq explores his bleak vision of a society in which genuine contact between people, whether sexual or otherwise, has become impossible. The book was a *succès de scandale* in France and elsewhere, and Houellebecq has followed it with several other novels which share its uncompromising outlook on life, love and sex. *Platform* tells the story of a sex tourist on a package holiday to Thailand who is drawn into an all-consuming affair that turns his previously controlled life upside down. *The Possibility of an Island* is a savagely funny dialogue between its two central characters, a scabrous, sex-obsessed comedian in the present and his cloned descendant, living in a Brave New World of the future.

Michel Houellebecq's other books include Whatever, Lanzarote *and* Against the World, Against Life *(a hybrid work, half-biographical and half critical, on one of his literary idols, the American horror writer of the 1920s and 1930s, H.P. Lovecraft).*

⬚Read on

◘ Georges Bataille, *The Story of the Eye*; Roberto Bolano, *The Savage Detectives*; Marie Darrieusecq, *Pig Tales*; ⟩⟩ Bret Easton Ellis, *American Psycho*.

HUGHES, Robert (born 1938)
Australian critic and historian

Robert Hughes's major work has been done as an art critic. *The Shock of the New* accompanied a TV series on modern art from Cubism to the 1980s but it was far from being the kind of bland pap so often associated with TV tie-in books. Rather, it was a trenchant, opinionated and intellectually rigorous history of art's attempts to reflect the disturbing experiences and upheavals of the twentieth century. *Goya*, the product of a lifetime's obsession with the work of the eighteenth-century painter and graphic artist, is a book that deftly combines biographical narrative with interpretation of Goya's dramatic and disturbing imagery. Hughes has also written historical works that move beyond the visual arts. *The Fatal Shore* (see below) is his contribution to the ongoing re-assessment of his own country's past. *Barcelona* is an idiosyncratic study of a city Hughes fell in love with when he was a student and mixes the political and cultural history of the Catalan capital with more personal memories.

THE FATAL SHORE (1987)
Written to reveal the true history of the convict settlement of Australia, a history Hughes felt his fellow Australians too often regarded with embarrassment and discomfort, *The Fatal Shore* brilliantly rescues from oblivion the experiences of thousands of men and women transported down under. Behind the conventional accounts of Australian history, according to Hughes, 'lurked the convicts, some 160,000 of them, clanking their fetters in the penumbral darkness' and this epic book is his attempt to do justice to their sufferings and their achievements.

Robert Hughes's other publications include American Visions *(a very personal look at the history of American art)*, Culture of Complaint *(a polemical assault on what he dislikes about American culture) and* A Jerk at the End *(a celebration of his love for fishing)*. Nothing If Not Critical *is a generous and wide-ranging selection of Hughes's criticism and reviews.* Things I Didn't Know *is a memoir.*

📖Read on

◘ to the art criticism: John Berger, *Ways of Seeing*; ≫ Simon Schama, *Rembrandt's Eyes*; ≫ John Updike, *Still Looking*.
◘ to *Barcelona*: ≫ Colm Tóibín, *Homage to Barcelona*.
◘ to *The Fatal Shore*: ≫ Thomas Keneally, *The Commonwealth of Thieves;* Siân Rees, *The Floating Brothel*.

HUGO, Victor (1802–85)
French novelist, poet and playwright

Although Hugo is famous in his native France as a poet and dramatist, he is best remembered in the English-speaking world for his panoramic historical novels. *The Hunchback of Notre Dame (Notre Dame de Paris)* (1831), set in medieval times, is about the beautiful foundling Esmeralda, the men who try to seduce her, and the deformed Quasimodo, bell-ringer at Notre Dame Cathedral, who loves her. The book's detail of Parisian low-life is matched in *Les Misérables*, about a noble-hearted convict and the corrupt policeman who persecutes him. Hugo's novels are long and prone to philosophizing, but they make up for it by the energy of their plots, the melodramatic attraction of their characters – not for nothing is *The Hunchback of Notre Dame* a Hollywood favourite – and the extraordinary feeling they give that every event, every story, is just one glimpse of the teeming anthill of human life.

Hugo's other novels include The Toilers of the Sea *(a story set in Guernsey where Hugo lived in exile from Napoleon III's France for many years)*, Ninety-Three *(set in the French Revolution) and* The Man Who Laughs. The Last Day of a Condemned Man *is a short novel, recounting the inner thoughts of a man facing the guillotine.*

📖Read on

◘ to *The Hunchback of Notre Dame*: Alessandro Manzoni, *The Betrothed (I promessi sposi)*.

◘ to *Les Misérables*: Heinrich Mann, *The Blue Angel*.
◘ to *The Toilers of the Sea*: G.B. Edwards, *The Book of Ebenezer Le Page* (a Guernsey-set novel of the twentieth century).
◘ to the more swaggering elements of Hugo's style: Lew Wallace, *Ben-Hur*; ➤➤ Alexandre Dumas, *The Man in the Iron Mask*; Mika Waltari, *The Egyptian*.

READ ON A THEME

THE HUMAN COMEDY
➤➤ Jane Austen, *Pride and Prejudice*
John Cheever, *The Wapshot Chronicle*
➤➤ David Lodge, *The British Museum is Falling Down*
➤➤ Alison Lurie, *Real People*
Armistead Maupin, *Tales of the City*
➤➤ Barbara Pym, *A Glass of Blessings*
➤➤ William Thackeray, *Vanity Fair*
➤➤ Barbara Trapido, *Brother of the More Famous Jack*
➤➤ Anne Tyler, *The Accidental Tourist*
➤➤ H.G. Wells, *Tono-Bungay*

HUXLEY, Aldous (1894–1963)
British novelist and non-fiction writer

Huxley's early books were glittering satires on 1920s intellectual and upper-class life, accounts of preposterous conversations at country-house costume parties and in such unlikely meeting places as publishers' offices or the Egyptian Room at the British Museum. His characters are intelligent, creative, fascinating and empty; haunted by the pointlessness of existence, they pass their time flirting, gossiping, swapping philosophical ideas and planning trivial alarms and excursions. In the 1930s, beginning with *Brave New World*, he changed his approach. Instead of focusing his satire on a single section of British society, he turned on the human race at large and wrote a series of increasingly bitter books demolishing all our ambitions to make a better society by science, philosophy, religion, socialism or (in the late 1950s, at the germination stage of flower power) hallucinatory drugs. His books are a witty, cold dazzle of ideas; enjoyable as you read them, they leave an acid aftertaste.

BRAVE NEW WORLD (1932)

In a soulless future world, genetic engineering programmes people from birth for their status in society, and removes all aggressive or unproductive instincts. Individuality, creativity and personality are sacrificed in the causes of material prosperity, good health and freedom from anxiety. Only a small group of 'savages' – people like us – survives, in a community in New Mexico, and one of them escapes and is brought into the 'real world', with tragic results. As in all his novels, Huxley tells this tale soberly and without comment: the flatness of his prose brilliantly intensifies the horror of what he is saying. Nothing truly terrible happens – and that is the most terrifying thing of all.

In chronological order, Huxley's novels are Crome Yellow, Antic Hay, Those Barren Leaves, Point Counter Point, Brave New World, Eyeless in Gaza, After Many a Summer, Time Must Have a Stop, Ape and Essence, The Genius and the Goddess *and* Island. Limbo, Mortal Coils, The Little Mexican, Two or Three Graces *and* Brief Candles *are collections of short stories.* The Devils of Loudun *is an historical study of an outbreak of supposed demonic possession in seventeeth century France.* The Doors of Perception *is Huxley's famous account of his experiences taking mescaline in the 1950s.*

🕮Read on

◆ *Ape and Essence* (about a California-dwelling group of survivors from the nuclear holocaust, primitives visited by a horror-struck scientist from New Zealand).
◘ to Huxley's social satires: ▶▶ F. Scott Fitzgerald, *The Beautiful and Damned* (from the 1920s); ▶▶ Anthony Powell, *Venusberg* (from the 1930s); ▶▶ Martin Amis, *Money* (from the 1980s).
◘ to *Ape and Essence*: ▶▶ Paul Theroux, *O-Zone*.
◘ to Huxley's later books: L.P. Hartley, *Facial Justice*; ▶▶ Michael Frayn, *Sweet Dreams*.

READ ON A THEME:

INDIA
Amit Chaudhuri, *A New World*
Anita Desai, *The Village by the Sea*
>> J.G. Farrell, *The Siege of Krishnapur*
>> E.M. Forster, *A Passage to India*
>> Amitav Ghosh, *The Hungry Tide*
Ruth Prawer Jhabvala, *Heat and Dust*
>> Rudyard Kipling, *Kim*
>> Rohinton Mistry, *A Fine Balance*
>> R.K. Narayan, *The Vendor of Sweets*
Arundhati Roy, *The God of Small Things*
>> Salman Rushdie, *Midnight's Children*
Paul Scott, *The Raj Quartet*
>> Vikram Seth, *A Suitable Boy*

READ ON A THEME:

IRELAND
Sebastian Barry, *The Secret Scripture*
>> Maeve Binchy, *Echoes*
Seamus Deane, *Reading in the Dark*
>> Roddy Doyle, *The Van*
>> J.G. Farrell, *Troubles*
Dermot Healy, *A Goat's Song*
>> James Joyce, *Portrait of the Artist as a Young Man*
John McGahern, *That They May Face the Rising Sun*
Edna O'Brien, *The Country Girls*
>> Flann O'Brien, *At Swim-Two-Birds*
James Plunkett, *Strumpet City*
Edward Rutherfurd, *Dublin*
>> Colm Tóibín, *The Blackwater Lightship*

IRVING, John (born 1942)

US novelist

Irving's novels are surreal black comedies, except that nothing that happens in them is unbelievable. His tales may lose nothing in the telling, but they are always plausible. The hero of *The World According to Garp* is a writer whose terror of death leads him to imagine appalling catastrophes for his loved ones – only to have even more, unimagined horrors actually occur. The family in *The Hotel New Hampshire* turns a derelict girls' school into a hotel (complete with dancing bear), and later, when business falls off, moves to Austria where the hotels are smaller, the bears are cleverer, and terrorists are threatening to take over the Vienna Opera. In *The Fourth Hand* a philandering journalist has his hand eaten by a lion live on TV and falls in love with the widow of the man whose hand is used by surgeons to replace his own. Irving, in his deadpan way, constantly implies – and who can deny it? – that there is nothing eccentric here, that he is recording the bizarreness of life itself.

THE CIDER HOUSE RULES (1985)

Homer Wells, brought up in a rural Maine orphanage and abortion clinic run by the saintly ether-addict Dr Larch, struggles against his destiny, which is to become a gynaecologist and take his mentor's place. He runs away, becomes the manager of a cider farm, falls in love with his best friend's wife and lives a life of confused obscurity – but he constantly feels the pull back to the clinic and to Melony, a homicidal feminist who hero-worships him and is waiting her chance to murder him.

Irving's other novels include The Water-Method Man, The 158-Pound Marriage, A Prayer for Owen Meany, A Son of the Circus, A Widow for One Year, Until I Find You *and* Last Night In Twisted River. The Imaginary Girlfriend *is a very idiosyncratic memoir, centred on Irving's joint passions for writing and for wrestling,* Trying to Save Piggy Sneed *a collection of shorter pieces mostly fictional.*

📖Read on

◆ *A Prayer for Owen Meany* (about the friendship of two boys, one of whom – Owen Meany – is a charming freak gifted with second sight and the ability to transform other people's lives).

▣ to *The Cider House Rules*: ›› Robertson Davies, *What's Bred in the Bone*.
▣ to Irving's work in general: ›› Salman Rushdie, *Midnight's Children*; ›› Thomas Pynchon, *The Crying of Lot 49*; ›› Don DeLillo, *White Noise*.

ISHERWOOD, Christopher (1904–86)
British/US writer of novels, screenplays and non-fiction

Isherwood was one of the Thirties' generation of writers of which the most conspicuous member was W.H. Auden. In 1939, in company with Auden, he moved to the USA and eventually settled in California where he worked as a teacher and Hollywood screenwriter. In the 1940s he became a follower of the Hindu mystic Swami Prabhavananda and several of his non-fiction works are on the subject of the Vedanta. His novels and stories are all based on personal experience. The best known (*Mr Norris Changes Trains, Goodbye to Berlin*) are set in 1930s Berlin, a seedy, decadent city haunted by the German defeat in the First World War and by the gathering power of Nazism. They are first-person stories, told by a naïve young language teacher amused, perplexed and vaguely terrified by the human tragi-comedy he reports. They have been filmed, made into a stage play (*I Am a Camera*) and a hit musical (*Cabaret*).

≋Read on
◆ *Prater Violet*; *Down There on a Visit*.
◘ to the Berlin novels: Klaus Mann, *Mephisto*; Alexander Döblin, *Berlin Alexanderplatz*.
◘ to Isherwood's work in general: Armistead Maupin, *Tales of the City*; Edward Upward, *Journey to the Border*; David Leavitt, *While England Sleeps*.

ISHIGURO, Kazuo (born 1954)
Japanese/British novelist

Ishiguro was educated in England and writes in English. His first two books are gentle, poetic studies of the effects on present-day Japanese of earlier twentieth-century events. The central character of *A Pale View of Hills*, a middle-aged woman living in England, is driven by her daughter's suicide to a prolonged reverie about her own childhood in Nagasaki, and her attempt to rebuild her life and her emotional relationships after the city's atomic destruction in 1945. Oni, the elderly protagonist of *An Artist of the Floating World*, was a prominent propagandist for Japanese militarism in the 1930s; now, in his sixties, he has to come to terms with the collapse of his professional life, his ostracism by younger colleagues, and the way his own children's moral values, typical of the new Japan, seem to deny everything he ever believed in or affirmed. Ishiguro's fiction has since become more expansive, although it has remained no less ambiguous and enigmatic. *The Unconsoled* is a long, ›› Kafkaesque account of the psychological disintegration of a famous concert pianist. *When We Were Orphans* tells the story of a famous detective from the 1930s who returns to Shanghai, where he grew up, to try to solve the mysteries surrounding his own parents. Playing cleverly with the conventions of mystery fiction, Ishiguro creates a book that is both a richly rewarding narrative and a subtle study of the way we all remake our pasts. *Never Let Me Go* does something similar to science fiction, taking motifs (cloning, genetic engineering) common to that genre and using them for very different purposes. Ishiguro's most recent book is *Nocturnes*, a collection of five very different stories united by a common musical theme.

THE REMAINS OF THE DAY (1989)

Ishiguro's Booker Prize-winning novel is a powerful study of emotional desiccation. Told in the first person by the humourless and pernickety English butler Stevens, it cleverly reveals the self-deceptions and moral cowardice of its narrator. Looking back on a life which has been busily self-important (his master was at the centre of dubious pro-appeasement negotiations in the late 1930s) Stevens cannot acknowledge that he has denied himself true human contact and the opportunity for emotional growth. His inability to deal with his attraction to the housekeeper Miss Kenton is only the most obvious example of personal failures which, somewhere beneath the cold formality of his prose, Stevens himself sadly, and movingly, half-recognizes.

⪦Read on

◻ ›› R.K. Narayan, *The English Teacher*; ›› Graham Greene, *The Quiet American*; ›› Ian McEwan, *Enduring Love*; ›› John Lanchester, *Fragrant Harbour*; Chang-Rae Lee, *A Gesture Life*.

READ ON A THEME:

ISRAEL

Lynne Reid Banks, *Children at the Gate*
Lionel Davidson, *A Long Way to Shiloh*
Linda Grant, *When I Lived in Modern Times*
David Grossman, *The Yellow Wind*
>> John Le Carré, *The Little Drummer Girl*
Amos Oz, *Black Box*
>> Philip Roth, *Operation Shylock*
Leon Uris, *Exodus*
A.B. Yehoshua, *The Lover*

JACOBSON, Howard (born 1942)
British novelist and critic

The anti-hero of Howard Jacobson's first novel, *Coming from Behind* (1983) is in a fictional tradition established at least as early as 1954 and the publication of Kingsley Amis's *Lucky Jim*. Stranded as an unwilling teacher of English literature in a dismal polytechnic in the Midlands, Sefton Goldberg is a character exhibiting a mixture of wit and disillusionment familiar in English comic fiction. The difference is that he is Jewish, which allows Jacobson to add extra layers of both alienation and comedy. He followed his debut novel with others, such as *Peeping Tom*, which similarly mixed erudite farce and erotic mishap. More recent novels, despatches from the front line of the battle between the sexes, have often been darker in tone. *No More Mr Nice Guy*, for example, follows Frank Ritz on the odyssey of sexual excess and comic embarrassments which engulf him when he is rejected by his partner. Tormented as well as defined by his raging libido, Frank becomes its despairing victim in a novel that pulls few punches in its depiction of a man using sex to fight off other fears.

THE MIGHTY WALZER (1999)
In 1950s Manchester, Oliver Walzer is entering adolescence, with all its potential for humiliation, armed only with a champion's skill at ping pong. Simultaneously celebrating and sending up both its central character and the Jewish community in

which he grows up, Jacobson's comic masterpiece draws on his own memories but transmutes them into a very funny, poignant coming-of-age story.

Howard Jacobson's other novels are Redback, The Very Model of a Man, Who's Sorry Now, The Making of Henry, Kalooki Nights *and* The Act of Love. In the Land of Oz *is a travel book about his journeys in Australia,* Roots Schmoots *examines Jewishness;* Seriously Funny *is an investigation into the nature of comedy and humour.*

📖Read on

◘ to the early novels: ›› Kingsley Amis, *Lucky Jim*; Malcolm Bradbury, *The History Man;* ›› David Lodge, *Changing Places*.
◘ to the later novels: ›› Philip Roth, *Everyman*.
◘ to *The Mighty Walzer*: ›› Mordecai Richler, *The Apprenticeship of Duddy Kravitz*.

JAMES, Clive (born 1939)
Australian writer and essayist

Clive James first came to the public's notice in the 1970s as the TV critic of *The Observer*. No one had ever written about television in the way that James did, treating it seriously as an artistic medium and yet revelling in the absurdity of its more schlocky manifestations. In 1980 he published the first volume of his autobiography, *Unreliable Memoirs*, a comic and poignant account of growing up in Sydney, the son of a single mother. Its combination of farcical accounts of childhood misadventures with precise recreation of the sights, sounds and smells of a vanished Australian suburbia made it one of the most memorable autobiographical works of the last thirty years. James followed it with further volumes (*Falling Towards England, May Week Was in June* and *North Face of Soho*) which recorded his pilgrimage to England, his experiences at Cambridge and his first ventures into the literary world respectively. Clive James has also written several novels, including *Brilliant Creatures*, set amid the glitterati of London's media and publishing world, *Brrm! Brrm!* and *The Silver Castle* but his finest creation remains the self-portrait he crafted for his memoirs.

James's other works include three mock heroic poems about life in the world of London's media and political elite (The Fate of Felicity Fark in the Land of the Media, Peregrine Prykke's Pilgrimage through the London Literary World *and*

Britannia Bright's Bewilderment in the Wilderness of Westminster), Fame in the
20th Century, *an insightful analysis of the corrosive effects of celebrity, and
collections of reviews and essays* (Snakecharmers in Texas, Even As We Speak,
The Meaning of Recognition, Cultural Amnesia *and others*). *His* Observer *TV
columns were collected in three volumes* – Visions Before Midnight, The Crystal
Bucket *and* Glued to the Box.

☰Read on

◆ *The Meaning of Recognition* (intelligent, thought-provoking essays on subjects
as diverse as Shakespeare, *The Sopranos* and Formula 1 motor racing).

◘ to the memoirs: Stephen Fry, *Moab is My Washpot*; ›› Germaine Greer, *Daddy,
We Hardly Knew You*; Barry Humphries, *My Life As Me*.

◘ to the essays: ›› Martin Amis, *The Moronic Inferno*, ›› Julian Barnes, *Something
to Declare*.

JAMES, Henry (1843–1916)
US/British novelist and short story writer

As well as novels, James wrote plays, essays, travel books, literary criticism and a
dozen volumes of short stories. In his fiction he returned again and again to the
same theme: the conflict between decadence and innocence. James identified
decadence with the 'old culture' of Europe, and innocence with the late nineteenth-
century USA; his books often depict visitors from one continent experiencing and
coming to terms with the other. Because he was not religious – he was brought up
as a rationalist – the moral struggle of his plots is usually less between overt good
and evil than between different standards and manners. He also liked to tease out
every strand of meaning in a situation, to explain and theorize about his characters'
motives and the possible outcome of each choice they make. Untangling this,
especially in his last three, most intricately stylized novels (*The Wings of the Dove,
The Ambassadors* and *The Golden Bowl*), is one of the chief pleasures of his work.

THE WINGS OF THE DOVE (1902)
Kate Croy lives with her snobbish aunt, who plans to make a 'great' marriage for
her. But Kate is secretly engaged to a penniless journalist, Merton Densher. Millie
Theale, a young, rich American, visits Kate's aunt to be introduced to London

society, and becomes Kate's friend. Millie is frail, and it is soon apparent that she is dying. She goes to Venice, where she welcomes all her friends in a decaying palazzo on the Grand Canal. Kate persuades Merton to try to comfort Millie's last months by pretending that he loves her. Kate hopes that Millie will then leave money to Merton which will enable them to marry. So everyone will be happy. But another of Millie's suitors, the unprincipled Lord Mark, tells Millie of Merton's and Kate's secret engagement – a revelation which brings tragedy to all three principal characters.

James's other novels include The Portrait of a Lady***,*** Roderick Hudson***,*** Washington Square***,*** The Bostonians***,*** The Spoils of Poynton***,*** What Maisie Knew ***and*** The Tragic Muse***. Of his hundred short stories and novellas, the best known are*** The Turn of the Screw ***(about two children haunted by a sinister dead couple),*** Daisy Miller ***and*** The Aspern Papers.

Read on

♦ ***The Portrait of a Lady*** (about the moral and social consequences of a young American's decision to settle in England and Italy); ***The Ambassadors*** (a long, ironical novel about how Europe changes a group of Americans, young and middle-aged, rich and poor, friends and strangers).

▫ ›› Marcel Proust, ***Swann's Way*** (Part One of ***Remembrance of Things Past***); ›› E.M. Forster, ***A Room With a View***; ›› Edith Wharton, ***The Reef***; ›› Muriel Spark, ***The Mandelbaum Gate***; ›› Stendhal, ***Scarlet and Black***; ›› Elizabeth Bowen, ***Eva Trout***.

JAMES, P.D. (Phyllis Dorothy) (born 1920)

British novelist

P.D. James writes like a cross between ›› Dorothy L. Sayers and ›› Patricia Highsmith. The crimes in her books are brutal, are committed by deranged, psychopathic people, and are described in chilling, unblinking prose, as objective as a forensic report. Her principal detective, Adam Dalgliesh, however, is a poet and aesthete, combining brilliant detective instincts with a liberal conscience and a dandyish distaste for what he does. Although the books at first seem long and leisurely, James racks tension inexorably tighter until her dénouement: not a cosy Christieish explanation round the library fire, but a scene of pathological, cathartic violence.

A TASTE FOR DEATH (1986)

A lonely spinster, taking flowers to decorate her local church, finds the throat-cut corpses of a tramp, Harry Mack, and a prominent Tory MP, Sir Paul Berowne. Berowne has been the subject of recent slanderous accusations, and Dalgliesh's investigation must begin by deciding whether he was murdered or committed suicide after killing Mack. The story gradually sucks in various members of Berowne's large and mutually hostile family, his servants and his mistress. As well as showing us this, and describing the police work in exact, unhurried detail, the book also concerns itself with the lives and preoccupations of Dalgliesh's assistants, especially Inspector Kate Miskin, the newest member of the team.

James's other crime novels are Cover Her Face, A Mind to Murder, Death of an Expert Witness, Unnatural Causes, Shroud for a Nightingale, An Unsuitable Job For a Woman *(which introduces James's female private investigator, Cordelia Gray),* The Black Tower, Innocent Blood, The Skull Beneath the Skin, Original Sin, Devices and Desires, A Certain Justice, Death in Holy Orders, The Murder Room, The Lighthouse *and* The Private Patient. Children of Men *is set in England in 2021, when there are no children and there is therefore no future.* Time To Be in Earnest *is a memoir.*

🕮 Read on

◆ *Death in Holy Orders* (an Anglican theological college on the East Anglian coast is the setting for one of James's most enthralling and mysterious narratives).

◘ ≫ Ngaio Marsh, *Surfeit of Lampreys*; ≫ Margery Allingham, *The Tiger in the Smoke*; ≫ Ruth Rendell, *A Sleeping Life*; ≫ Colin Dexter, *The Way Through the Woods*.

READ ON A THEME:

JAPAN
Alan Brown, *Audrey Hepburn's Neck*
James Clavell, *Shogun*
Shusako Endo, *Silence*
Arthur Golden, *Memoirs of a Geisha*
≫ Kazuo Ishiguro, *An Artist of the Floating World*
Yukio Mishima, *Confessions of a Mask*

>> Haruki Murakami, *The Wind-Up Bird Chronicle*
Kenzaburo Oe, *The Silent Cry*
Murasaki Shikibu, *The Tale of Genji*
Natsume Soseki, *Kokoro*
Banana Yoshimoto, *Goodbye, Tsugumi*

JARDINE, Lisa (born 1944)
British cultural historian and biographer

The daughter of the TV polymath Jacob Bronowski, Lisa Jardine has been one of the most stimulating of modern writers on sixteenth- and seventeenth-century European history, an academic able to reach general readers with her clear prose and narrative energy. *Worldly Goods* provides a new and thought-provoking interpretation of the Renaissance, emphasising the period's commercial vitality and trading power as much as its artistic achievements; *Ingenious Pursuits* investigates the intellectual revolution of the seventeenth century. *On a Grander Scale*, a biography of Sir Christopher Wren that places him firmly in the context of the intellectual revolution that was occurring in England after the restoration of Charles II, was followed by *The Curious Life of Robert Hooke*, an account of Wren's less well-known colleague in the reconstruction of London after the Great Fire. *The Awful End of Prince William the Silent* is a short but telling account of the assassination of the Dutch ruler and its consequences, showing how the first killing of a head of state with a hand gun has echoes that continue to sound to the present day.

Lisa Jardine's other books include Still Harping on Daughters *(a study of Shakespeare's women),* Erasmus: Man of Letters, Hostage to Fortune *(with Alan Stewart), a life of Sir Francis Bacon, and* Going Dutch, *a study of the close relationship between England and Holland in the second half of the seventeenth century.*

📖Read on

◘ to *Worldly Goods* and *Ingenious Pursuits*: John Brewer, *The Pleasures of the Imagination;* Vic Gatrell, *City of Laughter*; Roy Porter, *Enlightenment*.
◘ to the biographies: James Gleick, *Isaac Newton*; Adrian Tinniswood, *His Invention So Fertile: A Life of Christopher Wren*.

JEROME, Jerome K. (Klapka) (1859–1927)
British novelist and journalist

Jerome, an actor, wrote humorous pieces while waiting to go on stage, and after the success of *Three Men in a Boat* in 1889 he became a full-time writer. *Three Men in a Boat* is the story of a boating holiday on the Thames undertaken by three London clerks (to say nothing of the dog). The book's deadpan humour – what Jerome calls its 'hopeless and incurable veracity' – depends on magnifying life's small problems (such as opening a tin without a tin-opener, or being in the same house as a courting couple without embarrassing them) to epic proportions, and on losing no opportunity for reflections on life, liberty, the pursuit of happiness, and the heroes' invincible conviction that middle-class Victorian young Britons, such as themselves, are the goal to which all human evolution has been progressing.

✑Read on
◆ *Three Men on the Bummel* (the three protagonists of Jerome's most famous book take a cycling holiday through Germany's Black Forest); *My Life and Times* (autobiography).
◻ George and Weedon Grossmith, *The Diary of a Nobody*; Max Beerbohm, *Zuleika Dobson*; W.E. Bowman, *The Ascent of Rum Doodle*; H.F. Ellis, *The Papers of A.J. Wentworth, BA*; ›› P.G. Wodehouse, *The Luck of the Bodkins*.

JORDAN, Robert (1948–2007)
US novelist

Few fantasy worlds have been constructed with the same craft and skill shown by Robert Jordan in his Wheel of Time novels. Fans can, and do, exchange thoughts on the internet about the tiniest details of the alternative world he has created. The geography, peoples and mythology of RandLand, Jordan's setting for the books, have been carefully worked out. Yet the sequence never becomes bogged down in minutiae and has a sweeping, epic quality that matches, and sometimes surpasses, the best that other fantasy novelists supply. On the back of the kind of fundamental struggle between the forces of good and evil that a thousand fantasy writers have tackled, Jordan builds an intelligent and adult saga in which his central characters mature and develop from naïve children to wiser but world-weary protagonists. Fantasy fiction is often condemned, usually by those who have read little of it, as simple-minded and unsubtle. Jordan's monumental sequence of novels shows just how ambitious and rewarding the best work in the genre can be.

THE EYE OF THE WORLD (1990)

On a night of festival in his village, a woman claiming to be a magician wielding the One Power appears, a savage tribe of half-men, half-beasts attacks the village and the young Rand Al'Thor is propelled from his humdrum life into the quest that will shape his destiny in the first of the Wheel of Time novels. As Rand learns more of who he is and who he is to become, Jordan begins to unfold the rich world of his fantasy epic in which competing cultures struggle with one another and with the ancient, recurring forces of good and evil.

The Wheel of Time novels completed by Robert Jordan are, in order, The Great Hunt, The Dragon Reborn, The Shadow Rising, The Fires of Heaven, Lord of Chaos, A Crown of Swords, The Path of Daggers, Winter's Heart, Crossroads of Twilight *and* Knife of Dreams. *Jordan was working on* The Gathering Storm *at the time of his death and the book is due to be finished by Brandon Sanderson and published in the autumn of 2009.*

Read on

◘ ≫ J.R.R. Tolkien, *The Lord of the Rings*; George R.R. Martin, *A Game of Thrones* (and other books in A Song of Fire and Ice sequence); Terry Goodkind, *Wizard's First Rule* (and other books in The Sword of Truth series); Tad Williams, *Otherland*.

READ ON A THEME:

JOURNALISM
Colin Bateman, *Divorcing Jack*
Heinrich Böll, *The Lost Honour of Katharina Blum*
≫ Michael Frayn, *Towards the End of the Morning*
≫ George Gissing, *New Grub Street*
Andrew Martin, *Bilton*
≫ Jay McInerney, *Model Behaviour*
≫ William Thackeray, *Pendennis*
≫ Evelyn Waugh, *Scoop*

JOYCE, James (1882–1941)

Irish novelist and short story writer

Although Joyce exiled himself from his native land as a young man, he never left the Ireland of his memory: his work is a ceaseless exploration of Irish scenery, education, history, religion, habits of thought and patterns of daily life. His early writings – the short stories in *Dubliners* (1914) and the novel *A Portrait of the Artist as a Young Man* (1915), based on his own school and university life – are stylistically straightforward. They are also notable for precise evocation of sensation and atmosphere. By giving a mosaic of tiny impressions (the feel of wooden desks in a schoolroom, the taste of mud on a rugby field, the smell of gas lamps in student digs) Joyce builds up a detailed picture which is both factually and emotionally compelling. (>> Proust used a similar idea in the childhood sections of *Remembrance of Things Past*.) In his two long novels, *Ulysses* (see below) and *Finnegans Wake*, Joyce developed this mosaic structure further: *Ulysses* relates the events of a single day, *Finnegans Wake* a man's thoughts and dreams during a single night. Parts of these books are stream-of-consciousness monologues, a tumble of apparently unrelated sentences threading a path through the maze of one person's mind. Joyce often seems to be collapsing language itself: syntax splits apart; words blur into one another; each page is a kaleidoscope of puns, parodies, half-quotations, snatches of song and snippets from half a dozen languages. Some people find this style unreadable; for others it is endlessly rewarding, a mesmeric impression of the jumble of thought itself.

ULYSSES (1922)

The book follows two people, Leopold Bloom and Stephen Dedalus, from dawn to midnight on a single day in Dublin in 1904. At one level what they do is ordinary: they shave, go to the privy, eat, drink, argue in bars, go to a funeral, borrow money, flirt with girls on a beach, visit Dublin's red-light area. But Joyce also shows us their thoughts, the fragmentary responses and impressions evoked by each real incident. The book ends with a sixty–page 'interior monologue', the inconsequential, erotic reverie of Bloom's wife Molly as she lies beside him, drifting into sleep.

Joyce's works are Dubliners, Portrait of the Artist as a Young Man *(based on an earlier, unfinished novel,* Stephen Hero, *which has also been published),* Ulysses, Finnegans Wake, *and two collections of poetry,* Chamber Music *and* Pomes Penyeach.

Read on

◘ Ralph Ellison, *Invisible Man*; ➤➤ Malcolm Lowry, *Under the Volcano*; Dorothy Richardson, *Pilgrimage* (a multi-volume work which provides a female stream of consciousness to match the very male version served up by Joyce); Thomas Wolfe, *Look Homeward, Angel*. Both Joyce's experimental writing and the whole concept of Irishness are spectacularly sent up in ➤➤ Flann O'Brien's *At Swim-Two-Birds*.

KAFKA, Franz (1883–1924)
Czech novelist and short story writer

In the 1920s and 1930s people regarded Kafka as an unsmiling neurotic who depicted the human condition as a bureaucratic hell without explanation or compassion: 'Kafkaesque' was a synonym for 'nightmarish'. Kafka, by contrast, always regarded himself as a humorist, in the line of such surrealist East European jokers as ➤➤ Gogol. Each of his novels and stories develops a single idea to ludicrous, logical-illogical extremes. In 'Metamorphosis' a man has to cope with the fact that he has turned into a gigantic beetle overnight. The prison-camp commander of 'In the Penal Colony' is so eager to show off a newly invented punishment machine that he turns it on himself. In 'The Burrow' a creature designs a defence system of underground tunnels so complex and so perfect that it becomes the whole meaning of existence: it engulfs its own creator. The central figure of *The Trial (Der Prozess)* is arrested one morning although he has done nothing wrong, spends the book trying to discover the charges against him, and is finally executed without explanation. It is easy to treat such tales as psychological or political allegories. But it is also possible to read them as jokes, grimly funny anecdotes invented just for the hell of it. Perhaps keeping his face straight was Kafka's best trick of all.

THE CASTLE (DER SCHLOSS) (1926)

An ordinary, unremarkable man, K, arrives in a strange town to take up the post of land surveyor. He finds that no one is expecting him, that the town and the castle which dominates it are a labyrinthine bureaucracy where everyone is responsible only for passing the buck to someone else, and each favour done, each door opened, leads only to more confusion. K's efforts to reach the heart of the mystery, to be given some official confirmation of his existence, are doomed, hilarious and have the logic not of reality but of a very bad dream indeed.

Kafka's novels are The Trial, The Castle *and* America. *His short stories have been published in one-volume collected editions and in shorter collections such as* Metamorphosis and Other Stories *and* The Great Wall of China and Other Short Works. *Kafka's correspondence with the two women with whom he conducted complicated and soul-searching relationships gives fascinating insights into this most enigmatic of writers and has been published as* Letters to Felice *and* Letters to Milena.

ᗜRead on

◆ *The Trial, America* (the story of a naïve young German who goes to the USA thinking that its streets are paved with gold, and goes on believing it despite being cheated and betrayed by everyone he meets).

◘ echoing Kafka's dark humour: ▶▶ Joseph Heller, *Catch-22*; Nathanael West, *The Dream Life of Balso Snell*; Joe Orton, *Head to Toe*.

◘ echoing the idea of a Kafkaesque, nightmare society: Rex Warner, *The Aerodrome*; ▶▶ Alasdair Gray, *Lanark*; ▶▶ George Orwell, *Nineteen Eighty-four*.

KAPUSCINSKI, Ryszard (1932–2007)
Polish journalist and writer

Wars, coups, revolutions and political upheaval are the material from which Kapuscinski crafted some of the most remarkable reportage of the past half century. For many years Poland's only foreign correspondent, appointed by the Communist regime's press agency to report on the world's trouble spots, he travelled thousands of miles a year, usually from one war zone to the next, sending back despatches which, in one admirer's words, 'turned reportage into literature'. *Another Day of Life* records Kapuscinski's experiences in Angola in the 1970s as he watched the newly independent state dissolve into civil war and anarchy. *The Soccer War* takes its title from a short conflict between El Salvador and Honduras, which began with a dispute over a football match, but it is a more general study of many of the Third World disputes he has seen during his years as a foreign correspondent. *The Emperor* is an account of the dying days of Haile Selassie's rule as absolute monarch in Ethiopia, an astonishing portrait of an almost medieval court and its bizarre rituals. *Shah of Shahs* is another report on a despot in decline, chronicling the final years of the Shah's rule in Iran before the Ayatollah's revolution sent him into exile. *The Shadow of the Sun* is a collection of essays about his experiences in Africa covering more than forty years of Kapuscinski's career. *Travels with Herodotus*, a collection of personal impressions of places he knew mixed with lengthy quotations from the Greek historian of the title, is the nearest thing to a conventional autobiography that he wrote.

📖Read on

◻ James Cameron, *Point of Departure*; James Fenton, *All the Wrong Places*; Riccardo Orizio, *Talk of the Devil* (interviews with deposed dictators); John Pilger, *Hidden Agendas*; Michela Wrong, *In the Footsteps of Mr Kurtz*.

KEILLOR, Garrison (born 1942)

US novelist and broadcaster

In the United States, Keillor is known as much as a radio broadcaster as a writer – his show *A Prairie Home Companion* has been on air for more than thirty years – and his stories of small-town life gain much if they are heard in his homely Midwestern voice. (It is easy enough to find audiobooks of Keillor reading his own work.) *Lake Wobegon Days*, which first appeared in 1985, drew upon pieces he had produced for radio and was an amiable, humorous account of life in the fictional township of Lake Wobegon, Minnesota. He has followed it with a succession of other books which record the everyday adventures and misadventures of the people who live in the town. There are some harsh critics who see little but bland nostalgia in Keillor's stories but what lurks beneath the surface of his elaborate anecdotes and comic setpieces can often seem more like melancholic awareness of what is being lost than folksy celebration of small-town virtues. He is a steelier and less sentimental writer than initially he appears.

Keillor's other Lake Wobegon books are Leaving Home, We Are Still Married, Wobegon Boy, Lake Wobegon Summer 1956, Pontoon *and* Liberty. Radio Romance *is a non-Wobegon novel set in the 1930s Golden Age of Radio,* Love Me *a novel about a best-selling writer having a mid-life crisis,* The Book of Guys *a collection of comic short stories about men (and gods) in difficulties.* Homegrown Democrat *is a book which outlines his political and social values and beliefs.*

📖**Read on**

◆ *Pontoon* (a more recent entrant in the Lake Wobegon series in which octogenarian Evelyn Peterson passes away in the night, leaving idiosyncratic instructions for her funeral – her ashes are to be poured into a bowling ball and dropped into a lake– and a letter which reveals a secret life and a secret lover).

▢ Sherwood Anderson, *Winesburg, Ohio* (small town American life from an earlier generation); ›› Bill Bryson, *The Life and Times of the Thunderbolt Kid*; Sinclair Lewis, *Main Street*; Kent Haruf, *Plainsong*.

KENEALLY, Thomas (born 1935)

Australian novelist and playwright

Although Keneally has written books on many subjects, including the partly autobiographical *Three Cheers for the Paraclete* (about a young Roman Catholic losing his faith), he is best known for historical fiction. His books include *The Chant of Jimmie Blacksmith* (about racial confrontation in nineteenth-century Australia), *Confederates* (about Stonewall Jackson's campaigns in the American Civil War) and *The Playmaker* (see below). Among his more recent novels, *Bettany's Book*, ranges confidently from rural New South Wales in the nineteenth century to the story of a modern woman working for a charity in war-ravaged Sudan, while *The Tyrant's Novel* focuses on a successful writer's ambivalent relationship with a murderous Middle Eastern despot not entirely dissimilar to Saddam Hussein. *The Widow and her Hero* is the story of an elderly woman looking back to the time of the Second World War and uncovering uncomfortable truths about the heroic soldier she loved and lost. Keneally has also written several compelling non-fiction works, including *The Great Shame* (about the nineteenth-century Irish diaspora) and *The Commonwealth of Thieves*, the story of the founding of white Australia.

SCHINDLER'S ARK (1982)

Schindler is a bragging, boozing opportunist who makes a fortune in Poland during the Second World War German occupation, buying up the businesses of dispossessed Jews. We read about his black-market deals, his backslapping relationship with the authorities, his parties and his mistresses – and gradually discover that his lifestyle is a façade, that his true activity is saving thousands of Jews from the gas chambers. The novel is also known as *Schindler's List*, after the Steven Spielberg movie of the same name. Keneally has recently published a book entitled *Searching for Schindler*, a personal account of how he came to write the book.

⧉Read on
◆ *The Playmaker* (in which convicts transported to eighteenth-century New South Wales, under the guidance of a confused, would-be liberal army lieutenant, rehearse and perform – of all things – Farquhar's Restoration comedy *The Recruiting Officer*).

▣ to *Schindler's Ark*: John Boyne, *The Boy in the Striped Pyjamas*.

▣ to Keneally's historical fiction in general: ❯❯ Jane Rogers, *Promised Lands*; ❯❯ Peter Carey, *The True History of the Kelly Gang*; ❯❯ William Boyd, *An Ice-Cream War*; William Styron, *Sophie's Choice*.

LITERARY TRIVIA 8:

FIVE WRITERS WHO WERE KILLERS
François Villon
The fifteenth-century French poet, boozer and thief had to flee Paris in 1455 after a tavern brawl in which he had fatally stabbed a priest who had made the mistake of quarrelling with him over the nature of God.

Ben Jonson
In 1598, the poet and playwright killed an actor in a duel. Arrested and convicted, Jonson escaped hanging because he could claim 'benefit of clergy', an ancient legal privilege extended to the literate.

❯❯ William S. Burroughs
The American author of *The Naked Lunch* and *Junky* accidentally killed his wife during a drunken party game. He put a glass on her head and tried to shoot it off but missed the glass and hit his wife.

Thomas Griffiths Wainewright
A friend of several major figures in the English Romantic movement, including Hazlitt, Byron and Keats, Wainewright was an art critic who found that writing failed to support him in the style he wanted and turned to

murder to supplement his income. Almost certainly, he poisoned a number of relatives for their money but the evidence to convict him was inadequate. He was eventually found guilty of the lesser crime of forgery and transported to Australia for life.

Mary Lamb

The sister of the essayist Charles Lamb and co-author with him of *Tales from Shakespeare* suffered a severe mental breakdown in 1796 and stabbed her mother to death with a kitchen knife. It was decided that she had not been responsible for her actions and she was placed under the guardianship of her brother.

KENNEDY, A.L. (Alison Louise) (born 1965)
British novelist and short story writer

Other, usually male, writers in the recent renaissance of Scottish fiction have achieved more attention and been more regularly in the media spotlight but none has as strong and individual a voice as A.L. Kennedy. She writes of outsiders and grotesques, people who find it difficult or even undesirable to connect with others, people who march to the beat of very different drums and she does so in an edgy, blackly comic language. In her early short stories, published in *Night Geometry and the Garscadden Trains* and *Now That You're Back*, she had already found a distinctive voice. This has only become clearer, stronger and more confident in the novels that have followed. *Everything You Need* is a complex novel set largely on a small island which is a retreat for writers. The book centres on the developing relationship between Nathan Staples, a self-tormenting, self-obsessed middle-aged novelist and the young would-be writer Mary. Nathan knows Mary to be the daughter he has not seen since she was a small child. Mary does not know that the older mentor and teacher, for whom she has such ambivalent feelings, is her father. Through the relationship, Kennedy deals with difficult issues of love, pain and loss and the process of finding appropriate words to describe them.

SO I AM GLAD (1995)
So I Am Glad is a kind of bizarre, contemporary fairytale for grown-ups. Jennifer Wilson, the narrator, is a radio announcer whose unhappy upbringing has led her to

close down communication with others. She has chosen isolation and she works hard to maintain it and to keep buried the emotions, 'moles' she calls them, which are at work under the surface. Into her life comes a strange room-mate (is he fantasy or is he real?) who claims to be, and perhaps is, the ghost of Cyrano de Bergerac. The moles within Jennifer begin to stir and can no longer be ignored. A brief outline of *So I Am Glad* is sufficient to indicate the weirdness of Kennedy's imagination but can do little to demonstrate the power of the prose, its unique combination of grotesquerie, humour and poignancy. Only actually reading the book can do that.

A.L. Kennedy's other books include Original Bliss *(short stories),* Looking for the Possible Dance *(novel),* Indelible Acts *(short stories),* Paradise *(novel),* Day *(novel),* What Becomes *(short stories) and the non-fiction* On Bullfighting.

☜Read on
◆ *Day* (a remarkable novel which tells the story of a man blighted by his experiences in the Second World War who returns to them, four years after the war's end, as he plays an extra in a movie that echoes what he went through).
◻ to her novels: ≫ Alasdair Gray, *Lanark*; Janice Galloway, *The Trick Is to Keep Breathing*; ≫ Alan Warner, *The Sopranos*
◻ to her short stories: ≫ Ian McEwan, *First Love, Last Rites*; Laura Hird, *Nail and other stories*.

KEROUAC, Jack (1922–69)
US novelist

Born in Lowell, Massachusetts, Kerouac was from a French Canadian family and only learned English at primary school, a fact that must have contributed to the lifelong feeling of being an outsider that is so evident in his fiction. After a period in the US Merchant Marines and in the Navy Kerouac returned to Columbia University (which he had attended before his naval service) where he met a student named Allen Ginsberg. Ginsberg introduced him to a disparate group of like-minded spirits, united in little save an aversion to post-war America, and to the man who was to become his 'muse', Neal Cassady. *On the Road* (1957) is, and always will be, the archetypal Kerouac novel. This ground-breaking book was written (and rewritten) between 1948 and 1956. The story of Sal Paradise (Kerouac) and Dean Moriarty (Cassady) and their trans-coastal odysseys in an assortment of beat-up jalopies, fuelled on benzedrine, marijuana, wine and a hunger for kicks, is a tremendous, joy-filled paean to life and freedom amid the arid sterility of post-war America. A huge success, the book gave Kerouac the permanent label as leader of the 'Beat Generation'. Although it is generally agreed that he invented the term (playing on an association of 'beat', as in 'worn out', with a shortening of 'beatitude'), it was a title he never wanted. He has been revered by generations of would-be hipsters ever since, but Kerouac may well have been not so much a rebel as a rather weak-willed misfit who remained the outsider he felt he was as a child. Yet, in *On the Road* and (fitfully) in other works, he created a self-mythology and a prose style that have been culturally influential for nearly fifty years.

Kerouac's other novels include The Dharma Bums, Big Sur, Doctor Sax, The Subterraneans, Visions of Cody *and* Vanity of Duluoz. Lonesome Traveller *is a collection of meditations and essays triggered by his travels;* Satori in Paris *is his account of a journey to France.* Pomes All Sizes *is a collection of his poetry.*

ᗡRead on

◆ *The Dharma Bums* (beats and bohemians in San Francisco waver between asceticism and excess).
◻ Thomas Wolfe, *Look Homeward, Angel* (fictionalized autobiographical odyssey from an earlier American generation); ›› William S, Burroughs, *Junky*; John Clellon Holmes, *Go*; Herbert Huncke, *The Herbert Huncke Reader*.

KEYES, Marian (born 1963)
Irish novelist

Chick lit is often given a bad press. Often enough it deserves it. However, Marian Keyes is a writer who gives chick lit a good name. Since the publication of her first two novels, *Watermelon* and *Lucy Sullivan Is Getting Married*, in the mid 1990s, she has proved that it can be witty and engaging and that it can tackle serious issues (alcoholism, divorce, domestic violence) without becoming solemn or pompous. Keyes's heroines are typically single middle-class, thirtysomething women, unlucky with their men and over-indulgent in booze and recreational drugs, who struggle gamely to win first prize in the race for love and fulfilment but end up more frequently with the wooden spoon. Keyes chronicles their misadventures with great comic brio and, more often than not, allows them to triumph in the end.

Marian Keyes's other novels are Rachel's Holiday, Last Chance Saloon, Sushi for Beginners, No Dress Rehearsal, Angels, The Other Side of the Story, Anybody Out There? *and* This Charming Man. Under the Duvet *and* Further Under the Duvet *are collections of short comic pieces.*

☙Read on

◘ Cecelia Ahern, *P.S. I Love You*; Helen Fielding, *Bridget Jones's Diary*; Jane Green, *Second Chance*; Sophie Kinsella, *Confessions of a Shopaholic*; Jill Mansell, *Good at Games*.

KING, Ross (born 1962)
Canadian/British novelist and historian

Ross King originally made his name with two historical novels (*Domino*, set in eighteenth-century London, and *Ex Libris*, about a seventeenth-century bookseller in pursuit of an arcane volume which may hold the key to a series of mysteries), but his recent books have nearly all been gripping, non-fiction accounts of the creation of artistic masterpieces. *Brunelleschi's Dome* was the story of Filippo Brunelleschi, a paranoid, ill-tempered Renaissance architect, and his long struggle to build the still awe-inspiring dome of the cathedral of Santa Maria del Fiore in Florence. *Michelangelo and the Pope's Ceiling* (2002) takes the more familiar tale of the clashes between Michelangelo and Pope Julius II during the painting of the frescoes on the ceiling of the Sistine Chapel and provides it with a new vigour. *The Judgement of Paris* uses the careers of Ernest Meissonier, a French academic painter famous in his day but now largely forgotten, and Edouard Manet, the revolutionary 'father of Impressionism', as a means of analysing the changing fortunes of artistic reputations. King has also written a short biography of the Renaissance Italian philosopher and politician Niccolo Machiavelli.

☙Read on

◘ to the novels: Janet Gleeson, *The Grenadillo Box*; David Liss, *A Spectacle of Corruption*.
◘ to the non-fiction books: Martin Gayford, *The Yellow House: Van Gogh, Gauguin and Nine Turbulent Weeks in Arles*; Caroline P. Murphy, *The Pope's Daughter*; Witold Rybczinski, *The Perfect House: A Journey with the Renaissance Master Andrea Palladio*.

KING, STEPHEN (born 1946)

US novelist

Stephen King is one of the most popular novelists in the world and there can be few people who have not encountered his work in some form – either on the printed page, in one of the innumerable film and TV adaptations of his books or in his increasing experiments in writing specifically for the web. He is categorized, by those who like to place writers in categories, as a horror writer, but this label may well alienate some readers who would actually relish his fiction. King's strengths do not lie in the descriptions of blood, viscera and violence that characterize other horror writers (although his books are not for the squeamish or easily distressed). His great gift is for writing about ordinary, everyday fears and emotions in extraordinary ways. His first great success, *Carrie* (1974), describes an adolescent girl, bullied and tormented at school, who discovers telekinetic powers which she turns on her tormentors. But the power of the book comes not so much from the supernatural trappings of the story but from the precision with which King describes small-town nastiness and from the way he taps into everybody's fear of being an outsider, not one of the gang. The pages of *Bag of Bones* are packed with gory ghosts and visitors from other worlds but the book is concerned with love lost and found, mourning and recovery from grief as much as with haunting and horror. In the mammoth, one thousand-plus pages of *It*, the small Maine town of Derry is terrorized by the return of a supernatural killer. Seven friends who, as teenagers, experienced the horror of the first murderous spree return to confront the renewed nightmare. King ruthlessly dissects small-town life and gives to Derry a realism that is undermined and compromised by the horror. Who knows what lurks beneath the surface of the ordinary? That is the question King repeatedly asks in his fiction and he has provided some gripping and wildly imaginative answers in his string of bestsellers.

King's other novels include Salem's Lot, The Shining, The Stand, Pet Sematary, Misery, The Tommyknockers, Dolores Claiborne, Rose Madder, Dreamcatcher *and* Lisey's Story. The Dark Tower *is a series of seven books (so far) which chronicles the adventures of the Gunslinger in a bleak world parallel to ours.* The Green Mile *is a six-part sequence of short novels, set on the death row of a penitentiary in the 1930s. Short story collections include* Night Shift, Nightmares and Dreamscapes, Hearts in Atlantis *and* Just After Sunset. *King has also written fiction under the pseudonym Richard Bachman and collaborated with fellow horror novelist Peter Straub on* The Talisman *and* Black House. On Writing *combines recollections of King's own development as a writer with practical advice to budding novelists.*

⌷Read on
◆ *Misery, Pet Sematary.*
◘ Peter Straub, *Ghost Story*; James Herbert, *Sepulchre*; Dean Koontz, *Darkness Comes*; Clive Barker, *The Damnation Game.*

KINGSOLVER, Barbara (born 1955)
US novelist

Like the great nineteenth-century novelists, Barbara Kingsolver believes that fiction has a duty to engage with the real world. Her books are, in the best sense of the word, old-fashioned in that they grapple with political, social and moral issues. Where Victorian writers like ▶▶ Dickens, ▶▶ Eliot and Disraeli gave fictional form to debates about an England divided between the two nations of rich and poor, Kingsolver tackles contemporary concerns about colonialism, the rift between the developed and underdeveloped worlds and man's impact on the natural environment. And she does so in narratives that grip the reader with their imaginative depth and powerful characters.

THE POISONWOOD BIBLE (1999)
The Poisonwood Bible is, by some way, Barbara Kingsolver's most ambitious novel to date. Nathan Price, a narrow-minded Christian evangelist, arrives with his family in the Belgian Congo to serve as a missionary to African people to whom his message means little. The year is 1959 and great changes are on hand in the country but the messianic Price is as blind to these as he is to the real needs of his family and the people he has volunteered to 'save'. The narrative moves inexorably towards personal tragedy set amid the wider tragedy of a new nation still in thrall to the forces of economic imperialism. The story is told in the very different voices of Price's wife and his four daughters – pouting would-be prom queen Rachel, Leah (at first her father's greatest supporter but soon his fiercest critic), her twin sister Adah who suffers from hemiplegia but has her own idiosyncratic perspective on events, and the five-year-old Ruth May.

Barbara Kingsolver's other books include The Bean Trees, Animal Dreams, Pigs in Heaven, Prodigal Summer, Homeland *(a collection of short stories),* High Tide in Tucson *and* Small Wonder *(two volumes of essays and non-fiction writings), and* Animal, Vegetable, Miracle *(an account of her family's efforts to live a self-sufficient life on a farm in Virginia).*

🖘Read on
◆ *The Bean Trees* and its follow-up novel, *Pigs in Heaven*.
◘ ≫ Jane Smiley, *A Thousand Acres*; Louise Erdrich, *Love Medicine*; Alice Hoffman, *Seventh Heaven*; Ronan Bennett, *The Catastrophist* (another narrative set in Zaire; politically acute although very different from *The Poisonwood Bible* in its aims).

KIPLING, Rudyard (1865–1936)
British short story writer and poet

Kipling learned his craft working for English-language newspapers in India in the 1880s. He wrote reports, stories and poems about the British soldiers and administrators, their servants and the snake-charmers, fortune-tellers and other characters of the towns in which they lived. Later, during the Boer War, he worked as a correspondent in South Africa where he was a friend of Cecil Rhodes. In the circumstances, it would have been hard for him not to reflect the imperialist attitudes of his age, first sunny confidence and then the jingoistic panic which overtook it in late Victorian times. But he is a more rewarding writer than this suggests. His sympathies were always with subordinates – with private soldiers rather than generals, servants rather than employers, children rather than adults. He wrote well about all three: his stories for and about children, in particular, are magnificent. Something like half of each collection – most books contain both stories and poems – is nowadays hard to take, not least where he writes in baby-talk (as in the *Just-So Stories*, O best-beloved) or uses funny spellings to evoke Cockney or Irish speech. But every archness is balanced by a gem of insight or sensitivity. In this, too, he was characteristic of his time.

KIM (1901)
This episodic novel is the story of a British orphan brought up as a beggar in Lahore, who becomes first the disciple of a wandering Buddhist monk and then an agent of the British secret service. He travels throughout India, and Kipling uses his

adventures as a framework for descriptions of everyday scenes and characters, of 'such a river of life as nowhere else exists in the world'.

Kipling's collections include Barrack-room Ballads, The Seven Seas *and* The Years Between *(verse),* Plain Tales from the Hills, Soldiers Three *(stories), and the mixed prose-and-verse collections* Many Inventions, Traffics and Discoveries, A Diversity of Creatures *and* Debits and Credits. *His children's books include the* Just-So Stories, The Jungle Book, Puck of Pook's Hill *and the public-school yarn* Stalky and Co. Something of Myself *is a guarded autobiography.*

⮂Read on
◆ *Plain Tales from the Hills* (Kipling's first and, in some ways, most characteristic volume of short stories); *Debits and Credits* (a much later collection of verse and prose).
◘ to Kipling's stories about children: ►► Katherine Mansfield, *Bliss and Other Stories*.
◘ to his stories about colonial adults: Paul Scott, *The Raj Quartet*; many of ►► W. Somerset Maugham's short stories, collected in several volumes, deal with the English at large in the empire. John Masters, *Nightrunners of Bengal* and ►► J.G. Farrell, *The Siege of Krishnapur*, about the 1857 Indian 'Mutiny', match Kipling's insight into the heyday of the Raj.

KNEALE, Matthew (born 1960)
British novelist

Some of Britain's most gifted novelists turned to historical fiction in the 1990s and produced their finest works. In two novels Matthew Kneale has shown that his excursions into the past are fully as rewarding for the reader as those of, for example, ►► Rose Tremain, ►► Hilary Mantel or ►► Beryl Bainbridge. *Sweet Thames* is set in a superbly evoked early Victorian London and is probably the only novel ever written to have a sewage engineer as a hero. Joshua Jeavons (very loosely based on the real Victorian engineer, Sir Joseph Bazalgette) is a visionary who looks to a future London cleansed of the filth and shit and disease of its present – to what he calls 'the glory of a London unobstructed by effluent'. Working feverishly on his plans to transform the capital, Jeavons is swept into his own personal drama by the disappearance of his young wife. *English Passengers* weaves together many narrative voices to tell the story of an ill-fated voyage to Tasmania in the 1850s. The

Reverend Geoffrey Wilson is a fundamentalist clergyman determined to trump pretentious scientists by discovering the Garden of Eden in the southern hemisphere and thus proving the literal truth of the Bible. Accompanying him on his quixotic mission is a surgeon out to gain evidence for his own contentious theory of man's origins and a shipload of Manx smugglers who have agreed to transport the expedition to Tasmania for devious reasons of their own. Most ambitiously, Kneale allows some of the story to be told by a Tasmanian aboriginal called Peevay and his account is not one of Eden rediscovered but of the brutal destruction of his people and their culture.

Matthew Kneale's other books are Whore Banquets/Mr Foreigner, Inside Rose's Kingdom, Small Crimes in an Age of Abundance *(a collection of short stories) and* When We Were Romans.

⮂Read on

◘ to *Sweet Thames*: ➤➤ Peter Ackroyd, *Dan Leno and the Limehouse Golem*.
◘ to *English Passengers*: ➤➤ Rose Tremain, *The Colour*; ➤➤ J.G. Farrell, *The Singapore Grip*; ➤➤ David Malouf, *Remembering Babylon*.

KUNDERA, Milan (born 1929)
Czech novelist

Kundera's fiction is a giddy mixture of philosophical speculation, erotic intrigue and a sense of the wounding power history and politics have over the individual. His early fiction, culminating in *The Unbearable Lightness of Being* (see below) is shaped by his experiences as a writer and intellectual in a Czechoslovakia under a communist, Moscow-directed regime. *The Joke* plays a number of games with the word of its title. Its narrator, Ludvik, is condemned by the state for a joke sent on a postcard to his girlfriend. Years later he plots his revenge on the man who brought him down by means of an elaborate seduction and practical joke. History itself, Ludvik speculates, may be playing jokes on us all. Kundera has lived in France for many years – indeed several of his recent books were first written in French – and the fiction he has published after the Velvet Revolution in his home country has largely moved away from the political particularity of his early novels. *Immortality* juxtaposes a modern love triangle in Paris (two sisters love the same man) with the affairs of Goethe. Into this mixture Kundera typically introduces a whole range of his witty, occasionally melancholy diversions into philosophy and speculation. In heaven Goethe and Hemingway debate the meaning and value of literary immortality; aphorisms about love, death and fame abound.

THE UNBEARABLE LIGHTNESS OF BEING (1984)

Kundera's most characteristic novel is set in Prague at the time of the brief flowering of freedom in spring 1968. At its heart is the love affair and marriage between Tomas, a charming but incorrigible womanizer, and Tereza, a woman he meets when she is tending bar in a small town hotel. Tomas, a surgeon, is forced into exile and a menial job by the events of 1968 but continues his obsessive Don Juanism and his relationship with his mistress Sabina, herself entangled in another unhappy affair. *The Unbearable Lightness of Being* is at once an ironic story of the difficulties of sexual and romantic love and a novel of ideas, peppered with aphorisms, short digressions and meditations on the nature of human choice and the effects of mere chance and contingency on our plans and decisions.

Kundera's other novels include The Joke, The Book of Laughter and Forgetting, Life is Elsewhere, Immortality, Slowness, Identity *and* Ignorance. Laughable Loves *is a collection of short stories,* The Art of the Novel, Testaments Betrayed *and* The Curtain *are non-fiction works which bear witness to Kundera's belief in the transformative power of fiction.*

📖 Read on

◆ *Immortality*.

◘ Ivan Klima, *My Golden Trades*; Josef Skvorecky, *The Engineer of Human Souls*; ›› Gabriel García Márquez, *Love in the Time of Cholera*.

KUNZRU, Hari (born 1969)

British novelist

Hari Kunzru's first novel, *The Impressionist*, is set in the years of the Raj and its central character, its young anti-hero Pran Nath, is an embodiment of the contradictions and complexities of empire. Half-English and half-Indian, the boy is exiled from the comfortable life into which he was born when the truth about his parentage is revealed but he seizes upon a series of opportunities to reinvent himself, first as a streetwise denizen of the Bombay slums and eventually as an

English public schoolboy destined for an Oxford education. His story was a major success for Kunzru, an ambitious novel that combined exuberant comedy with a post-colonial investigation into self and identity. He has followed it with *Transmission*, a second novel which focused on America's Silicon Valley where a young Indian programmer arrives in search of success, *Noise*, a collection of short stories, and *My Revolutions*, in which a middle-aged Englishman finds his violent and politically radical past returns to haunt him.

⬚Read on

◘ Aravind Adiga, *The White Tiger*; David Davidar, *The Solitude of Emperor*s; Mohammed Hanif, *A Case of Exploding Mangoes*.

KUREISHI, Hanif (born 1954)
British novelist and screenwriter

Kureishi first came to notice as a dramatist and screenplay writer (*My Beautiful Laundrette*, *Sammy and Rosie Get Laid*) and his fiction has many of the qualities of his writing for film. It is witty and direct and celebrates the delights of popular culture. And, like his screenplays, Kureishi's novels are traditional enough in their form but they often encompass material that isn't usually found in mainstream 'literary' fiction. Ideas about ethnic and sexual identity and ambiguity, about what it means to be caught between competing cultures, are unpretentiously explored within lively, funny coming-of-age stories.

THE BUDDHA OF SUBURBIA (1990)
Karim is a teenager growing up in the suburbs in 1970s England, the son of an Indian father and an English mother. As well as the usual challenges adolescence imposes, he is also faced by those his family and his background provide. His father, after years of trying to be more English than the English, has chosen to become a New Age guru – the Buddha of the title – and leaves his wife for one of his glamorous admirers. Through his father's lover and her rock musician son, Karim is pitched into a new world of parties, drugs and bisexual opportunities. Moving with chameleon-like adaptability from one role to another, Karim searches for a more permanent sense of self and identity. Sexy, funny and sharply satirical in its mockery of many aspects of English society, *The Buddha of Suburbia* is a traditional English comedy of manners with very untraditional characters and settings.

Hanif Kureishi's other works of fiction are The Black Album, Intimacy, Gabriel's Gift *and* Something to Tell You *(novels) and* Love in a Blue Time, Midnight All Day *and* The Body and Other Stories *(short story collections).* Dreaming and Scheming *is a collection of essays.* My Ear at His Heart *is a moving family memoir which focuses on his father's failed attempts to become a writer.*

📖 Read on

◆ *The Black Album* (a young English Asian, torn between the glamour of modernity and the tempting certainties of conservative Islam, tries to make sense of his life).
◘ Meera Syal, *Anita and Me*; ▸▸ Zadie Smith, *White Teeth*; Michael Bracewell, *The Crypto-Amnesia Club*; Martin Millar, *Lux the Poet*; Farrukh Dhondy, *Bombay Duck*; Romesh Gunesekera, *Sandglass*.

LANCHESTER, John (born 1962)
British novelist

Lanchester's first two novels were both major achievements and, in very different ways, remarkable exercises in style and storytelling. *The Debt to Pleasure* begins with the narrator's archly ironic statement, 'This is not a conventional cookbook.' What follows is not a conventional first novel. Constructed around a sequence of menus, the book begins as an apparent memoir of its narrator, gourmet and aesthete Tarquin Winot, centred on his love and knowledge of food and cooking. Self-consciously erudite and civilized, Tarquin seems, at first, a harmless food snob with a fondness for heavy irony, arcane information and baroquely extravagant language. As the book progresses, however, Lanchester slowly and subtly allows his narrator to reveal a monstrous egotism lurking beneath the surface. By the time we reach the last pages we know we are in the company of a man whose selfishness and self-obsession have led to terrible deeds. Lanchester's second novel, *Mr Phillips*, could hardly have a more different central character. Mr Phillips is an accountant, just made redundant, who has not yet had the courage to tell his wife of his dismissal. Setting out as if for work, he spends his day idly wandering London, musing on life and sex and death and the humdrum occurrences that have made up his own existence. Written in a deliberately flat prose that is the reverse of Tarquin Winot's verbal acrobatics, Mr Phillips risks being as dull as his nondescript hero must appear to passers-by. Lanchester's triumph is that he succeeds in making his commuter-everyman a touching and comic character, an embodiment of our own ordinary failures, compromises and small pleasures. *Fragrant Harbour*, Lanchester's third novel, unfolds the history of Hong Kong in the twentieth century through a number of interconnecting first-person narratives.

⮥Read on

◘ to *The Debt to Pleasure*: ›› Vladimir Nabokov, *Lolita*; Patrick Süskind, *Perfume*; ›› Tibor Fischer, *The Collector Collector*.

◘ to *Mr Phillips*: ›› Virginia Woolf, *Mrs Dalloway* (different in style and period but also the thoughts of an ordinary person at large in London).

◘ to *Fragrant Harbour*: Timothy Mo, *An Insular Possession* (Hong Kong's earlier history told in a distinctly more rambunctious style than Lanchester's).

READ ON A THEME:

LARGER THAN LIFE
›› Anthony Burgess, *Earthly Powers*
›› Peter Carey, *Illywhacker*
›› Angela Carter, *Nights at the Circus*
›› Robertson Davies, *What's Bred in the Bone*
›› Howard Jacobson, *Redback*
   Robert Nye, *Falstaff*
›› François Rabelais, *Gargantua*
›› Laurence Sterne, *Tristram Shandy*

READ ON A THEME:

LATIN AMERICA
›› Isabel Allende, *Of Love and Shadows*
   Jorge Amado, *The War of the Saints*
   Machado de Assis, *Epitaph of a Small Winner*
›› Louis de Bernières, *The War of Don Emmanuel's Nether Parts*
   Alejo Carpentier, *The Lost Steps*
   Julio Cortazar, *Hopscotch*

Carlos Fuentes, *The Death of Artemio Cruz*
>> Malcolm Lowry, *Under the Volcano*
>> Gabriel García Márquez, *The General in His Labyrinth*
Manuel Puig, *Kiss of the Spider Woman*
>> Mario Vargas Llosa, *The Feast of the Goat*

LAWRENCE, D.H. (David Herbert) (1885–1930)
British writer of novels, short stories, plays and poems

For eighty years Lawrence's radicalism outraged as many people as it enthralled. He thought that every matter of concern to human beings, and moral and ethical issues in particular, could be settled by rational discussion, if people would only be honest about themselves. His novels deal with such matters as female emancipation, the class struggle, atheism, sexual liberation and pacifism – not explicitly but as part of an ongoing advocacy of nakedness, of people at their best when stripped of inhibition and convention. Lawrence regarded his plain speaking as a way of shedding light in dark corners, a return to the innocence of the Garden of Eden; his enemies thought it shocking. Nowadays, when his rawness seems less threatening, his books stand up not only for moral earnestness – they read at times like humourless, non-religious sermons – but for their acute presentation of people and society in turmoil, of attitudes to life which the Second World War and the nuclear age have made seem unimaginably remote.

SONS AND LOVERS (1913)

Paul Morel is the son of ill-matched parents, an ex-schoolteacher and an illiterate, alcoholic miner. Morel's mother is determined to help her son escape from the physical grind and intellectual atrophy of pit-village life and fulfil his ambition to be a painter. Her love for him is, however, a force for darkness not liberation. It inhibits both his self-discovery and his relationship with other people (especially the young farm girl Miriam, who encourages his artistic ambitions), and it is only when he breaks free of his mother – a protracted, agonizing process, a second birth – that he is able to fulfil the destiny she has planned for him.

Lawrence's other novels include The Rainbow *and its sequel* Women in Love, Aaron's Rod, Kangaroo, The Plumed Serpent *and* Lady Chatterley's Lover. *He also published poems, travel books* (Sea and Sardinia, Mornings in Mexico), *plays, books on history and literature, and collections of short stories* (England, My England; The Woman Who Rode Away).

⤷Read on
♦ *The Rainbow*.
◘ ⟩⟩ George Eliot, *Middlemarch*; ⟩⟩ Thomas Hardy, *Jude the Obscure* (especially close to *Women in Love* in its treatment of tensions between the sexes); David Storey, *Radcliffe*; ⟩⟩ Melvyn Bragg, *The Maid of Buttermere*; Henry Roth, *Call it Sleep*; and ⟩⟩ James Baldwin, *Go Tell it on the Mountain* all deal with Lawrentian themes in very different settings. Elaine Feinstein, *Lady Chatterley's Confession* is a sequel to – and a more searching novel than – *Lady Chatterley's Lover*.

LE CARRÉ, John (born 1931)
British novelist

For over a century, writers from ⟩⟩ Verne to ⟩⟩ Fleming depicted espionage as a swashbuckling, Robin Hood activity with clear rules, absolute moral standards and a penchant for flamboyance. But in the 1960s this view changed. The Cuban missile crisis all but led to world annihilation; the Berlin Wall was built; a series of well-publicized defections revealed that spies were secretive, unremarkable men, morally hesitant and trapped by their own profession. Betrayal, not derring-do, was their stock-in-trade; east, west, north, south, they were as indistinguishable as civil service clerks. This is the atmosphere of Le Carré's books. His characters are not James Bonds, swaggering forth to smash conspiracies of global domination; in dark back streets and rainy woods they nibble away at one another's loyalties, hardly even certain of their own. It is a world of remorseless moral erosion, and Le Carré chillingly shows how it functions for itself, inward-looking and self-perpetuating, with minimal relevance to real life. The end of the Cold War, which triggered creative collapse in lesser writers, led him to look for new ways of telling his stories and he has succeeded magnificently in reinventing himself as a novelist. In *The Night Manager* the focus is moral exhaustion, not in political life, but in late-twentieth-century society in general, and an international drugs-for-arms scandal in particular; *The Constant Gardener* is a devastating fictional indictment of the activities of large pharmaceutical companies in Africa.

A PERFECT SPY (1986)

Magnus Pym, the best of all agents, has gone missing, and Jack Brotherhood is desperately trying to track him down. Pym is in fact holed up in a tatty English seaside resort, writing his memoirs, and trying to discover his lost integrity as a human being. As the memoirs near completion, the hunt closes in . . .

Le Carré's other spy books are The Spy Who Came in From the Cold, The Looking Glass War, A Small Town in Germany, Our Game, The Russia House *and the four Smiley books* (Tinker Tailor Soldier Spy, The Honourable Schoolboy, Smiley's People *and* The Secret Pilgrim). *His other books are the detective stories* Call for the Dead *and* A Murder of Quality, The Naive and Sentimental Lover, The Little Drummer Girl, The Tailor of Panama, Single & Single, The Constant Gardener, Absolute Friends, The Mission Song *and* A Most Wanted Man.

ꙮRead on

◆ *The Russia House, The Constant Gardener.*
◘ to the spy stories: Eric Ambler, *Judgement on Deltchev*; ≫ Graham Greene, *The Human Factor*; ≫ Len Deighton, *Berlin Game* (and its follow-ups, *Mexico Set* and *London Match*).
◘ to *The Naive and Sentimental Lover*: ≫ John Fowles, *Daniel Martin*.
◘ to *The Constant Gardener*: ≫ Henning Mankell, *The Eye of the Leopard*.

LEE, Laurie (1914–97)
British poet and autobiographer

Laurie Lee grew up in a small Cotswolds village in the 1920s and *Cider With Rosie*, his evocative memoir of his childhood, bears witness to a rural way of life that seemed remote in 1959, when the book was first published, and has now completely vanished. Many such memoirs are self-indulgently nostalgic. One of the great strengths of *Cider With Rosie* is that it succeeds in resurrecting the charms and pleasures of Lee's early life without ever sentimentalizing the world in which he was brought up. Throughout his life, Laurie Lee thought of himself as primarily a poet and *Cider With Rosie* is filled with imagery and language that recreates the village and its inhabitants with the precision and originality of a poet's eye. Lee wrote two further memoirs. *As I Walked Out One Midsummer Morning* describes his departure from his village on a journey which took him to Spain on the brink of civil war. *A Moment of War* completed the trilogy with an account of Lee crossing the border back into Spain when the civil war was at its height.

📖Read on

◆ *A Rose for Winter* (Lee returns to the Spain he knew before the ravages of civil war changed it utterly).

◘ to *Cider With Rosie*: Winifred Foley, *A Child in the Forest*; Rosemary Sutcliff, *Blue Remembered Hills*; Flora Thompson, *Lark Rise to Candleford*.

◘ to the Spanish memoirs: Gerald Brenan, *South from Granada*; ≫ George Orwell, *Homage to Catalonia*.

LITERARY TRIVIA 9:

FIVE FAMOUS PEOPLE WHO WROTE A SINGLE NOVEL

Benito Mussolini

The Italian dictator harboured dreams of a literary career when he was a young man and wrote a novel entitled *The Cardinal's Mistress* in 1909. An overheated tale of murder and melodrama in the seventeenth century, the story was published in serial form in the socialist newspaper of which Mussolini was then assistant editor.

Winston Churchill

Although he won the Nobel Prize for Literature in 1953, Churchill was known for his work as a historian rather than an imaginative writer. His one novel, *Savrola*, published in 1900, is a story of political upheaval set in a North African state called Laurania.

Sarah Bernhardt

'The Divine Sarah', legendary actress and nineteenth-century celebrity, published a novel called *The Clouds* in 1878. Inspired by a balloon journey she had made the previous year, it's the story of four friends floating through the air over the French countryside and exchanging both idle gossip and philosophical debate.

Jean Harlow

The blonde bombshell of 1930s Hollywood wrote a risqué novel but her studio, MGM, refused to allow her to publish it. It only appeared many years after her death.

Joseph Goebbels

Hitler's sinister propaganda chief wrote a novel in diary form, clearly auto-biographical in much of its content, soon after gaining his PhD in literature at the University of Heidelberg. At the time no one was interested in publishing a mawkish story of a disillusioned soldier and student who sacrifices his life for the Volk but, by 1929, Goebbels was a major player in the Nazi Party, which was gaining ground in German politics, and the book appeared under the title *Michael*.

LE GUIN, Ursula K. (Kroeber) (born 1929)
US novelist

Le Guin made her name writing the prize-winning *Earthsea* novels, originally aimed at children but one of the great works of twentieth-century fantasy writing. Le Guin uses alternative-world fantasy to discuss social, ecological and political themes. Many of her other books are technically science fiction, set in the future and on other planets, but they explore questions of race and sexuality and politics which mainstream novelists have tackled and often do so with a good deal more elegance and style.

THE DISPOSSESSED (1974)

'An ambiguous utopia' as its subtitle calls it, tells the story of the different societies founded by humans on the verdant planet Urras and its barren moon Anarres. Anarres's society is a peaceful anarchy whose inhabitants have no possessions, live without laws and do not use the words 'I', 'me' and 'mine'; Urras is a capitalist meritocracy. Shevek, a mathematical genius from Anarres, travels to Urras where he is fêted as a success but is alienated by the class-ridden society of the planet. His involvement with a revolution on Urras is the backdrop to his theoretical mathe-matics which will ultimately lead to the invention of the Ansible, a device that will allow instantaneous contact with other planets, no matter how distant. But will Shevek let the materialistic society of Urras control and exploit the potential of the Ansible?

Le Guin's other novels include Rocannon's World, Planet of Exile, City of Illusions, The Lathe of Heaven, The Left Hand of Darkness, The Telling *and* Lavinia. The Wind's Twelve Quarters, The Birthday of the World *and* Changing Planes *are collections of short stories. The Earthsea Quartet is* A Wizard of Earthsea, The Tombs of Atuan, The Farthest Shore *and* Tehanu. Tales from Earthsea *is a collection of short stories and* The Other Wind *is a recent addition to the Earthsea canon.*

▽Read on
◆ *The Left Hand of Darkness.*
◘ to *The Dispossessed*: ❯❯ Margaret Atwood, *The Handmaid's Tale.*
◘ to Le Guin's work in general: ❯❯ Philip Pullman, *His Dark Materials* (a trilogy); Anne McCaffrey, *The Dragonriders of Pern*; Patricia McKillip, *Riddle-Master Trilogy.*

LEHANE, Dennis (born 1965)
US novelist

One of America's most compelling crime writers of the last two decades, Dennis Lehane began his career with a sequence of books featuring Boston private investigators Patrick Kenzie and Angela Gennaro. *A Drink Before the War*, the first of the books and typical of the series, sees the pair trying to uncover the whereabouts of a black cleaner and uncovering a network of extortion and abuse extending from the ghetto streets to the upper echelons of government. More recently, Lehane has chosen to write stand-alone novels of which the best-known (adapted for the movies by Clint Eastwood) is *Mystic River*, the story of three men who were friends as boys before something terrible happened to tear them apart and who are brought together again as adults to confront the past.

THE GIVEN DAY (2008)
Lehane changed direction again with this historical novel set in Boston at the end of the First World War. Built around events that led up to an infamous police strike in the city in 1919, *The Given Day* is the story of two families, one white and one

black, caught up in the turmoil of a city and a nation in the midst of change and unrest. It is an ambitious novel that clearly demonstrates Lehane's ability to write convincing fiction outside the confines of the crime genre.

The other Kenzie and Gennaro novels are Darkness, Take My Hand; Sacred; Gone, Baby, Gone *and* Prayers for Rain. Shutter Island *is set in the 1950s and is the story of a US marshal, despatched to a remote asylum to investigate the escape of a dangerous patient, who finds himself drawn into a plot as tangled as any Lehane has created before.*

📖Read on

◘ to *The Given Day*: E.L. Doctorow, *Ragtime*.
◘ to Lehane's fiction in general: ❯❯ Harlan Coben, *One False Move*; Robert Crais, *Demolition Angel*; George V. Higgins, *The Friends of Eddie Coyle*.

LEHMANN, Rosamond (1901–90)
British novelist

The ideas behind Lehmann's novels were strengthened by reading Jung and by psychic research after her daughter's death in the 1950s. She believed that we are not alone, that each person is part of a greater whole: the experience and knowledge of all human beings who have ever existed. We can enter into that experience, make use of it, during the rites of passage from one stage of existence to another – birth, adolescence, marriage, death – when the subconscious is particularly receptive. Lehmann's heroines are people on the brink of self-discovery; they are either innocents or victims of life, and the novels describe, in a lucid way far removed from the exoticism and mysticism of their events, how self-knowledge is achieved and how it changes the heroine's life, for bad or good.

THE BALLAD AND THE SOURCE (1944)
Ten-year-old Rebecca, picking bluebells in the garden of the old house beside the churchyard, is invited inside by the owner, Mrs Jardine, who knew Rebecca's grandmother. She and Rebecca become friends and Rebecca listens enthralled to Mrs Jardine's tales of 'the old days' – and the more terrible the stories (they are accounts of passion, adultery, betrayal and hatred in Mrs Jardine's own young life),

the more Rebecca is ensnared. Mrs Jardine is not so much like a witch casting a spell – though this is how Rebecca's alarmed mother sees her – as a sibyl from the remote past, revealing the true nature of human emotional existence.

Lehmann's other novels are Dusty Answer, Invitation to the Waltz *and its sequel* The Weather in the Streets, The Echoing Grove *and* A Sea-Grape Tree. The Gipsy's Baby *collects short stories, and* The Swan in the Evening *is an autobiographical memoir centring on her reactions to her daughter's death.*

☜Read on

◆ In *A Sea-Grape Tree* (the sequel to *The Ballad and the Source*) Rebecca, now grown-up and betrayed by men exactly as Mrs Jardine had been, goes to a Caribbean island to sort out her life and is affected not only by the people she meets there but by spirit-visitors from her past, including Mrs Jardine herself.

◻ Rose Macaulay, *The World My Wilderness*; ❯❯ Iris Murdoch, *The Philosopher's Pupil*; ❯❯ Alison Lurie, *Imaginary Friends*; Jane Gardam, *Crusoe's Daughter*.

LEIGH-FERMOR, Patrick (born 1915)
British travel writer

In 1933, as Europe was riven by the ideological divide between fascism and communism, the teenage Patrick Leigh-Fermor undertook an epic walk across the continent from the Hook of Holland to Istanbul. Nearly fifty years later, he drew on his memories and his journals of the trek to create two of the most memorable travel books of the twentieth century. *A Time of Gifts* and *Between the Woods and the Water* recreate his journey with a remarkable vividness, bringing back to life the sights he saw and the people he met. Travelling up the Rhine and down the Danube, Leigh-Fermor witnesses the last days of a particular kind of Mitteleuropa culture. The first volume takes him as far as Hungary; the second finishes as he arrives at the 'Iron Gates' that divide the Carpathian and Balkan mountains. Sadly a promised third volume, which will take Leigh-Fermor to the shores of the Bosphorus, has not yet appeared. As he is now in his nineties, it seems less and less likely that it ever will. The first two books, however, continue to provide an extraordinarily evocative portrait of a Central European world that was to be swept away by the Second World War.

Leigh-Fermor has also written a novel, The Violins of Saint Jacques, The Traveller's Tree *(about travels in the Caribbean), two volumes that recount his lifelong love affair with Greece* (Mani, Roumeli) *and* A Time to Keep Silence *(a short, scholarly and perceptive account of monastic life).*

📖Read on

◘ to *A Time of Gifts* and *Between the Woods and the Water*: Jason Goodwin, *On Foot to the Golden Horn*; Claudio Magris, *Danube*; Rebecca West, *Black Lamb and Grey Falcon*.

◘ to the Greek books: Dilys Powell, *An Affair of the Heart*; Patricia Storace, *Dinner with Persephone*.

LEON, Donna (born 1942)
American novelist

Donna Leon's crime novels are set in Venice and the calli and campi of the city provide the stage set on which the sympathetic figure of her central character, Commissario Guido Brunetti, conducts his investigations. Her evocation of Venice is very precise but she does not provide a sentimentalized version of the Pearl of the Adriatic. This is a city in which drugs, prostitution and corruption lurk in the shadows and through it all moves the thoughtful and humane Brunetti, honestly determined to get at as much of the truth as he can.

DEATH IN A STRANGE COUNTRY (1993)
A body is pulled out of a Venetian canal and proves to be that of a young American soldier from a base in the hills of the Veneto. Is he the victim of a casual mugging or is there a more sinister explanation for his death? Commissario Brunetti finds that his inquiries are leading him inexorably towards dirty linen that few people want to wash in public. Drugs are found in the young man's flat but they may have been planted there to divert attention from other lines of investigation that Brunetti might wish to pursue. Very powerful people indeed have a vested interest in ensuring that the truth about the American's death, and others that follow, should never emerge.

The other Brunetti novels include Death at La Fenice, A Venetian Reckoning, Acqua Alta, A Noble Radiance, Doctored Evidence, Blood from a Stone, Through a Glass Darkly, Suffer the Little Children, The Girl of his Dreams *and* About Face.

⬚**Read on**
- *Death at La Fenice* (the first of the Brunetti novels).
- ▢ Andrea Camilleri, *The Terracotta Dog*; ›› Michael Dibdin, *Dead Lagoon*; Magdalen Nabb, *Death of an Englishman*.

LEONARD, ELMORE (born 1925)
US novelist

In the 1990s Elmore Leonard became one of Hollywood's favourite novelists and perhaps the hippest of all American crime writers. Quentin Tarantino's film *Jackie Brown* was based on Leonard's novel *Rum Punch*. One of the roles which returned John Travolta to star status was that of Chili Palmer, the movie-loving gangster in the film version of Leonard's *Get Shorty*. And literary critics love Leonard's books, too. Even Martin Amis, often a difficult reader to please, described *Get Shorty* as a masterpiece. Leonard's status as America's most widely admired crime writer has been hard won. He began writing fiction in the 1950s, and his earliest books were westerns (the 1967 Paul Newman film *Hombre* is based on a Leonard novel) but it was when he turned to crime writing that he found a home for his finest gifts as a writer. Leonard writes the kind of dialogue that other writers would kill to achieve. His fast, funny stories – filled with low-life, weirdos and bad-assed villains – display a talent for expertly drawn action and a mastery of wisecracking and street-smart language that mark Leonard out as a king of crime writing.

Elmore Leonard's novels include The Big Bounce, City Primeval, Freaky Deaky, Glitz, Gold Coast, Killshot, La Brava, Out of Sight, Pronto, Be Cool, Cuba Libre, Split Images, Stick, Bandits, Tishomingo Blues, Mr Paradise, The Hot Kid *and* Up in Honey's Room. When the Women Come Out to Dance *is a collection of short stories which is like a crash-course introduction to Leonard's fictional world.*

⬚**Read on**
- *Be Cool* (Chili Palmer applies his particular talents to the music industry); *Cuba Libre* (not a crime novel but historical fiction set in Cuba as the Spanish-American War of 1898 is about to start).
- ▢ ›› Carl Hiaasen, *Double Whammy*; Robert B. Parker, *Night Passage*; ›› James Ellroy, *LA Confidential*; Richard Stark, *The Hunter*.

LESSING, Doris (born 1919)

British novelist and non-fiction writer

Lessing was brought up in Rhodesia (now Zimbabwe), but her involvement in progressive politics made it an uncomfortable place to live, and she moved to London in 1949. In the same year she published her first novel, *The Grass is Singing*, about relationships between the races. She followed it in 1952 with the semi-autobiographical *Martha Quest*, the first in a five-book series (the other volumes, published over the following seventeen years, are *A Proper Marriage, A Ripple From the Storm, Landlocked* and *The Four-gated City*). The sequence took her heroine from girlhood to marriage in white Rhodesia, from political virginity to radical activism, from Africa to London, from youth to age. Martha becomes a feminist; she samples and rejects the Swinging Sixties; she tries religion and mysticism; she watches, and reports on, the last hours of the human race as we writhe towards the apocalypse. The books are in a straightforward 'as-told-to' style: they have the power of documentary as much as fiction. Two other Lessing novels, *The Golden Notebook* (about an unhappy writer coming to terms with herself as a person and with her place in a male-dominated society) and *Briefing for a Descent into Hell* (about nervous breakdown), have similar intensity. Lessing's (Jungian) psychological interests, and her fascination with Sufi mysticism, influence much of her other work, especially the five-volume sequence *Canopus in Argus* (1979–83), which uses a science fiction format to explore ideas not so much of outer as of inner space, the alternative realities inside the mind.

The Canopus in Argus *novels are* Shikasta, The Marriage Between Zones Three, Four and Five, The Sirian Experiments, The Making of the Representatives for Planet 8 *and* Documents Relating to the Sentimental Agents in the Volyen Empire. Mara and Dann *is also a visionary fiction set in the future; it has a sequel in* The Story of General Dann and Mara's Daughter, Griot and the Snow Dog. *Lessing's other novels include* Memoirs of a Survivor, The Summer before the Dark, The Good Terrorist, Love, Again, The Fifth Child *and its sequel* Ben, in the World, The Sweetest Dream *and* The Cleft. *Two collections of African stories,* This Was the Old Chief's Country *and* The Sun Between Their Feet, *are full of remarkable writing.* Under My Skin *and* Walking in the Shade *are volumes of autobiography.* Alfred and Emily *is a recently published book which investigates the lives of her parents, two people damaged by the First World War, and the psychological legacy she inherited from them.*

Read on

■ to *Canopus in Argus*: Olaf Stapledon, *Last and First Men*.

■ to Lessing's work in general: Margaret Laurence, *A Jest of God*; ➤➤ Patrick White, *The Solid Mandala*; ➤➤ Margaret Drabble, *Jerusalem the Golden*; ➤➤ Nadine Gordimer, *July's People*; Simone de Beauvoir, *She Came to Stay*; H.H. Richardson, *The Fortunes of Richard Mahony*.

START POINT

LETTERS AND DIARIES

Fewer people write letters and diaries than did so even twenty years ago, but for centuries they were favourite forms of literature. Readers turned to them to find the writer's unguarded, private thoughts. Sometimes these were what they got – intimate documents meant only for personal use. In other cases, they got ideas selected and polished with the full intention of publication. (Politicians' diaries and letters, with the notable exception of Alan Clark's *Diaries*, are seldom 'private' documents.) The books selected here therefore contain some of the grandest, as well as the most revealing, of all literature.

Byron, Lord (1788–1824), *Selected Letters and Journals* (1984) (ed. Leslie Marchand). Byron's character revealed in all its complexity in letters and journals that sometimes read as if they were written yesterday instead of in the early nineteenth century.

Chesterfield, Lord (1694–1773), *Letters to His Son* (1774). Written to teach the young man the thoughts and manners of a gentleman. Politics, etiquette, religion, morals, the way of the world – each beautifully written letter is a glimpse into the eighteenth-century mind.

Clark, Alan (1928–99), *Diaries* (1993). Arch-cad of the Tory party reveals the gossip, bitchiness and backbiting of politics while also chronicling, with rueful, witty self-awareness, his own shortcomings and sexual escapades. Will be read long after most political memoirs have entered a decent oblivion.

Coward, Noël (1899–1973), *Diaries* **(1982)**. Coward demonstrates his talent to amuse, and his own inner doubts and self-questionings. The beautiful, the famous and the notorious of the twentieth century flit through its pages.

Frank, Anne (1929–45), *The Diary of Anne Frank* **(1947)**. Frank's own heartrending account of how she and her family hid from the Nazis in an attic – and of what it's like to spend one's formative years in such circumstances.

Goncourt, Edmond de (1822–96) and Jules de (1830–70), *The Goncourt Journal* **(1887–96)**. The Goncourts were at the hub of the Paris chattering class – actors, painters, writers, politicians, society folk – in the so-called Belle Époque, and wrote up these gossipy, malicious journals each night.

Kilvert, Francis (1840–79), *Kilvert's Diary* **(1938–40)**. Kilvert was a parson in rural Wales, and his *Diary* gives unsentimental pictures of country life one hundred and twenty five years ago.

Klemperer, Victor (1881–1960), *Diaries* **1933–1945**. Astonishing and moving record of a Jew who survived the war, although still living in Germany throughout it.

Partridge, Frances (1900–2004), *Diaries* **1939–1972 (2001)**. This selection from the diaries of the Bloomsbury Group's last survivor provides memories of ›› Virginia Woolf, ›› Lytton Strachey and others as well as Partridge's further recollections of her long life.

Pepys, Samuel (1633–1703), *Diary* **(1825)**. Not written for publication – it was even in code – Pepys's *Diary* tells of life in Restoration London, and of its happy, hard-working (and hard-playing) author. Shortened version advised, at least for first sampling.

Plath, Sylvia (1932–63), *Letters Home* **(1975)**. A moving mixture of domestic incident and despairing soul-searching in the letters Plath wrote, largely to her mother. Knowledge of the future, which we have but she doesn't, adds to the poignancy.

Van Gogh, Vincent (1853–90), *Letters* **(1963)**. The letters of the Dutch painter, mostly written to his long-suffering brother Theo, offer unique insights into his tormented personality and into the sources of his art.

>> **Waugh, Evelyn (1903–66),** *Letters* **(1980)**. Waugh's bilious wit and jaundiced view of the world and the people in it emerge entertainingly in his letters.

Kenneth Williams (1926–88), *The Diaries of Kenneth Williams* **(1993)**. In the Carry On films, on TV and on radio, Williams slipped into one outrageous character after another – and hated himself for doing so. In real life he was obsessive, lonely, bitchy and miserable. The broken-hearted clown is a showbiz cliché, but Williams's life gives it hypnotic, tragic power.

Also recommended: >> Kingsley Amis, *Letters*; Elizabeth Barrett and Robert Browning, *Letters, 1845–46*; Fanny Burney, *Diary*; John Evelyn, *The Diary of John Evelyn*; James Joyce, *Collected Letters*; Joe Orton, *Diaries*; Pliny the Younger, *Letters*; Oscar Wilde, *Letters*; Dorothy Wordsworth, *The Alfoxden and Grasmere Journals*.

HIDDENGEM:

JAMES BOSWELL – *LONDON JOURNAL* (1950)

'I own, sir, the spirits which I have in London make me do everything with more readiness and vigour,' James Boswell once told his mentor Dr Johnson and the proof is in his *London Journal*. In 1762, Boswell arrived in London as a young man in search of women, wine and the celebrities of the day. The *London Journal*, edited from private papers, first appeared nearly two hundred years after he wrote it and it provides not only a remarkable panorama of high and low life in the eighteenth-century city but also a self-portrait of endearing honesty. Boswell lives London life to the full – drinking, whoring, sightseeing, playgoing and then drinking some more. Self-reproach and vows to lead a better life are swiftly followed by further debauches. Few other personal journals are as entertaining for the reader as this one.

LEVI, Primo (1919–87)
Italian novelist and autobiographer

Primo Levi was a Jewish-Italian survivor of Auschwitz. For the rest of his life, he used his writings as a means of exorcising the demons that haunted him and of reminding others of the appalling realities of the Holocaust. In *If This is a Man* he describes, in clear and careful prose, the terrible events to which he was witness. As a humane testimony to monstrous inhumanity, it has its place among the most important and challenging books of the twentieth century. In *The Periodic Table*, Levi, a chemist by training, uses the elements of the periodic table as a means of organizing a sequence of autobiographical essays. Each of the twenty one chapters is given the title of one of the elements from the table; each one reflects something of Levi's life from his childhood through his experiences at Auschwitz to his career in post-war Italy. *If Not Now, When?* is a novel which follows the fortunes of a Russian Jew who joins a group of partisans fighting their way westwards behind the German frontline in the last years of the Second World War.

Primo Levi's other books include Moments of Reprieve, The Drowned and the Saved *and* The Wrench. The Voice of Memory *is a collection of interviews Levi gave to newspapers and magazines over a period of more than a quarter of a century.*

Read on
◆ *The Drowned and the Saved.*
◻ to *If This is a Man*: Roman Frister, *The Cap: The Price of a Life*; Wladsyslaw Szpilman, *The Pianist*; Elie Wiesel, *Night*.
◻ to *The Periodic Table*: ≫ Oliver Sacks, *Uncle Tungsten*.

LEVY, Andrea (born 1956)
British novelist

Andrea Levy's first novel, *Every Light in the House Burnin'*, drew on her own experiences as a black Briton in the story of Angela Jacob, an ordinary young woman brought up on a London council estate, forced to cope with the fear and anxiety of her father's painful struggle against cancer. As her life narrows to hospital visits and conversations with doctors, she finds her mind returning to her childhood in the 1960s. Levy followed her debut novel with two further books which explored the pleasures and dangers of being black in Britain. *Never Far From Nowhere* is the story, set largely in the 1970s, of two sisters whose lives take very divergent paths; in *Fruit of the Lemon*, the central character, a black Londoner, finds a new sense of her self and her past when she visits Jamaica. Levy's profile as a writer was raised significantly when her fourth novel, *Small Island* (see below), won the 2004 Orange Prize for fiction.

SMALL ISLAND (2004)

The year is 1948 and the first wave of immigrants from the Caribbean is arriving in London. Among them is Gilbert Joseph from Jamaica. Hortense, his new wife, soon follows but, armed with a teaching diploma and expecting an England similar to the fantasy land she has constructed in her mind, she is doomed to disappointment. Gilbert, with wartime experience of living in London, has more realistic expectations but is gradually worn down by the prejudice and misunderstandings he faces. In counterpoint to their lives, Levy shows us the world of Queenie Bligh, their formidable landlady, and her husband, Bernard, only recently returned to London after disappearing during the war. Her novel is a brilliant reconstruction of a vanished London and a memorable portrait of immigrants struggling to adapt to their new country.

❧Read on

◘ to *Small Island*: ›› Sarah Waters, *The Night Watch* (very different characters but a similarly exact recreation of 1940s London).

◘ to Levy's fiction in general: ›› Caryl Phillips, *Final Passage*; ›› Zadie Smith, *White Teeth*.

LEWIS, Norman (1908–2003)

British travel writer and novelist

Once described by ›› Graham Greene as 'one of the best writers, not of any particular decade, but of our century', Norman Lewis was one of the great travellers of his generation, drawn particularly to cultures where long-established ways of life were under threat from the encroachment of modernity. In unflamboyant but evocative prose he bore witness to the changes, often for the worse, that traditional societies from Spain to Indochina were undergoing and the effects these changes had on people. *A Dragon Apparent* describes his travels in Cambodia, Laos and Vietnam soon after the end of the Second World War when the French imperial project in Indochina was crumbling under the weight of its own contradictions. In *Golden Earth*, Lewis journeys through a Burma still scarred by the fighting in the Second World War; *Voices of the Old Sea* records the life of a Spanish fishing village on the Costa Brava in the years just before mass tourism changed the age-old rhythms of life irrevocably. Lewis also wrote memorably about Italy, its people and its history. *Naples '44* is the diary of Lewis's experiences in the country during the Second World War. *The Honoured Society* is a history of the Mafia's infiltration of every aspect of Sicilian life. *In Sicily*, published late in his long life, is a record of sixty years' fascination with the island and its people.

Norman Lewis's other books include The Missionaries *(an exposé of the damaging effects of American fundamentalist missionary work in Latin America and the Pacific),* The Tomb in Seville, A Goddess In the Stones *(travels in India) and* An Empire of the East. A View of the World *and* The Happy Ant-Heap *are both collections of shorter travel pieces.* Jackdaw Cake *and* The World, The World *are idiosyncratic volumes of autobiography. Lewis also wrote novels, including* The Day of the Fox, A Small World Made to Order *and* The Sicilian Specialist, *which have never gained the reputation of his travel books but are well worth reading.*

📖 Read on

◘ to the travel writing: Norman Douglas, *Old Calabria*; ›› Jan Morris, *A Writer's World*; Gavin Young, *Slow Boats to China*.

◘ to the Sicilian books: Peter Robb, *Midnight in Sicily*.

◘ to *Naples '44*: ›› Eric Newby, *Love and War in the Apennines*; Iris Origo, *War in Val D'Orcia*.

◘ to the autobiographies: ›› Michael Holroyd, *Basil Street Blues*.

LITT, Toby (born 1968)
British novelist

One of Granta's Best of Young British Novelists in 2003, Toby Litt is a writer whose spare and clever narratives can move easily from the sinister to the comic. His first novel, *Beatniks* (1997), is a cunningly contrived take on the Beat Generation and ›› Jack Kerouac's *On the Road*, transferring the action to provincial England in the

1990s where the protagonists, intent on reproducing the exploits of their beat heroes, find a world less ready for fantasies of escape and freedom. *Corpsing* is Litt's very individual and fast-paced version of an urban thriller in which the central character, Conrad, seeks the truth behind the apparently motiveless shooting of his girlfriend. *Ghost Story* focuses on a young, middle class couple, both suffering from the grief of the woman's miscarriage, who move into a new house where their relationship begins to unravel amid ambiguous hauntings and hallucinations. Prefaced by Litt's own account of his and his girlfriend's experiences of the pain of miscarriage, this is a strange and claustrophobic tale of loss and depression.

Toby Litt's other books are Deadkidsongs, Finding Myself, Hospital *and* Journey into Space *(all novels) and* Adventures in Capitalism, Exhibitionism *and* I Play the Drums in a Band Called Okay *(three collections of short stories).*

⮒Read on
◆ *Journey into Space* (Litt's venture into SF).
◘ to *Corpsing*: ›› Jake Arnott, *Johnny Come Home*; Matthew Branton, *The Hired Gun*.
◘ to Toby Litt's fiction in general: Nicholas Blincoe, *White Mice*; ›› Geoff Dyer, *Paris Trance*; Matt Thorne, *Pictures of You*.

LIVELY, Penelope (born 1933)
British writer

As well as for adults, Lively writes for children, and at least two of those books, *The Ghost of Thomas Kempe* and *A Stitch in Time*, are modern classics. Her adult novels share the same qualities – they are crisply written, strong on character and atmosphere, and have dazzlingly life-like dialogue. She is particularly good at evoking the emotional feel of a place and of its history, showing how these impinge on her characters. And the places and characters range widely, from the Oxfordshire village of *Judgement Day*, racked over fundraising for its historic (and slightly disreputable) church or the crumbling stately home of *Next to Nature, Art*, whose owner is trying to revitalize it as an arts centre, to the terrorist-threatened, age-old African state of *Cleopatra's Sister*. She works the convincing trick of lulling us by making us think the dilemmas and characters of her people are as familiar as our own – and then springing at least one major, sinister surprise.

MOON TIGER (1987)

Dying in hospital, Claudia Hampton reviews her whole past life, and in particular the wartime affair with a doomed young soldier in Egypt which both liberated her emotions and then (after his death) dried up her character even as it roused her to take up history, the profession at which she became so dauntingly successful.

Lively's other adult novels include The Road to Lichfield, According to Mark, Passing On, Heat Wave, The Photograph, Making it Up *(a curious cross between fiction and autobiography in which she imagines alternative life stories for herself and others) and* Consequences. *Her short story collections include* Pack of Cards *and* Beyond the Blue Mountains. Oleander Jacaranda *is a wonderfully evocative account of growing up in Egypt in the 1930s and 1940s and* A House Unlocked *a collection of memories awakened by the Somerset house in which her family have long lived.*

📖 Read on

♦ *The Photograph* (Glyn Peters' discovery of a photograph of his wife with another man heralds the unravelling of a marriage and the emergence of long-hidden truths).

▣ ≫ Anita Brookner, *A Closed Eye*; ≫ Susan Hill, *In the Springtime of the Year*; ≫ Joanna Trollope, *The Choir*; Shena Mackay, *The Artist's Widow*.

LODGE, David (born 1935)

British novelist

In the 1960s Lodge wrote half a dozen tragi-comic novels about young people perplexed by the pull between their Catholic upbringing and the urge of the Swinging Sixties; the funniest is *The British Museum is Falling Down*. In the 1970s he began to write campus comedies, many set in an imaginary Midlands university, Rummidge. These include *Changing Places* (in which an innocent Rummidge lecturer changes places for a year with brash, oversexed Maurice Zapp of Euphoria State University, USA), *Small World* (about a young man pursuing a beautiful girl at a succession of ludicrous academic conferences) and *Nice Work* (in which an uptight feminist lecturer and a chauvinist captain of industry are set to 'shadow' each other for a year). *Therapy* combines satire on modern literary preoccupations (such as writing unperformable screenplays or being a TV pundit) with a bleak

a middle-aged man discovering what existentialist angst is all about.
Thinks records the developing relationship of a middle-aged novelist and a media
don, set in familiar Lodge territory.

Lodge's other novels include Ginger, You're Barmy, How Far Can You Go?,
Paradise News, Author! Author! *and* Deaf Sentence. *He has also written academic
books, chiefly on the writing of fiction and on structuralism.*

⪧Read on
◘ to the Sixties' novels: ➤➤ Margaret Forster, *Georgy Girl*.
◘ to the campus comedies: Malcolm Bradbury, *The History Man*; ➤➤ Howard
Jacobson, *Coming From Behind*; Mary McCarthy, *The Groves of Academe*.

READ ON A THEME:

LONDON
➤➤ Jake Arnott, *The Long Firm*
   Alexander Baron, *Low Life*
➤➤ Peter Carey, *Jack Maggs*
   Justin Cartwright, *Look At it This Way*
   Esther Freud, *Peerless Flats*
   Anthony Frewin, *London Blues*
   Patrick Hamilton, *Hangover Square*
   Tobias Hill, *Undergound*
➤➤ Hanif Kureishi, *The Buddha of Suburbia*
   Colin MacInnes, *Absolute Beginners*
➤➤ Michael Moorcock, *Mother London*
➤➤ J.B. Priestley, *Angel Pavement*
➤➤ Iain Sinclair, *Downriver*
   Nigel Williams, *They Came From SW19*

282

LOPEZ, Barry (born 1945)

US essayist, naturalist and novelist

An original and compelling writer, Lopez has used many different literary forms, both fictional and non-fictional, to explore his fascination with the relationship between man and the natural world. His most famous book remains *Arctic Dreams*, first published in 1986. Subtitled 'Imagination and Desire in a Northern Landscape', *Arctic Dreams* is both a celebration of the frozen wilderness of the Canadian Arctic and a meditation on how landscape can shape our imaginations. Drawing on his own experiences of travelling in the Far North and on the insights of both the Inuit people who live there and the scientists of all kinds who study it, the book provides an astonishing portrait of a world that most people would see as hostile and inhospitable but in which Lopez discovers wonder and beauty.

Other books by Barry Lopez include Of Wolves and Men, Crossing Open Ground *and* About This Life. *He has also written a number of works of fiction, including* Light Action in the Caribbean *and* Resistance. Desert Notes, Field Notes *and* River Notes *are three volumes of short stories, most of which reflect Lopez's environmental interests and his ideas about the interaction of man and landscape.*

🕮Read on

◆ *Of Wolves and Men*.

◘ Edward Abbey, *Desert Solitaire*; Gretel Ehrlich, *This Cold Heaven*; ▸▸ Peter Matthiessen, *The Snow Leopard*; Piers Vitebsky, *Reindeer People*.

LOWRY, Malcolm (1909-57)

British novelist

Lowry began drinking at Cambridge, and by the time he was twenty he was irretrievably addicted. He spent the rest of his life bumming across the world, in rehabilitation clinics, or in self-imposed isolation while he struggled to turn his experiences into fiction. He published *Ultramarine* in 1933, soon after leaving Cambridge, but the only other novel published during his lifetime – it took him twenty years to write it – was *Under the Volcano* (1947). This tells of the last two days in the life of an alcoholic British consul in revolution-torn Mexico, and intertwines memory, dream and reality in the manner of ▸▸ Joyce's *Ulysses*. His posthumous novels are *Lunar Caustic*, set in a 'drying-out' clinic in New York, and *Dark As the Grave Wherein My Friend is Laid*, about a boozy, doom-ridden tour of Mexico. *Hear Us, O Lord, From Heaven Thy Dwelling Place* is a collection of shorter pieces.

⯒Read on

◘ ❯❯ Joseph Conrad, *Heart of Darkness*; ❯❯ F. Scott Fitzgerald, *Tender is the Night*; ❯❯ Fyodor Dostoevsky, *The Idiot*; ❯❯ Lawrence Durrell, *The Black Book*; ❯❯ Ernest Hemingway, *Islands in the Stream*.

LURIE, Alison (born 1926)
US novelist

The people in Lurie's novels are all terribly nice: well educated, well off, well dressed, liberal and compassionate. Their lives are like placid pools – and into each of them Lurie drops the acid of discontent (usually something to do with sex) and invites us to smile as the water seethes. Her funniest books are set on university campuses: *Love and Friendship* is about two people trapped in an affair (and what everyone else thinks about it); *The War Between the Tates* shows the gradual collapse of a 'perfect' marriage under threat from a combination of adultery and student politics. The people of *Imaginary Friends* are participants in or investigators of a bizarre religious cult. In *Foreign Affairs*, three Americans are visiting England: Vinnie, a fifty-four-year-old professor, Fred, a hunky young academic, and Chuck, a middle-aged, none-too-bright businessman on a package tour. The novel shows Vinnie's attempts to bring into the two men's lives the same kind of decorous, unflustered order she herself enjoys – and the way her own values crumple under the strain of real emotion.

Lurie's other novels are Real People, Only Children, Love and Friendship, Nowhere City *(a serious book about a woman trying to cope with unfocused psychological panic),* The Truth About Lorin Jones, The Last Resort *and* Truth and Consequences. Women and Ghosts *is a collection of supernatural stories.*

⯒Read on
◆ *The Truth About Lorin Jones* (about a woman writing the biography of a painter, whose life becomes totally entangled with the facts and emotions she is researching).

■ **>>** Anita Brookner, *Look At Me*; **>>** Carol Shields, *Larry's Party*; **>>** Anne Tyler, *Ladder of Years*; Alice Thomas Ellis, *The Birds of the Air*; Gail Godwin, *The Good Husband*.

McCALL SMITH, Alexander (born 1948)
British novelist

An African-born professor of Scottish law who became an expert on medical ethics, Alexander McCall Smith was in his forties before he turned his hand to crime fiction. But in *The No. 1 Ladies' Detective Agency* he introduced one of the most original and charming central characters in the genre. Precious Ramotswe runs the only female detective agency in Botswana. The mysteries she investigates are not the bloody murders of most crime fiction – she is more likely to confront ostrich rustlers and village witch-doctors than killers – but she applies her own resounding common sense and wide sympathies to the problems her clients bring her. The supporting characters (Mr J.L.B. Matekoni, kindly proprietor of Tlokweng Road Speedy Motors and Mma Ramotswe's fiancé, and secretary and assistant detective Mma Makutsi) are brilliant creations in themselves, the African setting is entirely convincing and the 'traditionally built' Mma Ramotswe, forever drinking her favourite red bush tea as she seeks the answers to life's difficulties, is an immensely appealing heroine.

The other Precious Ramotswe books are Tears of the Giraffe, Morality for Beautiful Girls, The Kalahari Typing School for Men, The Full Cupboard of Life, In the Company of Cheerful Ladies, Blue Shoes and Happiness, The Good Husband of Zebra Drive, Miracle at Speedy Motors *and* Tea Time for the Traditionally Built. *McCall Smith has also written a series of Edinburgh-set mystery novels featuring a middle-aged philosopher named Isabel Dalhousie (beginning with* The Sunday Philosophy Club) *and a number of episodic novels set in a building which houses a cross-section of Edinburgh society (the first took its title from the address,* 44, Scotland Street). The Two and a Half Pillars of Wisdom *is a collection of three comic novellas which detail the mishaps and misadventures of group of unworldly German academics.*

Read on
♦ *44 Scotland Street.*

◘ Sujata Massey, *The Salaryman's Wife* (one of another series of crime novels set in a non-Western culture – in this case, Japan); ❯❯ R.K. Narayan, *The Painter of Signs* (Narayan's novels set in the small Indian town of Malgudi are not crime fiction but they have the same charm and individuality as McCall Smith's books).

McCARTHY, Cormac (born 1933)
US novelist

Cormac McCarthy's portrayal of America is on a canvas that's dark and stained with blood. Celebrated primarily for his acclaimed *Border Trilogy*, comprising *All the Pretty Horses*, *The Crossing* and *Cities of the Plain*, he has written seven other novels, each one a powerful example of his stark and sombre vision. *Suttree*, for example, is a substantial and densely written book, which McCarthy worked at (on and off) for twenty years. Suttree abandons his middle-class life and family to live in a decaying houseboat on a Stygian river and hang out with thieves, drunks and a whole gallery of grotesque outcasts. The torpor of his existence on the rancid river is punctuated by outbursts of appalling violence and a doomed, traumatic love affair. The book resembles some kind of black parody of ❯❯ Steinbeck's *Tortilla Flat*. After being awarded the prestigious MacArthur Fellowship in 1981 (presiding over the judges was ❯❯ Saul Bellow who praised McCarthy's 'life-giving and death-dealing sentences'), he had time and freedom to concentrate on his next book. This was *Blood Meridian*, or *The Evening Redness in the West*, which many consider his masterpiece. The American West is utterly divested of any kind of mythology or heroism and depicted as an inferno. The book's two central characters are 'the kid', an orphan with no name but 'a taste for mindless violence', and a figure known as 'the judge', a shrewd, cunning psychopath who is to this sun-scorched domain what ❯❯ Melville's Captain Ahab is to the endless ocean. The cheapness of life envisaged in this hellish world was noted by a critic who calculated that, on average, there was a murder every fifth page. Although the *Border Trilogy* confirmed McCarthy's status commercially, *Blood Meridian* remains his key work, an extraordinary portrait of an apocalypse that destroys all, taking no prisoners save the reader, captured by McCarthy's rich and mesmeric prose.

📖Read on
◆ *No Country for Old Men*; *The Road* (a post-apocalyptic tale of a man and a boy struggling to survive in a landscape ravaged by future environmental disaster).

◘ to *Blood Meridian*: Ron Hansen, *Desperadoes*; Daniel Woodrell, *Woe to Live On*.

◘ to *The Road*: ❯❯ Margaret Atwood, *Oryx and Crake*; ❯❯ Russell Hoban, *Riddley Walker*.

◘ to McCarthy's fiction in general: ❯❯ William Faulkner, *Light in August*; ❯❯ Herman Melville, *Moby Dick*.

McCULLERS, Carson (1917–53)
US novelist

Reading McCullers sometimes seems like visiting a freak-show: her characters are repulsive but fascinating, macabre misfits set down in America's Deep South. The hero of *The Heart is a Lonely Hunter* is a deaf-mute, distracted by his inability to communicate either his sensitivity or his generosity of spirit. The awkward, ugly heroine of *The Ballad of the Sad Café* (1951) runs a haven in the Georgia swamps for tramps, lunatics and other social misfits – and her world is shattered when she falls in love with a malign homosexual dwarf. *Reflections in a Golden Eye* describes boredom and sexual obsession among the wives in a wartime army camp. *Clock Without Hands* is about racism. Only in one book, *The Member of the Wedding*, does McCullers transcend her more nightmarish imaginings. Her heroine is a young adolescent in a household bustling with preparations for a wedding: fascinated but totally ignorant about what is going on, she feels as locked out of 'real' (i.e. adult) society as the freaks and emotional cripples of McCullers's other books.

📖 Read on

◘ to *The Member of the Wedding*. ❯❯ Eudora Welty, *Delta Wedding*; Katherine Anne Porter, *The Leaning Tower* (short stories).

◘ to McCullers's books in general: Flannery O'Connor, *Wise Blood*; ❯❯ William Faulkner, *Intruder in the Dust*; Elizabeth McCracken, *The Giant's House*.

McCULLOUGH, Colleen (born 1937)
Australian novelist

Colleen McCullough first achieved a large, worldwide readership with her 1977 book *The Thorn Birds*, a sweeping multi-generational family saga set in the Australian outback which focused on the forbidden love affair between a young woman and a charismatic Roman Catholic priest and its consequences. A decade later, she changed direction dramatically and, with the publication of *The First Man in Rome*, embarked on a fictional journey through the history of the last days of Republican Rome that kept her occupied for many years. Nearly a thousand pages long, the book detailed the political struggle between two rival generals, Marius and Sulla, but it was only an introduction to a series which carried the story forwards to the campaigns of Pompey the Great (*Fortune's Favourites*), the rise of Caesar (*Caesar*) and, finally, the last great confrontation between Mark Antony and Octavian (*Antony and Cleopatra*). With the romances with which she started her career, Colleen McCullough proved herself a storyteller of remarkable gifts. When she directed these gifts to the recreation of some of the most dramatic events in the history of Ancient Rome, she produced a very different but no less enthralling kind of fiction.

The novels in the 'Masters of Rome' sequence, in chronological order, are The First Man in Rome, The Grass Crown, Fortune's Favourites, Caesar's Women, Caesar, The October Horse *and* Antony and Cleopatra. *Her other fiction includes* Tim *(her first novel – about an unexpected love affair),* An Indecent Obsession, The Ladies of Missalonghi, Morgan's Run *(a saga of convict settlers in the early years of white Australia),* The Touch *and* The Independence of Miss Mary Bennet *(which purports to tell the story of what happened to one of Elizabeth Bennet's sisters after the events of* Pride and Prejudice*).*

🕮Read on
◘ to *The Thorn Birds*: Barbara Taylor Bradford, *A Woman of Substance*; M.M. Kaye, *The Far Pavilions*.
◘ to 'Masters of Rome' series: ≫ Robert Graves, *I, Claudius*; Conn Iggulden, *The Gates of Rome*; Michelle Moran, *Nefertiti*; ≫ Steven Saylor, *A Murder on the Appian Way*.

McDERMID, Val (born 1955)
British novelist

Val McDermid has written some of the best British crime fiction of the last twenty years and has produced three series of books as well as a number of non-series titles. In her early career as a crime writer she created one of Britain's first lesbian investigators in Lindsay Gordon, a journalist drawn (often reluctantly) into webs of deceit and murder. In 1992, McDermid created her second series character, Kate Brannigan, a Manchester-based private detective. The Brannigan books are very recognizably set in the real world of contemporary Manchester, with its big-city crimes, computer fraud and get-rich-quick schemes out to con the gullible. A good example is *Dead Beat*, in which a friend of her rock journalist partner asks Kate to track down a missing songwriter, a trail which leads her into the seedier areas of several northern cities. In more recent years McDermid has published six novels, more complex in narrative and more willing to stretch the boundaries of the genre than either the Lindsay Gordon or Kate Brannigan books, which feature psychological profiler Tony Hill and his police colleague Carol Jordan. The first of these, *The Mermaids Singing*, in which they pursue a serial killer who targets gay men, established a style and characters that have proved successful in several follow-ups and a TV series, *Wire in the Blood*.

The Lindsay Gordon novels are Report for Murder, Common Murder, Final Edition, Union Jack, Booked for Murder *and* Hostage to Murder. *The Kate Brannigan books are* Dead Beat, Kick Back, Crackdown, Clean Break, Blue Genes *and* Star Struck. *McDermid's novels featuring Tony Hill and Carol Jordan are* The Mermaids Singing, The Wire in the Blood, The Last Temptation, The Torment of Others, Beneath the Bleeding *and* The Fever of the Bone. *She has also written half a dozen non-series titles including* A Place of Execution, The Grave Tattoo *and* A Darker Domain.

🐸Read on
♦ *A Place of Execution* (in the 1960s a schoolgirl disappears and a young detective is launched on an investigation that will shape his life); *The Grave Tattoo* (a stand-alone novel set in the nineteenth-century Lake District and featuring a woman drawn into investigating the death of a man who just might be the Bounty mutineer Fletcher Christian returned from exile on Pitcairn Island).
◻ to the Lindsay Gordon novels: Mary Wings, *She Came Too Late*; Kate Forrest, *Sleeping Bones*; Manda Scott, *Hen's Teeth*.

■ to the Kate Brannigan novels: Denise Mina, *The Field of Blood*; Cath Staincliffe, *Dead Wrong*.

■ to McDermid's other fiction: ➤➤ Ian Rankin, *The Black Book*; ➤➤ Peter Robinson, *In a Dry Season*; Jane Adams, *The Greenway*.

McEWAN, Ian (born 1948)

British novelist and short story writer

McEwan began his career writing short stories and short novels in which, in precise and glacially cool prose, he led his readers towards hidden horrors and terrible revelations. What, for example, is the secret of *The Cement Garden*, which only the children know? What unimaginable violence is to end the dream-like trip to Venice recounted in *The Comfort of Strangers*? Later novels are just as tense, but the characters are more sympathetic, the atmosphere is less claustrophobic and human warmth and humour leaven the pain. *Black Dogs*, for example, is about a man researching the life of his wife's parents ('borrowing them', so to speak, since his own parents died when he was young), and in particular trying to find out what was the horror (the Black Dogs of the title) they found on their honeymoon trip to France just after the Second World War. McEwan's more recent fiction has included a short but potent morality tale of love, death and deception (*Amsterdam*), and the story of a man whose comfortable middle-class life is arbitrarily disrupted by the obsessions and delusions of another man (*Enduring Love*). *Atonement*, his much-acclaimed novel of 2001, is an extended drama in three acts. In the first it is 1935 and a teenage girl, Briony Tallis, fatefully misinterprets events around her with terrible results for a young man named Robbie Turner. The other two parts of the book take place in 1940 and follow Robbie in the retreat to Dunkirk and Briony, striving to atone for her mistake and working as a probationary nurse in a Blitz-racked London. In a coda, set in 1999, Briony, now an old woman and a successful writer, looks back at her younger self, cleverly overturns our expectations and invites us to re-examine the 'atonement' she has presented to us.

McEwan's other books include First Love, Last Rites *and* In Between the Sheets *(short stories),* The Child in Time, The Innocent, Saturday *and* On Chesil Beach *(all novels) and the screenplay* The Imitation Game *(a psychological thriller about the code-breakers in Bletchley just after the Second World War).* The Daydreamer is a children's/adult's fantasy about a middle-aged MP catapulted back in time to his 1950s, 'Just William'-style childhood.

😴Read on

◆ *Saturday* (a compelling portrait of a successful neurosurgeon and one day in his life when the comforts of middle class contentment seem under threat).

◘ ≫ Barbara Vine (see ≫ Ruth Rendell), *A Fatal Inversion*; David Cook, *Crying Out Loud*; ≫ Beryl Bainbridge, *A Quiet Life*; ≫ Graham Swift, *The Light of Day*; ≫ Martin Amis, *London Fields*; ≫ Jonathan Franzen, *The Corrections*.

McGRATH, Patrick (born 1950)
British novelist

The word most frequently associated with the fiction of Patrick McGrath is 'grotesque'. Indeed one of his earlier novels, in which a cerebrally damaged lord of the manor watches in mute, enraged impotence as his new butler assumes control of his wife and home, is actually called *The Grotesque*. As a child, McGrath lived near Broadmoor Mental Hospital where his father was the medical superintendent for many years, an autobiographical fact that is often cited as the ultimate source of his grim and gothic sensibility. Certainly one of his best novels, *Asylum* (see below), the story of a forensic psychiatrist at a well-known psychiatric institution, was directly influenced by his father's experiences. Two more novels followed: *Spider* and *Dr Haggard's Disease*, a tale of sexual obsession (a recurring theme in McGrath's work), set in the medical profession in a superbly evoked 1930s England, just before the outbreak of war. *Martha Peake* is historical fiction set in eighteenth-century London and America. *Port Mungo* the story of a turbulent relationship between two artists, and *Trauma* records the disintegration of a New York psychiatrist as he faces demons from his past.

ASYLUM (1997)

Asylum once again dwells on sexual obsession, this time between the wife of a psychiatrist and one of her husband's patients. A beautiful and intelligent woman, Stella Raphael forms a destructive relationship with Edgar Stark, a mentally ill patient under the care of her husband Max; this is told by Peter Cleave, another psychiatrist, who knows the Raphaels well. McGrath is fond of using unreliable narrators, however, and Cleave, with his tale of Stella's terrible compulsion to love the decidedly dangerous Stark, is no exception.

Read on

♦ *Martha Peake* (unlike much of McGrath's work but just as memorable).
◘ ›› Ian McEwan, *The Cement Garden*; Patrick McCabe, *The Dead School*; Bradford Morrow, *Giovanni's Gift*.

McINERNEY, Jay (born 1955)
US novelist

Like a latter-day version of his hero ›› F. Scott Fitzgerald, McInerney exploded on to the American literary scene with his first novel, *Bright Lights, Big City* (1984), a slick, hilarious, semi-autobiographical tale of life in the Big Apple. The book's nameless narrator is fuelled by 'Bolivian marching powder', married to a beautiful model and just about holding down a cool job. Naturally, everything falls apart and McInerney chronicles the social and personal meltdown with detached wit and epigrammatic prose. The novel's success launched a 'bratpack' of similarly hip and cynical young novelists, including ›› Bret Easton Ellis, Tama Janowitz and Madison Smartt Bell. What distinguishes McInerney from his contemporaries is a solid gold wit that goes well beyond hip phrasemaking. Most of his other books have dealt with similar characters – Manhattanites in high jinks – and those that have attempted to break the mould have not been among his most successful. (*Ransom* is set around a group of expatriate young Americans in Japan and on the backpack trail around India and Nepal, and McInerney, like his characters, seems far from home.) *Story of My Life* returns to New York and the often very funny sex- and drug-filled social lives of another bunch of gilded youth – this time, women.

McInerney's other books include The Last of the Savages, Model Behaviour, The Good Life *(a kind of sequel to* Brightness Falls*),* How It Ended *(a collection of shorter fiction) and* Bacchus and Me *and* A Hedonist in the Cellar *(two collections of writings on wine).*

Read on

♦ *Brightness Falls* (an amusing and mostly effective satire on both the publishing world and the shark pool of high finance, low cunning and hostile takeover bids that is Wall Street).

◘ ➤➤ Bret Easton Ellis, *The Rules of Attraction*; ➤➤ F. Scott Fitzgerald, *The Great Gatsby*; Tama Janowitz, *Slaves of New York*; Ted Heller, *Slab Rat* (blistering satire on glitzy New York magazine world by Joseph Heller's son); David Handler, *The Man Who Would Be F. Scott Fitzgerald* (an amusing crime novel set in the New York literary scene which namechecks McInerney and the rest of the 'bratpack').

READ ON A THEME

MADNESS

➤➤ Margaret Forster, *The Bride of Lowther Fell*
Janet Frame, *Faces in the Water*
Janice Galloway, *The Trick is to Keep Breathing*
Charlotte Perkins Gilman, *The Yellow Wallpaper*
Lesley Glaister, *The Private Parts of Women*
➤➤ Susan Hill, *The Bird of Night*
Ken Kesey, *One Flew Over the Cuckoo's Nest*
Sylvia Plath, *The Bell Jar*
➤➤ Jean Rhys, *Good Morning, Midnight*
➤➤ Evelyn Waugh, *The Ordeal of Gilbert Pinfold*

See also: Depression and Psychiatry

MAHFOUZ, Naguib (1911–2006)
Egyptian novelist

Modern Arabic literature is little known in the West, and the loss is ours. Mahfouz was a Nobel prize-winning novelist, known worldwide for his *Cairo Trilogy* (1956–57). This is a panorama of life in the city during the first half of the twentieth century, and includes not only a family saga to rival ➤➤ Singer's *The Family Moskat* or ➤➤ Naipaul's *A House for Mr Biswas*, but also atmospheric studies of slum life, political satire and an absorbing description of a society trying to struggle free from centuries of religious and social stagnation into the modern, rational, democratic age. Mahfouz's style is leisurely, but the trilogy's span is enormous and repays time taken to get into it. The individual volumes are *Palace Walk, Palace of Desire* and *Sugar Street.*

Mahfouz's other novels include The Beginning and the End, Midaq Alley, Children of the Alley, The Thief and the Dogs, The Harafish, Karnak Cafe *and* Akhenaten, Dweller in Truth.

ᔥRead on
◆ *Akhenaten, Dweller in Truth* (Mahfouz wrote a number of novels set in Ancient Egypt and this fictional portrait of the heretical pharaoh of the eighteenth dynasty is one of the best of them).
◘ Ahdaf Soueif, *The Map of Love*; Nawal el Sadaawi, *God Dies by the Nile*; Robert Solé, *Birds of Passage.*

MAILER, Norman (1923–2007)
US writer

As well as novels, Mailer published both non-fiction (such as *Oswald's Tale*, an epic search for the truth behind Lee Harvey Oswald and the Kennedy assassination) and 'faction', a blend of real events and fiction (for example, *The Executioner's Song*, an examination of the character and crimes of the murderer Gary Gilmore). Most of his novels are set in the present day, and deal with a single theme: maleness. He regarded violence and competitiveness as essential components of masculinity, related to sexual potency – and claims, further, that capitalist society will only succeed if it models itself on the aggressive, cocky male. The world being what it is, Mailer was often forced – like ❯❯ Hemingway before him – to describe the failure of these macho fantasies, and because so many of his books are about the failure of the American Dream, despair gives his writing its stinging and continuing relevance. *The Naked and the Dead* (1948) is about the brutalization of a group of bewildered young airmen in the Second World War. In *Why Are We in Vietnam?* (1967), a savage Hemingway parody, a man takes his son on a bear-hunt as an eighteenth-birthday celebration, and this quintessential American manhood ritual is linked, in a devastating final paragraph, with the mindless, gung-ho crowing of the gook-slaughtering US army in Vietnam, into which the boy will be drafted now that he is adult. *An American Dream*, an equally pungent satire, shows a man at the end of his tether who commits murder and then tries to cudgel from his increasingly insane mind the reason why his country should have conditioned him to kill, why someone else's violent death should be the outcome of the American Dream.

A good sampler of Mailer's work is Advertisements for Myself, *an anthology of his early writings with a fascinating autobiographical commentary. His other novels include* Barbary Shore, The Deer Park, Ancient Evenings, *a dazzling and idiosyncratic reconstruction of Pharaonic Egypt, the thriller* Tough Guys Don't Dance, *the blockbusting* Harlot's Ghost, *an epic about the CIA,* The Gospel According to the Son, *a curiously mild take on the New Testament and* The Castle in the Forest, *published in the year he died, in which a demonic narrator tells the story of Adolf Hitler's family and upbringing.* The Spooky Art *is a collection of essays on writing and being a writer.*

☜Read on

◘ to Mailer's contemporary fiction: ❯❯ Ernest Hemingway, *For Whom the Bell Tolls*; ❯❯ Don DeLillo, *Underworld*; Henri de Montherlant, *The Bullfighters*; Robert Stone, *Dog Soldiers*; William Styron, *The Long March*.
◘ to *Ancient Evenings*: L.P. Myers, *The Near and the Far*; ❯❯ Thomas Mann, *Joseph and His Brothers*.
◘ to *The Executioner's Song*: Truman Capote, *In Cold Blood*.

MALOUF, David (born 1934)
Australian novelist and poet

Malouf has written novels set in a variety of historical and geographic settings (*An Imaginary Life*, for example, describes the exile of the Roman poet Ovid) but his most successful fiction explores, in prose of a rich and poetic range, the history of his native Australia. *Remembering Babylon* is set in Queensland in the nineteenth century and tells the story of Gemmy, who suddenly appears out of the bush at the edge of a small white settlement. Gemmy is himself white but, after a shipwreck, he has spent sixteen years living with the Aborigines. All the white characters in the novel are alternately fascinated and appalled by Gemmy's ambiguous status, the position he holds poised between two, for them mutually exclusive, categories, white and black. Gemmy may be white but his years with the Aborigines have marked him. He hardly remembers any English and his sense of self and the natural world belong to his adopted people. As the novel progresses and Gemmy moves towards the realization that, to save himself, he must return once more to the bush, one can only admire the skill and subtlety with which Malouf unfolds his story. *The Conversations at Curlow Creek* is also set in the nineteenth century. The date is 1827 and the novel takes the shape of the night-long conversation between Carney, an Irish bushranger who is to be hanged in the morning, and Adair, the police officer who is overseeing the hanging. As they talk the narrative moves back and forth in time through their memories as the forces that have shaped them both become clearer and connections are established between the criminal and the man deputed to punish him.

David Malouf's other novels include Johnno, Fly Away, Peter, Child's Play, Harland's Half Acre *and* The Great World. Dream Stuff *and* Every Move You Make *are volumes of short stories;* 12 Edmonstone Street *an idiosyncratic autobiography. Malouf has also published volumes of his poetry.*

🕮 Read on

◘ to *An Imaginary Life*: Christoph Ransmayr, *The Last World*.
◘ to the novels set in Australia's past: ›› Thomas Keneally, *The Chant of Jimmie Blacksmith*; ›› Patrick White, *Voss*; ›› Peter Carey, *The True History of the Kelly Gang*.

MANKELL, Henning (born 1948)
Swedish novelist and dramatist

Viewed from one perspective, Henning Mankell's status as a bestselling crime novelist is rather surprising. His books present a bleak view of his native Sweden as a country where welfare-state idealism has been destroyed. Immigrants are viewed with suspicion and even hatred; families are dislocated and dysfunctional; the values of tolerance and social inclusiveness are under permanent threat. Mankell paints a raw picture of modern life. Viewed from another perspective, his success is not so surprising. Mankell's chief protagonist, Inspector Kurt Wallander, is one of the most subtly realized figures in contemporary crime fiction. Struggling to maintain his personal and professional integrity in difficult circumstances, Wallander is a sympathetic and appealing character around whom Mankell builds his complex narratives of crime and injustice.

SIDETRACKED (1999)

A teenage girl commits suicide by burning herself to death. A serial killer with a taste for gruesome violence and an urge to scalp his victims is on the loose. Inspector Kurt Wallander, who has been a horrified witness to the girl's self-immolation, looks for a reason for her despair while also heading the police search for the killer. Like Mankell's other Wallander novels, this is not a conventional mystery story. Readers know the identity of the killer well before the book's conclusion. The emphasis is not on a puzzle that needs to be worked out but on character and on the contradictions and corruption of the Swedish society in which Wallander lives.

The other Kurt Wallander novels which have been translated into English are Faceless Killers, The Dogs of Riga, The White Lioness, The Man Who Smiled, The Fifth Woman, One Step Behind, Firewall *and* The Pyramid *(longish short stories about Wallander's early years as a cop). Before the Frost is the first novel in what Mankell intends to be a series of books featuring Wallander's daughter Linda, a recent graduate from police academy. Some of Mankell's non-Wallander novels, including* The Return of the Dancing Master, Kennedy's Brain *and* Chronicler of the Winds *have also appeared in English translations.*

📖 Read on

◘ Kerstin Ekman, *Blackwater*; Karin Fossum, *When the Devil Holds the Candle*; Arnaldur Indridason, *Jar City*; Pernille Rygg, *The Butterfly Effect*; Stieg Larsson, *The Girl with the Dragon Tattoo*.

MANN, Thomas (1875–1955)
German novelist and non-fiction writer

Although Mann was not a political writer, the themes of his work reflect northern European politics of the last one hundred years. His first great novel, *Buddenbrooks* (1901), shows the decline of a powerful German industrial family over three decades – and although it is superficially a Forsyte-like family saga, its strength comes from the persistent impression that the Buddenbrooks are characteristic of the decadent 'old Germany' as a whole. In *Joseph and His Brothers* (1933–43), based on the Bible and written under the shadow of Nazism, Joseph, the figure symbolizing progress, is a plausible rogue, a Hitler-figure, and his brothers, symbolizing barbarism, are as gullible as they are honest. The composer-hero of *Doctor Faustus* can unlock his creativity only by entering ever deeper into the morass of his own mind, and by accepting that to be 'ordinary' is to opt not for cultural calm but for chaos. The con-man central character of *The Confessions of Felix Krull, Confidence Man*, Mann's only comic novel, preys on the expectations of those who still believe in the old rules of religion, society and politics.

THE MAGIC MOUNTAIN (DER ZAUBERBERG) (1924)

Castorp, a rich, unimaginative young man, spends seven years in a Swiss tuber-culosis sanatorium. The sanatorium is full of endlessly talkative intellectuals, who educate Castorp in music, philosophy, art and literature. The book shows him growing in both knowledge and moral stature, until at last he is cured both of tuberculosis and of the greater disease (in Mann's eyes) of ignorant complacency. As the novel ends, however, he strides out to fight in the First World War – and Mann invites us, in the light of hindsight, to ponder his probable fate and that of the European culture he has so laboriously acquired.

Mann's shorter works include Mario the Magician *(about demonic possession),* Death in Venice *(about a writer galvanized by longing for a beautiful boy),* Lotte in Weimar *(a historical novel about the young* ≫ *Goethe), and* The Holy Sinner *(a beautiful – and poker-faced, despite the ridiculousness of its events – retelling of a medieval religious legend involving incest, communion with angels and magical transformations).*

⮒Read on

◆ *Buddenbrooks*; *The Confessions of Felix Krull, Confidence Man*.
◘ to *The Magic Mountain*: ≫ Johann Wolfgang von Goethe, *The Apprenticeship of Wilhelm Meister*; Robert Musil, *The Man Without Qualities*.
◘ to *Buddenbrooks*: ≫ I.B. Singer, *The Family Moskat*; ≫ Honoré de Balzac, *Cousin Bette*.
◘ to *Joseph and His Brothers*: ≫ Gustave Flaubert, *Salammbô*.

MANNING, Olivia (1908–80)
British novelist

Manning is best known for the six-novel *Fortunes of War* sequence: *The Balkan Trilogy* (1960–65) and *The Levant Trilogy* (1977–80). The central characters, Guy and Harriet Pringle, are English expatriates during the early years of the Second World War. They settle in Bucharest, where Guy teaches English; then, as the Axis powers advance, they move to Athens and from there to Cairo, where they 'hole up' during the desert campaign of 1942. Like the rest of Manning's characters, English, Middle Eastern or European, the Pringles dwell on the fringes, not at the centre, of great events; their lives are bounded by bread shortages, electricity cuts and squabbles over status. The civilization which bred them is collapsing, and they are themselves symbols of its decadence: they are effete and powerless, able only to run before events. None the less, Harriet's character does contain the seeds of change. When she marries Guy she is an unawakened personality, a genteel 1930s English rose. Events draw from her emotional and intellectual strength she didn't know she possessed – and the effects are to alienate the rest of the stuffy British community and to put stress on her marriage to the honourable but unimaginative Guy. At first sight Manning seems to be offering no more than a series of artless anecdotes about the muddle and horror of life in exotic cities engulfed by war. It is not until the mosaic is complete that her underlying scheme becomes apparent: the description of a whole culture in a state of unwished-for, panic-stricken change.

The novels in The Balkan Trilogy *are* The Great Fortune, The Spoilt City *and* Friends and Heroes; *those in* The Levant Trilogy *are* The Danger Tree, The Battle Lost and Won *and* The Sum of Things. *Manning's other novels include* School for Love, The Doves of Venus *and* The Rain Forest. Growing Up *and* A Romantic Hero *are collections of short stories.*

📖Read on
◘ ›› Elizabeth Bowen, *The Heat of the Day*; Jennifer Johnston, *The Captains and the Kings*; Isabel Colegate, *The Shooting Party*; ›› Evelyn Waugh, *Sword of Honour* trilogy (*Men at Arms, Officers and Gentlemen* and *Unconditional Surrender*).

MANSFIELD, Katherine (1888–1923)
New Zealand short story writer

Mansfield went to London at fourteen, and spent the rest of her life in Europe. When she wrote of New Zealand it was either with childhood nostalgia (for example in 'Prelude' and 'At the Bay') or with distaste for the lives its adults led in the outback ('Ole Underwood', 'The Woman at the Store') or in dingily genteel suburbs ('Her First Ball', 'How Pearl Button was Kidnapped'). She admired ›› Chekhov's stories, and sought to write the same kind of innocent-seeming anecdotes distilling single moments of human folly or aspiration. Her characters are often shallow, silly and desperate people: an unemployable film extra ('Pictures'), a snobbish mother and her unmarried daughters ('The Garden-Party'), a hen-pecked singing teacher ('Mr Reginald Peacock's Day'), expatriates on the continent ('The Man Without a Temperament', 'Je ne parle pas français'). She polished and refined her prose, often spending months on a single story – and the feeling of craftsmanship in her work, of slightly self-conscious artistry, greatly enhances the impression she seeks to give, that tragedies are not diminished because the lives they affect are small.

Mansfield's story collections are In a German Pension, Bliss, The Garden-Party and Other Stories, The Dove's Nest *and* Something Childish. *Her* Journals *give fascinating glimpses both of her character and of the events and conversations which she drew on in her work. Her* Letters *have also been published in several volumes.*

⬚Read on
◘ ›› Anton Chekhov, *The Lady With the Lap-Dog and Other Stories*; John Cheever, *Collected Stories*; Jean Stafford, *Collected Stories*; V.S. Pritchett, *Collected Stories*.

MANTEL, Hilary (born 1952)
British writer

Mantel is a varied writer. Her earlier novels, with the exception of *Eight Months on Ghazzah Street*, an account of women's lives in Saudi Arabia, are surrealist black farces. Her characters are obsessive, pathetic people trapped in situations which drive them over the edge of sanity and give them crazy, terrifying strength. What

READ ON A THEME: MANY GENERATIONS

they do is grotesque and awful but we pity them. In *Vacant Possession* Muriel Axon, whose intelligence seems to have been stunned by the terrible events of her childhood and adolescence, is released from a mental hospital. With devastating logic she sets to work to 'haunt' the places and people she remembers. More recently Mantel has turned to historical fiction, either in the relatively conventional form of *A Place of Greater Safety*, a story of the leaders of the French Revolution, or in the shape of oblique, suggestive narratives such as *The Giant O'Brien*. *Giving Up the Ghost* is an autobiographical mélange of fiction and non-fiction, in which short stories drawn from her own childhood experience are followed by more overtly factual memories. *Beyond Black* is a darkly comic and atmospheric tale of a medium haunted by visions of the past as well as the future.

⬦Read on

◆ *Fludd* (a mysterious stranger transforms the lives of Roman Catholics in a small northern town); *Wolf Hall* (Mantel's most recent novel is another large-scale historical narrative, set in the court of Henry VIII and focusing on the rise to power of Thomas Cromwell).

◻ ≫ Bernice Rubens, *Our Father*; ≫ Muriel Spark, *The Abbess of Crewe*; ≫ Beryl Bainbridge, *Master Georgie*; ≫ Kate Atkinson, *Emotionally Weird*; Alice Thomas Ellis, *The 27th Kingdom*.

READ ON A THEME

MANY GENERATIONS
≫ Isabel Allende, *The House of the Spirits*
≫ Kate Atkinson, *Behind the Scenes at the Museum*
Elizabeth Jane Howard, *The Light Years*
≫ Thomas Mann, *Buddenbrooks*
≫ Gabriel García Márquez, *One Hundred Years of Solitude*
Tim Pears, *In a Land of Plenty*
Rosamunde Pilcher, *The Shell Seekers*
≫ I.B. Singer, *The Family Moskat*

See also: Eccentric Families

MÁRQUEZ, Gabriel García (born 1928)

Colombian novelist and short story writer

In Márquez's invented South American town of Macondo, a place isolated from the outside world, magic realism rules: there is no distinction between magic and reality. At one level life is perfectly ordinary: people are born, grow up, work, cook, feud and gossip. But there is a second, irrational and surrealist plane to ordinary existence. The Macondans (unless they murder each other for reasons of politics, sex or family honour) live for 100, 150, 200 years. Although they are as innocent of 'real' knowledge as children – they think ice miraculous and they are amazed to hear that the world is round – they know the secrets of alchemy, converse with ghosts, remember Cortez or Drake as 'uncles'. Macondo is a rough-and-tumble Eden, a paradise where instinct rules and nothing is impossible – and Márquez spends his time either describing its enchantment or detailing the savage results when people from the outside world (jackbooted generals, con-men, lawyers, bishops) break through to 'civilize' it. For Márquez, Macondo stands for the whole of South America, and his stories are barbed political allegories. But he seldom lets this overwhelm the books. Instead of hectoring, he opens his eyes wide, puts his tongue in his cheek and tells us wonders.

ONE HUNDRED YEARS OF SOLITUDE (1967)

As Colonel Aureliano Buendía faces the firing squad, the whole history of his family flashes before his eyes. They begin as poor peasants in a one-roomed hut on the edge of a swamp. They proliferate like tendrils on a vine: Aureliano himself has seventeen sons, all called Aureliano. The family members absorb knowledge, people and property until they and Macondo seem indissoluble. Finally, led by Aureliano senior, they defend the old, innocent values against invasion by a government which wants to impose the same laws in Macondo as everywhere else, and the dynasty disappears from reality, living on only in fantasy, as a memory of how human beings were before the whole world changed.

Márquez's other novels are No One Writes to the Colonel, In Evil Hour, Chronicle of a Death Foretold, The Autumn of the Patriarch *(the stream-of-consciousness monologue of a dying dictator),* Love in the Time of Cholera *(a mesmeric love story spanning sixty years),* The General in His Labyrinth *(about the last days of Simón Bolívar),* Of Love and Other Demons *(about an eighteenth-century priest and the 'mad' girl he falls in love with) and* Memories of My Melancholy Whores. *His short story collections include* Leaf-storm and Other Stories, Strange Pilgrims *and* Innocent Erendira and Other Stories. *His non-fiction includes* The Fragrance of Guavas *(conversations with a fellow Colombian novelist),* News of a Kidnapping *(about the Colombian drugs wars and their effects on ordinary Colombians),* The Story of a Shipwrecked Sailor *and* Living to Tell the Tale, *the first of three planned volumes of autobiography.*

📖Read on

◆ *Love in the Time of Cholera*.

◘ ≫ Salman Rushdie, *Shame*; Carlos Fuentes, *Terra Nostra*; ≫ Mario Vargas Llosa, *The Storyteller*; Machado de Assis, *Epitaph of a Small Winner* (nineteenth-century Brazilian novel which is the grandfather of all Latin American magic realism).

MARSDEN, Philip (born 1961)
British travel writer and novelist

'If there is any wider purpose to our life,' Philip Marsden has written, 'it is to understand the world, to seek out its diversity, to celebrate its heroes and its wonders – in short, to witness it.' His travel books are the testaments to this credo. *The Crossing Place* records his journey into the Caucasus in search of the truth about the past and present of the Armenian people. *The Chains of Heaven* and an earlier book, *A Far Country*, record his fascination with the remote landscapes and resilient peoples of Ethiopia. In *The Spirit-Wrestlers* Marsden travelled well off the beaten path in Russia, encountering strange seekers after spiritual enlightenment, survivors of gulag imprisonment and a host of individuals whose lives seemed to be a tribute to an older Russia, one almost untouched by the upheavals and traumas of the Soviet era. Marsden is also a novelist. *The Main Cages*, set in a small fishing village in Cornwall in the 1930s, charts the tensions between an old way of life, dictated by the moods of the sea, and a new future promised by tourists and the invasion of the village by bohemian artists attracted by its apparent picturesqueness.

📖Read on

◆ *The Bronski House* (Marsden's journey with an ageing Polish poet to the village where she grew up is the starting point for a poignant reconstruction of a vanished world); *The Barefoot Emperor* (Marsden's most recent book is a biography of Theodore II, ninettenth-century emperor of Ethiopia and his tragic confrontation with the might of the British Empire).

◻ ❯❯ Bruce Chatwin, *In Patagonia*; Nicholas Griffin, *Caucasus*; ❯❯ Colin Thubron, *Among the Russians*.

MARSH, Ngaio (1899–1982)
New Zealand novelist

Few writers used 'classic' detective-story ingredients as magnificently as Marsh. Her murder methods are ingenious and unexpected. Her locations are fascinating: backstage (and onstage) at theatres; during a village-hall concert; in the shearing shed of a sheep farm; at a top-level diplomatic reception. Her characters are exotic and her detection is scrupulously fair, with every clue appearing to the reader at the same time as to Roderick Alleyn, Marsh's urbane and hawk-eyed sleuth. Above all, her books move at a furious pace, fuelled by her effervescent glee at the follies of humankind. Typical examples are *Artists in Crime*, in which a life-model meets an unfortunate end, *Enter a Murderer* (about a blackmailing actor done to death on stage) and *A Man Lay Dead*, about a weekend house party in which a murder game becomes all too real.

Marsh continued to publish until the early 1970s and her other books include Hand in Glove, Died in the Wool, Clutch of Constables, Overture to Death, Vintage Murder, Spinsters in Jeopardy, Surfeit of Lampreys, Black as He's Painted *and* Death in Ecstasy. Black Beech and Honeydew *is an autobiography, especially interesting on her childhood and her fascination with theatre.*

≋Read on
◆ *Overture to Death, Surfeit of Lampreys*.
◻ ❯❯ Margery Allingham, *The Beckoning Lady*; Caroline Graham, *The Killings at Badger's Drift*; Martha Grimes, *The Man With a Load of Mischief*; ❯❯ Dorothy L. Sayers, *The Unpleasantness at the Bellona Club*.

MATTHIESSEN, Peter (born 1927)
US naturalist and novelist

Novelist, travel writer, co-founder of the literary magazine *Paris Review* and Zen Buddhist priest, Peter Matthiessen is a man of diverse interests and gifts but all his writings, whether fiction or non-fiction, are animated by his concern for the natural world and man's relationship to it. *The Tree Where Man Was Born* is an account of his journeys in East Africa and his responses to the landscape and wildlife of the region and to sites such as Olduvai Gorge in Tanzania, home to some of our earliest ancestors. *The Snow Leopard* documents a journey Matthiessen made in Nepal in search of the elusive and rare creature which gives the book its title. The irony is that he never does see a snow leopard but the travels in quest of it come to have their own value and the book ends up recording a spiritual journey almost as much as a physical one. Matthiessen's finest fictional achievement comes in the shape of three novels which form a trilogy: *Killing Mr Watson*, *Lost Man's River* and *Bone by Bone*. Loosely based on real-life events in Florida a century ago, the books reconstruct the life, murder and legacy of a brutal, larger-than-life entrepreneur, using multiple narratives to build up a portrait of a complex man and the society in which he exercised power before allowing him, in the last volume, a voice of his own to tell his story. Matthiessen has recently revisited the story of Watson and has produced what he calls a 'new rendering' of it in *Shadow Country*, reworking the three novels into one long narrative.

Peter Matthiessen's other novels include At Play in the Fields of the Lord *and* Far Tortuga. *His other non-fiction includes* Indian Country, Under the Mountain Wall, Blue Meridian *(an account of a shark hunt which is said to have inspired Peter Benchley to write* Jaws*)*, In the Spirit of Crazy Horse, African Silences *and* The Birds of Heaven. Nine-Headed Dragon River *is a book of excerpts from journals detailing his increasing involvement with Zen Buddhist practices.*

Read on
◻ to the non-fiction: Dee Brown, *Bury My Heart at Wounded Knee*; Annie Dillard, *Pilgrim at Tinker Creek*; Elspeth Huxley, *The Flame Trees of Thika*; ›› Barry Lopez, *Arctic Dreams*; Henry David Thoreau, *Walden*.
◻ to the fiction: ›› Joseph Conrad, *Lord Jim*.

MAUGHAM, W. (William) Somerset (1874–1965)

British writer of novels, short stories and plays

A tireless traveller (especially in the Far East), Maugham wrote hundreds of short stories based on anecdotes he heard or scenes he observed en route. Many of them were later filmed: 'Rain', for example (about a missionary on a cruise-liner in Samoa struggling to reform a prostitute, and losing his own soul in the process), was made half a dozen times. Maugham's novels used true experience in a similar way, shaping it and drawing out its meaning but keeping close to real events. *Liza of Lambeth* is about a London slum girl tormented by her neighbours for conceiving a bastard child. *Of Human Bondage* is the story of an orphan, bullied at school because he has a club foot, who struggles to find happiness as an adult, is ravaged by love for a worthless woman, and settles at last to become a country doctor. The stockbroker hero of *The Moon and Sixpence* gives up career, wife and family to become a painter in the South Seas, as Gauguin did. *Cakes and Ale* is an acid satire about the 1930s London literary world; Maugham avoided libel suits only by claiming that every writer it pilloried was just another aspect of himself.

Maugham's other novels include The Trembling of a Leaf, The Casuarina Tree, The Razor's Edge *and* Catalina. *His* Complete Short Stories *and* Collected Plays *(from 1907 to 1932 he wrote two dozen successful plays, mainly comedies) were published in the 1950s.* A Writer's Notebook *and* The Summing Up *give fascinating insights into the balance between his life and work.*

⧉Read on

◘ to *Liza of Lambeth*: Arthur Morrison, *A Child of the Jago*.

◘ to *Of Human Bondage*: C.P. Snow, *Strangers and Brothers*.

◘ to *The Moon and Sixpence*: Joyce Cary, *The Horse's Mouth*.

◘ to *Cakes and Ale*: Rose Macaulay, *Crewe Train*; ≫ J.B. Priestley, *The Image Men*.

◘ to the short stories: ≫ Guy de Maupassant, *Boule de Suif*; ≫ R.L. Stevenson, *Island Nights' Entertainment*; ≫ Rudyard Kipling, *Wee Willie Winkie*; ≫ Paul Theroux, *World's End*.

MAUPASSANT, Guy de (1850–93)

French writer

De Maupassant's stories – over three hundred, from two-page sketches to full-length novels – have a scalpel ability to cut through pretension, hope, emotion and pretence to the bones of human experience. His best-known work is the long short story *Boule de Suif* (1880). A group of people travelling across France in a stagecoach includes Boule de Suif, a prostitute. The rest of the passengers despise her, but she gradually wins them over by her friendliness and humanity. Then the coach is held up by an army officer, who demands sex from her to let it continue. The other passengers beg her to agree – and when the journey continues, they reject her once more. The plot belongs to late nineteenth-century 'realism', but the way de Maupassant tells it, unsparingly, simply and apparently without inserting any authorial point of view, makes the stóry and the characters unforgettable.

☙Read on

◘ The stories of ❯❯ Anton Chekhov, ❯❯ Gustave Flaubert and V.S. Pritchett.

MELVILLE, Herman (1819–91)

US novelist

As a teenager, Melville educated himself by reading the Bible, Shakespeare, Milton and Sir Thomas Browne. He served at sea until he was twenty three, and later worked as a customs officer. His books take their style from the grand literature he read, and their stories from his own seafaring adventures or from travellers' tales. Many of his novels are long, and read at times as if Genesis or Job had been revised to include whaling, smuggling, shipwreck and naval war. But their epic thought and style easily match the magnificence of the books which influenced him.

MOBY DICK (1851)

Moby Dick is a huge sperm whale, and the novel tells of Captain Ahab's obsessive attempts to hunt it down and kill it. Melville's whaling lore is extensive, his action scenes are breathtaking, and he gives an unforgettable picture of Ahab: lonely, driven, daunting as an Old Testament patriarch, a fitting adversary for the monster he has vowed to kill.

Melville's other novels include Typee *and* Omoo *(based on his own experiences after being shipwrecked among cannibals in Polynesia),* Redburn: His First Voyage, White-jacket, or The World in a Man-o'-War, *the bitter satire* The Confidence Man *and* Billy Budd, *the story of an inarticulate young sailor who kills a sadistic petty officer. Two short works, of very different styles but both equally haunting, are* Bartleby, the Scrivener, *about a scrivener (copyist) who one day refuses to participate any longer in life, and* Benito Cereno, *a story centred on a mysterious slave ship.*

📖Read on

◘ ➤➤ Nathaniel Hawthorne, *The Scarlet Letter*; ➤➤ Victor Hugo, *Toilers of the Sea*; ➤➤ Joseph Conrad, *The Nigger of the Narcissus*.
◘ novels about dark obsessions of other kinds: ➤➤ Thomas Mann, *Doctor Faustus*; ➤➤ Norman Mailer, *An American Dream*; ➤➤ John Fowles, *The Collector*.

READ ON A THEME

THE MIDDLE AGES
➤➤ Italo Calvino, *Our Ancestors*
➤➤ Bernard Cornwell, *Harlequin*
➤➤ Umberto Eco, *The Name of the Rose*
    Ken Follett, *The Pillars of the Earth*
    John Fuller, *Flying to Nowhere*
➤➤ William Golding, *The Spire*
➤➤ Victor Hugo, *The Hunchback of Notre Dame*
➤➤ Thomas Mann, *The Holy Sinner*
    Rosalind Miles, *Guinevere: Queen of the Summer Country* (first of an Arthurian trilogy)
    Ellis Peters, *A Morbid Taste for Bones*
➤➤ Barry Unsworth, *Morality Play*
    Helen Waddell, *Peter Abelard*

See also: Other Peoples, Other Times; Renaissance Europe

MIÉVILLE, China (born 1972)
British novelist

Over the last decade, China Miéville has emerged as the leading writer of what has been termed the 'New Weird', a sub-genre of speculative fiction whose exponents turn their backs on the pastoral romanticism of much fantasy literature and instead create gritty urban settings for their stories. In New Crobuzon, the sprawling city where many of his stories take place, the streets are shared by humans and mutants and bizarrely alien life-forms. Khepri, human in body but equipped with the heads of insects, rub shoulders with cactus-people, the froglike, water-loving Vodyanoi, and Remades, men and women who have had weird prostheses, both organic and mechanical, attached to their bodies. And yet, unlike so many fantasy worlds, the one Miéville creates is, within its own terms, an entirely convincing one

PERDIDO STREET STATION (2000)
Into New Crobuzon comes Yagharek, one of a desert race of intelligent bird-men known as the garuda, who has had his wings sawn off as a punishment. He hates the city but he is in search of someone who can return the gift of flight to him and he approaches a renegade scientist named Isaac Dan der Grimnebulin. When Isaac undertakes research into flying creatures, he inadvertently sets in motion a terrible train of events. Amidst the menagerie he gathers in his laboratory is one curious and seemingly harmless caterpillar which eventually metamorphoses into a terrifying predator, intent on sucking the dreams and the consciousnesses from all of New Crobuzon's sentient citizens. Only Isaac and Yagharek and a motley crew of outcasts stands between the city and total devastation.

Miéville's other novels are King Rat, The Scar, Iron Council, Un Lun Dun *and* The City and the City.

☜Read on
♦ *King Rat* (Miéville's debut novel is an urban fantasy which draws on the story of the Pied Piper).
◻ Susanna Clarke, *Jonathan Strange & Mr Norrell*; Stephen Hunt, *The Court of the Air*; ≫ Mervyn Peake, *The Gormenghast Trilogy*; Steph Swainston, *The Year of Our War*; Jeff VanderMeer, *City of Saints and Madmen*.

MILLER, Andrew (born 1960)
British novelist

Andrew Miller's first two novels were both set in the eighteenth century. The central character in *Ingenious Pain* is James Dyer, a surgeon born with a freakish inability to feel pain and love. While travelling to Russia to treat the Empress Catherine the Great, Dyer encounters a witch-woman with supernatural powers whose gift of a 'heart' introduces him to the difficult realities of human emotions and the world of feeling. Miller followed this strange and unsettling first novel with *Casanova*, in which the legendary seducer, exiled from his home city of Venice, arrives in London and embarks on a doomed and obsessive love affair with the flirtatious Marie Charpillon. Miller then moved seamlessly from the Age of Reason to the present day for his next two novels. In *Oxygen*, two sons gather at their mother's deathbed. One is a fading actor reduced to auditioning for porn movies, the other a literary translator working on a play by a famous Hungarian writer. Miller's novel moves between the lives of the two brothers and that of the playwright, still haunted by his experiences in the 1956 Hungarian uprising, as it explores the meaning of love, courage and redemption. *The Optimists* focuses on a burnt-out war photographer, traumatized by witnessing a massacre of women and children in central Africa, who is struggling to regain his faith in humanity and to confront the demons which haunt him. Miller's most recent novel, *One Morning Like a Bird*, is set in Tokyo in 1940, as the country trembles on the brink of commiting itself to war.

📚Read on

◘ to the historical novels: ›› Ross King, *Domino*; David Liss, *The Coffee Trader*; Patrick Süskind, *Perfume*.
◘ to *Oxygen* and *The Optimists*: Andrew O'Hagan, *Our Fathers*; Rachel Seiffert, *The Dark Room*.

MILTON, Giles (born 1966)
British historian

Giles Milton has written a number of bestselling books which illuminate odd corners in the history of travel and exploration. His first book, *The Riddle and the Knight*, recounting his journeys in search of the medieval traveller Sir John Mandeville, was a delightful rescue act performed on a little-known figure, and the works that have followed have strayed off the beaten historical path with similar success. *Nathaniel's Nutmeg* (see below) unearths a forgotten story of the beginnings of English imperial expansion. *Big Chief Elizabeth* provides a vivid portrait of the first colonists who left Elizabeth I's England to attempt a new life in America; *Samurai William* tells the remarkable story of William Adams, an English seaman shipwrecked on the coast of Japan in 1600 who rose to become right-hand man to the Shogun; *White Gold* is the extraordinary story of an eighteenth-century Cornish cabin boy who was captured by Barbary corsairs and sold to the Sultan of Morocco. His most recent book, *Paradise Lost*, moves forward into the twentieth century to tell the terrible story of the destruction of the city of Smyrna in 1922.

NATHANIEL'S NUTMEG (1999)

In 1616, an Englishman called Nathaniel Courthorpe took possession of the island of Run in the East Indies and, with a few fellow adventurers, held it against besieging Dutch forces who were intent on achieving a monopoly on the supply of nutmeg, a spice which fetched fabulous prices back in Europe. So desperate were the Dutch to control the spice islands of the East that, fifty years after Courthorpe's death, they agreed to surrender another island in the New World as long as the British gave up Run. The other island was Manhattan. *Nathaniel's Nutmeg* vividly reconstructs the story of Nathaniel Courthorpe and his effect on the larger history of the world.

🕮 Read on

◆ *White Gold*.

◘ Ben Macintyre, *Josiah the Great: The True Story of the Man Who Would Be King*; Dean King, *Skeletons on the Zahara*; Lee Miller, *Roanoke: Solving the Mystery of the Lost Colony*; ›› Charles Nicholl, *The Creature in the Map*; Nathaniel Philbrick, *In the Heart of the Sea*.

MISTRY, Rohinton (born 1952)

Indian novelist

Born in Bombay, Mistry emigrated to Canada as a young man and it was there that he began to publish short stories. His stories attracted attention and won prizes from the very beginning and the novels he has gone on to publish have also been highly acclaimed by the critics. Mistry's appeal is not difficult to understand. His characters are ordinary men and women, with whom the reader can easily empathize, but the stories of their pains and pleasures are set in an India conjured up with a Dickensian richness and complexity. For Western readers especially, his combination of the everyday and the exotic is a winning formula. In *Such a Long Journey*, the central character, Gustad Noble, is a bank clerk whose quiet family life is disrupted when a request for help from an old friend leads him into troubled waters. *A Fine Balance* follows the fortunes of four very different characters whose lives intersect when they all become boarders in a small Bombay apartment; in *Family Matters* an ageing and ailing widower, haunted by the memories of a lifetime, is forced into changes and family crises that threaten everything he values. Mistry's novels have all the virtues of the English three-decker novel of the Victorian age – a vast and varied cast of characters, a backdrop of social change and upheaval, and a powerful blend of the comic and the tragic – but these have been transferred to the India of Indira Gandhi's years in power. Mistry has also published *Tales From Firozsha Baag* (1992) which is a collection of his short stories.

🐸Read on

◻ Vikram Chandra, *Red Earth and Pouring Rain*; Gita Mehta, *A River Sutra*; ⟫ Vikram Seth, *A Suitable Boy*; Manil Suri, *The Death of Vishnu*; Thrity Umrigar, *Bombay Time*.

MITCHELL, David (born 1969)
British novelist

From the very outset of his career, David Mitchell showed a determination to stray away from the paths of traditional linear narrative. In his first novel, *Ghostwritten* (1999), characters hand on the narrative baton as stories blossom and multiply, moving out from Japan and Hong Kong to the rest of the world and finally back to Japan. Beginning with a member of a cult which has launched a gas attack on the Tokyo Underground and including a quantum physicist and a teenage jazz buff, Mitchell creates a cast of characters as weirdly varied and intriguing as the stories they have to tell. Reality and fantasy collide and interact in *number9dream*, Mitchell's second novel, the story of a young man who arrives in Tokyo to search for his father. As his quest for the truth takes him into the underworlds of the city, his dreams and nightmares loom ever larger on the page. Reminiscent of the best fiction of ⟫ Haruki Murakami, the book has a haunting power all its own. *Cloud Atlas* (see below) was equally original in the way it told its tales but Mitchell's fourth and newest novel, *Black Swan Green*, turns its back on much of the narrative experimentation and expansiveness of his earlier books and tells a much simpler story of an adolescent boy growing up in a sleepy village in Worcestershire in the 1980s.

CLOUD ATLAS (2004)

Six stories are dazzlingly intertwined in Mitchell's ambitious third novel. From an American voyager in the Pacific in the mid-nineteenth century to a genetically engineered fast food waitress in a dystopian future, the lives of Mitchell's characters are linked in a narrative chain that moves back and forth through the centuries to create a novel combining intellectual adventure with the delight of great storytelling.

☜Read on

◘ to Mitchell's first three novels: Andrew Crumey, *Mobius Dick*; ≫ Haruki Murakami, *The Wind-Up Bird Chronicle*; Rupert Thomson, *The Five Gates of Hell*.
◘ to *Black Swan Green*: ≫ Jonathan Coe, *The Rotters' Club*; Mick Jackson, *Five Boys*.

LITERARY TRIVIA 10:

FIVE MEMORABLE BOOKS THAT NEVER EXISTED
Sherlock Holmes, *Practical Handbook of Bee Culture*
The fruit of the great detective's retirement, this book is mentioned by ≫ Conan Doyle in the story 'His Last Bow'.

Abdul Alhazred, *The Necronomicon*
The horror and fantasy writer H.P. Lovecraft refers to this blasphemous and dangerous book, 'the ghastly soul symbol of the forbidden corpse-eating cult on inaccessible Leng in Central Asia', in a number of his stories.

Oolon Colluphid, *Where God Went Wrong*
In ≫ Douglas Adams's The Hitchhiker's Guide to the Galaxy series, Oolon Colluphid is the author of this philosophical work. Sequels include *Who Is This God Person Anyway?* and *Well That About Wraps It Up for God*.

Sir Harry Flashman, *Twixt Cossack and Cannon*
One of the volumes of memoirs published by the legendary Victorian coward, cad and involuntary hero, according to his biographer, ›› George MacDonald Fraser.

X. Trapnel, *Profiles in String*
The *magnum opus* of the doomed novelist Trapnel in Anthony Powell's *Books Do Furnish a Room*. The manuscript is lost when it is thrown into the Regent's Canal by Trapnel's lover, Pamela Widmerpool.

MITCHELL, Margaret (1900–49)
US novelist

Gone with the Wind, Mitchell's only book (published in 1936; filmed three years later with Clark Gable and Vivien Leigh) was aptly described in its day as 'the greatest love story ever told'. In Atlanta, Georgia, at the outbreak of the 1860s American Civil War, Scarlett O'Hara falls in love with Ashley Wilkes, the foppish son of a neighbouring plantation owner. But he marries someone else, and she is heartbroken. She pours her love into her family's beautiful house and plantation, Tara. But as the Civil War proceeds, the South loses, Atlanta is burned, and to keep Tara Scarlett is forced to marry other men, including the cynical, rakish Rhett Butler. All fails, Tara is plundered, the devastation of war mirrors the suffering in Scarlett's heart – and when she tells Rhett of her hopeless love for Ashley, Rhett leaves her (with the blunt, oft-quoted 'Frankly, my dear, I don't give a damn'). Now, too late, she realizes that he (Rhett) was the man she loved all the time.

📖Read on
◻ Alexandra Ripley, *Scarlett* (authorized sequel, published in 1991) ›› Boris Pasternak, *Doctor Zhivago*; ›› Daphne Du Maurier, *Rebecca*; ›› Colleen McCullough, *The Thorn Birds*; M.M. Kaye, *The Far Pavilions*.

MITFORD, Nancy (1904–73)
British novelist and biographer

Like her friend ›› Evelyn Waugh, Nancy Mitford wrote cruelly witty novels set among the Bright Young Things and upper class families of Britain between the wars. Her own family, with its many aristocratic eccentricities, provided her with much of the material she reworked in her fiction. The Radlett girls in *The Pursuit of Love* – whose adventures are observed with a mixture of alarm and admiration by the book's narrator, their less flamboyant cousin Fanny Logan – are clearly modelled on the author and her sisters. The book's plot is largely concerned with Linda Radlett and her romantic misfortunes (marrying a pompous banker, falling for a succession of unsuitable charmers) but its strength lies as much in the supporting cast, particularly the bizarre patriarch of the family, Fanny's Uncle Matthew, as in the central narrative. *Love in a Cold Climate* reintroduces many of the characters and settings from *The Pursuit of Love* but focuses more on Polly Hampton, a young and beautiful heiress whose choice of husband sows dissension in her family. Both books are characterized by set-pieces of farcical misunderstandings between characters, richly comic dialogue and a healthily cynical view of the capacity of love to heal all wounds.

Nancy Mitford's other novels include Highland Fling, Pigeon Pie, The Blessing *and* Don't Tell Alfred. *She was also a skilful biographer who wrote lives of Madame de Pompadour, Louis XIV of France and Frederick the Great.* Voltaire in Love *is a portrait of the eighteenth-century philosopher's relationship with the aristocratic and intellectual Emilie du Chatelet.*

📖 Read on
♦ *Don't Tell Alfred*
◘ Jonathan Guinness, *The House of Mitford*; Jessica Mitford, *Hons and Rebels* (which describes the odd upbringing of the Mitford sisters that so influenced Nancy's fiction); ›› Evelyn Waugh, *Vile Bodies*.

READ ON A THEME

MONEY

›› Martin Amis, *Money*
  Po Bronson, *Bombardiers*
  Linda Davies, *Into the Fire*
  John Galsworthy, *The Forsyte Saga*
›› Jay McInerney, *Brightness Falls*
  Christina Stead, *House of All Nations*
›› Tom Wolfe, *The Bonfire of the Vanities*

MOORCOCK, Michael (born 1939)

British novelist

In the 1960s Moorcock edited the science fiction magazine *New Worlds*, pioneering and encouraging New Wave writing, which attempted to give science fiction a new social and political relevance to the time. Moorcock's own New Wave work is at its peak in his Jerry Cornelius books (including *The English Assassin* and *The Final Programme*), which are less straightforward novels than firework displays of ideas, magical mystery tours round one man's overheated brain. In later books Moorcock returned to a more sober style, still crammed with ideas but much easier to read. Many of his novels offer alternative versions of the present (*Warlord of the Air*, for example, imagines a twentieth century where the First World War never happened and the old nineteenth-century empires, British, Austrian, Russian and German, are still jockeying for power). Others (*Gloriana*, *The Jewel in the Skull*) are satires about societies which are dark and decadent perversions of our own. All of Moorcock's work, however, is interlinked at some level, a reflection of 'the multiverse' he has imagined, the interconnected, parallel universes through which his characters travel. Jerry Cornelius, Elric of Melnibone (doomed albino prince of a dying race in some of Moorcock's best sword-and-sorcery titles), Corum, Hawkmoon, Von Bek and others are all avatars of the Eternal Champion, Moorcock's Hero with a Thousand Faces.

Many of Moorcock's novels are grouped in series: The Chronicles of the Black Sword, The High History of the Runestaff, The Chronicles of Castle Brass, The Books of Corum, The History of the Eternal Champion. Byzantium Endures, The Laughter of Carthage *and* Jerusalem Commands *are three epic novels which follow the scheming Colonel Pyat through the story, real and imagined, of the twentieth century.* Mother London *and* King of the City *are non-science fiction novels, dazzling recreations of London lives past and present.*

❦Read on

◆ *Behold the Man* (time traveller arrives in Judaea at the time of Christ), *The Dancers at the End of Time.*

◘ to *Mother London*: ❭❭ Iain Sinclair, *Downriver*; Maureen Duffy, *Capital.*

◘ to other New Wave SF writers: Brian Aldiss, *Galaxies Like Grains of Sand*; ❭❭ J.G. Ballard, *The Terminal Beach.*

MOORE, Brian (1921–99)
Irish/Canadian novelist

Moore's novels explore personal anguish and unease in a similar way to ❭❭ Graham Greene's, though his characters are quite different. He is particularly good at describing feelings of rootlessness and sexual longing in lonely women (*The Lonely Passion of Judith Hearne, The Doctor's Wife, The Temptation of Eileen Hughes*), and the torments of firm Roman Catholic believers in threatening situations (*Catholics, I Am Mary Dunne, Black Robe*).

THE COLOUR OF BLOOD (1987)
Cardinal Bem, head of the Church in an unnamed eastern European communist state, survives an assassination attempt only to be taken into 'protective custody'. He must escape, to make a vital speech at a forthcoming religious celebration – and the book concerns his attempts to shed his physical identity in order to evade police checks, while maintaining the blazing religious and political certainty by which he has always lived his life.

Moore's other novels include Cold Heaven, The Great Victorian Collection, The Feast of Lupercal, The Mangan Inheritance, An Answer from Limbo, No Other Life, Lies of Silence *and* The Statement. *His final novel,* The Magician's Wife, *set in nineteenth-century French colonial Africa, where an illusionist uses his talents to demonstrate the supposed superiority of European power, shows Moore's ability to root political and religious ideas in absorbing narrative.*

📖 Read on

◆ *Black Robe* (Jesuit missionaries in seventeenth-century Canada suffer for their faith when they come into contact with Indian tribes).

◘ to *The Colour of Blood*: ≫ Saul Bellow, *The Dean's December*; Morris West, *The Clowns of God*; ≫ Arturo Pérez-Reverte, *The Seville Communion*.

◘ to Moore's work in general: ≫ Graham Greene, *The Power and the Glory*; ≫ William Trevor, *Death in Summer*; Ronan Bennett, *The Catastrophist*.

MORRIS, Jan (born 1926)
British travel writer and historian

For the first forty six years of her life Jan Morris was James Morris and, under that name, published a much-acclaimed three-volume history of the British Raj (*Heaven's Command, Pax Britannica* and *Farewell the Trumpets* appeared between 1968 and 1978) and became a well-known journalist, famous for accompanying the Everest expedition of 1953. Always aware that he was a female within a male body, Morris eventually underwent sex-reassignment surgery. *Conundrum* (1974) describes the life-changing transformation that made her a woman. Morris has travelled as widely as anyone living but she has a particular affinity with Venice. *Venice* was her earliest and most searching exploration of the city. *The Venetian Empire* records a journey along the sea routes used by Venetian merchants when the city's maritime possessions dominated the eastern Mediterranean. Other books have provided her own idiosyncratic and enlightening perspectives on cities from Oxford and New York to Sydney and Hong Kong. She has also gathered together a number of collections of her travel essays, most of them originally published in newspapers and magazines. Titles include *Cities, Destinations* and *Locations. Pleasures of a Tangled Life* is a collection of autobiographical essays that explore the enthusiasms that have shaped her life.

Jan Morris's other books include Manhattan '45, Coast to Coast, Wales: Epic Views of a Small Country, Fisher's Face *(an odd work which is part biography of the naval giant Jacky Fisher and part account of Morris's obsession with him) and* Trieste and the Meaning of Nowhere. A Writer's World *is a collection of her travel pieces written over the last fifty years;* Hav *and* Last Letters from Hav *describe visits to an imaginary city as intriguing as any of the real ones Morris has celebrated in her other works.*

Read on
- *Trieste and the Meaning of Nowhere.*
- to the British Empire trilogy: Lawrence James, *The Rise and Fall of the British Empire*; Dennis Judd, *Empire.*
- to the Venetian books: Christopher Hibbert, *Venice: The Biography of a City*; John Julius Norwich, *A History of Venice.*
- to the other travel writing: ≫ Paul Theroux, *The Pillars of Hercules*; ≫ Colin Thubron, *The Lost Heart of Asia.*

MORRISON, Toni (born 1931)
US novelist

Morrison's books explore the experience of black people in the USA, from slavery to the present day. She uses history, however, not as a main subject but as the backdrop to a sensitive and witty description of ordinary people's emotions and relationships. What happened to their ancestors, and to black people in general, only partly determines who they are today. Morrison's novels include *The Bluest Eye*, about an ill-treated girl's escape from reality into the fantasy that she has blue eyes; *Song of Solomon*, about a man's attempts to find meaning in his life by exploring the past history of his people; *Tar Baby*, whose background is the tension between today's 'successful' black people (who may, some of them think, have achieved success by compromising their racial heritage) and the poorer (possibly purer) fellow-citizens from whom they now feel alienated; and *Jazz*, set in 1920s Harlem. Since winning the Nobel Prize in 1993, she has published three further novels. *Paradise* is an enigmatic account of racial and cultural tension centred on an all-black township in Oklahoma, *Love* a startling narrative which explores the many meanings given to the word which provides its title, and *A Mercy* is a subtle and moving exploration of the roots of slavery set in seventeenth-century New England.

Read on
- *Beloved* (set during the period of national reconstruction after the Civil War), *Sula* (about the friendship of two black women growing up in Ohio in the 1920s and 30s).
- ≫ Alice Walker, *Meridian*; Zora Neale Hurston, *Their Eyes Were Watching God*; John Edgar Wideman, *Reuben*; ≫ James Baldwin, *If Beale Street Could Talk.*

MOSLEY, Walter (born 1952)

US novelist

Mosley has written a series of books featuring Ezekiel 'Easy' Rawlins, a black detective/fixer and his good friend, the entertaining, if psychopathically violent, Mouse. The first to be published was *Devil in a Blue Dress* (see below), filmed in 1995 with a Mosley screenplay and Denzel Washington as Easy Rawlins. This debut was followed by *A Red Death*, *White Butterfly*, *Black Betty* and *Little Yellow Dog*. In 1997, *Gone Fishin'*, a kind of prequel to the series originally written (and rejected by publishers) in 1988, finally appeared. It seemed to bring the series to a close but Mosley has returned to the character in the novels *Bad Boy Brawly Brown*, *Little Scarlet*, *Cinnamon Kiss* and *Blonde Faith*, and a collection of short stories, *Six Easy Pieces*.

DEVIL IN A BLUE DRESS (1990)

Although all the Easy Rawlins books are memorable, *Devil in a Blue Dress* remains the best. A racial inversion of ›› Raymond Chandler's classic noir novel *Farewell, My Lovely*, Mosley's tale sees a white man going into a Negro bar and enlisting the aid of a black man (Rawlins) to help find a missing white woman. Where Mosley's general approach differs is in the setting of Watts, the black area of Los Angeles, and its ubiquitous, if casual, threat of racially directed violence. As he searches for a white woman with a fondness for black jazz clubs, and jazz players, Easy Rawlins enters new realms of racial tension and violence, finding himself forced to straddle two worlds in order to survive, and Mosley provides a new update on Chandler's mean streets, viewed from a black perspective.

Walter Mosley's other books include Always Outnumbered, Always Outgunned *(the first collection of stories featuring a tough, wise ex-con named Socrates Fortlow) and its sequels,* Walkin' the Dog *and* The Right Mistake, *Fearless Jones,* Fear Itself *and* Fear of the Dark *(three books about a black investigator in 1950s LA),* RL's Dream *(the story of an old blues guitarist reminiscing about his meeting with the legendary Robert Johnson),* The Man in my Basement, *The* Wave *and* Fortunate Son.

📖 Read on

◘ ›› Raymond Chandler, *Farewell, My Lovely*; Chester Himes, *A Rage in Harlem*; Gary Phillips, *Bad Night is Falling*; Gar Anthony Haywood, *Fear of the Dark*; George Pelecanos, *Hell to Pay*; James Sallis, *The Long-Legged Fly*.

MUNRO, Alice (born 1931)

Canadian short story writer

Many of Munro's stories are set in the villages and small towns of British Columbia and Ontario, places she depicts as genteel, culturally negligible and bigoted, stagnant since the days of the Model-T Ford. Many of her characters are young people of spirit (usually women or girls), stretching the bounds of this environment. Although her themes are modern, her careful descriptions of the streets, houses, rooms and clothes of her people give the stories a strong nostalgic appeal. She is like one of the gentler Southern US writers (**>>** Eudora Welty, say) transported north.

Munro's story collections include Lives of Girls and Women, Friends of My Youth, Open Streets, The Love of a Good Woman, The Progress of Love, Dance of the Happy Shades, The Beggar Maid *(in which the stories are linked to form an episodic novel),* Runaway. The View from Castle Rock *and* Hateship, Friendship, Courtship, Loveship, Marriage, *a title which seemed to encompass all the relationships which form the bases for Munro's delicate and subtle observations of human behaviour.*

Read on

◘ **>>** Eudora Welty, *The Golden Apples*; **>>** Katherine Mansfield, *Collected Stories*; **>>** Helen Dunmore, *Love of Fat Men*; **>>** Raymond Carver, *Will You Please Be Quiet, Please*; William Maxwell, *All the Days and Nights: Collected Stories.*

MURAKAMI, Haruki (born 1949)

Japanese novelist

Murakami is, by a long way, the most popular contemporary Japanese novelist both in his own country and in the West. That he has become so popular in the West is no surprise. Unlike some other Japanese novelists, he draws unashamedly on Western culture. One of his bestselling books, *Norwegian Wood*, takes its title from a Beatles song and he is clearly obsessed by 1950s and 60s pop music and by jazz; he has translated American writers like **>>** Raymond Carver and **>>** John Irving into Japanese; elements of American detective fiction, movies, science fiction and comic books are woven into the multi-coloured tapestries that are his novels. Murakami's characters are unmistakably Japanese but they are at home (insofar as any of them are at home anywhere) in the global village of American-dominated culture. Murakami's fiction can be bizarre and unpredictably surreal. *A Wild Sheep Chase* has as its hero a thirtysomething advertising man drawn into the quest for a sheep with the power to bestow immortality. It can also be touchingly precise in its evocation of longing for an elusive contentment and for lost love. In *South of the Border, West of the Sun*, the narrator, married with children, is haunted by the memory of two lost loves and by thoughts of what might have happened had his life taken different paths. Meeting again with one of the loves from his past rekindles his emotional commitment to her but, as the novel makes clear, time past cannot be regained.

THE WIND-UP BIRD CHRONICLE (1997)

Toru Okada, the hero of Murakami's long and digressive novel, is a man who has opted out of the rat race of Japanese society. Content to live on the income of his magazine editor wife, he spends his days reading, cooking and pottering about their flat. Yet, when first his cat and then his wife disappear, Okada is drawn into a mad odyssey through alternative Tokyo worlds peopled by strange characters who may be real or may be just figments of his imagination. A mysterious woman keeps calling him and demanding phone sex. A precocious teenage neighbour shows him a dried-up well which appears to be a gateway into another world. A veteran of the Second World War recounts his dreadful experiences during that war. The mundane realities of Okada's everyday life are transformed into surreal revelations of his own half-acknowledged desires and of the hidden secrets of Japanese society.

Murakami's other novels include Sputnik Sweetheart, After the Quake, Dance, Dance, Dance *and* Kafka on the Shore. *Short story collections (Murakami is a master of the shorter fictional form) include* The Elephant Vanishes *and* Blind Willow, Sleeping Woman. Underground *is a haunting non-fiction examination of the lives affected by the 1995 gas attack on the Tokyo underground.* What I Talk About When I Talk About Running *is a memoir which focuses on Murakami's interest in long-distance running and marathons.*

🕮 Read on

◘ Kobo Abe, *The Box Man*; Banana Yoshimoto, *Kitchen*; ≫ John Irving, *The Fourth Hand*; David Foster Wallace, *Infinite Jest*; ≫ William Gibson, *Idoru*; Sujata Massey, *The Salaryman's Wife*.

MURDOCH, Iris (1919–99)

Irish/British novelist and philosopher

The subject of Murdoch's two dozen novels is personal politics: the ebb and flow of relationships, the way we manipulate others and are ourselves manipulated. The setting is the present day; the people are middle-class, professional, usually from the English home counties and they are all bizarre, possessed by a demon which blurs reality and dream into a single, mesmeric state. Seduction, mysticism and moral disintegration are favourite themes, and the innocent late adolescent (whose effect on other people's lives is often devastating) is a standard character.

THE BELL (1958)

Should we live our lives by the conventions of society or moment by moment, defining ourselves by our changing moods and enthusiasms? This question perplexes every character in *The Bell*: all are waiting for a sudden inspiration or discovery which will define their existence, show them how they should behave. The setting is a lay community housed in a former convent, a refuge for an eccentric collection of inmates whose peace is disturbed by the arrival of two amoral 'innocents', Dora and Toby. *The Bell* was popular in the hippie 1960s, and still seems to catch the wide-eyed, distracted mood of those times. But its story and characters are fascinating and its images (for example that of the naked, startlingly white-bodied Toby diving, like a fallen angel, into the murky convent lake to investigate a sunken bell) are as disturbing as they are unforgettable.

Murdoch's other novels include The Flight from the Enchanter, The Sandcastle, A Severed Head, The Red and the Green, The Time of the Angels, The Sea, the Sea, The Book and the Brotherhood, The Message to the Planet, The Green Knight *and* Jackson's Dilemma.

🐦Read on

◆ *The Green Knight.*
◘ ≫ A.S. Byatt, *The Virgin in the Garden*; Mary McCarthy, *A Charmed Life*; Alice Thomas Ellis, *The 27th Kingdom*; D.M. Thomas, *Birthstone*; Mary Flanagan, *Trust.*

MURPHY, Dervla (born 1931)

Irish travel writer

Dervla Murphy's first book, *Full Tilt* (1965), recorded her perilous journey on her bicycle from Ireland to India. Whether shooting a pistol at marauding wolves in Yugoslavia or defending herself from Azerbaijani bandits who coveted her bike, Murphy proved herself a daring and resourceful traveller and her book was a deserved bestseller. She followed it with a succession of other volumes chronicling her travels, usually by bike but occasionally accompanied by some troublesome beast of burden, in the remoter parts of the world. *In Ethiopia with a Mule* sees her engaged on a hazardous trek into the country's most hostile terrain; in *Muddling Through in Madagascar* she is joined by her teenage daughter in a journey through the island's spectacular landscapes. Not only is Murphy a dauntless traveller, who shrugs off misfortunes that would have defeated lesser mortals, she is also a sensitive one, always alert to the history and politics of the regions she visits and understanding of the problems faced by those who live there. Even in her seventies, she continues to roam the world. *Through Siberia by Accident* (2005) sees her heading for Ussuriland, the southernmost part of the Russian Far East but sidetracked by an injury which leaves her stranded in the vast and forbidding territories of Siberia.

Dervla Murphy's other travel books include On a Shoestring to Coorg, Where the Indus is Young, South From the Limpopo, One Foot in Laos, Through the Embers of Chaos, Silverland *and* The Island That Dared. Wheels Within Wheels *is an autobiography, telling of her odd upbringing in County Waterford.*

📖 Read on

◘ Gerald Durrell, *The Aye Aye and I* (an expedition in Madagascar); Anne Mustoe, *A Bike Ride: 12,000 Miles Around the World*; Bettina Selby, *Riding the Desert Trail* (another intrepid cyclist takes to her bike, in this case travelling to the source of the Nile); ›› Colin Thubron, *In Siberia*.

READ ON A THEME

MUSIC
- ➤➤ Anthony Burgess, *The Piano Players*
- ➤➤ Willa Cather, *The Song of the Lark*
- ➤➤ Hermann Hesse, *Gertrud*
- ➤➤ Kazuo Ishiguro, *Nocturnes*
  - David Leavitt, *The Page Turner*
  - Bernard MacLaverty, *Grace Notes*
- ➤➤ Thomas Mann, *Doctor Faustus*
  - H.H. Richardson, *The Getting of Wisdom*
- ➤➤ Vikram Seth, *An Equal Music*
  - Joseph Skvorecky, *Dvořák in Love*
- ➤➤ Rose Tremain, *Music & Silence*

MYERSON, Julie (born 1960)
British novelist

Few contemporary novelists have written about damaged lives and destructive, often obsessive relationships with the same mixture of intensity and psychological insight as Julie Myerson. Her novels have all been very different, ranging from a powerful study of a woman shaped by her relationship with a sadistic and tyrannical father (*Sleepwalking*) to a knowing exercise in recreating Victorian melodrama and sensation fiction for a modern readership (*Laura Blundy*). What they all share is a mercilessly close and unflinching observation of love-starved lives and the lengths to which people will go to escape the grip of their past histories.

ME AND THE FAT MAN (1998)
Amy, married but alienated from her husband, seeks erotic thrills in brief, anonymous encounters that simultaneously excite and repel her. The death of her mother, drowned when Amy was six, remains a disturbing memory and, when she meets a mysterious man named Harris who claims to remember her mother, she is prepared to accept much from him, even the way he forces her into a sexual relationship with another of his younger protégés, the fat man of the title.

Surprisingly, Amy and the fat man become true lovers but secrets from the past still need to be unearthed and, for both of them, they involve Harris, the Greek island where Amy's mother died and the deadening power of unacknowledged memories.

Julie Myerson's other novels are The Touch, Something Might Happen, The Story of You *and* Out of Breath. *Her non-fiction works include* Home *(in which she set about investigating the lives of all those people who had previously lived in her Victorian terraced house) and* The Lost Child, *a book which caused controversy with its revelations about her difficulties with her drug-taking teenage son.*

Read on
◆ *Laura Blundy*; *Something Might Happen* (an apparently random murder has a profound and unsettling effect on the small Suffolk seaside town where it takes place).
◻ Esther Freud, *The Sea House*; Zoë Heller, *Everything You Know*.

NABOKOV, Vladimir (1899–1977)
Russian/US novelist and short story writer

Nabokov wrote in Russian until 1940, when he settled in the USA; thereafter, he worked in English, and also translated and revised his earlier works. He was fascinated by language, and his books are firework displays of wit, purple-prose descriptions, ironical asides and multi-lingual puns: for his admirers, style is a major pleasure of his work. Several of his novels take the form of teasing 'biographies', revealing as much about their dogged biographers as their subjects. The hero of *The Defence* is a chess champion, crippled emotionally both by his profession and by his feeling of identity with the whole Russian cultural tradition. The heroes of *The Real Life of Sebastian Knight* and *Look at the Harlequins!* play ironical games with their would-be biographers: the more they seem to reveal themselves, the more elusive they become. *Pnin* is a sad comedy about an accident-prone Russian professor at an American university, trying to keep the customs of the Old Country in a baffling new environment. Humbert Humbert, the tragi-comic hero of Nabokov's most notorious novel, *Lolita*, is led by sexual infatuation for a twelve-year-old girl into a farcical kidnapping, a flight from the police through the motels and diners of grubby middle America, and finally to murder. The book's tone of obsessive erotic reverie is repeated in *Ada*, about an incestuous love affair between two rich, spoiled people in a mysterious country midway between nineteenth-century Russia and the 1930s USA.

PALE FIRE (1962)

Few novels can ever have had such an original form: a nine hundred and ninety nine-line poem with introduction and commentary. The poet is an exiled Eastern European king; the commentator is a fool who fantasizes that he is the real heir to the throne, and that he is writing under the shadow of an assassination plot. The effect is as if Anthony Hope had beefed up someone's PhD thesis: *Pale Fire* is funny, clever – and, despite its bizarre form, a delightfully easy read.

Nabokov's other novels include King, Queen, Knave, Despair, Glory, Invitation to a Beheading, Bend Sinister, Laughter in the Dark *and* The Gift. Nabokov's Dozen, Nabokov's Quartet, A Russian Beauty, Tyrants Destroyed *and* Details of a Sunset *are short story collections.* Speak, Memory *is a poetic account of Nabokov's privileged, pre-Revolutionary childhood.*

⊜Read on

◆ *Pnin*.

▫ to Nabokov's elegant, games-playing style: ›› Muriel Spark, *The Abbess of Crewe*; John Barth, *Giles Goat-boy*; Frederic Raphael, *California Time*; ›› Julian Barnes, *Flaubert's Parrot*.

▫ to his darker novels: ›› Franz Kafka, *The Trial*; Jerzy Kosinski, *The Painted Bird*; ›› Martin Amis, *Success*.

▫ to his short stories: Donald Barthelme, *City Life*.

NAIPAUL, V.S. (Vidiadhar Surajprasad) (born 1932)
Trinidadian novelist and non-fiction writer

A Trinidadian Indian who settled in England in his early twenties, Naipaul identifies exclusively with none of these three communities, and has written about all of them. His early novels (culminating in *A House for Mr Biswas*, see below) were gentle tragi-comedies, but from the late 1960s onwards his books grew darker. He wrote savage non-fiction about the West Indies, India, South America and the Middle East, a mixture of travel and harsh political and social analysis, and his novels dealt with totalitarian oppression and despair. *In a Free State* is about cultural alienation: its central characters are an Indian servant in Washington, a Trinidadian in racist London and two whites in a fanatical black-power Africa. *Guerrillas* is set in a Caribbean dictatorship, *A Bend in the River* in a 'new' African country, emerging from centuries of colonial exploitation into a corrupt, Orwellian state. *The Enigma of Arrival*, published in 1987, synthesizes most of his earlier themes. Its hero, a Trinidadian writer living near Salisbury, reflects on the way his ambitions and his art have changed as he has grown older, on the nature of friendship, on the passing of 'old England' and, generally, on the breakdown of the former order of the world. The book's tone is sombre, mellow and rueful; it seems more like autobiography than fiction. It is a unique and moving work.

A HOUSE FOR MR BISWAS (1961)

Mr Biswas is a free spirit shackled by circumstance. He is a poor Hindu in Trinidad, an educated man among illiterates, a good-natured soul who irritates everyone. He marries into an enormous extended family, the Tulsis, and spends the next twenty years trying to avoid being engulfed by their lifestyle, which he finds vulgar and ridiculous. The conflict – critics see it as an allegory about the absorption of political or ethnic minorities – is chiefly expressed in comedy. Mr Biswas is desperate to escape from the Tulsis's rambling mansion, thronged with disapproving relatives; his ambition is to live decently with his family in a home of his own. Although he succeeds, the book ends ironically and tragically: his victory, the vindication of all he stands for, turns to ashes even as he savours it.

Naipaul's other novels include The Suffrage of Elvira, *Mr* Stone and the Knights Companion, The Mystic Masseur, The Mimic Men, A Way in the World, Half a Life *and* Magic Seeds. *His non-fiction books include* The Middle Passage *(on the West Indies and South America),* An Area of Darkness *and* India: a Wounded Civilization *(two studies, a decade apart, of Indian life and politics) and* Among the Believers *and* Beyond Belief *(two investigations into the Islamic cultures of the Far East).* Miguel Street *and* A Flag on the Island *are collections of short stories.* Letters Between a Father and a Son *is the correspondence between Naipaul, studying at Oxford, and his father, working as a journalist in Trinidad and nursing his own literary ambitions. The correspondence is brought to a moving conclusion by the elder Naipaul's sudden death at the age of only forty seven.* A Writer's People *is a recent book which explore the writers and people who have mattered most to Naipaul in his career.*

Read on
- *The Enigma of Arrival*.
- to the social comedies: Shiva Naipaul (V.S.'s brother), *Fireflies*; >> R.K. Narayan, *The Printer of Malgudi*; Amos Tutuola, *The Palm-wine Drinkard*; Timothy Mo, *Sour-Sweet*; >> Rohinton Mistry, *Family Matters*.
- to Naipaul's political novels: >> Joseph Conrad, *Nostromo*; Christopher Hope, *Black Swan*.
- to *The Enigma of Arrival*: P.H. Newby, *Leaning in the Wind*.

NARAYAN, R.K. (Rasipuran Krishnaswami)
(1907–2001)

Indian novelist

Narayan's stories are set in the imaginary southern Indian town of Malgudi, or in the villages and farms of the nearby Mempi Hills. His characters are shopkeepers, peasant farmers, craftsmen, priests, money-lenders, teachers and housewives, and his theme is the way Hindu belief sustains them in the face of the bewildering or ridiculous events of daily life. Many of his books are comedies. In *The Maneater of Malgudi*, for example, a demented taxidermist works on a series of creatures of ever-increasing size until, to universal panic, he suggests killing and stuffing the town's sacred elephant. Other books replace knockabout with gentler, more bittersweet scenes from the human comedy. *The English Teacher/Grateful to Life and Death* is a beautiful story about a husband coping with grief after the death of his beloved wife.

Narayan's other novels include Swami and Friends *and* The Bachelor of Arts *(which with* The English Teacher *form a trilogy)*, Mr Sampath/The Printer of Malgudi, The Financial Expert, The Vendor of Sweets, A Tiger for Malgudi, The Painter of Signs, The Guide *and* Waiting for the Mahatma. Under the Banyan Tree *and* Malgudi Days *are short-story collections;* Gods, Demons and Others *is Narayan's retelling of stories from Hindu mythology;* My Days *is a placid autobiography.*

Read on
- *The Vendor of Sweets*.
- Rabindranath Tagore, *The Home and the World*; Anita Desai, *The Clear Light of*

Day; S.N. Ghose, *And Gazelles Leaping*; ➤➤ Kazuo Ishiguro, *An Artist of the Floating World*.

READ ON A THEME

NEW YORK
➤➤ Paul Auster, *The New York Trilogy*
Kevin Baker, *Dreamland*
E.L. Doctorow, *Ragtime*
➤➤ Henry James, *Washington Square*
Tama Janowitz, *A Certain Age*
➤➤ Jay McInerney, *Brightness Falls*
➤➤ Toni Morrison, *Jazz*
Henry Roth, *Call It Sleep*
Damon Runyon, *Guys and Dolls*
➤➤ J.D. Salinger, *The Catcher in the Rye*
Hubert Selby Jr, *Last Exit to Brooklyn*

NEWBY, Eric (1919–2006)
British travel writer

Eric Newby transformed the experiences of a varied life into comic and revealing memoirs in a succession of highly readable books. *Something Wholesale*, subtitled 'My Life and Times in the Rag Trade', describes his years working in his father's dress business; *The Last Grain Race* chronicles his 1938 journey as a teenage deck hand on one of the last clipper ships making the grain run from Europe to Australia and back. Probably his best (and best known) book is *A Short Walk in the Hindu Kush*, which turns what must have been a demanding and dangerous expedition in the peaks of Afghanistan into a laconically funny account of an apparently leisurely stroll through mountain scenery. Accompanied by an equally unfazed friend, Newby overcomes every obstacle the journey throws up with remarkable aplomb. One of the funniest passages of the book tells of their encounter with the formidable explorer and traveller ➤➤ Wilfred Thesiger who accuses the two of being 'pansies' when he sees that they propose sleeping on inflatable air beds. The meeting seems somehow emblematic of the conflict between two views of the purpose of travel – Thesiger's almost masochistic urge to escape the modern world and Newby's more relaxed desire to enjoy the places and peoples he encounters. Many readers will find their sympathies lie more with Newby.

Newby's other books include Love and War in the Apennines, The Big Red Train Ride, Slowly Down the Ganges *and* A Small Place in Italy. A Traveller's Life *is an autobiography written as a series of travel stories.*

Read on

♦ *Love and War in the Apennines* (Newby looks back on his experiences in Italy as an escaped PoW during the Second World War and his first meetings with the Italian woman who became his wife).

◘ to the travel books: ›› Robert Byron, *The Road to Oxiana*; Rory Maclean, *Stalin's Nose*; Rory Stewart, *The Places In Between*; ›› Paul Theroux, *The Great Railway Bazaar*.

◘ to *Something Wholesale*: ›› Edward Blishen, *Roaring Boys* (for tone of voice rather than subject).

NGOZI ADICHIE, Chimamanda (born 1977)
Nigerian novelist and short-story writer

In 2007, the Orange Prize for Fiction, awarded to what the judges believe to be the best novel by a woman writer in English each year, went to Chimamanda Ngozi Adichie for her book *Half of a Yellow Sun* a powerful story set amidst the horrors and upheaval of the civil war in Nigeria in the 1960s. The events of the war are seen through the eyes of her vividly realised characters, from Ugwu, the teenager employed as a houseboy by a charismatic university professor, to Olanna, the beautiful and well-educated Igbo woman who is the professor's mistress, as they find themselves swept up by historical forces beyond their control. It was a brilliant example of post-colonial fiction at its best and it was only the second book the thirty-year-old Nigerian had published. Her first novel, *Purple Hibiscus*, had appeared four years earlier and was the story of fifteen-year-old Kambili who leaves her privileged but religiously repressive family life behind her when her father is obliged to send her away to live with her aunt. Since winning the Orange Prize Ngozi Adichie has published a collection of short stories entitled *The Thing Around Your Neck*.

☜Read on

◘ Chinua Achebe, *Things Fall Apart*; Buchi Emecheta, *The Bride Price* (for Nigerian fiction of an earlier generation); Petina Gappah, *An Elegy for Easterly*; Jhumpa Lahiri, *Interpreter of Maladies*; Helen Oyeyemi, *The Icarus Girl*.

NICHOLL, Charles
British biographer and travel writer

Charles Nicholl is a travel writer who has published accounts of hair-raising journeys in South America (*The Fruit Palace*) and Burma (*Borderlines*) but he is best known for a number of books which combine the biography of a remarkable individual with an exploration of the world in which he lived. *The Reckoning*, for example, provides a compelling portrait of the Elizabethan underworld of spies and petty criminals in which the playwright Christopher Marlowe operated and unravels the mystery surrounding his murder. *Leonardo Da Vinci: The Flights of the Mind* aims to resurrect the real man behind the stereotyped image of the universal genius with which we are all familiar. 'The most relentlessly curious man in history', as Kenneth Clark described him, who was interested in everything from architecture to zoology, emerges from the myths and legends that have surrounded him. Leonardo's soaring 'flights of the mind' took off from the everyday realities of his life in the turbulent world of fifteenth- and sixteenth-century Italy and Nicholl's book reconstructs them with imagination and panache.

☜Read on

◆ *The Lodger* (Nicholl uses a 1612 London lawsuit as the starting point for an investigation into the life of one of the men who gave evidence in it – William Shakespeare).

◘ to *The Reckoning*: John Bossy, *Giordano Bruno and the Embassy Affair*; ❯❯ Anthony Burgess, *A Dead Man in Deptford* (novel); Dominic Green, *The Double Life of Doctor Lopez*.

◘ to *Leonardo Da Vinci: Flights of the Mind*: ❯❯ Ross King, *Michelangelo and the Pope's Ceiling*.

◘ to *The Lodger*: Jonathan Bate, *Soul of the Age*; ❯❯ Germaine Greer, *Shakespeare's Wife*.

NORFOLK, Lawrence (born 1963)

British novelist

Like an English version of ❯❯ Umberto Eco, Lawrence Norfolk writes big, baggy novels that raid history, mythology and philosophy in search of stories to entertain and educate the reader. *Lemprière's Dictionary* takes as its starting point the life of the classical scholar John Lemprière, author of an eighteenth-century dictionary of classical literature and the classical world. But Norfolk zigzags back and forth through the centuries, using the dark and tangled family history of the Lemprières and the subjects of John's scholarship to introduce stories from Greek and Roman mythology, the founding of the East India Company, the siege of La Rochelle and the crime-ridden streets of Georgian London. No reader could feel short-changed by the book's ebullient concoction of corruption, conspiracy, piracy, assassinations and murders, mismatched love affairs and the misdeeds of the past returning to haunt later generations. It was an explosive debut and was followed by another sprawling monster of a book, *The Pope's Rhinoceros*, which centred on sixteenth-century attempts to deliver a rhinoceros, an almost mythical beast at the time, to Pope Leo X. Again, this is just one of a whole gallery of interweaving stories about a Europe over which the shadow of the Reformation hangs. Norfolk's most recent book, *In the Shape of a Boar*, is shorter but, in many ways, more ambitious than his first two novels, in its linking of the mythological hunting of the Boar of Kalydon with an incident in Second World War Greece and its repercussions in the life of a Jewish poet.

✑Read on

◘ ❯❯ Umberto Eco, *The Island of the Day Before*; ❯❯ Rose Tremain, *Music & Silence*; ❯❯ Iain Sinclair, *Downriver*; ❯❯ Adam Thorpe, *Pieces of Light*; William T. Vollmann, *Argall*.

O'BRIAN, Patrick (1914–2000)
English novelist

O'Brian's Jack Aubrey novels, about an officer in the British Navy in Napoleonic times, chart his hero's progress up the ranks, and place him in great events and adventures of the time. The characters are three-dimensional (shown especially in the relationship between Aubrey and his friend, the ship's surgeon Stephen Maturin), the sailing and fighting are wonderfully described, the plots are exciting and the talk is multi-faceted, ironical and convincingly real. The novels are self-contained but add up to one of the most impressive of all works of naval fiction.

Starting with Master and Commander *in 1970, the novels that follow are* Post Captain, HMS Surprise, The Mauritius Command, Desolation Island, The Fortune of War, The Surgeon's Mate, The Ionian Mission, Treason's Harbour, The Far Side of the World, The Reverse of the Medal, The Letter of Marque, The Thirteen Gun Salute, The Nutmeg of Consolation, Clarissa Oakes, The Wine-Dark Sea, The Commodore, The Yellow Admiral, The Hundred Days *and* Blue at the Mizzen. The Road to Samarcand *is set in Asia in the 1930s;* The Golden Ocean *and* The Unknown Shore *are sea stories that predate the Aubrey/Maturin novels;* Collected Short Stories *were largely written in the 1950s.*

⮧Read on
◘ ≫ C.S. Forester, Hornblower novels; Alexander Kent, Bolitho novels, beginning with *Richard Bolitho, Midshipman*.

O'BRIEN, Flann (1911–66)
Irish novelist

Flann O'Brien was born Brian O'Nolan in County Tyrone, Northern Ireland, and moved to Dublin where he studied at University College. In 1935, he joined the Irish civil service, remaining there until ill-health forced him to retire in 1953. Civil servants were then forbidden to publish under their own names and his first novel, the surreal classic *At Swim-Two-Birds*, appeared under the name of Flann O'Brien in 1935. Praised by Samuel Beckett, James Joyce and Graham Greene (who had engineered its publication), the novel is a multi-faceted and highly comical analysis of both Irish culture and the art of fiction. His publisher rejected his second novel,

The Third Policeman, causing O'Brien's literary career to stall and leaving him so disappointed that he claimed the manuscript had been lost. The book only appeared, posthumously, in 1967. That same year, his third novel, originally published in Gaelic as *An Béal Bocht*, finally appeared in English as *The Poor Mouth*. Beginning in 1940, for over twenty five years O'Brien wrote a daily column in the *Irish Times* using the byline Myles na Gopaleen. These hilarious pieces appeared under the banner Cruiskeen Lawn (The Brimming Jug), and selections appeared in various volumes, including *The Best of Myles* in 1968 and *The Hair of the Dogma* in 1977. After his debut was reissued in 1960, O'Brien published *Hard Times* in 1962 and *The Dalkey Archive* two years later. Following his untimely, if rather fitting, death on April Fool's Day, his reputation as a great Irish author was secure, but, despite James Joyce declaring of him 'That's a real writer, with the true comic spirit', O'Brien privately felt that he had failed in his literary endeavours. For once, he was wrong.

Read on

◘ ➤➤ James Joyce, *Ulysses*; ➤➤ Samuel Beckett, *Murphy*; B.S. Johnson, *Christie Malry's Own Double-Entry*.

O'CONNOR, Joseph (born 1963)
Irish novelist

The Star of the Sea, a gripping novel in which refugees from the disaster of the Irish Potato Famine of the 1840s flee their ravaged native land for the hope and promise of the New World, won both critical and commercial success when it was first published in 2002. Its author was the Dublin-born writer Joseph O'Connor. O'Connor had already gained attention with a number of lively novels (*Cowboys and Indians*, *The Salesman*) set in his home city but *The Star of the Sea* was the first work of historical fiction he had attempted and travelling back into the past for his narrative seemed to free his imagination. He followed it with *Redemption Falls* in which a former hero of the Irish struggle against the British, later a flamboyant Union general in the American Civil War, struggles with whisky and self-recrimination in a godforsaken township on the Western frontier. Making use of all kinds of narrative material from letters and journals to transcripts of court proceedings and even wanted posters, *Redemption Falls* is an ambitious and inventive novel that confirms O'Connor's gifts as a historical novelist.

O'Connor's other novels include Desperadoes *and* Inishowen. True Believers *is a collection of short stories.* Sweet Liberty *is a book which chronicles O'Connor's journey through Irish America,* The Last of the Irish Males *gathers together non-fiction pieces, mostly humorous and mostly concerned with Irish life inside and outside Ireland.*

⮑Read on
◘ to the contemporary fiction: ➤➤ Roddy Doyle, *The Commitments*; Patrick McCabe, *The Dead School*.
◘ to the historical fiction: Pete Dexter, *Deadwood*; ➤➤ Roddy Doyle, *A Star Called Henry*; Michael White, *Soul Catcher*.

O'FARRELL, Maggie (born 1972)
British novelist

In her first novel, *After You'd Gone*, published in 2000, Maggie O'Farrell showed immediately a command of subtle narrative, convincing characterization and supple prose that marked her out as a major new voice in British fiction. The book's central character, Alice Raikes, returning to London after a strangely aborted journey to her native Scotland, steps out in front of a car. In a coma in hospital, the people and events of her past visit her and the mysteries surrounding her journey north and her entire life are slowly revealed. O'Farrell has followed this auspicious debut with three further novels. *My Lover's Lover* uses multiple narratives and settings to chart an ambivalent but passionate relationship haunted by the spectre of the previous partner of one of the lovers; in *The Distance Between Us*, two people, one in Hong Kong and one in London, are gradually brought together in a twisting narrative that moves back and forth between their past and present lives; *The Vanishing Act of Esme Lennox* is a story of family skeletons emerging from the cupboard as a young woman discovers a great aunt she never knew she had.

⮑Read on
◘ ➤➤ Helen Dunmore, *Talking to the Dead*; Lesley Glaister, *Now You See Me*; Zoë Heller, *Notes on a Scandal*; ➤➤ Julie Myerson, *Something Might Happen*.

O'HANLON, Redmond (born 1947)
British travel writer

Irresistibly drawn to the most inhospitable and inaccessible corners of the world, Redmond O'Hanlon returns from dicing with death and discomfort to write wonderfully funny and gripping narratives of his adventures. Amid all the fun and farce that O'Hanlon extracts from the misadventures of scholarly incompetents set loose in the wilds, his books are also filled with offbeat erudition, lyrical accounts of his encounters with flora and fauna, and a sensitive awareness that he is only a fleeting visitor to landscapes in which others are firmly at home. *Into the Heart of Borneo* told the story of his journey with the poet James Fenton in pursuit of a rare rhino only found in the heart of the country and how they (just) survived the perils of jungle life. *In Trouble Again* recounts a four-month trip up the Orinoco River and into the Amazon basin. In the absence of James Fenton – who tells O'Hanlon that he wouldn't travel with him from Oxford to High Wycombe – the author's companion is another old friend, a man even less suited than Fenton to the dangers and discomforts of the journey. In *Congo Journey*, O'Hanlon, inspired by legends of a dinosaur-like creature named Mokele-mbembe still lurking in the jungles of central Africa, sets out to track it down. His latest work, *Trawler*, records his experiences aboard a North Sea fishing boat. A seasick O'Hanlon flounders around the vessel, as much out of his depth as he has been on his jungle journeys and able only to record his admiration for the men whose daily work he is witnessing.

✒Read on
◘ Benedict Allen, *Mad White Giant*; ›› Peter Fleming, *Brazilian Adventure*; Eric Hansen, *Stranger in the Forest*; Jeffrey Tayler, *Facing the Congo*; John Wassner, *Espresso with the Headhunters*.

O'ROURKE, P.J. (born 1947)
American essayist

A living affront to political correctness, P.J. O'Rourke is a journalist and political commentator who flaunts his right-wing views, celebrates the pleasures of over-indulgence in booze, tobacco and yet more powerful intoxicants, and gleefully defies the liberal consensus on very nearly every political and social issue. *Republican Party Reptile* (1987), his first collection of essays, saw him pouring scorn on left-wing American tourists too eager to see the good in Soviet Russia, indulging in a high-speed car ride across the country and generally lambasting killjoys and busybodies intent on interfering with his right to go to the devil in his own sweet way. In *Holidays in Hell* O'Rourke deliberately chooses to visit some of the world's worst trouble spots and then, in essays with titles like 'A Ramble Through Lebanon' and 'Christmas in El Salvador', reports back on the inanities and insanities he has witnessed. In recent years, O'Rourke appears to have been tamed by a new domesticity and by fatherhood but he still retains some of the trenchant, hard-hitting, often cruel wit that marked his earlier books.

P.J. O'Rourke's other books include Give War a Chance, All the Trouble in the World, Eat the Rich, The CEO of the Sofa *and* Peace Kills.

☞Read on
◘ Michael Moore, *Stupid White Men* (different political perspective, same contempt for the powerful); Joe Queenan, *The Unkindest Cut*; ▶▶ Hunter S. Thompson, *Curse of Lono*.

LITERARY TRIVIA 11:

TEN WINNERS OF THE DIAGRAM PRIZE FOR THE ODDEST TITLE OF THE YEAR
Each year since 1978 this prize has been awarded to the book with the strangest and most bizarre title. Winners include:

Proceedings of the Second International Conference on Nude Mice (1978)
The Joy of Chickens (1980)
Oral Sadism and the Vegetarian Personality (1986)
How to Shit in the Woods (1989)
How to Avoid Huge Ships (1992)
Highlights in the History of Concrete (1994)
Living with Crazy Buttocks (2002)
The Big Book of Lesbian Horse Stories (2003)
Bombproof Your Horse (2004)
What to Do with People Who Don't Know They're Dead (2005)

ONDAATJE, Michael (born 1943)
Sri Lankan/Canadian novelist and poet

A poet before he was a novelist, Michael Ondaatje writes prose that is as rich, dense and allusive as poetry. Narrative is the bare bones on which Ondaatje hangs his often haunting and beautiful language and imagery. His early novels were resolutely experimental in form. Two are about real historical characters. *Coming Through Slaughter* tells the life of the legendary cornet player Buddy Bolden, allegedly the 'inventor' of New Orleans jazz, and does so in a mixture of poetry, prose, song lyrics and reminiscence. *The Collected Works of Billy the Kid* similarly presents a collage of poems, photographs and documentary evidence related to the life of, and, more significantly, the myth surrounding the teenage gunfighter. Both developed a certain cult status but were not major bestsellers. Only with *The English Patient* (see below) and the success of Anthony Minghella's film version of it has Ondaatje found the wide audience his fiction deserves. He has followed it with two further novels: *Anil's Ghost*, a searching tale of love and politics set in a Sri Lanka torn apart by civil war, and *Divisadero*, an intense and erotic story focused on the triangular relationship between a young man and two sisters.

THE ENGLISH PATIENT (1992)
As the Second World War drags towards its conclusion, a nurse and her patient, an Englishman burnt beyond recognition and swathed in bandages, are holed up in a villa near Florence after the retreat of the Germans. Two other damaged individuals, a Sikh bomb-disposal expert and a former criminal who has suffered torture, are now the villa's only other occupants. As the nurse and her two companions enter into complex relations of their own and speculate about the enigma of the English patient, he returns in his own mind to North Africa before the war and an intense but doomed love affair. Written in a prose that lingers on the details of the visible, tangible world and unfolding its story in a jigsaw of interlocking scenes, *The English Patient* is a hypnotic exploration of love, memory and desire.

✒Read on
◆ *Anil's Ghost*.
▫ Paul Bowles, *The Sheltering Sky*; ≫ Gabriel García Márquez, *Love in the Time of Cholera*; Romesh Gunesekera, *Heaven's Edge*; Alessandro Baricco, *Silk*.

ORWELL, George (1903–50)
British writer

George Orwell was the pseudonym of Eric Blair. In his twenties he worked for the colonial police in Burma (an experience he later used in the novel *Burmese Days*). He returned to England disgusted with imperialism and determined never again to work for or support 'the system'. In fact, most of his work thereafter was literary: articles, essays and books taking a jaundiced view of British society and attitudes. Commissioned to report on the industrial north of England, he wrote *The Road to Wigan Pier*, an indictment not only of unemployment and poverty but also of the failure of idealists, of all political parties, to find a cure. *Down and Out in Paris and London* is a description of the life of tramps and other derelicts; *Homage to Catalonia* is a withering account of the failure of the International Brigades in the Spanish Civil War. During the 1930s Orwell published three ❯❯ Wellsian novels about people dissatisfied with the constricting middle-class or lower-middle-class lives they led. It was not until 1945, when the Second World War seemed to have blown away forever the humbug and complacency which Orwell considered the worst of all British characteristics, that he published his first overtly political book, *Animal Farm*. In this Stalinist 'fairy story', pigs turn their farm into a workers' democracy in which 'all animals are equal, but some are more equal than others', and the rule of all quickly degenerates into the tyranny of the few. The success of *Animal Farm* encouraged Orwell to write an even more savage political fantasy, *Nineteen Eighty-four*.

NINETEEN EIGHTY-FOUR (1949)
In the totalitarian future, Winston Smith's job is to rewrite history, adding to or subtracting from the record people who are in or out of Party favour. He falls in love – a forbidden thing, because it arises from free will and not by order of the Party – and is betrayed to the Thought Police. He is tortured until he not only admits, but comes to believe, that the Party is right in everything: if it says that 2 + 2 = 5, then that is so. The book ends, chillingly, with the idea that Winston has won the victory over himself: he is happy because he has chosen, of his own free will, to have no choice.

Orwell's 1930s novels are A Clergyman's Daughter, Keep the Aspidistra Flying *and* Coming Up for Air. *His essays, letters and journalism have been collected in four volumes in paperback.*

Read on

◘ to the novels of the 1930s: Robert Tressell, *The Ragged Trousered Philanthropists*; ›› H.G. Wells: *The History of Mr Polly*.

◘ to the savage politics of *Nineteen Eighty-four*: Arthur Koestler, *Darkness at Noon*; ›› Franz Kafka, *The Trial*; ›› Vladimir Nabokov, *Bend Sinister*.

◘ future-fantasies of a similarly bleak kind: Yevgeni Zamyatin, *We*; ›› Aldous Huxley, *Brave New World*; ›› Anthony Burgess, *A Clockwork Orange* (Burgess also wrote *1985*, a right-wing riposte to *Nineteen Eighty-four*).

◘ ›› Mario Vargas Llosa, *The City and the Dogs/The Time of the Hero*, set in a Peruvian military academy, is that rare thing, an Orwellian political allegory which is also funny.

READ ON A THEME:

OTHER PEOPLES, OTHER TIMES
Historical novels set in remote or unusual times

    Jean M. Auel, *Clan of the Cave Bear* (prehistoric Europe)
›› Robert Edric, *The Book of the Heathen* (late nineteenth-century Belgian Congo)
    Shusako Endo, *Silence* (seventeenth-century Japan)
›› Gustave Flaubert, *Salammbô* (ancient Carthage)
›› Matthew Kneale, *English Passengers* (early nineteenth-century Tasmania)
›› Norman Mailer, *Ancient Evenings* (ancient Egypt)
    Naomi Mitchison, *Early in Orcadia* (prehistoric Orkneys)
›› Jane Rogers, *Promised Lands* (eigtheenth century Australia)
›› Jane Smiley, *The Greenlanders* (medieval Greenland)
    Sigrid Undset, *Kristin Lavransdatter* (fourteenth-century Norway)
›› Mario Vargas Llosa, *The War of the End of the World* (nineteenth-century Peru)

See also: Ancient Greece and Rome; The Bible

PALAHNIUK, Chuck (born 1962)
US novelist

Chuck Palahniuk writes visceral and disturbing fiction about people on the edge of violence, people alienated by consumer society, people who have been marginalized and made dangerous by their inability to conform. From a glamorous fashion model who becomes an 'invisible monster' when she is hideously disfigured in a mysterious accident to a sex addict and con-man who has devised an elaborate scam to support himself and his Alzheimer's-afflicted mother, his characters are outsiders and misfits. In writing about them, Palahniuk demonstrates a curious mixture of empathy and voyeuristic prurience. He is half fairground barker, inviting us inside the tent to watch the freaks, and half wise humanitarian reminding us that there are more things in heaven and earth than are dreamt of in our philosophy. The results are often unsettling but there is no doubt that Palahniuk is one of America's most daring and interesting writers.

FIGHT CLUB (1996)
Bored by consumerism and meaningless affluence, a group of male yuppies seek therapeutic release in a secret society devoted to bareknuckle fisticuffs. Their fight club gradually develops into an underground organisation intent on creating social mayhem.

Palahniuk's other novels are Survivor, Invisible Monsters, Choke, Lullaby, Diary, Haunted, Rant, Snuff *and* Pygmy. *His non-fiction, including essays about fame, real-life fight clubs and the circumstances surrounding the murder of his father was published in the UK with the unadorned title,* Non-Fiction.

🐟Read on
◆ *Haunted* (seventeen misfits join what they think will be a writer's retreat in Oregon, only to find themselves trapped in an abandoned theatre where each must tell a story in order to survive and escape).
◘ Charles Bukowski, *Factotum*; Katherine Dunn, *Geek Love*; ➤➤ Bret Easton Ellis, *American Psycho*; James Frey, *Bright Shiny Morning*; ➤➤ Irvine Welsh, *Filth*.

PAMUK, Orhan (born 1952)

Turkish novelist

Pamuk is Turkey's most famous contemporary novelist but, in many ways, his most revealing work is non-fiction, his recent *Istanbul: Memories of a City*, which is not only an evocative tribute to the city but a digressive memoir of his own childhood and adolescence. 'Istanbul's fate', Pamuk writes, 'is my fate: I am attached to this city because it has made me who I am.' He finds the key to Istanbul in *hüzün*, the melancholic sense of departed glories and spiritual loss that pervades a city long caught between the West and memories of a vanished Eastern empire. Chasing the feeling of *hüzün* down the decaying backstreets and hidden squares of an Istanbul fast disappearing beneath expansive modernization, he creates a remarkable, intertwined portrait of the city and of himself. Several of Pamuk's best novels draw on the history which haunts his later memoir. *The White Castle* is set in the seventeenth century and traces the relationship between two scholars, one a Turkish savant living in Constantinople, the other a Venetian captured and sold to him as a slave. The two men resemble one another physically and Pamuk uses this similarity as a metaphor to explore the intermingling of East and West that characterizes Turkish culture past and present. *My Name is Red* is also historical fiction, taking the mysterious murder of a miniaturist, engaged to produce a magnificently illuminated book for a sixteenth-century sultan, as the starting point for a book that cunningly combines a kind of detective story with a multi-stranded narrative of love and art and power.

Pamuk's other novels include The Black Book, The New Life *(the fastest-selling novel in Turkish history, a haunting fantasy of a man who grows obsessed by the magical powers of a book) and* Snow *(an exile returns to Turkey only to find himself stranded in a distant and wintry city and embroiled in the political struggle between secular nationalism and religious fundamentalism).*

☜Read on

◘ to the novels: Yashar Kemal, *Memed, My Hawk* (the greatest novel by a brilliant Turkish novelist of an earlier generation); Amin Maalouf, *Balthasar's Odyssey*; Elif Shafak, *The Flea Palace*.

◘ to *Istanbul: Memories of a City*: John Freely, *Istanbul: The Imperial City*; Joseph Mitchell, *McSorley's Wonderful Saloon* (Mitchell could scarcely have been a more different writer from Pamuk but he had a similarly intense and productive relationship with the city in which he wrote, in his case New York).

READ ON A THEME:

PARENTS AND CHILDREN
>> Iain Banks, *The Crow Road*
   Samuel Butler, *The Way of All Flesh*
   Justin Cartwright, *The Promise of Happiness*
>> Margaret Forster, *Private Papers*
   Esther Freud, *Hideous Kinky*
>> D.H. Lawrence, *Sons and Lovers*
   Shena Mackay, *The Orchard on Fire*
   Edna O'Brien, *Time and Tide*
   Dodie Smith, *I Capture the Castle*
>> Ivan Turgenev, *Fathers and Sons*
>> John Updike, *The Centaur*

See also: Adolescence; Eccentric Families; Many Generations; Teenagers

READ ON A THEME:

PAST AND PRESENT
Novels in which historical and contemporary stories meet and interact.

>> Peter Ackroyd, *The House of Doctor Dee*
Malcolm Bradbury, *To the Hermitage*
>> Tracy Chevalier, *The Virgin Blue*
David Ebershoff, *The 19th Wife*
Marina Fiorato, *The Glassblower of Murano*
Michael Gruber, *The Book of Air and Shadows*
James Robertson, *The Fanatic*
Rebecca Stott, *Ghostwalk*
Nigel Williams, *Witchcraft*

PASTERNAK, Boris (1890–1960)
Russian poet and novelist

In Russia Pasternak is remembered chiefly as a poet and translator (of ›› Goethe and Shakespeare). Western readers know him for his 1957 novel *Doctor Zhivago*, and for the savage reaction of the Soviet authorities of the time, who banned the book and made Pasternak renounce his Nobel Prize. *Doctor Zhivago* is about the doctor of the title and a teacher, Lara, caught up in the civil war which followed the 1917 Revolution. Although each is married to someone else and has a child, they fall in love – and the feverishness of their affair is increased by knowledge that neither it nor they will survive the war, since they come from a doomed class, the bourgeoisie. Horrified and powerless, they witness the brutality, class hatred and fury which precede the establishment of the USSR. Despite the reaction of the late-1950s authorities to all this, Pasternak was not really concerned with politics. He was more interested in the idea of people out of step with their time, star-crossed by destiny, and in the way Zhivago's and Lara's relationship was an emotional counterpart to the chaos and destruction all round them. The book ends with Zhivago's poems about Lara, like faded love-letters plucked from the rubble of the past.

⮑Read on
◻ ›› Leo Tolstoy, *Anna Karenina*; ›› Ernest Hemingway, *A Farewell to Arms*; ›› Elizabeth Bowen, *The Heat of the Day*; ›› Margaret Mitchell, *Gone With the Wind*; ›› Iris Murdoch, *The Red and the Green*.

PEACE, David (born 1967)
British novelist

From the very first pages of his very first novel David Peace showed himself to be a writer of uncompromising brutality and directness but one whose hypnotic and often expletive-laden prose had its own strange kind of dark poetry. *Nineteen Seventy-Four* followed a crime reporter returning to his native Yorkshire to investigate the story of a missing girl and finding himself entangled in a network of murder, depravity and corruption. Three further novels (*Nineteen Seventy-Seven*, *Nineteen Eighty* and *Nineteen Eighty-Three*) combined to form a series, known as the 'Red Riding Quartet'. *GB84* (about the miners' strike) and *The Damned United* (see below) followed, two novels in which real-life events and Peace's fictional re-imaginings of them mingled together. He has recently begun a new sequence of novels set not in the West Riding of Yorkshire but in Tokyo, where he now lives. It remains to be seen whether or not this can match the raw power and originality of the 'Red Riding Quartet'.

THE DAMNED UNITED (2006)

The late, great football manager Brian Clough is the focus of one of the most extraordinary novels about any sport ever published. Clough's brief period in charge of Leeds United in 1974 becomes the stage for his battles with the demons of success and failure. Imagined from the inside, Clough's battles with intransigent players, interfering chairmen and the soul-destroying unpredictability of the game itself develop an odd poignancy that echoes beyond the boundaries of sport. A football manager may seem an unlikely tragic antihero, but Peace's idiosyncratic imagination transforms Clough into something close to one.

⮐Read on

◆ *Tokyo Year Zero* (the first of Peace's novels to be set outside the West Riding of Yorkshire which tells the story of a Japanese detective searching for a serial killer in the aftermath of World War II).

◘ to *The Damned United*: David Storey, *This Sporting Life*.

◘ to Peace's fiction in general: Roberto Bolano, *2666*; Derek Raymond, *I Was Dora Suarez*.

PEAKE, Mervyn (1911–68)
British novelist and artist

Peake earned his living as an artist, drawing cartoons and grotesque, sombre illustrations to such works as *Treasure Island* and *The Hunting of the Snark*. He also made portraits of the main characters in his own novels: unsmiling freaks with distorted limbs and haunted eyes, violently cross-hatched as if with giant cobwebs. He admired ▶▶ Poe and ▶▶ Kafka, and his own work lopes gleefully – and hilariously – down the same dark passages of the imagination, peering into every corner and detailing the horrors that wait behind every moss-grown, rust-hinged door. The Gormenghast Trilogy (*Titus Groan*, *Gormenghast* and *Titus Alone*) takes place in a mist-shrouded, monstrous kingdom surrounding the crumbling Gothic castle of

Gormenghast. Evil broods, ever undefined but waiting to pounce. Everyone, from Lord Sepulchrave himself to the physician Prunesquallor, from Nanny Slagg to the demented scullion Steerpike, lives every second of each day by a precise, bizarre ritual, as compulsive and pointless as the movements of the insane. *Titus Groan* describes the fearful consequences when Steerpike, to further his own dark ambitions, starts fomenting social revolution. *Gormenghast* is about the growing-up of Titus, seventy seventh Earl of Groan: how he learns about his inheritance, uncovers the castle's secrets and begins to chafe against the rituals which choke its people's lives. In *Titus Alone* Titus breaks free of the castle and explores the country outside, an arrogant knight-errant on a terrifying, pointless quest.

Peake's only other novel, Mr Pye, is a gentler story about a man on Sark in the Channel Islands who shows distressing signs of turning into an angel. Peake's Progress*, an anthology of his poems, plays and drawings, is a splendid introduction to his work and includes an extra Gormenghast story, 'A Boy in Darkness'.*

📖Read on

◘ to *Gormenghast*; ❯❯ Mary Shelley, *Frankenstein*; ❯❯ Edgar Allan Poe, *The Fall of the House of Usher*; Stanislaw Lem, *Memoirs Found in a Bathtub*; ❯❯ Michael Moorcock, *Gloriana*.

PEARL, Matthew
US novelist

Matthew Pearl gained critical praise and commercial success with his very first novel, *The Dante Club* (see below). He followed it with a similar tale of nineteenth-century literary mystery. In *The Poe Shadow* an admirer of the author of *Tales of Mystery and Imagination* decides that the one person to investigate the circumstances surrounding his tragic death is the person on whom Poe modelled his famous fictional detective, C. Auguste Dupin. Problems arise when two candidates for the inspirational role make their separate claims. His most recent novel is *The Last Dickens*, set at a time when America is awaiting the latest instalment of the novel Charles Dickens was writing when he died. A young publisher's clerk is murdered and his employer is thrust into a mystery that takes him across the Atlantic in search of the truth about the 'last Dickens'. In all three of his novels so far published, Pearl has revealed an impressive ability to combine reconstruction of the past with page-turning narrative skills.

THE DANTE CLUB (2003)

A serial killer is stalking the streets of Boston in the year 1865. His victims meet terrible and bizarre deaths. A judge is struck on the head and left to be eaten alive by maggots. A church minister is buried upside-down in a pit and his feet set on fire. Only a small group of poets and scholars, including such famous men as Henry Wadsworth Longfellow and Oliver Wendell Holmes, recognize a method in the killer's apparent madness. Devotees of the Italian poet Dante (whose *Divine Comedy* Longfellow is translating into English), they realize that the killer is modelling his murders on the descriptions of hell's punishments in their idol's works and they must set about bringing him to justice.

⮐Read on

◻ Matthew Plampin, *The Street Philosopher*; Jed Rubenfeld, *The Interpretation of Murder*; Dan Simmons, *Drood*; Andrew Taylor, *The American Boy*.

PÉREZ-REVERTE, Arturo (born 1951)

Spanish novelist

In his home country, Pérez-Reverte is most famous for creating the character of Captain Alatriste, a swashbuckling seventeenth-century mercenary who has appeared in several novels, only some of which have been translated into English. Abroad, however, he is better known for a number of historical novels and thrillers which combine energetic action and page-turning readability with offbeat erudition and intellectual puzzles. *The Fencing Master*, set in a politically turbulent Spain in the 1860s, focuses on the ageing swordsman of the title, a man out of step with his times, who is drawn unwillingly into a world of deceit, intrigue and betrayal when a mysterious young woman appears on his doorstep and asks for fencing lessons. *The Flanders Panel* begins with an art historian spotting a curious inscription on a painting by a fifteenth-century Flemish master and gathers pace until the reader's head is spinning as much as the heroine's. Pérez-Reverte's novels are, in one sense, very old-fashioned. His love and admiration for writers like ⮞⮞ Alexandre Dumas, the ⮞⮞ Conan Doyle of the Brigadier Gerard stories and other purveyors of literary swash and buckle are clear in the elaborate narratives he creates. In another sense his books are post-modern games in which he teases his readers with riddling references to everything from chess (the murderer in *The Flanders Panel* signals his intentions with hints taken from the moves of a chess game) and treasure maps to theological controversies and the correct way to use a fencing rapier.

THE CLUB DUMAS (1996)

Lucas Corso is a professional book-hunter who hires himself out to rich bibliophiles in search of rare editions and obscure manuscripts. When he is asked to authenticate what seems to be a handwritten chapter from the original manuscript of Alexander Dumas's *The Three Musketeers*, he is drawn ever further into a dark mystery involving occult rituals, glamorous femmes fatales and a strange club whose members idolize the work of the nineteenth century French novelist.

The Alatriste novels published in English are Captain Alatriste, Purity of Blood, The Sun Over Breda, The King's Gold *and* The Man in the Yellow Doublet. *Pérez-Reverte's other novels include* The Seville Communion, The Nautical Chart, The Queen of the South *and* The Painter of Battles.

Read on

◆ *The Seville Communion* (a Vatican investigator arrives in the Spanish city to discover the truth behind two mysterious deaths in one of its churches).

▫ ➤ Alexandre Dumas, *The Three Musketeers*; ➤ Matthew Pearl, *The Dante Club*; Iain Pears, *The Dream of Scipio*; Rafael Sabatini, *Captain Blood*; Carlos Ruiz Zafón, *The Shadow of the Wind*.

PHILLIPS, Caryl (born 1958)

British novelist

Phillips was born on the island of St Kitts in the West Indies and moved to Britain with his family when he was still a small child, but several of his novels are set in the Caribbean. These novels often feature characters who struggle directly with the dark legacy of colonialism and the crises of identity that it can engender. In *A State of Independence* Bertram Francis has spent twenty years in Britain and returns to St Kitts, expecting to feel 'at home' in a way that he has not done for a long time. In a narrative that is both shrewdly observant and delicately comic, Phillips charts

Francis's homecoming to a place he no longer recognizes, caught as he is between two cultures. *Cambridge* deals overtly with slavery and its legacy. It uses two very different narrative voices – those of a nineteenth-century Englishwoman sent to visit her father's West Indies sugar plantation and of a gifted Christian slave, the eponymous Cambridge – to tell a chilling tale of an island society irredeemably tainted by the inhumanity on which it is built.

THE NATURE OF BLOOD (1997)

The central character in *The Nature of Blood* is Eva Stern, a young Jewish woman who first appears in the book as a traumatized survivor of the Nazi concentration camps which have claimed the lives of most of her family. Using Eva as the focus for his novel, Phillips then moves back and forth in time to encompass other narratives of the suffering inflicted by intolerance and the persistent human need to stigmatize 'otherness' and difference. One story is set in the Middle Ages and tells of hysterical anti-Semitism in a small Italian town, aroused by rumours that a Christian child has been ritually murdered. Another is Othello's own version of the events described in Shakespeare's play – although the narrator never explicitly identifies himself as the Moor of Venice. Phillips skilfully manipulates his varying narratives before bringing all the strands together in a surprising and compelling conclusion.

Phillips's other novels are The Final Passage, Higher Ground, Crossing the River, A Distant Shore, Dancing in the Dark *and* In the Falling Snow. Foreigners *is a volume of three novellas about three black Englishmen alienated by their experiences of racism.* A New World Order *is a collection of essays and* The Atlantic Sound *is an exploration of three places indelibly marked by their association with the slave trade.*

⏛Read on

◆ *Cambridge*.

▢ ≫ V.S. Naipaul, *The Mimic Men*; Fred D'Aguiar, *Feeding the Ghosts*; David Dabydeen, *The Counting House*.

PICOULT, Jodi (born 1966)
US novelist

Focusing on families in crisis, many of Jodi Picoult's novels seem to spring from a single provocative question. The narrative becomes a dramatization of imagined answers to that question. How would a teenager react to the knowledge that she had been genetically engineered to be a perfect match for her cancer-suffering sister? In *My Sister's Keeper*, teenager Anna brings a lawsuit against her own parents to prevent further medical demands on her body. How would two families react to a teenage suicide pact? In *The Pact*, her characters struggle to make sense of just such a pact. The Golds have to come to terms with their daughter's death; the Hartes see their son charged with her murder. In the hands of less skilled writers, the novels might seem tendentious and contrived but Picoult has the ability to transform them into stories that have their own life and vigour.

KEEPING FAITH (1999)
Is seven-year-old Faith in contact with God? As her parents' marriage breaks down, she sees visions, heals the sick and develops stigmata on her hands and feet. Doctors, priests and lawyers battle over the truth of Faith's experiences and a media circus descends on the family in a narrative that cleverly mixes psychology with spirituality.

Jodi Picoult's other novels include Songs of the Humpback Whale, Salem Falls, Vanishing Acts, The Tenth Circle, Nineteen Minutes *and* Handle with Care.

📖Read on
◆ *Salem Falls* (a man arrives in the small town of Salem Falls to escape the fallout from a wrongful conviction for sexual assault but his past re-surfaces when a precocious teenager accuses him of raping her).
◘ Kim Edwards, *The Memory Keeper's Daughter*; Sue Miller, *The Good Mother*; ≫ Anne Tyler, *Back When We Were Grown Ups*.

READ**ON**A**T**HEME:

PLACES

>> Melvyn Bragg, *The Maid of Buttermere* (English Lake District)

>> Emily Brontë, *Wuthering Heights* (Yorkshire moors)

>> Graham Greene, *The Comedians* (Haiti)

>> Thomas Hardy, *Jude the Obscure* (rural Wessex)

>> John Irving, *The Cider House Rules* (rural Maine)

>> Rudyard Kipling, *Kim* (rural India)

>> R.K. Narayan, *The Painter of Signs* (small-town India)

>> Graham Swift, *Waterland* (Norfolk fenlands)

See also: Australia; Canada; Deep South, USA; Egypt; Ireland; Israel; Japan; Latin America; London; New York; Russia; Scotland; Small-Town Life, USA; Village and Countryside; Wales; The Wilderness.

POE, Edgar Allan (1809–49)

US short story writer and poet

Poe's miserable life is almost as well known as his stories. He was an orphan whose foster-father hated him; he was thrown out of university, military college and half a dozen jobs because of the instability of his character; to earn a living he suppressed his real ambition (to be a poet) in favour of hack journalism and sensational fiction; he gambled, fornicated, and finally drank himself to death. He was like a man haunted by his own existence – and this is exactly the feeling in his macabre short stories, which are less about the supernatural than about people driven crazy by their own imagination. 'The Fall of the House of Usher' and 'The Premature Burial' recount the terrifying results when people are accidentally entombed alive. The murderer in 'The Tell-tale Heart' buries his victim under the floorboards, only to be haunted by what he takes to be the thud of the dead man's heartbeat. The hero of 'The Pit and the Pendulum' is psychologically tortured by the Spanish Inquisition, first by fear of a swinging, ever-approaching blade and then by the way the walls of his cell move inwards to crush him. As well as stories of this kind, Poe occasionally wrote lighter mysteries. The best-known of all ('The Murders in the Rue Morgue'; 'The Mystery of Marie Roget') centre on an eccentric investigator who solves crimes by meticulous reconstruction according to the evidence: they are the first-ever detective stories.

Poe's stories are normally collected nowadays as Tales of Mystery and Imagination. *His other writings include poetry ('The Bells'; 'The Raven') and vitriolic literary criticism, savaging such contemporaries as Longfellow.*

Read on

◘ to Poe's stories of the macabre: H.P. Lovecraft, *The Call of Cthulhu and Other Weird Tales*; M.R. James, *Ghost Stories of an Antiquary*; Roald Dahl, *Switch Bitch*; ›› Stephen King, *Nightmares and Dreamscapes*; Richard Marsh, *The Beetle*.

◘ to the detective stories: ›› Arthur Conan Doyle, *The Adventures of Sherlock Holmes*; Edgar Wallace, *The Four Just Men*.

READ ON A THEME

POLICE PROCEDURAL

›› Wilkie Collins, *The Woman in White* (Victorian ancestor of the subgenre)

Freeman Wills Crofts, *Death of a Train*

Martin Cruz Smith, *Gorky Park*

John Harvey, *Cold Light*

Bill James, *Eton Crop*

Quintin Jardine, *Skinner's Rules*

Stuart M. Kaminsky, *Lieberman's Law*

Ed McBain, *Killer's Choice*

›› Ruth Rendell, *A Guilty Thing Surprised*

Maj Sjöwall and Per Wahloo, *The Laughing Policeman*

Joseph Wambaugh, *Finnegan's Week*

READ ON A THEME

POLITICS

Chinua Achebe, *Anthills of the Savannah*
Jorge Amado, *The Violent Land*
Benjamin Disraeli, *Coningsby*
Michael Dobbs, *House of Cards*
Joe Klein, *Primary Colours*
Arthur Koestler, *Darkness at Noon*
>> George Orwell, *Animal Farm*
Amos Oz, *A Perfect Peace*
Howard Spring, *Fame is the Spur*
C.P. Snow, *The Corridors of Power*
>> Anthony Trollope, *Phineas Finn*
>> Gore Vidal, *Burr*

START POINT

POETRY

Even if we choose only from English poetry, the range is enormous. There are a thousand poets, a million poems. We may prefer book-long epics (such as Milton's *Paradise Lost*, recounting the Garden of Eden story of the Fall of Man), or short, lyric statements like the poems of Emily Dickinson or A.E. Housman. Our taste may be for ecstatic description and reflection (such as Shelley provides), gravely intellectual rumination (like that in Ezra Pound's or John Berryman's work) or joky nonsense (such as that of Ogden Nash or Pam Ayres). And because enjoying poetry depends so much on our mood and emotions, selecting what to read is more like choosing a piece of music to listen to than picking a novel or a travel book. For many people, browsing through anthologies is a good way to discover (or rediscover) poets: five minutes' work in the poetry section of a library or a bookshop can open Aladdin's Cave.

Auden, W.H. (1907–73). The personal and political explored in poetry of virtuoso technical ability, wit and intellectual range. It sometimes seems as if Auden could take any subject from the Spanish Civil War to the death of a lover and address it in any poetic form he chose.

Browning, Robert (1812–89). Browning's *Men and Women* (1855) provides lively verse 'snapshots' of grandees, artists, soldiers, monks, all telling us their stories in dramatic monologue. Easy-flowing, character-rich verse, full of quotable (and much quoted) lines and phrases.

Chaucer, Geoffrey (c 1343–1400). The twenty four tales in *The Canterbury Tales* (1387), purportedly told by pilgrims to Canterbury, are by turn, bawdy, wise, sad, chivalric and religious. In 'translation', fine; in Chaucer's own English, not impossible to understand – and wonderfully 'medieval' in flavour.

Donne, John (1572–1631). Religious poems; love lyrics. Highly personal reflections on the meaning of love (both sacred and profane), in beautiful Elizabethan English.

Duffy, Carol Ann (born 1955). Satirical, erotic, pessimistic, feminist poems on the tensions and evasions of modern life by the recently appointed Poet Laureate. Everyday details brought into sudden, startling focus, making you look again (and again) at what you thought you knew.

Eliot, T.S. (1888–1965). High-intellectual thought expressed in ravishing, simple images. *The Waste Land* (1922) is about psychological devastation and despair in a symbolic, ruined city. *Four Quartets* (1935–42) are meditations on how religious belief is possible for twentieth-century people. *Ash Wednesday* (1930) collects shorter, lyrical poems.

Frost, Robert (1874–1963). Lyric poems, with particularly fine descriptions of nature.

>> Graves, Robert (1895–1985). Lyric poems, including some magnificent love poetry.

Heaney, Seamus (born 1939). Richly pictorial poems about the countryside and human relations, especially good on the seasons and on old age.

Hopkins, Gerard Manley (1844–89). Religious lyrics, fizzing with ecstasy at the beauty of Creation. Exuberant, ever-surprising surge of language.

Hughes, Ted (1930–98). Comedians love to parody Hughes's doomy, Nature-red-in-tooth-and-claw imagery, and his poetry is grim and dark. But few writers better describe the weather, animals, trees, rocks and water.

Keats, John (1795–1821). 'To a Nightingale'; 'On a Grecian Urn'; 'To Melancholy' and other odes – romantic, ecstatic rhapsody at its headiest. Some of the best-loved lines in the language.

Larkin, Philip (1922–85). Short, sharp poems about ordinary British life since the Second World War: sad, funny and merciless.

Masefield, John (1878–1967). Neat rhythms, simple language, obvious rhymes – and a no-nonsense way with ballad and narrative. English schoolchildren once learned him by heart more than any other poet, and although critics turn up their noses, his verse is still some of the easiest, and most haunting, of the twentieth century.

McGough, Roger (born 1937). One of the 'Liverpool Poets' who became famous at the same time as the Beatles. Stand-up poetry: sly jokes about the human condition, in which the rhythms and the rhymes, comedian's patter crossed with song lyrics, are half the fun.

Owen, Wilfred (1893–1918). Compassionate, horrifying First World War poetry, achingly memorable.

Plath, Sylvia (1932–63). Macabre imagery and ironic wit combine in Plath's poetry of despair and female alienation. Obsession with the tragic drama of her life and death have often obscured the emotional power and technical skill of her poetry.

Tennyson, Alfred, Lord (1809–92). Victorian poetry, much of it inspired by Arthurian legend or by ancient Greece and Rome: sentimental, sometimes cringe-making, always eloquent.

Thomas, Dylan (1914–53). Great themes – love, Nature, ageing, death – in bardic, intoxicated language, a firework show of words.

Walcott, Derek (born 1930). Walcott examines, with immense intelligence and epic ambition, the tension between European culture and Afro-Caribbean culture and the difficulties of emerging from a colonial past with integrity and a genuine sense of self.

Whitman, Walt (1819–92). Hypnotic, free-rhythm poems on Nature, the Sublime and the Journey of Life. Grand thoughts; passionate language; a heady experience.

Wordsworth, William (1770–1850). Poems about Nature, the oddities of human life, memory ('emotion recollected in tranquillity'), in flowing, simple language: like diary jottings written up in verse.

Also recommended: Simon Armitage, *Selected Poems* (2001); John Betjeman, *Summoned by Bells* (1960); William Blake, *Songs of Innocence and Experience* (1794); John Clare, *The Shepherd's Calendar* (1827); Paul Farley, *The Ice Age* (2002); Robert Lowell, *Poems, 1938–1949*; Andrew Marvell, *Poems* (1681); Pablo Neruda, *Twenty Love Poems and a Song of Despair*, Don Paterson, *God's Gift to Women* (1997); Craig Raine, *A Martian Sends a Postcard Home* (1979); Christina Rossetti, *Goblin Market and Other Poems* (1862); William Shakespeare, *Sonnets*; Stevie Smith, *Selected Poems*; W.B. Yeats, *Collected Poems* (1933).

POWELL, Anthony (1905–2000)
British novelist

In the 1930s Powell wrote half a dozen novels satirizing the intellectual and upper classes of the time. The optimistic, aimless young people of *Afternoon Men* drift from party to party, trying to summon up enough willpower to make something of themselves. *From a View to a Death* sets the arts and foxhunting at each other's throats. The hero of *What's Become of Waring?* has to find someone to write the biography of a bestselling travel writer who has disappeared in circumstances which grow more mysterious, and more unsavoury, by the minute. After the Second World War, during which he produced no fiction, Powell abandoned single books for a twelve-novel sequence, *A Dance to the Music of Time*, a satirical portrait of seventy years of English high society and establishment life.

A DANCE TO THE MUSIC OF TIME (1951–75)

The sequence follows its characters from Edwardian schooldays to nostalgic, worldly-wise old age. The narrator, Nick Jenkins, discreet as a civil servant, goes everywhere, knows everyone, and writes of his contemporaries (notably the ambition-racked Widmerpool) in elegant, ironic prose. The books move imperturbably from farce to seriousness, from knockabout to reverie. The first three novels, *A Question of Upbringing*, *A Buyer's Market* and *The Acceptance World*, concern the characters' schooldays, their Oxbridge careers and their entry into the glittering smart set of 1920s London. *At Lady Molly's*, *Casanova's Chinese Restaurant* and *The Kindly Ones* are about first jobs, marriages and the establishment of a network of sexual, social, financial and political alliances which will bind their lives. *The Valley of Bones*, *The Soldier's Art* and *The Military Philosophers* take the characters through two world wars, and *Books Do Furnish a Room*, *Temporary Kings* and *Hearing Secret Harmonies* show them coming to terms with post-war austerity, the white heat of the technological revolution and flower power, reflecting on the change not only in themselves but in every aspect of British establishment life since their schooldays fifty years before.

Powell's other 1930s novels are Venusberg *and* Agents and Patients. *After finishing* A Dance to the Music of Time *he wrote an autobiography,* To Keep the Ball Rolling*, in four volumes and two other (unrelated) novels,* O, How the Wheel Becomes It *and* The Fisher King.

🕮Read on

◘ to Powell's 1930s books: ▸▸ Evelyn Waugh, *Vile Bodies*; Henry Green, *Party Going*; Rose Macaulay, *Crewe Train*.

◘ the mood of elegiac, upper-class malice characteristic of *A Dance to the Music of Time* is repeated in two other novel sequences – ▸▸ Marcel Proust, *Remembrance of Things Past (À la Recherche du temps perdu)* and Simon Raven, *Alms for Oblivion*. Henry Williamson's fifteen-volume *Chronicles of Ancient Sunlight* similarly takes its central character through many decades of his life, from late Victorian London to Devon in the 1950s but its atmosphere of intensity, tragedy and embittered nostalgia for lost happiness is worlds away from Powell's urbane irony. So, too, are Williamson's fascist political sympathies, which mar what is otherwise a striking sequence of novels.

POWYS, John Cowper (1872–1963)
British novelist and non-fiction writer

A university professor, Powys wrote books on ›› Dostoevsky, Homer and ›› Rabelais, dozens of articles, reviews and other non-fiction works, and a lively autobiography. His early novels (*Ducdame, Rodmoor, Wolf Solent*, all written before 1930) are sombre, ›› Hardyish stories about the farmers and fishermen of the English West Country. After he retired from teaching Powys wrote a series of completely different novels: long, mystical books influenced by Homer and the Old Testament and drawing on English legend and Dark Ages history. In *A Glastonbury Romance* modern inhabitants of the Glastonbury area (including worshippers and clergy at the Abbey) find their lives mysteriously affected by local legends of King Arthur and of the Holy Grail. In a similar way, *Maiden Castle* describes how unearthing the distant past – some of the characters are archaeologists working on a prehistoric site – disturbs the present.

🕮Read on
♦ *Weymouth Sands*; *Owen Glendower*.
▫ to Powys's early novels: ›› Victor Hugo, *Toilers of the Sea*; ›› George Eliot, *Silas Marner*; ›› Nathaniel Hawthorne, *The Scarlet Letter*.
▫ to the later fiction: ›› Peter Ackroyd, *English Music*; Lindsay Clarke, *The Chymical Wedding*; Charles Williams, *War in Heaven*.

Two of Powys's brothers were also novelists and *Mr Weston's Good Wine*, a strangely compelling religious allegory by Theodore, and *Love and Death*, a fictionalized autobiography by Llewellyn, are both still worth reading.

PRATCHETT, Terry (born 1948)

British novelist

Pratchett writes lunatic, farcical fantasy. His books are set on Discworld, a vast disc perched on the backs of four huge elephants. Discworld is the home of a thousand thousand species of creature, from trolls and elves to mysterious beings of wood, water, air, light, mud not to mention Mafia heavies, bimbos, winos, film directors, Death, the Three Witches from Macbeth, trombone-playing cows, talking trees, pyramid builders, opera singers and wizards of every degree from Arch-chancellor Wayzygoose to Rincewind (B.mgc, failed). Each book is self-contained, but characters bob in and out like participants in some particularly demented carnival.

The Discworld novels include: The Colour of Magic *(the first)*, The Light Fantastic, Equal Rites, Sourcery, Pyramids, Wyrd Sisters, Guards! Guards!, Moving Pictures, Witches Abroad, Men At Arms, Soul Music, Feet of Clay, Hogfather, Carpe Jugulum, The Thief of Time, Night Watch, The Wee Free Men, Monstrous Regiment, A Hat Full of Sky, Going Postal, Thud!, Wintersmith *and* Making Money.

☜Read on

◆ *Truckers*, *Diggers* and *Wings* (a trilogy of children's/adult fantasy books about a group of 'nomes' who live under the floorboards of a department store); *Good Omens* (a spoof of the horror genre, co-written with ➤➤ Neil Gaiman).

◘ Robert Asprin, Myth series (start with *Another Fine Myth*); Tom Holt, *Odds and Gods* (not fantasy but a farce about the gods and heroes of 'real' myth); Jasper Fforde, *The Eyre Affair* and its sequels; Robert Rankin, *The Hollow Chocolate Bunnies of the Apocalypse*.

PRIESTLEY, J.B. (John Boynton) (1894–1984)

British novelist and playwright

As well as plays and non-fiction books, Priestley wrote over sixty novels. They range from amiable satire (*Low Notes on a High Level*, sending up egghead BBC musicians) to sombre social realism (*Angel Pavement*, about a sleepy 1930s business firm galvanized into new activity and then destroyed by a confidence trickster). His best-loved novel, *The Good Companions*, tells of three people who escape from humdrum lives to join the Dinky Doos concert party in the 1920s. The novel follows the concert party's career in theatres and seaside resorts all over England, and ends with each of the main characters finding self-fulfilment in an entirely unexpected way. The book bulges with show-biz cliché – brave little troupers; lodging-house keepers with hearts of gold; leading ladies and their tantrums; cynical, hung-over leading men – and with warm-hearted nostalgia for the provincial England of the Good Old Days. It is an armchair of a novel, a book to wallow in – and if life was never really like that, so much the worse for life.

⬎ Read on

◆ *Lost Empires* is Priestley's own, darker story of life in the music halls.

◘ to *The Good Companions*: ≫ Beryl Bainbridge, *An Awfully Big Adventure* (set in a 1950s repertory company in Liverpool).

◘ to Priestley's books in general: ≫ H.G. Wells, *Tono-Bungay*; James Hilton, *Goodbye, Mr Chips*; Eric Linklater, *Poet's Pub*; ≫ George Orwell, *Keep the Aspidistra Flying*; Patrick Hamilton, *Twenty Thousand Streets Under the Sky*.

READ ON A THEME:

PRIVATE EYES

    Lawrence Block, *A Dance at the Slaughterhouse* (Matt Scudder)

    James Lee Burke, *Cadillac Jukebox* (Dave Robicheaux)

≫ Raymond Chandler, *Farewell, My Lovely* (Philip Marlowe)

    Max Allan Collins, *True Detective* (Nate Heller)

    Howard Engel, *Dead and Buried* (Benny Cooperman)

    Loren D. Estleman, *The Hours of the Virgin* (Amos Walker)

    Sue Grafton, *G is for Gumshoe* (Kinsey Millhone)

≫ Dashiell Hammett, *The Maltese Falcon* (Sam Spade)

    Stuart Kaminsky, *Murder on the Yellow Brick Road* (Toby Peters)

    Ross Macdonald, *The Drowning Pool* (Lew Archer)

    John Milne, *Dead Birds* (Jimmy Jenner)

    Robert B. Parker, *Small Vices* (Spenser)

See also: Classic Detection; Great (Classic) Detectives

PROULX, Annie (born 1935)
US novelist and short story writer

Annie Proulx did not begin writing fiction until she was in her fifties but almost immediately her original (often dark) imagination, her evocative use of landscape and setting, her quirky humour and arresting use of language brought her success. A collection of short stories, *Heart Songs* (1988), was followed by her first novel, *Postcards*, the tragic saga of an American farming family and one member of it, driven into exile by an act of violence. The narrative of harsh, bleak lives lived out against the backdrop of a succession of unforgiving landscapes is held together by the novel device of a sequence of postcards, carefully reproduced in the text, sent by and to the family. Her second novel, *The Shipping News* (see below) won the Pulitzer Prize for fiction. Since this success, Annie Proulx has published two further novels, *Accordion Crimes* and *That Old Ace in the Hole* and three collections of 'Wyoming' stories – *Close Range, Bad Dirt* and *Fine the Way It Is. Close Range* includes the successfully filmed novella, 'Brokeback Mountain', telling the poignant story of two Wyoming ranch-hands drawn into an intense sexual relationship. Their doomed struggle to accommodate their homosexual desire within a sense of self created by a macho culture is movingly portrayed.

THE SHIPPING NEWS (1993)
At the beginning of the novel Quoyle is an unsuccessful newspaperman in New York, still brooding on the humiliations of his marriage to a woman who first betrayed him and then was killed in an accident, leaving him with two small children. Accompanied by his young daughters and by a formidable maiden aunt, he returns to Newfoundland, his father's birthplace, and there he finds the fulfilment that eluded him in the city. He establishes himself at the local newspaper, finds himself drawn into the daily life of the community and emerges from the protective shell of loneliness to begin a new and rewarding relationship. More optimistic about human possibility than Proulx's other work ('And it may be that love sometimes occurs without pain or misery,' the book concludes) *The Shipping News* is saved from the banality that a mere outline of its plot might suggest by Proulx's wit, originality and skilful unravelling of events. Quoyle's transformation becomes an offbeat celebration of the potential people have for change.

☙Read on
◆ *Accordion Crimes* (stories of immigrants to the USA connected by possession of a button accordion).

◘ ❯❯ Carol Shields, *The Stone Diaries*; Jayne Anne Phillips, *Machine Dreams*; Joy Williams, *The Quick and the Dead*; Elizabeth McCracken, T*he Giant's House*.

PROUST, Marcel (1871–1922)

French novelist

Proust's *Remembrance of Things Past (À la Recherche du temps perdu)* (1913–27; magnificently translated by C.K. Scott Moncrieff and Terence Kilmartin) is in seven sections (*Swann's Way, Within a Budding Grove, The Guermantes Way, Cities of the Plain, The Captive, The Fugitive, Time Regained*). Each is as long as a normal novel and each can be read both on its own and as part of the whole huge tapestry. The book is a memoir, told in the first person by a narrator called Marcel, of a group of rich French socialites from the 1860s to the end of the First World War. It shows how they react to outside events – the Dreyfus case, women's emancipation, the First World War – and how, as the world moves on, their power and social position wane. Above all, it shows them reacting to each other, to friends, acquaintances and servants: the book is full of love affairs, parties (at which gossip is hot about who is 'in' or 'out' and why), alliances and betrayals. Through it all moves Marcel himself, good-natured, self-effacing, fascinated by beauty (both human and artistic: his accounts of music and literature are as deeply felt as those of people), and with a sharply ironical eye for social and sexual absurdity. Proust developed for the book a system of 'involuntary memory', in which each sensuous stimulus – the smell of lilac, the taste of cake dipped in tea – unlocks from the subconscious a stream of images of the past. Although this technique has structural importance in the novel – Proust believed that our present only makes sense when it is refracted through past experience – its chief effect for the reader is to provide pages of languorous, detailed descriptions, prose poems on everything from the feel of embroidery under the fingertips to garden sounds and scents on a summer evening. Proust likes to take his time: at one point Marcel spends nearly one hundred pages wondering whether to get up or stay in bed. But only the length at which he works allows him scope for the sensuous, malicious decadence which is the main feature of his work.

Proust's other writings include a collection of short stories and literary parodies, The Pleasures and the Days (Les Plaisirs et les jours)*, and* Jean Santeuil*, a draft of part of* Remembrance of Things Past. Against Sainte-Beuve and other Essays *is a collection of his literary criticism.*

📖Read on

◘ good parallels to the sensuous childhood evocations of the first part of *Remembrance of Things Past*: Alain-Fournier, *Le Grand Meaulnes*; ⟩⟩ James Joyce, *Portrait of the Artist as a Young Man*.

◘ echoing the hedonism and decadence of some of Proust's later sections: Joris-Karl Huysmans, *Against Nature (À Rebours)*.

◘ good on 'the texture of experience': Dorothy Richardson, *Pilgrimage*; ⟩⟩ Virginia Woolf, *The Waves*; John Dos Passos, *Manhattan Transfer*.

◘ novel sequences of comparable grandeur: ⟩⟩ Anthony Powell, *A Dance to the Music of Time*; Henry Williamson, *The Flax of Dreams*.

READ ON A THEME:

PUBLISH AND BE DAMNED

Writers; publishers; agents; readers; fans

⟩⟩ Margery Allingham, *Flowers for the Judge*
⟩⟩ Helen Dunmore, *Zennor in Darkness*
⟩⟩ P.D. James, *Original Sin*
    Wyndham Lewis, *The Apes of God*
⟩⟩ Anthony Powell, *What's Become of Waring?*
⟩⟩ Philip Roth, *Zuckerman Unbound*
    Bernhard Schlink, *The Reader*
⟩⟩ Tom Sharpe, *The Great Pursuit*
⟩⟩ Carol Shields, *Mary Swann*

PULLMAN, Philip (born 1946)
British novelist

The novels (*Northern Lights*, *The Subtle Knife* and *The Amber Spyglass*) which make up Philip Pullman's 'His Dark Materials' trilogy have gained a devoted following over the last decade. Film and stage adaptations have introduced yet more readers to a fictional universe (or multiverse) of memorable originality. At the heart of the story is Lyra, a young girl from an Oxford that resembles the university city of our own world in some ways and is radically different from it in others. At the beginning of **Northern Lights** (known as **The Golden Compass** in America and in the 2007 film adaptation), she is living in Jordan College where she has been placed by Lord Asriel, a man she believes to be her uncle. It is there that she first hears rumours of strange events taking place in the Arctic North, of the mysterious substance called 'Dust' and of the bogeymen known as the 'Gobblers', child-snatchers who prowl the city streets in search of prey. When her friend Roger disappears, apparently a victim of the Gobblers, Lyra embarks on a mission to rescue him which takes her first to London and then to the frozen North, and involves the glamorous but villainous Mrs Coulter, a truth-telling compass which few but she can interpret, a Texan aeronaut named Lee Scoresby and Iorek Byrnison, a giant armoured bear of great honour and intelligence. In the two books that followed, Pullman took Lyra and his readers into new worlds, slowly unfolding a narrative on an extraordinarily grand scale. Drawing on a remarkable range of sources, from classic literature and Norse mythology to particle physics and theology, Philip Pullman has created what may well be the most intelligent, dramatic and compelling work of fantasy fiction of modern times.

Lyra's Oxford *and* Once Upon a Time in the North *are short books connected to the Trilogy. Pullman's other books include a series of historical novels featuring a young woman in Victorian England named Sally Lockhart* (The Ruby in the Smoke, The Shadow in the North, The Tiger in the Well *and* The Tin Princess), *and a number of novels for children and young adults of which the most rewarding are* The Butterfly Tattoo, Clockwork *and* The Scarecrow and his Servant.

✎Read on
◆ *The Ruby in the Smoke.*
▢ Cornelia Funke, *Inkheart*; Philip Reeve, *Mortal Engines*; Jonathan Stroud, *The Amulet of Samarkand.*

PYM, Barbara (1913–80)
British novelist

Only ›› Jane Austen and Ivy Compton-Burnett wrote about worlds as restricted as Pym's – and she is regularly compared to both of them. Her books are high-Anglican high comedies; she is tart about the kind of pious middle-class ladies who regard giving sherry parties for the clergy as doing good works, and she is merciless to priests. Much of the charm of her books lies in their ornate, formal dialogue: her characters all speak with the same prissy, self-conscious elegance, like civil servants taught light conversation by Oscar Wilde.

A GLASS OF BLESSINGS (1958)

Wilmet Forsyth is rich, well-bred, happy and dim. She fills her mind with fantasies about the priests and parishioners at her local church, imagining that their lives are a whirl of hidden passions, ambitions and frustrations. She imagines herself in love with a handsome evening-class teacher, and assumes that he adores her too. As the book proceeds, every one of these assumptions is proved spectacularly, ludicrously mistaken.

Pym's other novels are Some Tame Gazelle, Excellent Women, Jane and Prudence, Less Than Angels, Quartet in Autumn, The Sweet Dove Died, Crampton Hodnett *and* An Academic Question.

☜Read on

◆ *Quartet in Autumn*.
◘ Ivy Compton-Burnett, *Pastors and Masters*; ❯❯ A.N. Wilson, *Kindly Light*; J.F. Powers, *Morte d'Urban*; ❯❯ Joanna Trollope, *The Choir*.

PYNCHON, Thomas (born 1937)
US novelist

Reading Pynchon's satires is like exploring a maze with an opinionated and eccentric guide. He leads us lovingly up every blind alley, breaks off to tell jokes, falls into reveries, ridicules everything and everyone, and refuses to say where he's going until he gets there. *The Crying of Lot 49* begins with Oedipa Maas setting out to discover why she has been left a legacy by an ex-lover, and what it is; but it quickly develops into a crazy tour of hippie 1960s California, an exploration of drugs, bizarre sex, psychic sensitivity and absurd politics, centring on a group of oddball characters united in a secret society determined to subvert the US postal system. *Gravity's Rainbow* is a much darker fable, a savage anti-war satire set in a top-secret British centre for covert operations during the Second World War. In a mad world, where actions have long ceased to have any moral point, where on principle nothing is ever explained or justified, the characters spend their working hours alternately doing what they are told and trying to find out the reason for their existence, and pass their leisure hours in masochistic, joyless sex. On the basis of his short stories and *The Crying of Lot 49*, Pynchon is sometimes claimed as a comic writer. But although *Gravity's Rainbow* is satirical, its jokes are knives, and its farce makes us scream with despair, not joy.

Pynchon's first and most experimental novel was V. *His other novels are* Vineland, Mason & Dixon *(a wild conflation of history and anachronism, loosely based on the two eighteenth-century surveyors who created the Mason–Dixon line),* Against the Day *and* Inherent Vice. Slow Learner *is a collection of short stories and novellas.*

📖Read on

♦ *Against the Day* (a huge slab of a novel, a thousand pages and counting, which provides Pynchon's unique take on the era between the 1890s and the First World War).

◘ the satirical fury of *Gravity's Rainbow* is most nearly matched in: ≫ Joseph Heller, *Catch-22*; William Gaddis, *J.R.* (about a deranged ten-year-old genius in a reform school who trades in stocks and shares and exploits other people's greed).

◘ Pynchon's more genial, loonier side is parallelled in: ≫ Mario Vargas Llosa, *Aunt Julia and the Scriptwriter*; Terry Southern, *The Magic Christian*; ≫ Kurt Vonnegut, *Breakfast of Champions*; John Barth, *The Sot-Weed Factor*.

RABAN, Jonathan (born 1942)
British travel writer and novelist

Raban's most successful travel books have described his varied encounters with America, where he has now made his home. *Old Glory* takes him on a voyage down the Mississippi, detailing his own achievement of a dream he had had since first reading Huckleberry Finn as a boy and recording the past and the present of those who live on the river's banks; *Hunting Mister Heartbreak* follows in the footsteps of Hector St John de Crevecoeur ('Mister Heartbreak'), a nineteenth-century French aristocrat turned American farmer, in an attempt to experience the reality of becoming or being an American in the late twentieth century. In *Passage to Juneau* Raban sails from Seattle to Alaska, accompanied only by the ghosts of his own past and of the men who made the journey before him. Raban has considered his relationship to his native land in both fiction and travel writing. The novel *Foreign Land*, the story of a man returning to Britain after years as an expatriate and finding that only his voyages on a small boat can reconcile him to the culture shock he experiences, prefigured in fictional form some of the ideas that found further expression in *Coasting*, a travel book that describes a journey he made around Britain, sailing the coastline and visiting the towns and resorts around it.

Jonathan Raban's other books include Soft City *(an analysis of urban life),* Arabia Through the Looking Glass *and* Bad Land *(travel books),* Waxwings *and* Surveillance *(novels), and* My Holy War *(a collection of essays and reflections on post-9/11 America).* For Love and Money *is a collection of reviews and essays.*

⪧Read on

◆ *Surveillance*.
◘ to the American books: ›› Bill Bryson, *The Lost Continent* (very different in style from Raban but a similarly unsentimental perspective on American life); Hector St John de Crevecoeur, *Letters from an American Farmer*; William Least-Heat Moon, *Blue Highways*; ›› John Steinbeck, *Travels with Charley* (the novelist goes in search of the real America in a 1962 journey).
◘ to *Coasting*: ›› Paul Theroux, *The Kingdom by the Sea*.

RABELAIS, François (c1494–1553)
French satirist

Renegade monk, doctor, scientist, philosopher and bon viveur – he led a crowded life – Rabelais began writing satire in his mid-thirties, and quickly acquired yet another scurrilous reputation. At heart his *Gargantua and Pantagruel* are simple fairytales: accounts of the birth and education of the giant Gargantua and of his son Pantagruel. But, in reality, he sends up every aspect of medieval knowledge and belief. The giants study philosophy, mathematics, theology and alchemy; they build an anti-monastery whose rules are not poverty, chastity and obedience but wealth, fornication and licence. Pantagruel's mentor is no dignified greybeard but the con-man Panurge, and the two of them go on a fantastic journey (through countries as fabulous as any of those visited by Sinbad or Gulliver) to find the answer to the question 'Whom shall Pantagruel marry?' Much of *Gargantua*'s first half is taken up with a fierce battle between the giants and their neighbours, and in particular with the exploits of the roistering, apoplectic Friar John of the Funnels and Goblets, who is later rewarded by being made Abbot of the Monastery of Do As You Like. Rabelais described his books as a 'feast of mirth', and their intellectual satire is balanced by celebration of physical pleasure of every kind: not for nothing has the word 'rabelaisian' entered the dictionary.

⮒Read on

◘ ≫ Laurence Sterne, *Tristram Shandy*; ≫ Jonathan Swift, *Gulliver's Travels*; Giovanni Boccaccio, *Decameron* (short stories); Anon, *A Thousand and One Nights/The Arabian Nights' Entertainment*.

RANKIN, Ian (born 1960)
British writer

So successful has Ian Rankin been as a crime writer in the last decade that he has established a whole new subgenre. According to one critic, Rankin, whose novels are set in Edinburgh, is 'the king of tartan noir'. Certainly he has been successful in portraying an image of Edinburgh very different from the traditional one. He shows the darker side of the city, the skull beneath the skin of the tourist façade. He takes us away from the Royal Mile and Princes Street and into a bleak and gritty Edinburgh of junkie squats, gangland wars and corruption in high places. Our guide through the mean streets of this other Edinburgh is the central character in most of Rankin's novels, Detective Inspector John Rebus. Rebus, although he owes something to crime fiction clichés of the lone-wolf investigator tormented by his own inner demons, is a genuinely original creation and has a complexity not often encountered in characters in 'genre' fiction. From the first novel, *Knots and Crosses* (1987), Rebus has been as interesting as the cases he investigates and, as the series has progressed, Rankin has developed the character with great skill. He has also shown increasing ambition in the subjects he covers. In *Dead Souls*, for example, the plot accommodates the human consequences of a paedophile scandal in a children's home, the return of a killer from the States to his native Scotland, Rebus's own return to his home town and the party-filled world of Edinburgh's *jeunesse dorée*. All the threads of the narrative are effortlessly woven into a satisfying whole.

BLACK AND BLUE (1997)

Bible John was the name given by the media to a serial killer in the 1970s. He was never caught. Now a copycat killer is at work. Rebus, struggling with a drink problem and unsympathetic superiors, has been sidelined. But, as another investigation takes him from Glasgow ganglands to Aberdeen and an offshore oilrig, he is drawn into the web of intrigue and corruption that surrounds the search for the killer dubbed by the media (with characteristic inventiveness) Johnny Bible.

The other Rebus novels are Hide and Seek, Tooth and Nail, Strip Jack, The Black Book, Mortal Causes, Let it Bleed, The Hanging Garden, Set in Darkness, The Falls, Resurrection Men, A Question of Blood, Fleshmarket Close, The Naming of the Dead *and* Exit Music. A Good Hanging *and* Beggars Banquet *are collections of short stories, many featuring Rebus. Rankin has also written three novels* (Witch Hunt, Bleeding Hearts *and* Cold Blood) *under the pseudonym Jack Harvey.*

☞Read on

◆ *The Hanging Garden*; *Exit Music*.

◘ ❯❯ Reginald Hill, *On Beulah Height*; ❯❯ Val McDermid, *The Wire in the Blood*; John Harvey, *Cutting Edge*; Quintin Jardine, *Skinner's Rules* (the first in a series of Edinburgh-set police procedurals); Denise Mina, *Garnethill*.

REICHS, Kathy (born 1950)

US novelist

One of the most successful sub-genres of crime fiction in recent years has been the forensic thriller in which readers get a front-row seat in the crime laboratory as investigators set about analysing blood spatter patterns and bone samples, using the tools of science to reconstruct what happened and point the finger at the bad guys. Since the publication of *Deja Dead* in 1997, Kathy Reichs has been amongst the most skilful practitioners in the field and her likeable heroine, the forensic anthropologist Temperance Brennan, has been the focus for some of its most intriguing mysteries. In her fiction, technical expertise serves the plot and science is married effectively to story.

MONDAY MOURNING (2004)

The skeletons of three young women are found beneath a basement floor. A nineteenth century button found with them suggests their age but Tempe Brennan is not so sure. If she's right the Montreal Homicide department has three new murders on its books.

The other Tempe Brennan books are Death du Jour, Deadly Decisions, Fatal Voyage, Grave Secrets, Bare Bones, Cross Bones, Break No Bones, Bones to Ashes, Devil Bones *and* 206 Bones.

Read on

◆ *Death du Jour* (past and present intertwine as Tempe Brennan investigates both the bones of a nineteenth century nun who is a candidate for sainthood and the victims of a recent and brutal arson attack).

◻ Simon Beckett, *The Chemistry of Death* (for a British version of Reichs's forensic mysteries); Tess Gerritsen, *The Surgeon*; James Patterson, *1st to Die*; Karin Slaughter, *Blindsighted*.

READ ON A THEME:

RENAISSANCE EUROPE

›› John Banville, *Kepler*
Sarah Dunant, *The Birth of Venus*
Dorothy Dunnett, *Niccolò Rising*
›› Umberto Eco, *The Island of the Day Before*
Carlos Fuentes, *Terra Nostra*
M.R. Lovric, *The Floating Book*
David Madsen, *Memoirs of a Gnostic Dwarf*
Stephen Marlowe, *The Memoirs of Christopher Columbus*
›› Lawrence Norfolk, *The Pope's Rhinoceros*
›› Salman Rushdie, *The Enchantress of Florence*
Irving Stone, *The Agony and the Ecstasy*

See also: The Middle Ages

RENAULT, Mary (1905–83)
South African novelist

A South African by birth, Renault went to London in her twenties, and served as a nurse during the Second World War. In her thirties and forties she wrote several novels about hospital and wartime life, culminating in *The Charioteer*, the moving story of a homosexual serviceman. In the 1950s she began writing historical novels about ancient Greece. *The King Must Die* (see below) and *The Bull from the Sea* are based on the myth of King Theseus of Athens, who killed the Cretan Minotaur; *Fire From Heaven*, *The Persian Boy* and *Funeral Games* are about Alexander the Great. Like ›› Robert Graves, Renault treats people of the past as though they were psychologically just like us, so that even the most bizarre political or sexual behaviour seems both rational and credible.

THE KING MUST DIE (1958)
Every year the Cretans demand tribute from Athens: seven young men and seven young women have to learn bull-dancing and be sacrificed to the Minotaur. One year, Prince Theseus takes the place of one of the young men, and sails to Crete to take revenge.

Renault's other Greek books are The Last of the Wine, The Mask of Apollo *and* The Praise Singer.

📖 Read on
♦ *The Bull From the Sea.*
◘ ›› Colleen McCullough, *The First Man in Rome*; ›› Robert Graves, *I, Claudius*; Tom Holt, *The Walled Orchard*; ›› Steven Saylor, *Roman Blood*; Naomi Mitchison, *The Corn King and the Spring Queen*; Steven Pressfield, *Last of the Amazons*.

RENDELL, Ruth (born 1930)
British novelist

Rendell's Chief Inspector Wexford novels are atmospheric murder mysteries in traditional style, set in the small towns and villages of the English Home Counties. Like ›› P.D. James, she spends much time developing the character of her detective, a liberal and cultured man appalled by the psychological pressures that drive people to crime. Those pressures are the subject of Rendell's other books (both under her own name and as Barbara Vine): grim stories of paranoia, obsession and inadequacy.

Rendell's Wexford books include From Doon With Death, Wolf to the Slaughter, A Guilty Thing Surprised, Some Lie and Some Die, Kissing the Gunner's Daughter, An Unkindness of Ravens, Harm Done, The Babes in the Wood, End in Tears *and* Not in the Flesh. *Her psychological novels include* The Face of Trespass, The Killing Doll, The Tree of Hands, Live Flesh, Talking to Strange Men, Going Wrong, The Crocodile Bird, A Sight for Sore Eyes, Thirteen Steps Down, The Water's Lovely *and* Portobello. Means of Evil, The Copper Peacock *and* Piranha to Scurfy *are collections of short stories. As Barbara Vine, Rendell has written* A Dark-Adapted Eye, A Fatal Inversion, The House of Stairs, Gallowglass, King Solomon's Carpet, Asta's Book, No Night is Too Long, The Brimstone Wedding, The Chimney-Sweeper's Boy, Grasshopper, The Blood Doctor, The Minotaur *and* The Birthday Present.

Read on

▪ to the Wexford books: ›› P.D. James, *Shroud for a Nightingale*; R.D. Wingfield, *Hard Frost*; ›› Reginald Hill, *Exit Lines*.
▪ to the psychological thrillers: ›› Patricia Highsmith, *The Glass Cell*; ›› Minette Walters, *The Dark Room*; Frances Fyfield, *Undercurrents*; Nicci French, *Killing Me Softly*.

READ ON A THEME

RESCUED LIVES
Biographies of people history had forgotten

Sarah Bakewell, *The English Dane* (Jorgen Jorgenson, 19th-century Danish adventurer and convict)
Sarah Gristwood, *Arbella: England's Lost Queen* (Arbella Stuart, claimant to the English throne)
Julia Keay, *Alexander the Corrector* (Alexander Cruden, 18th-century biblical scholar)
Ben Macintyre, *The Napoleon of Crime* (Victorian master-criminal Adam Worth)

Caroline P. Murphy, *The Pope's Daughter* (Felice della Rovere, daughter of Renaissance pope)

Miranda Seymour, *The Bugatti Queen* (pioneering woman racing driver Hellé Nice)

Dava Sobel, *Longitude* (the inventor and clockmaker John Harrison)

➤➤ Claire Tomalin, *The Invisible Woman* (Dickens's mistress, Ellen Ternan)

➤➤ Simon Winchester, *The Surgeon of Crowthorne* (William C. Minor, 19th-century lunatic and lexicographer)

Ben Woolley, *The Herbalist* (17th-century herbalist and physician Nicholas Culpeper)

READ ON A THEME:

REVISITING ONE'S PAST
➤➤ Margaret Atwood, *Surfacing*
➤➤ Anita Brookner, *A Start in Life*
➤➤ Michael Frayn, *Spies*
➤➤ David Guterson, *East of the Mountains*
Bernard MacLaverty, *Grace Notes*
➤➤ Hilary Mantel, *Vacant Possession*
➤➤ Bernice Rubens, *Our Father*
➤➤ Graham Swift, *Waterland*
➤➤ Paul Theroux, *Picture Palace*
➤➤ Virginia Woolf, *Mrs Dalloway*

READ ON A THEME:

REWRITING HISTORY
Novels where the past has changed

➤➤ Kingsley Amis, *The Alteration* (the Reformation hasn't taken place and England is still Catholic)

> » Michael Chabon, *The Yiddish Policemen's Union*
> » Philip K. Dick, *The Man in the High Castle* (the Axis powers have won the Second World War)
> » William Gibson & Bruce Sterling, *The Difference Engine*
> » Robert Harris, *Fatherland*
> Ward Moore, *Bring the Jubilee* (the South won the American Civil War)
> » Philip Roth, *The Plot Against America*
> Owen Sheers, *Resistance*

RHYS, Jean (1894–1979)
British novelist

All Rhys's novels and stories are about the same kind of person, the 'Jean Rhys woman'. She was once vivacious and attractive (an actress, perhaps, or a dancer) but she fell in love with some unsuitable man or men, was betrayed, and now lives alone, maudlin and mentally unhinged. In Rhys's first four novels (published in the 1920s and 1930s), the heroines are casualties of the Jazz Age, flappers crushed by life itself. In her last book, *Wide Sargasso Sea* (1966), the central character is a victim of the way men think (or fail to think) of women: she is a young Caribbean heiress in the early 1800s, who marries an English gentleman, Mr Rochester, and ends up as the demented creature hidden in the attics of Thornfield Hall in *Jane Eyre*.

GOOD MORNING, MIDNIGHT (1939)
Deserted by her husband after the death of their baby, Sasha would have drunk herself to death if a generous friend had not rescued her and paid for her to spend a fortnight in Paris. She 'arranges her little life', as she puts it: a cycle of solitary meals and drinks, barren conversations with strangers, drugged sleep in seedy hotel rooms. She is a damned soul, a husk – and then a gigolo, mistaking her for a rich woman, begins to court her, and she has to gather the rags of her sanity and try to take hold of her life once more.

Rhys's other novels are Quartet/Postures, After Leaving Mr Mackenzie *and* Voyage in the Dark. The Left Bank, Tigers are Better-looking *and* Sleep it Off, Lady *are collections of short stories.*

⧨Read on
◆ *Wide Sargasso Sea*.
◻ to *Good Morning, Midnight*: ⟩⟩ Brian Moore, *The Doctor's Wife*; ⟩⟩ Doris
Lessing, *The Golden Notebook*; Mary McCarthy, *The Company She Keeps*; ⟩⟩ Anita
Brookner, *Hôtel du Lac*.
◻ to *Wide Sargasso Sea*: Lisa St Aubin de Terán, *The Keepers of the House*.

THE RHYTHM OF NATURE
People in tune with or in thrall to the land

Pearl S. Buck, *The Good Earth*
Neil M. Gunn, *The Well at the World's End*
⟩⟩ Thomas Hardy, *Far From the Madding Crowd*
⟩⟩ Susan Hill, *In the Springtime of the Year*
Halldor Laxness, *Independent People*
Mikhail Sholokhov, *Virgin Soil Upturned*
⟩⟩ Jane Smiley, *A Thousand Acres*
⟩⟩ Adam Thorpe, *Ulverton*

See also: Village and Countryside

RICHARDSON, Samuel (1689–1761)
British novelist

A successful printer, Richardson was compiling a book of sample letters for all
occasions when he had the idea of writing whole novels in letter-form. He produced
three: *Pamela*, *Clarissa* and *Sir Charles Grandison*. They are enormously long
(over a million words each), and readers even at the time complained of boredom.
But the books were bestsellers – not, as Richardson imagined, because of their
high moral tone, but because his sensational theme (the way some people are
drawn irresistibly to debauch the innocent) guaranteed success.

CLARISSA, OR THE HISTORY OF A YOUNG LADY (1748)

To escape from her parents, who have shut her in her room until she agrees to marry a man she loathes, the hapless Clarissa Harlowe elopes with Mr Lovelace, a rake. He tries every possible way to persuade her to sleep with him, and when she refuses he puts her into a brothel, drugs and rapes her. She goes into a decline and dies of shame. The story is told by means of letters from the main characters, to one another, to friends and acquaintances. One of Richardson's triumphs – which some critics claim justifies the book's inordinate length – is to reveal Lovelace's villainy only gradually, as Clarissa herself discovers it.

⮏Read on

◆ *Pamela*.

◘ Pierre Choderlos de Laclos, *Les Liaisons dangereuses* is another letter-novel about moral predation, but shorter, wittier and less sentimental. A young aristocrat in pre-Revolutionary France, bored by the restrictions of polite society, devotes herself to the cynical, ice-cool shedding of all moral restraint. This book apart, Richardson's work has been more pilloried than parallelled. ❯❯ Henry Fielding, for example, in *Tom Jones*, mocks Richardson's moral earnestness: far from shrinking from the pleasures of seduction, Tom lives for them.

ROBERTS, Michèle (born 1949)

British poet and novelist

Michèle Roberts's novels combine a sensuous and poetic appreciation of the natural world with inventive imaginings and re-imaginings of history, religion, the relationships between men and women and those between mothers and daughters. *Daughters of the House* looks at several generations of women in an obsessively Catholic household in 1940s–50s provincial France. *Flesh and Blood* is an interlocking sequence of dark, magic-realist tales, spanning centuries, of the relationships between mothers and their daughters. *Impossible Saints* juxtaposes the fictional story of Saint Josephine with Roberts's retellings of the lives of actual Catholic women saints to create a portrait of female sexuality, intelligence and imagination battling through the centuries against the constraints imposed on them. *The Mistressclass* links a contemporary story of sibling rivalry and betrayal with the story of Charlotte Brontë's relationship with the Belgian teacher Constantin Heger.

THE BOOK OF MRS NOAH (1987)

This is a dazzling fantasy, set in the present day. A woman visiting Venice with her preoccupied husband fantasizes that she is Mrs Noah. The Ark is a vast library, a repository not only of creatures but of the entire knowledge and experience of the human race. She is its curator (or Arkivist), and her fellow voyagers are five Sibyls and a token male, the Gaffer, a bearded old party who once wrote a bestselling book (the Bible) and has now retired to a tax-heaven in the sky. Each Sibyl tells a story, and each story is about the way men have mistreated women down the centuries. Roberts channels feminist anger at male oppression into a witty and imaginative tour de force.

Roberts's other novels include The Wild Girl/The Secret Gospel of Mary Magdalene, In the Red Kitchen, Fair Exchange, The Looking Glass *and* Reader, I Married Him. *During* Mother's Absence *and* Playing Sardines *are collections of short stories;* Paper Houses *is a recently published memoir.*

➬Read on

◆ *The Wild Girl* (the gospel according to Mary Magdalene).

◘ ▶▶ Margaret Atwood, *The Handmaid's Tale*; ▶▶ Angela Carter, *The Infernal Desire Machines of Doctor Hoffman*; ▶▶ Virginia Woolf, *Orlando*; ▶▶ Margaret Forster, *The Memory Box*; Sara Maitland, *Three Times Table*.

ROBINSON, Marilynne (born 1943)

US novelist

In 1980, Marilynne Robinson published her first novel, *Housekeeping*, the story of two sisters and their eccentric upbringing in a small Midwestern town. Critics were enthralled by the carefully constructed cadences of its poetic prose and by its reworking of familiar motifs in American literature to tell an exclusively female coming-of-age story. *Housekeeping* attracted many awards and much acclaim but, for more than twenty years after its appearance, Robinson published no further novels. She finally broke her silence in 2004 with *Gilead* and readers were able once again to appreciate the beauty of her style and the subtlety of her intelligence. The elderly preacher John Ames, reviewing his life and marvelling over the late marriage and fatherhood that have provided him with unexpected happiness, worries over the return of his godson, the scapegrace Jack Boughton, to the small Iowa town that gives the book its title. Jack's arrival precipitates a sequence of events that disturbs Ames's ideas of both the past and the present. *Home*, which was published in 2008, examines some of the events in *Gilead* from a different perspective. We watch the return of the prodigal through his own eyes and through those of his sister Glory who has returned to the family home to care for their dying father. During Jack's extended visit to the home that he has not seen for so long, the siblings and their father are obliged to re-examine the ties that bind them. *Home*, like its two predecessors, has a grace and spiritual profundity that few modern novels can match.

⧉Read on

◻ Georges Bernanos, *The Diary of a Country Priest*; ≫ Penelope Fitzgerald, *The Blue Flower*; William Maxwell, *Time Will Darken It*; Per Petterson, *Out Stealing Horses*.

ROBINSON, Peter (born 1950)
British novelist

Over the last twenty years, Peter Robinson has written a series of book featuring Inspector Alan Banks, all set in the Yorkshire Dales and all combining the charm of old-fashioned English mysteries with a very contemporary concern with the realities of violence, desire and greed. As the series has progressed, Robinson's confidence and ambition have grown and the books are now among the most satisfying of all British police procedurals. Banks himself is a well-rounded character, of whom the reader learns more and more in each book, the supporting cast is well drawn and the plots, which often move between past and present, are complex but move smoothly towards convincing resolutions.

IN A DRY SEASON (1999)
The village of Hobb's End has been hidden beneath a reservoir for forty years. In the drought caused by an exceptionally hot summer, a secret from the village's past emerges in the shape of a human skeleton. Inspector Banks, in bad odour with his chief constable, is sent to head up what it is assumed will be a dead-end investigation but gradually he begins to unearth the truth about a death in the past that is still affecting the present.

Other Inspector Banks novels include Gallows View *(the first)*, A Dedicated Man, The Hanging Valley, Past Reason Hated, Innocent Graves, The Summer That Never

Was, Playing with Fire, Strange Affair, A Piece of My Heart, Friend of the Devil *and* All the Colours of Darkness.

🖉Read on
◆ *Past Reason Hated*.
◘ Stephen Booth, *The Dead Place*; Graham Hurley, *Deadlight*; ›› Val McDermid, *A Place of Execution*; Peter Turnbull, *After the Flood*.

ROGERS, Jane (born 1952)
British novelist

Jane Rogers's two finest novels are both historical fiction. *Mr Wroe's Virgins* (made into a memorable TV drama starring Jonathan Pryce), is the story of a charismatic fire-and-brimstone preacher in 1830s Lancashire who seizes upon a biblical text to persuade himself that he should live with seven virgins 'for comfort and succour'. Told in the very different voices of four of the virgins chosen from Mr Wroe's congregation, this is a novel that approaches the mysteries of faith and love with intelligence and humanity. *Promised Lands* interweaves the story of the First Fleet's journey to Australia and the largely uncomprehending responses of the men in it to a new land and new peoples with a modern story of a couple with very different ideas about the nature of their handicapped son. The modern and historical strands of the narrative occasionally seem inadequately connected, two novels struggling to emerge from one, but at its best *Promised Lands* uses both to consider ideas of innocence, idealism and the dangers of constructing stories to explain the lives of others.

Jane Rogers's other novels are Separate Tracks, Her Living Image, The Ice is Singing, Island *and* The Voyage Home. *She has also edited* The Good Fiction Guide.

🖉Read on
◆ *Island* (a woman abandoned as a baby traces her mother with the intention of killing her).
◘ ›› Margaret Atwood, *Alias Grace*; ›› Thomas Keneally, *The Playmaker*; ›› Matthew Kneale, *English Passengers*.

ROMAN CATHOLICISM

›› Kingsley Amis, *The Alteration*
Georges Bernanos, *Diary of a Country Priest*
›› Anthony Burgess, *Earthly Powers*
›› Graham Greene, *Monsignor Quixote*
›› Thomas Keneally, *Three Cheers for the Paraclete*
Patrick McCabe, *The Dead School*
›› Brian Moore, *Catholics*
J.F. Powers, *Morte d'Urban*
Frederick Rolfe, *Hadrian the Seventh*
›› Muriel Spark, *The Abbess of Crewe*
Morris West, *The Devil's Advocate*
›› Antonia White, *Frost in May*

ROTH, Philip (born 1933)
US novelist

One of the wriest and wittiest of all contemporary US novelists, Roth writes of Jewish intellectuals, often authors or university teachers, discomfited by life. Their marriages fail; their parents behave like joke-book stereotypes (forever making chicken soup and simultaneously boasting about and deploring their sons' brains); sexual insatiability leads them from one farcical encounter to another; their career success attracts embarrassing fans and inhibits further work; their defences of self-mockery and irony wear ever thinner as they approach unwanted middle age. In *Portnoy's Complaint*, Roth treats this theme as farce, heavy with explicit sex and Jewish mother jokes. The majority of his novels are quieter, the tone more rueful, and he generalizes his theme and makes it symbolize the plight of all decent, conscience-stricken people in a world where barbarians make the running. Many of Roth's novels feature a New York Jewish author, Nathan Zuckerman, who agonizes over his trade, writes an immensely successful (dirty) book, and is immediately harrassed by the way his fame both forces him to live the life of a celebrity, and makes him even more of an enigma to his family and friends. In the last decade

Roth has produced a sequence of startling and jaundiced examinations of American dreams and nightmares, which have shown that he has lost none of his power and range as a writer. *American Pastoral*, for example, is the story of Seymour 'Swede' Lvov, whose comfortable sense of himself and the America in which he lives is destroyed by events of the 1960s and by his own daughter's violent rejection of all he stands for. Other novels (a masterly exercise in alternative history entitled *The Plot Against America*, for example) have demonstrated how much Roth, as he reached his seventies, still has to say about contemporary America.

The Zuckerman books are: The Ghost Writer, Zuckerman Unbound, The Anatomy Lesson, The Prague Orgy, The Counterlife, I Married a Communist, The Human Stain *and* Exit Ghost. *Roth's other fiction includes* Goodbye, Columbus *(a novella and five stories, his first book, published in 1959),* The Great American Novel, Sabbath's Theatre, Operation Shylock, The Breast, The Professor of Desire *and* The Dying Animal *(three very different novels featuring an academic named David Kepesh),* Everyman *and* Indignation. The Facts: A Novelist's Autobiography *and* Patrimony: A True Story *are two slim and cunningly contrived volumes of memoirs which play games with simple notions of memory and truth.*

📖Read on

◆ *Operation Shylock* (a teasing, brilliant book, starting with a famous novelist called Philip Roth going to modern Israel – or its nightmare, Kafka-farce simulacrum – to track down an impostor called 'Philip Roth' and discover his true identity).

◻ Bernard Malamud, *Dubin's Lives*; ⟩⟩ Bernice Rubens, *Our Father*; ⟩⟩ Margaret Atwood, *Cat's Eye*; ⟩⟩ John Fowles, *Daniel Martin*; ⟩⟩ John Updike, *Marry Me*.

ROWLING, J. K. (Joanne Kathleen) (born 1965)
British writer

It is difficult to believe that, only a little over a decade ago, the name of Harry Potter was unknown to readers around the world. So enormous has been the success of J.K. Rowling's books and the films that have followed them that her boy wizard seems to have been around for ever. The character was introduced in *Harry Potter and the Philosopher's Stone* (1997) where he was first whisked away from dull suburbia and despatched via Platform Nine and Three Quarters at King's Cross to Hogwarts School of Witchcraft and Wizardry, there to learn just a little of the destiny which will eventually pit him against Lord Voldemort in a titanic struggle of good against evil. Since then another six books in the series have appeared and Harry Potter has become a global success of the most astonishing kind. Everyone has now heard of him and his friends. It has become almost impossible to separate the stories from the phenomenon but it is important to remember the fundamental reasons why the books have become so popular. They have done so largely because of Rowling's ever-fertile inventiveness and the narrative skills which have been on display from the very first chapter of the very first book.

The other Harry Potter books are Harry Potter and the Chamber of Secrets, Harry Potter and the Prisoner of Azkaban, Harry Potter and the Goblet of Fire, Harry Potter and the Order of the Phoenix, Harry Potter and the Half-Blood Prince, Harry Potter and the Deathly Hallows. The Tales of Beedle the Bard *is a collection of five fairy tales, supposedly the book which plays a role in the plot of* Harry Potter and the Deathly Hallows.

Read on
◻ Eoin Colfer, *Artemis Fowl*; Roald Dahl, *The Witches*; Eva Ibbotson, *The Secret of Platform 13*; Diana Wynne Jones, *Howl's Moving Castle*; Angie Sage, *Magyk*.

LITERARY TRIVIA 12:

FIVE CURIOUS BOOK DEDICATIONS
'To the inventor of the ice lolly'
Nikolaus Pevsner, the art critic and original creator of the Buildings of England series, saluted an unknown hero in his volume on Bedfordshire.

'To Lesley, for the use of her goat'
American novelist Larry McMurtry puzzles readers with the dedication to his book *Desert Rose*.

'To all those who lead monotonous lives in the hope that they may experience at second hand the delights and dangers of adventure'
>> Agatha Christie shows her low opinion of the excitement in her average reader's life in the dedication to one of her very early novels, *The Secret Adversary*.

> 'To the companion of my idle hours, the soother of my sorrows, the confidant of my joys and hopes, my oldest and strongest Pipe, this little volume is gratefully and affectionately dedicated'
> *Three Man in a Boat* author ➤➤ Jerome K. Jerome reveals himself as a possible Pipeman of the Year 1886 in the dedication to his *Idle Thoughts of an Idle Fellow*.
>
> 'To the most eminent and reverend Prince Giulio Poldo Pezzoli'
> Aubrey Beardsley's unfinished erotic tale 'Under the Hill' was dedicated to an entirely imaginary cardinal in the Roman Catholic Church.

RUBENS, Bernice (1927–2004)
British novelist

Rubens's heroes and heroines are people at the point of breakdown: her novels chart the escalation of tension which took them there or the progress of their cure. Some of the books are bleak: in *The Elected Member/The Chosen People*, for example, a man is driven mad by feeling that he is a scapegoat for the entire suffering of the Jewish people throughout history, and the story deals with his rehabilitation in a mental hospital. In other books, Rubens turns psychological pain to comedy, as if the only way to cope with the human condition were to treat it as God's black joke against the human race. God is even a character in *Our Father*: he pops up in the Sahara, in the High Street, in the parlour, in bed with the heroine and her husband, constantly nagging her to make up her mind about herself – and his persistence leads her to rummage through childhood memories (where it becomes clear that she completely misunderstood her parents' emotional relationship) and to redefine her life.

Rubens's other novels include Madame Sousatzka, I Sent a Letter to My Love, The Ponsonby Post, Sunday Best, Brothers, Birds of Passage, Spring Sonata, Mother Russia, Mr Wakefield's Crusade, Autobiopsy, The Waiting Game, I, Dreyfus, Nine Lives *and* The Sergeants' Tale.

📖Read on
◆ *Birds of Passage*; *I, Dreyfus* (in which a modern namesake of the Jewish officer wrongfully imprisoned in late nineteenth-century France suffers similarly).

◘ to *The Elected Member*: Paul Sayer, *The Comforts of Madness*.

◘ to Rubens's work in general: ➤➤ Paul Theroux, *Picture Palace*; ➤➤ Beryl Bainbridge, *A Quiet Life*; ➤➤ Rose Tremain, *Sacred Country*; Jane Gardam, *The Flight of the Maidens*.

RUSHDIE, Salman (born 1947)
Indian/British novelist and non-fiction writer

Rushdie's novels are magic realism: a mesmeric entwining of actuality and fantasy. *Midnight's Children* is the story of a rich Indian family over the past eighty years, and especially of Saleem, one of one thousand and one children born at midnight on 15 August 1947, the moment of India's independence from Britain. Saleem's birth time gives him extraordinary powers: he is, as Rushdie puts it, 'handcuffed' to India, able to let his mind float freely through its history and to share in the experience of anyone he chooses, from Gandhi or Nehru to the most insignificant beggar in the streets. In Saleem's experience (as relayed to us) time coalesces, 'real' politics blur with fantasy, a child's memories and magnifications are just as valid as newspaper accounts. The effect is to change reality to metaphor and Rushdie uses this to make several sharp political points. In 2008 *Midnight's Children* was voted Best of the Booker, as the finest novel awarded the Man Booker prize in the forty years of its existence. In 1988, Rushdie's fourth novel, *The Satanic Verses*, dramatized the conflict between good and evil in the persons of two actors, who fall out of an aeroplane and are transformed into the Angel Gibreel and Shaitan, the Devil. The book violently offended fundamentalist Muslims, who took Gibreel's sardonic, ironic dreams about the prophet Mahound in the fantasy city Jahilia as blasphemy against their religion. Copies of *The Satanic Verses* were burned, and a fatwa was issued against Rushdie by Ayatollah Khomeini of Iran — events whose surreal horror beggared anything in his fiction. *The Moor's Last Sigh*, written during his sentence of living death, is another hypnotic family saga, covering the lives of the Da Gama-Zogoiby dynasty, Portuguese-Indian pepper exporters in Bombay from the 1870s to the present. Since the lifting of the fatwa, Rushdie has published four further novels, including *The Ground Beneath Her Feet* (boldly mixing the mythologies of East and West with the modern iconography of rock in its story of two superstar musicians and their life and love across the decades) and *Fury*, a darkly comic tale of a disenchanted exile arriving in New York and finding his demons still in pursuit.

Rushdie's other works of fiction are Grimus, Shame, Haroun and the Sea of Stories, East, West *(a collection of short stories),* Shalimar the Clown *and* The Enchantress of Florence. The Jaguar Smile *is non-fiction, a politically savage look at the effect of US policies in Central America in general and Nicaragua in particular.* Imaginary Homelands *is a book of essays, chiefly on religion and literature, written during his enforced withdrawal from public life;* Step Across This Line *gathers together more of his non-fiction in a wide-ranging selection.*

⮞Read on
◘ to *Midnight's Children*: ❯❯ Vikram Seth, *A Suitable Boy*; ❯❯ Günter Grass, *The Tin Drum*.
◘ to *The Satanic Verses*: ❯❯ Angela Carter, *Nights at the Circus*; Lisa St Aubin de Terán, *Keepers of the House*.

READ**ON**ATHEME

RUSSIA (before, during and after the Soviet era)
   Andrei Bely, *Petersburg*
❯❯ Mikhail Bulgakov, *The Master and Margarita*
❯❯ Fyodor Dostoevsky, *The Brothers Karamazov*
❯❯ Nikolai Gogol, *Dead Souls*
   Andrey Kurkov, *Death and the Penguin*
   Victor Pelevin, *Babylon*
   Anatoli Rybakov, *Children of the Arbat*
   Mikhail Sholokhov, *And Quiet Flows the Don*

SACKS, Oliver (born 1933)
British neurologist and writer

Neurological illness might seem like an unlikely subject for a bestseller but *The Man Who Mistook His Wife for a Hat*, Oliver Sacks's collection of essays about patients lost in the strange worlds of their disorders, struck a chord with readers when it was first published in the 1980s and it continues to do so more than twenty years later. In his book Sacks unveils a series of portraits of people whose struggles with their peculiar and particular impairments shed new light on what it means to be human. From the music teacher whose visual confusion provides the book's title to the autistic savants who can make instant calendrical calculations far into the future, from the Tourette's sufferer to the 'lost mariner' who remembers nothing of his life since demob from the Navy after World War II, the individuals whom Sacks spotlights are far more than just the subjects of dry case histories. He brings their strange and exceptional experiences to life and allows us to enter their worlds. Before the publication of *The Man Who Mistook His Wife for a Hat*, Sacks was best-known for *Awakenings*, a book which chronicles a group of patients awaking after decades spent in a trance-like condition; his later books range from *Seeing Voices*, an investigation of the world of the deaf, to *Uncle Tungsten*, a memoir of his early life. In all his work, his wisdom and his empathy with those who are different are clearly evident.

Oliver Sacks's other books include Migraine, A Leg to Stand On, An Anthropologist on Mars, Oaxaca Journal *and* Musicophilia.

Read on
◆ *Uncle Tungsten*.
▫ Jean-Dominique Bauby, *The Diving Bell and the Butterfly*; Paul Broks, *Into the Silent Land*; Armand Marie Leroi, *Mutants: On the Forms, Varieties and Errors of the Human Body*; A. R. Luria, *The Mind of a Mnemonist*.

SALINGER, J.D. (Jerome David) (born 1919)
US novelist and short story writer

Salinger's only novel, *The Catcher in the Rye* (1951), is a rambling monologue by seventeen-year-old Holden Caulfield. He has run away from boarding school just before Christmas, and is spending a few days drifting in New York City while he decides whether to go home or not. He feels that his childhood is over and his innocence lost, but he detests the phoney, loveless grown-up world (symbolized by plastic Christmas baubles and seasonal fake goodwill). He thinks that to be adult is a form of surrender, but he can see no way to avoid it. He wanders the city, talking aimlessly to taxi-drivers, lodging-house keepers, bar-tenders, prostitutes and his own kid sister Phoebe, whom he tries to warn against growing up. Finally, inevitably, he capitulates – or perhaps escapes, since we learn that what we have just read is his 'confession' to the psychiatrist in a mental home. Salinger pursued the question of how to recover moral innocence in his only other publications, a series of short stories about the gifted, mentally unstable Glass family. 'Franny and Zooey', the most moving of the stories, shows Zooey Glass, an actor, talking his sister Franny out of a nervous breakdown. It is a performance of dazzling technical brilliance and full of loving kindness, but – and this is typical of Salinger's grim view of human moral endeavour – although it helps Franny momentarily, it contributes nothing whatever to the good of the world at large.

The Glass family stories are collected in Franny and Zooey, Nine Stories/For Esmé, with Love and Squalor *and* Raise High the Roofbeam, Carpenters.

📖Read on

◘ to *The Catcher in the Rye*: ≫ Carson McCullers, *The Member of the Wedding*; ≫ John Updike, *The Centaur*; Truman Capote, *Breakfast at Tiffany's*; ≫ Bret Easton Ellis, *Less Than Zero* (for a 1980s view of disenchanted preppy adolescence); S.E. Hinton, *The Outsiders* (adolescent angst recorded by a writer who was herself an adolescent when she wrote the book).

◘ to 'Franny and Zooey': Sylvia Plath, *The Bell Jar*; ≫ Susan Hill, *The Bird of Night*.

SANSOM, C.J. (Christopher John) (born 1952)
British novelist

C.J. Sansom has been one of the most critically and commercially successful British crime writers of the last few years and his creation, Matthew Shardlake, a hunchbacked lawyer who finds himself regularly entangled in the dangerous highways and byways of politics at the court of Henry VIII, is as intriguing as any character in recent fiction. Outwardly self-confident and yet inwardly self-doubting, the lawyer is an entirely convincing figure around whom Sansom has built his Tudor world and the novels which have followed the first, *Dissolution* (see below), have only served to enrich and expand the character.

DISSOLUTION (2003)
The novel that introduced Matthew Shardlake to readers is set in the year 1537. Henry VIII's Dissolution of the Monasteries has begun and Shardlake, a supporter

of Henry's ruthless chief minister Thomas Cromwell, has been sent to Scarnsea monastery on the Sussex coast to investigate the brutal killing of one of Cromwell's commissioners. As he investigates, and more murders take place, Shardlake is forced to question everything he believes and holds most dear. *Dissolution* makes clever use of the conventions of the classic English mystery and the enclosed community within which it takes place lends itself well to the kind of claustrophobic puzzle that characterises the genre but it is Sansom's central character, with his complexity and ambiguity of motive, who does most to sustain readers' interest.

The other Shardlake novels are Dark Fire, Sovereign *and* Revelation. Winter in Madrid *is a stand alone novel set in Spain in the early 1940s.*

🕮Read on

◆ *Winter in Madrid* (the intertwined stories of a British secret agent visiting the Spanish capital in the aftermath of the Spanish Civil War and a nurse searching for news of a lover lost on the battlefield several years earlier).

◘ to the Shardlake novels: Patricia Finney, *Firedrake's Eye*; Karen Maitland, *Company of Liars*; ➤➤ Hilary Mantel, *Wolf Hall* (for another fictional portrait of Cromwell); Leonard Tourney, *The Player's Boy Is Dead*.

◘ to *Winter in Madrid*: Robert Wilson, *The Blind Man of Seville*.

SARTRE, Jean-Paul (1905–80)

French novelist, poet and philosopher

The philosophy of existentialism, which Sartre developed in essays, plays, novels and monographs, says that Nothingness is the natural state of humanity: we exist, like animals, without ethics or morality. But unlike beasts we have the power to make choices, and these give moral status: they are a leap from Nothingness to Being. For some people, the choice is the leap of faith, and belief in God gives them moral status; for others the choice is to make no choice at all, to drift the way the world leads them without taking moral initiatives. For Sartre's characters, the leap into Being involved taking responsibility, making moral decisions from which there was no turning back. His vast novel *The Roads to Freedom (Les Chemins de la liberté)* (1945–49, in three volumes: *The Age of Reason, The Reprieve* and *Iron in the Soul*) tackles his theme exactly: the questions of what moral decisions to make and how to make them. It describes a group of young people trying to sort out their personal lives and at the same time to cope with the moral and intellectual challenges of fascism, communism, colonialism and the Second World War. Packed with intellectual, political and philosophical discussion and argument it is a complex read but few writings better give the intellectual 'feel' of the 1930s and 1940s.

Sartre's main philosophical monograph is Being and Nothingness. *His plays include* The Flies, Crime Passionel *and* Huis Clos/No Exit. Nausea *is an autobiographical novel about a young intellectual in the 1920s and 1930s.* Words *is a memoir of his childhood spent within the stifling confines of a small French town and describes how his upbringing permanently marked his life and thought.*

📖 Read on
◆ *Nausea*.
▫ ❯❯ Albert Camus, *The Plague (La Peste)*; Arthur Koestler, *Darkness at Noo*n.
▫ novels discussing similar personal dilemmas, but with different backgrounds and cultural conditions: ❯❯ Leo Tolstoy, *War and Peace*; ❯❯ Ford Madox Ford, *The Good Soldier*; ❯❯ Olivia Manning's *Levant trilogy*.

SAYERS, Dorothy L. (Leigh) (1893–1957)
British novelist

At various times, Sayers worked as an Oxford don, an advertising copywriter and a radio dramatist. She is best known, however, for a series of detective novels cruelly but accurately described (by the writer Colin Watson) as 'snobbery with violence'. The fascination of her books is not only in the solving of bizarre crimes in out-of-the-ordinary locations (an advertising agency, an Oxford women's college, an East Anglian belfry), but also in the character of her detective, the super-sleuth Lord Peter Wimsey. He is a languid, monocled aristocrat, whose foppish manner conceals the facts that he has a first-class Oxford degree, was in army intelligence during the First World War, collects rare books, plays the piano like Rubinstein, dances like Astaire and seems to have swallowed a substantial dictionary of quotations. He is aided and abetted by his manservant Bunter, a suave charmer adept at extracting confidences from the cooks, taxi-drivers, waitresses, barbers and vergers who would collapse in forelock-tugging silence if Wimsey himself ever deigned to speak to them. Several of the novels describe the unfolding relationship between Wimsey and the crime novelist Harriet Vane. Seldom have detective stories been so preposterous or so unputdownable.

The Wimsey/Vane romance is featured in Have His Carcase, Strong Poison, Gaudy Night *and* Busman's Honeymoon. *Sayers's other Wimsey books – which some admirers prefer to those involving Harriet Vane – include* Murder Must Advertise, Clouds of Witness *and* The Nine Tailors.

📖Read on

◆ *Gaudy Night.*

▢ Amanda Cross, *No Word From Winifred*; Michael Innes, *Hamlet, Revenge!*; Robert Robinson, *Landscape with Dead Dons*; ▶▶ P.D. James, *A Certain Justice*; ▶▶ Ruth Rendell, *Some Lie and Some Die.*

SAYLOR, Steven (born 1956)

US novelist

Very few of the many series of historical mysteries that have appeared over the last thirty years have the same unmistakable authority as Steven Saylor's books, set in the last decades of the Roman Republic. Where other writers have a rather stagey sense of their historical settings, Saylor's descriptions of the sights, smells and sounds of the crowded streets of Ancient Rome – based on wide ranging research – carry immediate conviction. His central character, Gordianus the Finder ('the last honest man in Rome', as another character calls him) is a tough, unsentimental but sympathetic hero, and we see him ageing and maturing as the series progresses and the dangerous politics of the period swirl around him, occasionally sweeping him up in conspiracy and murder. The real history of the dying days of the Roman Republic and the fictional narratives of Gordianus's casebook are brilliantly entwined.

ROMAN BLOOD (1991)

Based on a real case involving the Roman orator and politician Cicero, the first in the Gordianus series showed immediately Saylor's talent for blending real history with fictional mystery. The up-and-coming Cicero hires Gordianus to investigate the background to a murder case in which he is defending a man charged with killing his father. As Gordianus digs deeper, he finds that the case goes to the very heart of the political corruption and infighting in the Republic.

The other Gordianus the Finder books, best read in this order, are The House of the Vestals *and* A Gladiator Dies Only Once *(both volumes of short stories)*, Arms of Nemesis, Catilina's Riddle, The Venus Throw, A Murder on the Appian Way, Rubicon, Last Seen in Massilia, A Mist of Prophecies, The Judgement of Caesar *and* The Triumph of Caesar. A Twist at the End/Honour the Dead *is a novel set in late nineteenth-century Texas with the short-story writer O. Henry as chief protagonist.* Have You Seen Dawn? *is a contemporary mystery, set in Texas.*

ᏰRead on

◘ ›› Lindsey Davis, *The Iron Hand of Mars*; Ron Burns, *Roman Nights*; Joan O'Hagan, *A Roman Death*; Steven Pressfield, *Tides of War*; Valerio Massimo Manfredi, *Spartan*.

LITERARYTRIVIA13:

FIVE SPORTING WRITERS
›› Arthur Conan Doyle
As a young man, the creator of Sherlock Holmes excelled as a cricketer (he once bowled out W.G. Grace), a boxer and a skier. He was also the first goalkeeper of what became Portsmouth Football Club.

›› Samuel Beckett
The only Nobel Prize-winner to make an appearance in *Wisden Cricketer's Almanac*, the playwright and novelist was opening batsman for Dublin University in a 1925 match against Northamptonshire that was accorded first-class status.

›› Jack Kerouac
The author of *On the Road* and hero of the Beat Generation was a star sportsman at school and entered Columbia University on a football scholarship, later dropping out after rows with the team coach.

›› Albert Camus
The French existentialist writer attended the University of Algiers in the early 1930s and played in goal for the university football team. 'All that I know

most surely about morality and the obligations of man', he once wrote, 'I owe to football.'

Louis L'Amour
The writer of dozens of Westerns, and one of the most popular and bestselling American novelists of all time, L'Amour was a professional boxer in his youth. He fought in prizefights all across the country, winning fifty out of fifty nine professional bouts.

SCHAMA, Simon (born 1945)
British historian and essayist

Simon Schama is now a celebrity, a historian made famous by his epic TV series *A History of Britain*. The series and the assorted books that were spun off from it are evidence enough of Schama's gift for intelligent précis and the memorable phrase but the best of his work lies in those books he has written as an academic historian which none the less have much to appeal to general readers with an interest in the past. *The Embarrassment of Riches* is a grandly ambitious narrative which describes the sixteenth- and seventeenth-century transformation of the Dutch from an isolated people on the edge of Europe to a world power and what this has meant for their culture. This was followed by *Citizens*, which tells a story that has been told often enough but the book's fluent account of the bloody progress of the French Revolution, revisionist in its emphasis on the violence and ruthlessness of the revolutionaries, provided a new version in time for the bicentennial celebrations of the storming of the Bastille. A more recent work, *Rough Crossings*, tells the largely forgotten story of tens of thousands of black slaves who sought their freedom by fighting for the British, and shows his customary ability to resurrect the past in all its contradictions and confusions.

Schama's other books include Dead Certainties, Rembrandt's Eyes, The Power of Art *and* The American Future.

📖Read on
◘ to *The Embarrassment of Riches*: ›› Lisa Jardine, *Going Dutch*.
◘ to *Citizens*: Adam Zamoyski, *Holy Madness*.

▣ to Schama's work in general: Orlando Figes, *A People's Tragedy*; Adam Hochschild, *Bury the Chains*; Hugh Thomas, *The Slave Trade*.

READ**ON**A**THEME**:

SCHOOLS

›› Jonathan Coe, *The Rotters' Club*
›› Charles Dickens, *Nicholas Nickleby*
   James Hilton, *Goodbye, Mr Chips*
   Thomas Hughes, *Tom Brown's Schooldays*
›› James Joyce, *Portrait of the Artist as a Young Man*
›› John Le Carré, *Call for the Dead*
›› Muriel Spark, *The Prime of Miss Jean Brodie*
   Susan Swann, *The Wives of Bath*
›› John Updike, *The Centaur*
›› Evelyn Waugh, *Decline and Fall*

See also: Adolescence

STARTPOINT

SCIENCE FICTION AND FANTASY

The origins of science fiction have been hotly debated (some experts take them back to the ancient world) but it was the industrial revolution that led to the birth of modern SF and writers such as ›› Jules Verne and ›› H.G. Wells gave it its first mass audience. They took advantage of public interest in the discoveries of 'real' science to write stories featuring such topics as space travel, invasions from other planets and the exploration of 'worlds that time forgot'. Ever since, SF authors have exploited every new scientific discovery and, more seriously, have used the genre to examine such ideas as 'green issues', fascism or the ethics of colonization. Some write about not physical space but the worlds of dreams and the imagination. Fantasy literature has mushroomed after the success of ›› J.R.R. Tolkien's *The Lord of the Rings*

(1954–45) and has become one of the most popular of all genres of fiction in the last two decades.

>> **Asimov, Isaac, *I, Robot* (1950)**. Collection of linked future-detective stories in which the protagonists have to tackle crimes that may have been committed by robots.

>> **Banks, Iain M., *Consider Phlebas* (1987)**. First of Banks's space operas, traditional SF tales of galaxy-spanning empires and high intrigue, told in a refreshingly modern style.

Bester, Alfred, *Tiger! Tiger!/The Stars My Destination* (1956). High-energy story of revenge and transcendence told in a dazzling prose by a writer in love with the possibilities of language.

Brooks, Terry, *The Sword of Shannara* (1977). In a world where men co-exist with dwarves and trolls and gnomes, only the last descendant of an elven king can wield the Sword of Shannara and protect the forces of good against the evil Warlock Lord.

Card, Orson Scott, *Ender's Game* (1985). The world is under threat from loathsome aliens and junior geniuses train in war games to combat it.

Gemmell, David, *Legend* (1984). The Drenai Empire is threatened by invading armies and, as they converge on the mighty fortress of Dros Delnoch, only its legendary hero Druss can save it.

>> **Heinlein, Robert, *Stranger In a Strange Land* (1961)**. A new messiah is raised on Mars and his psychic powers lead him to the foundation of a new religion.

Holdstock, Robert, *Mythago Wood* (1984). A dark and particularly English fantasy in which mysterious Jungian archetypes haunt a Herefordshire forest.

Martin, George R.R., *A Game of Thrones* (1996). The first volume in Martin's epic cycle known as *A Song of Ice and Fire* introduces the quasi-medieval world of warring kingdoms where the action takes place.

Miller Jr, Walter M., *A Canticle for Leibowitz* (1959). In a post-holocaust America scraps of pre-war knowledge are treasured and preserved by guardians who no longer understand what they signify in this intelligent exercise in imagining the unimaginable future.

>> Pratchett, Terry, *Small Gods* (1992). This episode in Pratchett's hilarious and ever-increasing Discworld series tells of the Grand Inquisitor's secretary: a lad who never forgets anything, ever, and who has a unique and meaningful personal relationship with God (a very tiny turtle). All the Discworld books are self-contained; this is one of the funniest.

Priest, Christopher, *The Glamour* (1984). An enigmatic love triangle becomes a disturbing search for identity, as the three central characters all possess (or believe they possess) an uncanny quality that sets them apart.

Russell, Mary Doria, *The Sparrow* (1996). A clash of cultures brilliantly and movingly explored in this story of a Jesuit-sponsored mission to a distant planet and the unsettling mysteries of otherness and difference encountered among its inhabitants.

>> Vonnegut, Kurt, *The Sirens of Titan* (1959). Classic story of Niles Rumfoord, condemned by a scientific accident to live all moments of his life simultaneously and how, on a lunatic rollercoaster ride through the universe and time, he tries to shake off his condition.

Wolfe, Gene, *The Book of the New Sun* (1980–83). This classic four-book series uses fantasy form to explore ideas of the duality between good and evil, the nature of cruelty and the possibility of redemption. Severian, exiled to the mysterious, dying planet Urth, first explores, then exploits, then seeks to save it. Individual titles: *The Shadow of the Torturer, The Claw of the Conciliator, The Sword of the Lictor, The Citadel of the Autarch*.

Also recommended: Stephen Baxter, *Moonseed*; Greg Bear, *Blood Music*; James Blish, *A Case of Conscience*; Ray Bradbury, *Fahrenheit 451*; Jonathan Carroll, *The Land of Laughs*; Samuel R. Delany, *Nova*; Steven Erikson, *Gardens of the Moon*; Philip José Farmer, *A Feast Unknown*; Terry Goodkind, *Wizard's First Rule*; M. John Harrison, *Light*; >> Russell Hoban,

Riddley Walker; Daniel Keyes, *Flowers for Algernon*; » Ursula Le Guin, *The Left Hand of Darkness*; Stanislaw Lem, *Solaris*; Larry Niven, *Ringworld*; Tim Powers, *The Anubis Gates*; Kim Stanley Robinson, *Red Mars*; Joanna Russ, *The Female Man*; Norman Spinrad, *Bug Jack Barron*; Michael Swanwick, *The Iron Dragon's Daughter*; Vernor Vinge, *A Fire Upon the Deep*; Connie Willis, *Doomsday Book*.

See also: Atwood, Ballard, Clarke, Dick, Fantasy Adventure, Fantasy Societies, Feist, Gibson, Herbert, Jordan, Lessing, Rewriting History, Wyndham.

HIDDENGEM:

CHARLES G. FINNEY – *THE CIRCUS OF DR LAO* (1935)

Charles G. Finney was an American newspaperman who published a handful of novels in his lifetime, of which *The Circus of Dr Lao* was the first. The book takes place in Abalone, Arizona, an archetypal American small town where an advertisement appears in the local paper announcing the imminent arrival of a circus. However, the circus is unlike any other the townsfolk have seen. In place of the lions and tigers and elephants of ordinary circuses, Dr Lao has beasts of myth and legend. A millennia-old satyr, a Medusa with snakes instead of hair, a sphinx, a chimera – all these and more are members of his travelling menagerie. The stage is set for a series of encounters between the people of Abalone and the fantastic creatures from the circus. In fewer than one hundred and fifty pages, Finney moves elegantly from black humour to philosophical speculation, from the kind of textual playfulness that today gets labelled 'postmodernism' to satirical mockery of American provincialism. More than seventy years after it first appeared, *The Circus of Dr Lao* remains a fantasy novel like few others.

READ ON A THEME

SCIENCE WRITING

For the layman science can seem a bewildering subject in which its practitioners construct bizarre theories and conduct incomprehensible debates that no ordinary individual can grasp. Yet science sets out to answer the most basic questions about life that any thinking person might ask. To be ignorant of science today is to be intellectually crippled. Luckily there are plenty of scientists on hand, willing and able to explain the basic concepts of physics, genetics and other subjects in such a way that even the most baffled of scientific ignoramuses can begin to understand them.

>> Bryson, Bill, *A Short History of Nearly Everything* (2003). Bryson turns from comic travel books to popular science. Realizing, in his own words, that 'I didn't know the first thing about the only planet I was ever going to live on', he sets out on a voyage of discovery which he shares brilliantly with readers.

Capra, Fritjof, *The Tao of Physics* (1975). The surprising links between Eastern mysticism and the more mind-boggling theories of modern physics are explored in one of the first, and still one of the best, books to look for them.

>> Dawkins, Richard, *The Selfish Gene* (1976). Dawkins writes a book on evolutionary theory which argues that it works primarily at the level of the individual gene and coins a phrase in his title that has entered the language.

Fortey, Richard, *Life: An Unauthorised Biography* (1997). Fortey takes on the biggest subject of all – the four-billion-year history of life on earth – and makes it comprehensible to even the most scientifically challenged of readers.

>> Gould, Stephen Jay, *Wonderful Life* (1989). Gould uses the extraordinary fossils found on the Burgess Shale in the Canadian Rockies to illustrate his thesis that chance has played the major role in the evolution of life on Earth.

Greene, Brian, *The Elegant Universe* (1999). Superstring theory and other ideas at the cutting edge of modern physics are demystified for the general reader.

Gribbin, John, *Science: A History* (2003). An epic history of scientific discovery, peopled by the extraordinary individuals, both famous and forgotten, who have added to our understanding of the universe in which we live.

Jones, Steve, *Almost Like a Whale* (1999). Jones daringly borrows the structure of Darwin's landmark work, *The Origin of Species*, and rewrites what he calls 'the only bestseller to change man's conception of himself' with the benefit of another one hundred and fifty years of scientific research.

Pinker, Steven, *The Language Instinct* (1994). The more arcane mysteries of linguistics are satisfactorily and lucidly explained in a book that argues we are all born with an innate capacity for language.

Watson, James D., *The Double Helix* (1968). Watson's autobiographical account of the discovery of the structure of DNA has attracted much controversy (his dismissal of the contribution of Rosalind Franklin to the breakthrough is particularly questionable) but few books have described the realities of scientific research so vividly.

Also recommended: David Bodanis, $E=mc^2$; Paul Davies, *The Mind of God*; Jared Diamond, *The Rise and Fall of the Third Chimpanzee*; Richard Feynman, *Six Easy Pieces*; James Gleick, *Chaos*; Stephen Hawking, *A Brief History of Time*; Roger Osborne, *The Floating Egg*; Martin Rees, *Just Six Numbers*; Matt Ridley, *The Red Queen*; Ian Stewart, *Does God Play Dice?*; Edward O. Wilson, *The Diversity of Life*; Robert Wright, *The Moral Animal*.

READ ON A THEME

SCOTLAND

George MacKay Brown, *Greenvoe*
Lewis Grassic Gibbon, *A Scots Quair*
>> Alasdair Gray, *Lanark*
Neil M. Gunn, *Morning Tide*
James Hogg, *Confessions of a Justified Sinner*
James Kelman, *How Late it Was, How Late*
>> Walter Scott, *The Heart of Midlothian*
>> Robert Louis Stevenson, *Kidnapped*
Jeff Torrington, *Swing, Hammer, Swing*

>> Alan Warner, *Morvern Callar*
>> Irvine Welsh, *Trainspotting*

SCOTT, Sir Walter (1771–1832)
British novelist and poet

Scott began his career not with novels but with poems, in a style similar to Scottish folk ballads and the lyrics of Robert Burns. In 1814, piqued because his verse was outsold by Byron's, he turned instead to historical novels, and wrote twenty nine in the next eighteen years. They are swaggering tales of love, bravery and intrigue, many of them centred on events from Scottish history and set in the brooding landscapes of the highlands and islands.

ROB ROY (1817)
In the 1710s, Osbaldistone and Rashleigh are rivals for the hand of Diana Vernon. Rashleigh embezzles money and frames Osbaldistone. Osbaldistone escapes to the highlands of Scotland, where he seeks help from Rob Roy, an outlaw who (like Robin Hood centuries before him) robs the rich to help the poor, rights wrongs and fights a usurping power (in his case, the English) on behalf of an exiled, true royal prince (James Stuart, the Old Pretender). Osbaldistone's quest to clear his name becomes inextricably bound up with the Jacobite Rebellion, and it is not until Rashleigh (who, not unexpectedly, supports the English and betrays Rob Roy to them) is killed that justice prevails and Osbaldistone and Diana at last find happiness.

Scott's other novels include Waverley, Guy Mannering, Old Mortality, The Heart of Midlothian, The Bride of Lammermoor, Ivanhoe, Kenilworth, The Fortunes of Nigel, Quentin Durward, Redgauntlet *and* Castle Dangerous.

📖Read on
◆ *Ivanhoe, The Heart of Midlothian*.
▫ Harrison Ainsworth, *The Tower of London*; James Fenimore Cooper, *The Last of the Mohicans*; >> Victor Hugo, *The Hunchback of Notre Dame (Notre Dame de Paris)*; >> Alexandre Dumas, *The Man in the Iron Mask*; Nigel Tranter, *The Bruce Trilogy*.

SEBALD, W.G. (Winifred Sebald) (1944–2001)
German novelist and non-fiction writer

The death of W.G. Sebald in a car crash in 2001 robbed contemporary European literature of one of its most distinctive and original writers. His books, which have been gradually building up the readership they deserve, transcend and defy the limitations of genre. Are they novels or travel writing or exercises in biography and autobiography? They have elements of all three – as well as dashes of philosophy and history thrown into the mixture – but who cares about pedantic definition when the books themselves are so enthralling? Originally written in German, and translated into English under the careful supervision of Sebald, who lived and taught in Britain for half his life, they examine the displacements and disillusions of twentieth-century history with scrupulous exactness and melancholy irony. *The Emigrants* uses accounts of Jewish émigrés lives in Manchester, Norfolk, Austria and America – complete with illustrative black and white photographs – as a way of exploring notions of homeland and exile, of what it means to have roots in a place and a culture which the forces of history tear up. *Vertigo* gives the reader a series of very different narratives – including the story of Kafka's journey to Italy in search of health and Sebald's own account of a return to his childhood home – which move circuitously around questions of memory and the past.

THE RINGS OF SATURN (1998)
The most readily accessible of Sebald's books, this seems initially to be the account of a walking tour the author made around Suffolk in 1992. However, in Sebald's work, little remains what it seems and *The Rings of Saturn*, as it progresses through digression and diversion, becomes a multi-faceted meditation on identity, individuality and landscape. Sebald's own experiences on his journey mingle with memories and stories evoked by the places and people he sees

Sebald's other books include After Nature, On the Natural History of Destruction *and* Austerlitz. For Years Now *is a collection of short pieces by Sebald, each one paired with an image by the artist Tess Jaray.*

📖Read on
- to *The Emigrants*: Thomas Bernhard, *Extinction*; Sandor Marai, *Embers*.
- to *The Rings of Saturn* and *Vertigo*: Claudio Magris, *Danube*.

SELF, Will (born 1961)
British writer

Since first coming to attention with his 1991 collection of short stories *The Quantity Theory of Insanity*, Will Self has successfully maintained an ambivalent profile in contemporary fiction. On the one hand he is the perennial bad boy and outsider, a former heroin addict who writes with brutal directness about sex, drugs and urban violence. On the other, he is the Oxford-educated, middle-class satirist once described by Martin Amis as 'thrillingly heartless, terrifyingly brainy'. Like most satirists, much of Self's anger and indignation is directed at the hypocrisies and corruptions of the city. His fiction is mostly set in London and, in Self's work, London is an almost hallucinatory city in which no one and nothing is to be trusted, not even the ongoing humanity of its inhabitants. In *Great Apes* the artist Simon Dykes wakes after a night of dissipation to find that the human city has slipped away from him while he slept. His girlfriend has become a chimpanzee and so too have the rest of the inhabitants of London. Self is very definitely not a writer for the squeamish or the easily offended but for those who like their fiction to be thrillingly heartless and terrifyingly brainy, he is an essential read.

MY IDEA OF FUN (1993)
Ian Wharton has – or fantasizes that he has – eidetic powers, the ability to see into people's lives and minds as easily as into their pockets. Seeking to understand and control these powers, he becomes in thrall to 'Mr Broadhurst', alias 'Samuel Northcliffe', alias 'the Fat Controller', who leads him a Mephistophelean dance of alchemy, sexual fantasy and sadistic violence in return for his soul. The novel recounts Ian's twenty-year struggle to break free from the Fat Controller and his henchman Gyggle, a nightmare spiral through the underbelly of 1990s big-city Britain – or possibly through the drug-blasted synapses of his own imagination.

Self's other books include Cock and Bull, *two interlinked novellas which explore and undermine traditional ideas about male and female sexuality, the novels* How The Dead Live, Dorian *(a contemporary reworking of Wilde's* Picture of Dorian Gray*),* The Book of Dave *and* The Butt *and the four short story collections* Grey Area, Tough, Tough Toys for Tough, Tough Boys, Dr Mukti and Other Tales of Woe *and* Liver: A Fictional Organ with a Surface Anatomy of Four Lobes. Junk Mail, Feeding Frenzy *and* Psychogeography *are collections of his hard-hitting and witty journalism.*

📖Read on

◆ *The Book of Dave* (a lunatic London cabbie buries a book of his rantings and five hundred years later it is unearthed and becomes the sacred text of a weird, misogynistic religion).

◘ to *Great Apes*: John Collier, *His Monkey Wife*; ›› Peter Høeg, *The Woman and the Ape*.

◘ to *My Idea of Fun*: ›› William S. Burroughs, *The Naked Lunch*.

◘ to Self's work in general: ›› Martin Amis, *Dead Babies*; ›› Irvine Welsh, *Marabou Stork Nightmares*; Christopher Fowler, *Spanky*.

READ ON A THEME:

SEQUELS

'What happened next' to characters from famous novels of the past

Elaine Feinstein, *Lady Chatterley's Confession* (after *Lady Chatterley's Lover*)

›› George MacDonald Fraser, *Flashman* (after *Tom Brown's Schooldays*)

Lin Haire-Sargeant, *Heathcliff* (after *Wuthering Heights*)

›› Susan Hill, *Mrs de Winter* (after *Rebecca*)

Nikos Kazantzakis, *The Odyssey* (after Homer's *Odyssey*)

Bjorn Larsson, *Long John Silver* (before and after *Treasure Island*)

Valerie Martin, *Mary Reilly* (after *Doctor Jekyll and Mr Hyde*)

Alexandra Ripley, *Scarlett* (after *Gone With the Wind*)

John Spurling, *After Zenda* (after *The Prisoner of Zenda*)

Emma Tennant, *Pemberley* and *An Unequal Marriage* (after *Pride and Prejudice*)

Angela Thirkell, *High Rising* (after Anthony Trollope's Barsetshire novels)

SETH, Vikram (born 1952)

Indian writer

Could two contemporary novels by the same author be more different in form and content than *The Golden Gate* and *A Suitable Boy*? *The Golden Gate* is a novel in verse, a sequence of nearly seven hundred sonnets telling of the loves and lives of a group of twentysomething professionals in California. *A Suitable Boy* is a huge fifteen hundred-page book which sets the stories of four families in newly independent India against the backdrop of the social and political changes that independence has brought. Yet both are the work of Vikram Seth. What links two such different books are Seth's easy wit, his readability and his acute eye for manners and mores both in 1980s California and in Nehru's new India. Seth's only other novel is *An Equal Music*, in which a classical violinist struggles to revitalize a love he thought he'd lost and to find artistic fulfilment through his music.

Vikram Seth has also written several volumes of poetry, a book about his travels in Sinkiang and Tibet, From Heaven Lake*, a family memoir entitled* Two Lives *and a collection of animal fables,* Beastly Tales From Here and There.

⮑Read on

◘ to *A Suitable Boy*: ›› Salman Rushdie, *Midnight's Children*; Arundhati Roy, *The God of Small Things* (for two very different ways of treating post-independence India in fiction); ›› Rohinton Mistry, *A Fine Balance* (another epic of Indian lives caught up in wider social change, this time set in the 1970s).
◘ to *An Equal Music*: Bernard MacLaverty, *Grace Notes*.

READ ON A THEME

SEX
›› Nicholson Baker, *Vox*
›› J.G. Ballard, *Crash*
   Georges Bataille, *The Story of the Eye*
   T. Coraghessan Boyle, *The Inner Circle*
›› D.H. Lawrence, *Lady Chatterley's Lover*
   Henry Miller, The Rosy Crucifixion trilogy (*Sexus*, *Plexus*, *Nexus*)
   Anaïs Nin, *Delta of Venus*
   Pauline Reage, *The Story of O*
   D.M. Thomas, *The White Hotel*

SHARPE, Tom (born 1928)
British novelist

If, as many foreigners maintain, British humour is obsessed with the functions of the lower body, then Sharpe is our comic Laureate. In each of his books he chooses a single target – polytechnic life, publishing, Cambridge University, the landed gentry – and demolishes it magnificently, comprehensively, by piling slapstick on crudity like a demented circus clown. Sharpe's heroes live in a state of unceasing, ungovernable panic, and are usually crippled by lust, forever tripping over their own erections. His old men are gluttonous, lecherous and senile, prone to perversion and prey to strokes and heart attacks; his matrons are whooping, whip-wielding Boadiceas, scything down every beddable male in sight. If your humorous fancy is for penises trapped in briar patches, condoms ballooning above Cambridge spires or maniacs burying sex-dolls in wet cement, Sharpe's books are for you.

Sharpe's books include Wilt *and its sequels* The Wilt Alternative, Wilt on High *and* Wilt in Nowhere; Riotous Assembly *and* Indecent Exposure, *two darkly comic farces set in apartheid-era South Africa:* The Throwback; Porterhouse Blue *and its sequel* Grantchester Grind; Ancestral Vices, Vintage Stuff *and* The Midden.

📖 Read on
◆ *Indecent Exposure*; *Porterhouse Blue*.
▣ Colin Douglas, *The Houseman's Tale*; ▶▶ Howard Jacobson, *Peeping Tom*; J.P. Donleavy, *The Ginger Man*.

SHELLEY, Mary (1797–1851)
British novelist

After the death of her husband (the poet) in 1822, Shelley developed a literary career of her own, editing her husband's work, writing essays, journals and travel books, and publishing short stories and novels. Her best-known book is *Frankenstein, or the Modern Prometheus*, about a man who tries to prove the superiority of scientific rationality to the supernatural by usurping God's function and creating life. Although, thanks to Hollywood, Frankenstein's monster has nudged his creator from centre-stage, even the worst Frankenstein films keep to one of Shelley's most fascinating ideas: that the monster is an innocent, as pure as Adam before the Fall, and that its ferocity is a response learned by contact with 'civilized' human beings. Shelley developed the theme of the contrast between innocence and the corruption of civilization in other books, most notably the future-fantasy *The Last Man*, set in a world where all human beings but one have been destroyed by plague, and the survivor wanders among the monuments of the glorious past like a soul in Hell.

⮒Read on

◆ to *Frankenstein*: ≫ H.G. Wells, *The Island of Doctor Moreau*; ≫ Bram Stoker, *Dracula*; Gerald Du Maurier, *Trilby*; Brian Aldiss, *Frankenstein Unbound*; Theodore Roszak, *The Memoirs of Elizabeth Frankenstein*.

◘ to *The Last Man*: ≫ Daniel Defoe, *Robinson Crusoe*; Bernard Malamud, *God's Grace*; David Markson, *Wittgenstein's Mistress*.

SHIELDS, Carol (1935–2003)
US/Canadian novelist and short story writer

In most of her novels Carol Shields wrote about very ordinary people who lead lives that might be considered narrow and restricted by outside observers. Yet she had a gift for locating the extraordinary that lurks within apparently ordinary people. She could highlight an individuality that is not only hidden from other characters in the novel but may even be hidden from the person herself. Her novels have been varied in subject matter but all have had at their core people working through the maze of life in search of an elusive sense of self at its heart.

THE STONE DIARIES (1993)

The Stone Diaries is the story of an 'ordinary' woman's life from birth in rural Canada to her death in a Florida nursing home ninety years later. Daisy Goodwill Flett, as the chapter headings of the book (Birth, Childhood, Marriage, Love etc) ironically underline, lives in one sense a conventional life as (in her son's words at her memorial service) 'wife, mother, citizen of our century'. In another sense her life is most unconventional, including elements that might not have looked out of place in a magic-realist novel. Her mother dies in childbirth without even realizing she is pregnant. A neighbour returns to his native Orkney Islands and lives to the age of one hundred and fifteen, proud of his ability to recite *Jane Eyre* from memory. And the novel in which Daisy's life is told is far from being conventional. It mimics the form of a non-fiction biography with family tree, photographs of family members, excerpts from letters, journals, newspaper articles and so on. In a poignant, funny and knowing narrative, Carol Shields carefully unfolds the extraordinary story of the ordinary 'wife, mother and citizen of the century'.

Carol Shields's other books include Happenstance, The Box Garden, Small Ceremonies, The Republic of Love, Larry's Party, Unless *and* A Celibate Season *(a collaboration with Blanche Howard). Her* Collected Stories *were published posthumously. She also wrote a biography of »* Jane Austen.

⩗Read on
◆ *Mary Swann* (the story of four very different people whose lives are linked by an obsessive interest in the work and life of a Canadian poet unrecognized before her violent death).
▫ to the novels: ⟩⟩ Margaret Atwood, *The Blind Assassin*; ⟩⟩ Anne Tyler, *Breathing Lessons*; ⟩⟩ Jane Smiley, *Moo*; ⟩⟩ Anita Shreve, *The Pilot's Wife*.
▫ to the short stories· ⟩⟩ Alice Munro, *Dance of the Happy Shades*.

READONATHEME:

SHIPS AND THE SEA
⟩⟩ Joseph Conrad, *The Nigger of the Narcissus*
   Paul Gallico, *The Poseidon Adventure*
⟩⟩ William Golding, *Rites of Passage*
⟩⟩ Herman Melville, *Moby Dick*
   Nicholas Monsarrat, *The Cruel Sea*
⟩⟩ Patrick O'Brian, *Master and Commander*
⟩⟩ Barry Unsworth, *Sacred Hunger*
⟩⟩ Jules Verne, *Twenty Thousand Leagues Under the Sea*
   Herman Wouk, *The Caine Mutiny*

READ ON A THEME:

SHIPWRECK
R.M. Ballantyne, *The Coral Island*
>> Daniel Defoe, *Robinson Crusoe*
>> William Golding, *Pincher Martin*
>> Muriel Spark, *Robinson*
>> Kurt Vonnegut, *Galápagos*
>> Patrick White, *A Fringe of Leaves*
Marianne Wiggins, *John Dollar*

READ ON A THEME:

SHORT STORIES
John Cheever, *The Stories of John Cheever*
Junot Diaz, *Drown*
>> Helen Dunmore, *Ice Cream*
Nathan Englander, *For the Relief of Unbearable Urges*
Aleksander Hemon, *The Question of Bruno*
>> James Joyce, *Dubliners*
>> Franz Kafka, *Metamorphosis and Other Stories*
Jhumpa Lahiri, *Interpreter of Maladies*
Ring Lardner, *Collected Short Stories*
William Maxwell, *All the Days and Nights: Collected Short Stories*
Lorrie Moore, *Birds of America*
>> Alice Munro, *Hateship, Friendship, Courtship, Loveship, Marriage*
Flannery O'Connor, *Everything That Rises Must Converge*
Saki, *The Complete Stories*
Helen Simpson, *Four Bare Legs in a Bed*

See also: Borges, Calvino, Carver, Chekhov, Doyle, Fitzgerald (F. Scott), Hemingway, Mansfield, Maugham, de Maupassant, Poe, Stevenson, Taylor (Elizabeth), Trevor, Updike, Welty, Wilson (Angus), Wyndham

SHREVE, Anita (born 1946)
US novelist

Read a précis of the plot of any of Anita Shreve's novels and she sounds remarkably like a writer of soap opera stories and undemanding weepies. Begin to read one of the novels, rather than a précis of it, and her skill at depicting the nuances of troubled relationships, her expertise in navigating the treacherous waters of love and passion and her gift for creating memorable and multi-faceted characters are immediately apparent. Take her 2003 novel, *All He Ever Wanted*, as an example. This is the story of a man who becomes obsessed by a woman he first sees as he flees from a hotel fire and the life with her which this chance meeting begins. Even the title suggests a romantic melodrama. Nothing could be further from the truth. *All He Ever Wanted* is a subtle and moving portrait of a man who mixes passion with cold possessiveness and a hauntingly exact depiction, over several decades, of a relationship far removed from the comforting clichés of romance. Like all of Shreve's novels it delivers far more than it says on the tin.

THE WEIGHT OF WATER (1997)
At the centre of *The Weight of Water* is a nineteenth-century murder in which two women living isolated lives on one of a group of islands off the coast of New Hampshire are brutally killed and a third is left to hide, terrified, from the unknown assailant. A modern magazine photographer journeys to the islands to produce a photo-essay on what has become a famous case. As she unearths new evidence about the murders, her own marriage is falling apart around her and her husband is becoming dangerously involved with one of their companions on the sailing trip to the islands. *The Weight of Water* shows how skilfully Shreve can take almost melodramatic plots and invest them with subtlety and insight.

Anita Shreve's other novels include Fortune's Rocks, Eden Close, Strange Fits of Passion, The Pilot's Wife, The Last Time They Met, Light on Snow, A Wedding in December, Body Surfing *and* Testimony.

📖 Read on
◆ *The Pilot's Wife* (a newly bereaved wife discovers her husband's secret life).
❑ ➤ Margaret Atwood, *Alias Grace*; ➤ Carol Shields, *Mary Swann*; ➤ Anne Tyler, *Back When We Were Grown-ups*; Ann Patchett, *The Magican's Assistant*.

SIMENON, Georges (1903–89)
Belgian novelist

Simenon began work as a seaman, then as a journalist, and finally began writing in his twenties. He produced over five hundred books, sometimes writing them in a week or less. In his most productive year as a hack writer of potboilers he produced no fewer than forty four books. Simenon is best known for some one hundred and fifty crime stories featuring the pipe-smoking, Calvados-drinking Commissaire Maigret of the Paris police. The books are short and spare; they concentrate on Maigret's investigations in bars, lodging houses and rain-soaked Paris streets, and on his casual-seeming, fatherly conversations with suspects and witnesses. But Simenon is a far more substantial writer than this, and his relentless productivity, suggest. Many of his non-Maigret novels are compelling studies of people distracted by fear, obsession, despair or hate. *Act of Passion* is the confession of a madman who kills his lover to keep her pure, to prevent her being contaminated by the evil which he feels has corroded his own soul. The hero of *The Man Who Watched the Trains Go By*, outwardly placid and controlled, is in fact so gnawed by the sense of his own inadequacy that he chooses murder as the best way to make his mark on the world. *Ticket of Leave* is about a woman who falls in love with a paroled murderer. All these books are written in a sinewy, unemotional style, as plain as a police report.

⌾Read on
◻ to the Maigret books: Nicolas Freeling, *Love in Amsterdam*; Maj Sjöwall and Per Wahlöö, *The Laughing Policeman*; Friedrich Dürrenmatt, *The Quarry*.
◻ to the non-Maigret books: Benjamin Black, *Christine Falls*; ❯❯ Ruth Rendell, *Adam and Eve and Pinch Me*.

SINCLAIR, Iain (born 1943)
British writer

For the last thirty years, Iain Sinclair has been conducting his own intense, idiosyncratic, fictional study of the topography, history and inhabitants of his adopted city, London. His work does not often make easy reading. In Sinclair's imagination there are interconnections between the most disparate phenomena and the city is a network of links between people (past and present), buildings, sites of numinous significance, books, rituals and power structures. This, and his highly wrought, linguistically inventive prose, make demands on the reader but the rewards are considerable. *Lud Heat*, influential on ›› Peter Ackroyd's *Hawksmoor*, is a mixture of prose and poetry which centres on the London churches of the architect Nicholas Hawksmoor. Sinclair's first novel *White Chappell, Scarlet Tracings* (1987) follows the antics of a group of seedy, unscrupulous book dealers as they try to track down arcane editions of Victorian novels and joins to this a sequence of meditations and revelations about the Whitechapel murders of Jack the Ripper. Sinclair's finest novel to date is *Downriver*, as ambitious to encompass the possibilities of London as ›› Joyce's *Ulysses* is to memorialize Dublin. Built around twelve interlocking tales centred on the Thames and the life surrounding it, and incorporating characters from Victorian boatmen and visiting Aboriginal cricketers to Sixties' gangsters and nuclear-waste train-drivers, *Downriver* is an extraordinary, ebullient celebration of the splendours and squalor of the city.

Sinclair's other novels are Radon Daughters, Landor's Tower *and* Dining on Stones. Lights Out for the Territory *is a collection of essays,* London Orbital *an account of walks around the M25,* Hackney, That Rose-Red Empire *an exploration of the area of London in which he has long lived.* Rodinsky's Room *(written in collaboration with the artist Rachel Lichtenstein) looks at the Jewish East End and focuses on the mysterious disappearance of a reclusive scholar from his room above a synagogue in Princelet Street.*

🐟Read on

◆ *Landor's Tower* (Sinclair deserts his usual setting of London in a story set entirely in the borderlands of England and Wales).

◻ ›› Peter Ackroyd, *Hawksmoor*; ›› Michael Moorcock, *Mother London*; Paul West, *The Women of Whitechapel*; Chris Petit, *Robinson*; Nicholas Royle, *The Matter of the Heart*; Maureen Duffy, *Capital*.

SINGER, I.B. (Isaac Bashevis) (1904–91)
Polish/US novelist and short story writer

Singer wrote in Yiddish and maintained that, even when he translated his work himself, English diluted its force. His characters are either Middle European Jews – merchants, yeshiva-students, gravediggers, rabbis, drunks – from the ghettos and peasant villages of the seventeenth to nineteenth centuries, or (in several of his finest stories) present-day settlers in Israel or the USA. They struggle to lead decent lives, uplifted or oppressed by the demands of orthodox Jewish belief and ritual. They are haunted by outside forces beyond their control: supernatural beings – several stories are narrated by dybbuks, ghosts and even the Devil himself – or mindless, vicious anti-Semitism. Singer's finest novel is *The Family Moskat*, a warm, multi-generation story about a large Jewish family in Warsaw. The focus is on the human relationships within the family, magnificently and movingly described; but the novel's edge comes from the constant intrusion of grim outside reality, the tormented history of Poland between the Congress of Vienna in 1815 and the Nazi storming of the Warsaw ghetto in the Second World War.

Singer's other novels include Satan in Goray, The Magician of Lublin, The Manor, The Estate, The Golem, Enemies, The King of the Fields *and* Shadows on the Hudson. Collected Stories *is a fat anthology of his short stories.* In My Father's Court *is a memoir of Singer's Warsaw days as the son of a rabbi, a theological student and a budding writer.*

☙Read on

◘ to the short stories: S.Y. Agnon, *The Bridal Canopy*; Isaac Babel, *Odessa Tales*.
◘ to *The Family Moskat*: I.J. Singer (I.B.'s brother), *The Brothers Ashkenazy*.
◘ to Singer's other novels: Bernard Malamud, *The Fixer*; Nikos Kazantzakis, *The Greek Passion*; ›› Mario Vargas Llosa, *The War of the End of the World*; Jerzy Kosinski, *The Painted Bird*.

SINGH, Simon (born 1964)
British writer

The best popular science opens our eyes to new worlds of knowledge and meaning and Simon Singh has, over the last decade, proved himself to be one of the best writers in Britain when it comes to making abstruse scientific and mathematical ideas accessible to a general readership. His first book, *Fermat's Last Theorem* (1998) provided a fascinating survey of three centuries of failure and of one mathematician's ultimate success in proving a mathematical theorem originally formulated by Pierre de Fermat in the seventeenth century. Tantalisingly, Fermat had claimed that he had a 'truly marvellous proof' of his theorem but he didn't have the space to write it down. It wasn't finally and fully proven until the 1990s. Singh followed his success with *Fermat's Last Theorem* with *The Code Book*, a book about the long history of cryptography which managed to cover topics as diverse as the Enigma machine and the decipherment of Linear B, and *Big Bang*, one of the most lucid and comprehensible of many accounts of Big Bang theory and the origins of the Universe. His latest book, written in collaboration with the physician and professor of complementary medicine Edzard Ernst, is *Trick or Treatment*, a critical examination of the often extravagant claims of alternative medicines and therapies.

🐟Read on
◘ ❯❯ Bill Bryson, *A Short History of Nearly Everything*; Ben Goldacre, *Bad Science*; Paul Hoffman, *The Man Who Loved Only Numbers*; Michio Kaku, *Parallel Worlds*; Marcus du Sautoy, *The Music of the Primes*.

READ ON A THEME:

THE SIXTIES
T. Coraghessan Boyle, *Drop City*
Richard Brautigan, *In Watermelon Sugar*
Richard Farina, *Been Down So Long It looks Like Up to Me*
Ken Kesey, *One Flew Over the Cuckoo's Nest*
❯❯ Thomas Pynchon, *The Crying of Lot 49*
Terry Southern, *The Magic Christian*

READ ON A THEME:

SLAVES AND THE SLAVE TRADE
Russell Banks, *Cloudsplitter*
Fred D'Aguiar, *Feeding the Ghosts*
Charles Johnson, *Middle Passage*
Edward P. Jones, *The Known World*
Valerie Martin, *Property*
❯❯ Toni Morrison, *Beloved*

>>   Caryl Phillips, *Cambridge*
       Harriet Beecher Stowe, *Uncle Tom's Cabin*
       William Styron, *The Confessions of Nat Turner*
>>   Barry Unsworth, *Sacred Hunger*

READ ON A THEME:

SMALL-TOWN LIFE, USA

Louisa May Alcott, *Little Women*
Russell Banks, *Affliction*
John Cheever, *Bullet Park*
>> John Irving, *The Cider House Rules*
>> Garrison Keillor, *Lake Wobegon Days*
Larry McMurtry, *The Last Picture Show*
William Maxwell, *Time Will Darken It*
Jayne Anne Phillips, *Machine Dreams*
Dawn Powell, *My Home Is Far Away*
Richard Russo, *The Risk Pool*

See also: Deep South, USA

SMILEY, Jane (born 1951)
US novelist

A story set in the Midwest that echoes the events described in *King Lear* (*A Thousand Acres*); a satire on the academic pretensions of a small college (*Moo*); a historical novel of immense ambition that takes place in the battleground between pro- and anti-slave factions that was Kansas in the 1850s (*The All-True Travels and Adventures of Lydie Newton*) – Jane Smiley's fiction is immensely varied. Her novels have few common denominators beyond the subtlety of her intelligence and the supple flexibility of her prose, which she can adapt to whatever requirements her story demands. In *The All-True Travels and Adventures of Lydie Newton* the idealistic settlers of Kansas Territory find that they have to face not only the belligerence of their pro-slave neighbours but the intransigence of a land that is far from being the one of milk and honey that they imagined. The women of the book face the challenges more realistically than the men. (Smiley's fiction is full of strong women who get on with the daily tasks of life while the men have a tendency to make fine speeches and adopt noble postures.) Yet even the likeable and resourceful heroine Lydie is caught up in forces she cannot understand. Her husband is killed by pro-slavers and her attempt to make her own stand for his ideals (by helping in the escape of a slave) turns to tragedy.

Jane Smiley's other novels include Horse Heaven, The Greenlanders *(an epic set in medieval Greenland),* Barn Blind, Duplicate Keys, At Paradise Gate, Ordinary Love, Good Faith *and* Ten Days in the Hills. The Age of Grief *is a collection of short stories.* Thirteen Ways of Looking at the Novel *is about the pleasures of reading fiction.*

Read on
• *A Thousand Acres.*
>> Annie Proulx, *Accordion Crimes*; >> Barbara Kingsolver, *The Bean Trees*; >> Carol Shields, *The Stone Diaries*; Jane Hamilton, *A Map of the World.*

SMITH, Wilbur (born 1933)
South African novelist

Smith's novels, set in southern Africa, are swaggering adventure yarns in the tradition of >> H. Rider Haggard. Their backgrounds are war, mining and jungle exploration; their heroes are free spirits, revelling in the lawlessness and vigour of frontier life. *Shout At the Devil* is typical: the story of lion-hunting, crocodile-wrestling, ivory-poaching Flynn O'Flynn whose Robin Hood humiliations of the sadistic German commissioner Fleischer take a serious turn when war is declared – this is 1914 – and he falls into a German trap.

Smith's other novels include A Falcon Flies, Men of Men, The Angels Weep, The Leopard Hunts in Darkness *(four books about the Ballantyne family and its role in the colonial history of Rhodesia),* Eagle in the Sky, Cry Wolf, Hungry as the Sea *and* Elephant Song. *The 'Courtney' novels, which trace the fortunes of a white South African family across several generations, include* When the Lion Feeds,

The Sound of Thunder, A Sparrow Falls, Rage, Birds of Prey, Monsoon, The Triumph of the Sun *and* Assegai. River God *is set in ancient Egypt and has been followed by three other books with a similar setting,* The Seventh Scroll, Warlock *and* The Quest.

📖Read on

◆ *River God* (the first of Smith's Ancient Egyptian blockbusters).

▣ Hammond Innes, *Campbell's Kingdom*; ≫ H. Rider Haggard, *King Solomon's Mines*; Bryce Courtenay, *The Power of One*.

▣ to the Egyptian novels: Christian Jacq, *Ramses: The Son of the Light*.

SMITH, Zadie (born 1976)
British novelist

Few first novelists gain the attention that Zadie Smith did with her debut *White Teeth* (2000). For several months before and after its publication Smith and her book were omnipresent in the media. *White Teeth* went on to win very nearly every literary prize for which it was eligible. For once the hype and the hoopla were justified. The novel is an ambitious and generous story of different generations of two families in London which takes on, with confidence and humour, the question of what it means to be English in a post-colonial world. Archie Jones is a working-class Englishman who meets Samad Iqbal, a Muslim, during the Second World War and begins a lifelong friendship with him. *White Teeth* traces the progress of that friendship through several decades, through marriage and parenthood and through the dramatically changing social landscape of post-war Britain. The story moves into the next generation with Irie (daughter of Archie and his Jamaican second wife) and the twins Millat and Magid (sons of Samad's arranged marriage). Packed with energy and inventiveness and alive with the details of London life, *White Teeth* moves back and forth through the decades to create a vivid portrait of cultures mixing and melding in the city. Smith followed this astonishing debut with *The Autograph Man*, the story of Alex-Li Tandem, a man who makes his money out of our never-ending modern hunger for a connection with celebrity. Alex buys, sells (and occasionally fakes) autographs. Haunted still, after many years, by the death of his father and obsessed by an obscure 1940s movie star whose autograph is legendarily hard to acquire, he sets off on a hectic odyssey that brings him face to face with his own fears and the perilous nature of fame.

📖Read on

◆ *On Beauty* (Zadie Smith's third novel, modeled on ❯❯ E.M. Forster's *Howards End*, is the story of two generations and two families of middle-class academics struggling to connect with one another).

◘ ❯❯ Monica Ali, *Brick Lane*; ❯❯ Hari Kunzru, *The Impressionist*; ❯❯ Salman Rushdie, *The Ground Beneath Her Feet*; Arundhati Roy, *The God of Small Things*.

SOLZHENITSYN, Alexandr (1918–2008)

Russian novelist and non-fiction writer

Denounced for treason in 1945 (he was a Red Army soldier who criticized Stalin), Solzhenitsyn spent eight years in a labour camp where he developed stomach cancer, and after nine months in a cancer hospital was sent into internal exile. He turned this bitter experience into novels: the prison-camp books *One Day in the Life of Ivan Denisovich* and *The First Circle*, and *Cancer Ward*, a story of patients in a Soviet hospital. Their publication outside the USSR made him one of the most famous of the 1960s Soviet dissidents. He was finally expelled from the USSR in 1974, for writing an exhaustive description of the location, history and methods of the Russian prison camp system, *The Gulag Archipelago*. Few writers have ever surpassed Solzhenitsyn as a chronicler of human behaviour at its most nightmarish: his personal history authenticates every word he wrote.

Solzhenitsyn's only other fiction is the vast (and partially untranslated) 'Red Wheel' sequence of which August 1914 *and* November 1916, *about the stirrings of the Russian Revolution, are two volumes.* Invisible Allies *is a memoir and a tribute to those people who kept his work alive in Russia when to do so was to risk imprisonment.*

📖Read on

◘ ❯❯ Fyodor Dostoevsky, *Notes from the House of the Dead*; Arthur Koestler, *Darkness at Noon*; ❯❯ Vladimir Nabokov, *Bend Sinister*; ❯❯ André Brink, *Looking on Darkness*; ❯❯ Thomas Pynchon, *Gravity's Rainbow*; William Styron, *Sophie's Choice*.

READ ON A THEME:

SOUTH AFRICA

>> André Brink, *Imaginings of Sand*
>> J.M. Coetzee, *Disgrace*
   Bryce Courtenay, *The Power of One*
>> Nadine Gordimer, *Burger's Daughter*
>> H. Rider Haggard, *King Solomon's Mines*
   Bessie Head, *When Rain Clouds Gather*
   Alan Paton, *Cry, The Beloved Country*
   Sol Plaatje, *Mhudi* (first novel in English by a black South African)
   Olive Schreiner, *The Story of an African Farm*
>> Tom Sharpe, *Riotous Assembly*
   Anthony Sher, *Middlepost*
>> Wilbur Smith, *Rage*

SPARK, Muriel (1918–2006)
British novelist

Spark made her name in the 1960s: her tart black comedies seemed just the antidote to the fey optimism of the time. Her books' deadpan world is a distorted mirror image of our own, a disconcerting blend of the bland and the bizarre. In *Memento Mori* old people are mysteriously telephoned and reminded that they are about to die. In *Robinson* a plane-load of ill-assorted people (among them the standard Spark heroine, a 'Catholic With Doubts') crashes on an island where laws and customs are hourly remade at the whim of the sole inhabitant. In *The Prime of Miss Jean Brodie* an Edinburgh schoolmistress tries to brainwash her pupils into being nice, non-conforming 'gels'. The hero of *The Only Problem*, a scholar working on the Book of Job, finds its events parallelling those in his own life. Spark develops these ideas not in farce but in brisk, neat prose, as if they were the most matter-of-fact happenings in the world. The results are eccentric, unsettling and hilarious.

THE GIRLS OF SLENDER MEANS (1963)
A group of young ladies lives in a rundown London club for distressed gentlefolk. It is 1945, and there is rumoured to be an unexploded bomb in the garden. The girls are

excited by the possibility of imminent destruction: they find it almost as thrilling as the thought of sex. They bustle about their busy, vapid lives: pining after film stars, writing (unanswered) letters to famous writers, bargaining for black-market clothing coupons. The book is an allegory about seedy-genteel, self-absorbed Britain under the threat of nuclear extinction; for all Spark's breezy humour, the novel is haunted by the questions of where we'll be and how we'll behave when the bomb goes up.

Spark's other novels include The Mandelbaum Gate *(her most serious book, about a half-Jewish Catholic convert visiting Jerusalem at the height of Arab-Israeli tension),* The Driver's Seat, The Ballad of Peckham Rye, A Far Cry from Kensington, Symposium, Loitering With Intent, Reality and Dreams, Aiding and Abetting *and* The Finishing School. The Complete Short Stories *gathers together all her previously published stories and some that have not appeared before.* Curriculum Vitae *is autobiography.*

🕮Read on
◆ *The Ballad of Peckham Rye, The Bachelors.*
◘ Ronald Firbank, *The Eccentricities of Cardinal Pirelli*; Rose Macaulay, *The Towers of Trebizond*; Christopher Hope, *Serenity House*; ›› Hilary Mantel, *Beyond Black*; Elizabeth Jolley, *Miss Peabody's Inheritance.*

READ ON A THEME:

SPIES AND DOUBLE AGENTS
Eric Ambler, *Epitaph for a Spy*
James Buchan, *Heart's Journey in Winter*
›› Joseph Conrad, *The Secret Agent*
›› Frederick Forsyth, *The Fourth Protocol*
›› Alan Furst, *Night Soldiers*
›› Graham Greene, *The Honorary Consul*
›› W. Somerset Maugham, *Ashenden*
›› John Le Carré, *A Perfect Spy*
Gavin Lyall, *Spy's Honour*
Anthony Price, *The Labyrinth Makers*
›› Ruth Rendell, *Talking to Strange Men*

See also: High Adventure, War: Behind the Lines

READONATHEME:

SPORTING TALES

   J.L. Carr, *How Steeple Sinderby Wanderers Won the FA Cup* (football)
>> Tibor Fischer, *Under the Frog* (basketball)
>> John Grisham, *Bleachers* (American football)
>> George MacDonald Fraser, *Black Ajax* (bareknuckle boxing)
   Bernard Malamud, *The Natural* (baseball)
>> David Peace, *The Damned United* (football)
   Lionel Shriver, *Double Fault* (tennis)
   David Storey, *This Sporting Life* (rugby league)

STARK, Freya (1893–1993)
British travel writer

Described in her obituary in *The Times* as 'the last of the Romantic travellers', Freya Stark was a throwback to the days of formidable Victorian women like Mary Kingsley, who left their comfortable London lives to venture into the unknown. Most of Stark's travels took place in the Middle East, well-trodden destinations for many writers, but she often visited places where Western women had rarely, if ever, been seen. *The Valleys of the Assassins* (1934) chronicles several journeys in what are now Iraq and Iran, including an attempt to visit Alamut, the stronghold of the eleventh-century leader of the Islamic sect known as the Assassins, which met with formidable obstacles. ('One of them was that I could not find it on my map,' Stark laconically notes.) *The Southern Gates of Arabia* (1936) is her description of a journey into the interior of Arabia in search of the ruins of Shabwa, a legendary city associated with the Queen of Sheba, *Riding to the Tigris* (1959) an account of travels on horseback through some of the remotest parts of Turkey and on towards the Tigris river. Stark was still travelling at an age when most people would have resigned themselves to drinking cocoa by their own firesides and *Minaret of Djam* (1970) describes an excursion into some of the least accessible parts of Afghanistan.

Freya Stark's other travel books include Alexander's Path, The Lycian Shore, East is West *and* A Winter in Arabia. Traveller's Prelude, Beyond the Euphrates, The Coast of Incense *and* Dust in the Lion's Paw *are described as autobiographies but necessarily include much about her travels.*

📖 **Read on**

◆ *Traveller's Prelude.*

□ Gertrude Bell, *The Desert and the Sown*; Mary Kingsley, *Travels in West Africa*;

≫ Wilfred Thesiger, *The Marsh Arabs.*

STEINBECK, John (1902–68)

US novelist

Until Steinbeck settled to writing in 1935, he moved restlessly from one job to another: he was a journalist, a builder's labourer, a house painter, a fruit picker and the caretaker of a lakeside estate. This experience gave him first-hand knowledge of the dispossessed, the unemployed millions who suffered the brunt of the US Depression of the 1930s. Their lives are his subject, and he writes of them with ferocious, documentary intensity and in a style that seems exactly to catch their habits of both mind and speech. The ruggedness of his novels is often enhanced by themes borrowed from myth or the Old Testament. *Tortilla Flat* about 'wetbacks' (illegal Mexican immigrants to California) uses the story of Arthur, Guinevere and Lancelot from British myth. *East of Eden* is based on the story of Cain and Abel. Though Steinbeck never thrusts such references down his readers' throats, they add to the grandeur and mystery which, together with documentary grittiness, are the overwhelming qualities of his work.

THE GRAPES OF WRATH (1938)

The once-fertile Oklahoma grain fields have been reduced to a dust-bowl by over-farming, and the Joad family is near starvation. Attracted by leaflets promising work in the fruit plantations of California, they load their belongings into a battered old car and travel west. In California they find every plantation surrounded by destitute, desperate people: there are a thousand applicants for every job. The plantation owners pay starvation wages and sack anyone who objects; the workers try to force justice by strike action – and are beaten up by armed vigilantes. When Tom Joad, already on the run for murder, is caught up in the fight for justice and accidentally kills a man, it is time for Ma to gather the family together again and move on. There must be a place for them somewhere; there must be a Promised Land.

Steinbeck's shorter novels include Of Mice and Men, Cannery Row, The Pearl *and* The Short Reign of Pippin IV. *His short stories, usually about wetbacks, share-*

croppers and other victims of the system, are in The Red Pony *and* The Long Valley. The Acts of King Arthur and his Noble Knights *is a straightforward retelling of British myth;* Travels with Charley *an account of his journeys around America in 1960.*

📚Read on
◆ *Of Mice and Men* (a tragedy about the friendship between two ill-matched farmworkers, Lennie – a simple-minded giant of a man – and the weedier, cleverer George).
◘ Erskine Caldwell, *God's Little Acre*; ➤ Edith Wharton, *Ethan Frome*; ➤ William Faulkner, *The Hamlet*; Upton Sinclair, *The Jungle*; Frank Norris, *McTeague*; James T. Farrell, *Studs Lonigan*.

STENDHAL (1783–1842)
French novelist and non-fiction writer

Stendhal was a pseudonym used by the French diplomat Henri-Marie Beyle. As well as fiction (four novels; a dozen short stories) he published essays on art, literature and philosophy and several autobiographical books. Unlike most early nineteenth-century writers – even ➤ Balzac and ➤ Dickens – who concentrated on surface likenesses, painting word-pictures of events, people and places without intro-spection, Stendhal was chiefly interested in his characters' psychology. The main theme of his novels was the way outsiders, without breeding or position, must make their way in snobbish, tradition-stifled society by talent or personality alone. His books give the feeling that we are watching the evolution of that personality, that we are as intimate with his people's psychological development as if they were relatives or friends.

SCARLET AND BLACK (LE ROUGE ET LE NOIR) (1830)
The book is a character study of Julien Sorel, a carpenter's son who rises in the world by brains, sexual charm and ruthlessness. He becomes, first, tutor to the children of the local mayor, then the mayor's wife's lover, and finally secretary to an artistocratic diplomat whose daughter falls in love with him. In ten years he has travelled from humble origins to the verge of a dazzling marriage and a brilliant career. But then the mayor's wife writes a letter denouncing him as a cold-hearted adventurer, his society acquaintances reject him, and he returns to his native town to take revenge.

Stendhal's other completed novels are Armance, The Abbess of Castro *and* The Charterhouse of Parma. The Life of Henri Brûlard *and* Memoirs of an Egoist *are fictionalized autobiography.* Love *is a collection of reflections on the subject, prompted by the failure of one of Stendhal's many unrequited passions.*

📖Read on

◆ *The Charterhouse of Parma* (set in Italy in the early nineteenth century, this is Stendhal's most perceptive account of the disorienting power of sexual passion and the harsh reality of politics).

◘ to *Scarlet and Black*: ≫ André Gide, *Strait is the Gate (La Porte étroite)*; ≫ Nikolai Gogol, *Dead Souls*; ≫ George Eliot, *Middlemarch*; ≫ Honoré de Balzac, *Lost Illusions*.

◘ to *The Charterhouse of Parma*: ≫ Umberto Eco, *The Name of the Rose*.

STEPHENSON, Neal (born 1959)
US novelist

When he first began to publish his fiction in the 1980, Stephenson found his work described as SF but, as the years have passed, it has become clear that he has as much (if not more) in common with writers of post-modern fiction like ≫ Thomas Pynchon and ≫ Don DeLillo as he does with the cyberpunk authors with whom he was initially classified. His books are gigantic grab-bags packed with whatever ideas, jokes, offbeat erudition and weird stories have come to his attention. Readers may sometimes despair of their meandering plots ever arriving at a destination but the journey on which Stephenson takes them is always exhilarating and exciting. *Cryptonomicon* cuts between two narratives, one involving World War II code-breakers and one set in the present day as a group of West Coast techno-geeks work to create a 'data haven' in the (fictional) South-East Asian island sultanate of Kinakuta. 'The Baroque Cycle' (*Quicksilver, The Confusion* and *The System of the World*) is a vast saga set in the seventeenth and eighteenth centuries in which real-life historical figures, from Charles II and Samuel Pepys to Isaac Newton and the pirate Blackbeard, mingle with Stephenson's own creations, many of them the ancestors of the characters who appear in *Cryptonomicon*.

Stephenson's other novels are The Big U, Zodiac, Snow Crash, The Diamond Age *and* Anatham. *He has also published* Interface *and* The Cobweb, *two novels* written in collaboration with his uncle, the historian George Jewsbury, which originally appeared under the pseudonym of Stephen Bury.

⫘Read on

◆ *Snow Crash* (Stephenson's early novel set in a near-future America where the nation-state has disintegrated into a patchwork quilt of retailing franchises run by organizations like the Mafia, gated estates known as 'burbclaves', multi-lane freeways and vast airports, and where those who are able to do so spend long periods of time in virtual reality).

◫ to the 'Baroque Cycle': ⧸⧸ Thomas Pynchon, *Mason & Dixon*; William T. Vollmann, *The Ice Shirt*; David Foster Wallace, *Infinite Jest*.

◫ to Stephenson's fiction in general: Mark Z. Danielewski, *House of Leaves*; ⧸⧸ William Gibson, *Virtual Light*; Charles Stross, *Accelerando*.

STERNE, Laurence (1713–68)
British novelist

Sterne was a Yorkshire clergyman and a lover of wine, good talk, travel and song. His only novel, *The Life and Opinions of Tristram Shandy, Gentleman* (1760–77) is less a story than a gloriously rambling conversation. Tristram sets out to tell his life story (beginning with the moment of his conception, when his mother's mind is less on what she is doing than on whether his father has remembered to wind the clock). But everything he says reminds him of some anecdote or wise remark, so that he constantly interrupts himself. It takes three hundred pages, for example, for him to get from his conception to the age of seven, and in the meantime we have had such digressions as a treatise on what the size and shape of people's noses tell us about their characters, an explanation of how the boy came to be called Tristram by mistake for Trismegistus (and what each name signifies), accounts of the Tristapaedia (the system devised for Tristram's education), the curse of Ernulphus of Rochester and the misfortunes of Lieutenant le Fever; we have also had the novel's preface (placed not at the beginning but as the peroration to Book III), and many musings on life, love and the pursuit of happiness by Tristram's father, Uncle Toby and Corporal Trim. The reader is constantly exhorted, nudged and questioned; there is even a blank page in case you have urgent thoughts of your own to add. We never know how Tristram's life turns out; instead, we are copiously informed about Uncle Toby's love affairs, Tristram's travels in France and the adventures of the King of Bohemia. Sterne himself called Tristram Shandy 'a civil, nonsensical, good-humoured book'; it is the most spectacular shaggy-dog story ever told.

Sterne's other writings include sermons and A Sentimental Journey, *a discursive, half-fictionalized account of the towns and people he saw and the tales he heard during six months' travelling in France.*

📖 Read on

◘ ⟩⟩ François Rabelais, *Gargantua*; Miguel de Cervantes, *Don Quixote*; Tobias Smollett, *The Expedition of Humphry Clinker*; John Kennedy Toole, *A Confederacy of Dunces*; ⟩⟩ Flann O'Brien, *At Swim-Two-Birds*; ⟩⟩ Saul Bellow, *Henderson the Rain King*.

STEVENSON, R.L. (Robert Louis) (1850–94)
British writer of novels, short stories and non-fiction

Apart from the brief psychological thriller *Dr Jekyll and Mr Hyde*, about a man who uses drugs to change himself from kindly family doctor to deformed killer and back again, Stevenson's chief works are historical adventure stories. It is often assumed that these are books for children, but (except perhaps in *Treasure Island*) there is also plenty to interest adults: Stevenson's evocation of scenery (especially Scotland), the psychological complexity of his characters, and the feeling that each human life is part of a vast historical, moral and cultural continuum.

KIDNAPPED (1886)

Kidnapped takes place in 1751. The Jacobite Rebellion and Bonnie Prince Charlie's first triumphal and then tragic progress through the Highlands are only six years in the past. Scotland is still a country in upheaval where dangers lurk and betrayal is a constant threat. Stevenson's heroes are sixteen-year-old David Balfour and the fiery Jacobite Allan Breck who join forces to evade the redcoats searching for them after they are wrongly believed to be responsible for the murder of a hated government agent in the Highlands.

Stevenson's other novels include The Master of Ballantrae, The Wrong Box, Catriona *(a sequel to* Kidnapped*) and* Weir of Hermiston *(unfinished at his* *death).* New Arabian Nights *and* Island Nights' Entertainment *are collections of short stories.* Travels with a Donkey *is the account of Stevenson's journey as a young man through an area of southern France.*

🕮Read on

◆ *The Master of Ballantrae.*

▣ to *Dr Jekyll and Mr Hyde*: ≫ H.G. Wells, *The Invisible Man*; Gaston Leroux, *The Phantom of the Opera*; James Hogg, *Confessions of a Justified Sinner*; James Robertson, *The Fanatic.*

▣ to the adventure stories: ≫ George MacDonald Fraser, *The Candlemass Road*; ≫ Walter Scott, *The Heart of Midlothian*; ≫ John Buchan, *Castle Gay*; ≫ Arthur Conan Doyle, *The Valley of Fear*; J. Meade Falkner, *Moonfleet*; Bjorn Larsson, *Long John Silver.*

STOKER, Bram (1847–1912)

Irish writer

Forget all sendups and tawdry horror-film exploitation. *Dracula* is still one of the most blood-curdling novels ever written. The reader may begin by counting off the clichés – foggy cemeteries, vaults under the madhouse, the blazing crucifix, the bat-count climbing down the castle walls – but the sheer power of the story, its conviction and its exotic (and erotic) eeriness soon grip like tiny pointed teeth. Stoker was not a genius, but *Dracula* is a work of genius, the gothic novel (written in the form of diaries and letters to give added authenticity) to end them all.

🕮Read on

≫ Edgar Allan Poe, *Tales of Mystery and Imagination*; Sheridan Le Fanu, *Carmilla*; ≫ Stephen King, *Salem's Lot*; Anne Rice, *Interview With the Vampire*; Tom Holland, *Supping with Panthers* (contemporary pastiche/homage to the classic vampire story).

STRACHEY, LYTTON (1880–1932)
British biographer and critic

A pivotal member of the Bloomsbury Group, Strachey gained fame (and notoriety) with *Eminent Victorians*, a collection of historical and psychological case-studies (of Florence Nightingale, Cardinal Manning, Thomas Arnold and General Gordon) which, in their witty and iconoclastic analyses of their subjects' failings and eccentricities, came to epitomize the Bloomsbury generation's dismissal of Victorian values. He followed this book with an equally irreverent biography of Queen Victoria and with *Elizabeth and Essex*, a short account of the relationship between the Tudor queen and one of her most powerful courtiers. Strachey's method – pithy and aphoristic rather than long-winded and deferential – revolutionized the art of biography. Appropriately enough, ›› Michael Holroyd's two-volume life of Strachey, published in the 1960s, has also been seen as marking a turning point in the history of biographical writing.

⮩Read on
▫ Piers Brendon, *Eminent Edwardians*; Gretchen Gerzina, *Carrington*; ›› Michael Holroyd, *Lytton Strachey*.

SWIFT, Graham (born 1949)
British novelist

Swift's novels centre on apparently ordinary people – shopkeepers, housewives, clerks – under psychological stress. They have reached turning points in what have seemed boring, routine lives, and the novels show them mentally rerunning the past to find explanations for their feelings, either to themselves or to others. In *Waterland* the main character is an elderly history teacher, and the event he is remembering is the discovery, forty years before, of a boy's body in a drainage ditch in the English fens. In front of a bored, cheeky class, he begins thinking aloud about the reasons for the boy's death – and his monologue ranges through the history of the remote, enclosed world of the fens, the story of several generations of his own family and, not least, an account of the rivalry between his mentally subnormal brother Dick and Freddie Parr, the boy found drowned.

Swift's other novels are The Sweet Shop Owner, Shuttlecock, Out of This World, Ever After, Last Orders, The Light of Day *and* Tomorrow. Learning To Swim *is a collection of short stories,* Making an Elephant *a recently published volume of essays, poetry and interviews.*

≋Read on

◆ *Last Orders* (a deceptively simple story of four ageing men on a journey to the coast where they plan to scatter the ashes of an old friend in the sea which forces them all into reassessments of their own lives and relationships).
◘ ≫ Ian McEwan, *The Child in Time*; ≫ Julian Barnes, *Staring at the Sun*; Peter Benson, *The Levels*; ≫ Jane Rogers, *Promised Lands*.

SWIFT, Jonathan (1667–1745)
British/Irish satirist and journalist

Swift was a savage satirist, pouring out poems, articles and essays attacking the follies of his time. *Gulliver's Travels* differs from his other work only in that the edge of its satire is masked by fairytale – indeed, the satire and scatology are often edited out so that the book can be sold for children. Gulliver is a compulsive explorer, despite the moral humiliation he suffers after every landfall. In Lilliput the people (who are six inches high) regard him as an uncouth, unpredictable monster – particularly when he tells them some of the ideas and customs of his native England. In Brobdignag he becomes the pet of giants, and tries without success to convince them of the value of such civilized essentials as lawcourts, money and guns. He visits Laputa and Lagado, cloud-cuckoo-lands where science has ousted common sense; on the Island of Sorcerers he speaks to great thinkers of the past, and finds them in despair at what has become of the human race. Finally he is shipwrecked among the Houynhyms, horses equipped with reason who regard human beings as degenerate barbarians, and who fill him with such distaste for his own species that when he returns to England he can hardly bear the sight, sound or smell of his own family. Throughout the book, Gulliver doggedly preaches the glories of European 'civilization' (that is, the customs and belief of the Age of Enlightenment), and arouses only derision or disgust.

≋Read on
◘ Voltaire, *Candide*; Samuel Butler, *Erewhon*; Nathanael West, *A Cool Million*.

◘ to equally lacerating satires on aspects of late twentieth-century life: ⟩⟩ Michael Frayn, *A Very Private Life*; ⟩⟩ Thomas Pynchon, *The Crying of Lot 49*; ⟩⟩ Angela Carter, *The Passion of New Eve*.

TAN, Amy (born 1952)
US novelist

In Amy Tan's best-known and bestselling novel, *The Joy Luck Club*, two generations of Chinese-American women share stories of their lives and struggle to understand the choices that have made them who they are. Poetic and imaginative, the book celebrates the lives of mothers and daughters and their triumphs over pain and loss. Tan has followed her success with *The Joy Luck Club* with a number of other novels, most of which explore the difficult interactions between generations and between the demands of traditional Chinese culture and those of modern American society. In *The Kitchen God's Wife* an ageing Chinese woman reveals the bitter secrets of her past to her American daughter. *The Bonesetter's Daughter* begins with a woman in San Francisco discovering manuscript memoirs written by her mother and then moves back in time to the mother's life growing up in a remote Chinese village in the 1920s. Tan's most recent novel, *Saving Fish From Drowning*, moves her work in a new direction as it tells the story of a group of American tourists visiting Myanmar for the holiday of a lifetime who are kidnapped and carried into the mountains by tribesmen convinced that one of the Americans is an incarnation of a tribal god. *The Opposite of Fate* is a collection of essays on her life and her writing career.

Read on
♦ *The Hundred Secret Senses* (two sisters, one brought up in China and the other in America, struggle to make contact across the cultural divide).
◘ Patricia Chao, *Monkey King*; Louise Erdrich, *Love Medicine*; Jhumpa Lahiri, *The Namesake*; Adeline Yen-Mah, *Falling Leaves* (a personal memoir which reflects many of the same experiences that Tan uses in her fiction).

TARTT, Donna (born 1963)
US novelist

In 1992 Donna Tartt made one of the most successful debuts in American fiction for decades with her novel *The Secret History*, triumphantly acclaimed by critics and reviewers, but she then discovered that there are few tasks more daunting in literature – particularly in American literature, for some reason – than providing a successful encore to a remarkable debut. It was ten years before she published her second novel *The Little Friend*. *The Secret History* tells the story of Richard Papen, who arrives as a classics student at a prestigious New England college. His fellow students all appear sophisticated and worldly beyond their years and all are in some way in thrall to their mentor, Julian Morrow. Slowly Richard is drawn into the inner circle where he learns the secret that binds them together and that the group's interest in Dionysiac frenzy in Greek religion has gone beyond scholarly speculation. *The Little Friend* is set in the Deep South (Tartt comes from Mississippi) and again centres on a murder and its consequences. The heroine, Harriet Dusfresnes, is a twelve-year-old girl in a small town whose short life has been haunted by the even shorter life of her brother. Robin Dusfresnes was found hanging from a tree when Harriet was a baby, the victim of a murderer who has never been caught. Harriet believes she knows who the murderer is – one of a bunch of unsavoury rednecks called the Ratliffes – and sets out to prove it. In doing so, she enters territory for which her fantasies about unearthing the truth have ill-prepared her.

📖Read on

◘ to *The Secret History*: Jeffrey Eugenides, *The Virgin Suicides*; Carol Goodman, *The Lake of Dead Languages*; Jody Shields, *The Fig Eater*.
◘ to *The Little Friend*: Harper Lee, *To Kill a Mockingbird*; Joe R. Lansdale, *The Bottoms*; Flannery O'Connor, *The Violent Bear It Away*.

TAYLOR, D.J. (David John) (born 1960)
British writer

D.J. Taylor has been one of the most versatile of British writers of the last twenty years, moving readily from fiction to biography and from history to literary criticism. His first novel, *Great Eastern Land*, was published in 1986 and has been followed by more than half a dozen others. *Kept*, subtitled 'A Victorian Mystery', is an ingenious reworking of a nineteenth-century novel by a twenty-first century sensibility. His most recent novel, *Ask Alice*, moves from the Edwardian era to the 1930s as it tells the story of the rise of a socially ambitious adventuress. Taylor has also written successful biographies of ›› George Orwell and ›› William Makepeace Thackeray, and *Bright Young People*, a study of the proto-celebs who enlivened 1920s gossip columns and were immortalized in the novels of ›› Evelyn Waugh, demonstrates his skills as a social historian.

D.J. Taylor's other novels are Real Life, English Settlement, Trespass *and* The Comedy Man. After Bathing at Baxter's *is a collection of short stories,* After the War *an examination of British fiction in the last sixty years and* On the Corinthian Spirit, *a short and witty examination of the decline of amateurism in sport.*

Read on

◘ to the novels: Michael Cox, *The Meaning of Night* (like *Kept* a novel of Victorian life); Sadie Jones, *The Outcast*; Mark Mills, *The Savage Garden*.
◘ to the biographies and non-fiction: ›› Victoria Glendinning, *Leonard Woolf*; Virginia Nicholson, *Among the Bohemians*

TAYLOR, Elizabeth (1912–75)
British novelist and short story writer

A large part of Taylor's art consists of appearing to have no art at all: few authors have ever seemed so self-effacing in their work. As each novel or story begins, it is as if a net curtain has been drawn aside to reveal ordinary people in a normal street. The setting is the outskirts of some large English town; the people are housewives, bus conductors, labourers, schoolchildren; there seems to be no drama. But as the story proceeds, an apparently unfussy chronicle of ordinary events and conversations builds up enormous psychological pressure, which Taylor then releases in a shocking or hilarious happening which opens wide speculation about whatever will happen when the book is closed. Her artistry – subtle, gentle and unsettling – is at its peak in short stories; her novels, thanks to larger casts, more varied settings and longer time schemes, tend more to wry social comedy than to the sinister.

THE DEVASTATING BOYS (1972)

The people in this story collection are typical Taylor characters: an elderly couple in the countryside who decide to offer a holiday to two black children from the city slums; a young West Indian, utterly alone in London on the eve of his birthday; an eleven-year-old child taking a bus home from a hateful piano lesson; a blue-rinsed widow with an orderly routine of life. Something unexpected happens to each of them, a psychological bombshell. They were as unremarkable as our neighbours – but after these stories, our neighbours will never seem the same again.

Dangerous Calm *is an aptly titled selection from Taylor's short stories. Her novels include* Angel, At Mrs Lippincote's, A View of the Harbour, The Wedding Group, Blaming, A Wreath of Roses, Mrs Palfrey at the Claremont *and* The Soul of Kindness.

⮂Read on

◆ *Dangerous Calm*; *The Wedding Group*.

▣ to the stories: ›› William Trevor, *Angels at the Ritz*; Mary Gordon, *Temporary Shelter*.

▣ to the novels: ›› Susan Hill, *A Change for the Better*; ›› Barbara Pym, *Excellent Women*; ›› Angus Wilson, *Late Call*.

READ ON A THEME

TEENAGERS
›› Julian Barnes, *Metroland*
   S.E. Hinton, *The Outsiders*
›› John Irving, *A Prayer for Owen Meany*
›› Hanif Kureishi, *The Buddha of Suburbia*
›› J.D. Salinger, *The Catcher in the Rye*
   Sue Townsend, *The Secret Diary of Adrian Mole, aged 13½*
   Alan Warner, *The Sopranos*
›› Jeanette Winterson, *Oranges Are Not the Only Fruit*

See also: Adolescence; Children

READONATHEME:

TERRORISTS/FREEDOM FIGHTERS

Jerzy Andrzeyewski, *Ashes and Diamonds*
>> Tom Clancy, *Patriot Games*
>> Joseph Conrad, *Under Western Eyes*
>> John Le Carré, *The Little Drummer Girl*
>> Doris Lessing, *The Good Terrorist*
>> Primo Levi, *If Not Now, When?*
Frederic Raphael, *Like Men Betrayed*

See also: Spies and Double Agents, War: Behind the Lines

THACKERAY, William Makepeace (1811–63)
British novelist and journalist

Until the success of *Vanity Fair* (see below) when he was thirty six, Thackeray earned his living as a journalist and cartoonist (especially for *Punch* magazine) and as a humorous lecturer. His first intention in his novels was to write 'satirical biographies', letting the reader discover the follies of the world at the same time as his naïve young heroes and heroines. But the characters took over, and his books now seem more genial and affectionate than barbed. He invented characters as grotesque as >> Dickens's, caricatures of human viciousness or folly, but he wrote of them with a kind of disapproving sympathy, a fellow-feeling for their humanity, which Dickens lacks. Humbug, ambition and the seven deadly sins are Thackeray's subjects and so are friendship, kindness and warm-heartedness. At a time when many English novels were more like sermons, clamorous for reform, he wrote moral comedies, showing us what fools we are.

VANITY FAIR (1847–48)

The book interweaves the lives of two friends, gentle Amelia and calculating, brilliant Becky Sharp. Becky is an impoverished orphan determined to make her fortune; Amelia believes in love, marriage and family life. Each of them marries; Amelia's husband has an affair with Becky and dies at Waterloo with her name on his lips; Becky's husband finds her entertaining a rich, elderly admirer and abandons her. In the end, each girl gets what she longed for, but not in the way she hoped. Amelia, after ten years pining for her dead husband, is cruelly told by Becky of his infidelity and turns for comfort to a kind man who has worshipped her from afar and who now offers her marriage, a home and all the comforts of obscurity. Becky's son inherits his father's money and gives her an annuity on condition that she never speaks to him again; we see her at the end of the book, queening it in Bath, an idle, rich member of the society she has always aspired to join and whose values Thackeray sums up in the title of the book.

Thackeray's other books include Pendennis *(the story of a selfish young man, spoilt by his mother, who goes to London to make his fortune as a writer) and its sequel* The Newcomers, Henry Esmond *and its sequel* The Virginians, *and* Barry Lyndon.

⏚Read on
◆ *Pendennis*.
❯❯ Jane Austen, *Emma*; ❯❯ Arnold Bennett, *The Card*; ❯❯ H.G. Wells, *Tono-Bungay*; ❯❯ Eudora Welty, *The Ponder Heart*; ❯❯ Barbara Pym, *No Fond Return of Love*.

THEROUX, Paul (born 1941)
US novelist and non-fiction writer

Some of Theroux's most enjoyable books are about travelling: *The Great Railway Bazaar, The Old Patagonian Express, The Kingdom by the Sea, Riding the Iron Rooster, The Happy Isles of Oceania, The Pillars of Hercules, Dark Star Safari* and, most recently, *Ghost Train to the Eastern Star*. In all of them the narrator, the writer himself, feels detached, an observer of events rather than a participant – and the same is true of the people in Theroux's novels. They live abroad, often in the tropics; like the heroes of ❯❯ Graham Greene (an author Theroux often resembles) they feel uneasy both about the society they are in and about themselves; they fail to cope. The hero of *Saint Jack*, an American pimp in Singapore, hopes to make a fortune providing rest and relaxation for his servicemen compatriots, but the pliability of his character makes him the prey for every con-man and shark in town. In *The Mosquito Coast* an ordinary American citizen, depressed by life, uproots his family and tries to make a new start in the Honduran jungle, with tragic, farcical results. *Honolulu Hotel* is an episodic novel set in a rundown hotel in Hawaii. The manager is an unsuccessful writer, battling with the personal demons that beset so many of Theroux's characters, who acts as witness to the tragi-comedies and mini-dramas that unfold in the seedy rooms of the hotel.

Theroux's other novels include Waldo, The Family Arsenal, Doctor Slaughter, Picture Palace, *an acid science fiction fantasy* O-Zone, My Secret History, Chicago Loop, Millroy the Magician, My Other Life, Kowloon Tong *and* Blinding Light. The Consul's File, The London Embassy *and* The Stranger at the Palazzo d'Oro *are collections of short stories.* Fresh Air Fiends *is a collection of travel essays;* Sir Vidia's Shadow *is a memoir of Theroux's 30-year friendship (now ended) with »* V.S. Naipaul, horribly compelling in its revelations of the insecurities and jealousies of the literary life.

Read on
◆ *My Secret History*.

◘ to Theroux's fiction: P.H. Newby, *Leaning in the Wind*; Timothy Mo, *Sour-Sweet*; ›› William Boyd, *Stars and Bars*.

◘ to the travel books: ›› Jonathan Raban, *Coasting*; ›› Colin Thubron, *Behind the Wall*; ›› V.S. Naipaul, *Among the Believers*.

LITERARY TRIVIA 14:

TEN NOBEL LAUREATES FEW PEOPLE NOW READ

R.F.A. Sully-Prudhomme – French poet and first Nobel Laureate (1901)
Jose Echegaray y Eizaguirre – Spanish dramatist (1904)
Henrik Pontoppidan – Danish novelist (1917)
Carl Friedrich Georg Spitteler – Swiss poet (1919)
Wladyslaw Stanislaw Reymont – Polish novelist (1924)
Erik Axel Karlfeldt – Swedish poet (1931)
Frans Eemil Sillanpää – Finnish novelist (1939)
Par Fabian Lagerkvist – Swedish novelist and poet (1951)
Salvatore Quasimodo – Italian poet (1959)
Yasunari Kawabata – Japanese novelist (1968)

Among the rather better-known writers who were nominated for the prize but didn't win were: ›› Joseph Conrad, ›› Henry James, ›› Marcel Proust, ›› F. Scott Fitzgerald, ›› Virginia Woolf and ›› Graham Greene.

THESIGER, Wilfred (1910–2003)

British travel writer

A throwback to an earlier and more heroic era of exploration rather than mere travel, Wilfred Thesiger was a man lost in the modern world, only at home when he could escape its irritations and journey into the desert. Few other writers have so memorably combined travel writing, autobiography and almost mystical philosophical musings, and his blend of 'Lawrence of Arabia' heroics and lyrical accounts of the landscapes through which he travelled is unique. ***Arabian Sands***, the accounts of his journeys across the Empty Quarter of the Arabian Peninsula with the Bedouin, is one of the great travel books of the twentieth century and a moving tribute to a world which was dying when he encountered it and has now disappeared forever. ***The Marsh Arabs*** describes his encounters with the peoples who lived in the marshlands of southern Iraq.

Wilfred Thesiger's other books include Among the Mountains***,*** The Danakil Diary***, and*** My Kenya Days***. Thesiger was as fine a photographer as he was a writer and*** A Vanished World ***is a collection of his portraits of the tribespeople he encountered during his travels.***

Read on

- ***The Life of My Choice*** (autobiography).

▫ Michael Asher, ***In Search of the Forty Day Road***; C.M. Doughty, ***Arabia Deserta***; T.E. Lawrence, ***The Seven Pillars of Wisdom***; Gavin Maxwell, ***A Reed Shaken by the Wind***; Laurens van der Post, ***The Lost World of the Kalahari***.

THOMPSON, Hunter S. (Stockton) (1937–2005)

American essayist and journalist

High priest of 'gonzo' journalism, the very personalized style of reportage that came to the fore in the 1960s and 1970s, Thompson is most notorious for his 1971 book, ***Fear and Loathing in Las Vegas***, a hallucinatory, partly fictionalized account of a drink- and drug-fuelled odyssey in search of an American dream that was turning into a nightmare. Narrator Raoul Duke and his attorney, Dr Gonzo, recklessly ingesting improbable amounts of illicit substances as they race from California to Las Vegas, symbolic heart of American consumerism, become unlikely spokesmen for a generation of outsiders disillusioned with the way the country is heading. Thompson had previously written *Hell's Angels*, a brilliantly bizarre narrative of riding with the outlaw motorcycle gangs of California, but nothing had prepared the reading public for the venomous surrealism of *Fear and Loathing in Las Vegas*. Thompson followed it with *Fear and Loathing on the Campaign Trail*, a jaundiced vision of the madness of American politics produced by witnessing the 1972 presidential campaign at close hand. Among assorted collections of his work, *The Great Shark Hunt* includes not only sections from the *Fear and Loathing* books but also 'The Kentucky Derby is Decadent and Depraved', a piece of sports writing unlike any other ever published, and brutal, ranting attacks on those public figures, particularly Richard Nixon, whom Thompson found offensive. In Thompson's later years, when he was trading on his legendary reputation, he was always likely to lapse into self-parody. Books like *Kingdom of Fear* and *Better Than Sex* are monstrously self-indulgent and crying out for the editor's blue pencil but they still contain passages of diamond-sharp invective that only he could have written.

Hunter S. Thompson's other books include The Rum Diary *(a novel he wrote in the late 1950s, finally published in 1999),* The Curse of Lono, Generation of Swine, Songs of the Doomed *and* The Proud Highway *(a first volume of his anarchic and chaotic correspondence).*

☞Read on
◘ *The Proud Highway.*
◘ Lester Bangs, *Psychotic Reactions and Carburettor Dung* (gonzo meets rock criticism); ≫ P.J. O'Rourke, *Republican Party Reptile*; ≫ Tom Wolfe, *The Electric Kool Aid Acid Test*.

THORPE, Adam (born 1956)
British novelist and poet

Thorpe began his writing career as a poet and his novels show a poet's sensitivity to the subtleties and nuances of language but they are not the delicate miniatures that many other poets create when they turn to fiction. Thorpe's novels are bold and ambitious – almost epic in scale. His first novel, *Ulverton* (see below), is an attempt to invent an entire history for an imagined village. His second novel, *Still*, is the eve-of-the-millennium confession of failed ex-pat British film director Ricky

Thornby, for which Thorpe draws on every resource of the language to let Ricky tell his story. The result is an extraordinary five hundred-plus page mélange of voices from inside Ricky's head, those of ex-wives and lovers, long-dead relations and mentors and of the masters of the cinema whose work he has idolized but not matched. An exuberant stream-of-consciousness – dense, allusive and often very funny – spills across the pages. *Still* becomes Ricky's last and best work of art, premièred for the readers of the novel.

ULVERTON (1992)

Thorpe imagines the West Country village which gives the book its title and then, in twelve very different narratives, peoples it with individuals from several centuries of its history. These narratives take different forms, from a seventeenth-century sermon through a dialect monologue delivered by a nineteenth-century farm labourer to the TV script for a documentary about a greedy, unimaginative property developer and his battle with conservationists. Each chapter works as an individual story but they weave together to form the longer story of Ulverton across three hundred years. The reader is shown the change and the continuity in one English community as it is shaped by time. *Ulverton* is a bravura performance, in which Thorpe recreates and re-imagines the voices of the past. It is a demanding, sometimes difficult read but a very rewarding one.

Adam Thorpe's other novels are Pieces of Light *(partly set in Africa and partly in an Ulverton which has its own hearts of darkness),* Nineteen Twenty One*,* No Telling*,* The Rules of Perspective*,* Between Each Breath*,* The Standing Pool *and* Hodd. Shifts *and* Is This the Way You Said? *are collections of short stories,* Birds with a Broken Wing *the latest of Thorpe's five volumes of verse.*

ᗺ Read on

◆ *Hodd* (Thorpe's version of the Robin Hood story in which a medieval manuscript rescued fom a ruined church in the aftermath of the First World War reveals a very different character to the loveable hero of the greenwoods we all know).

◘ ≫ Graham Swift, *Waterland*; ≫ William Boyd, *The New Confessions*; ≫ Anthony Burgess, *Earthly Powers*.

START POINT

THRILLERS

Thrillers grew out of the adventure novels of the nineteenth century, such as
>> Jules Verne's *Twenty Thousand Leagues Under the Sea* or >> H. Rider
Haggard's *King Solomon's Mines*. >> Rudyard Kipling's *Kim* (1901) and
Erskine Childers' *The Riddle of the Sands* (1903) were among the first
novels to add politics to adventure – a blend which has dominated thrillers
ever since. The many wars of the twentieth century, in particular the (non-
fighting) Cold War, gave thriller writers exciting backgrounds and ready-
made 'good guys' and 'bad guys'. 'Their' chaps are out to use any trick, wile
or murderous plot to control the world, and are thwarted only by the grit and
pluck of 'our' chaps. In subtler thrillers (pioneered by >> Graham Greene in
his 1940s 'entertainments', and since the 1960s by >> John Le Carré) writers
dealt not in moral blacks and whites but in myriad shades of grey. During the
Cold War anti-communist feeling in the West led to a mass of thrillers casting
the former USSR as the villain and Soviet thrillers returned the compliment
by blackening the West. But since the early 1990s thrillers of this kind have
become as dead as dodos and writers either set their stories in the past (for
example in the Second World War), or find new enemies (such as terrorists,
serial killers, organized crime or religious fundamentalists), and leave
East–West politics alone.

Ambler, Eric, *The Mask of Dimitrios* (1939). A writer on holiday in Turkey
sees the body of a criminal in the morgue and sets out, despite all attempts
to stop him, to discover his story.

>> Clancy, Tom, *The Sum of All Fears* (1991). In the near future, Palestinian
terrorists get control of nuclear weapons.

>> Deighton, Len, *City of Gold* (1992). In Cairo, during the 1942 Desert War,
someone in Allied High Command is feeding Rommel military secrets, and
must be stopped.

>> Furst, Alan, *The World at Night* (1997). Film producer becomes involved
in the dark and dangerous world of resistance to the Nazis in wartime
France.

>> Grisham, John, *The Pelican Brief* (1992). A young law student is the only person in the USA to see a connection between two simultaneous political assassinations, on the right and the left. From that moment on her life is in deadly danger.

Harris, Thomas, *The Silence of the Lambs* (1990). Hannibal Lecter, the favourite film bogeyman of the 1990s, leads FBI agent Clarice Starling a merry dance as she tries to track down a serial killer.

Higgins, Jack, *Thunder Point* (1993). Secret Second World War documents, found in a sunken U-boat in the Caribbean fifty years later, reveal a conspiracy to keep Nazism alive after the war and implicate many of those still in power in the 1990s.

Hunter, Stephen, *Point of Impact* (1993). An expert sniper and assassin, who learned his trade in the jungles of Vietnam, is brought out of retirement for one last mission but discovers that he is meant to be the fall guy in a labyrinthine conspiracy.

Kerr, Philip, *A Philosophical Investigation* (1992). Detective in the not-so-distant future pits his wits against a serial killer with a fondness for Wittgenstein.

>> Le Carré, John, *The Quest for Karla* (1974–90). Classic quartet of Cold War, house-of-mirror novels, involving George Smiley's search not just for Soviet agents but also for traitors in his own service, the ironically named 'Circus'. Individual titles: *Tinker Tailor Soldier Spy*, *The Honourable Schoolboy*, *Smiley's People* and *The Secret Pilgrim*.

Ludlum, Robert, *The Road to Omaha* (1992). Amerindian fighter for justice defends the interest of the Wopotami people against Strategic Air Command, who have taken over their land and are prepared to fight dirty to keep it.

Pattison, Eliot, *The Skull Mantra* (2000). Original and moving thriller in which a disgraced Chinese investigator is drawn into the mystery surrounding a headless corpse found on a Tibetan mountainside.

Price, Anthony, *Other Paths to Glory* (1975). When events from the First World War seem to have a continuing relevance in the present day, a young military historian is recruited into the murky world of Cold War espionage.

>> Smith, Wilbur, *Elephant Song* (1991). Action adventure in Zimbabwe, as film-maker and anthropologist try to thwart a conspiracy involving ivory-poaching, international business interests and the projected elimination of an entire country and its people.

Also recommended: David Baldacci, *Absolute Power*; Dan Brown, *The Da Vinci Code*; >> Lee Child, *Killing Floor*; Richard Condon, *The Manchurian Candidate*; >> Michael Connelly, *The Poet*; >> Bernard Cornwell, *Storm Child*; Martin Cruz Smith, *Gorky Park*; Clive Cussler, *Dragon*; Jeffery Deaver, *The Vanished Man*; Ken Follett, *Night Over Water*; Colin Forbes, *Cross of Fire*; Jonathan Kellerman, *Time Bomb*; Richard North Patterson, *The Outside Man*; Henry Porter, *Remembrance Day*; John Sandford, *Rules of Prey*.

See also: Buchan, Forsyth, Harris (Robert), High Adventure, Spies and Double Agents, Terrorists/Freedom Fighters

HIDDENGEM:

GEOFFREY HOUSEHOLD – *ROGUE MALE* (1939)

An unnamed Englishman stalks an unnamed Continental dictator with the aim of assassinating him. (The book first appeared in the 1930s and the dictator seems remarkably similar to Hitler.) He is caught and tortured but miraculously escapes and returns to England. Even here he is not safe. His pursuers are still after him and he is transformed into little more than a hunted animal as he struggles to stay out of their clutches. *Rogue Male* is seventy years old but it remains one of the most exciting and nerve-wrenching thrillers ever published.

THUBRON, Colin (born 1939)

British travel writer and novelist

Long one of the most elegant and erudite of British travel writers, Thubron published several books (*Mirror to Damascus*, *The Hills of Adonis*) about the Middle East in his early career but more recently his finest works have been his mournfully perceptive and gracefully written records of his journeys through the ruins of the Soviet Empire. *Among the Russians* (1983) was published before the disintegration of that empire but Thubron's travels through Brezhnev's Russia not only revealed the cracks in the Soviet façade but took him to places and people where older traditions of life still survived. *The Lost Heart of Asia* (1994), written shortly after the break up of the old Soviet satrapies in Central Asia and their re-emergence as independent republics, provides prescient insights into the troubles that the fragmentation of the region have created. *In Siberia* (1999) records Thubron's travels in the vast landscapes of Russia's Wild East. All three books are characterized by his curiosity about the people he meets, his alertness to the changes that history has imposed on the countries he visits and his appreciation of the landscape amid which he travels.

Colin Thubron's other travel books include The God in the Mountain, The Silk Road, Behind the Wall *(about China) and* Shadow of the Silk Road. *He has also written a number of novels including* Emperor *(an historical novel set in the fourth-century Roman Empire),* A Cruel Madness *and* Turning Back the Sun.

≋Read on

◆ *Behind the Wall*.

◘ to the travel books: Jason Elliot, *An Unexpected Light*; Philip Marsden, *The Spirit-Wrestlers*; ▸▸ Paul Theroux, *Riding the Iron Rooster*.

◘ to the novels: ▸▸ Bruce Chatwin, *Utz*; ▸▸ Patrick McGrath, *Asylum*.

TÓIBÍN, Colm (born 1955)
Irish writer

In his fiction Colm Tóibín has used an unobtrusive, undemonstrative but highly effective prose style to tell stories largely about Irish people, both past and present, caught in emotional dilemmas and crises in their lives. *The Blackwater Lightship* (see below) is, arguably, the novel in which his economic, unflamboyant use of language is most movingly deployed. His first novel, *The South*, is set in 1950s and 1960s Spain. A young Irishwoman, an aspiring painter, arrives in Barcelona in flight from her family in Ireland. Her relationship with a Spanish painter, at odds with Franco's régime, moves towards a tragic conclusion. His most recent novel, *Brooklyn*, tracks the fortunes of a young woman from a small Irish town in the 1950s as she struggles to create a new and more expansive life for herself in America.

THE BLACKWATER LIGHTSHIP (1999)
Declan O'Doherty is a young man dying of AIDS. He asks to be taken to the isolated house by the sea where his grandmother lives and which he remembers from his childhood. Three generations of the women in his family – grandmother, mother and sister – join him there, as do two gay friends, who have known of his illness far longer than his family. Mutual antagonism and estrangement have characterized all the relationships between the women in the family and unresolved conflicts simmer beneath the surface, occasionally breaking out in harsh exchanges, as they all try to come to terms with Declan's illness and with one another.

Tóibín's other novels are The Heather Blazing, The Story of the Night *and* The Master. Mothers and Sons *is a collection of stories on the mother–son relationship. His non-fiction books include* Bad Blood *(travels along the border between the Republic and Northern Ireland),* The Sign of the Cross *(travels in Catholic Europe),* Homage to Barcelona *and* Love in a Dark Time *(essays on gay writers and gay creativity). He has also edited* The Penguin Book of Irish Fiction.

Read on
◆ *The Master* (Tóibín deftly mixes fiction and fact in telling the story of five crucial years in the life of the novelist Henry James).
◘ Seamus Deane, *Reading in the Dark*; John McGahern, *Amongst Women*; David Leavitt, *The Page Turner*; ≫ John Banville, *Eclipse*; Niall Williams, *Four Letters of Love*; Dermot Bolger, *Father's Music*.

TOLKIEN, J.R.R. (John Ronald Reuel) (1892–1973)
British novelist

In 1937 Tolkien, a teacher of Anglo-Saxon literature at Oxford University, published a children's book, about a small furry-footed person who steals a dragon's hoard: *The Hobbit*. Bilbo Baggins was the hobbit of the title and his quest was the prologue to an enormous adult saga in which elves, dwarves, wizards, ents, human beings and hobbits unite to destroy the power of evil (embodied by the Dark Lord Sauron and his minions the Ring-wraiths and the Orcs). The three volumes of *The Lord of the Rings*, published in the mid-1950s, were the starting point for the vast expansion of interest in fantasy over the last half-century which has spread worldwide and taken in films and computer games as well as fiction. Tolkien still outstrips nearly all his innumerable imitators not so much because of his plot (which is a simple battle between good and bad, with the moral issues explicit on every page) as thanks to his teeming professorial imagination. He gave his made-up worlds complete systems of language, history, anthropology, geography and literature. Reading him is like exploring a library; his invention seems inexhaustible.

Although The Hobbit *and* The Lord of the Rings *are self-contained, Tolkien published several other volumes filling in chinks of their underlying history, explaining matters only sketched in the main narrative, and adding even more layers of linguistic, historical and anthropological fantasy. The chief books are* The Silmarillion *and* Unfinished Tales. Lost Tales *(three volumes) and* The History of Middle Earth *(five volumes) contain notes and drafts, chiefly of interest to addicts.* Farmer Giles of Ham *and* The Adventures of Tom Bombadil *are shorter stories for children.*

☜Read on

◘ Stephen Donaldson, *The Chronicles of Thomas Covenant*; Piers Anthony, *A Spell for Chameleon*; David Eddings's *Belgariad Quintet*; ▸▸ Raymond E. Feist's *Riftwar Saga*. *Bored of the Rings* is a best-selling spoof first published in the 1960s and still going strong.

TOLSTOY, Leo Nikolaevich (1828–1910)
Russian novelist

In his sixties and beyond Tolstoy became famous as a kind of moral guru or secular saint: he preached the equal 'value' of all human beings, and suited actions to words by giving away his wealth, freeing his serfs and living an austere life in a cottage on the edge of his former estate. A similar view underlies his fiction. His ambition was to enter into the condition of each of his characters, to show the psychological complexity and diversity of the human race. His books are not tidily organized, with every event and emotion shaped to fit a central theme, but reflect the sprawl of life itself. The result was a psychological equivalent of ›› Balzac's 'snapshots' in *The Human Comedy (La Comédie Humaine)*. Whether Tolstoy is showing us a coachman who comes and goes in half a page, or a major character who appears throughout a book, he invites us to feel full sympathy for that person, makes us flesh out his or her 'reality' in terms of our own.

WAR AND PEACE (1869)
The book begins with people at a St Petersburg party in 1805 discussing the political situation in France, where Napoleon has just been proclaimed emperor. Tolstoy then fills one hundred pages with seemingly random accounts of the lives and characters of a large group of relatives, friends, servants and dependants of three aristocrats, Andrey Bolkonsky, Pierre Bezuhov and Natasha Rostov. Gradually all these people become involved both with one another and with the gathering storm as Napoleon's armies sweep through Europe. The story culminates with the 1812 French invasion of Russia, Napoleon's defeat and his retreat from Moscow. The war touches the lives of all Tolstoy's people, and in particular resolves the triangle of affection between his central characters. The effects of war are the real subject of *War and Peace* It contains five hundred and thirty nine characters the range is from Napoleon to the girl who dresses Rostov's hair, from Bolkonsky to an eager young soldier sharpening his sword on the eve of battle – and Tolstoy shows how their individual nature and feelings are both essential to and validated by the vast tapestry of human affairs of which they are part.

Tolstoy's other fiction includes Anna Karenina *(in which an adulterous and tragic love affair is used to focus a picture of the stifling, morally incompetent aristocratic Russian society of the 1860s),* The Death of Ivan Illich, The Cossacks, The Kreutzer Sonata, Master and Man *and* Resurrection. *His autobiographical books include* Childhood, Boyhood, Youth *and* A Confession.

▷Read on
◆ *Anna Karenina*.
▯ to *War and Peace*: ≫ Émile Zola, *The Downfall (Le Débâcle)*; ≫ I.B. Singer, *The Family Moskat*; ≫ Bernice Rubens, *Mother Russia*.
▯ to *Anna Karenina*: ≫ Ivan Turgenev, *On the Eve*; ≫ George Eliot, *Romola*; ≫ Gustave Flaubert, *Madame Bovary*; Theodor Fontane, *Effi Briest*; ≫ Boris Pasternak, *Doctor Zhivago*.

TOMALIN, Claire (born 1933)
British biographer

The subjects of the biographies that Claire Tomalin has published in the last thirty years have been diverse but many of her books have shown her interest in gifted women who have defied society's conventions in their search for intellectual and emotional fulfilment. *The Life and Death of Mary Wollstonecraft*, first published in 1974, was one of the earliest books to give due credit to the feminist pioneer for the courageous choices she made in her life and her work. *The Invisible Woman* looks at the story of Charles Dickens and Ellen Ternan, the young actress with whom he conducted a long, clandestine relationship and rescues Ternan from the invisibility which society demanded of her at the time and which posterity has also imposed on her. *Mrs Jordan's Profession* is another book which recreates the life of a marginalized woman, in this case Dora Jordan, a leading Regency actress who was also the mistress of the future William IV and mother to his ten illegitimate children.

Claire Tomalin has also written biographies of ≫ Katherine Mansfield, ≫ Jane Austen, Samuel Pepys and, most recently, ≫ Thomas Hardy. Several Strangers *is a collection of her essays and articles.*

▷Read on
◆ *Samuel Pepys: The Unequalled Self*.
▯ Juliet Barker, *The Brontës*; Amanda Foreman, *Georgiana, Duchess of Devonshire*; ≫ Margaret Forster, *Elizabeth Barrett Browning*; Hermione Lee, *Virginia Woolf*.

TRAPIDO, Barbara (born 1942)
South African/British novelist

Trapido's novels begin quietly, establishing a handful of characters (usually young, usually middle-class) and a setting (school, university, big house in a quiet street). But then she springs surprises on her characters – a new arrival, unexpected love, a visitor from long ago – and watches them squirm. Her books turn Aga-saga to high comedy: her witty style, the characters' likeability and foolishness and the bubbly good humour and invention keep you reading to the end. Her novels are *Brother of the More Famous Jack, Noah's Ark, Temples of Delight* and its sequel *Juggling* (about the same characters twenty years on but just as delightfully confused), *The Travelling Hornplayer* and *Frankie & Stankie*.

Read on
◆ *Frankie & Stankie* (Trapido's most recent novel marks a new direction in her writing as she draws on her own experiences of growing up in 1950s South Africa to create a memorable portrait of her heroine's life lived in the shadow of the politics of her country).
◻ ≫ Mary Wesley, *The Vacillations of Poppy Carew*; ≫ Anne Tyler, *Ladder of Years*; Elizabeth Jolley, *The Newspaper of Claremont Street*.
◻ to *Frankie & Stankie*: ≫ Nadine Gordimer, *Burger's Daughter* (for a darker version of a coming-of-age story set in South Africa).

READ A THEME

TRAINS
≫ Agatha Christie, *Murder on the Orient Express*
≫ Graham Greene, *Stamboul Train*
≫ Jaroslav Hašek, *The Good Soldier Svejk*
≫ Patricia Highsmith, *Strangers on a Train*
  Bohumil Hrabal, *Closely Observed Trains*
  Andrew Martin, *The Necropolis Railway*
  John Masters, *Bhowani Junction*

STARTPOINT

TRAVEL

Travel writing has a long history. Some two and a half thousand years ago Herodotus travelled widely in the Middle East and Egypt, researching his *History of the Persian War*, and wrote up the unexpected peoples and customs he encountered. Six centuries later Pausanias walked every kilometre of Greece, recording local legends and customs in a guidebook which, incredibly, can still be used today. Some eleven hundred years later still, the Venetian Marco Polo produced, in *Travels* (1298), one of the first travel bestsellers, a wide-eyed account of the wonders of medieval Asia. Travel writing has flourished ever since. For the reader it has a double attraction: we hear about exotic places and people, and the writer takes all the strain. Nowadays, when so much of the world is documented, it is often this last feature, the personal spin each author puts on familiar experience, which gives a book life: personal grouchiness, comedy, fine descriptive prose, interesting reflections, or (in the best books of all) all four.

Burton, Richard, *A Personal Narrative of a Pilgrimage to Al-Madinah and Mecca* (1855). Burton, disguised as an Arab, was the first European to visit the holy places of Islam, and tells the tale as if he were writing an adventure novel.

Durrell, Gerald, *The Bafut Beagles* (1953). Funny account of animal-collecting in Africa, by the author of *My Family and Other Animals*. Also: *Three Singles to Adventure, A Zoo in My Luggage, The Whispering Land*.

Elliot, Jason, *An Unexpected Light* (1999). Neither the Soviet occupation of the country nor the rise of the Taliban can deter Elliot from his journeys in Afghanistan, a country which had fascinated him from his childhood.

Heyerdahl, Thor, *The Kon-Tiki Expedition* (1948). Across the Pacific on a huge balsa-wood raft to show that Polynesians may have been settlers from ancient South America.

Kingsley, Mary, *Travels in West Africa* (1897). Unflappable Victorian lady walks and rides through jungles, crosses rivers, climbs mountains, camps near hostile villages and savours every moment.

>> Matthiessen, Peter, *The Snow Leopard* (1978). Matthiessen travels into the Himalayas in search of one of the world's most elusive creatures. He never sees one but his book becomes a record of a remarkable spiritual journey as much as an account of a physical one.

McCarthy, Pete, *The Road to McCarthy* (2002). McCarthy proves an amiable and amusing guide as he travels around the world, from Ireland to a remote Alaskan township, in search of those who share his surname.

Moorhouse, Geoffrey, *Om* (1993). Well-known travel writer tours south India, looking for enlightenment. Fascinating places and people and a thoughtful account of the author's spiritual journey.

>> Naipaul, V.S., *An Area of Darkness* (1964). West Indian Hindu writer spends a year in India and writes dazzling, caustic account.

Simon, Ted, *Jupiter's Travels* (1979). Simon takes a four-year journey around the world on a motorbike and discovers, amid the dangers and adventures, a freedom of spirit which he thought he had lost.

>> Stark, Freya, *Riding to the Tigris* (1959). One of the most formidable of all women travellers takes a horseback ride through the wilder parts of Turkey and on to the Tigris river.

>> Theroux, Paul, *The Old Patagonian Express* (1979). Splendidly grumbly novelist specializes in horrendous train journeys. This one takes him from Boston, Massachusetts, all the way to Patagonia and back. A modern classic.

>> Thubron, Colin, *Behind the Wall* (1987). Modern China, its landscape, its people and its uneasy links with a glorious past.

Also recommended: Gerald Brenan, *South from Granada*; >> Robert Byron, *The Road to Oxiana*; Charlie Connelly, *Attention All Shipping*; Alexander Frater, *Chasing the Monsoon*; Martha Gellhorn, *Travels with Myself and Another*; Che Guevara, *The Motorcycle Diaries*; Heinrich Harrer, *Seven Years in Tibet*; >> Norman Lewis, *Dragon Apparent*; Rory Maclean, *Stalin's Nose*; Claudio Magris, *Danube*; >> Philip Marsden, *The Spirit-Wrestlers*; >> Dervla

Murphy, *Full Tilt: Ireland to India on a Bicycle*; ❯❯ P.J. O'Rourke, *Holidays in Hell*; Jeremy Seal, *A Fez of the Heart*; ❯❯ John Steinbeck, *Travels With Charley*; Chris Stewart, *Driving Over Lemons*.

HIDDENGEM:

APSLEY CHERRY-GARRARD – *THE WORST JOURNEY IN THE WORLD* (1922)
This is a classic account, using letters, diaries and the author's own polar experience, of Captain Scott's doomed final expedition in the 1910s. Cherry-Garrard described polar exploration as 'the cleanest and most isolated way of having a bad time which has yet been devised' and his book goes a long way towards proving his point. But it is also filled with an old-fashioned heroism that can still stir the hearts of armchair travellers and his account of his own 'worst journey', through the Antarctic winter with two of the men who would later die on the way to the Pole, remains an intensely moving study of comradeship in terrible circumstances.

TREMAIN, Rose (born 1943)
British writer

Early success as a radio writer taught Tremain the skill of showing people's emotions and attitudes in their own words and without a wasted syllable. Her early novels (*Letter to Sister Benedicta, The Swimming Pool Season*) are outstanding at showing people developing emotionally, coming to understand and to change themselves. These are contemporary, but her richest work has been historical. *Restoration* is set in the England of Charles II and is told by Robert Merivel, an ambitious nonentity who is favoured by Charles, falls from grace by his own foolishness, and then gradually discovers, through suffering, the inner strength of his own character. The book's settings are Charles's court, Bidnold House in Norfolk (for Merivel, a kind of earthly paradise), New Bedlam lunatic asylum in Whittlesea, and a rundown house in Cheapside, London, in the months leading up to the Great Fire. *Restoration* engulfs the reader, its gusto never flagging, but its underlying theme – how Merivel first damns and then redeems himself – and its beautiful ending, give it the depth and sadness characteristic of all Tremain's work. In *Music & Silence* Peter Claire, an English lutenist, travels to the court of the seventeenth-century king of Denmark, Christian IV. Christian, a charismatic man fallen into melancholy, depends on music to raise his fallen spirits. His wife hates music and longs only for the energetic attentions of her German lover. Claire, in flight from a love affair with an Italian-born Irish countess, is drawn to one of the Queen's ladies-in-waiting, herself an escapee from a dark family background. Told in a variety of voices, *Music & Silence* harmonizes them all into a powerful and sensuous narrative.

Tremain's other novels include The Cupboard, Sacred Country, The Way I Found Her, The Colour *and* The Road Home. *Her short stories are collected in* The Colonel's Daughter, The Garden of the Villa Mollini, Evangelista's Fan *and* The Darkness of Wallis Simpson.

Read on

◆ *The Road Home* (a migrant worker from Eastern Europe struggles with a new life in London).

◘ to *Restoration* and *Music & Silence*: ›› Robert Graves, *Wife to Mr Milton*; ›› Jeanette Winterson, *Sexing the Cherry*; ›› Tracy Chevalier, *Girl With a Pearl Earring*; ›› Jane Rogers, *Mr Wroe's Virgins*.

◘ to Tremain's other books ›› Anita Brookner, *Lewis Percy*; Jane Gardam, *The Queen of the Tambourine*.

TREVOR, William (born 1928)

Irish writer

Trevor worked briefly as schoolteacher (history and art), sculptor and advertising copywriter before becoming a full-time writer in 1964. He is a leading author of short stories, many of which have been adapted for TV with outstanding success. He writes of sad, unfulfilled and remorselessly ordinary people, trapped by age, unattractiveness, miserable marriages or dead-end jobs and struggling to make sense of lives in seedy, rundown cities and out-of-season holiday resorts. The world is in a state of creeping, half-genteel decay – and only the glimmer of ambition in his people's minds, flaring sometimes into obsession, keeps them from surrender.

Trevor's many short story collections include The Day We Got Drunk on Cake, Angels at the Ritz, After Rain, The Hill Bachelors, A Bit on the Side *and* Cheating at Canasta. *His novels include* The Old Boys, Elizabeth Alone, The Children of

Dynmouth, Mrs. Eckdorf in O'Neill's Hotel, The Love Department, Other People's Worlds, The Silence in the Garden, Felicia's Journey *and* Death in Summer. *A number of books* (Fools of Fortune, The News From Ireland, Family Sins, The Story of Lucy Gault) *deal more specifically than his other work with the difficult effects of Irish history in the twentieth century on Irish individuals.*

Read on

◆ *The Children of Dynmouth* (about a disturbed teenager terrorizing a rundown seaside town); *The Story of Lucy Gault* (a melancholic, beautifully written chronicle of one woman's life and missed opportunities of happiness).

◘ to Trevor's short stories: ›› Susan Hill, *A Bit of Singing and Dancing*; V.S. Pritchett, *The Camberwell Beauty and Other Stories*; Mary Lavin, *In a Cafe: Selected Short Stories*.

◘ to his novels: ›› John Banville, *Eclipse* ›› Angus Wilson, *The Middle Age of Mrs Eliot*; ›› Mary Wesley, *A Dubious Legacy*; ›› Anita Brookner, *Look At Me*.

TROLLOPE, Anthony (1815–82)

British novelist

Until Trollope was fifty two he worked for the Post Office, travelling in Europe, the USA, north Africa and all over the British Isles. He turned his foreign experience into travel books, and used his British observations in forty seven novels, many of them written, in the fashion of the time, for serial publication in magazines. His style is genial and expansive, and his books deal with such characteristic Victorian themes as class, power, money and family authority. His favourite characters are the upper middle class of small towns and the surrounding estates. His plots involve the exercising of authority by the older generation and, by the young, all kinds of pranks, kicking over the traces, unsuitable love affairs and mockery of their elders' stuffiness. Trollope's best-loved novels are in two six-book series, the Barsetshire books (1855–67), about intrigue and preferment in a cathedral city, and the Palliser books (1864–80), about politics on the wider stages of county and country. Each novel is self-contained, but recurring characters and cross-references between the books, added to Trollope's easy-going style, give the reader a marvellously comfortable sensation, as of settling down to hear about the latest scrapes of a group of well-loved friends.

BARCHESTER TOWERS (1857)

The second novel in the Barsetshire sequence is high comedy. Imperious Mrs Proudie, wife of the timid new Bishop of Barchester, brings the Reverend Obadiah Slope into the Palace to help dominate her husband and run the diocese. But Slope is a snake in the grass, determined to make a rich marriage for himself, to win preferment in the church, even to defy Mrs Proudie if that will advance his cause. Their power struggle is the heart of the book, a stately but furious minuet which soon sweeps up all Trollope's minor characters: rich, pretty Widow Bold, apoplectic Archdeacon Grantly, flirtatious Signora Vesey-Negroni, saintly Mr Harding, bewildered Parson Quiverful and his fourteen squalling brats.

The Barsetshire novels are The Warden, Barchester Towers, Doctor Thorne, Framley Parsonage, The Small House at Allington *and* The Last Chronicle of Barset. *The Palliser novels are* Can You Forgive Her?, Phineas Finn, The Eustace Diamonds, Phineas Redux, The Prime Minister *and* The Duke's Children. *Trollope's other novels include* The Bertrams, Orley Farm, The Belton Estate, The Way We Live Now *and* Mr Scarborough's Family.

Read on

◆ *The Way We Live Now* (Trollope's 'state-of-the-nation' novel is a scathing attack on the commercial values of the Victorian age as embodied in the person of the financier Augustus Melmotte).

◘ to the Barsetshire books: ❯❯ Joanna Trollope, *Parson Harding's Daughter*; Angela Thirkell, *High Rising* (first of a series set in Barsetshire and borrowing Trollope's characters); Elizabeth Goudge, *Cathedral Close*; Susan Howatch, *Absolute Truth*; ❯❯ Barbara Pym, *Crampton Hodnett*.

◘ to the Palliser books: John Galsworthy, *The Forsyte Saga*; Benjamin Disraeli, *Coningsby*; Christina Stead, *House of All Nations*.

TROLLOPE, Joanna (born 1943)

British novelist

In 1980 Trollope's *Parson Harding's Daughter*, a sequel to her forebear ❯❯ Anthony Trollope's *The Warden*, was garlanded as the Historical Novel of the Year. She has also written a modern 'Barsetshire chronicle': *The Choir*, set among the musicians in a squabble-filled Anglican cathedral close. But she is best known for a series of novels about the lives and problems of ordinary contemporary people. She is particularly good at describing the ebb and flow of relationships, between siblings, parents and children, husband and wives. Her evocations of 'village Britain' – especially the gossip and machinations under the serene soap-opera surface – are much admired.

A SPANISH LOVER (1993)

Lizzie, an Earth Mother with four lively children, an 'artistic' husband and a career to juggle, relies on the detached strength of her twin Frances – particularly at Christmas. But one year Frances announces that she is spending the holiday in Spain, and both women's lives start to unravel, until they learn to stand on their own feet without their sibling to support them.

Trollope's other novels include A Village Affair, A Passionate Man, The Rector's Wife, The Men and the Girls, The Best of Friends, Next of Kin, Other People's Children, Marrying the Mistress, Girl from the South, Brother and Sister, Second Honeymoon *and* Friday Nights. *She has also written period romances (as Caroline Harvey), and a non-fiction account of women in the British Empire,* Britannia's Daughters.

✥Read on

◆ *Marrying the Mistress*.

◘ ➤➤ Margaret Forster, *The Battle for Christabel*; ➤➤ Penelope Lively, *According to Mark*; Penelope Mortimer, *The Pumpkin Eater*; ➤➤ Joanne Harris, *Coastliners*; Elizabeth Jane Howard, *The Light Years* (and other books in the Cazalet Chronicle); Angela Lambert, *Love Among the Single Classes*.

TURGENEV, Ivan Sergeevich (1818–83)

Russian novelist and playwright

A rich man, Turgenev spent much of his life travelling in Europe, and was welcomed abroad as the leading Russian writer of his time. He was less popular in Russia itself. Although his limpid style (influenced by his friend ➤➤ Flaubert) and his descriptions of nature were admired, his wistful satire, treating all human endeavour as equally absurd, won favour with neither conservatives nor radicals. His favourite characters are members of the leisured class, and his stories of disappointed ambition, failed love affairs and unfocused dissatisfaction anticipate not so much later revolutionary writings as the plays of ➤➤ Chekhov.

FATHERS AND SONS (1861)

Arkady, a student, takes his friend Bazarov home to meet his father. The old man is impressed by Bazarov's vigorous character and outspoken views – which are that none of the old moral and social conventions have intrinsic validity, and that people must decide for themselves how to live their lives. (This attitude to life, nihilism, was widespread among Russian intellectuals in the 1860s and 1870s.) The novel soon leaves politics to explore the effects of Bazarov's character on his own life. He falls in love and disastrously misinterprets his beloved's wish for friendship as the proposal of a 'free' liaison; he visits his parents, who cannot reconcile their admiration for their son with bewilderment at his ideas; he quarrels with the traditionalist Pavel, Arkady's uncle, and fights an absurd duel with him; he nurses serfs during a typhus epidemic and becomes fatally infected. Although Bazarov always regarded his own existence as futile, after his death it becomes apparent that he has changed the lives and attitudes of every other person in the story.

Turgenev's fiction includes Rudin, *A Nest of Gentlefolk,* Torrents of Spring, *On the Eve,* Smoke *and* Virgin Soil. *A Hunter's Notes/A Sportsman's Sketches contains short stories and poetic descriptions of country scenes. A Month in the Country, a Chekhovian comedy, is his best-known play.*

☙Read on

◆ *Torrents of Spring* (the story of a man torn by love for two women, a beautiful girl and the wife of an old school friend).

◘ ≫ Gustave Flaubert, *A Sentimental Education*; L.P. Hartley, *The Go-Between*; ≫ Willa Cather, *The Professor's House*; ≫ Anton Chekhov, *The Lady With the Lapdog and Other Short Stories.*

TWAIN, Mark (1835–1910)

US novelist and journalist

Mark Twain was the pseudonym of Samuel Clemens. A former steamboat captain on the Mississippi, soldier, goldminer and traveller, he wrote breezy, good-humoured accounts of his experiences, with an eye for quirky customs, manners and characters. His favourite form was the short story or comic, factual 'sketch' of half a dozen pages, and several of his books are collections of such pieces. *The Prince and the Pauper* is about a beggar-boy changing places with King Edward VI of England, his exact double; *A Connecticut Yankee in King Arthur's Court* focuses on a man, transported back in time, who startles Camelot with such 'magic' items as matches, a pocket watch and gunpowder. In Twain's best-loved books, *The Adventures of Tom Sawyer* and *The Adventures of Huckleberry Finn*, he wove reminiscences of boyhood and of life on the Mississippi into an easy-going, fictional form. *Tom Sawyer* is about the scrapes, fancies and fears of boyhood. The heroes of *Huckleberry Finn*, a boy and a runaway slave, pole a raft down the Mississippi, beset by con-men, bounty-hunters and outraged citizens, and fall into slapstick adventures each time they land.

Twain's satires include Pudd'nhead Wilson *and* The Mysterious Stranger. Tom Sawyer Abroad *and* Tom Sawyer Detective *are novels that follow Tom's adventures in adult life. Twain's short stories are collected in* The Celebrated Jumping Frog of Calaveras County and Other Sketches *and* The Man That Corrupted Hadleyburg. *His books of travel and reminiscence include* The Innocents Abroad, Roughing It, A Tramp Abroad *and* Life on the Mississippi.

⬚Read on

◘ to *Huckleberry Finn*: Alphonse Daudet, *Tartarin of Tarascon*; ›› Henry Fielding, *Tom Jones*; H.E. Bates, *The Darling Buds of May*.

◘ to Twain's travel books: ›› Robert Louis Stevenson, *Travels With a Donkey in the Cévennes* (and its sibling, ›› John Steinbeck, *Travels With Charley*); ›› Laurence Sterne, *A Sentimental Journey*; ›› Laurie Lee, *As I Walked Out One Midsummer Morning*.

TYLER, Anne (born 1941)
US novelist

Tyler writes, in cool, stylish prose, of the anguish of people caught up in the pains of everyday emotional life. She is especially good on relationships: between husbands and wives, brothers and sisters, parents and children. Her plots are as simple as those of any romantic novelist: people finding one another, drifting apart, coming together again. But the elegance of her writing, and the extraordinary life-likeness of her characters, take her into the literary company of ›› Lurie or ›› Updike, worlds away from most romance.

THE ACCIDENTAL TOURIST (1985)

Ethan, the twelve-year-old son of Macon and Sarah Leary, is brutally murdered, and his death destroys his parents' marriage. The story centres on Macon, a writer of rueful travel books, as he struggles against the need to rebuild his life, and in particular against the possibility of finding happiness with Helen (a dog-trainer many years his junior). Just as emotional scar tissue begins to form, Sarah comes back into his life, reopening the wound and confronting him once more with the need for choice.

Tyler's other novels include The Clock Winder, Celestial Navigation, Dinner at the Homesick Restaurant, Breathing Lessons, Saint Maybe, Earthly Possessions, Ladder of Years, A Patchwork Planet, Back When We Were Grown-ups, The Amateur Marriage *and* Digging to America.

≋Read on

◆ *The Amateur Marriage.*

▫ ≫ Alison Lurie, *The War Between the Tates*; ≫ Anita Shreve, *Strange Fits of Passion*; ≫ Carol Shields, *Larry's Party*; Alice Hoffman, *Turtle Moon*; Douglas Kennedy, *State of the Union.*

UGLOW, Jenny

British biographer and historian

Jenny Uglow began her career as a feminist scholar, rescuing from potential oblivion the lives and achievements of gifted women in works like the *International Dictionary of Women's Biography*, but she has achieved a wider success in the last ten years with books that explore the richness and variety of eighteenth-century culture in Britain. *Hogarth: A Life and a World*, as its subtitle suggested, was not only an account of the life of the artist but also an ambitious, wide-ranging portrait of the society in which he lived and which provided the inspiration for the vibrant images of London he created. *The Lunar Men* is a collective biography of a number of remarkable men, including the engineer James Watt, the scientist Joseph Priestley and Charles Darwin's polymathic grandfather Erasmus, who were members of an informal group known as the Lunar Society (because it met at each full moon). Uglow's book provides both a panoramic portrait of intellectual life in the second half of the eighteenth century and new insights into the ways the Lunar Men shaped the future of the industrial revolution which was just beginning when they first met.

Jenny Uglow's other works include Elizabeth Gaskell: A Habit of Stories *and* George Eliot *(two biographies of Victorian novelists),* Nature's Engraver *(a biography of Thomas Bewick) and* A Little History of British Gardening.

⮾Read on

◘ Linda Colley, *Britons*; ›› Victoria Glendinning, *Trollope*; Liza Picard, *Dr Johnson's London*; Roy Porter, *Enlightenment*.

UNSWORTH, Barry (born 1930)
British novelist

Unlike some historical novelists who impose contemporary ideas and psychologies on their characters, Unsworth gets under the skin of the past, showing us not merely long-ago manners and ways of behaviour but a whole philosophical and ethical outlook, sometimes as remote from today as if his characters came from other planets. *Morality Play*, for example, is a spare and moving story in which the leading character is a fourteenth-century priest who leaves his vocation because of boredom and takes up with a company of strolling actors – only to find that they are creating a play about a recent child-murder whose perpetrator may next turn on them. *Sacred Hunger*, which shared the Booker Prize in 1992, is an epic story about the Atlantic slave trade. *Losing Nelson* cleverly fuses past, present and the present's interpretation of the past in the story of a man obsessively researching a biography of Nelson. As he struggles to reconcile what he learns with what he wants to believe about the great naval hero, he slowly begins to lose his grip not only on his idea of Nelson but on his own sense of self.

Unsworth's other novels include Pascali's Island, The Rage of the Vulture, Stone Virgin, Sugar and Rum, After Hannibal, The Songs of the Kings, The Ruby in her Navel *and* Land of Marvels.

⮾Read on

◆ *Stone Virgin* (a conservationist working in Venice finds his life mysteriously affected by the statue he is restoring); *The Songs of the Kings* (the story of the Trojan War told from a distinctly twenty-first-century perspective).

◘ to *Sacred Hunger*: David Dabydeen, *A Harlot's Progress*; Fred D'Aguiar, *Feeding the Ghosts*.

◘ to Unsworth's fiction in general: ›› William Golding, *Rites of Passage*; ›› Thomas Keneally, *The Playmaker*; ›› Brian Moore, *Black Robe*; ›› Rose Tremain, *Restoration*.

UPDIKE, John (1932–2009)
US novelist and short story writer

Updike's short stories (most of them written for the *New Yorker*) are witty anecdotes about the snobberies and love affairs of ambitious Long Island couples, or single, brilliant jokes (for example treating bacteria under a microscope as if they were guests at a trendy cocktail party). Some of his novels are in a similarly glittering, heartless style. In *Couples* a small group of bored Connecticut commuters changes sex-partners as carelessly as if playing a party game. In *The Witches of Eastwick* three bored young widows set themselves up as a coven of amateur witches, only to become sexually ensnared by a devilishly charming man. The hero of *A Month of Sundays* is a 'progressive' clergyman tortured by lust. Updike's other novels are deeper, concentrating more on the underlying pain than on the ludicrous surface of his characters' lives. The Rabbit books (*Rabbit, Run*; *Rabbit Redux*; *Rabbit is Rich*; *Rabbit at Rest*, 1960–90) follow the life of a former school sports champion who finds emotional maturity and happiness almost impossible to grasp. The hero of *Roger's Version*, a middle-aged professor, is thrown into moral turmoil by the possibility of devising a computer program to prove the existence of God. Updike's more recent novels have included *Gertrude and Claudius,* an ambitious and witty retelling of events familiar from *Hamlet, Toward the End of Time,* set in 2020, in which a typical Updikean man muses on his life, *Seek My Face,* the story of an encounter between a grande dame of American art and a young interviewer, and *Villages,* in which a serial adulterer vainly pursues happiness in the beds of his New England neighbours.

Updike's other novels include The Poorhouse Fair, Of the Farm, The Centaur, The Coup, S, *the savage black farce* Memories of the Ford Administration *and three which are constructed from linked stories about a neurotic writer:* Bech, a Book, Bech is Back *and* Bech at Bay. Brazil *is an unusual, and unusually rich, departure: a love story retelling the myth of Tristan and Isolde and set in South America. His story collections include* The Same Door, Pigeon Feathers, Museums and Women, The Music School, Trust Me, The Afterlife, Licks of Love (*which also contains an intriguing coda to the Rabbit saga) and the posthumous* My

Father's Tears. Self-consciousness *contains six autobiographical essays, fascinating background to his fiction.* Due Considerations *is a large collection of essays and reviews written by Updike in the last years of his life.*

Read on

◘ ➤➤ Philip Roth, *The Ghost Writer;* ➤➤ Anne Tyler, *Dinner at the Homesick Restaurant;* ➤➤ Brian Moore, *The Great Victorian Collection;* ➤➤ Jonathan Franzen, *The Corrections.*

VARGAS LLOSA, Mario (born 1936)
Peruvian novelist

An admirer of ➤➤ Gabriel Garciá Márquez, Vargas Llosa uses magic realism to give an even more biting view of South American life and politics. *The Time of the Hero* is a satire on fascism set in a gung-ho, brutal military academy. *The War of the End of the World* is about the oppression, by the authorities, of a nineteenth-century utopian community for derelicts and dropouts, deep in the magic wilderness. *The Storyteller* is set among a fast-disappearing tribe of Amazonian Indians, whose stories are their history – and, as the book progresses, their only real existence. *The Feast of the Goat* is a remarkable and unflinching analysis of despotism in the grotesque shape of Rafael Trujillo, the longtime dictator of the Dominican Republic. Few other writers can match Vargas Llosa for insights into the corruptions of power and few recent novels have turned real events of twentieth-century history into such compelling fiction.

AUNT JULIA AND THE SCRIPTWRITER (1977)
Mario, a student, works part-time for a decrepit radio station, and idolizes the extraordinary man who writes and stars in half a dozen daily soap operas. Mario's own life is complicated by his love affair with his aunt, Julia. The book alternately gives us extracts from the soap operas, as weird as dreams, and Mario's own farcical story, as romantic and over-the-top as any soap.

Vargas Llosa's other novels include The Green House, Who Killed Palomino Molero, The Time of the Hero, In Praise of the Stepmother, Death in the Andes, The Notebooks of Don Rigoberto, The Way to Paradise *and* The Bad Girl. The Perpetual Orgy *is a book-length musing about* ➤➤ *Flaubert's* Madame Bovary, *part literary criticism, part reconstruction, part anthology – it is magic realism and non-fiction, hand in hand.* The Temptation of the Impossible *does much the same for* ›› *Victor Hugo's* Les Miserables. A Fish in the Water *is the story of Llosa's own involvement in Peruvian politics, often as surreal as the events of his fiction.*

☙Read on

♦ *The Notebooks of Don Rigoberto* (an erotic fantasia in which the protagonist, recording his sexual longings and memories, draws himself and the reader into a world of uncertainty and transgression).

◘ ›› Louis de Bernières, *Señor Vivo and the Coca Lord*; ›› Isabel Allende, *Eva Luna*; Augusto Roa Bastos, *I, the Supreme*; ›› Gabriel García Márquez, *The General in his Labyrinth*.

◘ to *The Perpetual Orgy*: ›› Julian Barnes, *Flaubert's Parrot*.

VERNE, Jules (1828–1905)
French novelist

Verne began writing in the 1860s, the heyday of both exploration and popular science – and his inspiration was to mix the two. His stories mimic the memoirs of real-life explorers of the time, fabulous adventures narrated in sober, business-like prose – and, by stirring in scientific wonders impossible or unlikely at the time, he tips them into fantasy. His heroes are not tethered to the surface of the Earth: they tunnel towards its core (*Journey to the Centre of the Earth*), live underwater (*Twenty Thousand Leagues Under the Sea*) and ride rockets into space (*From the Earth to the Moon; Round the Moon*). Alternately with these 'scientific' adventure stories, Verne produced tales of more orthodox derring-do: *Michel Strogoff*, for example, is a gentleman-adventurer whose bravery saves Civilisation As We Know It; in *Round the World in Eighty Days* Phileas Fogg embarks on a crazy journey to win a bet. Modern science has outstripped most of Verne's inventions, but few later science fiction writers have bettered him for straight-down-the-line, thrill-in-every-paragraph adventure.

☙Read on

◘ ›› Arthur Conan Doyle, *The Lost World*; ›› H.G. Wells, *The First Men in the Moon*; ›› H. Rider Haggard, *She*; Edgar Rice Burroughs, *Pirates of Venus*; ›› Kurt Vonnegut, *The Sirens of Titan*.

READ ON A THEME: VICTORIAN ENGLAND

READONATHEME

VICTORIAN ENGLAND
As seen by writers of the times

>> Charles Dickens, *Hard Times*
   Benjamin Disraeli, *Sybil, or the Two Nations*
>> Mrs Gaskell, *North and South*
>> George Gissing, *The Nether World*
   George and Weedon Grossmith, *The Diary of a Nobody*
>> William Thackeray, *Pendennis*
>> Anthony Trollope, *The Warden*

VICTORIAN ENGLAND
As seen by modern writers

>> Peter Carey, *Jack Maggs*
   Michael Cox, *The Meaning of Night*
>> Michel Faber, *The Crimson Petal and the White*
>> John Fowles, *The French Lieutenant's Woman*
   John Maclachlan Gray, *The Fiend in Human*
   Jane Harris, *The Observations*
>> Julie Myerson, *Laura Blundy*
   Charles Palliser, *The Quincunx*
>> D.J. Taylor, *Kept: A Victorian Mystery*
   Harry Thompson, *This Thing of Darkness*
>> Sarah Waters, *Fingersmith*
   James Wilson, *The Dark Clue*

VIDAL, Gore (born 1925)
US novelist and non-fiction writer

Vidal made his name as a tart-tongued, witty commentator on 1960s and 70s life, a favourite chat-show guest. Whatever the topic, from the rotation of crops to the horror of Nazi concentration camps, from zen to flower-arranging, he had something interesting to say. The same protean brilliance fills his novels. Whether their subject is homosexuality (*The City and the Pillar*), the excesses of the film industry (*Myra Breckinridge*) or US politics (the series *Burr*; *Lincoln*; *1876*; *Empire*; *Hollywood*; *Washington DC* and *The Golden Age*), they are original, stimulating and engrossing. This is particularly so in his historical novels, where he makes his alternative view of past events seem more attractive than reality itself. *Julian* is a study of the last pagan Roman emperor, who tried to stop the rush of Christianity in the name of (as Vidal sees it) the more humane, more generous Olympian religion. *Creation* is the memoirs of an imaginary Persian nobleman of the fifth century BC, who went as ambassador to India, China and Greece and knew Confucius, Buddha and Socrates.

Vidal's other novels include Williwaw, Myron, Kalki, Live from Golgotha, Messiah *and* Duluth. *He has also written detective stories under the name Edgar Box.* A Thirsty Evil *is a collection of short stories.* Palimpsest *is a malicious, gossipy memoir which occasionally surprises the reader by the poignancy of Vidal's recollections, particularly of his grandfather and of a lover killed in the Second World War.* Point to Point Navigation *is a memoir of more recent decades.* United States *is a massive selection of Vidal's often brilliant essays, written in the decades from 1952 to 1992;* The Last Empire *collects more recent non-fiction in which Vidal rides his hobby horses with greater enthusiasm than the reader can usually feel.*

☜Read on

◆ *Duluth*.

◘ to Vidal's historical novels: Peter Green, *The Sword of Pleasure* (set in republican Rome); John Hersey, *The Wall* (about American missionaries in China); ›› Rose Tremain, *Restoration* (set in 1660s Britain).

◘ to Vidal's novels in general: ›› Kingsley Amis, *The Alteration*; ›› Patrick White, *The Twyborn Affair*; ›› Muriel Spark, *The Ballad of Peckham Rye*.

READ ON A THEME

VILLAGE AND COUNTRYSIDE
›› Bruce Chatwin, *On the Black Hill*
   Isabel Colegate, *The Shooting Party*
   Christopher Hart, *The Harvest*

>> V.S. Naipaul, *The Enigma of Arrival*
   Tim Pears, *In the Place of Fallen Leaves*
>> Graham Swift, *Waterland*
>> Adam Thorpe, *Ulverton*
>> Joanna Trollope, *A Passionate Man*

See also: The Rhythm of Nature; Small-Town Life, USA

VONNEGUT, Kurt (1922–2007)
US novelist

Vonnegut's views of the world and of humanity were profoundly shaped by his experiences when he served in the American forces in Europe during World War Two. Captured by the Germans, he was present in Dresden in February 1945 when the city was firebombed by the Allies and tens of thousands lost their lives. Vonnegut survived but the bombing of the city scarred him for the rest of his life. In some sense, all his later writing can be seen as a response to the destruction of Dresden and as an attempt to explain his own chance survival. His most famous novel, *Slaughterhouse-5* tells the story of Billy Pilgrim whose wartime experiences echo those of Vonnegut but who has also become 'unstuck' in time, moving through his life randomly rather than chronologically. Only through his contacts with the strangely fatalistic aliens from the planet Trafalmadore does Billy begin to sense the underlying truth about life that can set him free. Life has no meaning, purpose or structure. It simply is. Vonnegut's fiction in the years after the publication of *Slaughterhouse-5* made him famous continued to blend disguised autobiography, science fiction, jokes and a deep philosophical pessimism into a unique style.

Vonnegut's other novels include Player Piano, The Sirens of Titan, Cat's Cradle, Breakfast of Champions, Deadeye Dick, Galapagos *and* Hocus Pocus. Welcome to the Monkey House *and* Bagombo Snuff Box *are collections of shorter fiction.* A Man Without a Country, *published in 2005, is an idiosyncratic volume of essays, recollections and opinions that was the nearest Vonnegut came to an autobiography.*

📖Read on
■ to *Slaughterhouse-5*: >> Martin Amis, *Time's Arrow*; >> Joseph Heller, *Catch-22*.
■ to Vonnegut's fiction in general: >> Philip K. Dick, *The Three Stigmata of Palmer*

Eldritch; Ken Kesey, *One Flew Over the Cuckoo's Nest*; ▶▶ Thomas Pynchon, *The Crying of Lot 49*.

WALKER, Alice (born 1944)

US novelist, poet and non-fiction writer

The background to Walker's books is the struggle for equal rights in the USA over the past forty years, first by blacks and then by women. Radical politics are not, however, her main concern. She writes wittily, ironically, about the follies of human life, and she is as merciless towards her idealistic, college-educated activists as she is to their slobbish, mindless opponents. *Meridian*, Walker's second novel, is the splendidly ironical study of a southern black activist, educated to be a 'lady' (in the 1920s white meaning of the term), who becomes a leader in the equal rights movements of the 1960s. When we see Meridian years later, all battles won, holed up in the small southern town of Chickokema, where apart from the coming of equality, nothing momentous has ever happened, she is totally confused about where all her energy, her driving force, has gone. Was this really what her life was for? Her best-known book, *The Color Purple*, uses a number of imaginative narrative devices to tell the story of Celie, a black woman in the segregated Deep South who has known nothing but abuse and exploitation until she meets Shug Avery, a female singer who offers her the chance of love and emotional support.

Walker's other novels include The Third Life of Grange Copeland, Possessing the Secret of Joy, The Temple of My Familiar, By the Light of My Father's Smile *and* Now is the Time to Open Your Heart. In Love and Trouble, You Can't Keep a Good Woman Down *and* The Way Forward is With a Broken Heart *are short story collections. She has also published poetry* (Horses Make a Landscape Look More Beautiful; Willie Lee, I'll See You in the Morning *and others*) *and three books of essays:* In Search of Our Mother's Garden, Living by the Word *and* Anything We Love Can Be Saved. The Same River Twice *is autobiography.*

📖Read on

◆ *Possessing the Secret of Joy* (about African tribal women facing a horrific initiation into adult life).
▢ to Walker's elegant, tart style: Mary McCarthy, *The Group*; ▶▶ Muriel Spark, *The Girls of Slender Means*.

◘ to her view of the bizarreness lurking inside perfectly ordinary-seeming human beings: ›› John Irving, *The World According to Garp*; Tove Jansson, *Sun City*.

◘ to her politics: Gayl Jones, *Corregidora*; Ralph Ellison, *Invisible Man*.

READONATHEME:

WALES
Trezza Azzopardi, *The Hiding Place*
A.J. Cronin, *The Citadel*
Peter Ho Davies, *The Welsh Girl*
Emyr Humphreys, *Flesh and Blood*
Richard Llewellyn, *How Green Was My Valley*
Malcolm Pryce, *Aberystwyth Mon Amour*
Kate Roberts, *Feet in Chains*
John Williams, *Cardiff Dead*

WALTERS, Minette (born 1949)
British novelist

Like so many of the best contemporary writers of crime fiction (›› Ruth Rendell, Frances Fyfield, Andrew Taylor) Minette Walters produces books that are less 'whodunits' than 'whydunits'. Our interest is held not so much by the twists and turns of a convoluted, puzzle-like plot but by the way the narrative progressively reveals more and more about the psychology and hidden depths of her characters. This has been the case since her first novel *The Ice House*, about three women who may or may not have got away with murder ten years before the book opens, was published in 1992. Her second novel, *The Sculptress*, introduced the kind of pairing of disparate characters that has recurred in later books. The obese, unloved Olive Martin, imprisoned for the apparent murders of her mother and sister, represents a terrible enigma, an affront almost, to the middle-class complacency of the woman intent on writing a book about her crimes. In her more recent novels Minette Walters has increasingly concentrated on stories which gradually unveil the hidden motivations of her characters. In *The Shape of Snakes* a teacher refuses to accept that the death of an alcoholic neighbour is an accident. For twenty years she obsessively amasses evidence to prove that murder took place. Narrated by the teacher and reproducing many of the documents that constitute her evidence, the book moves relentlessly towards the revelation of dark, unsettling and moving truths about its characters. Retaining its tension and mystery until its last page, it is the best example yet of Minette Walters's ambition to press forward into territory not usually occupied by writers of crime fiction.

Minette Walters's other novels are The Scold's Bridle*,* The Echo*,* The Breaker*,* The Dark Room*,* Acid Row*,* Fox Evil*,* Disordered Minds*,* The Devil's Feather *and* The Chameleon's Shadow*.* The Tinder Box *and* Chickenfeed *are novellas.*

⮒Read on
◆ *The Dark Room.*
◘ Barbara Vine (see ➤➤ Ruth Rendell), *A Fatal Inversion*; Nicci French, *The Safe House*; ➤➤ Val McDermid, *Killing the Shadows*; Andrew Taylor, *The Barred Window*; Frances Fyfield, *Seeking Sanctuary*.

READ ON A THEME:

WAR: BEHIND THE LINES
  Noel Barber, *A Woman of Cairo*
➤➤ Elizabeth Bowen, *The Heat of the Day*
➤➤ Louis de Bernières, *Captain Corelli's Mandolin*
➤➤ Sebastian Faulks, *Charlotte Gray*
➤➤ Jaroslav Hašek, *The Good Soldier Svejk*
➤➤ Ernest Hemingway, *A Farewell to Arms*
➤➤ Thomas Keneally, *Schindler's Ark*
➤➤ Leo Tolstoy, *War and Peace*

See also: Terrorists/Freedom Fighters

WARNER, Alan (born 1964)
British novelist

In the five novels he has published, the Scottish writer Alan Warner has created a fictional world that is immediately recognizable as uniquely his own: a version of his home country that is simultaneously real and surreal. Often set in an imaginary Scottish town known only as the Port, his books feature a ragbag of weirdly memorable characters – ex-British Rail trolley-girls, crazed snowboarders, sybaritic members of a corrupt and corrupting aristocracy, strangely erudite drifters and drinkers. Warner's writing is uncompromisingly direct, shot through with deviant sexuality and demented humour, but there is often tenderness (and a surprising lyricism) at the heart of the fierce and alienated world he commits to paper.

MORVERN CALLAR (1995)
Warner's first novel tells the story of its eponymous heroine, a strangely affectless young woman, a supermarket employee in a remote Highland sea port, who wakes one morning to find that her boyfriend has committed suicide on the kitchen floor. Largely unperturbed, Morvern hides the body, takes possession of the manuscript of a novel he had been writing and passes it off as her own. Financially buoyed by an advance from a publisher, she attempts to escape her dead-end life by travelling to the rave scene of the Mediterranean where she throws herself into its world of Ecstasy, music and casual sex before returning, pregnant, to Scotland to face an uncertain future. Short on plot, Morvern Callar comes alive through the memorable first person narrative voice of its central character. Warner succeeds in creating a 'heroine' who reacts with deadpan amorality to all that happens around her but who none the less engages the sympathies of readers allowed to glimpse the enormous longings behind her blank exterior.

Warner's other novels are These Demented Lands, The Sopranos, The Man Who Walks *and* The Worms Can Carry Me to Heaven.

🕮Read on
◆ *The Sopranos* (five feisty girls from a Catholic school choir descend on the bright lights of the big city).
◻ Janice Galloway, *The Trick is to Keep Breathing*; ≫ A.L. Kennedy, *Everything You Need*; ≫ Irvine Welsh, *Glue*.

WARNER, Marina (born 1946)
British cultural historian and novelist

Much of Marina Warner's non-fiction work has concentrated on the ways in which society creates its images of femininity and ideal womanhood and has often analyzed folklore, fairytales and mythology and their continuing influence on art and culture. *Alone of All Her Sex* investigates the cult of the Virgin Mary in the Catholic Church, finding in it both echoes of female deities in other religions and restricting images of what women are or should be. *Monuments and Maidens* takes a number of allegorical uses of the female form, from the Statue of Liberty to newspaper images of Margaret Thatcher and tries to show what they say about our culture's notions of the female. *No Go the Bogeyman* scours folklore, history, literature and the visual arts in search of evidence of what scares us and how we master our fears by translating them into art and stories. In all these books, and others, Warner demonstrates a range of reference and an ability to make links between the most disparate of cultural phenomena that is both exhilarating and thought-provoking. She has also written several novels, of which the most challenging and original is *The Lost Father*, shortlisted for the Booker Prize in 1988.

Marina Warner's other non-fiction works include From the Beast to the Blonde, Managing Monsters, Fantastic Metamorphoses, Other Worlds, Signs and Wonders *and* Phantasmagoria. *Her other novels include* In a Dark Wood, The Skating Party, Indigo *and* The Leto Bundle. Mermaids in the Basement *and* Murderers I Have Known *are collections of short stories.*

📖Read on
◆ *From the Beast to the Blonde* (an investigation into fairytales and the roles they allot women)
▢ to the non-fiction: Karen Armstrong, *A Short History of Myth*; Bruno Bettelheim, *The Uses of Enchantment*.
▢ to the fiction: ❯❯ Michèle Roberts, *Impossible Saints*.

WATERS, Sarah (born 1966)

British novelist

A TV adaptation of *Tipping the Velvet* in 2002 brought new readers to Sarah Waters but she already had an appreciative audience for her lively fictional excursions into the lesbian sub-culture of Victorian Britain. *Tipping the Velvet* is the story of Nan Astley's voyage of self-discovery through a riotous demi-monde of music-hall entertainers, Sapphic aristos and cross-dressing gender benders, all brought to vivid life by Waters's exuberant prose. Nan begins as the respectable daughter of a restaurant owner but is propelled into new worlds by her encounter with Kitty Butler, a male impersonator treading the boards at the local music hall. In two further novels Waters introduces the reader to some of those other Victorians who the history books don't always mention. For the heroine of *Affinity*, Margaret Prior, her *coup de foudre* takes place not in a music hall but in Millbank prison. She is visiting the prison as part of the duties of a socially concerned, middle-class spinster but is completely unprepared for the effect upon her of the beautiful spiritualist, Selina Dawes, imprisoned for fraud. Alternating between Margaret's journal and Selina's account of her life, *Affinity* chronicles the developing relationship between the two women. Waters's third novel, *Fingersmith*, shortlisted for the 2002 Man Booker, begins in the thieves' dens of 1860s Southwark and expands into an elaborate story of cross and double-cross centred on a suave con-man's attempt to use the heroine in a plot to defraud a wealthy heiress. All three of Waters's novels take the themes and motifs of classic Victorian literature but put them to new uses in creating characters and settings that her nineteenth-century predecessors firmly excluded from their fiction. Much more than pastiche, her books are some of the most adventurous and enjoyable historical novels of the last few years.

📖Read on

♦ *The Night Watch* (Sarah Waters's first venture outside the Victorian era is set during and immediately after the Second World War and traces the intertwining lives of a group of characters whose secret histories slowly emerge in the course of the narrative); *The Little Stranger* (her most recent novel, a ghost story set in a decaying country house just after the war).

◘ ≫ Angela Carter, *Nights at the Circus*; ≫ Michel Faber, *The Crimson Petal and the White*; Sheri Holman, *The Dress Lodger*; Emma Donoghue, *Slammerkin*.

WAUGH, Evelyn (1903–66)
British novelist

Waugh's main work was a series of tart satires on 1930s attitudes and manners. His vacuous, amiable heroes stumble through life, unsurprised by anything that happens. By chance, they land in the centre of affairs (political, business and sexual) and their presence triggers a sequence of ever more ludicrous events. Innocence is their only saving grace: Waugh's views were that the world is silly but dangerous, and that those who think they understand it are the most vulnerable of all. He was particularly venomous about British high society, depicting the ruling class as a collection of alcohol-swilling Hooray Henries or Henriettas, whose chief pastimes are partying (if young) and interfering in public life (if old). That class apart, the range of his scorn was vast. *Decline and Fall* sends up (among other things) the English prep school system, *Black Mischief* mocks tyranny in an African state emerging from colonialism, *Scoop* satirizes gutter journalism and *The Ordeal of Gilbert Pinfold* mercilessly details the hallucinations of an alcoholic author on a detestable ocean cruise. The Second World War trilogy *Sword of Honour* sets Waugh's foolish heroes in the context of truly dangerous, genuinely lunatic real events, and *Brideshead Revisited* is a more serious book still, the study of an aristocratic Catholic family collapsing under the weight of centuries of unconsidered privilege.

A HANDFUL OF DUST (1934)
The book begins with standard Waugh farce: a pin-headed society wife, Brenda Last, takes a lover to occupy her afternoons. But the effect on her husband Tony and son John is devastating, and the book moves quickly from farce to tragedy. Waugh never abandons the ridiculous – no one else would have placed his hero in impenetrable tropical jungle, the slave of a megalomaniac who makes him read Edwin Drood aloud – but he also writes with compassion for his characters, involving us in their loneliness as his more farcical novels never try to do.

Waugh's other novels are Vile Bodies, Put Out More Flags *and* The Loved One. *His travel books include* Remote People *and* Waugh in Abyssinia. *His* Diaries, *his* Letters *and his autobiography* A Little Learning *are a revealing blend of pity for himself and mercilessness to others. Like all his work, they are also very funny.*

Read on
◆ *Scoop*.

◻ >> William Boyd, *A Good Man in Africa*; >> Anthony Powell, *Afternoon Men*; >> Anthony Burgess, *The Complete Enderby*; Malcolm Bradbury, *Eating People is Wrong*; >> David Lodge, *How Far Can You Go?*; P.H. Newby, *The Picnic at Sakkara*.

READ**ON**A**THEME**:

WEEPIES
    Jeannie Brewer, *A Crack in Forever*
>> Charlotte Brontë, *Jane Eyre*
>> Louis de Bernières, *Captain Corelli's Mandolin*
>> Daphne Du Maurier, *Rebecca*
    Nicholas Evans, *The Horse Whisperer*
>> Margaret Mitchell, *Gone With the Wind*
>> Boris Pasternak, *Doctor Zhivago*
    Erich Segal, *Love Story*
    Robert Waller, *The Bridges of Madison County*

WELDON, Fay (born 1931)
British novelist and screen-writer

A former advertising executive and TV dramatist, Weldon writes novels in short, screenplay-like scenes full of dialogue: her books are like sinister sitcoms turned into prose. In the 1970s she was regarded as a leading feminist writer, and 'women's experience' is a major theme in all her books. Her heroines are ordinary people resisting the need to define themselves as someone else's wife, lover or mother, and missing the traditional cosiness such roles afford. Individuality can only be bought at the cost of psychic discomfort – and this is often intensified by the malice of others and by the hostility of the environment: witchcraft and the venomousness of nature regularly add spice to Weldon's plots. Her books are fast, funny and furious; but their underlying ideas are no joke at all.

PUFFBALL (1980)
Liffey, married to boring, ambitious Richard, longs to live in a country cottage; Richard wants a child. They strike a bargain, move to the wolds near Glastonbury

and do their best to get Liffey pregnant. Almost at once the idyll turns to nightmare. The cottage has few facilities; there are no commuter trains to London; their neighbour is a child-beater and an amateur witch. As the baby grows in Liffey's womb and Richard, alone in London for five days a week, consoles himself, Mabs (the neighbour) tries every trick of witchcraft, from potions to pin-stuck wax models, to make Liffey abort her child. *Puffball* is a romantic novel for grown-up people – and the games Weldon plays with our longing for a happy ending give the plot some of its most devastating, satisfying twists.

Weldon's other novels include Down Among the Women, Female Friends, Little Sisters, Praxis, Watching Me Watching You, The Life and Loves of a She-Devil, The Heart of the Country, The Fat Woman's Joke, Rhode Island Blues, She May Not Leave, The Spa Decameron *and* The Stepmother's Diary. A Hard Time to Be a Father *and* Nothing to Wear and Nowhere to Hide *are the two most recent of her collections of short stories.* Godless in Eden *is a selection of essays,* Auto da Fay *an autobiography,* Mantrapped *a curious hybrid of fiction and memoir.*

🕮 Read on

◆ *Darcy's Utopia*.

◘ ►► Margaret Atwood, *Life Before Man*; Marge Piercy, *The High Cost of Living*; Mary Gordon, *The Company of Women*; Penelope Mortimer, *Long Distance*; Alice Thomas Ellis, *Unexplained Laughter*; Maggie Gee, *Light Years*.

WELLS, H.G. (Herbert George) (1866–1946)
British writer of novels, short stories and non-fiction

Wells's early novels were science fantasies, imagining what it would be like if people could travel in time (*The Time Machine*) or space (*The First Men in the Moon*), or how the Earth might defend itself against extraterrestrial attacks (*The War of the Worlds*). Like ►► Verne, Wells predicted many inventions and discoveries now taken for granted: in *The War in the Air* (1908), for example, he forecast fleets of warplanes and bombers in the days when the Wright brothers were still headline news. For all their scientific wonders, these novels are full of pessimism about society: wherever people go, they find barbarism, oppression and misery. *The Island of Doctor Moreau*, about a mad scientist hybridizing humans and animals on a lonely island, brings the pessimism nearer home. Side by side with such morbid fantasies, Wells wrote a series of utterly different books. These are genial social comedies, about ordinary people (shop-assistants, clerks) who decide that the way to find happiness is to break out and 'make a go of things'. Sometimes (as in *Ann Veronica*, about a girl determined on emancipation despite the wishes of her family) Wells's message is polemical, but most of the books – *Love and Mr Lewisham*, *Kipps*, *The History of Mr Polly* – replace propaganda with an indulgent, enthusiastic view of human enterprise.

TONO-BUNGAY (1909)

George Ponderevo goes to live with his uncle Teddy. He helps Teddy market a marvellous new elixir, Tono-Bungay: it is the answer to the world's problems, the health, wealth and happiness of humankind in a bottle. The Tono-Bungay fortune swells by the minute – and then George discovers that the product is ninety-nine per cent distilled water. The discovery presents George with unresolvable moral dilemmas of all kinds. Does it matter what Tono-Bungay is made of, if it does what it claims to do? Is Teddy a crook or does he genuinely believe he is benefiting humankind? How can George bankrupt those he loves – and in the process destroy his own chances of a happy marriage and a prosperous home? He puts off the decision, and in the meantime continues his hobby: pioneer aviation. In the end, technology – the lighter-than-air-machine itself – comes to the rescue: a charming example of Wells's view that all moral and social dilemmas can be solved by science.

Wells's other science fantasies include When the Sleeper Wakes*,* The Food of the Gods *and the story collections* Tales of Space and Time *and* The Country of the Blind and Other Stories*. His other novels include* A Modern Utopia*,* The New Machiavelli *and* Mr Britling Sees it Through*.*

☜Read on

◙ to Wells's science fiction: ⟫ Jules Verne, *Twenty Thousand Leagues Under the Sea*; Brian Aldiss, *Moreau's Other Island* (Wells's nightmare vision transplanted to space).
◙ to his social comedies: ⟫ Arnold Bennett, *The Card*; Hugh Walpole, *Mr Perrin and Mr Traill*; ⟫ J.B. Priestley, *The Good Companions*.

LITERARY TRIVIA 15:

TEN FICTIONAL PLACES

Ankh-Morpork
The city state at the centre of many of the adventures in ❯❯ Terry Pratchett's Discworld novels.

Gondor
One of the countries of Middle Earth in ❯❯ Tolkien's *The Lord of the Rings*.

Isola
The city, not unlike New York, in which Ed McBain's 87th Precinct crime novels are set.

Lake Wobegon
The fictional town in Minnesota which is the setting for ❯❯ Garrison Keillor's stories.

Llareggub
The town in Dylan Thomas's play *Under Milk Wood* which sounds a plausible Welsh place name but is actually 'bugger all' backwards.

Malgudi
The fictional town somewhere in South India where the majority of ❯❯ R.K. Narayan's novels are set.

Maycomb, Alabama
The small town in which the action of Harper Lee's novel *To Kill a Mockingbird* takes place.

Shangri-La
The isolated Himalayan valley where peace and harmony reign in James Hilton's novel *Lost Horizon*.

St Mary Mead
The village in which ❯❯ Agatha Christie's spinster detective Miss Marple lives.

> **Yoknapatawpha County**
> The fictional county in Mississippi in which most of ❯❯ William Faulkner's
> novels are set.

WELSH, Irvine (born 1958)
British novelist

Revealing an Edinburgh at odds with the tourist image of tartan tweeness,
Trainspotting (1993), Irvine Welsh's portrait of heroin users on bleak council
estates, was a landmark in Scottish (and British) fiction and, through a successful
film adaptation, became a cult book for a generation. Welsh adopts no easy tone
of moral condemnation. Heroin is presented simply as an everyday part of the lives
of his characters – source of pleasure as well as desolation – and even the most
shocking descriptions of cheap sex, violence and the desperate urge to score are
shot through with dark humour. Told in energetic, phonetically reproduced Scots
language, awash both with obscenity and accidental poetry, *Trainspotting* is a
black but utterly compelling narrative. Welsh followed the book with *Marabou
Stork Nightmares*, an ambitious attempt to fuse another story of blighted, violent
lives with excursions into the fantasy world of its central character. Roy Strang lies
in a coma in hospital. As his real past, as both victim and perpetrator of sexual
violence, unfolds in his mind, so too does a surreal safari through a half-imagined,
half-remembered Africa where Strang, re-cast as some kind of gentleman explorer,
hunts the marabou stork. *Glue* is once again set in the now-familiar Welsh terrain
of Edinburgh slum estates and is again told in the now-familiar vernacular but, in
carrying the story of four friends through three decades of their lives, he stretched
his range as a writer.

Welsh's other fictional works are Filth *(a novel),* Ecstasy *(a collection of three
novellas),* The Acid House *(short stories),* Porno *(a return to the characters first
seen in* Trainspotting*),* The Bedroom Secrets of the Master Chefs*,* Crime *and* If You
Liked School, You'll Love Work*.*

🔖Read on
◻ James Kelman, *A Chancer*; ❯❯ Alan Warner, *Morvern Callar*; John King, *The
Football Factory*; Laura Hird, *Born Free*.

WELTY, Eudora (1909–2001)
US novelist and short story writer

Unlike such writers as ›› Faulkner or ›› McCullers, who saw the southern states of the USA as a kind of hell tenanted by freaks and degenerates, Welty treats them as paradise. The countryside is lush; birds and animals teem; all nature is in harmony. Human beings are at the heart of the idyll – and Welty shows them as uncomprehending innocents. The Negroes – she is writing about times long gone – are children of nature, at peace with their environment. *The White Folks*, by contrast, feel edgy. They sense that they are corrupt, that their presence threatens Eden, but they have no idea why this should be so, and all they can do is live as they always have and hope that things will be all right, that nothing will change. The surface events in Welty's books are a mosaic of ordinariness – parties, children's games, chance meetings in town or at the bathing station – but underlying them all is a sense of fragility, of impending loss. Her characters are living in a dream, comfortable and comforting, but it is only a dream, and already we, and they, sense the first chill of wakefulness.

DELTA WEDDING (1946)
In the 1920s, nine-year-old Laura travels to her uncle's plantation in the Mississippi delta, to help in preparations for her cousin's wedding. She revels in the eccentric, affectionate rough-and-tumble of cousins, great-aunts, visitors (and dozens of blacks, as friendly and unconsidered as household pets); she climbs trees, bakes cakes, guesses riddles, listens to gossip as the wedding dress is sewn. Welty also shows the preparations through the eyes of the bride's parents, the bride and groom themselves, and an assortment of servants, friends and neighbours. The wedding brings a whole community into focus – and we are shown, with persistent, gentle irony, that it is not just the bride and groom who must undergo a rite of passage, but the South itself.

Welty's other novels are The Robber Bridegroom, The Ponder Heart, The Optimist's Daughter *and* Losing Battles. *Her short stories are collected in* A Curtain of Green, The Wide Net, The Golden Apples *and* The Bride of Innisfallen. One Writer's Beginnings *is a series of essays, originally lectures, that describe the people and places that shaped her development as a writer.*

☜Read on
◆ *The Optimist's Daughter.*

◘ Randall Jarrell, *Pictures From an Institution*; L.P. Hartley, *The Go-Between*; ➤➤ Evelyn Waugh, *Brideshead Revisited*; Robert Penn Warren, *All the King's Men*.

WESLEY, MARY (1912–2002)
British novelist

Wesley's first adult novel, *Jumping the Queue*, was published when she was seventy. The story of a middle-aged woman, a would-be suicide, who gives refuge to a charming murderer, and finds that his presence makes her life flower anew, it was a great success. Mary Wesley was launched on a late career as a bestselling novelist. In several of her novels she writes of elegant elderly people, usually women, whose efficient outward lives depend on unsuspected and eccentric thoughts, rituals or long-held secrets. Her stories tell what happens when some chance event – often falling in love with a younger person – brings eccentricity to the surface, rippling the apparently tranquil pool in ways which are bizarre, hilarious, often joyously sexy, and very, very sad. In others (*The Camomile Lawn*, for instance) she looks back at the Second World War, not for nostalgic purposes, but to examine, often astringently, the lives and loves of ordinary young people caught up in larger events.

Wesley's other books include Harnessing Peacocks, The Vacillations of Poppy Carew, Not That Sort of Girl, A Sensible Life, Second Fiddle *and* Part of the Furniture.

🕮Read on
◆ *Not That Sort of Girl*.
◘ Elizabeth Jolley, *Palomino*; ➤➤ Joanna Trollope, *A Village Affair*; Jenny Diski, *Happily Ever After*; ➤➤ Joanne Harris, *Five Quarters of the Orange*.

READONATHEME:

THE WEST (THE GREAT AMERICAN FRONTIER)
Desmond Barry, *The Chivalry of Crime*
Thomas Berger, *Little Big Man*
Michael Blake, *Marching to Valhalla* (fictionalized version of Custer's career)
Pete Dexter, *Deadwood*
E.L. Doctorow, *Welcome to Hard Times*
Thomas Eidson, *St Agnes' Stand*
Zane Grey, *Riders of the Purple Sage*
Ron Hansen, *Desperadoes*
Larry McMurtry, *Lonesome Dove*
» Jane Smiley, *The All-True Travels and Adventures of Lydie Newton*
Guy Vanderhaeghe, *The Last Crossing*

WHARTON, Edith (1862–1937)
US writer of novels, short stories and non-fiction

A society hostess, Wharton caused outrage by writing with ironical rage about the complacency and shallowness of her own class. (She later described high society as 'frivolous ... able to acquire dramatic significance only through what its frivolity destroys'.) In 1907 she moved to Europe and broadened her scope, writing two » Hardyesque rural tragedies (*Ethan Frome, Summer*), several books set in Europe and some atmospheric ghost stories. But she regularly returned to her favourite theme, the stifling conventions of 1870s–1920s New York high life – and it is on this that her reputation rests. Her enemies put her down as a clumsy imitator of James. But whereas he showed his characters' psychological innerness, she was interested in manners, in events. She also wrote shorter, wittier sentences, and crisper dialogue. Except that her subject matter is so sombre, she is more like Oscar Wilde than James.

THE HOUSE OF MIRTH (1905)
Lily Bart, a beautiful, sharp-witted girl, has been conditioned to luxury from birth. Unfortunately she is an orphan, living on a small allowance. She gambles at cards, loses, and because of her moral scruples (she refuses to pay off her debts by

becoming the mistress of a wealthy creditor), she ends up poorer and more desperate than ever. Faced with the choice of marrying either a rich man she despises (not least because he is a Jew, something her WASPish upbringing has taught her to abhor) or the penniless man she loves, she chooses neither – and soon afterwards, as the result of scandalous accusations, loses her position in society. She moves into cheap lodgings and sinks into despair. She has achieved moral integrity, broken free of her upbringing, but in the process, because of that upbringing, she has destroyed herself.

Wharton's other novels include The Custom of the Country, The Age of Innocence, Old New York *and* The Reef. *Her short stories, published originally in several volumes, have been collected in one volume.* A Backward Glance *is autobiography, interesting on her friendship with Henry James.*

⮺Read on
◆ *The Custom of the Country.*
◘ Ellen Glasgow, *Barren Ground*; Louis Auchincloss, *A World of Profit*; ≫ George Eliot, *Middlemarch*; ≫ Elizabeth Taylor, *The Wedding Group*; ≫ Mary Wesley, *Not That Sort of Girl.*

WHITE, Antonia (1899–1979)
British novelist

A journalist and translator, White is remembered for four deeply felt auto-biographical novels. *Frost in May* is the story of a child at a grim convent boarding school. The nuns' mission is to 'break' each pupil like a horse – to tame her for Christ – and the book remorselessly charts the series of small emotional humiliations they inflict on the heroine, which have entirely the opposite effect from the one intended. In the later novels White's heroine works as an actress (*The Lost Traveller*), tries to combine serious writing with work as a copywriter (*The Sugar House*), and finally (*Beyond the Glass*), in the course of a terrifying mental illness, exorcises the ghosts of Catholicism and her relationship with her father, the influences which have both defined and deformed her life.

White's other books include the short story collection Strangers, *and* The Hound and the Falcon, *an account in letter form of her return to Catholicism.*

Read on

◘ to *Frost in May*: ❯❯ James Joyce, *Portrait of the Artist as a Young Man*; Jane Gardam, *Bilgewater*; ❯❯ Thomas Keneally, *Three Cheers for the Paraclete*.

◘ to *Beyond the Glass*: Sylvia Plath, *The Bell Jar*; Janet Frame, *Faces in the Water*.

◘ to White's work in general: ❯❯ Rosamond Lehmann, *Dusty Answer*; Rose Macaulay, *The World My Wilderness*.

WHITE, Edmund (born 1940)
US novelist, biographer and critic

In his fiction, Edmund White has charted the trajectory of a generation of gay men from the joyful promiscuity of the pre-AIDS era to the more sombre realities of lives overshadowed by the threat of death and disease. *A Boy's Own Story*, still his most famous book, works in a long tradition of the coming-of-age novel but re-imagines it from a gay perspective. Growing up in a small American town in the 1950s, White's nameless narrator has to struggle with his emotional isolation from his parents and his peers and with his growing realization of his homosexuality. *The Beautiful Room is Empty* takes the story further as the narrator leaves school for college, half-enjoying, half-despising the life of one-night stands and guilt-ridden sex before finding a new self-acceptance in the wake of the Stonewall riots and the emerging gay liberation movement. *The Farewell Symphony*, taking its title from the Haydn symphony in which players leave the stage one by one until only a single violinist remains, sees the narrator in the 1990s taking a journey back into his past, mourning the losses of friends and lovers but affirming the value of the experiences, sexual and social, which have made him the writer he is. Although each book is self-contained, the three novels read together provide not only a remarkable panorama of the lives of gay men over several decades but also a moving portrait of one man's journey through life.

Edmund White's other novels are Forgetting Elena, Nocturnes for the King of Naples, Caracole, The Married Man, Fanny: A Fiction *and* Hotel de Dream. *He has also written biographies of Jean Genet, ❯❯ Marcel Proust and Arthur Rimbaud,* The Flaneur *(a non-fiction book subtitled 'A Stroll Through the Paradoxes of Paris') and* My Lives, *a book which revisits the personal experiences of life as a gay man on which he drew for his fiction.* Arts and Letters *is a collection of pen portraits of artists and writers who have influenced his life and work;* The Burning Library *is a volume of essays.*

📚**Read on**
◆ *The Married Man.*
◘ ≫ James Baldwin, *Giovanni's Room*; ≫ Alan Hollinghurst, *The Swimming-Pool Library*; David Leavitt, *The Lost Language of Cranes*.

WHITE, Patrick (1912–90)
Australian novelist and playwright

White was interested in Nietzsche's idea of 'superbeings', people endowed with qualities or abilities which set them apart from the rest of the human race. But White's characters are cursed, not blessed, by difference: their chief attribute is a cantankerous individuality which makes it impossible for them to adjust to society or it to them. In some books (*Riders in the Chariot*, about anti-Semitism, or *The Vivisector*, about a convention-defying painter) the 'enemy' is the stifling gentility of lower-middle-class Sydney suburbanites. In others, such as *The Tree of Man*, about a young farmer in the 1900s, or *A Fringe of Leaves*, the battle is symbolic, against the wilderness itself. But wherever conflict takes place, it is of epic proportions: White's craggy prose puts him in the company of such past writers as ≫ Melville or ≫ Conrad, and in the twentieth century only ≫ Golding equals his blend of fast-paced storytelling and brooding philosophical allegory.

VOSS (1957)
In 1857, financed by a group of Sydney businessmen, a group of explorers sets out to cross Australia. The expedition is led by the German visionary Voss: physically awkward, ill-at-ease in towns and houses, speaking a tortured, poetic English which sounds as if he learned it by rote, phrase by painful phrase. The other members include an ex-convict and a dreamy Aboriginal boy, Jackie, torn between the white people's culture and his own. White balances reports of the expedition's struggle against the desert and to understand one another with accounts of the life of Laura Trevelyan, a young woman fascinated by Voss (at first as a larger-than-life character, an epic personality, and then as a vulnerable human being) as she waits in Sydney, like a medium hoping for spirit-messages, for news of him.

White's other novels are Happy Valley, The Living and the Dead, The Aunt's Story *(a comedy about an indomitable spinster travelling alone),* The Solid Mandala, The Eye of the Storm *and* The Twyborn Affair. The Burnt Ones *and* The Cockatoos *are collections of short stories.* Flaws in the Glass *is an autobiography, good on White's own battles against the wilderness (he was an outback farmer) and against the conventions of his day (he was homosexual).*

Read on

♦ *A Fringe of Leaves* (about a woman shipwrecked in Queensland in the 1840s, who is captured by Aborigines and brought to terms not only with an alien culture but with her feelings about the 'civilization' she knew before).

◘ to *Voss*: ›› William Golding, *Darkness Visible*; H.H. Richardson, *The Fortunes of Richard Mahony*; ›› Peter Carey, *Oscar and Lucinda*; Paul Bowles, *The Sheltering Sky*; ›› Joseph Conrad, *The Nigger of the Narcissus*.

◘ to *A Fringe of Leaves*: ›› D.H. Lawrence, *The Plumed Serpent*; Katharine Susannah Prichard, *Coonardoo*; ›› David Malouf, *Remembering Babylon*.

◘ to White's work in general: Christina Stead, *The Man Who Loved Children*; Joyce Cary, *The Horse's Mouth*; ›› Elizabeth Taylor, *Blaming*.

READ ON A THEME

THE WILDERNESS
   Andrea Barrett, *The Voyage of the Narwhal*
›› Willa Cather, *Death Comes for the Archbishop*
›› Joseph Conrad, *Heart of Darkness*
   James Fenimore Cooper, *The Last of the Mohicans*
   Charles Frazier, *Cold Mountain*
›› Brian Moore, *Black Robe*
›› Paul Theroux, *The Mosquito Coast*
›› Patrick White, *Voss*

WILSON, Angus (1913–91)

British novelist and short story writer

Wilson was a post-Second World War successor to the great Victorian novelists. His plots are expansive, his pages teem with characters and his style is pungently satirical. His middle-class heroes and heroines, often members of the professions, have large, quarrelsome families; adultery, homosexuality, shady dealing and the conflict between public and private duty shape their lives. The 'public' plot of *Hemlock and After* is about a novelist trying to establish a writers' centre in a large, old house; the 'private' plot concerns his anguish about his own homosexuality. In *Anglo-Saxon Attitudes*, a successful academic with a shambolic personal life reflects on the triumphant archaeological discovery of his youth, when he unearthed an obscene pagan statue in the grave of a seventh-century Christian missionary. Was it, he wonders, a hoax and, if so, is this yet another of the lies on which he has built his life? As well as his novels, Wilson's short stories are much admired. They are sharp anecdotes of emotional ineptness, often involving the clash between middle-aged parents and their children or between ill-matched lovers.

Wilson's other novels are The Middle Age of Mrs Eliot, The Old Men at the Zoo, No Laughing Matter, Late Call, As If By Magic *and* Setting the World on Fire. The Wrong Set, Such Darling Dodos *and* A Bit Off the Map *are collections of short stories.*

⤳Read on

◆ *The Old Men at the Zoo* (a satire set in a future Britain threatened by a united Europe and defeated by its own penchant for replacing action with committee rhetoric).

▣ to Wilson's novels: ❯❯ Iris Murdoch, *The Sandcastle*; ❯❯ Willa Cather, *The Professor's House*; Peter Taylor, *A Summons to Memphis*.

▣ to the short stories: V.S. Pritchett, *The Camberwell Beauty and Other Stories*; Mary Gordon, *Temporary Shelter*.

WILSON, A.N.

WILSON, A.N. (Andrew Norman) (born 1950)
British novelist and historian

Wilson began his career as a novelist and his early works (*The Sweets of Pimlico, Unguarded Hours*) were comic novels in the style of ›› Evelyn Waugh, and just as funny. Later fiction, while still firmly within the tradition of the English comic novel, was tinged with a more melancholic understanding of human failures and foibles. A sequence of five novels (*Incline Our Hearts, A Bottle in the Smoke, Daughters of Albion, Hearing Voices* and *A Watch in the Night*) follows the life of an actor and writer, Julian Ramsay, through many decades and traces the ways in which it intertwines with the history of an eccentric upper class family, the Lampitts. In recent years, Wilson, long a skilful biographer, has had more success as a writer of non-fiction than as a novelist. *The Victorians, After the Victorians* (see below) and *Our Times* are large-scale, ambitious and idiosyncratic works of social history which, taken together, move from the 1830s to the present day.

AFTER THE VICTORIANS (2005)
To write a history of Britain and the world which takes readers from the death of Queen Victoria to the coronation of Elizabeth II and encompasses everything from major subjects like women's suffrage, the decline of the Raj, two world wars and the birth of the welfare state to less weighty ones like the rise of the crossword puzzle, the bizarre career of the Rector of Stiffkey and the popularity of detective fiction demands an author with great confidence in his own powers of narrative and synthesis. Wilson rises to the challenge in a book that neatly mixes anecdote and analysis.

Wilson's other novels include The Healing Art, Wise Virgin, Love Unknown, Dream Children *and* Winnie *and* Wolf. He has written biographies of ›› Sir Walter Scott, John Milton, Hilaire Belloc, ›› Tolstoy, C.S. Lewis and John Betjeman. Jesus: A Life *and* Paul: The Mind of an Apostle *are investigations of the historical facts behind Biblical accounts.*

📖Read on
◘ to Wilson's non-fiction: Piers Brendon, *The Decline and Fall of the British Empire*; Andrew Marr, *A History of Modern Britain*; Jerry White, *London in the Nineteenth Century*.
◘ to Wilson's fiction: ›› Hilary Mantel, *Beyond Black*; Allan Massie, *Change and Decay in All Around I See*; ›› Anthony Powell, *A Dance to the Music of Time*.

WINCHESTER, Simon (born 1944)
British travel writer and historian

A former foreign correspondent for British newspapers, Winchester gained short-lived and undesirable fame when he was one of the journalists held captive by the Argentine forces during the Falklands War. In the 1980s he wrote several travel books of which the most enjoyable was *Outposts*, an account of his experiences while visiting the far-flung islands that constituted the last remaining relics of the British Empire. In 1998 he achieved, perhaps unexpectedly, bestseller status with *The Surgeon of Crowthorne*, a short but compelling narrative that told the extraordinary tale of Dr William C. Minor, an American doctor who was incarcerated in Broadmoor Lunatic Asylum after being convicted of murder but who became one of the most valued freelance contributors to the first edition of the massive Oxford English Dictionary. Combining an offbeat human interest story with insights into subjects as diverse as the history of lexicography and the American Civil War (Minor served as an army surgeon in the war), *The Surgeon of Crowthorne* deserved its success. Winchester has followed it with a number of other books which tell forgotten but intriguing stories. *The Map That Changed the World* chronicles the life of William Smith, the self-educated scientist who became the founding father of modern geology; *Krakatoa – The Day the Earth Exploded* is about the cataclysmic volcanic eruptions around the South-East Asian island of Krakatoa in 1883; *A Crack in the Edge of the World* describes the 1906 San Francisco earthquake. His most recent volume, *Bomb, Book and Compass*, is a biography of Joseph Needham, a remarkable British accademic and polymath who became one of the western world's greatest experts on China.

⏎Read on

◆ *A Crack in the Edge of the World*.

◘ Deborah Cadbury, *The Dinosaur Hunters*; John Keay, *The Great Arc*; Peter Morgan, *Fire Mountain* (dramatic story of the volcanic eruption on the Caribbean island of Martinique in 1902); K.M. Elisabeth Murray, *Caught in the Web of Words* (a biography of James Murray, founding editor of the OED); Roger Osborne, *The Floating Egg*.

WINTERSON, Jeanette (born 1959)

British novelist

Several of Winterson's early novels are tart, magic-realist fables which set characters with modern sensibilities in riotously chaotic historical settings: Noah's Ark (filled with grumbling women) in *Boating for Beginners*, the rank back-canals of Venice and the battlefields of Napoleonic France in *The Passion*, the mudflats and brothels of seventeenth-century London in *Sexing the Cherry* (see below). Her more recent books have continued to use all the resources of myth, fairytale and language itself to construct ever more daring and demanding fictions. *The Powerbook*, for example, flits between Capri and Paris, London and cyberspace in a series of interlocking narratives that invite the active participation of the reader in creating their stories.

SEXING THE CHERRY (1989)

The place is London, in the grip of Puritans whose Christian fervour has no truck with compassion or even with simple truth. A giantess known as the Dog Woman rescues an infant from the Thames, names him Jordan and brings him up until he is apprenticed to the naturalist John Tradescant and starts to travel the world in search of exotic plants. Jordan's dreams of far countries, and of a princess who exists beyond the grasp of gravity, are intertwined, page by page, with his mother's account of her brutal daily life, as fundamentalist to its violent principles as the Puritans she preys on are to theirs.

Winterson's other fiction includes Oranges Are Not the Only Fruit *(about a young girl who escapes a harsh Plymouth Brethren upbringing by asserting her lesbian identity),* Written on the Body *(a bizarre love story in which the book we are reading is the body, and the body is the book),* Art and Lies, Gut Symmetries, Lighthousekeeping, Weight *and* The Stone Gods. Art Objects *is a collection of characteristically impassioned essays on writing and writers.* Tanglewreck *is an inventive tale about time and treasure written for children.*

📖Read on

◆ *The Passion*.

◻ ≫ Michèle Roberts, *The Book of Mrs Noah*; ≫ Angela Carter, *The Magic Toyshop*; ≫ Italo Calvino, 'The Cloven Viscount' (in *Our Ancestors*); ≫ Iain Sinclair, *Radon Daughters*.

WINTON, Tim (born 1960)
Australian novelist

Tim Winton is the most admired Australian novelist of his generation, twice shortlisted for the Booker Prize, and it is not difficult to see why. He began publishing his fiction when he was in his early twenties (his award-winning first novel, *An Open Swimmer*, was published in 1981) and his books have grown in their ambition and scale ever since. Haunted by the landscape in which he grew up and fascinated by the complex interactions of families and family life, he has written a series of novels that explore Australian lives with an honesty and imagination that few other writers have matched. In *The Riders*, the first of his novels to be up for the Booker Prize, he mixes psychological suspense with a devastating love story in the account of a displaced Australian, unhappily ensconced in Ireland, who sets out to explain the mystery of his wife's disappearance. Powerful, lyrical and emotionally charged, *The Riders* shows clearly why Winton is so highly praised.

DIRT MUSIC (2001)
Set amid the wonderfully evoked landscape of the west coast of Australia, *Dirt Music* is a compelling story of a strange triangular relationship between the widowed owner of a lobster fishery, the woman he lives with and a poacher-cum-musician in flight from the tragedies of his past. Half love story, half exercise in Australian gothic, the book provides memorable portraits of three people in thrall to their personal histories yet struggling to reinvent themselves.

Tim Winton's other novels are Shallows, That Eye, the Sky, In the Winter Dark, Cloudstreet, Blueback *and* Breath. The Turning *is a recent collection of short stories.*

⮒Read on
◆ *Cloudstreet* (a generous and humane story of two contrasting families in Western Australia and the way their lives intertwine through the years).
◻ Murray Bail, *Eucalyptus*; Richard Flanagan, *Death of a River Guide*; ≫ Kate Grenville, *The Idea of Perfection*.

WODEHOUSE, P.G. (Pelham Grenville) (1881–1975)
British novelist

In the 1920s and 1930s Wodehouse wrote Broadway shows, and he once described his novels as 'musical comedy without the music'. There are over a hundred of them, gloriously frivolous romps set in high society 1920s England or among dyspeptic American newspaper magnates and film tycoons. Wodehouse's gormless heroes are in love with 'pips' and 'peacherinos'. Before they can marry they must persuade dragon-like relatives (usually aunts) to give reluctant consent or to part with cash – and the persuasion often involves stealing valuable jewels (to earn undying gratitude when they are 'found' again), smuggling the girl into the house disguised (so that the radiance of her personality will charm all opposition) or blackmail (threatening to reveal embarrassing secrets of the relative's misspent youth). There are two main novel-series, the Jeeves books (in which Bertie Wooster consistently makes an ass of himself, usually by being the fall-guy in Jeeves's machiavellian schemes), and the Blandings books (in which Lord Emsworth's prize pig bulks large). Other books tell of the multifarious members of the Mulliner family and the Drones Club, of golfers, cricketers and incompetent crooks; in all of them the season is high summer, every cloud is lined with silver, and happy endings are distributed 'in heaping handfuls' (to quote Wodehouse's own immortal phrase).

Wodehouse's Blandings books include Galahad at Blandings, Heavy Weather, Pigs Have Wings *and* Uncle Fred in the Springtime. *His Jeeves books include* Joy in the Morning, Carry On, Jeeves, The Inimitable Jeeves, Jeeves in the Offing, Much Obliged, Jeeves, Right Ho, Jeeves, Stiff Upper Lip, Jeeves *and* The Code of the Woosters. *His other novels include* Money in the Bank, Uncle Dynamite, The Luck of the Bodkins *and* Quick Service. The Man Upstairs, The Clicking of Cuthbert, Eggs and Crumpets *and* Meet Mr Mulliner *are short story collections, and* Performing Flea *is autobiography.*

📖Read on

◘ Richard Gordon, *Doctor in the House*; Patrick Dennis, *Auntie Mame*. The same kind of gormless farce, transplanted to California, updated to the 1980s and set among incompetent crooks and gangsters is in Donald E. Westlake's Dortmunder books, such as *Bank Shot* or *Who Stole Sassi Manoon?*

WOLFE, Tom (born 1931)
US journalist and novelist

The 1960s creator and practitioner of New Journalism (non-fiction writing that ignored traditional attempts at objectivity and impersonality in favour of an exuberant adoption of many of the techniques of fiction), Tom Wolfe had long hinted that he would one day turn his attention to the novel. When *The Bonfire of the Vanities* finally arrived in 1987 it fulfilled most of the expectations advance publicity had aroused. It is a big and bold novel, attempting to do for 1980s New York what Dickens had done for 1840s London – provide an all-encompassing vision of urban society from its richest citizens to the dwellers in its ghettos. Sherman McCoy is a wealthy Wall Street investment banker, one of the 'Masters of the Universe', as Wolfe ironically calls him. His life seems an embodiment of the American Dream until, driving his Mercedes through the Bronx, he hits a black pedestrian. From that point dream turns rapidly to nightmare and Sherman is pitched into a world of politicians on the make, sleazy media hacks and the assorted lowlife caught up in a legal system that offers its own strange versions of 'justice'. Alive with satirical observation, peopled by a rich cast of over-the-top characters and narrated in the pyrotechnic language that Wolfe had perfected in his non-fiction, *The Bonfire of the Vanities* is a highly entertaining study of a status-mad society.

Wolfe's other two novels are A Man in Full *and* I Am Charlotte Simmons. *His non-fiction books include* The Right Stuff *(the story of the early years of the American space programme),* The Electric Kool-Aid Acid Test *(classic 1960s account of Ken Kesey, his Merry Pranksters and their bus ride across America),* The Kandy-Kolored Tangerine-Flake Streamline Baby *and* From Bauhaus to Our House. Hooking Up *is a collection of essays that also includes a novella, 'Ambush at Fort Bragg'.*

📖 Read on
■ to the fiction: ➤➤ Don DeLillo, *Underworld*; ➤➤ John Irving, *A Prayer for Owen Meany*.
■ to the non-fiction: ➤➤ Hunter S. Thompson, *Fear and Loathing in Las Vegas*; ➤➤ Norman Mailer, *The Executioner's Song*.

WOOLF, Virginia (1882–1941)

British novelist and non-fiction writer

As well as novels, Woolf published two dozen non-fiction books: biographies (one of Flush, Elizabeth Barrett Browning's pet dog), diaries, essays on feminism and on literature. She was fascinated by psychology, and her nine novels set out to show, in prose, the workings of the subconscious mind. Instead of narrating strings of events she lets her characters run on in a stream-of-consciousness style which gradually builds a clear picture of their personalities. She tells us the jumble of thoughts and memories in ordinary men and women, and she is particularly good at showing moments of radiant inner happiness. *Mrs Dalloway*, the interior monologue of a middle-class woman preparing to give a dinner party, reveals her feelings about herself and her past as well as the urgent claims of the coming evening. In *To the Lighthouse* a group of adults and children is shown on a summer holiday – the trip to the lighthouse is a promised birthday treat for one of the children – and then in the same place ten years later, when the trip is finally made. Despite war and death in the intervening years, the influence of the dead mother is as strong as in her lifetime. *The Waves*, Woolf's most complex book, traces six people's reactions to experiences from childhood to maturity, showing how apparently small 'real' past events continue to affect the personality as waves shape and reshape the shore.

Woolf's other novels are The Voyage Out, Night and Day, Jacob's Room, Orlando, The Years *and* Between the Acts. Haunted House *and* Mrs Dalloway's Party *are collections of short stories. Her* Diaries *have been published in five volumes and her* Letters *in six.*

📖 Read on

◘ ≫ Marcel Proust, *Swann's Way* (Part One of *Remembrance of Things Past*); ≫ Jean Rhys, *Good Morning, Midnight*; Dorothy Richardson, *Pilgrimage*; Anaïs Nin, *Seduction of the Minotaur*; ≫ Margaret Atwood, *Surfacing*; Gertrude Stein, *Three Lives*; ≫ Iris Murdoch, *The Sea, The Sea*; Michael Cunningham, *The Hours* (novel that pays homage to Mrs Dalloway while creating its own narrative voices in three interconnected stories).

WYNDHAM, John (1903–69)

British novelist and short story writer

John Wyndham was one of the pseudonyms of John Wyndham Lucas Beynon Harris, who wrote straightforward science fiction and thrillers under the names John Wyndham Parkes and Lucas Beynon. The John Wyndham novels are less science fiction than thrillers with science fiction overtones: he called them 'logical fantasies'. In *The Midwich Cuckoos* an alien race seeks to colonize Earth not by force of arms but by fertilizing women – and the story begins, in the quiet English countryside (a favourite Wyndham location) as the half-alien children approach puberty. In *Chocky* a small boy has an invisible confidant – not a figment of his imagination, but a being from outer space. *The Day of the Triffids* begins with two simultaneous disasters, the sudden blinding of almost all human beings and the growth of enormous, mobile, predatory plants; the novel concerns the hero's attempts to organize resistance and save the human race.

Wyndham's other novels include The Chrysalids, The Kraken Wakes *and* Trouble With Lichen. *His short stories are collected in* The Seeds of Time, Consider Her Ways *and* Web.

☙Read on
◆ *The Chrysalids* (set in a post-apocalyptic future where society banishes all those with genetic mutations to a badlands known as the Fringes).
◻ Ray Bradbury, *Fahrenheit 451*; John Christopher, *The Death of Grass*; Nevil Shute, *On the Beach*; ≫ H.G. Wells, *The Time Machine*.

ZOLA, Émile (1840–1902)

French novelist and non-fiction writer

Zola won scandalous fame at twenty seven with his novel *Thérèse Raquin*, about a pair of lovers who murder the woman's husband. The book's financial success let him take up fiction full-time, and he began a twenty-novel series designed to show – in a scientific way, he claimed, as species are described – every aspect of late nineteenth-century French life. Although each novel is self-contained, their main characters are all members of the two families which give the series its name, The

Rougons and the Macquarts. Zola's scheme echoed ❯❯ Balzac's in *The Human Comedy (La Comedie Humaine)*, and like Balzac he was interested in exact description, what he called 'naturalism'. But his morbid and pessimistic nature led him to concentrate on the harsher aspects of human existence, so that his characters often seem less like real human beings than the people dragged into sermons to illustrate the effects of drink, lust or poverty. Outside France, Zola's best-known books are *Germinal* (about conditions in the coalmines, and including a strike and a major accident), *Earth (La Terre)* (about subsistence farming) and *The Boozer (L'Assommoir)*.

NANA (1880)

The subject is sex. Nana's mother was a country girl who went to Paris to seek her fortune, became a laundress but was destroyed by drink – this is the story of *The Boozer*. Nana grows up as a street urchin, and later becomes an actress and singer. She is beautiful but corrupt, morally brutalized by her childhood. She sets out systematically to destroy men: Zola thinks of her first as one of the Sirens in myth, drawing men irresistibly to her by the beauty of her voice, and then as a spider, preying on them even as she mates with them. He pities neither Nana nor her victims: like his other novels, this panorama of big city life is painted entirely in shades of black.

Other books in the series include The Human Beast (La Bête humaine) *(about the gangs of navvies who built railroads),* The Belly of Paris (Le Ventre de Paris) *(about the food markets of the city),* For Women's Delight (Pour le bonheur des dames) *(about the staff and customers of a department store),* Money *(set among financiers) and* The Downfall (Le Débâcle) *(a devastating picture of the 1870 Commune and siege of Paris, which Zola saw as a cleansing operation, ridding the city of the corruption which had led to the misery described in his other books). In his last years he finished the first three books of another series,* The Four Gospels: *their titles are* Fertility, Work *and* Truth.

🕮 Read on

◆ *Thérèse Raquin*.
◻ ❯❯ W. Somerset Maugham, *Liza of Lambeth*; Theodor Fontane, *Effi Briest*; Frank Norris, *The Pit*; Theodore Dreiser, *An American Tragedy*; ❯❯ George Gissing, *New Grub Street*.

PRIZELISTS

THE BIG READ

This is the list of the UK's favourite 100 titles, as voted for in the BBC's 2003 nationwide poll.

The Alchemist by Paulo Coelho
Alice's Adventures in Wonderland by Lewis Carroll
Animal Farm by George Orwell
Anna Karenina by Leo Tolstoy
Anne of Green Gables by L.M. Montgomery
Artemis Fowl by Eoin Colfer
The BFG by Roald Dahl
Birdsong by Sebastian Faulks
Black Beauty by Anna Sewell
Bleak House by Charles Dickens
Brave New World by Aldous Huxley
Brideshead Revisited by Evelyn Waugh
Bridget Jones's Diary by Helen Fielding
Captain Corelli's Mandolin by Louis de Bernières
Catch-22 by Joseph Heller
The Catcher in the Rye by J.D. Salinger
Charlie and the Chocolate Factory by Roald Dahl
A Christmas Carol by Charles Dickens
The Clan of the Cave Bear by J.M. Auel
Cold Comfort Farm by Stella Gibbons
The Colour of Magic by Terry Pratchett
The Count of Monte Cristo by Alexandre Dumas
Crime and Punishment by Fyodor Dostoevsky
David Copperfield by Charles Dickens
Double Act by Jacqueline Wilson
Dune by Frank Herbert
Emma by Jane Austen
Far From the Madding Crowd by Thomas Hardy

Girls in Love by Jacqueline Wilson
The God of Small Things by Arundhati Roy
The Godfather by Mario Puzo
Gone With the Wind by Margaret Mitchell
Good Omens by Neil Gaiman and Terry Pratchett
Goodnight Mister Tom by Michelle Magorian
Gormenghast by Mervyn Peake
The Grapes of Wrath by John Steinbeck
Great Expectations by Charles Dickens
The Great Gatsby by F. Scott Fitzgerald
Guards! Guards! by Terry Pratchett
Harry Potter and the Chamber of Secrets by J.K. Rowling
Harry Potter and the Goblet of Fire by J.K. Rowling
Harry Potter and the Philosopher's Stone by J.K. Rowling
Harry Potter and the Prisoner of Azkaban by J.K. Rowling
His Dark Materials by Philip Pullman
The Hitchhiker's Guide to the Galaxy by Douglas Adams
The Hobbit by J.R.R. Tolkien
Holes by Louis Sachar
I Capture the Castle by Dodie Smith
Jane Fyre by Charlotte Brontë
Kane and Abel by Jeffrey Archer
Katherine by Anya Seton
The Lion, the Witch and the Wardrobe by C.S. Lewis
Little Women by Louisa May Alcott
Lord of the Flies by William Golding
The Lord of the Rings by J.R.R. Tolkien
Love In the Time of Cholera by Gabriel García Márquez
The Magic Faraway Tree by Enid Blyton
Magician by Raymond E. Feist
The Magus by John Fowles
Matilda by Roald Dahl
Memoirs of a Geisha by Arthur Golden
Middlemarch by George Eliot
Midnight's Children by Salman Rushdie
Mort by Terry Pratchett
Night Watch by Terry Pratchett
Nineteen Eighty-four by George Orwell

Noughts and Crosses by Malorie Blackman
Of Mice and Men by John Steinbeck
On the Road by Jack Kerouac
One Hundred Years of Solitude by Gabriel García Márquez
Perfume by Patrick Süskind
Persuasion by Jane Austen
The Pillars of the Earth by Ken Follett
A Prayer for Owen Meany by John Irving
Pride and Prejudice by Jane Austen
The Princess Diaries by Meg Cabot
The Ragged Trousered Philanthropists by Robert Tressell
Rebecca by Daphne Du Maurier
The Secret Garden by Frances Hodgson Burnett
The Secret History by Donna Tartt
The Shell Seekers by Rosamunde Pilcher
The Stand by Stephen King
The Story of Tracy Beaker by Jacqueline Wilson
A Suitable Boy by Vikram Seth
Swallows and Amazons by Arthur Ransome
A Tale of Two Cities by Charles Dickens
Tess of the D'Urbervilles by Thomas Hardy
The Thorn Birds by Colleen McCullough
To Kill a Mockingbird by Harper Lee
A Town Like Alice by Nevil Shute
Treasure Island by Robert Louis Stevenson
The Twits by Roald Dahl
Ulysses by James Joyce
Vicky Angel by Jacqueline Wilson
War and Peace by Leo Tolstoy
Watership Down by Richard Adams
The Wind in the Willows by Kenneth Grahame
Winnie the Pooh by A.A. Milne
The Woman in White by Wilkie Collins
Wuthering Heights by Emily Brontë

THE MAN BOOKER PRIZE

Still the most prestigious literary prize in Britain, the Man Booker Prize (once just the Booker Prize) attracts much media attention and hot debate.

1969	P.H. Newby – *Something to Answer For*
1970	Bernice Rubens – *The Elected Member*
1971	V.S. Naipaul – *In a Free State*
1972	John Berger – *G.*
1973	J.G. Farrell – *The Siege of Krishnapur*
1974	Nadine Gordimer – *The Conservationist*
	Stanley Middleton – *Holiday*
1975	Ruth Prawer Jhabvala – *Heat and Dust*
1976	David Storey – *Saville*
1977	Paul Scott – *Staying On*
1978	Iris Murdoch – *The Sea, The Sea*
1979	Penelope Fitzgerald – *Offshore*
1980	William Golding – *Rites of Passage*
1981	Salman Rushdie – *Midnight's Children*
1982	Thomas Keneally – *Schindler's Ark*
1983	J.M. Coetzee – *The Life and Times of Michael K.*
1984	Anita Brookner – *Hôtel du Lac*
1985	Keri Hulme – *The Bone People*
1986	Kingsley Amis – *The Old Devils*
1987	Penelope Lively – *Moon Tiger*
1988	Peter Carey – *Oscar and Lucinda*
1989	Kazuo Ishiguro – *The Remains of the Day*
1990	A.S. Byatt – *Possession*
1991	Ben Okri – *The Famished Road*
1992	Michael Ondaatje – *The English Patient*
	Barry Unsworth – *Sacred Hunger*
1993	Roddy Doyle – *Paddy Clarke Ha Ha Ha*
1994	James Kelman – *How Late it Was, How Late*
1995	Pat Barker – *The Ghost Road*
1996	Graham Swift – *Last Orders*
1997	Arundhati Roy – *The God of Small Things*
1998	Ian McEwan – *Amsterdam*
1999	J.M. Coetzee – *Disgrace*

2000	Margaret Atwood – *The Blind Assassin*
2001	Peter Carey – *True History of the Kelly Gang*
2002	Yann Martel – *Life of Pi*
2003	D.B.C. Pierre – *Vernon God Little*
2004	Alan Hollinghurst – *The Line of Beauty*
2005	John Banville – *The Sea*
2006	Kiran Desai – *The Inheritance of Loss*
2007	Anne Enright – *The Gathering*
2008	Aravind Adiga – *The White Tiger*

THE PULITZER PRIZE FOR FICTION

The Pulitzer Prize for Fiction is the most prestigious such prize in America and has been awarded each year since 1918 (originally under the title of the Pulitzer Prize for the Novel) to the writer of what the judges believe to be the most distinguished work of American fiction in a given year. Here is a list of all the winners of the prize since 1980:

1980	Norman Mailer – *The Executioner's Song*
1981	John Kennedy Toole – *A Confederacy of Dunces*
1982	John Updike – *Rabbit is Rich*
1983	Alice Walker – *The Color Purple*
1984	William Kennedy – *Ironweed*
1985	Alison Lurie – *Foreign Affairs*
1986	Larry McMurtry – *Lonesome Dove*
1987	Peter Taylor – *A Summons to Memphis*
1988	Toni Morrison – *Beloved*
1989	Anne Tyler – *Breathing Lessons*
1990	Oscar Hijuelos – *The Mambo Kings Play Songs of Love*
1991	John Updike – *Rabbit at Rest*
1992	Jane Smiley – *A Thousand Acres*
1993	Robert Olen Butler – *A Good Scent From a Strange Mountain*
1994	E. Annie Proulx – *The Shipping News*
1995	Carol Shields – *The Stone Diaries*
1996	Richard Ford – *Independence Day*
1997	Steven Millhauser – *Martin Dressler: The Tale of an American Dreamer*
1998	Philip Roth – *American Pastoral*

1999	Michael Cunningham – *The Hours*
2000	Jhumpa Lahiri – *Interpreter of Maladies*
2001	Michael Chabon – *The Amazing Adventures of Kavalier and Clay*
2002	Richard Russo – *Empire Falls*
2003	Jeffrey Eugenides – *Middlesex*
2004	Edward P. Jones – *The Known World*
2005	Marilynne Robinson – *Gilead*
2006	Geraldine Brooks – *March*
2007	Cormac McCarthy – *The Road*
2008	Junot Diaz – *The Brief Wondrous Life of Oscar Wao*
2009	Elizabeth Strout – *Olive Kittredge*

THE COSTA AWARDS (formerly THE WHITBREAD AWARDS)

Launched in 1971 as the Whitbread Awards, these are given in a number of different categories. The winners of the award for best novel have been:

1971	Gerda Charles – *The Destiny Waltz*
1972	Susan Hill – *The Bird of Night*
1973	Shiva Naipaul – *The Chip Chip Gatherers*
1974	Iris Murdoch – *The Sacred and Profane Love Machine*
1975	William McIlvanney – *Docherty*
1976	William Trevor – *The Children of Dynmouth*
1977	Beryl Bainbridge – *Injury Time*
1978	Paul Theroux – *Picture Palace*
1979	Jennifer Johnston – *The Old Jest*
1980	David Lodge – *How Far Can You Go?*
1981	Maurice Leitch – *Silver's City*
1982	John Wain – *Young Shoulders*
1983	William Trevor – *Fools of Fortune*
1984	Christopher Hope – *Kruger's Alp*
1985	Peter Ackroyd – *Hawksmoor*
1986	Kazuo Ishiguro – *An Artist of the Floating World*
1987	Ian McEwan – *The Child in Time*
1988	Salman Rushdie – *The Satanic Verses*
1989	Lindsay Clarke – *The Chymical Wedding*

1990	Nicholas Mosley – *Hopeful Monsters*
1991	Jane Gardam – *The Queen of the Tambourine*
1992	Jeff Torrington – *Swing Hammer Swing*
1993	Joan Brady – *Theory of War*
1994	William Trevor – *Felicia's Journey*
1995	Salman Rushdie – *The Moor's Last Sigh*
1996	Beryl Bainbridge – *Every Man for Himself*
1997	Jim Crace – *Quarantine*
1998	Justin Cartwright – *Leading the Cheers*
1999	Rose Tremain – *Music and Silence*
2000	Matthew Kneale – *English Passengers*
2001	Patrick Neate – *Twelve Bar Blues*
2002	Michael Frayn – *Spies*
2003	Mark Haddon – *The Curious Incident of the Dog in the Night-Time*
2004	Andrea Levy – *Small Island*
2005	Ali Smith – *The Accidental*
2006	William Boyd – *Restless*
2007	A.L. Kennedy – *Day*
2008	Sebastian Barry – *The Secret Scripture*

THE ORANGE PRIZE

The Orange Prize was created in 1996 and is given to the best original full-length novel by a female novelist writing in English. It has rapidly become one of the country's most prestigious literary prizes.

1996	Helen Dunmore – *A Spell of Winter*
1997	Anne Michaels – *Fugitive Pieces*
1998	Carol Shields – *Larry's Party*
1999	Suzanne Berne – *A Crime in the Neighbourhood*
2000	Linda Grant – *When I Lived in Modern Times*
2001	Kate Grenville – *The Idea of Perfection*
2002	Ann Patchett – *Bel Canto*
2003	Valerie Martin – *Property*
2004	Andrea Levy – *Small Island*
2005	Lionel Shriver – *We Need to Talk About Kevin*
2006	Zadie Smith – *On Beauty*

2007   Chimamanda Ngozi Adichie – *Half of a Yellow Sun*
2008   Rose Tremain – *The Road Home*

THE RICHARD AND JUDY
BOOK CLUB CHOICES 2006

Nicole Krauss, *The History of Love*
Kate Mosse, *The Labyrinth*
Richard Benson, *The Farm*
Martin Davies, *The Conjuror's Bird*
Julian Barnes, *Arthur and George*
Eva Rice, *The Lost Art of Keeping Secrets*
Andrew Smith, *Moondust*
Geraldine Brooks, *March*
Anchee Min, *Empress Orchid*
Michael Connelly, *The Lincoln Lawyer*

THE RICHARD AND JUDY
BOOK CLUB CHOICES 2007

Jed Rubenfeld, *The Interpretation of Murder*
Lori Lansens, *The Girls*
William Boyd, *Restless*
Catherine Ryan Hyde, *Love in the Present Tense*
Chimamanda Ngozi Adichie, *Half of A Yellow Sun*
Griff Rhys Jones, *Semi-Detached*
James Robertson, *The Testament of Gideon Mack*
A.M. Homes, T*his Book Will Save Your Life*

THE RICHARD AND JUDY
BOOK CLUB CHOICES 2008

Khaled Hosseini, *A Thousand Splendid Suns*
Danny Scheinmann, *Random Acts of Heroic Love*
Katharine McMahon, *The Rose of Sebastopol*

R.J. Ellory, *A Quiet Belief in Angels*
Patric Gale, *Notes from an Exhibition*
Joshua Ferris, *Then We Came to the End*
Mark Slouka, *The Visible World*
Lloyd Jones, *Mister Pip*
Tim Butcher, *Blood River*
Peter Ho Davies, *The Welsh Girl*

THE RICHARD AND JUDY BOOK CLUB CHOICES 2009

Jesse Kellerman, *The Brutal Art*
Kate Summerscale, *The Suspicions of Mr Whicher*
Andrew Davidson, *The Gargoyle*
Kate Atkinson, *When Will There Be Good News?*
David Ebershoff, *The 19th Wife*
Frances Osborne, *The Bolter*
Joseph O'Neill, *Netherland*
Beatrice Colin, *The Luminous Life of Lilly Aphrodite*
Elizabeth H. Winthrop, *December*
Steven Galloway, *The Cellist of Sarajevo*

INDEX

This is a selective index of the featured authors in the guide and their works where described in detail.

2001: A Space Odyssey 88

2010: Odyssey Two 88

44 Scotland Street 285

About a Boy 225

Acceptance World, The 358

Accidental Tourist, The 457

Accordion Crimes 362

Ackroyd, Peter 5–6, 411

Act of Passion 410

Ada 326

Adams, Douglas 6

Adamson, Gil 1

Adventures of Augie March, The 42

Adventures of Huckleberry Finn, The 456

Adventures of Tom Sawyer, The 456

Affinity 470

African Queen, The 159

After the Victorians 485

After You'd Gone 336

Afternoon Men 357

Against the Day 367

Age of Iron 92

Age of Kali, The 107

Air and Angels 213

Akhenaten, Dweller in Truth 294

Akunin, Boris 8

Alchemist, The 91

Alentejo Blue 9

Alexandria Quartet, The 131

Ali, Monica 9

Alias Grace 22

Alienist, The 73, 74

All He Ever Wanted 409

All of Us 76

All Tomorrow's Parties 174

All-True Travels and Adventures of Lydie Newton, The 414

Allende, Isabel 9–10, 112

Allingham, Margery 10–11

Alone of All Her Sex 469

Amateur Marriage, The 457

Amazing Adventures of Kavalier and Clay, The 79

Ambassadors, The 238

American Dream, An 294

American Gods 169

American Pastoral 382

American Psycho 137, 138

American Tabloid 140

Americana 116

Amis, Kingsley 12–13

Amis, Martin 13–14

Among the Russians 442

Amsterdam 290

Ancestor's Tale, The 110

Angel Pavement 360

Angelica's Grotto 221

Angelou, Maya 15–16

Angels and Insects 68

Anglo-Saxon Attitudes 484

Anil's Ghost 339

Animal Farm 340

Ann Veronica 474

Anna Karenina 446

Another Country 32

Another Day of Life 246

Another World 39

Antony and Cleopatra 288

Any Human Heart 54

Ape and Essence 231

Arabian Nights, The 196

Arabian Sands 436

Arcadia 101

Archangel 199

Arctic Dreams 283

Armadillo 54

Arnott, Jake 17
Arthur and George 40
Artist of the Floating
 World, An 234
Artists in Crime 304
As I Walked Out One
 Summer Morning 265
Asimov, Isaac 18–19, 87
Ask Alice 431
Asylum 291–292
At Freddie's 153
At Lady Molly's 358
At Swim-Two-Birds 334
Atkinson, Kate 19–20
Atomised 227
Atonement 290
Atwood, Margaret 21
Aunt Julia and the
 Scriptwriter 460
Austen Jane 22–23, 171,
 365
Auster, Paul 24
Autograph Man, The 416
Awakenings 387
Awful End of Prince
 William the Silent, The
 241
Awfully Big Adventure, An
 30

Babel Tower 67
Bad Dirt 362
Bag of Bones 254
Bainbridge, Beryl 29–30,
 257
Baker, Nicholson 31
Baldwin, James 32

Balkan Trilogy, The 299
Ballad and the Source,
 The 269–270
Ballad of Peckham Rye,
 The 419
Ballad of the Sad Café,
 The 287
Ballard, J.G. 33
Balzac, Honoré de 34–35,
 122, 153, 422, 445, 493
Banks, Iain [M.] 35–36
Banville, John 36–37
Barcelona 228, 229
Barchester Towers 453
Bardin, John Franklin 103
Barker, Nicola 37–38
Barker, Pat 38–39
Barnes, Julian 40–41
Baron in the Trees, The
 69
Barrow's Boys 155
Basil Street Blues 224,
 225
Baudolino 133
Bayonets to Lhasa 157,
 158
Be Cool 272
Béal Bocht, An 335
Bean Trees, The 256
Bear and the Dragon, The
 87
Beatniks 279
Beautiful and Damned,
 The 152
Beautiful Room is Empty,
 The 481
Beckett, Samuel 40–41

Beevor, Antony 41
Before She Met Me 39
Behind the Scenes at the
 Museum 19
Behind the Wall 442
Behindlings 38
Behold the Man 317
Being Dead 101
Bell, The 323
Bellow, Saul 42–43
Beloved 319
Bend in the River, A 328
Bennett, Arnold 43–44,
 126
Berlin – The Downfall 41
Best of Myles, The 335
Bettany's Book 248
Better Than Sex 437
Between the Woods and
 the Water 270, 271
Beyond Black 301
Beyond the Glass 480, 481
Big Bang 413
Big Sleep, The 81
Binchy, Maeve 45–46
Birds of Passage 384
Birds Without Wings 112
Birdsong 146
Birthday Boys, The 29
Black Album, The 261
Black and Blue 370
Black Betty 320
Black Dahlia, The 140
Black Dogs 290
Black Mask 80
Black Mischief 471
Black Robe 317, 318

Black Swan Green 313

Blackburn, Julia 49

Blackwater Lightship, The 443

Bleak House 122

Blind Assassin, The 21

Blind Watchmaker, The 110

Blishen, Edward 50

Blithedale Romance, The 201

Blood Meridian 286, 287

Bloody Chamber, The 74

Bluest Eye, The 319

Boating for Beginners 487

Body Farm, The 99

Bomb, Book and Compass 486

Bomber 116

Bone by Bone 305

Bonecrack 164

Bonesetter's Daughter, The 429

Bonfire of the Vanities, The 490

Book of Colour, The 49

Book of Dave, The 403

Book of Evidence, The 16

Book of Imaginary Beings 50

Book of Mrs Noah, The 378

Book of the Heathen, The 134, 135

Books Do Furnish a Room 358

Border Crossing 39

Border Trilogy (All the Pretty Horses, The Crossing and *Cities of the Plain)* 286

Borderlines 332

Borges, Jorge Luis 52

Boswell, James 276

Bottle in the Smoke, A 485

Bottle-factory Outing, The 29

Boule de Suif 307

Bowen, Elizabeth 52–53

Boy's Own Story, A 481

Boyd, William 53–54

Bragg, Melvyn 55

Brave New World 230, 231

Brazilian Adventure 157

Brick Lane 9

Brideshead Revisited 471

Bridge, The 35

Briefing for a Descent into Hell 273

Bright Lights, Big City 292

Bright Young People 431

Brightness Falls 292

Brighton Rock 189

Brilliant Creatures 237

Brink, André 56–57, 182

British Museum is Falling Down, The 281

Broken Lands, The 134

Bronski House, The 303

Brontë, Charlotte 57–58, 171

Brontë, Emily 57–58

Brookmyre, Christopher 58–59

Brookner, Anita 59–60

Brooks, Geraldine 60–61

Brother of the More Famous Jack 447

Brothers Karamazov, The 122, 123

Brrm! Brrm! 237

Brunelleschi's Dome 253

Bryson, Bill 61–62

Buchan, John 62–63, 97, 189

Buddenbrooks 297, 298

Buddha of Suburbia, The 260

Bulgakov, Mikhail 63–64

Bull from the Sea, The 372

Burgess, Anthony 64–65

Burmese Days 340

Burning Bright 83

Burroughs, William S. 66–67

Business, The 35

But Beautiful 131

Buyer's Market, A 358

Byatt, A.S. 59, 67–68, 126

Byron, Robert 68–69, 107

Cabal 119

Cack-Handed War, A 50

Caesar 288

Cairo Trilogy (Palace Walk, Palace of Desire, Sugar Street) 293

Cakes and Ale 306

Call If You Need Me 76
Calvino, Italo 69–70
Cambridge 350
Camomile Lawn, The 4/8
Camus, Albert 70–71
Cancer Ward 417
Candlemass Road, The 166
Captain Corelli's Mandolin 112
Card, The 44
Carey, Peter 72–73, 92
Carr, Caleb 73–74
Carrie 254
Carter, Angela 74–75
Carver, Raymond 76, 321
Casanova 310
Casanova's Chinese Restaurant 358
Case Book of Sherlock Holmes, The 124
Case Histories 19, 20
Casebook of Victor Frankenstein, The 5
Castle of Crossed Destinies, The 69
Castle, The (Der Schloss) 245
Cat Who Walks Through Walls, The 202
Cat's Eye 21, 22
Catch-22 144. 200, 203
Catcher in the Rye, The 387, 388
Cathedral 76
Cather, Willa 77–78
Catholics 317

Caves of Steel, The 19
Cement Garden, The 290
Chabon, Michael 79
Chains of Heaven, The 303
Chandler, Raymond 79–80, 320
Changing Places 281
Chant of Jimmie Blacksmith, The 248
Charioteer, The 372
Charlotte Gray 146
Charterhouse of Parma, The 423
Chatterton 5
Chatwin, Bruce 81
Chekhov, Anton 82, 454
Cherry-Garrard, Apsley 450
Chevalier, Tracey 82–83
Child, Lee 83–84
Children of Dynmouth, The 452
Chocky 492
Chocolat 198
Choir, The 453
Christie, Agatha 80, 85
Chrysalids, The 492
Cider House Rules, The 233
Cider With Rosie 265, 266
Circus of Dr Lao, The 397
Citizens 393
City and the Pillar, The 463
City of Djinns 107
City of Glass 24

City of the Beasts 10
Clancy, Tom 86–87
Clarissa, or The History of A Young Lady 376, 377
Clarke, Arthur C. 87–88
Clayhanger 44
Clear and Present Danger 87
Cleopatra's Sister 280
Client, The 194
Clock Without Hands 287
Clockwork Orange, A 65
Close Range 362
Closed Circle, The 90
Closing Time 203
Cloud Atlas 312, 313
Cloudstreet 488
Club Dumas, The 349
Clubbable Woman, A 212
Coasting 368
Coben, Harlan 89–90
Cocaine Nights 33
Code Book, The 413
Coe, Jonathan 90–91
Coelho, Paul 91–92
Coetzee, J.M. 92–93
Coleridge: Darker Reflections 223
Coleridge: Early Visions 223
Collected Works of Billy the Kid, The 339
Collector, The 163
Collector Collector, The 151
Collins, Wilkie 93–94
Color Purple, The 465

Colour of Blood, The 317, 318

Comfort of Strangers, The 290

Coming From Behind 236

Coming Through Slaughter 339

Commitments, The 125

Commonwealth of Thieves, The 248

Concrete Island 33

Confederates 248

Confessions of Felix Krull, Confidence Man 298

Confidential Agent, The 189

Congo Journey 337

Connecticut Yankee in King Arthur's Court, A 456

Connelly, Michael 95

Conrad, Joseph 96–97, 482

Consolations of Philosophy, The 113

Constant Gardener, The 264, 265

Continent 101

Conundrum 318

Conversations at Curlow Creek, The 296

Cookson, Catherine 97

Cornish Trilogy, The 108

Cornwell, Bernard 98

Cornwell, Patricia 99

Corpsing 280

Corrections, The 165

Count Zero 174

Country of the Blind 59

Coupland, Douglas 100

Couples 459

Cowboys and Indians 335

Crabwalk 186

Crace, Jim 101

Crack in the Edge of the World, A 486

Cranford 171

Crash 33

Creation 463

Credo 55

Crime and Punishment 122, 123

Crimson Petal and the White, The 141

Crossing Place, The 303

Crossing the Line 55

Crying of Lot 49, The 366, 367

Cryptonomicon 423

Crystal Rooms 56

Curé of Tours, The 35

Curious Life of Robert Hooke, The 241

Custom of the Country, The 480

Daddy, We Hardly Knew You 191

Daisy Bates in the Desert 49

Dalkey Archive, The 335

Dalrymple, William 107

Damned United, The 345, 346

Dan Leno and the Limehouse Golem 5

Dance to the Music of Time, A 358

Dangerous Calm 432

Daniel Martin 163

Dante Club, The 347, 348

Darcy's Utopia 473

Dark Room, The 467

Dark Star Safari 434

Daughters of Albion 485

Daughters of the House 377

David Copperfield 121

Davies, Robertson 108

Davis, Lindsey 109

Dawkins, Richard 110

Day 251

Day of Creation, The 33

Day of the Jackal, The 162

Day of the Triffids, The 492

De Bernières, Louis 112

De Botton, Alain 113

Dead Beat 289

Dead Cert 164

Dead Lagoon 119

Dead Souls (Gogol) 179, 180

Dead Souls (Ian Rankin) 369

Deadly Percheron, The 103

Deakin, Roger 111

Deal Breaker 90

Death at La Fenice 172

Death Comes for the Archbishop 78
Death du Jour 371
Death in a Strange Country 271
Death in Holy Orders 240
Death of Sweet Mister, The 106
Death of the Heart, The 53
Death to the French 159
Debt to Pleasure, The 261, 262
Decline and Fall 471
Defence, The 326
Defoe, Daniel 114–115
Deighton, Len 115–116
Deja Dead 370
Delillo, Don 116–117, 423
Delta Wedding 477
Deportees, The 125
Deptford Trilogy, The 108
Devastating Boys, The 432
Devil in a Blue Dress 320
Devil May Care 146
Devil's Paintbrush, The 17
Dexter, Colin 118
Dharma Bums, The 252
Dibdin, Michael 118–119
Dick, Philip K. 120
Dickens 5
Dickens, Charles 121–122, 153, 171, 206, 255, 422, 433
Diggers 360
Dirk Gently's Holistic Detective Agency 6

Dirt Music 488
Dirty Tricks 119
Discomfort Zone, The 165
Discworld novels 360
Disgrace 92–93
Dispossessed, The 267–268
Dissolution 388–389
Distance Between Us, The 336
Disturbance Fee, The 50
Divisadero 339
Do Androids Dream of Electric Sheep? 120
Doctor Copernicus 36
Doctor Faustus 298
Doctor Zhivago 345
Don't Read This Book If You're Stupid 150
Don't Tell Alfred 315
Dostoevsky, Fyodor 122–123, 359
Double Vision 39
Down and Out in Paris and London 340
Down Under 62
Downriver 411
Doyle, Arthur Conan 123–124, 348
Doyle, Roddy 125
Dr Haggard's Disease 291
Dr Jekyll and Mr Hyde 425, 426
Dr Johnson and Mr Savage 224

Drabble, Margaret 67, 126–127
Dracula 426
Dragon Apparent, A 279
Drink Before the War, A 268
Drowned and the Saved, The 277
Drowned World, The 33
Dry White Season, A 56
Du Maurier, Daphne 129
Dubliners 244
Ducdame 359
Duel and Other Stories, The 82
Duluth 463
Dumas, Alexandre 127–128, 348
Dune trilogy 207
Dunmore, Helen 129–130
Durrell, Lawrence 130–131, 163
Dyer, Geoff 131–132

Earth (La Terre) 493
Earthly Powers 65
Earthsea Quartet 267
East of Eden 421
Eco, Umberto 132–133, 333
Edric, Robert 134–135
Effective Affinities 179
Egyptian, The 217
Eight Months on Ghazzah Street 300
Elected Member/The Chosen People, The 384

Electricity 178

Elephant and Other Stories 76

Eliot, George 126, 136–137 171, 255

Elizabeth and Essex 427

Ellis, Bret Easton 137–138, 292

Ellroy, James 139–140

Elysium 134

Embarrassment of Riches, The 393

Emigrants, The 401

Eminent Victorians 427

Emma 23

Emotionally Weird 19

Emperor, The 246

Emperor's Last Island, The 49

Empire of the Sun 33

Empire Trilogy 147

Enderby's Dark Lady 64

Enduring Love 290

Endzone 116

England, England 40

Engleby 146

English Assassin, The 316

English Passengers 257

English Patient, The 339

English Teacher/Grateful to Life, The 329

Enigma of Arrival, The 329

Enright, Anne 140–141

Enter a Murderer 304

Equal Music, An 404

Erik Bright-Eyes 196

Error World, The 170

Essays in Love 113

Ethan Frome 479

Eva Luna 9

Evening Redness in the West, The 286

Every Light in the House Burnin' 277

Every Man For Himself 30

Everything You Need 250

Ex Libris 253

Executioner's Song, The 294, 295

Eye in the Door, The 38

Eye of the World, The 243

Faber, Michel 141, 142

Fall, The (La Chute) 70, 71

Falling Angels 83

Falling Towards England 237

Family Matters 312

Family Moskat, The 293, 412

Family Romance, A 60

Far Country, A 303

Far From the Madding Crowd 197

Farewell Symphony, The 481

Farewell to Arms, A 204

Farewell to the Trumpets 318

Farewell, My Lovely 80, 320

Farrell, J.G. 144

Fatal Shore, The 228, 229

Father and Son 29

Fatherland 199

Fathers and Sons 455

Faulkner, William 144–145, 477

Faulks, Sebastian 145–146

Fear and Loathing in Las Vegas 436, 437

Feast of the Goat, The 460

Feist, Raymond E. 147

Female Eunuch, The 191

Fencing Master, The 348

Fermat's Last Theorem 412, 413

Fermata, The 31

Fever Pitch 226

Fiancé and Other Stories, The 82

Fielding, Henry 148–149

Fifth Queen, The 158

Fight Club 342

Final Programme 316

Fine Balance, A 312

Fine the Way It Is 362

Fingersmith 470

Finnegans Wake 244

Finney, Charles G. 397

Fire From Heaven 372

Fire Gospel, The 142

Fire Next Time, The 32

Fires 76

Firm, The 194

First Circle, The 417

First Man in Rome, The 288

First Men in the Moon, The 473

Fischer, Tibor 150–151

Fit, The 207

Fitzgerald, F. Scott
151–152, 292

Fitzgerald, Penelope 153

Flanders Panel,
The 348

Flashman and the Angel
of the Lord 166

Flaubert, Gustave 153–154,
454

Flaubert's Parrot 39, 40

Fleming, Fergus 155

Fleming, Ian 83, 155–156,
264

Fleming, Peter 157–158

Flesh and Blood 377

Flight 178

Flounder, The (Der Butt)
186

Fludd 301

Folding Star, The 223

Fool's Alphabet, A 146

Footsteps 224

Ford, Ford Madox 158

Foreign Affairs 284

Foreign Land 368

Forester, C.S. 98, 159

Forster, E.M. 159–160

Forster, Margaret
161–162

Forsyth, Frederick 162

Fortune's Favourites
288

Fortunes of War 299

Foucault's Pendulum
133

Foundation Saga, The
(*Foundation,*
Foundation and
Empire, Second
Foundation) 18–19

Four-Gated City, The 273

Fourth Hand, The 233

Fowles, John 141, 163–164

Fragrant Harbour 262

Francis, Dick 164

Frankenstein, or the
Modern Prometheus
405, 406

Frankie & Stankie 447

Franzen, Jonathan 165

Fraser, George MacDonald
166

Frayn, Michael 166–167

French Lieutenant's
Woman, The 141, 163,
164

Frenchman's Creek 129

Fringe of Leaves, A 482,
483

From a View to a Death
357

From Russia with Love 156

From the Beast to the
Blonde 469

From the Earth to the
Moon 461

From the Holy Mountain
107

Frost in May 480, 481

Fruit of the Lemon 278

Fruit Palace, The 332

Full Tilt 324

Funeral Games 372

Furst, Alan 168

Further Adventures of
Robinson Crusoe, The
115

Fury 385

Gaiman, Neil 169

Game, The 67

Garfield, Simon 170–171

Gargantua and
Pantagruel 368

Garrick Year, The 127

Gaskell, Mrs 171–172

Gate of the Angels, The
153

Gathering, The 141

Gaudy Night 391

GB84 345

Generation X 100

Gentlemen and Players
198

Georgy Girl 161

Germinal 493

Gertrud 208

Gertrude and Claudius
459

Get Shorty 272

Ghosh, Amitav 173

Ghost of Thomas Kempe
280

Ghost Road, The 38

Ghost Story 280

Ghost Train to the Eastern
Star 434

Ghosts 24

Ghostwritten 312

Giant O' Brien, The 301
Gibson, William 174
Gide, André 175
Gift of Stones, The 101
Gilead 378, 379
Giovanni's Room 32
Girl at the Lion d'Or, The
146
Girl with a Pearl Earring
82
Girlfriend in a Coma 100
Girls of Slender Means,
The 418–419
Gissing, George 177
Given Day, The 268–269
Giving Up the Ghost 301
Glass Bead Game,
The/Magister Ludi (Das
Glasperlenspiel) 208
Glass Lake, The 45
Glass of Blessings, A 366
Glass Palace, The 173
Glastonbury Romance, A
359
Glendinning, Victoria 178
Gloriana 316
Glue 476
Go Tell It on the Mountain
32
God Delusion, The 110,
111
God's Own Country 3
Goethe, Johann Wolfgang
von 178–179, 345
Gogol, Nikolai Vasilevich
179–180, 245
Golden Bowl, The 238

Golden Child, The 153
Golden Earth 279
Golden Gate, The 403
Golden Notebook, The
273
Golding, William 180–181,
482
Gone Away World, The
1–2
Gone With the Wind 314
Good Companions, The
360, 361
Good Man in Africa, A 54
Good Morning, Midnight
375
Good Omens 169
Good Soldier Svejk, The
200
Good Soldier, The 158
Goodbye to Berlin 234
Gordimer, Nadine
182–183
Gormenghast Trilogy, The
(Titus Groan,
Gormenghast and Titus
Alone) 346
Gosse, Edmund 29
Gould, Stephen Jay
183–184
Government Inspector,
The 179
Grahame, Kennedy
184–185
Grand Babylon Hotel, The
44
Grand Man, A 97
Grapes of Wrath, The 421

Grass is Singing, The 273
Grass, Günter 185–186
Graves, Robert 186–187,
372
Gravity's Rainbow 366,
367
Gray, Alasadair 188–189
Great Apes 402, 403
Great Eastern Land 430
Great Expectations 72,
121
Great Gatsby, The 152
Great Jones St 116
Great Railway Bazaar, The
434
Great Shame, The 248
Great Shark Hunt, The 437
Green Knight, The 323
Greene, Graham 69,
189–190, 278, 318, 434
Greenmantle 63
Greer, Germaine 191
Gregory, Philippa 192
Grenville, Kate 193
Grisham, John 194
Grotesque, The 291
Ground Beneath Her Feet,
The 385
Grown-Ups, The 178
Guerrillas 328
Gulag Archipelago, The
417
Gulliver's Travels 178,
428
Gun for Sale/This Gun for
Hire, A 189
Gun, The 159

Guterson, David 195

Haggard, H. Rider 196, 415
Hair of the Dogma, The 335
Half of a Yellow Sun 331
Hammett, Dashiell 196–197
Handful of Dust, A 53, 471
Handmaid's Tale, The 21, 22
Hanging Garden, The 370
Hard Times 335
Hardy, Thomas 55, 197–198
Harkaway, Nick 1–2
Harris, Joanne 198–199
Harris, Robert 199
Harry Potter and the Philosopher's Stone 382
Hašek, Jaroslav 200
Haunted 342
Hawksmoor 5, 411
Hawthorne, Nathaniel 200–201
He Kills Coppers 17
Headlong 167
Hearing Secret Harmonies 358
Hearing Voices 485
Heart is a Lonely Hunter, The 287
Heart of Darkness 96
Heart of the Matter, The 190
Heart Songs 362

Heat of the Day, The 53
Heaven's Command 318
Heinlein, Robert 202
Hell's Angels 437
Heller, Joseph 144, 203–204
Hemingway, Ernest 204–205
Hemlock and After 484
Henderson the Rain King 42
Hensher, Philip 206
Herbert, Frank 207–208
Herzog 43
Hesse, Hermann 208
Hey Nostradamus 100
Hiaasen, Carl 209–210
High Fidelity 225
High Rise 33
Highsmith, Patricia 211, 239
Hill, Reginald 212
Hill, Susan 213
Hills of Adonis, The 442
Hired Man, The 55
His Dark Materials trilogy (Northern Lights, The Subtle Knife and The Amber Spyglass) 364
History Maker, A 188
History of Mr Polly, The 474
History of the World in 10½ Chapters, The 39, 40
Hitchhiker's Guide to the Galaxy, The 6
Hoban, Russell 221

Hobbit, The 444
Hodd 438
Hogarth: A Life and a World 457
Hold Tight 89–90
Holidays in Hell 338
Hollinghurst, Alan 222–223
Holmes, Richard 223–224
Holroyd, Michael 126, 224–225, 427
Homage to Catalonia 340
Home 379
Honolulu Hotel 434
Honoured Society, The 279
Hornby, Nick 225–226
Hosseini, Khaled 226–227
Hot Rock, The 94
Hôtel du Lac 60
Hotel New Hampshire, The 233
Houellebecq, Michel 227–228
House for Mr Biswas, A 293, 327, 328
House of Mirth, The 479–480
House of Sleep, The 91
House of the Seven Gables, The 201
House of the Spirits, The 9, 10
Household, Geoffrey 441
Housekeeping 378
How Proust Can Change Your Life 113

How to Be Good 226
Howards End 160
Høeg, Peter 222
Hughes, Robert 228–229
Hugo, Victor 229–230
Human Comedy, The (La Comedie Humaine) 34, 445, 493
Human Croquet 19, 20
Human Factor, The 190
Human Traces 146
Humboldt's Gift 42–43
Hunchback of Notre Dame (Notre Dame de Paris) 229
Hundred Secret Senses, The 429
Hungry Tide, The 173
Hunt for Red October, The 86
Hunting Mister Heartbreak 367
Huxley, Aldous 230–231

I Am Mary Dunne 317
I, Claudius 187
I Know Why the Caged Bird Sings 16
I, Robot 19
I Will Fear No Evil 202
I'm the King of the Castle 213
Ice House, The 466
Ice-Cream War, An 54
Idea of Perfection, The 193
Idiot, The 122, 123
Idoru 175

If Not Now, When? 275
If on a Winter's Night a Traveller 69
If This is a Man 277
Illywhacker 72
Imaginary Friends 284
Imaginary Life, An 295, 296
Imaginings of Sand 56
Immoralist, The 175
Immortality 258, 259
Impossible Saints 377
Impressionist, The 259
In a Dry Season 379
In a Free State 327
In Desolate Heaven 134
In Ethiopia with a Mule 324
In Patagonia 81
In Siberia 442
In Sicily 279
In the Kitchen 9
In the Shape of a Boar 333
In the Springtime of the Year 213
In Trouble Again 337
In Xanadu 107
Incline Our Hearts 485
Indecent Exposure 405
Ingenious Pain 310
Ingenious Pursuits 241
Inheritors, The 181
Innocence 153
Inside Mr Enderby 64
Instant in the Wind 56
International Dictionary of Women's Biography 457

Into the Heart of Borneo 337
Invisible Woman, The 446
Ipcress File, The 115
Iron Hand of Mars, The 109
Irving, John 233, 321
Isherwood, Christopher 234
Ishiguro, Kazuo 234–235
Island 380
Island of Doctor Moreau, The 473
Island of the Day Before, The 133
Istanbul: Memories of a City 343
It 254
Italian Secretary, The 74
Ivanhoe 400

Jack Maggs 72
Jackie Brown 272
Jacobson, Howard 236–237
James, Clive 237–238
James, Henry 238
James, P.D. 239–240, 372
Jane Eyre 57–58
Jardine, Lisa 241
Jazz 319
Jerome, Jerome K. 242
Jewel in the Skull, The 316
Job 202
Johnny Come Home 17
Joke, The 258
Jonathan Swift 178

Jones, Sadie 2
Jordan, Robert 242–243
Joseph and His Brothers 297
Joseph Andrews 148
Josh Lawton 55
Journey into Space 280
Journey to the Centre of the Earth 461
Joy Luck Club, The 429
Joyce, James 244–245, 283, 411
Judgement Day 280
Judgement of Paris, The 253
Juggling 447
Jumping the Queue 478
Junky 66

Kafka, Franz 52, 69, 92, 122, 179, 245–246, 346
Kapuscinski, Ryszard 246–247
Kate Hannigan's Daughter 97
Keeping Faith 351
Keillor, Garrison 247–248
Keneally, Thomas 72, 248–249
Kennedy, A.L. 250–251
Kepler 36
Kept 431
Kerouac, Jack 100, 251–252, 279
Keyes, Marian 252–253
Kidnapped 425
Killing Dragons 155

Killing Floor 83
Killing Mr Watson 305
Kim 256–257
Kindly Ones, The 358
Kindness of Women, The 33
King Must Die, The 372
King Rat 309
King Solomon's Mines 196
King, Ross 253
King, Stephen 254–255
Kingdom Come 55
Kingdom of Fear 437
Kingdom of the Wicked, The 64
Kingsolver, Barbara 255–256
Kipling, Rudyard 256–257
Kipps 474
Kiss and Other Stories, The 82
Kiss and Tell 113
Kitchen God's Wife, The 429
Kitchen Venom 206
Kite Runner, The 226
Kneale, Matthew 257–258
Knots and Crosses 369
Krakatoa – The Day the Earth Exploded 486
Kundera, Milan 258–259
Kunzru, Hari 259–260
Kureishi, Hanif 260–261

Lady and the Unicorn, The 83

Lady in the Lake, The 81
Lady with a Lap Dog, The 82
Lady's Maid 161
Lake Wobegon Days 247
Lanchester, John 261–262
Landlocked 273
Landor's Tower 411
Last Act in Palmyra 109
Last Dickens, The 347
Last Grain Race, The 330
Last Mughal, The 107
Last Sherlock Holmes Story, The 119
Laura Blundy 325, 326
Lawrence, D.H. 55, 263–264
Le Carré, John 264–265
Le Guin, Ursula 267–268
Leaven of Malice 108
Lee, Laurie 265–266
Left Hand of Darkness, The 268
Lehane, Dennis 268–269
Lehmann, Rosamond 269–270
Leigh-Fermor, Patrick 270–271
Lemprière's Dictionary 333
Leon, Donna 271–272
Leonard, Elmore 272
Leonardo Da Vinci: The Flights of the Mind 332
Leper's Companions, The 49
Les Misérables 229, 230

Less Than Zero 137
Lessing, Doris 273
Letter to Sister Benedicta 450
Levant Trilogy, The 299
Levi, Primo 277
Levy, Andrea 277–278
Lewis, Norman 278–279
Libra 117
Life and Death of Mary Wollstonecraft, The 446
Life and Opinions of Tristram Shandy, Gentleman, The 424
Life and Times of Michael K, The 92
Life and Times of the Thunderbolt Kid 62
Life Before Man 21
Life Class 39
Life of My Choice, The 436
Light in August 145
Lillian's Story 193
Line of Beauty, The 223
Lion of Boaz-Jachin and Jachin-Boaz, The 221
Litt, Toby 279–280
Little Friend, The 430
Little Yellow Dog 320
Lively, Penelope 280–281
Liza of Lambeth 306
Locked Room, The 24
Lodge, David 281–282
Lodger, The 333
Lolita 326
London Journal 276

London: A Biography 5
Lonely Passion of Judith Hearne, The 317
Long Dark Teatime of the Soul, The 6
Long Firm, The 17
Longitude 170
Look at Me 60
Look at the Harlequins! 326
Look to the Lady 11
Lopez, Barry 283
Lord of the Flies 180, 181
Lord of the Rings, The 444
Losing Nelson 458
Lost Continent, The 61
Lost Empires 361
Lost Father, The 469
Lost Heart of Asia, The 442
Lost Lady, A 77
Lost Man's River 305
Lost Traveller, The 480
Love 319
Love and Friendship 284
Love and Mr Lewisham 474
Love and War in the Apennines 331
Love in a Cold Climate 315
Love in the Time of Cholera 303
Low Notes on a High Level 360
Lowry, Malcolm 283–284
Lucky Jim 12, 23

Lucy Sullivan is Getting Married 252
Lud Heat 411
Lud-in-the-Mist 143
Lunar Men, The 457
Lurie, Alison 284–285, 456
Lyre of Orpheus, The 109

Madame Bovary 154
Maggot, A 163
Magic Mountain, The (Der Zauberberg) 298
Magic Toyshop, The 74
Magus, The 164
Mahfouz, Naguib 293–294
Maid of Buttermere, The 55
Maiden Castle 359
Mailer, Norman 294–295
Main Cages, The 303
Malayan Trilogy, The 64
Mallen Trilogy, The (The Mallen Girl, The Mallen Litter and *The Mallen Streak)* 97
Maluuf, David 295–296
Man in the High Castle, The 120
Man in the Picture, The 213
Man Lay Dead, A 304
Man on a Donkey 217
Man Who Mistook His Wife for a Hat, The 386, 387

Man Who Watched the Trains Go By, The 410
Maneater of Malgudi, The 329
Mankell, Henning 296
Mann, Thomas 297–298
Manning, Olivia 299
Mansfield, Katherine 300
Mansfield Park 23
Mantel, Hilary 257, 300–301
Mantissa 163
Mao II 117
Map That Changed the World, The 486
Marabou Stork Nightmares 476
March 60
Marital Rites 161
Márquez, Gabriel García 9, 113, 302–303, 460
Married Man, The 482
Marrying the Mistress 454
Marsden, Philip 303–304
Marsh Arabs, The 436
Marsh, Ngaio 304
Martha Peake 291, 292
Martha Quest 273
Mary Barton 171–172
Mary Swann 407
Master, The 443
Master and Margarita, The 63–64
Master of Ballantrae, The 426
Master of Petersburg, The 93

Matthiesson, Peter 305
Maugham, W. Somerset 306
Maupassant, Guy de 307
Mauve 170
May Week Was in June 237
Mayor of Casterbridge, The 198
McCall Smith, Alexander 285–286
McCarthy, Cormac 286–287
McCullers, Carson 287, 477
McCullough, Colleen 288
McDermid, Val 289–290
McEwan, Ian 290–291
McGrath, Patrick 291–292
McInerney, Jay 292–293
Me and the Fat Man 325–326
Meaning of Recognition, The 238
Melville, Herman 307–308, 482
Member of the Wedding, The 287
Memento Mori 418
Memoirs of Sherlock Holmes, The 124
Mercy, A 319
Meridian 465
Mermaids Singing, The 289
Methuselah's Children 202

Metroland 39
Mezzanine, The 31
Michel Strogoff 461
Michelangelo and the Pope's Ceiling 253
Middlemarch 136–137
Midnight's Children 385, 386
Midwich Cuckoos, The 492
Miéville, China 309
Mighty Walzer, The 236–237
Military Philosophers, The 358
Mill on the Floss, The 137
Miller, Andrew 310
Milton, Giles 310–311
Minaret of Djam 420
Mirrlees, Hope 143
Mirror to Damascus 442
Misery 255
Miss Smilla's Feeling for Snow 222
Missing of the Somme, The 131
Mist in the Mirror, The 213
Mistressclass, The 377
Mistry, Rohinton 311–312
Mitchell, David 312–313
Mitchell, Margaret 314
Mitford, Nancy 315
Mixture of Frailties, A, 108
Moby Dick 307
Moment of War, A 266

Mona Lisa Overdrive 174
Monday Mourning 371
Money 14
Monsignor Quixote 189
Montezuma's Daughter 196
Month of Sundays, A 459
Monuments and Maidens 469
Moo 414
Moon and Sixpence, The 306
Moon Tiger 281
Moonstone, The 94
Moor's Last Sigh, The 385
Moorcock, Michael 316–317
Moore, Brian 317–318
Morality Play 458
Morris, Jan 318–319
Morrison, Toni 319
Morvern Callar 468
Mosaic 225
Mosley, Walter 320
Mosquito Coast, The 434
Mother Can You Hear Me? 161
Mother London 317
Mr Norris Changes Trains 234
Mr Phillips 261, 262
Mr Wroe's Virgins 380
Mrs Dalloway 491
Mrs de Winter 213
Mrs Jordan's Profession 446
Muddling Through in Madagascar 324

Mulberry Empire, The 206, 207
Munro, Alice 321
Murakami, Haruki 312, 321–322
Murder at the Vicarage 85
Murder is Announced, A 85
Murdoch, Iris 323
Murphy, Dervla 324
Music & Silence 450, 451
Muther and Walking Spirits 109
My Antonia 77
My Beautiful Laundrette 260
My Dark Places 139
My Idea of Fun 402, 403
My Life as a Fake 72
My Lover's Lover 336
My Name is Red 343
My Revolutions 260
My Secret History 435
My Sister's Keeper 351
Myerson, Julie 325–326
Myra Breckinridge 463
Mysteries of Pittsburgh, The 79
Mysterious Flame of Queen Loana, The 133
Mystic River 268

Nabokov, Vladimir 326–327
Naipaul, V.S. 293, 327–328
Naïve and Sentimental Lover, The 265

Naked and the Dead, The 294
Naked Sun, The 19
Name of the Rose, The 133–134
Nana 493
Naples '44 279
Napoleon Symphony, The 64
Narayan, R.K. 329–330
Nathaniel's Nutmeg 311
Nature of Blood, The 350
Nausea 390
Neither Here Nor There 61
Neuromancer 174
Never Far From Nowhere 278
Never Let Me Go 235
Neverwhere 169, 170
New Confessions, The 54
New Grub Street 177
New York Trilogy, The 24
Newby, Eric 330–331
News From Tartary 157
Newton Letter, The 36
Next to Nature, Art 280
Ngozi Adichie, Chimamanda 331–332
Nice Work 281
Nicholas Nickleby 122
Nicholl, Charles 332
Night Geometry and the Garscadden Trains 250
Night Manager, The 264
Night Soldiers 168
Night Watch, The 470
Nights at the Circus 75

Nineteen Eighty-Four 340
Nineteen Seventy-Four
  345
Ninety Degrees North 155
No Country for Old Men
  286
No Go the Bogeyman 469
No Heroics Please 76
No More Mr Nice Guy
  236
No Name 94
No Name in the Street 32
*No. 1 Ladies' Detective
  Agency, The* 285
Noah's Ark 447
Nocturnes 235
Noise 260
Norfolk, Lawrence 333
North and South 172
Northern Clemency, The
  207
Norwegian Wood 321
Not That Sort of Girl 478
Not the End of the World
  19
*Notebooks of Don
  Rigoberto, The* 461
*Notes From a Small
  Island* 62
Notes of a Native Son 32
Nothing like the Sun 64
Now That You're Back 248
Number of the Beast 202
number9dream 312
Numquam 131

O'Brian, Patrick 334
O'Brien, Flann 334–335

O'Connor, Joseph 335–336
O'Farrell, Maggie 336
O'Hanlon, Redmond 157,
  337
O'Rourke, P.J. 337–338
Obstacle Race, The 191
Odessa File, The 162
Of Human Bondage 306
Of Love and Shadows 9,
  10
Of Mice and Men 422
Of Wolves and Men 283
Offshore 153
Oh, Play That Thing 125
Old Devils, The 12, 13
Old Glory 367
*Old Goriot (Le Père
  Goriot)* 34
Old Man and the Sea, The
  205
Old Men at the Zoo, The
  484
Old Wives' Tale, The 44
Old Women, The 178
On a Grander Scale 241
On Beauty 417
On Beulah Height 212
On Green Dolphin Street
  146
On the Black Hill 81
On the Road 251, 252,
  279
Ondaatje, Michael 339
*One Day in the Life of
  Ivan Denisovich* 417
*One Fine Day in the
  Middle of the Night* 59
One Good Turn 19

*One Hundred Years of
  Solitude* 9, 302
One Morning Like a Bird
  420
Only Problem, The 418
Open Swimmer, An 488
Operation Shylock 382
Optimist's Daughter, The
  477
Optimists, The 310
*Ordeal of Gilbert Pinfold,
  The* 471
Orwell, George 340–341,
  431
Oscar and Lucinda 72
Oswald's Tale 294
Other Boleyn Girl, The 192
Other Lulus 206
Other Queen Mary, The
  192
Our Ancestors 69
Our Father 384
Our Hidden Lives 171
Our Man in Havana 189
Our Mutual Friend 121
Our Times 485
Out of Sheer Rage 131
Outcast, The 2
Outland 1
Outposts 486
Outsider, The (L'Étranger)
  70
Overture to Death 304
Oxygen 310

Pact, The 351
Paddy Clarke Ha Ha Ha
  125

Painted House, A 194

Palahniuk, Chuck 342

Pale Fire 327

Pale View of Hills, A 234

Pamela 376, 377

Pamuk, Orhan 343

Parade's End 158

Paradise 319

Parson Harding's Daughter 453

Partisan's Daughter, A 112

Passage to India, A 159, 160, 161

Passage to Juneau 367

Passion, The 487

Passion of New Eve, The 74, 75

Past Reason Hated 380

Pasternak, Boris 345

Patriot Games 87

Pattern Recognition 174

Paula 9

Pax Britannica 318

Payment Deferred 159

Peace, David 345–346

Peake, Mervyn 346–347

Pearl, Matthew 347–348

Pebble in the Sky 19

Peeping Tom 236

Pendennis 434

People of the Book 61

People Who Knock on the Door 211

Peppered Moth, The 127

Pérez-Reverte, Arturo 348–349

Perfect Spy, A 265

Periodic Table, The 277

Perpetual Orgy, The 461

Persian Boy, The 372

Persuader 83

Pesthouse, The 101

Pet Semetary 255

Phillips, Caryl 349–350

Photograph, The 281

Pickwick Papers 121

Picoult, Jodi 351

Pilgermann 221

Pilot's Wife, The 409

Place of Execution, A 289

Place of Greater Safety, A 301

Plague, The (La Peste) 70–71

Plain Murder 159

Plain Tales from the Hills 257

Platform 227

Players 117

Playmaker, The 248, 249

Pleasure of Eliza Lynch, The 141

Pleasured 206

Plot Against America, The 382

Pnin 326, 327

Poe, Edgar Allan 74, 352–353, 346

Poe Shadow, The 347

Point of Origin 99

Poisonwood Bible, The 255

Polish Officer, The 168

Pontoon 248

Poor Mouth, The 335

Poor Things 188

Pope's Rhinoceros, The 333

Port Mungo 291

Portnoy's Complaint 381

Portrait of a Lady, The 239

Portrait of the Artist as Young Man, A 244

Possessing the Secret of Joy 465

Possession 67

Possibility of an Island, The 227

Post Mortem 99

Postcards 362

Powell, Anthony 357–358

Power and the Glory, The 190

Powerbook, The 487

Powys, John Cowper 359

Pratchett, Terry 169, 360

Prater Violet 234

Prayer for Owen Meany, A 233

Prescott, H.F.M. 217

Prester John 63

Pride and Prejudice 22–23

Priestley, J.B. 360–361

Prime of Miss Jean Brodie, The 418

Prince and the Pauper, The 455

Private Papers 161, 162

Promised Lands 380

Proper Marriage, A 273

Proud Highway, The 437

Songlines, The 81

Sons and Lovers 265

Sopranos, The 468

*Sorrows of Young
 Werther, The (Die
 Leiden des Jungen
 Werthers)* 179

Sorry, Dad 50

Sound and the Fury, The
 144–145

South, The 443

*South of the Border, West
 of the Sun* 322

*Southern Gates of Arabia,
 The* 420

Spanish Lover, A 454

Spark, Muriel 418–419

Spell, The 223

Spell of Winter, A 130

Spider 291

Spies 167

Spire, The 181

Spirit-Wrestlers, The
 303

Spook Country 174

Sport of Nature, A 183

Squeeze Play 24

SS-GB 116

Stalingrad 41

Stamboul Train 189

Star Called Henry, A 125

Star of the Sea, The 335

Stark, Freya 420–421

Stars like Dust, The 19

Starship Troopers 202

*State of Independence,
 A* 349

Station, The 69

Steinbeck, John 286,
 421–422

Stendhal 422–423

Stephenson, Neal
 423–424

Sterne, Laurence 424–425

Stevenson, R.L. 224,
 425–426

Still 438

Still Life 67

Stitch in Time, A 280

Stoker, Bram 426

Stone Diaries, The 406

Stone Virgin 458

Story of My Life, The 292

Storyteller, The 460

Strachey, Lytton 427

Strait is the Gate 175

*Stranger in a Strange
 Land* 202

Such a Long Story 312

Sugar House, The 480

Suitable Boy, A 403, 404

Sum of All Fears, The 87

Sum of Our Days, The
 10

Summer 479

Super-Cannes 33

*Surgeon of Crowthorne,
 The* 486

Surveillance 368

Suttree 286

Sweet Dreams 167

Sweet Thames 257, 258

Sweets of Pimlico, The
 485

Swift, Graham 427–428

Swift, Jonathan 428

*Swimming Pool Season,
 The* 450

*Swimming-Pool Library,
 The* 223

Sword and the Cross, The
 155

Sword of Honour 53, 471

Symons, A.J.A. 48

Take a Girl Like You 12, 13

Tales From Firozsha Baag
 312

Talking to the Dead 130

Tan, Amy 429

Tar Baby 319

Tara Road 45

Tartt, Donna 430

Taste for Death, A 240

Taylor, D.J. 430–431

Taylor, Elizabeth 431–432

Tell No One 89

Tempest-tost 108

Temples of Delight 447

Temporary Kings 358

*Temptation of Eileen
 Hughes, The* 317

Thackeray, William
 Makepeace 431,
 433–434

That Old Ace in the Hole
 362

Therapy 281

Thérèse Raquin 492, 493

Theroux, Paul 434–435

Thesiger, Wilfred 330, 436

Thinks 281

Third Man, The 189

Third Policeman, The 335

Thirty-nine Steps, The
  62–63
Thompson, Hunter S.
  436–437
Thorn Birds, The 288
Thorpe, Adam 437–438
Thought Gang, The 151
Thousand Acres, A 414,
  415
Thousand Splendid Suns,
  A 227
Three Cheers for the
  Paraclete 248
Three Men in a Boat 242
Three Men on the
  Bummel 242
Three Musketeers, The
  128
Three Stigmata of Palmer
  Eldritch, The 120
Through Siberia by
  Accident 324
Thubron, Colin 442
Ticket of Leave 410
Tilly Trotter 97
Time Enough to Love 202
Time Machine, The 473
Time of Gifts, A 270, 271
Time of the Hero, The
  460
Time to Kill, A 194
Time's Arrow, Time's
  Cycle 184
Tin Drum, The (Die
  Blechtrommel) 185
Tin Men, The 167
Tipping the Velvet 470
Titus Alone 347

Titus Groan 347
To the Lighthouse 491
Tóibín, Colm 443
Toilers of the Sea, The
  230
Tokyo Year Zero 346
Tolkien, J.R.R. 444
Tolstoy, Leo Nikolaevich
  206, 445–446
Tom Jones 148
Tomalin, Claire 446
Tono-Bungay 474
Torrents of Spring 455
Tortilla Flat 286, 421
Tourist Season 209
Toward the End of Time
  459
Towards the End of
  Morning 166
Trainspotting 476
Transmission 260
Trapido, Barbara 447
Trauma 291
Traveller's Prelude 421
Travelling Hornplayer,
  The 447
Travels with Herodotus
  247
Travels with my Aunt
  189
Trawler 337
Treasure Island 425
Tree of Man, The 482
Tree Where Man Was
  Born, The 305
Tremain, Rose 257,
  450–451
Trevor, William 451–452

Trial, The (Der Prozess)
  245, 246
Trick of the Light, A 146
Trick or Treatment 413
Trieste and the Meaning
  of Nowhere 319
Trollope, Anthony 171, 176,
  452–453
Trollope, Joanna 453
Troubles 144
Troublesome Offspring of
  Cardinal Guzman, The
  112
Truckers 360
True History of the Kelly
  Gang, The 72, 73
Truth About Lorin Jones,
  The 284
Tunc 131
Turgenev, Ivan Sergeevich
  454–455
Twain, Mark 455–456
Twenty Thousand
  Leagues Under the Sea
  461
Two for the Lions 109
Tyler, Anne 456–457
Typhoon 96
Tyrant's Novel, The 248

Uglow, Jenny 457–458
Ultramarine 283
Ulverton 437, 438
Ulysses 68, 244, 283, 411
Unbearable Lightness of
  Being, The 258, 259
Uncle Tungsten 387
Unconsoled, The 235

Under the Frog 151
Under the Volcano 283
Underworld 117
Unguarded Hours 485
Unreliable Memoirs 237
Unsworth, Barry 458–459
Untouchable, The 37
Unweaving the Rainbow 110
Updike, John 456, 459–460

Vacant Possession 301
Valis 120
Valley of Bones, The 358
Valleys of the Assassins, The 420
Vanishing Act of Esme Lennox, The 336
Vanity Fair 433–434
Vargas Llosa, Mario 460–461
Various Haunts of Men, The 213
Vendor of Sweets, The 329
Venetian Empire, The 318
Venice 318
Verne, Jules 264, 461–462, 473
Veronika Decides to Die 92
Vertigo 401
Viceroy of Ouidah, The 81
Vidal, Gore 462–463
Villages 459

Vine, Barbara: *see* Rendell, Ruth
Virgin Blue, The 82
Virgin in the Garden, The 67
Vivisector, The 482
Voices of the Old Sea 279
Vonnegut, Kurt 202, 464–465
Voss 482, 483
Vows of Silence, The 213
Vox 31
Voyage to the End of the Room 151

Walk in the Woods, A 62
Walker, Alice 465–466
Waltari, Miki 217
Walters, Minette 466–467
War and Peace 445, 446
War Between the Tates, The 284
War in the Air, The 473
War of Don Emmanuel's Nether Parts, The 112
War of the End of the World, The 460
War of the Worlds, The 473
Warden, The 453
Warlord of the Air 316
Warner, Alan 468
Warner, Marina 469
Wasp Factory, The 35
Waste Land, The 68
Watch in the Night, A 485
Waterland 427
Waterlog 111

Watermelon 252
Waters, Sarah 470
Waugh, Evelyn 53, 68, 315, 431, 471–472
Waves, The 491
Way We Live Now, The 453
Weight of Water, The 409
Weldon, Fay 472–473
Wells, H.G. 202, 473–474
Welsh, Irvine 476
Welty, Eudora 477–478
Wesley, Mary 478
Westlake, Donald E. 94
Weymouth Sands 359
Wharton, Edith 479–480
What a Carve Up! 90–91
What We Talk About When We Talk About Love 76
What's Become of Waring? 357
What's Bred in the Bone 109
Wheel of Time novels 243
When We Were Orphans 235
When Will There Be Good News 19
Where Angels Fear to Tread 160
Where I'm Calling From 76
Whistling Woman, A 67
White Butterfly 320
White Chappell, Scarlet Tracings 411
White Company, The 123
White Goddess, The 186

White Gold 311
White Mughals 107
White Noise 117
White Teeth 416
White, Antonia 480–481
White, Edmund 481–482
White, Patrick 72, 482–483
Whole Woman, The 191
Why Are We in Vietnam? 294
Wide Open 38
Wide Sargasso Sea 375
Widow and Her Hero, The 248
Wig My Father Wore, The 140
Wild Boys 67
Wild Girl, The 378
Wild Sheep, A 322
Wildwood 111
Wilhelm Meister 179
Will You Please Be Quiet, Please 76
Wilson, A.N. 485

Winchester, Simon 486
Wind in the Willows, The 184, 185
Wind-up Bird Chronicles, The 322
Wings 360
Wings of the Dove, The 238–239
Winter in Madrid 389
Winter King, The 98
Winter Queen, The 8
Winterson, Jeanette 487
Winton, Tim 488
Wise Children 75
Witches of Eastwick, The 459
With Your Crooked Heart 130
Wodehouse, P.G. 79, 489
Wolf Solent 359
Wolfe, Tom 490
Woman and the Ape, The 222
Woman in Black, The 213

Woman in White, The 93
Woman Who Walked Into Walls, The 125
Wonder Boys 79
Wonderful Life 183
Woodrell, Daniel 106
Woolf, Virginia 491
Workers in the Dawn 177
Works on Paper 224
World According to Garp, The 233
Worldly Goods 241
Worst Journey in the World, The 450
Wrestling, The 170
Wroblewski, David 4
Wuthering Heights 58
Wyndham, John 492

Years of Wonder 60
Young Adolf 29

Zola, Émile 492–493